florence
& tuscany

FODOR'S TRAVEL PUBLICATIONS
NEW YORK • TORONTO • LONDON • SYDNEY • AUCKLAND

WWW.FODORS.COM

Contents

KEY TO SYMBOLS

✚ Map reference
✉ Address
☎ Telephone number
🕐 Opening times
💷 Admission prices
🚌 Bus number
🚉 Train station
⛴ Ferry/boat
🚗 Driving directions
ℹ Tourist office
🎫 Tours
📖 Guidebook
🍴 Restaurant
☕ Café
🏬 Shop
🚻 Toilets
🛏 Number of rooms
🚭 No smoking
❄ Air conditioning
🏊 Swimming pool
🏋 Gym
❓ Other useful information
🏬 Shopping
🎭 Entertainment
🍸 Nightlife
🏀 Sports
⭐ Activities
❤ Health and Beauty
😊 For Children
▷ Cross reference
★ Walk/drive start point

HOW TO USE THIS BOOK

Understanding Tuscany is an introduction to the region, its geography, economy and people. **Living Tuscany** gives an insight into the area today, while **The Story of Tuscany** takes you through the region's past.

For detailed advice on getting to Tuscany—and getting around once you are there—turn to **On the Move**. For useful practical information, from weather forecasts to emergency services, turn to **Planning**.

Out and About gives you the chance to explore Tuscany through walks and drives.

The **Sights**, **What to Do** and **Eating and Staying** sections are divided geographically into four regions, which are shown on the map on the inside front cover. These regions always appear in the same order. Towns and places of interest are listed alphabetically within each region.

Map references for the **Sights** refer to the atlas section at the end of this book or to individual town plans. For example, Lucca has the reference ➕ 283 D4, indicating the page on which the map is found (283) and the grid square in which Lucca sits (D4).

UNDERSTANDING TUSCANY

Tuscany is probably the most visited region in Italy and its capital, Florence, is up there with Rome and Venice as one of the most popular destinations in the country. But the wealth of art and architecture in the city is only half the story. There is an extraordinary concentration of smaller art towns across Tuscany. Chianti is an area of great natural beauty. The shopping—from designer fashions to handmade paper—is excellent. There is some of the best food and wine in the country. There are mountains and beaches, and many places to go sailing, walking, skiing, diving and to play golf. With this comes a seductively easy-going lifestyle and a sense that here, there is always plenty of time.

A vineyard in the Chianti district, famed for its red wine

Detail of a carved figure on a fountain in the Giardino di Boboli

LANDSCAPE
Tuscany is an extraordinarily diverse region. Florence lies to the north on the River Arno; the wide river basin that runs due west and into the sea near Pisa is probably the flattest part of the region. Elsewhere, with the exception Val di Chiana, hills and mountains dominate the terrain. Chianti is famous for its characteristic rolling hills dotted with olive trees and cypresses, striped with vines and littered with villas, farmhouses and castles. However, there's more to Tuscany than hills and vales: the heavily-wooded Casentino; the barren landscapes of the Val d'Orcia and the Crete Senese; the verdant Mugello, with its alpine feel in parts; Elba, Giglio and Capraia, the principal islands of the Tuscany archipelago; the gentle hills and Etruscan sites of the Maremma. You can swim off the wide, safe beaches of the Riviera di Versilia, dive off the rocky coast of Monte Argentario, ski on the Appenine slopes near Abetone and walk the paths of Monte Amiata, Tuscany's highest mountain.

CLIMATE
Florence is in a basin, surrounded on three sides by hills, which gives it an unpredictable climate. It is likely to be among the coldest places in winter and the hottest in summer, and humidity levels, particularly in July and August, can be unbearable.

Once out of the city, things improve, but other Tuscan towns such as Siena, Lucca, Pisa and Arezzo also suffer from extremes of temperature. In high summer, head for the hills; even some height above sea level will make all the difference. Areas such as the Casentino and the Alta Versilia will stay cool, at least at night, when the rest of the region is sweltering. The best months to visit are May, June, September and October.

POLITICS
In Italy, elections are held on four different levels: national, regional, provincial and communal or municipal. So, in theory, while Italy might be under the rule of a right-wing government, a particular region could be governed by the left, one of its provinces by the right and the principal town of that province by something in between. Tuscany has a long history of left-wing politics, so while President Silvio Berlusconi's right-wing Forza Italia party has made inroads into various left-wing strongholds, Tuscany on the whole has remained staunchly left or centre-left.

THE ECONOMY
Agriculture provides the backbone of Tuscany's economic existence: Tuscan olive oils and wines are exported throughout the world. However, tourism is playing an increasingly important role.

On an industrial level, Prato is important for the manufacture of textiles and Arezzo is famous for its gold jewellery; every year it exports some €2 billion of the stuff. Tuscany is known for leather goods and has many factories making shoes, clothing and accessories. This, however, is changing fast as many designers move to countries where manufacturing costs are much lower.

GETTING THE BEST FROM YOUR STAY

Tuscany has an incredible amount for the visitor: great art, fabulous scenery, arguably the best food and wine in the country, remote hilltop towns and villages, good beaches, and a variety of activities, from cooking or language courses to horseback riding and sailing. Given that the road network is good and public transport is excellent, it's possible to fit a lot into your stay. If you want to concentrate on seeing art and are not worried about the weather, the best months to come are November and February, when there will be fewer people about. If you want a mixture of rural relaxation and city culture, May, June and September are good months as it's not too hot for either. Avoid the coastal resorts in July and August as this is when Italian families take their holidays. If you are based in the country and want to spend the day in Florence, use public transport to get there as parking is very difficult. Florence, Siena and other popular towns like San Gimignano become very busy during the summer, so make sure you arrive early in the morning or late in the afternoon, when the crowds have thinned out.

Try to catch one of the many traditional festivals that take place in Tuscany annually. The biggest are the *Giostra del Saracino* in Arezzo (▷ 190), the *Palio* in Siena (▷ 183), the *Scoppio del Carro* in Florence (▷ 172) and the *Gioco del Ponte* in Pisa (▷ 180). However, there are many smaller festivals held in towns throughout the summer, and a few hours spent at one of these is a great way to sample country life in Tuscany.

Whatever you choose to do, allow plenty of time and don't expect opening hours to be exactly what they say they are. You can always go and have lunch while you wait.

View from Monte Oliveto Maggiore

Looking out over the rustic tiled rooftops of Volterra

Villa surrounded by steep vineyards near Camigliano

BEST TUSCAN EXPERIENCES

Enjoy a lazy, al fresco lunch involving *bistecca* (steak) and a glass of Chianti at a simple countryside *trattoria*.

Cross the Ponte Vecchio in Florence at sunset on a golden summer evening.

Watch one of the major festivals such as the *Palio* in Siena or the *Giostra del Saracina* in Arezzo.

Take in the view from the top of the Campanile in Florence.

Hear Gregorian chants at the abbey of Sant'Antimo.

Go for an early morning walk in the magnificent Giardino di Boboli in Florence.

Taste a *rustic fettunta* (toasted bread rubbed with garlic and drizzled liberally with oil) made with new olive oil in December.

Pisa's Campo dei Miracoli is a remarkable sight with its Romanesque buildings in gleaming white marble.

Visit the Galleria degli Uffizi in Florence—the greatest collection of Renaissance art in the world.

Il Campo in Siena is arguably the most beautiful square in Tuscany and a great place to sit and watch the world go by.

A climb into Brunelleschi's dome (right) at Florence's Duomo is the best way to appreciate the extraordinary feat of engineering it took to build it.

Watch a performance of Italian opera at Florence's Teatro del Maggio for a taste of theatrical magic.

THE PROVINCES OF TUSCANY

The region of Tuscany (Toscana) covers an area of nearly 23,000sq km (8,970sq miles) and is divided into ten provinces. These enjoy a certain amount of administrative independence, but are ultimately answerable to the central Italian government.

Provincia di Firenze Florence is the regional capital and the place that most visitors to Tuscany are likely to spend time in given its extraordinary artistic wealth. Its province extends north through the green and little-visited area of the Mugello to the border with Emilia-Romagna, west a little way along the Arno valley, south and west to include much of the Chianti area and east to the wooded slopes of the Vallombrosa.

Provincia di Siena After Florence, many visitors head south to Siena, capital of possibly the richest province in Tuscany in terms of things to see. Covering a large area that stretches from San Gimignano in the northwest to the borders of Lazio in the southeast, the area has fascinating towns and villages, gorgeous scenery, some of the best wine growing areas in Italy and richly fertile agricultural land.

The Fountain of Neptune in Florence's Piazza della Signoria

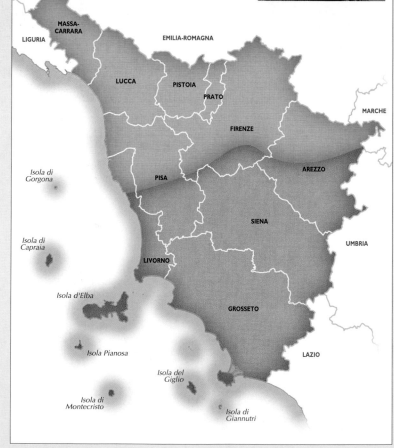

THE PROVINCES OF TUSCANY

Provincia di Arezzo The wealthy town of Arezzo is known for its production of gold jewellery. It is more or less in the middle of its surrounding province, which borders Chianti to the west and Umbria to the east. To the north are the relatively unknown high, wooded hills of the Casentino, which borders Emilia-Romagna.

Provincia di Prato Tuscany's newest and smallest province dates from 1992 and has prosperous, industrial Prato at its heart. Although this lively town is dedicated to the manufacture of cloth, it also has historical and artistic significance. The province is made up of a narrow strip running north to south.

Provincia di Pistoia The town of Pistoia has an abundance of art and refreshingly few visitors. The province reaches north into the Appenine mountain range (where, at Abetone, Florentines flock to ski in winter) and includes the two spa towns of Monsummano Terme and Montecatini Terme.

Provincia di Lucca The lovely walled town of Lucca lies between Florence and the sea. The province has dramatic contrasts: To the west it borders the sea where the beaches of the Versilia coast are a popular holiday destination for Italians; inland from here is the wooded Alta Versilia, dotted with tiny villages clinging to the mountains and popular with walkers; north and west of the town of Lucca is the verdant Garfagnana.

The Ponte Vecchio (Old Bridge), Florence (left), Florentine bookbinder (middle), Pisa's distinctive Leaning Tower, Duomo and Baptistery (right)

Provincia di Massa-Carrara This province is bordered by Liguria in the north and west and by Emilia-Romagna in the northeast. The marble industry dominates life along the coast, which is overshadowed by the dramatic and rugged Alpi Apuane. Michelangelo chose the marble for some of his greatest works from a quarry near Carrara and the local near-white marble (with its characteristic dark grey vein) is still quarried and exported around the world. Many artists and sculptors live along the coast from Carrara to Pietrasanta. The beautiful Lunigiana, to the northwest, is one of the most remote corners of Tuscany.

Provincia di Pisa Pisa is world-famous because of its iconic Leaning Tower, though there is much more to the town than just this. It sits in the north of its province; the southern part is characterized by rolling hills and some pretty country villages. The magnificent Etruscan town of Volterra lies to the south.

Provincia di Livorno Livorno has the feel of the hard-working port that it is. It's one of the biggest container ports in Europe, but is not without charm and is full of wonderful fish restaurants. Its province is made up of a narrow strip of coast that runs south, and one of its most attractive features is the Isola d'Elba, off the south coast. Inland, rolling hills form part of the north and there are some interesting archaeological sites in the area.

Provincia di Grosseto Grosseto is the chief town of the Maremma, an area of reclaimed swamp that was ravaged by malaria during the Middle Ages. Today its long beaches and coastline, particularly rugged Monte Argentario, are popular with glamorous Florentines and Romans. At Alberese a beautiful national park begins and runs south along the coast, delightfully unspoilt due to severe restrictions on the number of visitors allowed to enter. Inland, the rolling hills are relatively empty in spite of many remarkable towns. To the east is Monte Amiata, the highest mountain in Tuscany at 1,738m (5,700ft). To the south is a lonely and remote area of great archaeological importance because of its Etruscan sites. It includes the towns of Pitigliano, Sorano and Sovano.

BEST TOWNS FOR ART

Florence's Duomo (left); The Holy Family, by Michelangelo, in the Uffizi Gallery (below)

Arezzo (▷ 131) This wealthy town has several good museums and is home to *The Legend of the True Cross* by Piero della Francesca (see Best Fresco Cycles).

Florence (▷ 60–96) The best city in the world to see Renaissance art and architecture.

Lucca (▷ 102–105) A lovely walled town with rich pickings in its galleries and churches.

Pisa (▷ 106–109) There is much more to see in Pisa than just its most famous monument, the Leaning Tower.

Siena (▷ 112–127) The Sienese school of painting in the early 14th century produced many masterpieces, all set in a beautiful medieval city.

Detail of ceramic in San Gimignano (right); the impressive skyline of San Gimignano (below)

BEST HILL TOWNS

Montalcino (▷ 137) This small walled town is beautifully surrounded by olive groves and vineyards, the latter producing its most famous asset, Brunello wine.

Montepulciano (▷ 139) A handsome town dominating the Val di Chiana in southeast Tuscany.

Monteriggione (▷ 140) A tiny, perfectly formed hill town enclosed by perfectly preserved walls.

Pienza (▷ 141) Built by Pope Pius II and a perfect example of Renaissance town planning.

Pitigliano (▷ 140) Dramatically built on an outcrop in the southern Maremma, Pitigliano has Etruscan origins and is known for its excellent dry white wine.

San Gimignano (▷ 142–145) This town has managed to preserve its medieval atmosphere in spite of huge numbers of visitors.

Volterra (▷ 148) A rather austere medieval town in a magnificent position, famous for its production of alabaster.

BEST PLACES TO EAT

Beccofino, Florence (▷ 219) Modern Italian food at its best in contemporary surroundings.

Caffè Rivoire, Florence (▷ 220) A famous bar that was once a chocolate factory overlooking Piazza della Signoria.

Il Carlino d'Oro, San Regolo, Gaiole in Chianti (▷ 235) The essence of a simple country *trattoria*; a great place to sample great home cooking.

Zuppa di fagioli—*Tuscan bean soup*, baccalà—*salted cod* and ceci—*chickpeas (below)*

Cibreo, Florence (▷ 221) This is one of Florence's most famous restaurants, serving excellent food and wine.

La Darsena, Viareggio (▷ 230) Informal *trattoria* hidden away among the boatyards serving excellent fish and seafood.

Enoteca Pinchiorri, Florence (▷ 221) One of Italy's best known restaurants and one of the few in the country to possess three Michelin stars.

Il Falconiere, Cortona (▷ 236) Elegant, Michelin-starred restaurant in lovely surroundings.

Gambero Rosso, San Vincenzo (▷ 239) Michelin-starred fish restaurant overlooking the sea with a delightful unstuffy atmosphere.

Osteria dei Cavalieri, Pisa (▷ 229) Excellent, imaginative Tuscan food and a good wine list in the old town.

Vivoli, Florence (▷ 225) This ice cream parlour changes its flavours to suit the seasons.

The magnificent façade of Siena's Duomo

BEST CHURCHES

Duomo, Pisa (▷ 108) One of Italy's most celebrated Romanesque churches and an example of typical Pisan church architecture.

Duomo, Siena (▷ 120–123) Siena's Gothic Duomo dates from the 13th century and has a fabulous marble pavement.

Sant'Antimo, near Montalcino (▷ 129) The beautiful Romanesque church of Sant'Antimo, partly built in luminous alabaster from Volterra, has an incomparable, isolated setting.

Santa Croce, Florence (▷ 93) A Franciscan church, Santa Croce was rebuilt starting in 1294; it contains the tombs of many notable Florentine citizens and much important art.

Santa Maria Novella, Florence (▷ 95) This major Gothic church begun by the Domincans in 1246 houses some extraordinary frescoes and has a beautiful symmetrical marble façade by Alberti.

San Miniato al Monte, Florence (▷ 96) This Romanesque church dominates Florence from its position high on a hill just south of the river.

BEST LANDSCAPES

Inside Siena's Duomo (above)
Vineyards near the little town of Greve in Chianti (right)

Alpi Apuane (▷ 98) The tall, jagged mountains that rise above the Versilia coast provide some dramatic scenery; white scars left by the marble quarries are easily mistaken for snow.

Casentino (▷ 98) Chestnut woods, pine forests, pastoral meadows, isolated monasteries and little-visited towns characterize this peaceful region.

Chianti (▷ 132–133) The classic image of the Tuscan landscape with vineyards, olive groves, cypresses, crenelated towers and villas adorning rolling hills.

Crete Senese (▷ 135) A strange lunar landscape of exposed chalk cliffs to the north towards Asciano.

Mugello (▷ 110) This lovely, hilly region was popular with the powerful Reniassance family, the Medici, who built weekend retreats here; it's an excellent area for walking.

Val d'Orcia (▷ 204) The remote valley of the River Orcia in the southeastern corner of Tuscany is dominated by Monte Amiata and dotted with tiny fortified hill towns and castles.

Painted houses in the Mugello region (below)
Sunset over wooded hillsides in the Casentino (right)

THE BEST OF TUSCANY

BEST FRESCO CYCLES

Brancacci Cappella, Florence (▷ 64) The frescoes illustrating the life of St. Peter by Masaccio and Masolino are considered masterpieces that profoundly influenced the course of Florentine Renaissance art.

Cappella dei Magi, Florence (▷ 79) This tiny chapel in the Palazzo Medici-Riccardi is decorated with delightful frescoes by Benozzo Gozzoli.

Collegiata, San Gimignano (▷ 143) This church is decorated with important fresco cycles by Taddeo di Bartolo, Ghirlandaio and masters from the workshop of Simone Martini.

Duomo, Prato (▷ 110) The choir stalls of Prato's striped cathedral is decorated with beautiful frescoes by Filippino Lippi.

Monte Oliveto Maggiore, near Asciano (▷ 129) Frescoes illustrating the life of St. Benedict by Sodoma and Luca Signorelli adorn the walls of the great cloister of this monastery.

Museo Civico, Siena (▷ 116–118) Frescoes by artists of the famous Sienese school of painting: Simone Martini, Sodoma and Ambrogio Lorenzetti.

Sant'Agostino, San Gimignano (▷ 144) Scenes from the life of St. Augustine by Benozzo Gozzoli and assistants decorate the choir of this 13th-century church.

Santa Croce, Florence (▷ 93) Look out for Giotto's frescoes in the Bardi and Peruzzi chapels and Agnolo Gaddi's painting in the Sanctuary of this vast Franciscan church.

San Francesco, Arezzo (▷ 131) *The Legend of the True Cross*, by Piero della Francesca, is one of the greatest of all Italian fresco cycles.

Santa Maria Novella, Florence (▷ 95) There are a number of great frescoes in Florence's Gothic church, including cycles by Filippino Lippi, Ghirlandaio, Nardo di Cione and Andre di Buonaiuto.

The main chapel in Santa Croce, Florence's most majestic church

Fresco by Ghirlandaio in the Capella Tornabuoni in Santa Maria Novella, Florence (above)

BEST PLACES TO STAY

Antica Torre, Siena (▷ 252) Stay in a 16th-century medieval tower, with views over Siena and the hill beyond.

Albergo Pietrasanta, Pietrasanta (▷ 250) This hotel, in an elegant palace in the heart of town, makes a good base for exploring the mountains and beaches of the Versilia.

Locanda l'Elisa, Lucca (▷ 249) An elegant villa just outside Lucca, which has an excellent restaurant.

Loggiato dei Serviti, Florence (▷ 245) A beautiful hotel in an ex-convent opposite Brunelleschi's famous Ospedale.

Palazzo Ravizza, Siena (▷ 253) This comfortable and atmospheric hotel comes with a lovely garden.

Royal Victoria, Pisa (▷ 250) The style here recalls the days of the Grand Tour on the River Arno.

Scoti, Florence (▷ 247) Simple, inexpensive and friendly with a surprisingly smart location.

Tornabuoni Beacci, Florence (▷ 247) Writers and academics have been attracted to this hotel since the late 1920s.

Villa Il Poggiale, San Casciano Val di Pesa (▷ 251) A refined villa in a pretty setting with surprisingly reasonable prices.

Villa San Michele, Fiesole (▷ 248) Exclusive and luxurious hotel in an ex-monastery overlooking Florence.

The cloisters at Sant'Agostino, San Gimignano (above)
Locanda l'Elisa, Lucca (left)

Helvetia & Bristol Hotel, Florence (above)
La Cisterna Hotel, San Gimignano (left)

Living Tuscany

Sunflowers are grown as a crop in Tuscany (far left); the rolling hills of Greve in Chianti (left) and Buonconvento (right)

Ornate ironwork in Arezzo (below)

A modern statue in Montefienali (left); Helena Bonham Carter and Julian Sands in *A Room with a View* (right); scuba diving in Livorno (below left); Lago di Bilancino (bottom)

The Landscape of
Tuscany

Tuscany's beauty is matched by only a few places on Earth. The region is a natural marvel of ever-changing scenery: golden meadows of sunflowers with cypress trees on the horizon, green rolling hills, dusty grey olive groves and glistening Mediterranean waters under an azure sky. Inspiring artists and writers for centuries, no other region in Europe conjures images so evocative nor is spoken of in such terms that it can often seem like a country all of its own.

But Tuscany is more than sweeping countryside, as its villages and spectacular hilltop towns also contribute to its distinctive character. Life in rural Tuscany continues to be based on tradition and agriculture, a fact reflected in rural events, often promoting local customs or simply celebrating the region's breathtaking natural wonders.

The Fake Lake

Following the 1966 flood of the Arno (▷ 37), a plan was drawn up to build a dam that would regulate the flow of the River Sieve, one of its tributaries, and hopefully prevent a similar disaster. So the vast Lago di Bilancino, a few kilometres outside the town of Barberino di Mugello, was created. The lake is just over 31m (100ft) at its deepest point with a total surface area of 5sq km (1.95sq miles). For many Tuscans it has become a popular alternative to going to the coast. Indeed, this artificial seaside has numerous sandy beaches and a variety of water sports. It's also a must for birdwatchers—the lake forms a large part of the World Wildlife Fund's Gabbianello Nature Reserve, which is directly on the migration route between Europe and Africa.

Towns like Arezzo (above) and Anghiari (below) are a feature of the landscape

The Maremma national park (above)
A farm outside San Gimignano (right)

In Bloom

Tuscany may be famed for its wine-making and olive oil production, but few realise that the cultivation of flowers accounts for approximately 30 per cent of saleable agricultural production in the region, 15 per cent of national production and 6 per cent of all EU production. Around 4,700 companies are devoted to this blooming industry, most of which are based in and around Pistoia, 'the city of plants in the land of gardens'. Pistoia's flower growing pedigree was rewarded when it was chosen to represent Italy at Floriade 2002, the world's most important flower show, held in the Netherlands once every ten years. Plans are underway to establish a Denomination of Protected Flowers for Pistoia. This EU award recognizes the flowers' origins and quality, and the town eventually hopes to secure the prestigious title of European Capital of Flower Growing.

On Location

Film-makers have long been enchanted by Tuscany. But it was the huge success of James Ivory's *A Room with a View* (1985) that catapulted the area to stardom. In the 1990s Tuscany almost became as common a location on the silver screen as Manhattan or Hollywood. One of the latest releases set against this gorgeous backdrop is Audrey Wells' *Under the Tuscan Sun*, adapted from Frances Mayes' bestseller and shot in the hills of Cortona. Now, in recognition of Tuscany's influence on the world of cinema, the Florence City Council has created *Firenze tra cinema e ville* (Florence as seen through cinema and villas), a series of screenings of films set in the region. Appropriately for such a celebration of Tuscany's landscape, each screening takes place in one of the area's grandiose villas, where a seminar discussing the location follows each movie showing.

A Village Restored

If pieces of art and even entire villas can be completely restored, then why not a whole village? This is exactly what happened in Borgo Montefienali, a small village in the borough of Gaiole in Chianti. The tiny hamlet sat abandoned and forgotten for more than 45 years, until a palace owned by the Albizi family, a rich and powerful Renaissance family, was discovered. The entire village was given a makeover by Germana Costruizioni, a Tuscan specialist construction company that had already given a new lease of life to several similarly derelict villages in Siena, Castellina in Chianti and Barberino Val d'Elsa. An inauguration ceremony was held for Montefienali's official rebirth, a ceremony that included the symbolic delivery of keys to the owners of each property.

Burnt Siena

The Sienese countryside has provided more for painters than just inspiration. The town's buildings and surrounding fields are distinctive for their orange and red tones, which are at their best in the autumn, when the ploughed fields reveal a warm brown palette, baked by the sun. This earth is the origin of the painting pigment burnt Siena, which is taken from the very soil of the area, *terre di Siena*. A mixture of iron oxide and clay, it was one of the first paint pigments to be used by man and is found in many cave paintings. The Renaissance painters found it the best medium to translate the warmth of the Tuscan landscape onto canvas. These days, you won't find real earth in the paint, but its name and colour will always conjure images of Tuscany.

One of the *contrades*, or neighbourhoods, getting ready for Siena's *Palio* (left)

Keeping up with the news (left)

Enjoying a night out in Siena (above and left)

The Culture of Tuscany

Tuscans are among Italy's greatest individualists, proud of their region and its traditions. They consider themselves Tuscans first, Italians second. This strong feeling of regionalism, felt by most Italians, is known as *campanilismo*. The word derives from campanile, or bell tower, meaning that everything of significance happens within the sound of the bells of your local church. It is loyalty to the region, not country, that is important. Tuscans refuse to be influenced by the trends that are closely followed by the rest of Italy. As a consequence, Tuscany's cultural and artistic output in the fields of cinema, music and entertainment often reflect an individual attitude.

However, this does not mean the region has abandoned what went before, and often events or institutions combine modernity with tradition—the Chianti League, for example. Tuscany continues to respect and draw on its cultural independence, its history, its beauty, and its position as an important focus for art, study, business, fashion and tourism.

The Italian national flag (above left)
There is still much respect for traditional ways of life, especially in agriculture (right)

Capital of Culture
The city of Florence is considering a bid for the title of European Capital of Culture for the year 2008. Having witnessed the cultural success and economic benefits the award has bestowed upon other Italian cities (Bologna in 2000, Genoa in 2004), Florence feels it too is worthy of this proud recognition. The proposal was launched in June 2004 by the city council in conjunction with a local cultural-political newspaper, *Rosso Fiorentino*. A previous bid failed in 1986, but Florence now feels the timing is right, and that the ambitious City of Galileo project—an initiative underway to promote the city as Europe's most important scientific and museum centre—will swing votes their way.

CONSORZIO DEL MARCHIO STORICO · CHIANTI CLASSICO ·

A Chianti road sign (left)
The old quarter in Livorno
celebrating a festival (below)

Florence, city of culture
and nightlife (right)
Martina Stella (far right)

Chianti's League

The Chianti League is a promotional association designed to celebrate the history, culture and natural beauty of the region. It was set up in 1384 and was originally intended to settle disputes between Florence and Siena. The new association closely resembles its 14th-century counterpart. The league's head, known as the Capitano Generale, presides over its members, each of whom wears a special hand-sewn robe and hat—red for those who live in the Chianti region, yellow for those who come from outside. Upon entering the league, members must partake in a swearing-in ceremony, promising 'to love nature, to give my life religious motivation, to see the world with optimism and love.' Unsurprisingly, one of the League's principal activities involves the promotion and cultivation of the region's world-famous wine.

Seven-Day Party People

Alessandro Palma has been a model, PR consultant and even insurance clerk, but he now makes a living having fun—or rather, making sure other people do. Palma is the founder of a travel agency (Sotto la Palma, or Under the Palm) that arranges private events throughout Tuscany and trips around the world, which he describes as 'a seven-day-long party'. Palma is also artistic director at several of the region's hottest clubs, and he still finds time to promote special evenings at many other venues. But Palma believes the public is becoming increasingly hard to impress. 'There has to be some kind of spectacle with real artists and musicians,' he says. 'I think in the future we'll see a return to live music. People are no longer satisfied by a single DJ standing behind a turntable.'

Toscana Pride

Tuscany has created its own manifesto for sexual equality. Toscana Pride is organized by Pride Nazionale GLBT (Gay, Lesbian, Bisexual and Transsexual) and celebrates 'the right to be different, because to be different is every citizen's right.' For two weeks in June a variety of events, including debates, concerts and cinema screenings, take place in Florence, Lucca and Pistoia. The 2004 festival saw a deliberate effort to expand the promotion of gay pride away from the major cities and into Tuscany's provinces, where the main focus of the event was Grosseto, one of the region's lesser known towns. The finale, 'Rainbow Party', featured a rare performance by Patty Pravo, the legendary Italian singer of the 1960s and gay icon.

A Stella is Born

Even the region's actresses have a certain Tuscan attitude for independence. Martina Stella was born in Florence in 1984, and made her film debut in 2001's *L'Ultimo Bacio* (The Last Kiss), in which she plays a schoolgirl who begins an ill-judged affair with an older man. The film won a handful of David di Donatellas (the Italian equivalent of Oscars) and an audience award at the US Sundance Film Festival 2002. Since that performance, young Stella has successfully shifted between cinema, theatre and television with effortless grace. Now, with 2004's hit TV wartime drama *Le Stagioni del Cuore* (The Seasons of the Heart) behind her, she's planning to go from strength to strength. 'I come from a family of women,' she says by way of explanation. 'All the men have either died, run off or been kicked out.'

THE CULTURE OF TUSCANY 15

Design in all forms, with
ceramics from Tinacci Tito & M. Grazia's
store in San Gimignano (above middle)

A window display
at the Roberto
Cavalli store in
Florence (right)

Tuscan Style

Italy has always been synonymous with style, and even
though you might think of Milan or Rome first, Tuscany
contributes in its own way. Style can be traced back to the
Etruscans, who were pioneers in the ceramic arts. By the
Renaissance, Florence was making great developments in
paper and textiles, creating many designs and techniques that
are still used today. It was perhaps inevitable that an Italian
fashion revolution should take place in Tuscany: Florence
hosted Italy's earliest fashion shows in the 1950s, and
innovative designers Salvatore Ferragamo,
Guccio Gucci and Emilio Pucci made
their fortunes within the city's
medieval palaces. The city
becomes the fashion world's
focus twice a year during Pitti
Immagine week, and today's
youngest designers and
manufacturers continue
to take inspiration from the
region's rich heritage and
knack for originality. Meanwhile
Tuscany's crafts, such as pottery,
continue to thrive thanks to their
popularity with visitors and the
hard work of local artisans.

Fashion is at the forefront of
Tuscan style

I Feel Pitti

On 12 February
1951, Giovanni
Battista Giorgini
created the modern
notion of Italian fashion
overnight. During a party
in the ballroom of his
home on Florence's Via
dei Serragli, Italian ladies'
outfits were presented
to select buyers and
journalists. An instant
success, it was the first
fashion show of its kind
in Italy, and in 1952
the event moved to
the Palazzo Pitti, where
over the next 30 years
it helped catapult many
Italian names to global
stardom. Since 1982
the bi-annual event
has taken place at the
Fortezza di Basso trade
complex, yet retains its
Pitti name. The 2004
summer Pitti Immagine
fair while showcasing
new brands and design-
ers, also featured a
homage to Salvador Dalí,
a video installation by
Anglo-Nigerian designer
Ozwald Boateng, exhibits
dedicated to film-maker
Wim Wenders, and pho-
tographs published in
Vogue Sport.

A young girl takes part in the 2004 Pitti Immagine (left); mopeds are part of the style package (above); designer marbled paper from Florence (below)

Italian Stallion

Where can you find cowhide in Florence? The answer: Roberto Cavalli. Florence's most celebrated contemporary designer, Cavalli first found success in the 1960s when he patented a process for printing on leather. He's now a leading player in fashion circles, and leather continues to dominate his designs for jackets, bags, trousers and shoes, but he believes it shouldn't be considered a precious material. 'Don't be afraid to ruin it or scratch it,' he says. 'Leather is much nicer with a vintage look.' Cavalli's flagship store is on the corner of Via Tornabuoni, with the adjacent café incorporating calfskin stools. The Spring 2004 collection featured one of the designer's hobbies—horseback riding. Which is perhaps unsurprising, given that *cavalli* is the Italian word for 'horses'.

Tuscan Textiles

Embroidery has been a Tuscan craft ever since the times of the *barulli* (peddlers), who would journey around the region selling cloths and fabrics from door to door, carried on their shoulders or with the help of a mule. The textiles left to the peasant wives would then be converted into elegant tablecloths, sheets and towels for the local gentry. The owners of the Gallianino shop in the tiny village of Galliano claim to have real *barulli* amongst their ancestors. They also have the most renowned laceworks in the region and continue to produce the same quality cloths and linens. Today the seamstresses of Galliano still travel throughout the Mugello area to each of the region's weekly markets, giving the people of other local towns the opportunity to take home an original piece of Gallianino embroidery.

Pots of Style

Though for centuries an important craft in the region, Tuscan-style ceramic works are becoming increasingly hard to find. You have to know where to look. On the road between Borgo San Lorenzo and Ronta in the Mugello valley, the Ceramiche Franco Pecchioli workshop is one of the few remaining places where you can witness the craftsmanship necessary to create authentic Tuscan ceramics. Here, Vieri Chinis and his sons, Cosimo and Mattia, produce home furnishings, plates and vases using traditional firing methods and decorated in blues, greens and yellows. Many original Chini pieces are on display in the Villa Pecori Giraldi museum in Borgo San Lorenzo. It was perhaps inevitable that the Chinis should adopt this craft, as they are descendants of Galileo Chini: painter, ceramicist and an exponent of Italy's art nouveau movement in the early 1900s.

The Paper Makers

The production of paper has been a skill since the rule of the Medicis. Now, there are many traditional Florentine paper stores across the region, as well as innumerable market sellers offering decorative notebooks and writing paper. Each claims to be a Florentine original, but one shop continues to leave all others in its wake: the Giannini Giulio & Figlio store in Piazza Pitti. The Giannini family has been creating paper products since 1856. Their leather-bound diaries are hand-sewn, their address books are marbled, and their classic Florentine correspondence paper (where each leaf of the paper's decorative motif is echoed in the matching envelope) continues to outsell the rest. And in this age of email there's still no greater pleasure than receiving a hand-written letter on a sheet of Giannini's writing paper.

Stopping for lunch in Siena (below)

Montepulciano is famed for its wine (above and right)

A *Taste of* Tuscany

Italian food holds a special place in the hearts of millions around the world, and many of the dishes originate from Tuscany. Tuscan cuisine is often praised for its rural simplicity and the use of the finest, freshest ingredients. The key, however, to a dish's success lies in its olive oil. With miles of dry olive groves, Tuscany is the leading region in Italy's olive oil production, and the area's perfect growing conditions also mean an abundance of fruit and vegetables. The Tuscans are jokingly called 'bean-eaters' by other Italians, a reference to their indifference to pasta dishes and preference for pulse-based soups and stews. But many Tuscan delicacies, including an enormous range of cheeses and cured meats, are known throughout the country and proudly celebrated around the region. And that's without even mentioning the wine: While a Tuscan meal in itself can be an unforgettable experience, don't miss the chance to wash it down with a bottle of vintage Chianti.

Tips for Tripe

Historian Leo Coducci spoke of 'the refinement of tripe', or *trippa*, and though tripe may no longer feature heavily in the diets of many, Florentines continue to devour it with gusto. Not only is tripe an important ingredient on the menu of Florence's restaurants, it is also sold by outdoor vendors, satisfying everyone from children in need of an after-school snack to hungry workers on their lunch break. The pale dish is displayed on a bed of cheesecloth. You can buy a single portion, prepared simply with oil, salt, pepper and garlic, although the classic recipe for *trippa alla fiorentina* involves cooking the tripe before adding it to a rich tomato sauce.

Chestnuts (above)
Cappuccino (right)

Honey from Lucca
(above)

Cantuccini biscuits
(below)

Panforte, a typical Sienese
product (above)
Ice cream in Florence
(right)
Pecorino from Acciaiolo
(below)

Etruscan Sacrifice

Chiusi was a thriving town during the time of the Etruscans. Today the people of Chiusi may not have much in common with their ancestors—except when it comes to food, certain gastronomic traditions are not easily forgotten. Take the recipe and special preparation of *brustico*. *Brustico*, meaning roasted, is an ancient fish dish directly derived from an Etruscan recipe. Small fish, usually rudd, pike or perch, are cooked on a grill (which, for the Etruscans, would have been the sacrificial altar) over a fire of reeds from the nearby lake. After being fully roasted, the darkened fish are scaled, seasoned and drizzled in olive oil, before being washed down with a complimenting dry white wine. And in keeping with Etruscan conventions, the fish is always eaten with the fingers.

The Cream of Tuscany

Many Florentines claim that ice cream was the brainchild of Ruggeri, chef to Catherine de' Medici (1519–89) and the world's first professional ice cream maker. So Florence is probably the ideal place to learn more about this fine art. Gelati Fantasiosi is an ice cream making course that is held from time to time at Cordon Bleu, a prestigious school of culinary art on a tiny Florence side street. During the afternoon lessons, ice cream expert Palmiro Bruschi demonstrates the preparation of a variety of ice creams inspired by the tastes of the region; evening classes teach the delicate marrying of flavours in combination with a whole meal. Students learn from the best, as Bruschi knows his sorbet from his *semi-freddo* (semi-frozen dessert). He owns the famous Ghignoni *gelateria* in Sansepolcro and is a member of the Italian Ice Cream Academy.

The Bread Tree

Over the centuries chestnuts were an irreplaceable source of food for many Tuscans, to such an extent that the chestnut tree was known as 'the bread tree', since the nut's flour was used to prepare bread, pasta and polenta. Today Tuscany is still home to some of Italy's largest chestnut groves. The best chestnuts, including the Amiata from the provinces of Siena and Grosseto, and the Mugello Marron, are sold and eaten boiled or roasted, while the smaller ones become flour. The flour-making process takes place in a stone building, where on the lower floor a chestnut wood fire is kept slowly burning, over which the chestnuts are dried on a mat upstairs for around 30 days. The chestnuts are then roasted for a further 10 hours, before being stone-milled and sieved into flour, which is the best product to make *Castagnaccio Toscano*, a Tuscan chestnut cake.

Loyal to their Oil

Not only is olive oil a vital ingredient for all Tuscan cooking, it is also appreciated in its purest form. Olive oil sampling sessions are now almost as common as the more renowned meetings for wine. Experts can distinguish between brands and their types, such as *extra vergine* (extra virgin) or *delicato* (a finer extra virgin), as easily as a wine connoisseur can separate Brunello from Barolo. Strict procedures are followed at such tastings. First, the palate must be cleansed with apple. Then the oil is poured into a dark container (so the taster is not influenced by its colour) warmed in the hands and gently swirled to release its full aroma and subtle flavours. Eventually, the delicate qualities of the oil are savoured in small sips.

Postcards for sale in Florence (below)

Taking a break on a visit to Tuscany (above, below left); Ponte Vecchio (below)

A sculpture in the Parco di Pinocchio, a popular place to visit (right)
A poster for the Lippi/Botticelli exhibition (below right)

Botticelli
Filippino

Tuscany and Tourism

More than 10 million visitors descend on Tuscany every year in search of culture and history—especially that of the Renaissance. Florence in particular recognizes the importance of its most celebrated epoch. It now devotes itself to the preservation and promotion of Renaissance masterpieces, often at the expense of the growth of the modern city—for example, an underground metro system was shelved in the 1980s when excavators kept unearthing priceless pieces of art. Although the region has been cunning in exploiting its number one industry, many Tuscans feel it is ill-equipped to deal with the endless flow of visitors, as the resulting over-crowded cities and traffic-clogged streets testify. Florence has become one of the most expensive cities in Italy, and many Florentines lament the commercialization of their town and its surroundings, fearing it will soon resemble a Renaissance theme park, with Michelangelo's *David* as its mascot.

The Weight of Love

Anyone passing over Florence's Ponte Vecchio in recent years will have noticed a mass of pad-locks tied to two metal cables projecting from the bridge into the River Arno. This tradition was originated by military academy students who left the padlocks of their lockers on the bridge on finishing their course. The rite soon grew popu-lar with young lovers, who fastened a padlock to the cables before tossing the keys into the Arno as a gesture of everlasting love—much like the Etruscans, who threw amulets into the river. This custom was soon adopted by visitors to Florence. That was until it became apparent that the weight of the padlocks was damaging the cables and putting stress on the bridge. Fearing an overload on St. Valentine's Day, on 13 February 2004 the municipal police removed the padlocks, much to the dismay of romantics, as they will have to find another way to pledge their devotion.

Botticelli's Blockbuster

A major exhibition of the work of Filippino Lippi (1406–69) was organized in Florence to commemorate the fifth centenary of his death. But it was the far more popular Sandro Botticelli (1445–1510), his friend and teacher, who stole the show. It was Botticelli who appeared on the banners and posters all over the city, and even on the carriages of the intercity trains. Filippino continued to play a sup-porting role inside the magnificent Palazzo Strozzi, where the art-works were displayed: Just 16 of his paintings, compared to 26 of Botticelli's, were on show. The pulling power of a big-name Renaissance artist was the bankable option and the event was a huge success, as more than 30,000 tickets were sold before it even opened.

Restorer Cinzia Parnigoni at work on Michelangelo's
statue *David* (above)
Too Much Tuscan Sun gives one local's view (left)

Castagno's Confessions

Many writers throughout history have recounted the trials and tribulations they faced when visiting Tuscany. Native Dario Castagno decided to reverse this trend by reporting events from the viewpoint of a resident. Castagno is perhaps in a better position than most to comment on the attitude of tourists to Tuscany, having worked as a tour guide for more than 12 years. Entitled *Too Much Tuscan Sun: Confessions Of A Chianti Tour Guide*, the anecdotal book affectionately pokes fun at the cultural differences between Italians, Americans and the British. On sale in 250 stores throughout Tuscany and in English-language bookshops in Italy's major cities, the book has also been published in the UK and US, and the film rights have already been sold.

David's Dusting

Michelangelo's statue *David* has had an eventful life. The figure's toe was accidentally chiselled off with a hammer, it lost an arm when a chair was thrown by rioters, and it has been struck by lightning. In 2004 the statue underwent restoration to celebrate 500 years as Western art's most revered male beauty. But the work was hampered by controversy, resulting in the chief restorer storming out after an argument over techniques. Her replacement, Cinzia Parnigoni, confessed to being daunted by the responsibility. 'Sometimes it was hard to find the inner strength,' she admitted at the unveiling of the new and improved *David*. Yet she confounded critics who felt she wasn't up to the task. 'The doubts and second thoughts weren't so much to do with technique,' Parnigoni explained, 'as with having to measure up to Michelangelo.'

The British Experience

Tuscany is one of Europe's most popular destinations for people who want to study abroad. But many students are tired of the classroom atmosphere, and wish to learn in a more informal setting. The region is teeming with schools designed especially for visitors, and the British Institute of Florence is the leader in this field. Originally founded in 1917 to improve cultural relations between the UK and Tuscany, 'il British' offers the study of the Italian language and even more popular study courses and social events. After all, why sit behind a desk when you can cook in a Tuscan kitchen, learn to sing opera, understand fresco painting or create your own masterpiece in a Tuscan meadow? Ironically, as increasing numbers of students come to Tuscany, more and more Italian graduates are seeking their fortune abroad, a trend that could have serious consequences for the country's economy.

Tuscany has courses on everything from windsurfing to drawing (above, below)

Two teams battle for possession of the ball during the *Calcio Storico* (below); the opening of *Calcio Storico* (right)

Fiorentina, in purple, against Sampdoria in a Serie A match (right)

People's Passion

In Italy *calcio*, or soccer, is a national obsession, built on local pride and sporting fervour. Nowhere is this more apparent than in Tuscany, where a prevailing sense of regionalism means that support for its teams is particularly intense. Yet the Florentines were for many years the only fans with anything to shout about. Famous for their purple strip, Fiorentina is the only Tuscan club to have achieved any kind of success. But Fiorentina (or La Viola, the team's new nickname) has suffered a turbulent recent history, and smaller Tuscan teams have started to make an impact. Despite the relegation of Empoli, the top flight survival of Siena, promotion of Livorno and last-gasp return of Fiorentina means that for the first time since 1987 Tuscany was represented by three different cities in 2004 Serie A championship, a feat matched only by the northern giants of Lombardy. It was a proud moment for the region, but when the Tuscan sides meet, expect one or two medieval feuds to resurface on the soccer pitch.

Tod's Team

In the late 1990s Fiorentina was doing well in European soccer. But in 2001 it was discovered that team president Vittorio Cecchi Gori had been using the club's money for his own business ventures. Fiorentina was banished to Serie C2 (Italy's lowest professional division) and forced to start the 2002 season with the new name of Fiorentia Viola 1926. After gaining promotion to C1, in summer 2003 La Viola was pulled up a further division after a shake-up in the league system. Under the patronage of Tod's shoes mogul Diego Della Valle, Fiorentina won back its original name. In June 2004 Fiorentina beat Perugia in a play-off to regain its place in Serie A. La Viola is the only team in history to go from the first to the fourth division and back in two years.

The Roots of the Game

As early as the 16th century Florence had developed its own version of *calcio*. Groups of aristocrats and youths chased a ball and each other around the squares of Florence. This medieval scene is recreated by the Florentines every summer in a sand-covered Piazza Santa Croce in *Calcio Storico* (Soccer in Costume). Players are selected as early as Easter, and four teams of 27 players (all in historical dress) take part, each side representing a different area of the city. Before each game a formal procession parades from Santa Maria Novella to Santa Croce, where a flag-throwing display then precedes the main event. But some traditions have been abandoned: the decapitated head has been replaced by a ball.

The Story of Tuscany

The Birth of a Region

Tuscany was first settled on a large scale by tribes from present-day Emilia-Romagna in the 10th century BC. It was then inhabited by the Etruscans, a mixture of indigenous peoples and settlers from Greece and Asia Minor. They established many settlements that exist to this day, notably Fiesole, Arezzo, Cortona and Volterra, where extensive tombs, statues and jewellery bear witness to their passing. The Etruscans were overrun by the Romans, who consolidated the original towns and founded new ones—Florence being the most famous.

After the fall of Rome in 410AD, the region was subject to a series of invasions from the north, culminating in the arrival of Charlemagne, the leader of the Franks, in 774AD. Tuscany then became part of the Franks' Carolingian Empire, later the Holy Roman Empire, but was increasingly ruled on behalf of Charlemagne's northern-based emperors by a succession of Lucca-based princes known as the margraves. In time, the margraves became more independent, transferring their allegiance from the distant emperors in Lucca to the popes in Rome. This allowed the emergence of some of the towns and city states, such as Siena, Pisa and Florence, that would grow rich through trade and banking, and which would dominate Tuscan and Italian history for some 500 years.

The Defeat of Fiesole

By 283BC Fiesole was under the control of Rome, but until 60BC it continued to enjoy relative independence. In that year, according to legend, a spirited fugitive and renegade soldier, Cataline, assumed control of the town. Rome dispatched a force under General Fiorino to dislodge the upstart. The general decided against a frontal attack on the hilltop town, the position bequeathed it by its Etruscan founders. Instead, he chose to starve the inhabitants into submission from a nearby base on the Arno—present-day Florence. Fiorino's tactics won the day, though Cataline escaped, eventually being defeated near Pistoia in 62BC. Fiorino's fate is less clear. Some say he died in a raid on his camp, others that he never existed.

A fresco at the abbey of Sant'Antimo in Montalcino, said to have been founded by Charlemagne in the 8th century

Charlemagne (742–814), Holy Roman Emperor

900BC

An Etruscan bronze chimera found in Arezzo

Roman remains at Volterra (right)

What's in a Name?

It's one of Europe's most celebrated cities, but nobody knows how Florence (Firenze) came by its name. Some claim it derives from Fiorino, the Roman commander sent to subdue Fiesole in the 1st century (see The Defeat of Fiesole). Others say that it comes from *fluentia*, either after the River Arno that 'flows' through the city, or the 'confluence' of the Arno and nearby Mugnone river. Many see its origin in the word flowers (*fiori* in Italian), and in particular the *giaggiolo*, or *Iris florentia*, a purple iris that grows in the hills around Florence. The flower is still the symbol of the city and of the Virgin Mary, and the cathedral's formal name is Santa Maria del Fiore.

Acius and Senius

The She-Wolf was the mythical creature that suckled the twins Romulus and Remus, legendary founders of Rome. But why is this same She-Wolf, along with the suckling twins, depicted so often in the statues and paintings around Siena? The answer is overlapping myth, for the Sienese took the story of Romulus and Remus one stage further. Apparently the brothers could not agree on a name for their settlement, and after one dispute Remus was killed by Romulus, whose choose Roma as the name. Remus had two sons, Senius and Acius, who went forth from the city to found a settlement of their own, a place which took the name of the former: Senius, hence Siena.

The Move to Florence

Tuscany's 10th-century rulers, the margraves, were originally based in Lucca, but in 978 the widow of the Margrave Uberto, Willa, founded the Benedictine Badia Fiorentina in Florence in honour of her husband. Willa's son, the Margrave Ugo, shared her fondness for the city and he transferred the region's capital to Florence in 1001. He also continued the story of the Badia, endowing it in the wake of a vision in which he saw 'black and deformed men…damned souls all' and was informed that his own soul was similarly damned unless he repent it. Repent he did, selling many of his lands and funding the Badia, an institution that would become Florence's focal point for centuries. Its bell tolled the divisions of the city's day and its cells housed one of its first hospitals.

The Price of a Port

The story of the Leaning Tower of Pisa reflects the story of the city itself. The tower was started in 1173, and such an expensive project was contemplated thanks to the city's considerable wealth, the result of its port and the maritime trade it allowed. Many of the motifs and architectural ideas on the tower reflect the breadth of this trade and the scope of Pisa's empire, which embraced Corsica, Sardinia and the Balearic Islands. But the fact that the tower started to lean almost from the moment it was begun was a hint of Pisa's fate. The lean was caused by the area's sandy subsoil, created when an area is under or close to the sea. Pisa's port eventually silted up, and the city—tower and all—eventually fell to Florence.

The myth of Romulus and Remus (left) developed into the story of Acius and Senius Florence's coat of arms (right)

1207

Florence was founded by the Romans (right) Abbey of Sant'Antimo in Montalcino (far right)

Richly carved Romanesque font in San Frediano, Lucca (left); Etruscan necropolis on the Tyrrhenian coast (below)

Etruscan plate from the museum in Chiusi (above)

An Age of Trade and Conflict

The 13th century was the start of Florence and Tuscany's golden age, a period that laid the foundations of its artistic, cultural and economic supremacy. Florence's prosperity was founded primarily on textiles, and on wool in particular, that in turn encouraged the development of banking and other industries. As trade blossomed, so the city developed a system of guilds, or *arti*, the leading lights of which often rose to positions of administrative power. Wealth and power inevitably lead to conflict, both between individuals and rival banking families, but also between supporters of the two major powers of the day: the papacy and Charlemagne's imperial descendants, known as the Holy Roman emperors. Supporters of the pope were Guelphs and supporters of the emperors were Ghibellines.

Florence was not alone in its success, nor in the benefits and problems it created. Towns across Tuscany and beyond evolved into dynamic and independent city states, bolstered by trade and able to flourish in the power vacuum created by the weakness of the papacy and the emperors. As the prosperity of cities such as Pisa, Lucca and Siena increased, so the cities and their citizens wished to make conspicuous displays of their new wealth. As a result, both the cities' ruling councils *(comunes)* and rich individuals began to commission works of art from ever-more sophisticated and adventurous artists.

Florence's Florin

Banking was one of the pillars of the Florentine economy, the business that made the Medici and other families their fortunes. But before banking and trade could flourish, a stable and trustworthy currency was required. In 1252 the Florentines created the gold *fiorino*, or florin, a coin that bore the likeness of St. John the Baptist (the city's patron saint) on one face and the city's name, Florentia, and a fleur-de-lis floral symbol on the other. To prevent the coinage becoming debased, high standards were applied at the city's mint. By the 15th century, when the coin was accepted across Europe, some two million had been minted.

Towns like Colle were part of the Guelphs/Ghibellines struggle (left); a gold florin from 1252 (right)

1208

Poster announcing the Giostra del Saracino, held in Arezzo (right) Wall relief on Orsanmichele (below) of the *arti* at work

Detail of *Dante and his Worlds* by Domenico di Michelino in the Duomo in Florence (above)

A Way with Wool

During the 12th and 13th centuries, groups of Benedictine monks from Lombardy in northern Italy began to move south to Florence. The Umiliati, as they were known, were skilled in the weaving of woollen cloth, and Florence had all that was needed for a thriving textile industry. They settled first on the banks of the River Arno, whose water they used to wash and rinse finished cloth. In time they became a mainstay of the district, and in 1256 founded a church in the area, Ognissanti, which survives to this day. It was the start of an industry that was soon employing 30,000 people, a third of the city's population, and which processed raw wool imported from as far afield as northern England. The monks became so wealthy that they were able to commission Giotto's great *Maestà* altarpiece for their church, now in the Uffizi.

Dubious Duties

St. Francis had encouraged peaceful principles in his followers. But this didn't stop 13th-century Franciscans of Florence, who were based in the church of Santa Croce, from taking over the duties of the feared papal Inquisition in 1254. The Dominicans proved equally zealous, making a pun of their name—*domines canes*, or the hounds of the Lord—to underline their dogged determination in matters of doctrine. Two armed friars would roam the city in the company of a lawyer, hunting down heretics. Confessions were often extracted with torture, and those found guilty could be fined or burned at the stake. One third of the fines went to the papacy and Inquisition, one third to the city (the money was used to build the walls) and one third towards the building and upkeep of Santa Croce and Santa Maria Novella, the Dominicans' church in Florence.

A Conflict in Black and White

Factions and conflicts were a way of life in Tuscan cities. All it took in Pistoia to create bloody discord, for example, was an accident. A child, so the story goes, was sent by his parents to apologize for hurting his friend while playing with a sword. The friend's father chopped off the child's hand, saying 'Iron, not words, is the remedy for sword wounds.' The punishment immediately divided Pistoia into rival camps—the Neri and Bianchi (the Black and White), the ancestral names of the families concerned. The same names were eventually taken up by different factions of Florence's ruling papal, or Guelph supporters. Dante, for example, was a White sympathiser, and the power of the rival Black faction one of the reasons he was exiled from Florence in 1302.

A Saint's Life

Santa Fina, one of San Gimignano's much-loved patron saints, led a strange life, even by the standards of medieval saints. Born in the village in 1238, she was only 10 when she vehemently repented her sins after contracting a serious illness. One of her worst transgressions had been to accept an orange from a boy. She passed the next five years on a wooden board awaiting her death, which had been announced to her by St. Gregory in a vision. At the same time she worked the miracles that would bring her sainthood: She restored a choirboy's sight, healed her nurse's paralyzed hand and caused angels to ring the bells of the cathedral. At her death, violets blossomed from her board and flowers sprang from the walls of San Gimignano's towers.

The poet Dante (1265–1321) was born in Florence and there are a number of images of him across the city (right)

1305

Coats of arms of the Republic of Florence outside the Palazzo Vecchio (above)

Codex in Santa Croce (above); detail from Pisa's Duomo pulpit (right); mosiac in San Miniato al Monte in Florence from 1297 (far right)

The Rise of the Medici

Life in medieval Tuscany was often turbulent, and never more so than in the 14th century, when the continued prosperity enjoyed by cities and the artistic and cultural awakening of the period were tempered by catastrophes such as the collapse of major Florentine banks like the Peruzzi and Bardi in 1339, and the Black Death in 1348. Civic unrest also continued to be a problem, and it was against this background that the Medici, in the shape of the dynasty's founding father, Giovanni di Bicci de' Medici (1360–1429), first began to make their presence felt.

It was also in this period that the process of artistic and other cultural change gathered pace as new artists built on the work of early innovators such as Cimabue and Giotto di Bondone in Florence, and Duccio and Simone Martini in Siena. Painters, writers and scholars such as Donatello and Piero della Francesca began to make Florence their home. One of the wealthiest cities in the known world, it was a sophisticated and cosmopolitan place in which a freethinking and febrile atmosphere fostered creativity and innovation.

Statue of the painter Giotto
(c1267–1337) in the main square in
Vicchio in the Mugello region (left)

1306

Law and Order

As Tuscan city states became more sophisticated they made attempts to rule and regulate themselves. Florence's approach, based on a written constitution, was typical. Names of selected guild members were drawn from eight leather bags every two months (the short time span was designed to prevent their power becoming entrenched). The nine men drawn become Priori, or Signori, and formed a government called the Signoria. They consulted numerous committees and other elected councils, and had to take heed of permanent officials such as the Podestà, a chief magistrate brought in from outside to guarantee his impartiality. During their period of office, the members of the Signoria were kept virtual prisoners, but were waited on hand and foot, and kept entertained by a professional joke-teller, the Buffone.

Cosimo de' Medici

Cosimo de' Medici (1389–1464), also known as Cosimo il Vecchio (Cosimo the Elder), was the man whose business sense and political acumen laid the foundations for more than 300 years of Medici dominance in Tuscany. Cosimo's father, Giovanni, had built up a textile and banking business from the humble beginnings of just two wool workshops, but Cosimo increased the family fortune tenfold. At the same time he was careful to avoid ostentation and overt political interference, knowing that his powerful rivals could destroy him at any time. Yet he also gave considerable amounts to charity and commissioned numerous works of art and buildings. Pope Pius II would describe him as 'master of the country' and 'king in everything but name'.

The Black Death

The Black Death arrived in Italy in 1347 or early 1348. In Florence, the plague inspired Giovanni Boccaccio (1313–75), a merchant, man of letters and diplomat, to write the *Decameron*, a masterpiece of medieval European literature. It begins in the Cappella di Filippo Strozzi in the city's church of Santa Maria Novella. Here, one Tuesday after Mass, seven ladies decide to leave the plague-ravaged city for the safety of the countryside to 'hear the birds sing, and see the green hills, and the plains and the fields covered with grain.' Over 10 days they would tell the 100 stories that form the basis of Boccaccio's literary monument to 'the most deadly pestilence, which, either because of the movement of the heavenly bodies or because of our sinful deeds provoked the righteous wrath of God.'

The Baptistery Doors

The Renaissance had no distinct beginning. Rather it was a gradual process of cultural evolution that spanned at least two centuries. Many commentators, however, have identified the year of 1401 as the moment that it finally burst into life. This was the year that a competition was announced in Florence to design the doors for the Baptistery. The judges could not decide between the entries of two young goldsmiths, Filippo Brunelleschi and Lorenzo Ghiberti. Asked to collaborate, the pair fell out: Brunelleschi went off to Rome in a sulk, but would eventually design Florence's great cathedral dome, while Ghiberti remained to work on the project, a task that would take almost 25 years and produce one of the masterpieces of the Florentine Renaissance.

Baptisms and Birthrate

The Annunciation—the announcement of the Incarnation to the Virgin by the angel Gabriel—was long a popular subject for Florentine painters, not least because the Feast of the Annunciation (March 25) marked New Year's Day in the old Florentine calendar. It was also the day on which a mass-baptism of children born each year in Florence took place in the city's Baptistery. When a child was born, a counter was placed in an urn in the Baptistery—black for a boy, white for a girl—and the data recorded. By this means, historians have been able to calculate that the average birthrate in Florence during the 14th century was about 6,000 births annually out of a city population of 90,000.

Cosimo de' Medici, who built on his father's work to establish the Medici as a political and financial dynasty

Medal of Pius II, born in Pienza in 1405 and who drew up plans to redevelop the entire town

1434

Andrea Pisano's south doors (1336) on Florence's Baptistery (above); the Florentine Lion, with the city's coat of arms (far left); a reproduction of *The Triumph of Death* at Pisa, painted in the wake of the Black Death (left)

Detail of one of the bronze panels of the Gates of Paradise at the Baptistery in Florence. It was made by Lorenzo Ghiberti and the original is now in the Museo dell'Opera del Duomo

The Golden Age

Cosimo de' Medici's son, Piero de' Medici (1416–69), enjoyed a brief period in the Florentine limelight, a prelude to the arrival of the most famous of the Medici: Lorenzo de' Medici (1449–92), better known as Lorenzo the Magnificent. Lorenzo's life coincided with the height of the Renaissance, an era during which many of the region's most celebrated artists and sculptors—Leonardo da Vinci, Michelangelo, Sandro Botticelli and others—were creating their best-known work.

Lorenzo, like his predecessors, controlled affairs from behind the scenes—few Medici ever held public office. Florence and the rest of the region enjoyed a period of relative peace and prosperity, though Lorenzo did arouse the enmity of rivals. After his death in 1492, however, the fortunes of Florence began to change. Turmoil followed his demise, and a weakened city found itself a pawn in a much larger power struggle between France, the papacy (two popes of the period were from the Medici line) and Holy Roman Emperor Charles V. Charles' sack of Rome in 1527 would mark a watershed in Tuscan and Florentine affairs. From then on, the city and the region would largely be ruled by foreign powers.

The painter Raphael (1483–1520) was born in Urbino and later worked in Florence

Detail of a 15th-century bust of Piero de' Medici, housed in the Palazzo del Bargello

1435

Bothered Botticelli

Botticelli (1445–1510) was a man with ingenuity when affronted. Life in his studio was interrupted when a weaver moved in next door and set up eight looms. The resulting noise and vibrations forced the painter out of his studio. His pleadings with the weaver—who claimed he could do as he wished in his own home—were to no avail. Botticelli's response was to have a boulder winched to the top of his own house, which overlooked the weaver's lower property. He then balanced the stone as precariously as he could, so it appeared that any tremour would send it crashing into his neighbour's house. The weaver appealed to Botticelli, who merely said he could do as he pleased in his home. The weaver had no option but to remove his looms.

Savonarola

Reformer Girolamo Savonarola was born in Padua in 1452, moving to Florence, where he achieved high rank in the Dominican order. A strange but charismatic figure, his stirring sermons drew crowds of 10,000, including Michelangelo, who claimed in old age that he could still hear the monk's speeches ringing in his ears. Following Lorenzo de' Medici's death in 1492, as the armies of France advanced on Italy, Savonarola gained effective control of Florence, encouraging its cowed citizens, among other things, to burn their more decadent possessions in a great bonfire in Piazza della Signoria. By 1497, unsettled by plague, poor harvests and war with Pisa, the people turned against him, and he was burned as a heretic in the same square.

Machiavelli

Niccolò Machiavelli (1469–1527) came from impoverished noble stock, but still rose to prominence in the Florentine republic, which he first served as a diplomat. He visited several Italian and European courts, acquiring a first-hand knowledge of the machinations of princes and other rulers. He had the ear of the city's de facto ruler at a time when the Medici had been replaced. But after 1512, when the Medici returned, he fell from favour, retiring for a while to write books, notably *The Prince*, for which he is best known. These were masterpieces of political analysis, skilfully linking political science with the study of human nature. Machiavelli himself was not 'Machiavellian'—the term was coined later by the French to denigrate not the writer, but all things Italian.

Michelangelo's Genius

Michelangelo (1475–1564) was born not in Florence but in the remote village of Caprese, about 96km (60 miles) east of the city. In later life he became convinced that the reason he acquired his sculptural acumen was his wet-nurse, a woman who came from the Carrara region, part of the Alpi Apuane mountains in northwest Tuscany. The area was known for its stone and the marble for Michelangelo's *David* came from the region. Michelangelo fondly imagined it was the marble dust in his nurse's milk that accounted for his genius as a sculptor. He would also claim to have introduced the art of quarrying to the region, and made pilgrimages to distant parts of the mountains in search of perfect marble.

Artist and architect Leonardo da Vinci (1452–1519)

Niccolò Macchiavelli, author of *The Prince*

1527

Duomo, Florence (below)
Carrara marble quarries (right)

Adoration of the Magi by Ghirlandaio (above)

The Birth of Venus by Botticelli, in the Uffizi (left)

Funerary figures on the tomb of Giuliano de' Medici by Michelangelo (right)

The Fall of the
Medici

After the Sack of Rome in 1527 by the Holy Roman Emperor Charles V, Florence and the Medici lost any real power on the wider European stage. Instead they were minor players in a game dominated by Austria and Spain. When Florence's nominal ruler, Alessandro de' Medici, who Charles V arranged to marry to his daughter, was murdered in 1537, there was no obvious successor. Charles and his imperial advisors installed Cosimo de' Medici (1519–74), a member of an obscure branch of the family. Despite his ostensible role as a stooge, Cosimo I, the first of Tuscany's self-styled Grand Dukes, managed a long and autocratic rule while being careful not to antagonize his imperial masters.

His successors, however, were less able, and a string of ever-more feeble Medici descendants presided over a period of decline, dissipating the family's proud heritage, and with it the last vestiges of Florentine and Tuscan power. The family struggled on for more than 150 years after Cosimo's death, the Medici line finally petering out with its last member, Anna Maria, who died in 1743, thus bringing to an end almost 300 years of continuous Medici power and influence in the region.

Bronze monument to Cosimo de' Medici (right)
The Medici family crest on the façade of the Church of Ognissanti in Florence (below left)

The Origins of Opera

Many scholars trace the origins of opera to Florence, and in particular to the *intermedii* of Florentine weddings—displays of dance, singing and static performance. Members of the city's Camarata, a cultural academy, were inspired by these entertainments and began to combine their musical elements with portions of Greek drama. From here it was a short step to *Dafne*, produced in 1597 by two of the academy's members, Jacopo Peri and Ottavio Rinucci. This piece is generally considered to be the first ever opera. They also created *Euridice*, the first opera to survive in its complete form, performed in the city's Palazzo Pitti as part of the celebrations of the marriage of Maria de' Medici to the French king, Henri IV. Such performances continued to be part of Florentine and Tuscan life during the 18th century, paving the way for the region's pre-eminent 19th-century composer, Giacomo Puccini (1858–1924).

1528

A ceiling at Palazzo Medici-Riccardi, home to the Medici until 1540 (right)

Three Toes Short of Perfection

Benvenuto Cellini's great bronze statue of Perseus was nearly ruined before it was started. Cellini (1500–71) was outraged when Cosimo I, the man who commissioned the statue but whom Cellini despised, suggested that the plaster model could never be cast in bronze. Cellini, in a rage, stoked his furnaces so high that the heat gave him a fever, forcing him to bed. When an assistant allowed the bronze to start cooling, the project was at risk as the mould would not be filled properly. Cellini was back in action, throwing every available piece of metal into the furnace. His roof caught fire, but the bronze was cast. Two days later, when the metal cooled, the statue was found to be perfect, except for three missing toes, which were put on later.

Strange Deaths

Grand Duke Francesco I of Tuscany had a problem. His second marriage to Bianca Cappello, who had left her Venetian lover to be with him, was going well. Unfortunately, his first wife managed to ban Bianca from Florence itself, a city whose Catholic citizens also took a dim view of second marriages, and who further ostracized the duke's new wife. As a result, Bianca became a social outcast, and Francesco was forced to build her a special apartment at Poggio a Caiano, one of the Medici's old villas just outside Florence. The refuge was not enough to save Bianca, nor Francesco, for both died in 1587. Some claim they succumbed to a virulent illness, but the fact that they died within a few hours of each other suggests the more sinister explanation of poison.

Siena's Last Stand

After hundreds of years of fighting with Florence, the proud Sienese Republic was brought to its knees—but not before a rousing last stand. A two-year siege of Siena (1554–55) left only 8,000 of the 40,000 population alive. After the city fell about 700 families fled south to Montalcino, determined to keep the Republic's flag flying. Here, with the support of the French, they survived the almost constant onslaught of the Medici and Spanish armies for four years. Surrender was only countenanced when the Spanish and French signed a treaty in 1559. This last stand is still commemorated today at the *Palio* in Siena, when the Montalcino group takes pride of place at the head of the opening procession under a medieval banner proclaiming 'The Republic of Siena in Montalcino'.

A Celebrated Experiment

Pisa-born Galileo Galilei (1564–1642), one of the world's first scientists, insisted on the use of experiment to prove or disprove a theory. One of his most famous came in about 1590, when, in front of his students from Pisa University, he is said to have dropped a cannon ball and a wooden ball from the top of the Leaning Tower to disprove Aristotle's assertion that an object falls at a speed proportional to its weight. If this were true, a 10kg (22 lb) ball should fall ten times faster than a 1kg (2.2 lb) ball. The scientist also asked his students to imagine a brick falling from the tower: as it falls, he said, it breaks in two. Will it, he asked, suddenly slow down to half the speed, as Aristotle's theory suggests, or will the two pieces continue falling side by side?

Cellini's *Perseus* holding the severed head of Medusa, on the cover of a 1930s brochure (left)

Galileo Galilei

1743

Statue of the *Rape of the Sabine Women* (1583) in the Piazza della Signora in Florence (left)
Scuola Normale Superíore on Piazza dei Cavalieri, Pisa (below), with the exterior by Giorgio Vasari (1511–74)

Towards Nationhood

After the death of Anna Maria de' Medici, Florence and most of Tuscany passed by treaty to the House of Lorraine, whose members were cousins of the Austrian Habsburgs. The first Lorraine duke, the future Francis I of Austria, brought stability and reform to the region, ushering in a period of resurgence that was interrupted by the arrival of Napoleon, who defeated Austria in 1799. Napoleon lingered briefly in Italy, including a period of exile on Elba, though his troops remained in the region until his ultimate defeat at Waterloo in 1815. The House of Lorraine, and by implication Austria—which held sway over much of Italy—was then returned to power, remaining in control until removed by the Risorgimento, a series of revolutionary uprisings in Italy during the 1850s. These uprisings culminated in the unification of Italy in 1860, after which Florence briefly became the country's capital, as Rome remained occupied by French and papal troops until 1870.

Political unrest aside, the 18th and 19th centuries were periods of cultural renewal, particularly in music, when opera flourished. It was also the time of the Grand Tour, the ritualized trip around Europe, including Italy, made by the wealthy.

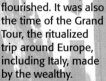

The Tuscan island of Elba where Napoleon Bonaparte spent his exile

Aristocratic Largesse

Florence's 19th-century aristocracy lacked for nothing in the way of hospitality, as Thomas Trollope's account of the grand balls held in the Palazzo Pitti makes clear. 'Guests,' observed the writer in *From What I Remember* (1887), 'used to behave abominably. The English would seize the plates of bonbons and empty the contents bodily into their coat pockets…I have seen huge portions of fish, sauce and all, packed up in newspaper and deposited in a pocket. I have seen fowls and ham share the same fate, without any paper at all. I have seen jelly carefully wrapped in an Italian countess's laced mouchoir…I never saw an American pillaging the supper table; though I may add that American ladies accepted any amount of bonbons from English blockade-runners.'

1744

Folly with statuary in the formal 18th-century gardens of Villa Garzoni in Collodi (above)

A Difficult Relationship

Lucca-born composer Giacomo Puccini (1858–1924) had an almost lifelong friendship with the conductor Toscanini. It started with the premiere of *La Bohème* in 1896, which Toscanini was chosen to conduct, despite the fact that he was just 28. The two musicians continued to work together, but regularly fell out over questions of art and interpretation. On one occasion when they were on bad terms, Puccini sent the conductor a *panettone* cake at Christmas. Then he remembered they were not speaking, and dispatched a telegram: 'Panettone sent by mistake.' Toscanini's reply came back: 'Panettone eaten by mistake.' Yet Toscanini would be Puccini's only real enduring friendship, and it was fitting that the former should conduct the premiere of the composer's last, unfinished opera, *Forzano*, in 1926. He brought the performance to a close, saying 'the opera finishes here for at this point the Maestro died'.

Napoleon on Elba

Napoleon arrived in exile on Elba, a place he claims he chose for the gentleness of its climate and its inhabitants, on 4 May 1814. On his way to the island he spent the journey musing over plans for his pocket principality, and doodling designs for a new island flag: a red diagonal on a white background—a deliberate echo of the Medici banner—plus the bees of his own imperial emblem. On arrival in the island capital, Portoferraio, he was offended by the stench, and virtually his first act was to give the town drains. This was one of many public works he instigated, partly to occupy and help pay for the 500-strong Napoleonic Guard that had stuck with him.

Napoleon in famous pose (above)

Shelley's Funeral

English poet Percy Bysshe Shelley (1792–1822) was one of many Grand Tourists to visit Tuscany. His sojourn would end in tragedy, however, for he drowned off the Tuscan-Ligurian coast, his body washing ashore near Viareggio. His friends, including writers Edward Trelawny, Leigh Hunt and Lord Byron, conducted a Greek-style funeral on the desolate beach. Trelawny called the ceremony 'beautiful and distressing', describing how the pyre burned yellow with the wine and frankincense poured on the body as libations. In a final twist, Trelawny noticed that among the detritus left as the flames subsided—little more than fragments of jaw and skull—Shelley's heart had remained entire. Trelawny plunged his hand into the embers to 'snatch this relic from the fiery furnace'.

English poets Shelley (left), Browning (middle) and Byron (right) all visited Tuscany

Modigliani's Last Laugh

Artist Amedeo Modigliani was born in Livorno in 1884, and studied at art school there before spending much of the rest of his life in Paris. He returned to the city towards the end of his life, and announced that he was going to drink himself to death. This he did, dying at the age of just 35. Before doing so he asked the students of his old art school where he might store some of his work. 'Throw it in the canal,' they allegedly replied. In 1984, on the 100th anniversary of his birth, Livorno's council acted on the story and dredged the old canal around the city. They were delighted to find three Modigliani sculptures, but less delighted when three schoolboys appeared on Italian television and demonstrated how they had created the so-called originals with power tools.

1913

Cover of the score of Puccini's *La Bohème* (above); Hall of Jupiter in the Palazzo Pitti, Florence, scene of much extravagance (left)

Portrait of a young lady by Modigliani

The Modern Age

Italy was a largely reluctant participant of World War I (1914–18), but paid as high a price as other combatant countries—a fact confirmed by the sombre war memorials in many of Tuscany's towns and villages. The region also suffered in the political and economic chaos that followed the war, and in the ensuing period of Fascist rule under Mussolini. Many of the region's hill towns, however, provided some of the most resolute of the *partigiani*, or partisans, who fought Italian fascism and then the Nazis during World War II (1939–45). The region also saw its share of action as the Nazis withdrew, not least in Florence, where all but one of the city's bridges were destroyed.

After the war, Tuscany was part of the economic miracle of the 1950s, when Italy, then still largely an agricultural and undeveloped country, was transformed in a few short years into one of the world's leading industrial nations. While the region retained its rural and agricultural traditions, many thousands of smallholders or landless peasants abandoned the land for jobs in the service sector, fashion and textiles, or in the small family businesses that have been the motor of economic change in Italy for more than 50 years.

A Changing Face

It is easy when visiting central Florence to be so blinded by the medieval and Renaissance city that you miss the changes that considerably altered its architectural face during the 20th century. The most obvious is the controversial Santa Maria Novella railway station (1935), which owes an obvious debt to the Fascist and other architecture of the 1930s. Similar influences can be seen in the Campo di Marte stadium (1932), now declared a national monument. The station's chief architect, Giovanni Michelucci, also designed the striking Cassa di Risparmio bank building (1957) at Via Bufalini 6. On the River Arno, the graceful Vespucci bridge was built from scratch after the war, while among the art nouveau creations is the lovely house squeezed between old buildings at Borgo Ognissanti 26.

The Mille Miglia (thousand miles) rally was held between 1927–57. Revivals are still held and pass through Florence

1914

RIVIERA della VERSILIA
VIAREGGIO
LIDO DI CAMAIORE
MARINA DI PIETRASANTA
FORTE dei MARMI

Vespa Championship races on town roads from Florence to Grosseto and back in June 1961

Hosiery by Tuscan-based Emilio Cavallini (right)
Travel brochure from the 1930s (left)

Guccio Gucci

Milan may be modern Italy's fashion capital, but Florence can claim one of the biggest designer names of all: Guccio Gucci (1881–1953). Gucci opened a small workshop and his first saddlery store in Florence in 1921, selling leather goods to horsemen and women; Gucci's bit-and-stirrup motif dates from these early days, while the distinctive red webbing (introduced in the 1950s) is also taken from its original place on a saddle girth. The success of this store meant Gucci expanded, and as horses gave way to cars, began to sell luggage, bags and other leather goods. In 1938 he opened a shop on Rome's prestigious Via Condotti. In the year of his death in 1953, Gucci opened a store in New York, marking the start of the company's association with high-class chic.

The 1966 Flood

The River Arno has flooded throughout its history, but the flood of 1966 that followed 40 days of rain was of a different order. Just before dawn on 4 November, 500,000 tonnes of mud, water and debris crashed through the Arno's breached banks, killing 35 people, destroying hundreds of homes and damaging untold numbers of paintings (including 8,000 in the cellars of the Uffizi), manuscripts, sculptures and other works of art. In some places the water was 6m (20ft) above street level. Helicopters winched women and children from rooftops, water and power failed for several days, and bread and milk had to be distributed from the Palazzo Vecchio. Volunteers poured in to help, not least with restoration, which continued for many years.

The Death of a Village

Today the Tuscan village of Sant'Anna di Stazzema is almost deserted because of a tragedy that occurred more than 60 years ago. It began when Mussolini was deposed in 1943, and an armistice was signed. The German army then poured into the breach left by the Italians in southern and central Italy. A year later, as the Allies pushed up the peninsula, Italian partisans began harrying the retreating Nazi troops. In northern Tuscany the 16th Division of the SS (the Schutzstaffel or special police) was clearing villages to deny the partisans support. When villagers in Sant'Anna heard that the SS was approaching, some of the village's men fled, little thinking that women and children would be harmed. They were wrong. The Nazis rounded up, killed and then burned 560 people, mainly women, children and the elderly.

A Bridge Too Far

In 1944, as the American Fifth Army advanced towards Florence from the south, the defending Germans reneged on a promise to demilitarize the city, which would have saved its buildings and artistic heritage from bombing and other attack (Rome had successfully been protected in a similar way a few months earlier). Instead, all the bridges across the River Arno were destroyed on 4 August to hamper the Allied advance. All the bridges save one, that is. Field Marshall Kesselring, commander of the German forces, spared the Ponte Vecchio, almost certainly on the direct orders of Hitler, who was swayed by its historical importance. However, many precious medieval buildings on both banks of the river and the Ponte Santa Trinità were razed to prevent easy access to the surviving bridge.

Audrey Hepburn in a Gucci shop (far left), and one of Gucci's desirable creations (left)

1966

Summer, one of the rescued Four Seasons statues from the Ponte Santa Trinità (left)

A Ferragamo sandal in 18-carat gold—his first workshop was in Florence (below)

Goering, Mussolini, second from left, Hitler and Count Ciano, then Italian foreign minister

A Region Reborn

Since the 1960s Tuscany has shared Italy's economic and social transformation, but also suffered the political up-heavals and left- and right-wing terrorism of the 1970s and early 1980s. However, these have done little to derail the resurgence of fashion, design and textiles as major industries, both in and around Florence and farther afield. Nor have they damaged Tuscany's artistic heritage, a heritage that has proved a mixed blessing since the advent of mass tourism. On the one hand it has attracted millions of visitors to Florence and the rest of the region, with all the economic benefits that accrue, but on the other the sheer number of visitors threat-ens the very works of art they come to admire, placing an enormous strain on Tuscany's already burdened infrastructure.

Architect Renzo Piano is working on a project for Grosseto

A Tuscan Turnaround

The town of Montalcino in the 1950s was an impoverished commu-nity; a place that was officially the second-poorest *comuni* in the province of Siena. It had been making wine for centuries: In the 1660s, the British king, Charles II, had praised the 'Mont Alchin' wine. But by 1960 its Brunello wines were only known locally, if at all. This changed in 1966, when it acquired official DOC recognition (Italy's wine classification system). By 1980, it became the first Italian wine to be awarded the rare and elevated DOCG status. The effect on Montalcino was profound, as agricul-tural and other tourist initiatives paid dividends. Almost one million people a year visit the village, which is now the second-richest of the province's *comuni*.

Uffizi Bombing

Tuscany had been largely free of the terrorism that had ravaged Italy in the 1970s and 80s, so the country was stunned when an enormous bomb planted in central Florence exploded in the early hours of the morn-ing on 27 May 1993. The blast, close to the Uffizi gallery, killed five people, including the gallery curator and her family, destroyed three (relatively minor) Renaissance paintings, and damaged some 200 other works of art. The Vasari Corridor was also damaged, along with the Gregoriophilius library. To this day, no-one has claimed responsibility for or been charged with the outrage, though there has been no short-age of theories, ranging from Mafia agents to government conspiracy. More than five years later, in December 1998, the damage was finally fully repaired, and new areas of the gallery were opened after a substan-tial refurbishment.

1967...

Sport, such as racing at Ippodromo delle Mulina near Florence, are big tourist attractions

Crowds outside the Uffizi (left)
Motorsport at Tuscany's Mugello circuit (below)

On the Move

ARRIVING

ARRIVING BY AIR

A large percentage of visitors to Italy arrive by air, the number increasing steadily with the growing popularity of short breaks and the choice of budget airlines for Europeans. Most visitors heading for Florence will find themselves landing at Pisa, an hour or so from the city. Florence has its own airport and there are plans to extend the runway, but only visitors who can afford regular airline fares fly to Florence directly. Those wanting inexpensive flights go to Pisa or Bologna.

If you are flying from outside Europe you will probably arrive at Rome or Bologna. You can catch connecting flights from either airport to Pisa, but the distance from Bologna to Tuscany is such that you might decide to rent a car and drive yourself (▷ 41–42).

Alternatively, you could fly to London Heathrow for a direct flight to Tuscany. Many US visitors coming to Florence and Tuscany fly to Germany and catch a flight to Florence from there.

There are two main airports within the region: Florence and Pisa (see map on page 48 for the location of airports).

Florence's airport, **Amerigo Vespucci** (FLR), is 4km (2.5 miles) northwest of the city. You may also hear it called Peretola, which is its old name. It handles mainly domestic flights, with a limited number of daily departures to other European cities. There are two terminal buildings: a smaller one for arrivals with tourist information, car rental, banking services

The check-in desks at Amerigo Vespucci airport just outside Florence

and a bar, and a larger one for departures with a café-bar, left luggage, banking services and some shops.

Pisa Galileo Galilei (PSA) is the region's main entry point, 2km (1 mile) outside Pisa and 91km (56.5 miles) west of Florence. It has good road and train connections to Florence, and handles domestic and European flights. The

TRANSFERS FROM AIRPORTS		
	AIRPORT (CODE)	
	FLORENCE AMERIGO VESPUCCI (FLR)	**PISA GALILEO GALILEI (PSA)**
DISTANCE TO CITY	4km (2.5 miles) to Florence	2km (1 mile) to Pisa
TAXI	Price: €15; journey time: 15 min	Price €6–€8; journey time: 10–20 min
TRAINS	n/a	n/a
BUS	SITA buses to Santa Maria Novella (SMN) station Frequency: every 30 min between 5.30am and 8.30pm; every hour after 8.30pm Price: €4 Journey time: 20 min or Vola In Bus to Piazza Adua (next to SMN) Frequency: every 30 min between 6am and 11.30pm Price: €4 Journey time: 20 min	CPT No. 3 from Pisa airport to Pisa city Frequency: every 15 min Price: €0.50 Journey time: 10–15 min
CAR	Journey time: 30 min	Journey time: up to 30 min

USEFUL TELEPHONE NUMBERS AND WEBSITES

AIRPORTS

	Telephone		Website
General			www.worldairportguide.com
Florence	055 306 1300		www.safnet.it
Pisa	050 849300		www.pisa-airport.com
Bologna	051 647 9615		www.bologna-airport.it
Rome Fiumicino	06 65951		www.adr.it

AIRLINE CONTACTS

	UK	Italy	Website
Alitalia	0870 544 8259	8488 65643	www.alitalia.co.uk
British Airways	0870 850 9850	199 712266	www.ba.com
Easyjet	0871 750 0100	848 887766	www.easyjet.com
Meridiana	020 7839 2222	199 111 333	www.meridiana.it
Ryanair	08871 246 0000	899 899844	www.ryanair.com
Virgin Express	0870 730 1134	843 390109	www.virgin-express.com
	US		Website
Alitalia	800/223-5730		www.alitaliausa.com
American Airlines	800/433-7300		www.aa.com
Continental	800/231-0856		www.continental.com
Delta	800/241-4141		www.delta-air.com
KLM	870/243-0541		www.klm.com
Lufthansa	212/479-8800		www.lufthansa.com
Northwest Airlines	800/447-4747		www.nwa.com
United	800/538-2929		www.ual.com
US Airways	800/428-4322		www.usairways.com

one spacious terminal has information desks, an adjoining rail station and ticket office, banks, bureau de change, left-luggage facilities and car rental desks, as well as a bar, a restaurant and a number of shops. There is a building project to help the airport cope with increased visitor numbers.

Two other airports you might fly to are outside Tuscany.

Bologna's **Guglielmo Marconi** (BLQ) is 105km (65 miles) northeast of Florence in the Emilia-Romagna region. It handles a large volume of European charter and scheduled flights, as well as budget airline flights. From the airport you have to catch a bus to the main rail station, then it's a rail journey of about an hour to Florence. Alternatively you can rent a car

and drive yourself into the region. The airport has banking and exchange services, car rental desks, a bar and a small number of shops.

Rome's **Leonardo Da Vinci Fiumicino** (FCO), usually abbreviated to Fiumicino, is 32km (20 miles) west of central Rome and about 425km (264 miles) from Florence. If your flight lands here and you don't wish to catch a connecting flight, then you can rent a car to drive to Tuscany. Alternatively you can catch a train to Florence, but you have to get a train into Rome (Termini station) itself first.

The airport has three terminals: A for domestic flights, B for domestic and international, and C for international flights only. A satellite terminal is connected to the main terminal C building by monorail. All three terminals are big, so allow plenty of time for connections. Fiumicino has airport information desks, a tourist information office, a hotel reservation desk, a lost-luggage office, car rental desks, shops, banks, restaurants and left-luggage facilities. There are interactive touch-screen information points in both the arrival and departure areas.

CAR RENTAL
The major groups are all represented in the region and have offices at airports, rail stations and in the bigger cities. You will get a better deal if you shop around before you leave home and book from your own country. Smaller, local companies will often have airport pickup points, but you may be unable to book them in advance from home. If you book with a tour operator, they will be able to arrange car rental in advance.

Before you leave, check your car insurance and see if you will need any additional coverage. You will need a credit card to act as a deposit when you pick up the car, and it's rare to pay additional charges for car rental with anything else.

TRANSFERS BETWEEN CITIES

PISA TO FLORENCE

DISTANCE	91km (56.5 miles)
TRAINS	Pisa airport through to Florence Santa Maria Novella Frequency: every hour Price: €4.60 Journey time: 1 hour
BUS	Terravision from the airport to outside Santa Maria Novella in Florence Frequency: 9 per day Price: €4.90 one way Journey time: 1 hour
CAR	Journey time: 1 hour 15 min

CAR RENTAL COMPANIES

You can book your rental car before you leave home through one of the major international rental groups.

	UK	USA
Alamo	0870 400 4562 www.alamo.co.uk	800/462-5266 www.alamo.com
Avis	08700 100 287 www.avis.co.uk	800/230-4898 www.avis.com
Budget	08701 539 170 www.budget.co.uk	800/527-0700 www.budget.com
Hertz	08708 448844 www.hertz.co.uk	800/654-3131 www.hertz.com
National	0870 400 4581 www.nationalcar.co.uk	800/227-7368 www.nationalcar.com

BUS INFORMATION

Journey time from London:
Florence 28 hours
Siena 28.5 hours
Ticket prices:
Florence £65, Siena £55
Journey time from Berlin:
Florence 18 hours
Ticket price:
€109
Eurolines services:
US: tel 800/327-6097
www.britishtravel.com
France: tel 892 89 90 91
www.eurolines.fr
Italy: tel 055 35 71 10
www.eurolines.it
Germany: tel 069 790 350
www.deutsche-touring.com

You should also check that the car comes with a warning triangle and a reflective waistcoat, as these must be used in case of an accident or a breakdown.

Drivers of rental cars must be over 21 or 25, depending on the individual rental company, and have a valid driver's licence. If there is to be more than one driver you must specify this when you pick up the car. Any additional drivers may also have to sign the rental agreement.

If you intend to go off public roads, check that the insurance covers this. You will be offered the choice of returning the car filled with fuel; it is less expensive to fill it up yourself just before you return it. Before driving off, be sure to check thoroughly both inside and outside the vehicle for any damage. If you find any, report it at once and get a company representative to make a note. See pages 48–52 for more information on driving.

ARRIVING BY BUS
You can catch a long-distance bus to Tuscany from most European countries. Buses from the UK are run by National Express Eurolines (tel 08705 808080, www.eurolines.co.uk). They operate from London Victoria three or five times a week, depending on the time of year, and go to Florence, Pisa and Siena. However, this may involve changing at Paris.

Pisa rail station has a smart exterior and approach

Visitors from outside the UK can also make use of the Eurolines service, with information on the website above, or check the details given in the panel. There are a limited number of services, operating mostly from Germany.

The majority of long-distance buses arrive at and depart from the Autostazione SITA, which is across the road from Florence's Santa Maria Novella rail station. From here you can catch a

TIP
Bus fares will be less expensive the earlier you can book them.

regional service to other Tuscan cities (▷ 53–55).

ARRIVING BY RAIL
If you arrive by train you will come into either Florence or Pisa. There are direct services from across Europe, including Amsterdam, Basel, Brussels, Frankfurt, Munich and Paris. If you travel from London Waterloo

RAIL INFORMATION

Eurostar
EPS House, Waterloo Station, London
SE1 8SE
tel 08705 186 186
www.eurostar.com

Rail Europe
179 Piccadilly, London W1V 0BA;
International Rail Centre, Victoria
Station, London W1V 1JY
tel 0870 584 8848
www.raileurope.co.uk

Italian State Railways (Trenitalia)
tel 020 7724 0011
www.trenitalia.com

French Rail Network, SNCF
tel 0892 353 535
www.voyages-sncf.com

via Eurostar, you will need to change at either Brussels or Paris. Changing at Brussels may be a better option as the route via Paris involves a change of train station at Paris, crossing the city from Gare du Nord to Gare de Bercy. Trains then run direct to Florence.

Both Eurostar and other fast European services include:
- 1st- and 2nd-class seating.
- Bar/restaurant cars.
- Trolley service on day trains.
- Baby-changing facilities on day trains.
- Air-conditioning.
- Telephone booths.
- Toilets in each carriage, including some that are accessible to wheelchairs.
- Sleepers are available from Paris on direct routes to Florence. Accommodation varies from 3-, 4- and 6-berth couchettes to single and double sleepers with private shower and toilets.

Rail Passes
- Interail Passes are valid for 1 month's unlimited rail travel within a specific zone; Italy is in Zone G together with Turkey, Greece and Slovenia. You must be a European citizen or have lived in Europe for 6 months to be eligible. The full fare is around €315 for adults and €275 for those under 26. The ticket gives

you discounts on cross-Channel services, including Eurostar.
- Eurail passes are available for North American visitors. They allow several days' consecutive travel, or a certain number of days with a fixed time period in up to 17 countries. There are many combinations to choose from; visit www.raileurope.com.
- Before you invest in a pass, bear in mind that train travel in Italy is not expensive. If you're only planning to go on one or two train journeys during your stay, it is likely to work out cheaper to buy individual tickets.

ARRIVING BY CAR
Florence is on the A1, Italy's main motorway (expressway)—the Autostrada del Sole. It links Bologna in the north and Arezzo and Rome in the south. The A11 off the A1 at the exit of Firenze—Nord takes you to Prato, Pistoia and Lucca. The best exits to take for the city of Florence are Firenze—Certosa or Firenze—Signa.

From the UK, you can cross the Channel either by car ferry or through the Channel Tunnel. The main routes south run through France, Switzerland and Germany. All cross the Alps; the main passes are the St. Gotthard, the Great St. Bernard, Frejus

If you travel by rail to Tuscany, you will arrive at either Pisa or Florence

and the Mont Blanc tunnel. The St. Gotthard tunnel is free, the others cost between €15 and €25. To reach these from Calais (where the car ferry arrives from England) take the E15 and E17 to Reims, then pick up the roads towards the different passes.

There are toll roads (turnpikes) all along the route. You should allow between 11 and 14 hours' driving time to reach the north Italian border.

You will need the following documents when driving to Italy: valid driver's licence, original vehicle registration document, car insurance certificate (at least third-party insurance is compulsory) and passport.

ARRIVING BY BOAT
Livorno is Tuscany's main port, but it is unlikely that you will arrive in the region by boat, as there are no services from other countries. The port is used mostly for local routes to and from the surrounding islands.

If you do arrive at Livorno then you are probably on a cruise around the Mediterranean and there will be organized tours into the countryside or the major cities.

GETTING AROUND

The best way to see the Tuscan countryside is by car—exploring the narrow roads is one of the highlights of visiting the region. If you are planning to spend most of your time in Florence you will not need a car, as the city is compact and there are good public transport links.

The biggest problem when driving in Tuscany is parking. The middle of the towns and cities are often walled and closed to traffic, or the roads are very narrow; parking is therefore likely to be on the outskirts, where designated parking areas have been built. At busy times of the year there may well be a shortage of spaces.

You can choose to rely on public transport, which is good between the larger towns and major sights, such as Siena and Pisa. In these cases you can get away without driving. However, getting to the smaller towns is less easy, while rail services and bus connections are non-existent for the national parks, hills and the valleys.

Driving is the best way to visit to smaller towns, such as Carrara

FLORENCE

The Tuscan capital has no metro or subway system, but the historic part of town is largely traffic-free, and can be crossed on foot in 30 minutes.

There are conventional bus services, but none of the routes are allowed to enter the traffic-free zone. These buses are useful, however, if you're staying on the outskirts of the city, or for getting around to the more outlying sights, such as the Piazzale Michelangelo (▷ 90).

In addition to the normal bus service there are four bus routes that do enter the traffic-free zone. These are powered by electricity to keep down the amount of pollution.

Azienda Trasporti Area Fiorentina (ATAF) is responsible for public transportation in Florence. Visit the website at www.ataf.net, both in Italian and English, for details on routes and services.

See pages 45–47 for more information on getting around in Florence.

TUSCANY

Most of the cities and towns in Tuscany are not large, making them easy enough to walk around, which is the best way to see them. If you need a map of the town, the local tourist office should be able to supply you with one.

The best way of getting to the most remote parts of the region is by car (▷ 48–52), but you may be lucky enough to find a bus route suitable for where you want to go (▷ 56).

Most roads and routes in Tuscany are scenic, but particular bus journeys worth a mention are Florence to Siena and Montalcino to Montepulciano.

Getting Around in Florence

The best way to see Florence is on foot. A large number of the major sights are in the heart of the city, which is closed to cars. There is no metro system, but buses are useful for getting to the outskirts of town. The electric buses act as unofficial tour buses, as they cut through the traffic-free zone.

BUSES

The ATAF information desks at Piazza San Marco and Piazza della Stazione (both open Mon–Fri 8–7, Sat 8–noon) provide timetables, details of routes and sell tickets.

The city's orange buses do not run through the pedestrian-only zone, but can be useful for getting to your hotel after a day's sightseeing or for returning to your car if it's parked on the outskirts. Most lines either originate at or pass the bus station (next to Santa Maria Novella rail station) or the Piazza del Duomo. Services run from around 6am to midnight, after which the night buses take over (▷ 46).

Routes are not always the same on the return leg so check the map at the bus stop (*fermata*) to be sure you can get off at the stop of your choice.

TIP
You board a bus through the front or rear door, but exit through the middle ones.

Tickets
● Tickets are sold at *tabacchi* (tobacconists), bars and newsstands displaying ATAF signs and at ATAF offices (see above).
● All tickets must be validated by inserting the ticket into the orange machine behind the driver.
● Tickets can be bought from the driver for an extra €0.50.
● Your ticket becomes valid from the time it is stamped on board the bus. This is because tickets are not bought on the basis of how many trips you want to make, but how long you want to use your ticket for (see Types of Tickets on this page).

● Both the city buses and the electric buses (see below) use the same ticketing system.

Types of Tickets
● A single ticket costs €1.
● The **60 minuti** (60-minute) ticket is valid for 1 hour, from the first time that it is stamped on the bus, and costs €1. You can then use as many different bus routes as you choose within the hour. You don't need to validate your ticket each time you change buses with this ticket—just the first time you board.
● The **3 ore** (3-hour) ticket works in the same way as the 60-minute ticket, but for three hours. It costs €1.80.
● The **multiplo** (multiple) gives you four 60-minute tickets, costing €3.90. Although the financial savings aren't great, it is very useful to have the tickets to hand, rather than having to find a shop to buy them in. And because they are only valid once they are stamped on board a bus, you can store them up to use during your visit.

TIPS
● Children travel free if they are less than 1 metre (3.28ft) in height. Their height is checked against the box that you validate your ticket in—it's at 1 metre (3.28ft), so below this line your child travels free.
● Smoking is not allowed on buses.
● A limited number of buses are adapted for passengers with disabilities.

● The **24 ore** (24-hour) ticket works in the same way as the 60-minute ticket, but for 24 hours. It costs €4.50 and is a good option if you are visiting the outer edges of the city.
● You can also buy tickets for two days, three days and seven days, costing €7.60, €9.60 and €16 respectively.
● All the above passes can be shared as long as a ticket is stamped for each person. For example, four different people can use the tickets that you get with a *multiplo*, but each of the tickets is only valid for the one hour, so if four of you go through the system at once, that's the *multiplo* used up.

ELECTRIC BUSES
Four orange single-decker, environmentally friendly buses run through the middle of town and are offically known as

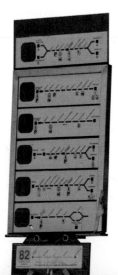

USEFUL ROUTES AND MAJOR STOPS

7	Stazione–Duomo–San Marco–Fiesole
10	Stazione–Duomo–San Marco–Settignano
12	Duomo–Porta Romana–San Miniato al Monte
13	Stazione–Duomo–Piazzale Michelangelo

Bussini Ecologici. Each bus is identified by a letter—A, B, C or D. Bus D runs south of the River Arno to Palazzo Pitti, which is useful for tired legs.

The map opposite shows these routes around the city; Trenitalia routes are rail connections to other cities; and Vola In Bus is a bus connection to Florence airport (see Transfers table on page 40).

A bright tour bus does the rounds in Florence

MAIN STOPS

The main stops along the routes are:

Bus A: Santa Maria Novella–Palazzo Strozzi–Orsanmichele–Piazza della Repubblica

Bus B: Ognissanti–Santa Trinità–Piazza del Limbo–Uffizi

Bus C: Piazza de San Marco–Museo Archeologico–SS Annunziata–Sant'Ambrogio–Santa Croce

Bus D: Santa Maria del Carmine–Santo Spirito–Palazzo Pitti

NIGHT BUSES

Only one bus, No. 70, runs through the night until 5am. The main stops are: Santa Maria Novella, Duomo, Piazza San Marco, Piazzale Donatello, Piazza Beccaria, Campo di Marte, then back to Santa Maria Novella via Piazza Indipendenza. Fares are the same as on the day buses.

SIGHTSEEING BUSES

If you really want to avoid any leg work, or want to get an overview of how the city is laid out, take an open-top bus ride with City Sightseeing (tel 055 264 5363, www.city-sightseeing.it). You buy a ticket on the bus or at an appointed agent, which is valid for 24 hours from the first time you get on. You are then free to hop on and off any number of times at designated stops. Each bus has a commentary in Italian, English, French, Spanish, German, Portuguese and Japanese.

Line A starts at the rail station, Santa Maria Novella, and Line B at Porta San Frediano, which is south of the Arno, and includes Fiesole. You can use your ticket

on both routes. Tickets cost €20 for adults, €10 for children (5–15) and €60 for 2 adults and 3 children. The buses operate April through to September.

DRIVING

It really is not worth driving around Florence. Much of the city is closed to traffic, there is a one-way system and parking is difficult. If you have a rental car, try to book a hotel with parking.

TAXIS

Taxis in Florence are white with a yellow design and are expensive. There is a set fee already on the

PARKING AREAS

Parcheggio di Piazza Stazione
Tel 055 230 2655
Open 24 hours
Built under the square outside Santa Maria Novella. Pay at a cash machine (credit cards are not accepted) before leaving, or at the cash desk if open. First two hours €2, then every following hour €3; 5-day ticket €140 payable before parking

Parcheggio Oltarno
Tel 055 223274
Piazza Tassa 24
Open Mon–Sat 7–midnight, Sun 10–10
Entrance is alongside Porta Romano in Piazza del Calza
Each hour €1.50; €15 for 24 hours

meter when you get in the taxi, then an additional €1.45 per kilometre is added inside the city limits. Rates for journeys farther out must be agreed before starting your journey.

There are also a number of surcharges: for journeys between 10pm and 6am (€4), travel to and from the airport, travel on a Sunday or public holiday, and for carrying luggage (each piece is €0.65).

Taxi stands are at Piazza della Repubblica, Santa Maria Novella, Piazza della Stazione, Piazza del Duomo, Piazza San Marco, Piazza Santa Croce and Piazza di Santa Trinità.

You can hail taxis in the street—the light indicates they are available. But there are relatively few cabs in the city, and you may wait a long time before one passes you.

If you call for a taxi, be aware that you will be charged from the moment it sets off, not from when you get in. For radio taxis call 4390, 4798, 4242 or 4386.

Only some taxis are adapted for passengers with disabilities, and they should be booked ahead on one of the telephone numbers above.

Smoking is at the discretion of the driver.

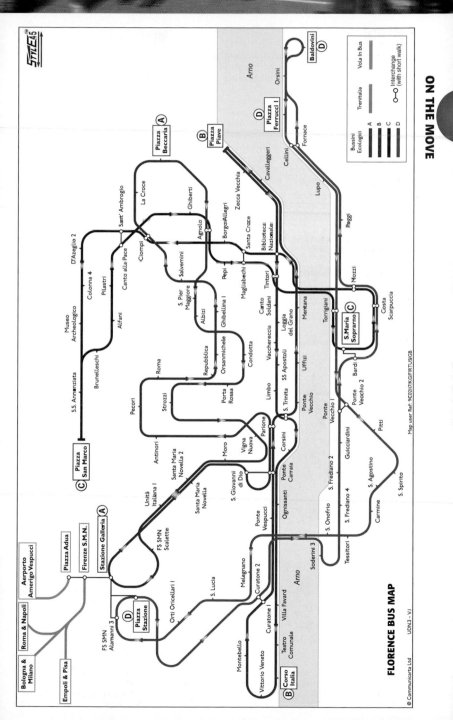

FLORENCE BUS MAP

© Communicarta Ltd   UDN3 - VI

Map user Ref: 9CD2II7/KGIFIRTU5/GB

Driving

Tuscany's road system ranges from motorways (expressways) and dual-carriageways (divided highways) all the way down to narrow, winding country lanes. Driving around the region outside the towns and cities is easy and a pleasure.

A car is ideal if you are concentrating on visiting the smaller towns and cities and rural areas. Tuscan drivers are fairly safe and cautious—Siena has the lowest rate for insurance in Italy—but be prepared for traffic jams in August, when the whole of Italy is on holiday and everyone heads for the roads, particularly on Saturdays and Sundays.

The best bet is to steer clear of cities. One-way systems, narrow streets, lack of parking, traffic congestion and the occasional bit of aggression make city driving stressful.

BRINGING YOUR OWN CAR

Before you leave:

● Well before your departure, check out what you must do to adjust headlights for driving on the right. For many newer cars, this adjustment may have to be made by a dealer for your make of vehicle.

● Remove any device to detect radar speed traps as they are banned in most European countries. Even if not in use, possession of such a device will incur a fine and may result in confiscation of the car.

● Contact your car insurer or broker at least one month before taking your car to Italy.

● Have your car serviced and check the tyres.

● Ensure you have adequate breakdown assistance cover. Contact driving organizations

MAIN ROAD NETWORK AND AIRPORTS

HOW TO NAVIGATE A ROUNDABOUT

- When you come to a roundabout (traffic circle), you must give way to traffic approaching from the left.
- If road markings allow you to approach without giving way, proceed, but look left before joining.
- Always look forward before moving onto the roundabout to check traffic is moving.
- To take the first exit, signal right, approach in the right-hand lane, keep right and continue signalling right.
- To take the intermediate exit, select the appropriate lane, signalling as necessary, stay in this lane and signal right after you pass the exit before the one you want.
- To take the last exit or go full circle, sign a left, approach in the left-hand lane, keep left until you need to exit and signal right after you pass the exit before the one you want.

Road signs in Tuscany are clear and easy to follow

such as the AA in the UK, tel 0800 444500, www.theAA.com.

You will need with you:
- A valid driving licence (if you have a UK photocard licence, you'll need this as well as the counterpart).
- The original vehicle registration document or certificate.
- A car insurance certificate; at least third-party (liability) insurance is compulsory.
- A warning triangle.
- A distinguishing nationality sticker (but this is unnecessary if you have euro-plates and are not motoring outside the EU).
- A reflective waistcoat to wear in case of emergencies (this is compulsory).
- A set of replacement bulbs is recommended.
- If you're driving in winter you may need winter tyres or snow chains, depending on where you want to go.

DOCUMENTS

Carry documents with you whenever you are driving. If you are stopped by the police they will want to see them.

The American Automobile Association (AAA) and the Canadian Automobile Association (CAA) advise holders of US and Canadian driving licences to always carry an International Driving Permit (IDP), together with their national licence.

RULES OF THE ROAD

- Drivers must be at least 18 (or older to drive a rented car) and hold a full driver's licence.
- Drive on the right and give way to traffic from the right. However at intersections displaying a precedence sign (an inverted triangle with the words *dare precedenza*) give way to traffic approaching from both the left and right.

- Seat belts must be worn in the front of a vehicle and (where fitted) in the back.
- Children under 4 must have a suitable restraint system and babies under nine months a specially adapted rear-facing front seat (but not in cars with airbags). Children aged between 4 and 12 cannot travel in the front of the car without a fitted restraint system.
- It is now compulsory to have dipped headlights on at all times when driving on all roads outside built-up areas.

SPEED LIMITS

Built-up areas: 50kph (31mph)
Outside built-up areas: 70kph (44mph) to 110kph (68mph)
Four-lane highways *(superstrade)* without an emergency lane: 90kph (56mph)
Four-lane highways with an emergency lane: 110kph (68mph)
Motorways/expressways *(autostrade)*: 130kph (81mph)
Motorways/expressways *(autostrade)* in bad weather conditions: 110kph (68mph)

TRANSLATIONS OF ITALIAN ROAD SIGNS

Accendere Switch on lights	**Parcheggio** Parking
Accendere i fari Switch on headlights	**Parcheggio autorizzato** Parking allowed
Banchina non Keep off hard shoulder	**Passaggio a livello** Level crossing
Caduta massi Falling rocks	**Pericolo** Danger
Crocevia Crossroads (intersection)	**Rallentare** Slow down
Curva pericolosa Dangerous bend	**Senso unico** One way
Discesa pericolosa Dangerous downhill	**Senso vietato** No entry
Divieto di accesso No entry	**Sosta autorizzata** Parking permitted
Divieto di sorpasso No overtaking	**Svolta** Bend
Divieto di sosta No parking	**Uscita** Exit
Entrata Entry	**Vietata ingresso veicoli** No entry
Incrocio Crossroads	for vehicles

ROAD SIGNS

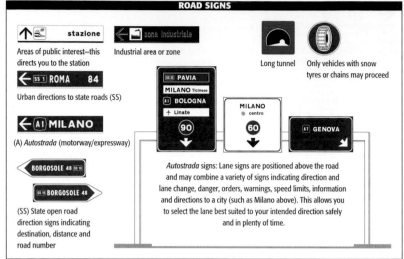

Areas of public interest—this directs you to the station

Industrial area or zone

Long tunnel

Only vehicles with snow tyres or chains may proceed

Urban directions to state roads (SS)

(A) *Autostrada* (motorway/expressway)

(SS) State open road direction signs indicating destination, distance and road number

Autostrada signs: Lane signs are positioned above the road and may combine a variety of signs indicating direction and lane change, danger, orders, warnings, speed limits, information and directions to a city (such as Milano above). This allows you to select the lane best suited to your intended direction safely and in plenty of time.

- Dipped headlights are only necessary in built-up areas when it's dark.
- There are severe penalties for drinking and driving. The legal level is below 0.05 per cent of alcohol in the bloodstream. You should never drive under the influence of alcohol.
- Italy uses international road signs.

Driving outside the main cities is a pleasure

TOLL ROADS AND MOTORWAYS (TURNPIKES AND EXPRESSWAYS)

- As you approach the *autostrada* take the ticket from the automatic box to the left of the car or press the red button to get one. The barrier will lift. Keep your ticket safe, as you will need it to pay when you leave the *autostrada*.
- Cash payment is normally made to the official in the booth; the amount is displayed on a screen outside the pay window. If you are using a pass or paying by credit card, follow the signs into the Viacard booth.
- Slip roads (entrance and exit ramps) on to and off Italian *autostrade* are short. You may have to stop and wait for traffic to pass before you can join.
- Only use the outer lanes for overtaking and be prepared to move to allow faster drivers behind you to overtake.

TUSCANY'S ROADS

- The region has three main *autostrade*:
A1 (Rome–Florence–Bologna); A11 (Lucca–Florence); and A12 (Livorno–Genova).
- The SS1 Via Aurelia runs up the coast from Rome and becomes the A12 just south of Livorno. Much work has been done to make this a highway and it will probably become a motorway (expressway).
- The Via Cassia runs from Rome, passing through Bagno Vignoni, Buonconvento and Siena before going on to Florence. For almost all its length, the road has only two lanes.
- The four-lane Superstrada del Palio was built in the 1960s and links Florence and Siena.
- The newest road, some of which is still being widened, is the much needed cross-Italy route. In Tuscany it goes through Grosseto, Siena and Arezzo and to Sansepolcro before crossing the Apennines and ending at Faro. For most of its length the road has just two lanes, but the plan is for it to have four.

PROBLEMS

- If your car breaks down outside built-up areas, turn on your hazard warning lights, put on the reflective jacket and place the warning triangle 50m (164ft) behind the vehicle on ordinary roads, and 100m (328ft) on motorways. Your rental car should come with both a waistcoat and triangle.
- If you are driving your own car on non-motorway roads, you can obtain assistance from the Automobile Club d'Italia (ACI) by calling 803 116 or, if using a foreign network mobile, 800 116 800. This is not a free service, so it is a good idea to arrange breakdown cover with a motoring organization before you

JOURNEY TIMES AND DISTANCES

This chart gives the distances in kilometres (green) and duration in hours and minutes (blue; hours given in the larger number) of a car journey between key towns. The times are based on average driving speeds using the fastest roads. They do not allow for delays or rest breaks.

Distances (km) from each town, reading across the top triangle:

Arezzo: 230, 215, 239, 035, 059, 210, 205, 139, 123, 051, 059, 156, 122, 159, 114, 134, 043, 114, 152, 158
Barga: 140, 021, 251, 146, 302, 134, 055, 311, 250, 258, 122, 128, 357, 137, 223, 307, 233, 118, 223
Carrara: 122, 234, 128, 227, 059, 048, 253, 233, 241, 050, 112, 339, 121, 201, 250, 216, 035, 153
Castelnuovo di Garfagnana: 258, 149, 309, 143, 103, 318, 257, 305, 128, 133, 404, 144, 232, 313, 240, 124, 229
Cortona: 119, 206, 225, 159, 109, 037, 047, 216, 141, 149, 134, 142, 100, 109, 212, 159
Firenze: 208, 118, 050, 144, 118, 126, 106, 032, 226, 024, 058, 135, 107, 103, 121
Grosseto: 152, 208, 059, 139, 123, 156, 225, 122, 217, 144, 241, 114, 208, 154
Livorno: 041, 236, 221, 229, 027, 105, 303, 115, 126, 237, 204, 041, 118
Lucca: 216, 156, 204, 028, 035, 303, 044, 130, 212, 139, 024, 128
Montalcino: 041, 025, 235, 201, 123, 153, 120, 153, 050, 232, 137
Montepulciano: 016, 215, 141, 122, 133, 139, 122, 106, 211, 156
Pienza: 222, 148, 112, 141, 132, 130, 102, 219, 149
Pisa: 051, 306, 100, 119, 229, 155, 029, 112
Pistoia: 246, 026, 112, 155, 121, 047, 136
Pitigliano: 240, 231, 228, 200, 318, 247
Prato: 104, 147, 113, 058, 128
San Gimignano: 209, 043, 139, 034
Sansepolcro: 144, 227, 232
Siena: 154, 059
Viareggio: 133

Durations, reading across the lower triangle:

181
206, 61
193, 14, 49
30, 212, 230, 223
78, 106, 123, 115, 107
133, 217, 205, 230, 140, 149
165, 85, 73, 96, 194, 90, 138
150, 37, 55, 48, 179, 71, 183, 50
73, 209, 226, 220, 66, 114, 55, 185, 174
54, 215, 232, 226, 33, 110, 91, 196, 180, 37
61, 222, 239, 233, 46, 117, 77, 203, 187, 23, 14
177, 65, 56, 76, 206, 98, 160, 23, 30, 203, 209, 216
119, 78, 96, 84, 148, 40, 180, 91, 44, 145, 151, 158, 71
141, 300, 274, 312, 127, 197, 70, 206, 267, 80, 73, 67, 226, 234
101, 89, 108, 100, 130, 22, 161, 102, 55, 127, 133, 140, 82, 22, 219
119, 153, 133, 165, 110, 60, 109, 83, 120, 75, 98, 91, 75, 86, 148, 69
39, 220, 237, 227, 69, 115, 167, 201, 185, 109, 86, 93, 212, 152, 190, 135, 156
65, 170, 187, 180, 72, 75, 76, 151, 135, 41, 61, 57, 162, 102, 114, 85, 36, 100
175, 63, 33, 74, 204, 96, 184, 50, 28, 201, 207, 214, 31, 66, 250, 81, 108, 209, 162
141, 105, 142, 119, 123, 83, 112, 74, 70, 89, 112, 104, 64, 109, 162, 92, 29, 175, 50, 118

Scooters are a useful means of negotiating narrow streets

leave home. On motorways, you must use the emergency telephones to obtain assistance.
● If your rental car breaks down, call the rental company on the emergency number included with the car's paperwork.
● If you have an accident call the police (113), but do not admit liability. Witnesses should make statements and exchange details.
● If you are stopped by the police, they will want to see your papers. They may give no reason for stopping you, in which case it is likely to be a random spot check. The commonest offence is speeding, for which there is a substantial on-the-spot fine. The police are legally obliged to issue fined drivers with a receipt.

SAFETY
In the countryside be aware of animals, slow-moving agricultural vehicles, soft roadsides and unsurfaced roads, which can be hazardous in long spells of drought or heavy rain.

Motorcycle police in Pisa

PARKING
Parking is often difficult, as towns and villages were not built to accommodate vehicles.
● Invest in a parking dial; in permitted parking areas these are displayed on your windscreen to indicate when you arrived.
Rental cars are normally equipped with one; otherwise they are available at tourist offices.
● Many cities have parking zones: Blue zones (with blue lines) have a maximum stay of 4 hours. Pay the attendant or at the meter. White zones (with white lines) are free and unlimited in some cities, but reserved for residents in others. Yellow zones (with yellow lines) are generally for residents only.
● Traffic-free zones allow cars in to deposit luggage—you may have to obtain a permit first from your hotel.
● A *zona di rimozione* is a tow-away zone.

BUYING FUEL
There are two grades of unleaded fuel *(senza piombo)*, 95 and 98 octane, diesel *(gasolio)* and LPG. Leaded petrol (gasoline) is virtually unobtainable; you will have to buy lead-substitute additive.

Motorway (expressway) service areas and petrol (gas) stations in major towns accept credit cards. If you need fuel at night, you will need to find a petrol (gas) station with a 24-hour *(24 ore)* automatic pump. These take €5, €10 and €20 notes. Feed in the money; the fuel stops when the money runs out. These can be temperamental and often reject old notes.

SCOOTERS
Most large towns and holiday resorts have scooter rental outlets—ask at a tourist office for details. To rent a scooter you must be over 21 and hold a full driver's licence. You need to leave your passport and/or a credit card as a deposit. Crash helmets are compulsory.
There are more scooters in Florence than in any other Italian city. Because Florence has less traffic than some other cities, the roads can be less dangerous. But scooters are not for the faint-hearted. If you have never ridden one in a big city, don't start in Florence. However, in quieter areas, a scooter is economical and easier to park than a car. Italian scooter drivers weave in and out of the traffic; unless you are experienced, do not be tempted to copy them.

Trains

Italy has one of Europe's cheapest and most efficient rail networks, and if you're planning to cover a lot of ground without a car, trains are the best option. There are a number of good links to Tuscan towns, and Florence's Santa Maria Novella station acts as a hub.

Trenitalia, the state railway system, covers the whole country. Its trains run on time, with clean and comfortable carriages. Trenitalia is also known as Ferrovia dello Stato (FS), which is its older name and the FS logo can still be seen at smaller stations.

TYPES OF TRAIN
● **Eurostar Italia (ES)** A super-fast (250kph/155mph) service connecting the main Italian cities (eg Rome to Florence). First-class tickets are available and include newspapers and refreshments. All trains have a restaurant car and trolley service. You should book ahead, especially for a weekend journey (book at stations; via Trenitalia agents; by telephone on 892021; or on-line at www.trenitalia.com).
● **Intercity (IC)** High-speed trains connecting the main Italian cities and important regional towns. Almost all trains have restaurant/trolley facilities. Advance reservations are advisable (see above).
● **Treni Espressi (E)** Long-distance express trains connecting major cities and towns all over Italy. Espressi services include overnight trains, and seats and sleeping compartments can be reserved in advance (see above).
● **Diretti (D)** Similar to Treni Espressi, they call at larger stations. No seat reservations.
● **Regionale (R)** Local trains operating within 100km (62 miles) of their departure station. They stop at every station and can be very slow. There are no seat reservations available and smoking is not permitted.

TICKETING AND FARES
● Italian trains have first- and second-class tickets, which can be purchased on-line

(www.trenitalia.com), at railway stations or through a Trenitalia agent.
● Train fares are calculated by the kilometre. A single second-class fare between Siena and Florence costs about €5.50.
● Supplements are charged for the faster services, such as Eurostar, Intercity and Espressi. You are issued with a separate ticket for the supplement. (A supplement means you are basically paying for a faster service, or in the case of Eurostar, all its extra facilities.)
● There are no discounts for return (round-trip) journeys.
● Children aged 4–12 travel at 50 per cent of the normal fare; children under 4, not occupying a seat, travel free.
● Tickets are valid for up to two months, but must be used within six hours of being validated (see below).

BUYING A TICKET
● Large stations have separate ticket windows for advance booking, and sometimes for first- and second-class travel. Major city stations may also have a travel office for enquiries and advance bookings.
● Ask for either *andata* (one

Santa Maria Novella rail station in Florence, where you can catch trains to other parts of Tuscany

way) or *andata e tornata* (return/round trip). The kilometres and price are displayed on an electronic board next to the booking clerk. Specify which train you are taking in case there is a supplement to pay. This can be paid directly to the ticket inspector on the train, but it is cheaper to pay it in advance.
● Payment can be made in cash or by credit card, though credit cards are often not accepted for low-cost tickets.
● Once you have purchased your ticket it must be validated before you board the train. Do this by inserting your ticket into one of the yellow boxes found at various points in the station and on platforms. If you fail to do this, you are liable to an on-the-spot fine of around €16. Your ticket is inspected during your journey.

TIP
There are two very helpful information desks at Santa Maria Novella in Florence, both open daily 7am–10pm.

RAIL PASSES

● Trenitalia Pass (for Europeans): This is the best discount pass for non-Italians who plan to use the train a lot. It is valid for 4–10 days' travel within a two-month period and is issued for first- and second-class travel. It can be purchased through Trenitalia in your own country up to six months in advance, or up to two months in advance once you arrive in Italy. You must specify the number of days' travel required when you buy the pass, which also gives discounts on the journey to Italy. Before your pass is used for the first time, it must be validated at any Italian station ticket window or information office. The staff

LOCATIONS OF RAIL STATIONS	
CITY (NEAREST STATION)	**DISTANCE TO CITY**
Arezzo	on edge of old city
Cortona (Camucia)	6km (4 miles)
Lucca	on edge of old city
Montepulciano	10km (6 miles)
San Gimignano (Poggibonsi)	11km (7 miles)
Siena	2km (1.2 miles)
Viareggio	on edge of town; 1 km (0.5 mile) to seafront
Volterra (Saline di Volterrra)	9km (6 miles)

will stamp it and write the first and last day of validity and your passport or ID number on the ticket.

● Other versions of the above are the Trenitalia Pass Youth for 12 to 25-year-olds and the Trenitalia Pass Saver for groups of up to five people.

● Eurail Pass is available for US and Canadian visitors. It allows 15 days' rail travel in a two-month period for US$498, but there is a complicated fare structure with many options.

● Eurail Select Pass is valid for

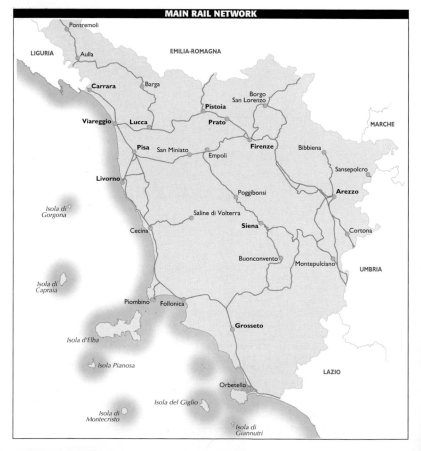

MAIN RAIL NETWORK

Pontremoli
LIGURIA
Aulla
EMILIA-ROMAGNA
Carrara
Barga
Borgo San Lorenzo
Pistoia
Viareggio
Lucca
Prato
MARCHE
Pisa
San Miniato
Firenze
Bibbiena
Empoli
Livorno
Sansepolcro
Isola di Gorgona
Poggibonsi
Arezzo
Saline di Volterra
Cecina
Siena
Cortona
Buonconvento
Montepulciano
UMBRIA
Isola di Capraia
Piombino
Follonica
Isola d'Elba
Grosseto
Isola Pianosa
LAZIO
Isola di Montecristo
Orbetello
Isola del Giglio
Isola di Giannutri

train and ferry travel on Eurail group transport for periods of 15 or 21 days and one, two or three months. It's useful if you're coming to Europe for a long trip and plan to move around a lot. The similar Eurail Flexipass is valid for 15 or 21 days within a two-month period.

INFORMATION

- There are several ways to obtain train and timetable information: on-line at www.trenitalia.com or tel 892021.
- Travel agents displaying the Trenitalia logo have up-to-date timetables, and you can also book tickets there.
- Visit www.raileurope.com for more on rail passes.
- Stations display departure and arrival times in the entrance hall. In addition there are timetables for arrivals *(arrivi)* and departures *(partenze)* from the station displayed on boards on every platform.

POINTS TO REMEMBER

- For lost property, call the station at either your departure or arrival point.
- If you have a connection to make, head for the timetable board on the platform where your train has pulled in. Find your connection by looking for the train number, its final destination, or its departure time from the station where you are. The platform will be listed under *binario*.
- All Italian stations, except for very small ones, have a ticket office, bookstall, bar, toilets and left luggage.
- Station bars sell food to take out; in larger stations there are also trolleys selling drinks, water, sandwiches and snacks.
- Luggage trolleys (baggage carts) are few and far between, even at major stations.
- Announcements are clear, but are in Italian only, except for airport train announcements at Florence, which are also in English.
- All trains have on-board toilets.
- There are smoking carriages on all trains except Regionale.

RAIL JOURNEY TIMES

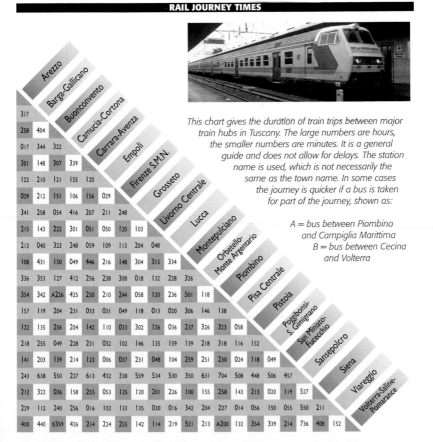

This chart gives the duration of train trips between major train hubs in Tuscany. The large numbers are hours, the smaller numbers are minutes. It is a general guide and does not allow for delays. The station name is used, which is not necessarily the same as the town name. In some cases the journey is quicker if a bus is taken for part of the journey, shown as:

A = bus between Piombino and Campiglia Marittima
B = bus between Cecina and Volterra

	Arezzo	Barga-Gallicano	Buonconvento	Camucia-Cortona	Carrara-Avenza	Empoli	Firenze S.M.N.	Grosseto	Livorno Centrale	Lucca	Montepulciano	Orbetello-Monte Argentario	Piombino	Pisa Centrale	Pistoia	Poggibonsi-S. Gimignano	San Miniato-Fucecchio	Sansepolcro	Siena	Viareggio
Barga-Gallicano	317																			
Buonconvento	258	404																		
Camucia-Cortona	017	344	322																	
Carrara-Avenza	301	148	307	339																
Empoli	122	210	121	155	120															
Firenze S.M.N.	029	212	151	106	156	029														
Grosseto	341	258	054	416	207	211	248													
Livorno Centrale	215	143	222	301	051	050	120	103												
Lucca	213	040	323	248	059	109	113	204	048											
Montepulciano	108	431	150	049	446	216	148	304	315	334										
Orbetello-Monte Argentario	336	353	127	412	256	238	308	018	132	228	326									
Piombino	354	342	A226	425	250	210	244	058	120	236	501	118								
Pisa Centrale	157	119	204	231	033	031	049	118	013	020	306	146	138							
Pistoia	122	135	256	204	142	110	033	302	126	036	237	326	323	058						
Poggibonsi-S. Gimignano	218	255	049	228	231	032	102	146	135	159	139	218	318	116	152					
San Miniato-Fucecchio	141	203	139	214	123	006	037	231	048	104	259	251	230	024	118	049				
Sansepolcro	243	638	550	227	613	432	338	559	534	530	350	631	704	508	448	506	457			
Siena	212	322	026	158	255	053	125	120	201	226	100	155	258	143	213	020	119	527		
Viareggio	229	112	240	256	016	102	133	135	030	016	342	204	227	014	056	150	055	550	211	
Volterra-Saline-Pomarance	400	440	B359	426	214	224	255	142	114	219	521	213	A200	132	354	339	214	736	408	152

Buses

Italy has no single national long-distance bus company. Buses are operated by several different companies who mainly run services within their own region, though there are a few that operate outside their own immediate area.

With the low cost of rail travel, longer journeys are often less expensive by train. For example SENA run buses from Siena to Rome (eight per day, costing €17) and Milan (three per day, costing €24). However, buses can be much more useful for reaching smaller places.

INTER-TOWN SERVICES
● Buses that run between major towns are known as pullman or *corriere*. They link such places as Pisa, Lucca, Siena and Florence.
● It is rare to find a dedicated bus station apart from in Florence and Siena. Services tend to depart from the rail station or the main square.
● If there is a bus station it is likely to have a newsstand, toilets, a bar and lost-property office.
● Inter-town buses are almost always blue.

Buses are a useful way of getting to remote villages

RURAL BUSES
Rural buses link outlying small towns and villages with the main regional towns or the larger local towns.
● Buses stop at designated places, either at points along the route or in the main piazzas of the villages.
● Services are geared to the local population's needs, so many buses operate to suit working and school hours and are drastically reduced on Saturdays and Sundays and during school holidays.

CITY-BASED BUSES
● Services that operate specifically around a town or city are called *autobus*.
● Most of the cities have bus services, but these are largely aimed at bringing workers and schoolchildren from the suburbs to the heart of the city, and their schedules are set according to these demands.
● Once you are in the historic part of a town you will find there are few buses. For example, in Siena there is no bus that runs around the Campo. In some towns, such as Montepulciano, there is a shuttle service that runs around inside the town, useful for taking you from the bottom to the top of a steep hill.
● See pages 45–47 for services in Florence.

INFORMATION
● You can get timetables and information from the bus company office or the tourist information office.
● Tickets are available from bus station ticket offices or on board.
● Seat reservations are not generally available.
● Air-conditioning is generally available.
● Smoking is not permitted.

Taxis

Taxis are available in all towns and cities. Government-regulated vehicles are predominantly white. Always check that the taxi is registered and that the meter is running—avoid taxis without a meter, as they may not be insured. All charges should be listed on a rate card displayed inside the vehicle. It can be difficult to hail a cab, so it is often better to go to a stand or book over the phone. Supplements are added for telephone bookings, luggage and additional passengers. Rates are higher at night and on Sundays and public holidays. Many city taxis have set rates from airports to cities, so confirm the price before you begin your journey.
● Taxi stands can always be found outside the rail station and in the main city squares.
● For radio taxis call Florence (tel 055 4390, 055 4798, 055

SAMPLE FARES		
Florence to	Siena	€6.50
	San Gimignano	€5.90
	Volterra	€6.95
Siena to	San Gimignano	€5.20
	Montepulciano	€4.40
	Montalcino	€3

BUS COMPANIES IN TUSCANY	
ATAF	Piazza della Stazione, Florence: tel 800 424500, www.ataf.net
SENA	Piazza Gramsci (underneath bus station), Siena: tel 0577 247934, www.eurolines.it
SITA	Piazza Gramsci (underneath bus station), Siena; for local and regional services: tel 055 834651, 055 478 2250, www.sita-on-line.it
LAZZI	Lazzi Via Mercadante 2, Florence: tel 055 363041, www.lazzi.it
CAP	Largo Fratelli Alinari 9, Florence; for services in northern Tuscany: tel 055 230 2855, www.capautolinee.it
TRA-IN	Piazza Gramsci (underneath bus station), for services in Siena and the Siena province: tel 0577 204111, www.trainspa.it

4242, 055 4386), Siena (tel 0577 49222), Lucca (tel 0583 495575, 0583 492691, 0583 494989).

● The maximum number of passengers a taxi will take is four.

Domestic Flights

Domestic flights within Tuscany are non-existent, but you can fly from Pisa or Florence to a number of other cities such as Milan, Rome and Bologna. Tickets for domestic flights are relatively expensive, but advance booking may secure you one of the limited number of inexpensive seats available on each flight. If you fly to Italy with Alitalia (www.alitalia.it) you are eligible for a Visit Italy Pass, which allows you to take three domestic flights for around €125.

Domestic Ferries

Tuscany has three main islands that you are likely to visit. Elba, Giannutri and Giglio are served by ferries from the mainland. It is essential to book ferries and accommodation in advance for the summer months of July and August. Out-of-season services are drastically reduced, or even nonexistent. See the table below for more details.

A ferry docked in Livorno

Bicycles

Cycling around the Tuscan countryside is a real pleasure and is a good way to see the national parks. In many of the more rural areas, such as Garfagnana, Alpi Apuane, Crete, Monte Amiata and Monti dell'Uccelina, there are marked trails for mountain bikes. Ask at the nearest tourist office for further information. Safety helmets are not obligatory, but it might be wise to bring your own if you are planning to do a lot of cycling.

There are few city-based bike routes, but you can go more or less anywhere; one good example is along the top of the walls of Lucca. Cycling in Florence is more of a lottery, thanks to the fast-moving traffic and the fact that other vehicles use bicycle lanes. However, you are allowed to cycle in the traffic-free zone. See panel right for more information.

BICYCLE COMPANIES

FLORENCE

Florence by Bike
Tel 055 488992
www.florencebybike.it
A growing company that rents out bikes and scooters within the city and has a cycling tour of Chianti. Bicycle rental is €2.50 per hour for use in the city; €18 a day for a mountain bike; rental also available for three days, five days and a week.

Alinari
Via Guelfa 85r, 50129 Florence
Tel 055 280500
www.alinarirental.com
Scooters and bicycles available for rental—prices range from €12 per hour to €47 a day.

SIENA

D.S. Bike
Via Massentana Romana 54
Tel 0577 271905
www.dsbike.it
Bicycle rental is €15 per day.

DOMESTIC FERRIES			
	ISOLA D'ELBA	**ISOLA DEL GIGLIO**	**ISOLA DEL GIANNUTRI**
MAINLAND PORT	Piombino	Porto Santo Stefano	Porto Santo Stefano
ARRIVAL PORT	Portoferraio	Giglio Porto	Giannutri
JOURNEY TIME	1 hour	1 hour	1.5 hours
FERRY COMPANY	**Moby**, Nuova Stazione Marittima, Piombino, tel 0565 225211 or Via Ninci 1, Portoferraio, tel 0565 9361, www.mobylines.it **Toremar**, Nuova Stazione Marittima, Piombino, or **Calata Italia** 23, Portoferraio, tel 199 123199, www.toremar.it	**Mareggiglio**, Porto Santo Stefano, tel 0564 812920, www.mareggiglio.it **Toremar**, Porto Santo Stefano, tel 0564 810803, www.toremar.it	**Mareggiglio**, Porto Santo Stefano, tel 0564 812920, www.mareggiglio.it **Toremar**, Porto Santo Stefano, tel 0564 810803, www.toremar.it
COST (one-way only)	A car and two passengers €47–€68	A car and two passengers (no cars in Aug) €40.40–€50.40	Foot passengers only €8 (service runs Easter to end Oct)

VISITORS WITH A DISABILITY

ON THE MOVE

There is a mixed overall picture of facilities in Tuscany for those with disabilities. The major problems are often not with transport, accommodation or public buildings, but with the layout and nature of the cities and towns themselves. Many of the region's medieval, walled towns present difficulties for those in a wheelchair, with their cobbled streets and hill-top locations.

Things are progressing, particularly with regard to public transport and access to museums and galleries. It is now the law in Italy that hotels, restaurants and bars must provide disabled facilities. However, with some key exceptions, facilities have not yet caught up with those in northern European countries and North America.

FLORENCE
● There are a number of green/grey buses that are adapted for wheelchair use, as is the D electric bus (▷ 45–46).
● Many of the larger museums have ramps, elevators and specially adapted toilets.
● Santa Maria Novella station is adapted for disabled people.

RAIL TRAVEL
There are Centro Assistenza Disabili (Customer Assistance) offices in more than 180 stations across Italy, where you will be given help and advice on your journey, plus help to board and leave trains at stations with these offices. You should call at least 24 hours in advance if you require this particular service. The offices are open 7am to 9pm, with the same number for all stations: 199 303060. This service is available at all big cities if you want to travel outside Tuscany.
● If you have a disability, plan carefully or consider booking your holiday with a specialist tour operator.
● You should contact your airline in advance of your date of travel. They will let the airports know what assistance you will need.
● The airports in the region are modern, or in the process of being upgraded, so you should find good facilities. They are

---

TUSCAN STATIONS WITH ASSISTANCE DESKS

Arezzo; Campiglia; Empoli; Florence (Santa Maria Novella); Grosseto; Livorno; Lucca; Massa Centro; Montecatini; Piombino; Pisa; Pistoia; Prato; Siena; Viareggio

---

TIP
The telephone number 199 303060 can be called from anywhere in the country, and the operator will be able to help or advise you on rail travel.

---

small enough for visitors not to have to walk long distances between gates.
● Only some Tuscan buses have been adapted for visitors with disabilities; if you are unsure, call one of the numbers on page 56.
● Trains sometimes have wheelchair access, and this is indicated on the timetable by a wheelchair symbol. If you need assistance at the station, contact them 24 hours in advance (3 hours notice is sufficient from big city to big city).
● Taxis can take wheelchairs folded and stored in the boot (trunk), but Italian taxis are saloon (sedan) cars and getting in and out may be difficult. There are some taxis that are converted for wheelchairs, but you will need to book well ahead. Ask when calling.
● If you are driving and from the UK, you can use your blue Disabled Person's Parking Badge in Italy.
● Major pedestrian crossings in cities have a sound signal for the visually impaired.
● An increasing number of public places and some museums have information in braille.

● Book well in advance and be specific about your requirements when reserving accommodation.
● For a more relaxed Italian holiday, steer clear of the major cities and use a car to explore rural areas and smaller towns and villages of artistic or architectural interest.
● Contact the local tourist office for more details (▷ 274).

USEFUL CONTACTS

IN ITALY
Unione Italiana dei Ciechi
(Italian Society for the Blind)
Unione Italiana dei Ciechi, Via Borgognona 38, 00187 Roma
tel 06 699881, fax 06 678 6815
www.uiciechi.it

Accessible Italy
(Regency San Marino srl)
Via C. Manetti 34, 47891 Dogana Borgomaggiore
Repubblica di San Marino 47031
tel 0549 941108, fax 0549 907189
www.accessibleitaly.com

ABROAD
Australia: The Disability Information and Resource Centre Inc, 195 Gilles Street, Adelaide SA 5000
tel (08) 8223 7522; www.dircsa.org.au

Canada: The Easter Seals Society, 1185 Eglinton Avenue East, Suite 800, Toronto ON M3C 3C6
tel 800-668-6252; www.easterseals.org

New Zealand: Disabled Persons Assembly (DPA), PO Box 27–524, Wellington 6035
tel 644 801 9100; www.dpa.org.nz

UK: RADAR, 12 City Forum, 250 City Road, London EC1V 8AF
tel 020 7250 3222; www. radar.org.uk

US: SATH, 347 5th Avenue, Suite 610, New York City, NY 10016
tel 212/447-7284; www.sath.org

This chapter is divided geographically into four sections, which are shown on the map on the inside front cover. Places of interest are listed alphabetically within each section. Major sights are listed at the start of each section.

The Sights

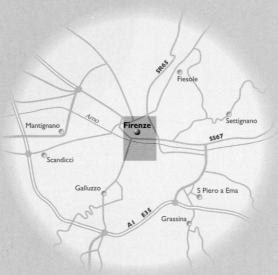

FLORENCE

Florence was the birthplace of the Renaissance
and the creative hub for some of the world's
greatest artistic talents. The city's churches
and museums contain masterpieces and its
narrow streets are lined with splendid palaces
and elegant shops.

MAJOR SIGHTS

Florence

✚ 284G5 🚹 Via Cavour 1r (five minutes walk north of the Duomo), Mon–Sat 8.30–6.30, Sun 8.30–1.30; tel 055 290832
🚉 Santa Maria Novella
www.firenzeturismo.it • The official site of the tourist board in Tuscany (in English and Italian)

A close-up view of the Duomo's roof from the Campanile (right); a satyr, part of the base of the Fountain of Neptune by Bartolomeo Ammanati, found in Piazza della Signoria (below)

SEEING FLORENCE

The best way to see Florence is to stay for a while, punctuating some serious sightseeing with simply wandering the streets or relaxing at a café table. If you're coming in for the day from elsewhere in Tuscany, the train and bus stations are less than a 15 minute walk northwest of the historic hub, and, with some planning, it's feasible to experience the city's glories in a day.

Most of the highlights lie within a traffic-free zone on the north bank of the River Arno, an area split by the Via dei Calzaiuoli. This runs south from the stunning Duomo complex to the Piazza della Signoria, Florence's main square and home to the Palazzo Vecchio. Just off here is the Uffizi, one of the world's greatest galleries, while south lies the famous Ponte Vecchio.

North of the Duomo is San Lorenzo, the Medici church, which stands within easy reach of the Galleria dell'Accademia, housing Michelangelo's *David*, and the monastery of San Marco. East from the Piazza della Signoria is Santa Croce, burial place of the city's great and good. Other major churches and museums are scattered throughout the city.

Crossing the river, you'll come to the Oltrarno district; its major draws are the Palazzo Pitti and its galleries, Santa Maria del Carmine and some beguiling artisan shops.

The best way to explore all this is on foot, starting at either the Duomo or the Piazza della Signoria, though you may want to hop on a bus to visit the more outlying sights.

BACKGROUND

The Romans founded the colony of Florentia in 59BC, which quietly prospered until the fall of Rome in AD410. Florence only re-enters the history books during the 13th-century struggle between supporters of the papacy and the Holy Roman Empire. From this, individual city-states emerged, and by the 13th century Florence had a civic leader, the Podestà, and a number of *arti* (guilds) that represented the interests of the merchant and banker classes. From the latter emerged the Medici, a dynastic family that controlled Florence during the crucial years of the Renaissance and were patrons of scholarship and the arts. By the 16th century the Medicis were the Grand Dukes of Tuscany, continuing their patronage of the arts, but a duchy that was in steady economic decline. In 1737 Medici rule ended and Florence fell into the hands of the Austrian Lorraine dynasty, which, except during the Napoleonic years, ruled Tuscany until 1859. In 1860 Florence became part of united Italy, serving as the capital briefly in 1861. Today it is capital of one of Italy's richest regions.

THE SIGHTS

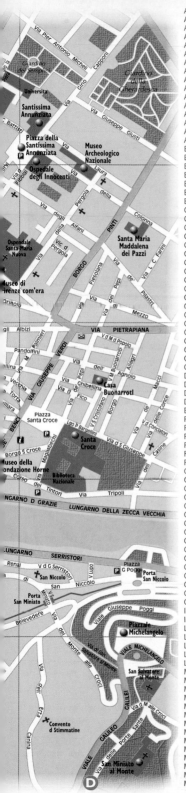

THE SIGHTS

Certosa di Firenze was founded in the 14th century

CAPPELLA BRANCACCI

This chapel is embellished by a fresco cycle that marks a watershed in the development of painting and is among the earliest true Renaissance works.

✚ 62 A3 • Piazza del Carmine, 50125 ☎ 055 238 2195 🕐 Mon, Wed–Sat, 10–5, Sun 1–5; last entrance 4.30 💰 Adult €4, under 18 €1.50 🚇 D ❓ Combined ticket with Palazzo Vecchio available: Adult €8, under 18 €3 www.museoragazzi.it

RATINGS	
Historic interest	●●●○
Photo stops	●●●○
Value for money	●●●○

The walls in the chapel are covered with frescoes, including Masaccio's Tribute Money *(top) and Lippi's* Raising the Emperor's Son *(bottom)*

This small chapel, entered via a separate entrance, lies at the end of the right transept of the Church of Santa Maria del Carmine, has some of the most significant works of the Florentine Renaissance. Although the church's exterior is dull—a rough stone façade was rebuilt after a fire in 1771—the frescoes survived and, thanks to restoration carried out in the 1980s, are vibrant once again. Advance reservation here is now compulsory for much of the year, so call ahead to book tickets.

THE FRESCOES

Rich merchant Felice Brancacci commissioned the frescoes in 1424. Masolino and his apprentice Masaccio began the work a year later. Both died before the cycle could be completed and, since the patron Brancacci was exiled by Cosimo de' Medici after 1436, the frescoes were untouched for 50 years. They were eventually finished by Filippino Lippi (1457–1504), who copied the style of his two predecessors.

The chapel (which can only accommodate 30 people at one time) is covered from top to bottom with paintings. The entire cycle, apart from two paintings, depicts scenes from St. Peter's life. In particular, look for Masaccio's dramatic *Expulsion of Adam and Eve* and *Tribute Money*, probably the most famous of the images and the first monumental Renaissance fresco painting. In contrast to the two-dimensional portrayals characteristic of Masaccio's predecessors, the depiction of Adam and Eve in their anguish is particularly moving and forms a striking contrast to Masolino's depiction of the same event. Other highlights are *St. Peter Healing the Sick* and *Distribution of Alms*.

CASA BUONARROTI

✚ 63 D3 • Via Ghibellina 70, 50122 ☎ 055 241752 🕐 Wed–Mon 9.30–2 💰 Adult €6.50 🚇 A, 14 🏛

www.casabuonarroti.it

The Casa Buonarroti, once a Renaissance townhouse, is now the Michelangelo museum, providing an insight into the life of one of the world's most famous artists. Michelangelo Buonarroti (1475–1564) bought the house in 1508. On his death he left the property and several works of art to his nephew Leonardo, who in turn left it to his son, also named Michelangelo. This Michelangelo was an art collector and in 1612 he turned part of the house into a gallery dedicated to his great-uncle. The museum is not packed with works, but you can see several portraits of the great artist, and the marble bas-relief of *The Madonna of the Steps*, his earliest known work.

CERTOSA DI FIRENZE

✚ 284 G5 • Certosa di Galluzzo, Via Buca di Certose, 50124 ☎ 055 204 9226 🕐 Tue–Sun 9.15–1.15, 3.15–5.15 💰 Free 🚌 Guided tours only

This great Carthusian monastery was once occupied by 18 monks, who lived silent lives in self-contained, three-room apartments. They had individual gardens around the stunning Chiostro Grande, a cloister that is decorated with tondi by brothers Andrea (1435–1525) and Giovanni (c1469–1529) della Robbia. The visit includes the Palazzo degli Studi, which holds the great *Scenes from the Passion* frescoes, executed by Pontormo while he was sheltering there during the 1522 plague outbreak. Brutally and unsuccessfully restored in the 1970s, they are ghosts of what they were, though nothing can detract from the power of the composition.

CAPPELLE MEDICEE

The Medici family's monumental private chapels are remarkable for their scale—visible proof of the dynasty's tremendous wealth.

The chapels are at the eastern end of the Church of San Lorenzo (▷ 94) and consist of the crypt, the Cappella dei Principi (Chapel of Princes) and the Sagrestia Nuova (New Sacristy). Most members of the Medici family are buried within the chapels, the minor ones interred in the vaulted crypt where there are numerous tombstones. Glass cases display gold and silver objects from the church treasury, including a beautiful 16th-century pearl-encrusted mitre.

CAPPELLA DEI PRINCIPI

Stone steps lead from the crypt to this chapel, the Grand Dukes' (▷ 32) octagonal mausoleum. It was begun in 1604 and is entirely lined with marble and gems. It is a magnificent example of *pietre dure* craftsmanship (a technique of inlaying stones) at which the Florentines of the time were particularly skilled. The massive sarcophogi set high around the walls contain the remains of the most illustrious of the Medici: (from left to right) Fernando II, Cosimo II, Fernando I, Cosimo I, Francesco I and Cosimo III. The huge, gilded bronze statues (1626–42) above two of the tombs are by Pietro and Ferdinando Tacca.

SAGRESTIA NUOVA

The Sagrestia Nuova is totally different in style from its predecessor. The grey *pietra serena* (stone taken from the hills of Fiesole, ▷ 99) against white marble and the classical lines are a sober contrast to the extravagance of the Cappella dei Principi. Work is thought to have been begun by Giuliano da Sangallo in 1491, and was continued (though never completed) by Michelangelo between 1520 and 1533. Inspired by Brunelleschi's Old Sacristy (access through the main church), it was used as a funeral chapel for the Medici family. Here you will find two superb examples of tombs and statues by Michelangelo. The tomb of Lorenzo, Duke of Urbino and grandson of Lorenzo Il Magnifico, is on the left of the entrance and is decorated with the reclining figures of *Dawn* and *Dusk*. The corresponding statues on the tomb opposite, that of Giuliano, Duke of Nemours, represent *Day* and *Night* and are considered among Michelangelo's finest. The beautiful statue of the *Madonna and Child* (1521) is also by Michelangelo, along with the two carved candelabra on the altar.

RATINGS	
Historic interest	● ● ● ●
Photo stops	● ● ● ● ●
Value for money	● ● ●

BASICS

✚ 62 B2 • Piazza Madonna degli Aldobrandini 2, 50123

☎ 055 238 8602

🕐 Daily 8.15–4.30; closed 2nd and 4th Sun and 1st, 3rd and 5th Mon of each month

💶 Adult €6, under 18 free

🚌 A, 1, 17

🎧 Audiotours in English and Italian for €4.65

📖 A wide selection is available, the official book is €8, plus an inexpensive leaflet for €1.55

🏬 Sells the usual books, guides, postcards, calendars, posters and gift items

🚻 Found off the stairs into the chapel

❓ Advance booking not required but advisable in high season

www.firenzemusei.it

The Cappella dei Principi (top); the Cappelle Medicee are in the church of San Lorenzo (above)

Galleria dell'Accademia

The gallery is home to Michelangelo's *David*, one of the world's best-known sculptural pieces, and to other works by this Renaissance artistic giant.

A close-up of the feet of David

A corridor containing the Slaves *leads you to Michelangelo's* David

RATINGS	
Cultural interest	●●●●○
Historic interest	●●●●○
Specialist shopping	●●●○○
Value for money	●●●○○

BASICS

✚ 62 C1 • Via Ricasoli 60, 50122
☎ 055 238 8612
🕐 Tue–Sun 8.15–6.50 (hours often extended in summer); Easter Sun and Mon 8.15am–10pm; 1 May 8.15–8
💶 Adult €6.50, under 18 free
🚌 1, 6, 7, 11, 17
🎧 Audiotours in English, French, Spanish, German, Japanese, Italian, €4.65 for a single, €6.20 for a double. For organized guided tours, tel 055 294883
📖 Shorter book for €9.50, and another for €14 with more photos
🏛 A selection of art books, posters, postcards, gifts and stationery

www.sbas.firenze.it/accademia
A useful site with a floorplan to help you plan your visit

A detail from one of the Slaves *(top);* David *confirmed Michelangelo as a leading sculptor of the time (right)*

SEEING THE GALLERIA DELL'ACCADEMIA

The Accademia, second only to the Uffizi in visitor numbers, contains several sculptures by Michelangelo, but it is his *David* that is the main attraction, drawing a constant stream of people. In summer, you'll have to wait for hours if you haven't booked ahead; advance booking, whatever the time of year, will save you much time and frustration. The entrance to the gallery is by way of the large Sala del Colosso, from where you'll pass through to the gallery containing the *David*, protected (since an attack in 1991) by glass in a specially built alcove. The Accademia also has Michelangelo's four *Slaves* and *St. Matthew*, which you'll see in the corridor leading to the *David*, and a large collection of 13th- to 16th-century Florentine paintings.

HIGHLIGHTS

DAVID

Liberated, if only temporarily, from the shackles of the Medici rulers and the fanatical religious reformer Girolamo Savonarola (▷ 31), the city fathers decided to commemorate this rebirth of civil liberty with a large public statue. In 1501 the group that looked after the Duomo, the Opera del Duomo, chose the subject of David the Giant-Killer as a suitable theme to invoke Florence's success against more powerful forces, and commissioned Michelangelo, then only 26, to carve the piece. The block of marble available was huge (more than 4m/13ft), misshapen, cracked and thin; it had already defeated sculptors including Jacopo Sansovino and Leonardo da Vinci. Where they failed, Michelangelo succeeded, producing an amazing display of virtuosity, and turning the stone's defects into strengths. The statue shows the young David in meditative pose as he prepares for his fight with Goliath, aware that the salvation of his people depends upon him.

Bear in mind that the statue wasn't intended to be seen in the confined interior space it now occupies, but as a public sculpture to be viewed from below in a large open piazza. In this context, the huge head and over-large hands fall into proportion. It took 40 men four days to move the finished work into the Piazza della Signoria, where it became a symbol of republican liberty.

Tobias with the archangels Michael, Raphael and Gabriel by Domenico di Michelino

THE SLAVES

The four *Slaves*—unfinished marble pieces in which the figures appear trapped in the stone—were carved between 1519 and 1536, and originally intended for the tomb of Pope Julius II (1443–1513) in St. Peter's, Rome. Michelangelo held the theory that sculpting was a process of liberating the subject from the stone and started work by cutting the figure in deep relief into the block. This process was often carried out by his assistants, Michelangelo then stepping in to 'set free' the three-dimensional figure. These works are a perfect example of the process, and may also have been intended to act as an illustration of the 'imprisonment' of the arts following Julius' death. Julius' tomb was never assembled in its intended form, so the *Slaves* remained in Florence. There were originally six figures; two are now in the Louvre. The four in the Accademia were moved there in 1909 from the Giardino de Boboli (▷ 74), where they had been placed by the Medici in 1564.

OTHER HIGHLIGHTS

The figure of *St. Matthew* by Michelangelo is in the same corridor as the *Slaves*. It was intended to be the first of a set of all twelve apostles; this is the only one ever started. The *Cassone Adimari*, a painted panel from a marriage chest, shows a lively and much-reproduced wedding scene of the mid-15th century taking place in front of the city's baptistery. *Madonna of the Sea* is an early Botticelli (also known as *Madonna and Child with the Young St. John and Two Angels*). *Venus and Cupid* is an early work by Pontormo, probably painted using a Michelangelo cartoon.

BACKGROUND

Florence's first drawing academy was founded in the 1560s. In 1764 it moved to the Via Ricasoli, its current home, where its role expanded to cover the visual arts generally. Named the Accademia di Belle Arti, it obtained its own gallery in 1784, quickly building up a teaching collection of art, used to aid students working on all aspects of art—painting, drawing and sculpture. It was augmented with numerous paintings during the 19th century and became the home of the *David* in 1873, when the statue was moved indoors from the Piazza della Signoria.

Galleria degli Uffizi

This is one of Europe's oldest art galleries, displaying priceless paintings and sculptures from the world's most important collection of Renaissance art. It attracts more than 1.5 million visitors every year.

The Uffizi is the most popular gallery in Florence

A section of the Adoration of the Magi by Gentile da Fabriano

SEEING THE GALLERIA DEGLI UFFIZI

Whatever you do, set aside plenty of time to see the Uffizi—there is so much art of such importance that a flying visit is out of the question. The gallery is laid out on the second floor of the u-shaped Palazzo degli Uffizi, with works arranged in chronological order in a series of interconnecting rooms down each long wing. Don't attempt to see the entire collection in one day, but use your first visit to concentrate on Rooms 1 through 18 in the East Corridor, which present major Florentine, Tuscan Gothic and Renaissance works. Return to tackle 16th-century and later artists in the remainder of the East Corridor and the rooms along the West Corridor. Only 660 people are allowed in at any one time, so you should pre-book your visit by telephone, for which there is a small booking fee; you will be allocated an entrance time and booking number. Collect your tickets at Entrance 2 in the west ground-floor arcade. The alternative is to wait, but this might be hours in the summer. It's a long climb to the galleries so take the lift to save your legs before walking around.

HIGHLIGHTS

MADONNA RUCELLAI

Painted by Duccio di Buoninsegna for the Rucellai Chapel in Santa Maria Novella in 1285, this watershed painting came to the Uffizi in 1937. Though heavily influenced by the work of Cimabue (born c1240), it breaks new ground stylistically with the introduction of delicate Gothic overtones and brilliant colours, features that were to become the hallmark of Sienese painting. These are strongly evident in the rendition of the throne, with its Gothic pointed shapes, and the supporting angels all gazing devoutly at the Virgin, a totally new concept—formerly, they would have been background figures. The roundels in the lower section contain images of saints revered by the Dominicans, the commissioners of the work.

ADORATION OF THE MAGI

This altarpiece, epitomizing the intricacy and richness of International Gothic, was commissioned in 1423 by Palla di Strozzi for the family

The Niobe room displays Roman statues about the myth of Niobe, who was destroyed by Apollo and Diana

RATINGS	
Cultural interest	● ● ● ● ●
Good for kids	● ●
Specialist shopping	● ● ● ● ●
Value for money	● ● ● ●

Head of Young Girl, a pencil sketch by da Vinci (top); a detail of the Madonna from Madonna with Child and Two Angels by Filippo Lippi (opposite)

The Uffizi's management have long been aware of its shortage of display areas and visitor facilities. In the first years of the 21st century a huge redevelopment plan was launched, which will eventually almost double the museum's space, as well as provide much-needed visitor infrastructure in the shape of better access, more cloakrooms and refreshment facilities. Works in storage will emerge, and the aim is to open up on a regular basis the Corridoio Vasariano (▷ 91), which links the Uffizi with the Palazzo Pitti. Work will continue throughout the first decade of the century; while it's in progress the museum will remain open as usual, although some galleries will close on a rotating basis.

family chapel in Santa Trinità (▷ 96). It was painted by Gentile da Fabriano and Strozzi's culture, learning and wealth are reflected in the richness of detail and lavish use of gold in the Magi procession. The panels above the altar showing the *Nativity*, the *Rest on the Flight into Egypt* and the *Presentation*, move stylistically towards the Renaissance, as can be seen by the realistically blue sky.

THE DUKE AND DUCHESS OF URBINO
This double portrait was painted in 1465 by Piero della Francesca. It has an allegorical scene on the reverse and was completed two years after the death of the Duchess, Battista Sforza. It shows the sitters in profile; the Duke, Federigo da Montefeltro, lost his right eye in battle and was always portrayed from the left. Piero painted few portraits and it is worth comparing this with his religious works in Arezzo (▷ 131) and Sansepolcro (▷ 146). The town behind Battista is Gubbio, the place of her death in childbirth.

PRIMAVERA
Probably dating from around 1477, this instantly familiar painting by Sandro Botticelli (1445–1510) is associated with the nuptials of Lorenzo di Pierfrancesco de' Medici, cousin of Lorenzo the Magnificent: It was placed outside the wedding chamber. The symbolism of this picture celebrates fecundity and new life through

the freshness of spring. The identities of the figures reflect the Renaissance interest in the classical world; on the right Zephyrus, the wind god, pursues the nymph Cloris, who is transformed into Flora, the pregnant goddess of spring. The central figure is Venus, goddess of love, flanked by the Three Graces with Cupid above and Mercury fending off stormy winter clouds. Art historians have argued for years over the exact meaning of all this, but the picture probably ·celebrates the triumph of Venus, typified by the burgeoning of spring after winter.

THE BIRTH OF VENUS

This is another of Botticelli's instantly recognizable pictures and the last of his mythological works. It was painted about 1484 for the villa of Pierfrancesco de' Medici, which also housed the *Primavera*. Its theme is often interpreted as the myth of Venus' birth, which taught that the goddess was born from the sea after it had been impregnated by the castration of Uranus, an allegory for the creation of beauty. Zephyrus, god of the west wind, accompanied by the nymph Cloris, blows the goddess ashore to be clothed by Hora, daughter of Aurora, goddess of dawn. The liberties taken with anatomy—note the unnatural length of Venus' neck and shoulders and the awkward left arm—serve to add to the beauty of the central figure, creating a dreamlike picture of grace and harmony.

Diptych of the Duke and Duchess of Urbino

TIPS

● Advance booking is highly recommended; waiting times for entrance, even in the quieter winter months, can be up to 3 hours.
● Plan what you want to see before you start and remember that backtracking is difficult.
● Be patient, the highlights are often blocked by large groups, making them virtually invisible.
● There are frequently long waits for the toilets; go before you come or after you leave.
● The audioguides will help you get more out of your visit.

The Doni Tondo is the only example of a painting by Michelangelo in Florence

ANNUNCIATION

Previous depictions of the Archangel Gabriel announcing the news of her pregnancy to the Virgin Mary were almost all interior scenes, laid out on the vertical. This early Leonardo da Vinci departs from the convention, showing the Virgin and angel against a lovingly detailed background of both architecture and landscape, where soft light falls on the distant mountains and water and every detail is observed with the greatest precision. It was probably painted about 1475, when Leonardo was still a pupil of Andrea del Verrocchio.

THE TRIBUNA

The octagonal room 18, known as the Tribuna, once held some of the greatest of the Medici treasures. It is still home to important classical sculptures, notably the *Medici Venus*, a first-century BC Greek copy of the Aphrodite of Cnidos. The walls are hung with some of the Uffizi's most compelling portraits, depictions of the ruling Medici and their children by Agnolo Bronzino. Ice-cold and perfect, they epitomize the power and wealth of the family at its zenith. High on one wall you can also see Rosso Fiorentino's *Musical Cherub*.

THE HOLY FAMILY

Michelangelo created this painting, also known as the *Doni Tondo*, between 1504 and 1505 for the marriage of Agnolo Doni and Maddalena Strozzi. It's his only completed easel painting, and a precursor to the Sistine Chapel frescoes at the Vatican Museums in Rome. The composition is perfectly aligned with the shape of the picture, an eye-satisfying series of circular forms.

THE RAPHAEL PAINTINGS

Several important works hang in room 26, including the luminous *Madonna del Cardellino*, a self-portrait and the portrait group *Leo X*

Prints for sale outside the gallery

with *Giulio de' Medici*, a wonderfully sinister group of clerics, painted shortly before Rapahel's death.

Primavera by Botticelli

THE VENUS OF URBINO

This sensual, earthy nude was painted *c*1538 by Tiziano Vecellio, better known as Titian (*c*1488–1576). This is no idealized female beauty, but a warm-blooded, provocative woman who serves as an allegory for the delights of married love. It's a superbly composed piece, the relaxed figure gazing out with a mischievous expression, while the domestic touches of the servants in the background and the little dog lend the whole scene a feeling of temporal reality.

MADONNA DAL COLLO LUNGO

The Uffizi is rich in Mannerist paintings and none better illustrates the genre than the *Madonna of the Long Neck*, a sinuous and eccentric composition, full of elongated forms and brittle refinement. Painted for a church in Parma by Francesco Parmigianino (1504–40), it's actually unfinished, which may explain discrepancies such as the extraordinary row of shadows caused by a single column and the odd, three-legged scroll.

BACKGROUND

The Palazzo degli Uffizi was originally intended to be government offices *(uffizi)* of the Grand Duchy of Tuscany and was built between 1560 and 1574 by Giorgio Vasari, under the orders of Cosimo I de' Medici. His son, Francesco I (1541–87), had the upper floor converted to house his art collections, which were available for public inspection from 1591, making the Uffizi one of the oldest museums in Europe. Succeeding Medici dukes added to the collections, which were bequeathed to the people of Florence by the last member of the family, Anna Maria Lodovica, in 1737, on the condition that the works never leave the city. In the 19th century much of the sculpture and the archaeological collections were transferred elsewhere, making the Uffizi essentially a painting gallery with some classical sculptures. In 1993 a terrorist bomb killed five people and caused great damage, and partly as a result of this, the gallery has undergone major reorganization. The Uffizi continues to acquire paintings and drawings but, with space at a premium, a huge development project is scheduled to take place over the next few years (see panel on page 70).

BASICS

✚ 62 C3 • Piazzale degli Uffizi, 50122

☎ 055 238 8651

🕐 Tue–Sun 8.15–6.50 (hours usually extended in summer); booking in advance Mon–Fri 8.30–6.30, Sat 8.30–12.30, tel 055 294883

💶 Adult €9.50, under 18 free, free to all in Cultural Week (24–30 May)

🚌 B, 23

🎧 Audiotours in English, French, Spanish, German, Japanese, Italian from €6.50

📖 Official guidebook from €4.50

☕ Good, if expensive, café serving drinks and snacks at the end of the West Corridor. It has a superb terrace overlooking Piazza della Signoria

🏛 A good book and gift shop, selling art books and guidebooks, posters, prints, and the usual gift items

🚻 At the far end of the West Corridor, at the opposite end from where you start

www.firenzemusei.it

One of the many fountains in the Giardino di Boboli

Museo delle Porcellane, as seen from the Giardino di Boboli

A painted sarcophagus at the Museo Archeologico Nazionale

THE SIGHTS

GIARDINO DI BOBOLI

✚ 62 A5 • Palazzo Pitti, Piazza Pitti, 50125 ☎ 055 265 1838 🕓 Daily 8.15–7.30, Jun–end Aug; 8.15–6.30, Apr–end May; 8.15–5.30, Mar, Sep, Oct; 8.15–4.30, Nov–end Feb; closed 1st and last Mon of each month 🎫 Adult €2, under 18 free. Combined ticket available with Museo degli Argenti in the Pitti Palace, valid for 3 days, for €3 🚌 D, 11, 36, 37 🚻 ♿

This green space in the middle of Florence, a cool oasis on a hot summer's day, is the perfect fresh-air antidote to the many indoor sights in the city. Even at the height of summer the warren of small lanes and pathways provides a welcome refuge with elaborate fountains, grottoes, elegant buildings, formal gardens, lichen-covered statues and secluded glades.

The gardens are laid out on a hillside behind Palazzo Pitti (▷ 80–81) and stretch from the palace up to Forte Belvedere (▷ 197). They were designed by Niccolò Tribolo (1500–50) for Cosimo I de' Medici and were opened to the public in 1766. Near the main courtyard of Palazzo Pitti is the magnificent Grotta Grande. In each of the four corners are copies of Michelangelo's unfinished *Slaves*; the originals are in the Galleria dell'Accademia (▷ 67). Walk up the terraces to the Neptune fountain (1571), where you can either take a detour to the elegant pavilion Kaffeehaus, for wonderful views and refreshments, or continue up to

Cosimo I's court jester was captured as Bacchus for this fountain

the top of the garden to the large statue, *Abundance*.

Off the beaten track, follow the magnificent Viottolone, a wide, steep path lined by cypress trees and statues leading to the lower part of the garden. At the bottom is the magical Isolotto, an island surrounded by an oval moat, adorned with statues, lemon trees and the Oceanus fountain. You can reach the Museo delle Porcellane (the Porcelain Museum, ▷ 81) from the top of the gardens. **Don't miss** Before you leave, be sure to see the Bacchus fountain.

MUSEO ARCHEOLOGICO NAZIONALE

✚ 63 D2 • Via della Colonna 38, 50121 ☎ 055 23575 🕓 Mon 2–7, Tue, Thu 8.30–7, Wed, Fri–Sun 8.30–2 🎫 Adult €2, under 18 free 🚌 21, 22 www.comune.firenze.it

The Museo Archeologico Nazionale has an excellent collection of art and ancient objects, including one of the most important Etruscan and Egyptian collections in Italy. One of the museum's highlights is the restored bronze *Idolino*, which is exhibited in a room on the ground floor. The torso of this statue of

a young man, probably once used as a lampstand, is thought to date from the first century BC. The Etruscan collection includes the famous bronze *Chimera*, part lion, part goat and part snake, dating from the late fifth to the early fourth century BC. Here also is the monumental *Arringatore*, or *Orator*, dating from the Hellenistic period (the fourth to first century BC), and a statue of Minerva.

The Egyptian collection includes mummies, statuettes, sarcophagi and vases, along with a 14th-century BC Hittite chariot made of bone and wood. On the second floor is a collection of vases dating from the sixth and fifth centuries BC. Outstanding among these is the François Vase. Made in Athens around 570BC, this huge, highly decorative piece is one of the earliest examples of its kind.

MUSEO BARDINI

✚ 62 C4 • Piazza de' Mozzi 1, 50125 ☎ 055 234 2427 🕓 Closed for restoration

Art collector and antiques dealer Stefano Bardini (1836–1922) built Palazzo Bardini in 1883 to house his vast and eclectic art collection. It's a rewarding museum to visit for the huge variety of art on show and it is well organized. The collections include paintings, medieval and Renaissance sculpture, furniture, ceramics, arms and armour and musical instruments. In addition, Bardini was particularly fond of reclaiming doorways, staircases and ceilings from demolished buildings and many of these architectural bits and pieces have been incorporated into the palazzo. On his death, he bequeathed the house and its entire contents to the city. The Museo has been closed for restoration for some years.

The Pianta della Catena map at Museo di Firenze com'era, which is in the former convent of the Oblate order

Statues on display at the Anthropology Museum

MUSEO DELLA CASA FIORENTINA ANTICA

✚ 62 B3 • Via Porta Rossa 13, 50122 ☎ 055 238 8610 ⏰ Daily 8.15–1.50; closed 1st and 2nd Sun and 1st, 3rd and 5th Mon of the month 🎫 Free www.sbas.firenze.it

This stately 14th-century palace, also known as the Museo del Palazzo Davanzati, has been closed since 1995 for renovation. The former home of the wealthy Davizzi family was converted into a museum, giving a rare and vivid insight into the life of city merchants, artists and noblemen during the Middle Ages. The exterior is typical of a house of its period, with three floors rising above arches. The interior, including the furnishings, tapestries, ceramics, paintings and domestic objects, are all typical of a Florentine house built between the 15th and 17th centuries.

The only part of the palazzo presently on view to the public is the spacious entrance hall, temporarily housing furniture and other objects. Once the museum reopens, additional rooms on the third floor will be on view for the first time.

MUSEO DI FIRENZE COM'ERA

✚ 63 C2 • Via dell'Oriuolo 24, 50122 ☎ 055 261 6545 ⏰ Fri–Wed 9–1.30 🎫 Adult €2.60, under 17 €1 🚌 14, 23 www.comune.firenze.it

The Museum of Florence As It Was gives you a glimpse of what the city actually looked like at the various stages of its development through maps, plans, engravings and paintings, beautifully illustrating how many of the city's old landmarks have survived intact. The Pianta della Catena map is an outstanding exhibit. The original dates from 1490, and what

you see is a copy that fills a wall in the first room and shows the city at the height of the Renaissance. The bridges are all marked, and most of the churches are there, as are many of the streets and piazzas. It also shows an idyllic scene of fishermen hauling their catch from the Arno. The series of lunette paintings (1599) of Medici villas is by the Flemish painter Giusto Utens. Other illustrations show Florence as it was before the 19th-century demolition of the medieval buildings and streets around the Mercato Vecchio (the old market), the area now filled by Piazza della Repubblica (▷ 90).

MUSEO DELLA FONDAZIONE HORNE

✚ 63 C3 • Via de' Benci 6, 50122 ☎ 055 244661 ⏰ Mon–Sat 9–1 🎫 Adult €5, child (6–16) €3, under 6 free 🚌 B, C, 23

English art historian and collector Herbert Percy Horne (1864–1916) lived in Florence from 1904 and bought the Renaissance Palazzo Corsi to house his collection of paintings, furniture and sculpture. He carefully restored the building and lived on the top floor for the last months of his life. On his death, he left the palazzo and its contents to the people of Italy.

The collection is arranged on three floors of the building, which has an attractive courtyard and a decorated frieze. In one of the rooms off the courtyard is a portrait of Horne along with a copy of his book on Botticelli. Another room contains an excellent collection of drawings including works by Raphael, Bernini, Giulio Romano, Guido Reni and Rubens. Other important pieces in the museum include an age-darkened *Deposition* by Benozzo Gozzoli (c1421–97) and a *Holy Family*

by Domenico Beccafumi (1486–1551) in an elaborate gilt frame.

A beautiful depiction of the young St. Stephen by Giotto (c1267–1337), one of his most important paintings, is the highlight of the collection. There is a striking array of Renaissance furniture, including some splendidly inlaid chests, and several of the rooms have fine fireplaces. Also on display is a good collection of household objects and utensils.

MUSEO NAZIONALE DI ANTROPOLOGIA E ETNOLOGIA

✚ 62 C2 • Via del Proconsolo 12, 50122 ☎ 055 239 6449 ⏰ Mon, Wed–Sat 9–1 🎫 Adult €4, child (6–25) €2, under 6 free 🚌 A, 14

The anthropological museum, founded in 1869, was the first of its kind in Europe and is the most important anthropological and ethnological museum in Italy. The museum occupies the magnificent Palazzo Nonfinito, begun in 1593 by Buontalenti, but not finished, hence the name *nonfinito*. It is one of the finest on a street of exceptionally fine Renaissance palaces.

The 35 rooms are filled with old-fashioned showcases displaying a huge variety of items: Peruvian mummies collected in 1883, objects from Oceania probably gathered by the explorer Captain James Cook on his last voyage in 1776–79, shrunken heads from Ecuador, articles made by the Ainu people from Japan, items from places as far apart as Sumatra, Eritrea and North Pakistan, as well as musical instruments from all over the world.

Don't miss The museum holds a rare collection of material from the extraordinarily rich Kafiri culture of North Pakistan.

RATINGS

Cultural interest	●●●○
Historic interest	●●●○
Value for money	●●●●

BASICS

🞧 62 C3 • Via del Proconsolo 4, 50122
☎ 055 238 8606
🕐 Daily 8.15–1.50; closed 1st, 3rd and 5th Sun, and 2nd and 4th Mon of every month
🎫 Adult €4, under 18 free
🚌 A, 14
📖 Official guidebook €7.50
🏪 Small bookshop selling art books, museum guides, posters and gifts
🚻 On the ground floor
www.sbas.firenze.it

The Annunciation *in terracotta by Andrea della Robbia (above); a bust of Piero di Lorenzo de' Medici from the late 15th century on display at the museum (below)*

MUSEO NAZIONALE DEL BARGELLO

Come here to get an overview of Florentine sculpture through important works by Donatello, Ghiberti, Michelangelo and Cellini, fine Della Robbia terracottas and Mannerist bronzes.

The forbidding, crenellated Palazzo del Bargello, home to the Bargello Museum, was built in 1255 as the Palazzo del Popolo, the seat of the city's government. In the 16th century the police headquarters were here, along with a prison, which was in use until 1858. The museum was first opened to the public in 1865.

GROUND FLOOR

Begin in the Gothic courtyard with its statues and sculptures. Until 1786, executions were carried out here, and condemned prisoners spent their last night in the chapel on the first floor. Off the court-yard, the hall contains the gallery's most celebrated sculptures by Michelangelo and his contemporaries. Michelangelo's works include an early *Drunken Bacchus* (c1497)—a humorous portrayal of the god of wine—and the marble tondo of the Madonna and Child with the infant St. John, known as the *Pitti Tondo* (c1503). Important works by Benvenuto Cellini (1500–71) include *Narcissus*, carved from a block of Greek marble, and *Apollo and Hyacinth*. There is also a life-size preliminary bronze cast of his famous *Perseus*.

FIRST FLOOR

The loggia has bronze birds by Giambologna (1529–1608), while the Gothic Salone del Consiglio Generale has works by Donatello (1386–1466) and his contemporaries. Donatello's *Marzocco Lion*, the symbol of Florence, is the focus of the room, although his *St. George* and the sexually ambivalent bronze *David* are far more important artistically. On the walls hang two of the trial bronze panels made by Lorenzo Ghiberti and Filippo Brunelleschi for the Baptistery doors (▷ 88), a marble relief of the *Madonna and Child with Angels* by Agostino di Duccio (1418–81) and a number of attractive glazed terracottas Madonnas by Luca della Robbia (1400–82).

DECORATIVE ARTS

There are several rooms dedicated to European and Middle Eastern decorative art, including carpets and clocks. The Renaissance bronzes on display here form the most important collection of its kind in Italy.

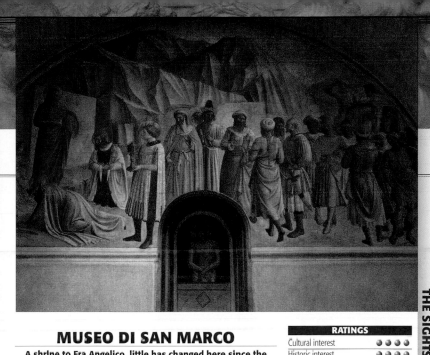

MUSEO DI SAN MARCO

A shrine to Fra Angelico, little has changed here since the 1400s, and it is a chance to see the Dominican friar's spiritual paintings in their original context.

The Convent of San Marco, home to the museum, is next to the church of the same name. The original convent on the site was of the Silvestrine Order, but it was given to the Dominicans by Cosimo 'il Vecchio' de' Medici, who commissioned the expansion of the existing buildings. Fra Angelico (c1387–1455), also known as Beato Angelico, lived here from 1436 to 1447, during which time he painted these ethereal images, full of endlessly fascinating detail. The museum was founded in 1869, and in 1921 most of Fra Angelico's panel paintings were transferred here from other museums in Florence.

THE CLOISTERS AND THE PILGRIMS' HOSPICE

A visit starts in Michelozzo's peaceful Cloister of Sant'Antonio. In the middle is an old cedar of Lebanon and at each corner is a small lunette fresco by Fra Angelico. The Pilgrims' Hospice is off this cloister, a long room full of beautiful paintings, glowing in bright jewel shades and gold leaf. At one end of the room is the superb *Deposition from the Cross* (c1435–40), and at the other the *Linaiouli Tabernacle* (1433) with its saints and enthroned Madonna; the border consists of musical angels, often reproduced on Christmas cards. This room also contains the great *Last Judgement* altarpiece (1431) and a series of reliquary tabernacles in gold frames showing 35 tiny scenes from the life of Christ.

There are paintings here by Fra Bartolomeo, Giovanni Sogliani and Lorenzo Lippi, among others. Before climbing the stairs to the monks' quarters, visit two more frescoes: Fra Angelico's large *Crucifixion and Saints* (1441–42) in the Chapter House and Domenico Ghirlandaio's *Last Supper* in the small refectory.

THE MONKS' CELLS

At the top of the stairs to the dormitory is one of Angelico's most famous frescoes, the *Annunciation* (1442). Each of the 44 tiny cells where the monks lived has a shuttered window and a small fresco by Fra Angelico or one of his assistants. Those by the master himself are in cells one to nine—look for the beautiful angel in cell three and the nativity scene in cell five. Famous inhabitants of the cells include Girolamo Savonarola (▷ 31), the rebel priest, who was prior in 1491, and the painter Fra Bartolomeo, who was a friar.

RATINGS	
Cultural interest	● ● ● ○
Historic interest	● ● ● ○
Value for money	● ● ● ○

TIP

● Only 120 people are allowed up to the dormitories at one time, so book your visit in advance (tel 055 294883), arrive early in the morning, or be prepared to wait.

BASICS

✚ 62 C1 • Piazza San Marco 1, 50121
☎ 055 238 8608
🕒 Mon–Fri 8.15–1.50, Sat–Sun 8.15–7; closed 1st, 3rd and 5th Sun and 2nd and 4th Mon of each month
💶 Adult €4, under 18 free
🚌 1, 6, 7
📖 Official guidebook €7.50
🏪 Small shop selling guidebooks to this and other museums, some art books, good reproductions of paintings, postcards, book marks and gift items
♿ On the ground floor
www.sbas.firenze.it

One of a large number of frescoes at the museum, this one depicting the Adoration of the Magi

The city's Science Museum has exhibits dedicated to Galileo

A section of the beautiful frescoes on the ceiling of the Ognissanti (All Saints), founded by the order of the Umiliati

THE SIGHTS

MUSEO SALVATORE FERRAGAMO

✚ 62 B3 • Via Tornabuoni 2, 50123
☎ 055 336 0456 ◷ Mon–Fri 9–1, 2–6
🎫 Free 🚇 A ♿
www.salvatoreferragamo.com

This unusual museum is heaven for footwear fetishists. Salvatore Ferragamo's life story is a classic tale of rags to riches. Born in a small village near Naples in 1898 and one of 14 children, he emigrated to the US at the age of 16 and soon began designing shoes to be worn by actors in movies. In 1927 he moved back to Italy and opened his workshop in Palazzo Spini Ferone in Florence, which is still the company's business headquarters as well as the museum. Ferragamo shod some of the world's most famous feet, and shoes made for such glamorous names as Judy Garland, Lana Turner, Lauren Bacall, Audrey Hepburn, Marilyn Monroe and Eva Perón are on display.

Marilyn Monroe's stilettos were entirely covered in red Swarovski crystals

They are all exquisite and some are totally fantastical, decorated with intricate beadwork, rhinestones and ostrich feathers or stacked on enormously high platform soles in bands of suede. Each pair of shoes is accompanied by an anecdote about the owner from Ferragamo himself, which is a great way of supplying an intimate glimpse of celebrities from the past.
Don't miss Marilyn Monroe's red stilettos are beautifully made

from satin. You should also look out for the sandals made from 18-carat gold chain for the wife of an Australian tycoon.

MUSEO DI STORIA DELLA SCIENZA

✚ 62 C3 • Piazza dei Giudici 1, 50121
☎ 055 265311 ◷ Mon, Wed–Fri 9.30–5, Tue, Sat 9.30–1, Jun–end Sep; Mon, Wed–Sat 9.30–5, Tue 9.30–1, rest of year 🎫 Adult €6.50, child (7–14) €3, under 7 free 🚌 B, 23
www.imss.fi.it

This absorbing and informative museum explores the history of physics, chemistry, astronomy and medicine through scientific and mathematical instruments, many of them both practical and beautifully decorated. As you look at the exhibits, the significant contribution made by Florence and Tuscany to the history of science becomes clear.

Room IV is dedicated to Galileo Galilei (1564–1642), who was born in Pisa and died in Florence, having spent years in the service of the Medici family. One of his many achievements was the perfection of the telescope, and here you can see the instrument through which he observed Jupiter's four moons for the first time. The museum also charts the progressive improvement of the telescope from Galileo's first examples, made in 1610.

Another room in the museum, Room XII, is dedicated to the development of the mechanical clock, with beautiful examples of pocket watches. Room XVIII has some gruesome 18th-century anatomical waxworks and terracotta models that demonstrate possible complications of childbirth, along with sets of surgical instruments from that time, including one for amputation. If you are of a nervous disposition, it might be best to move quickly through the room.

OGNISSANTI

✚ 62 A2 • Borgo Ognissanti, 50123
☎ 055 239 8700 ◷ Church: Daily 7.30–12.30, 4–7.30; Convent and Cloister: Mon, Tue, Sat 9–noon 🎫 Free 🚌 B, 12

The principal reason to visit this church to the west of the city is to see Domenico Ghirlandaio's (c1448–94) celebrated *Cenacolo*, which is actually in the convent next door.

But the church, which dates from the 12th century, has a few riches of its own. The elaborate exterior in travertine, a light-coloured stone, positively glows; there is an attractive lunette of the *Coronation of the Virgin* above the door. Inside there are a few paintings and a couple of tombs of note, including that of Botticelli, whose tombstone lies in the south transept, and of the explorer Amerigo Vespucci (1451–1512), whose family lived on Borgo Ognissanti; their family tombstone is in the floor to the left of the altar. It is said that Amerigo gave his name to the New World. Look for Ghirlandaio's early frescoes above the second altar on the south side; Botticelli's fine *St. Augustine in his Study* (1480); and a fresco of St. Jerome (1480) by Ghirlandaio.

Ghirlandaio's *Cenacolo* (a depiction of the Last Supper) is in the vaulted convent refectory to the left of the church. He painted four such scenes in Florence, of which this one, dating from 1480, is the best and said to have inspired da Vinci's *Last Supper*. The familiar scene is set against the background of a garden with charming details such as birds, flowers and fruit trees. The *Annunciation* by the same artist dates from 1369.
Don't miss The beautiful high altar in the church has marble and mother-of-pearl inlay.

Two saints' statues in a niche on the façade of the Orsanmichele

Fountain outside the Ospedale degli Innocenti

The ceiling of the gallery in Palazzo Medici-Riccardi

ORSANMICHELE

✚ 62 C3 • Via Arte della Lana, 50122
☎ 055 284944 ⏱ Closed for restoration

The Orsanmichele was built as a grain market in 1337, and the original building had a granary on the upper floor. When the market was moved in 1380, the ground floor became a church. The city's guilds commissioned some of the best artists of the day to make statues of patron saints to sit in the canopied niches, and so created a permanent outdoor exhibition of 15th-century Florentine sculpture. These statues are being removed one by one for restoration and copies are being put in their places; some of the original statues are still here, including Lorenzo Ghiberti's bronzes of St. Matthew (1419–22) and St. Stephen (1427–28). Inside, frescoes of patron saints decorate the walls, but the church's focal point is the Gothic tabernacle, a large decorative work commissioned by the survivors of the Black Death in 1349. Even though the church is closed for restoration, classical music concerts are held here. Check with the tourist office.

OSPEDALE DEGLI INNOCENTI

✚ 63 D1 • Piazza della Santissima Annunziata, 50122 ☎ 055 249 1708 ⏱ Thu–Tue 8.30–1.30 💶 Adult €2.60, child (6–18) €1.60 🚌 C, 6

The Ospedale degli Innocenti opened as a foundling hospital in 1445. It was the first of its kind in Europe and remained open as an orphanage until 2000. It was home to the first school of obstetrics in Italy, and ground-breaking research into nutrition and vaccination was carried out

One of the tondi on the exterior of the Ospedale

here. The building, an important architectural landmark because of its beautiful portico by Filippo Brunelleschi (1377–1446), is an early Renaissance masterpiece.

A portico with nine arches borders Piazza della Santissima Annunziata (▷ 90) and is adorned with blue-and-white tondi (glazed terracotta medallions) of babies in swaddling clothes by Andrea della Robbia (1435–1525). At the other end of the portico is the window-wheel where babies were left anonymously by their mothers. Brunelleschi also designed the two cloisters. The Chiostro degli Uomini, reserved for men, is rather sober, whereas the Chiostro delle Donne, the women's cloister, is beautiful—a slim oblong in shape, with a low loggia above. From the Chiostro degli Uomini, stairs lead up to the Museo dello Spedale, a long room with a timbered ceiling where some fine paintings are hung, including Domenico Ghirlandaio's vivid *Adoration of the Magi* (1488). At one end of the room is a poignant collection of identification tags left by mothers in the hope that one day they might see their children again.

PALAZZO MEDICI-RICCARDI

✚ 62 C2 • Via Cavour 3, 50129
☎ 055 276 0340 ⏱ Thu–Tue 9–6.30 💶 Adult €4, child (6–12) €2.50, under 6 free 🚌 1, 7, 17 🔖

The massive Palazzo Medici-Riccardi was built by Michelozzo some time after 1444 as a town mansion for Cosimo il Vecchio, and was the residence of the Medici until 1540. The Riccardi family bought the palace in 1659 and enlarged it. It is now the headquarters of the provincial government. The Medici-Riccardi's surprise, after the slightly rugged and stately exterior, is one of the most pleasant little spaces in Florence, the Cappella dei Magi. Renovation work is going on here, but the palace is still open.

The main, columned courtyard is suitably noble, and the adjacent gardens are filled with lemon trees in huge terracotta pots. The principal staircase off the courtyard leads to the chapel, which is covered by Benozzo Gozzoli's restored frescoes of the *Procession of the Magi to Bethlehem* (1459–63). The glorious colours used have tremendous immediacy and the clothes are particularly splendid—you can almost feel the textures of the rich fabrics. Gozzoli dotted the scene with members of the Medici family and other well-known people of the day; the beautifully dressed young ruler on a horse on the right-hand wall is believed to be an idealized portrait of Lorenzo Il Magnifico. The gallery is a large and elaborate baroque room decorated with mirrors, plasterwork and ceiling frescoes by Luca Giordano (1683). Look for the *Madonna and Child* by Filippo Lippi in the smaller adjoining room.

Palazzo Pitti

Florence's largest and most opulent palace was once the main seat of the Medici. It now contains the Galleria Palatina with Florence's most important picture collection after the Uffizi.

Ceiling detail from the Hall of Mars (top), and the Room of the Iliad (above), Galleria Palatina

SEEING THE PALAZZO PITTI

The Pitti's collections are vast: There are eight museums and galleries in all. It makes sense to concentrate on the Galleria Palatina, a suite of 26 rooms, with walls covered with paintings. The works are displayed much as they were in the 17th century, covering the walls from floor to ceiling in no discernible chronological order. Allow 2–3 hours to fully appreciate the paintings before moving on to another gallery that takes your fancy. Be prepared for crowds, and also for sections or collections to be closed; you can book ahead to avoid disappointment (tel 055 294883). There is much to see, but make sure you leave time to relax afterwards in the Giardino di Boboli behind the palace (▷ 74). Combined tickets can be bought (see Basics).

HIGHLIGHTS

APPARTAMENTI REALI

The royal apartments have been expertly and sensitively restored to their 19th-century condition. From the 17th century they were the residence by turn of the Medici, the dukes of Lorraine and the Savoy family, including Italy's first monarch, King Umberto I. They are hard to beat in terms of extravagance, with their gilding and stuccowork, rich damask hangings, vast chandeliers, enormous gilt mirrors, period furnishings, paintings and sculptures.

THE COURTYARD

The main entrance to the palace leads you through to a grand courtyard (1560–70), an excellent example of Florentine Mannerist architecture by Bartolomeo Ammanati (1511–92), best known for the Ponte Santa Trinità (▷ 90). It was used as a stage for lavish spectacles between the 16th and 18th centuries, and is still the venue for concerts and ballet in the summer.

GALLERIA PALATINA

Madonna and Child (Sala di Promoteo)

Painted in 1452 and known as the *Pitti Tondo*, Filippo Lippi's famous work perfectly combines exquisite painting and intense spirituality. The eye is drawn to the pure face of the Virgin, who forms the central point, and the Christ Child lying on her knee; around her are scenes from the life of her mother, St. Anne.

Madonna della Seggiola (Sala di Saturno)

Raphael painted this tondo in Rome in 1514, and it has been in the Pitti since the 18th century. Although heavily influenced by Venetian painting, evident in its use of light and shade, the painting follows a strictly Florentine form, its shape emphasizing the tender curves of the Virgin and Child.

Pietro Aretino (Sala di Apollo)

Portraiture gained importance during the High Renaissance as the Church lost its control over subject matter, and new money brought self-made men to prominence. Titian painted this portrait of the

satirical poet Pietro Aretino in 1545, after Aretino had moved from Mantua to Venice, Titian's native city.

Sleeping Cupid (Sala dell'Educazione di Giove)
This plump little sleeping Cupid is full of allegorical references to passion and lost love. Caravaggio painted it when he was in Malta in 1608. By this time he had already lived in Rome, where he had studied and grasped the fine details of human anatomy, and was beginning to concentrate on the development of chiaroscuro, the contrast of light and dark, a technique he expertly employed in his later work.

MUSEO DEGLI ARGENTI
In a series of sumptuous state rooms, this museum concentrates on luxury items amassed by the Medici dukes. There is a huge range, including antique vases collected by Lorenzo Il Magnifico, stunningly worked figurines and a vast number of inlaid pieces.

BACKGROUND
Construction began on the Palazzo Pitti in 1457, supposedly to a design by Filippo Brunelleschi. It was originally the private residence of the banker Luca Pitti, a rival of the Medici family, and his descendants, but in 1549 the family funds dried up and it was purchased by Cosimo I's wife, the Grand Duchess Eleonora. It became the official residence of the Grand Dukes and was occupied by ruling families until 1919, when it was presented to the state by Vittorio Emanuele III. Under Medici ownership it was repeatedly enlarged, notably in the 16th century, when Ammanati lengthened the façade and built the courtyard; the side wings were added in the 18th and 19th centuries. The Medici family began decorating and amassing the collections in the 17th century. The main galleries opened to the public in 1833 and the Galleria d'Arte Moderna, Florence's modern art museum, joined the gallery complex in 1924.

A Concert by Paganini, painted by Annibale Gatti (1827–1909), in the Galleria d'Arte Moderna

GALLERY GUIDE
Galleria Palatina: The main collection, strong on 16th-century works; in wing of main palace.
Galleria d'Arte Moderna: Works spanning the mid-18th to mid-20th centuries; in main building on the floor above the Palatina.
Museo degli Argenti: Objects, gold and jewellery from the Medici collections; accessed from the main courtyard.
Museo del Costume: Rotating exhibitions of clothing from the early 18th to mid-20th centuries; in Palazzina Meridiana in the south wing.
Museo delle Porcellane: French, Italian, German and Viennese porcelain and ceramics; in a pavilion at the top of the Boboli Gardens.
Appartamenti Reali: Lavishly decorated state apartments following on from the Palatina.
Collezione Contini Bonacossi: A picture collection on long-term loan; next to the Museo del Costume in the Palazzina Meridiana.
Museo delle Carozze: Carriage collection—closed at present.

Venus Italica in the Sala di Venere (Hall of Venus) in the Palatina

RATINGS	
Cultural interest	● ● ● ○
Good for kids	● ● ● ○
Historic interest	● ● ● ●
Photo stops	● ● ● ●

BASICS

✚ 62 C3 • Piazza della Signoria, 50122
☎ 055 276 8465; 055 276 8224 to book an activity (see Tip)
🕐 Fri–Wed 9–7, Thu 9–2
💶 Adult €6, under 18 €2
🚌 A, B
🎧 Audioguides in Italian and English €4.30
📖 Different formats for €11 and €4.65
📚 A good bookshop selling books for children, art books, posters, postcards and gift items
🏛 On the ground floor next to the ticket office
www.comune.fi.it
www.museoragazzi.it

TIP

• A number of activities now make a visit to the palazzo more entertaining. For example, you can be taken on a guided tour by costumed actors, or take the children to a themed games room. To take part, €2 are added to the entry fee, or buy a family ticket for 4 at €14, or for 5 at €16.

A copy of Putto *by Andrea del Verracchio tops the fountain in the courtyard—the original is inside the palace (top); the tower is easily recognizable around the city (above)*

PALAZZO VECCHIO

This is the grand embodiment of Florentine civic purpose dating from the 14th century, with both elaborately decorated public rooms and intimate private apartments.

Florence's town hall stands on the site of the medieval Palazzo dei Priori, which was demolished and rebuilt at the beginning of the 1300s. The Palazzo Vecchio was built as the seat of the government, and the bell in the tower summoned the citizens to the piazza below for public meetings in times of trouble. The Palazzo Vecchio is still home to the City of Florence council offices.

THE COURTYARD

The courtyard, reconstructed by architect Michelozzo in 1453, is beyond the main entrance. It was elaborately decorated by Giorgio Vasari in 1565 to celebrate the marriage of the son of Grand Duke Cosimo I to Joanna of Austria.

FIRST FLOOR

The largest room is the Salone dei Cinquecento, a meeting room for the 500-member Consiglio Maggiore (Grand Council). Vasari painted the frescoes here to celebrate Cosimo I's triumphs over Pisa and Siena. The most notable sculpture is Michelangelo's *Victory*. Next door, the tiny, windowless Studiolo di Francesco I has allegorical paintings by Vasari helped by a team of assistants. It was here that the melancholic son of Cosimo I pursued his interest in alchemy. On the same floor, Vasari and his assistants decorated the Quartiere di Leone X with ornate illustrations of the history of the Medici family.

SECOND FLOOR

Access to the private apartments of Cosimo I's wife, Eleonora di Toledo, is via a balcony across the end of the Salone dei Cinquecento. This gives you a close up-view of the ceiling. The chapel is decorated with frescoes of various saints. The Sala dei Gigli owes its name to the lily *(giglio)* motif, a symbol of the city; here you can see Donatello's bronze statue, *Judith and Holofernes* (1455). The political writer Niccolò Machiavelli used the Cancellaria next door as an office from 1498 to 1512, when he was a government secretary.

PIAZZA DELLA SIGNORIA

Florence's most noble and famous piazza is a vast, open-air, traffic-free sculpture gallery with elegant cafés and restaurants.

This wide, open square next to the Galleria degli Uffizi (▷ 68–73), marks the heart of the *centro storico* (old town). The Piazza della Signoria has been the political focus of Florence since the Middle Ages. Surrounded by tall buildings, notably the grand, austere Palazzo Vecchio (see opposite), this is where the ruling city elders called open-air public assemblies in times of crisis. The crowd was often provoked by speeches from the *arringhiera* (oration terrace), a raised platform, and the gatherings frequently degenerated into violence. The area in front of the Palazzo Vecchio was named Piazza del Popolo in 1307.

THE SCULPTURES

The enormous Loggia dei Lanzi (also known as the Loggia della Signoria) was designed to be used by dignitaries for formal meetings and ceremonies. It was completed in 1382 and has been used as an open-air sculpture museum since the late 18th century.

The front is dominated by Benvenuto Cellini's Mannerist bronze *Perseus* (1545). Considered his greatest work, it shows Perseus triumphantly holding aloft the severed head of Medusa. Near it is Giambologna's (1529–1608) last work, the *Rape of the Sabine Women*, completed in 1583. Donatello's *Judith and Holofernes* was the first of the statues to be placed in the piazza, but what you see is a copy—the original is in the Palazzo Vecchio.

In front of the main entrance to the Palazzo Vecchio stands a copy of Michelangelo's *David* (the original is in the Accademia, ▷ 66). The other large statue near by is Baccio Bandinelli's *Hercules and Cacus* (1534), described by his rival Cellini as an 'old sack full of melons'. At the corner of the Palazzo Vecchio is Bartolomeo Ammanati's massive fountain (1575), with the undignified figure of Neptune. The watery theme is said to reflect Cosimo I's naval ambitions. The large equestrian bronze, Giambologna's monument to Cosimo I (1595), shows detailed scenes of the Grand Duke's coronation and his victory over the Sienese.

The plaque in the pavement in front of the fountain marks the spot where Girolamo Savonarola was burned at the stake as a heretic and traitor on 23 May 1498 (▷ 31). A ceremony to mark his death is held in the square annually on this day.

RATINGS

Cultural interest	●●● ○
Good for kids	●● ○
Historic interest	●●●● ○
Walkability	●●● ○

BASICS

🔲 62 C3 • Piazza delle Signoria, 50122
🎫 Free
🚌 A, B

TIPS

● An elegant (if expensive) table at the Café Rivoire is a good place to people watch. Otherwise, perch on a stone bench under the Loggia dei Lanzi.
● Free open-air concerts are held here in summer.

Cellini's Perseus *stands at 3.2m (10.5ft) and was placed here in 1554 (top); Neptune, as portrayed by Ammanati in his* Fountain of Neptune *(above)*

Piazza del Duomo

Florence's cathedral, bell tower and baptistery form one of the most important early Renaissance architectural complexes in Italy. Brunelleschi's mighty freestanding dome is a masterpiece of early engineering.

The Last Judgement *fresco* inside the dome of the Duomo

A Roman temple is said to have stood on the site of the *Battistero*

A Duomo-styled umbrella on sale as a gift

SEEING THE PIAZZA DEL DUOMO

The sublime complex of the Duomo, Campanile, Battistero and Museo dell'Opera del Duomo lies just north of the Piazza della Signoria and the River Arno and less than 20 minutes' walk east from the rail station. The Duomo (cathedral), the Battistero (baptistery) and Campanile (bell tower) stand in their own square. It's constantly busy with visitors, so get here early in the day to beat the crowds. Many of the best artworks are displayed in the Museo dell'Opera del Duomo, behind the east end of the Duomo. The entrance to the dome is by the Porta dei Canonici on the south side of the Duomo.

RATINGS	
Good for kids	● ● ● ●
Historic interest	● ● ● ● ●
Photo stops	● ● ● ● ●
Value for money	● ● ● ● ●

TIP

● You will not be allowed into the Duomo wearing skimpy shorts or a sleeveless top.

HIGHLIGHTS

THE DUOMO'S EXTERIOR

The Duomo of Santa Maria del Fiore, to give it its full name, is huge—there is room inside for 20,000 people. Walk all the way around its green- and-white striped marble exterior to appreciate the vast proportions. The marble came from all over Tuscany: white from Carrara, red from the Maremma and green from Prato. Several doors punctuate the walls, the most elaborate being the Porta della Mandorla with its relief of the Assumption sculpted by Nanni di Banco in 1420. Also look out for the late 14th-century Porta dei Canonici and the unfinished gallery round the base of the dome. Work on this ceased after Michelangelo disparagingly described it as a 'cricket's cage'. The ornate Gothic-style façade dates from the 19th century; the original was destroyed in the late 1500s.

THE DUOMO'S INTERIOR

Compared with the outside, the interior of the cathedral is remarkably austere. Over the years many of the finest artworks have been moved to the Museo dell'Opera del Duomo, leaving the Duomo relatively bare. But you are better able to appreciate the soaring space beneath the Gothic arches, the patterned marble flooring, the scale of the dome itself and the superb mid-15th-century stained-glass windows,

Detail of the mosaic depicting the Annunciation *(top) and a 14th-century relief (above) on the exterior of the Duomo; the dome of the Duomo is one of the iconic images of Florence (opposite)*

Marble figures depicting the virtues Temperance (right) and Fortitude (below right) on the Campanile; a sculpted figure in one of the portals on the exterior of the Duomo (below)

which are among Italy's finest. There are two equestrian memorials in fresco dedicated to two of Florence's most famous *condottieri* (mercenary soldiers): Niccolò da Tolentino (1456) by Andrea del Castagno, and a far sharper-edged portrait (1436) of Englishman Sir John Hawkwood, by Paolo Uccello. Terracotta reliefs by Luca della Robbia (1400–82) decorate both north and south sacristy doors, and a superb bronze reliquary urn by Lorenzo Ghiberti stands in the central apse.

Steps to the crypt of Santa Reparata lead down from the south aisle. The church was excavated in the 1960s and dates from anywhere between the sixth and 12th centuries. This space has archaeological finds dating from Roman times and including paleo-Christian and Romanesque elements, as well as mosaics and early frescoes. It's a confusing and complicated maze, so it might be better, and certainly more inspiring, to take in the tomb of Filippo Brunelleschi (1377–1446), architect of the cathedral's remarkable dome. You'll find this behind a grille to the left of the bottom of the steps.

INSIDE THE DOME

Climbing the rather claustrophobic 463 steps of the dome *(cupola)* is a must; not only will you be rewarded with some of Florence's best views from the top but you'll also get an insight into the construction of Brunelleschi's great plan. He beat Ghiberti in a competition to win the commission—a reversal of the Baptistery doors competition (see below). First stopping point is the gallery that runs round the interior of the dome, with vertiginous views to the street beneath and close-ups of the stained-glass roundels. From here up, you're climbing between the inner and outer shells of the dome itself, all slanting space, arches and brickwork, a fine example of the sophistication of Renaissance building techniques and the genius of the architect.

KEY TO FLOOR PLAN OF THE DUOMO
1. L'Assunta window by Ghiberti Incoronazione di Maria
2. Equestrian painting of Niccolò da Tolentino, by A. del Castagno
3. Equestrian figure of Giovanni Acuto (John Hawkwood) painted by Uccello
4. 14th-century window, and below, *Dante and the Divine Comedy* by D. di Michelino
5. Marble altar (Buggiano)
6. In the door, lunette, *Risurrezione*, by Luca della Robbia
7. New sacristy
8. Above the altar, two angels (Luca della Robbia), below the altar reliquary of St. Zenobius by Ghiberti
9. Lunette, *Risurrezione*, terracotta by Della Robbia
10. Old sacristy
11. Altar by Michelozzo
12. Entrance to the dome
13. Bust of Brunelleschi, by A. Cavalcanti
14. Stairs to the Cripta di Santa Reparata

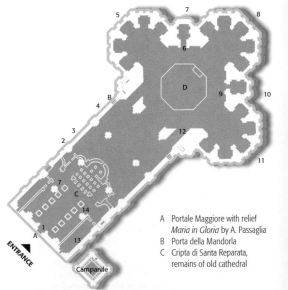

A Portale Maggiore with relief *Maria in Gloria* by A. Passaglia
B Porta della Mandorla
C Cripta di Santa Reparata, remains of old cathedral

THE SIGHTS

MUSEO DELL'OPERA DEL DUOMO

The Museo dell'Opera del Duomo contains the sculptures and paintings from the Duomo complex, too precious to be left to the mercy of modern pollution. The building, behind the east end of the Duomo, is also home to the workshops that are responsible for the maintenance of the fabric of the cathedral and its works of art. Ghiberti's Gates of Paradise (see below) probably steal the show, but the collection as a whole provides a splendid overview of the best of Florentine sculpture, with works by many of the city's most outstanding sculptors.

Luca della Robbia

Don't miss the *cantoria* by this artist, a superb contrast to that by Ghiberti. The frame of this choir loft is inscribed with the words from

A detail of a dancing choir, one of the panels from Luca della Robbia's cantoria *originally above the door of the Sacristy of the Masses in the Duomo and now in the Museo*

THE SIGHTS

Psalm 33, 'Praise the Lord with harp, sing unto him with psaltery and the instrument of ten strings', and the solemn young sculpted musicians follow this command perfectly.

Donatello

The collection contains several works by Donatello (1386–1466), the greatest of Michelangelo's predecessors. He was involved with sculpting the 16 statues that once stood in the niches of the Campanile, and created the powerful figure of the prophet Habbakuk. It is so realistic he is said to have seized it, crying 'Speak, speak!' He was also responsible for the wood carving of the gaunt and bedraggled Mary Magdalene, while his lighter side emerges in the choir gallery *(cantoria)* from the Duomo, where he carved capering infants and cherbubs.

Arnolfo di Cambio

This artist (active mid-13th century) sculpted figures for the earlier façade of the Duomo, demolished in 1587. These, which include a Madonna, are displayed in the first rooms. One of these is of Santa Reparata, who is one of Florence's patron saints and gave her name to the first church on the site of the Duomo.

Michelangelo

The sculptor was 80 when he created his *Pietà*, said to be his last work. He intended it for his own tomb, but never finished it; the figure of Nicodemus is traditionally believed to be a self-portrait.

Michelangelo's Pietà *depicts the mourning of Christ's death*

Christ Enthroned is the focal point of the Battistero's golden mosaic cupola by Jacopo de Torrita (far right); one of the sculptural group from the Baptism of Christ in the museum (below right)

GHIBERTI'S BAPTISTERY DOORS

Having finished the north doors in the baptistery in 1424 (see below), Ghiberti set to work on the doors for the east side, a work of such beauty that Michelangelo named them the Gates of Paradise. Completed in 1452, they are made up of 10 relief panels of biblical subjects, exquisitely carved in low relief and high-lighted in gold to give wonderful perspective and pictorial effects. Their artistic importance is in their use of perspective, extending

the scenes far into the background, which was a totally new concept at the time that became typical of work produced during the Renaissance. The composition is far more naturalistic than in the earlier baptistery doors, with figures grouped so as to intensify the drama of each scene. The subjects are taken from the first books of the Bible, and each panel contains several scenes from each selected story, while the border panels show Old Testament figures, busts, vegetation and flowers, inhabited by insects, frogs and lizards.

Moses receiving the Ten Commandments is a scene from one of the bronze panels on the Battistero's Gates of Paradise (above)

The panels read left to right, top to bottom, starting with Adam and Eve and the story of their creation, temptation and expulsion from Eden. Next is a panel devoted to the murder of Abel by Cain; this is followed by the story of Noah and his ark—look out for the quirkily observed animals, which include an elephant. This is followed by the tale of Abraham and Isaac, then Jacob and Esau, and, finally, Joseph and his brothers, three panels that tell complex stories and are rich in detail. The next panel is essentially a single scene, showing Moses on Mount Sinai receiving the tablets of the Ten Commandments from God, while the frightened people gather below. This contrasts with Joshua's story, the next relief, which shows the crossing through the dried-up River Jordan and the walls of Jericho tumbling down. The final two scenes are devoted to the story of David and Goliath and the visit by the Queen of Sheba and her retinue to King Solomon. Look on the frame of the left-hand door for Ghiberti's self-portrait—the rather smug-looking, bald-headed man. The doors, restored after they were damaged by the 1966 floods, are now on display at the Museo dell'Opera del Duomo—those on the Battistero are replicas.

THE BATTISTERO

The octagonal baptistery, entirely encased in green and white marble, is one of Florence's oldest buildings, probably dating from around the sixth to seventh century, and remodelled in the 11th century. It is most famous for its three sets of bronze doors, the south set dating from the 1330s by Andrea Pisano, and the north and east by Lorenzo Ghiberti. Ghiberti, aged 20, won the commission for the north doors in a competition and worked on them from 1403 to 1424, embarking on his finest achievement, the east set (see above), immediately afterwards. The panels in the doors here are reproductions; the originals are kept away from pollution in the Museo dell'Opera del Duomo.

The interior of the dome glitters with Florence's only mosaic cycle, the earliest dating from 1225. Look above the entrance door and follow the history of the world from the Creation to John the Baptist, before taking in the main image of Christ and the Last Judgement, together with the Apostles and the Virgin.

The fresco of the statute of Sir John Hawkwood in the Duomo (above); the Campanile is 85m (278ft)

THE CAMPANILE

Giotto designed the campanile in 1334, but died before it was completed. Both Andrea Pisano, who took over after Giotto's death in 1337, and Francesco Talenti altered the original design considerably, strengthening the walls and adding large windows. The building is covered with bands of green, white and pink marble and is decorated with copies of sculptures and reliefs showing prophets and scenes from the Old Testament; the originals are in the Museo dell'Opera del Duomo. There are 414 steps to the top of the bell tower, which commands 360-degree views of Florence and the surrounding hills. The empty octagon marks the original site of the city's font, in which every child born over the previous year was once baptised on New Year's Day.

BACKGROUND

The sixth- to seventh-century baptistery was originally Florence's cathedral, later to be replaced by the Church of Santa Reparata, whose remains lie beneath the present Duomo. In the 13th century the city fathers decided to build a new cathedral, largely to flaunt the city's political clout and growing wealth and size. In 1294 the project was entrusted to Arnolfo di Cambio, and work continued throughout the 14th century, with various architects realizing Arnolfo's plan. The Duomo's campanile was finished by 1334 and by 1418 the nave and tribunes were complete. The building awaited the massive dome planned for the crossing, because nobody had yet worked out how it would be built. The architect Filippo Brunelleschi (1377–1446) offered his services, refusing to explain his solution, but exuding confidence. The building committee finally gave him the job, insisting that he work with his rival Lorenzo Ghiberti (1378–1455), who was responsible for the baptistery doors. In 1436 the first freestanding dome since Roman times was completed, and the cathedral consecrated. The lantern was finally finished in the 1460s.

BASICS

Duomo
✚ 62 C2 • Piazza del Duomo, 50122
☎ 055 230 2885 ☉ Mon–Wed, Fri 10–5, Thu 10–3.30, Sat 10–4.45, Sun 1.30–4.45 ✋ Free ☐ 1, 7, 17 Free guided tours in English, French, German, Spanish, Italian, Mon–Sat 10–12.30, 3–5, Sun 3–5; audioguide in English, French, Spanish, Italian for €1 📖 Guidebooks cover the whole complex, in Italian, English, French, German and Spanish for €10 📷 Bookshop sells guidebooks, art books, gifts and posters

Cupola
✚ 62 C2 • Piazza del Duomo, 50122
☎ 055 230 2885 ☉ Mon–Fri 9–7, Sat 10–4.45 (last entry 40 min before closing); closed 1st Sat of each month

Battistero
✚ 62 B2 • Piazza del Duomo, 50122
☎ 055 230 2885 ☉ Mon–Sat noon–6.30, Sun 8.30–1.30 ✋ Adult €3, under 6 free Audioguide for €2

Museo dell'Opera del Duomo
✚ 62 C2 • Piazza del Duomo, 50122
☎ 055 230 2885 ☉ Mon–Sat 9–7.30, Sun 8.30–1.30 ✋ Adult €6, under 6 free Audioguide €4 📷 Sells art books, postcards, gifts and posters

Campanile
✚ 62 C2 • Piazza del Duomo, 50122
☎ 055 230 2885 ☉ Daily 9–7 ✋ Adult €6, under 6 free

www.operaduomo.firenze.it

Piazza della Santissima Annunziata

Piazzale Michelangelo, set above the River Arno, commands impressive views over the city with the Duomo on the right

THE SIGHTS

PIAZZA DELLA REPUBBLICA

✚ 62 B3 • Piazza della Repubblica, 50123 🖐 Free 🚌 A, 22

This is not Florence's prettiest square, but it is traffic-free, one of the few open spaces at the heart of the city, and bustling with activity. It stands on the site of the Roman forum which, by the Middle Ages, was occupied by a market square and the Jewish ghetto. The Mercato Vecchio (old market), as it was known, was pulled down in the late 19th century in a wave of urban renewal; this is generally considered to have been a grave error of judgement on the part of the authorities of that time. Lined with important-looking buildings—nowadays largely banks and insurance company headquarters—Piazza della Repubblica is also a place to find outdoor cafés, street vendors and street performers. Dominating the western side is a vast triumphal arch and opposite this is the Savoy Hotel (▷ 246). On the corner of Via Roma is the lovely belle-époque Caffè Gilli, a great place for a rather expensive cappuccino.

PIAZZA DELLA SANTISSIMA ANNUNZIATA

✚ 63 D1 • Piazza della Santissima Annunziata, 50122 🖐 Free 🚌 C, 6

This space, arguably the loveliest piazza in Florence, remains much as it was when built. Designed by Filippo Brunelleschi (1377–1446), it is surrounded on three sides by graceful porticoes. The church of Santissima Annunziata (▷ 91) has elegant, neoclassical arches. To the right of the church is the Ospedale degli Innocenti (▷ 79), its portico adorned with Andrea della Robbia's blue and white

tondi of swaddled babies. The later portico of Antonio Sangallo and Baccio d'Agnolo (1516–25) is to the left, mirroring the Ospedale across the square, on which they based their design. In the middle of the piazza is a large equestrian statue of Grand Duke Ferdinand I by Giambologna, the artist's final work. The south side of the piazza is open, which means there are fine views of the cathedral dome (▷ 85–86). The wide steps under the left and right porticoes are a good vantage point, and they are often full of people chatting, eating or simply taking a break.

PIAZZALE MICHELANGELO

✚ 63 D4 • Piazzale Michelangelo, 50125 🖐 Free 🚌 12, 13

It is worth making the climb, or taking a bus, to Piazzale

Michelangelo on a hillside south of the Arno, for the unrivalled views over Florence. There's a huge replica of Michelangelo's *David* in the middle of the square, and terraces well placed for the panoramic views, which on a clear day extend beyond the city to the surrounding hills. The sunsets are glorious and on Sunday afternoons the piazza is packed with everyone taking advantage of the city's best photo opportunity. Piazzale Michelangelo is halfway along the broad, leafy road that winds through this part of the city, where traffic can be heavy at peak times.

PONTE SANTA TRINITÀ

✚ 62 B3 • Piazza Santa Trinità, 50123 🖐 Free 🚌 A, B www.firenzeturismo.it

The original Santa Trinità bridge was destroyed by bombs in 1944 during World War II, along with all the other bridges in Florence except the Ponte Vecchio (see opposite). It was carefully reconstructed using stone from the original quarries and what you see today is a faithful replica of Bartolomeo Ammanati's (1511–92) bridge of 1567. With three wide, graceful arches, it links the elegant Via Tornabuoni on the north bank of the Arno to the Oltrarno on the south side of the river. At each of its four corners stands one of the original *Four Seasons* statues, which fell into the river during the bombing, but were salvaged and reassembled; the last piece, the head of Spring, was fished out in 1961.

Ponte Santa Trinità is also where you get the best view of the Ponte Vecchio.

Spring, one of the Four Seasons *on the Ponte Santa Trinità, originally dating from 1608*

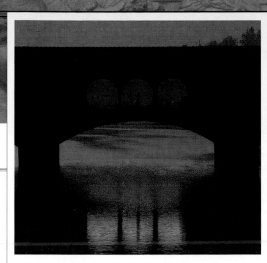

The Ponte Vecchio as silhouetted by a fiery sunset

A fresco showing scenes from the Life of St. Philip Benizzi

PONTE VECCHIO

The medieval bridge over the Arno, with its line of overhanging shops, is one of the immediately recognizable emblems of Florence.

✚ 62 B3 • Ponte Vecchio, 50123
🎟 Free 🚌 B, D

RATINGS	
Historic interest	●●●○
Photo stops	●●●●●
Specialist shopping	●●●○

If you can ignore the crowds and the many modern stores selling gold and jewellery, the Ponte Vecchio gives you a taste of what medieval Florence was like—as well as a good view of the River Arno, its palaces and the next bridge along the river, the Ponte Santa Trinità (see opposite).

The present bridge was built in 1345, a reconstruction of an earlier structure (until 1218 the only crossing of the river) washed away by a flood. At the end of the 16th century Grand Duke Ferdinand I replaced the evil-smelling hog-butchers' shops that lined the bridge with gold- and silversmiths, and the trade has prevailed here ever since. The bridge has survived two major traumas in recent history: In 1944, while all the other bridges in Florence were destroyed by bombing, the Ponte Vecchio was preserved on Hitler's orders; and in 1966 the waters of the Arno rose to such a level that a fortune in gold was washed away in the floods.

Small shops and houses line the bridge on both sides, supported on brackets that overhang the river. They are painted in mellow shades of yellow, and with their wooden shutters, wrought-ironwork and awnings have retained their medieval appearance. Clearly visible running over the top of the eastern shops is the Corridoio Vasariano, a passageway designed by Giorgio Vasari in 1565 as a secret route for Cosimo I. It joins the Galleria degli Uffizi (▷ 68–73) and the Palazzo Pitti (▷ 80–81).

Don't miss The sun sets directly downriver from the bridge, and the golden tones of the structure itself are magical on a good evening.

Wooden shutters are still used to close up some of the shops on the bridge

SANTISSIMA ANNUNZIATA

✚ 63 D1 • Piazza della Santissima Annunziata, 50122 ☎ 055 239 8034
🕐 Daily 7–12.45, 4–6.30 🎟 Free

In the mid-15th century this large, grand building was one of the most important churches in Florence. It was founded in 1250 to protect a miraculous picture of the Virgin (said to have been painted by a monk with help from an angel), and expanded between 1444 and 1481 by Michelozzo. He also designed the Chiostrino dei Voti in front of the church, an unusual glass-roofed atrium decorated with frescoes by Andrea del Sarto (1486–1531) and some of his contemporaries.

The church stands on the north side of Piazza Santissima Annunziata, its façade made up of a graceful portico that leads into the Chiostrino dei Voti. On the right are frescoes by Rosso Fiorentino of the Assumption and to the left is Jacopo Pontormo's *Visitation*. The dim interior is lavishly decorated with marble and gold leaf. The tabernacle commissioned by the Medici family in the 15th century contains the painting of the Virgin mentioned above. The large apse behind the main altar is entered by way of a triumphal arch, clearly influenced by Roman architecture.

Notable works of art in the main body of the church include, in the left aisle, an *Assumption* by Perugino (c1450–1523) and *The Holy Trinity with St. Jerome* by Andrea del Castagno (c1421–57). The splendid organ in the nave, built between 1509 and 1521, is the oldest in the city and the second oldest in Italy.

The Chiostro dei Morti is to the left of the church and houses del Sarto's *Madonna del Sacco*, one of his most famous works.

THE SIGHTS

The Last Supper by Andrea del Castagno in Sant'Apollonia

A detail from the altarpiece of Santa Felicità

The frescoed trompe l'oeil ceiling at Santa Maria

THE SIGHTS

SANT'APOLLONIA

✚ 62 C1 • Via XXVII Aprile 1, 50129
☎ 055 238 8607 🕔 Daily 8.15–1.30; closed 1st, 3rd, 5th Sun and 2nd, 4th Mon of each month 🎟 Free 🚌 1, 6, 7

There is only one reason to come here—but it's a strong one. Andrea del Castagno's *Last Supper*, or *Cenacolo* (1447), is housed in the refectory of the former convent of Sant'Apollonia and is one of the finest paintings of that subject in Florence. Few visitors make time to see it, so you may well have the place to yourself. The painting shows Christ's table in the unusual surroundings of a marble loggia. The predominant dark greens, browns, blues and reds are sombre while the faces of the disciples are vivid. Above the *Cenacolo* is a faded fresco of the Crucifixion also by Castagno, and on the opposite wall of the long room is the *sinopia*, the rough outline on plaster that the artist followed. The lunette frescoes are also by Castagno.

SANTA FELICITÀ

✚ 62 B4 • Piazza Santa Felicità, 50125 ☎ 055 213018 🕔 Mon–Sat 9.30–12.30, 3–6, Sun 9–1 🎟 Free 🚌 D

Santa Felicità, off the busy Via Guicciardini, often gets over-looked by visitors hurrying between the Ponte Vecchio and the Pitti Palace. The church itself is not outstanding, its chief allure lying in the harmonious use of the local grey stone *pietra serena*, but it has a long history. It is thought to be one of the city's oldest churches, founded by Syrian Greek merchants in the second century. Since then it's been rebuilt several times, notably in 1565 by Vasari, who added a portico to accommodate his *corridoio*, the covered passage linking the Uffizi and the

Palazzo Pitti; you can see a window into the passageway high in the church's interior. The present façade dates from 1736.

To the right of the main door is the Cappella Capponi containing Jacopo Pontormo's extraordinary painting of the *Deposition* (1528). The chapel itself was designed in the 1420s by Brunelleschi, and frescoed a century later by Pontormo and his adopted son, Bronzino. The right wall has an *Annunciation*; under the cupola are four tondi of the Evangelists, but it is the *Deposition* that draws the eye. The composition makes this one of the greatest of all Mannerist works. Scale means nothing here—note the Virgin and her attendants—and all the usual elements of this subject are lacking: Where are the cross, the soldiers, the mourners? The virulent tones (their acidic quality is caused by low light levels) light up the chapel with pinks, blues, lime-green, oranges and reds and form a luminous contrast to the monotonous grey elsewhere in the building. Make sure you have a €1 coin for the light box that illuminates the painting.

SANTA MARIA MADDALENA DEI PAZZI

✚ 63 D2 • Borgo Pinti 58, 50121
☎ 055 247 8420 🕔 Daily 9–12, 5–9 🎟 Church: free; Perugino: donation 🚌 C, 6

The convent of Santa Maria Maddalena dei Pazzi was named after a Carmelite nun, famed for her religious devotion of covering herself in boiling wax; she lived from 1566 to 1607 and was canonized in 1669. The entrance to the church is through a large, plain and rather sober cloister, but the church itself is built to grand dimensions, with a lavishly frescoed trompe l'oeil ceiling and a series of chapels under

beautifully carved arches. The main chapel surrounding the altar was built in extravagant and vibrant marble in 1675 in homage to Santa Maddalena herself. However, the main reason for visiting the church lies in the chapter house, entered by passing through the crypt under the church. Here you'll find Perugino's superb fresco of the *Crucifixion and Saints*, painted between 1493 and 1496, considered one of his masterpieces. The picture's strength lies as much in its peaceful rural background as in the Crucifixion itself—a continuous panorama across the wall of a beautiful spring landscape around Lake Trasimeno in Umbria.

SAN MARTINO DEL VESCOVO

✚ 62 C3 • Piazza San Martino, 50122
☎ 055 281259 🕔 Mon–Sat 10–12, 3–5 🎟 Donation 🚌 A

The tiny oratory of San Martino del Vescovo, right in the heart of medieval Florence, is a rewarding stop-off. A church founded on the site in the 10th century was the poet Dante's parish church. It was rebuilt in 1479 and became the headquarters of the Compagnia dei Buonomini di San Martino, a charitable institution. Inside, a series of lunette frescoes by the workshop of Domenico Ghirlandaio decorates the upper walls. These illustrate scenes from the life of St. Martin and acts of charity, and show Florentines going about their daily business. There are also two lovely paintings of the Madonna on the walls, one Byzantine and the other attributed to a close follower of Perugino. Near the latter is a small, blocked window marked with a plaque; from here bread was distributed during the Black Death in 1348.

SANTA CROCE

The largest Franciscan church in Italy, reputedly founded by St. Francis himself, incorporates one of Brunelleschi's most important works, the early Renaissance Cappella dei Pazzi

In the heart of one of Florence's most attractive areas, Santa Croce was begun in 1294 and completed in the 1450s. The original plain front was replaced in the 19th century with an elaborate neo-Gothic façade. The interior is vast, with a wide nave and superb stained-glass windows by Agnolo Gaddi (c1300–66). Some of the frescoes are in a disappointing condition, but there are some exceptional works.

THE LEFT (NORTH) AISLE
Lorenzo Ghiberti (1378–1455) is buried under the tomb-slab with the eagle on it. There is also a monument to Galileo (1564–1642), the great scientist, who spent his last years in Florence.

THE EASTERN END
The polygonal sanctuary in the eastern end is covered with vivid frescoes by Gaddi. On either side are small chapels, each dedicated to an eminent Florentine family of the day, with frescoes by Giotto (c1267–1337). The Bardi di Libertà Chapel has frescoes by Bernardo Daddi, a contemporary of Giotto, and an altarpiece by Giovanni della Robbia (c1469–1529). The Bardi di Vernio Chapel has frescoes (c1340) by Maso di Banco, while Donatello's wooden crucifix hangs in the Bardi Chapel in the north transept. The frescoes in the Castellani Chapel are by Gaddi, whose father was responsible for the beautiful paintings in the Baroncelli Chapel. Next to the Baroncelli Chapel a passage leads to the Medici Chapel by Filippo Brunelleschi.

THE RIGHT (SOUTH) AISLE
In the right aisle are the tombs of Michelangelo (designed by Vasari, 1511–74), the poet Dante and the political writer Niccolò Machiavelli.

CAPPELLA DEI PAZZI, THE CLOISTERS AND MUSEUM
You can access the Cappella from the right aisle and through the 14th-century cloister. Brunelleschi was still working on this tranquil masterpiece when he died in 1446. Inside, the grey stone, simply carved in classical lines, is set against a white background. At the base of the elegant dome, 12 terracotta roundels by della Robbia depict the Apostles. There are more fine works of art in the Museo dell'Opera di Santa Croce, the entrance to which is off the cloister.

RATINGS	
Cultural interest	●●●○
Historic interest	●●●○
Value for money	●●●○

BASICS
✚ 63 D3 • Piazza Santa Croce, 50122
☎ 055 244619
⏰ Church, Cappella, Museum: Mon–Sat 9.30–5.30, Sun 1–5.30
💶 Adult €4 (also covers cappella and museum), child (11–18) €2, under 11 free
🚌 B, C
🎧 Free tours in English, French, German, Spanish, Italian Mon–Sat 10–12.30, 3–5, Sun 3–5 (tours given by volunteers, so times and availability of languages may vary). Audioguides at fixed points: English, French, Spanish, Italian €1
📖 Official book €8
🛍 One shop sells gifts, books, posters and postcards; another sells leather goods, which you can watch the artisans making
www.firenzeturismo.it

The green, white and pink marble exterior of Santa Croce (top); a statue of Dante in the Piazza Santa Croce (above)

RATINGS

Good for kids	●●
Historic interest	●●●●
Value for money	●●●●

BASICS

✚ 62 B2 • Piazza San Lorenzo, 50123
☎ 055 216634
🕐 Church: Mon–Sat 10–5.30. Cloister: Mon–Sat 10–6, Sun 9–1
💶 Adult €2.50, under 6 free
🚌 1, 6, 17, A
🎧 Free tours Mon–Sat 10–12.30, 3–5, Sun 3–5 in English, French, German, Spanish, Italian (tours given by volunteers, so times and availability of languages may vary). Audioguides at fixed points in English, French, Spanish, Italian €1
📕 Official guide €8
🎫 Small bookshop selling guides
🚻 In the Sacristy

The Cloisters of San Lorenzo (top); terracotta relief showing St. Cosmas and St. Damian by Donatello in the Sagrestia Vecchia (above)

SAN LORENZO

The Medici family church is a superb example of archetypal Renaissance architecture.

The basilica that originally stood on the site of San Lorenzo was consecrated in AD393 and is thought to have been the oldest church in Florence. The Medici family commissioned Filippo Brunelleschi to rebuild it in 1425, enlisting Michelangelo's expertise for certain projects. There are fewer important works of art here than elsewhere in Florence, but the church is a wonder in itself and houses the Cappelle Medicee, the family mausoleum (▷ 65).

THE CHURCH
The interior is mainly grey shades of *pietra serena* stone columns, with a grey-white marble floor designed by Brunelleschi. The overall affect is elegant, as the wooden ceiling, painted white and gold, creates a feeling of light. The aisles are lined with chapels, and paintings to look out for include Rosso Fiorentino's *Marriage of the Virgin* (1523) in the second chapel on the right and the enormous, flesh-toned fresco of the Martyrdom of St. Lawrence by Bronzino along the left aisle. The most important works within the church are Donatello's massive rectangular pulpits in the nave, which were his last work.

SAGRESTIA VECCHIA
The left transept leads you to the Sagrestia Vecchia (Old Sacristy) by Brunelleschi, a partner to the Sagrestia Nuova (New Sacristy) in the Cappelle Medicee. The vault with terracotta tondi is by Donatello, who also made the bronze doors. The small dome above the altar is decorated with frescoes of the zodiac in midnight-blue and gold. The tomb in the middle of the room is of Giovanni and Piccarda, founders of the Medici wealth. You can wander out of the main door on the left into the graceful two-tiered cloisters that frame the garden.

BIBLIOTECA LAURENZIANA
The Biblioteca Laurenziana is on the first floor and is entered via a hall dominated by an extraordinary freestanding staircase, built to a design by Michelangelo. The long reading room is full of closely packed desks and has a beautiful carved wooden ceiling. None of the library's collection of great manuscripts is on permanent display. A selection is brought out twice a year for periods of roughly three months.

Don't miss Filippino Lippi's *Annunciation* is in the left transept.

SANTA MARIA NOVELLA

This is one of the great Florentine churches, full of superb artworks and with the advantage of being relatively uncrowded.

The Gothic church with its adjoining museum complex is immediately striking thanks to the remarkable black-and-white marble exterior. Inside it has outstanding stained glass and important frescoes, while the museum includes unusual cloisters decorated by Paolo Uccello.

THE INTERIOR

The church is entered through the old cemetery, via the side door. Its lofty interior, with high stone vaulting decorated with stripes, is calm and uncluttered. One of the first things you notice is Giotto's crucifix (c1300) hanging dramatically in the middle of the nave. Opposite the door is the church's most famous fresco, Masaccio's *Trinità* (c1425), remarkable for its use of perspective; it depicts the Virgin and St. John with the painting's sponsors above a skeleton. The sanctuary is decorated with frescoes (1485–90) by Domenico Ghirlandaio, illustrating the lives of the Virgin Mary, John the Baptist and the Dominican saints. Next to it is the Filippo Strozzi Chapel that contains frescoes by Filippino Lippi on the lives of St. Philip and St. John.

MUSEO DI SANTA MARIA NOVELLA

There are yet more important frescoes in the Museo within the convent of the church. Here the first cloister, known as the Chiostro Verde, takes its name from the greenish hues that characterize the great but fading frescoes by Paolo Uccello. His scenes from the book of Genesis cover the walls straight in front of the entrance. At the far end of the cloister is the entrance to the Cappellone degli Spagnoli (Spanish Chapel), so called because the Spanish members of Eleonora di Toledo's court used it in the 16th century. It was once the headquarters of the Inquisition. The vault and walls are covered in vivid frescoes (1365–67) by a relatively unknown artist called Andrea di Buonaiuto who chose as his subject matter the Dominican cosmology.

Other rooms in the museum contain fresco fragments, holy vestments and 16th- and 17th-century reliquaries. The Chiostro Grande is occupied by a military school and is not open to the public.

Don't miss There is an enchanting little nativity scene by Botticelli over the main door inside the church.

RATINGS

Good for kids	●●
Historic interest	●●●●
Value for money	●●●●

BASICS

✚ 62 B2 • Piazza Santa Maria Novella, 50123

☎ Church: 055 215918. Museum: 055 282187

🕐 Church: Mon–Thu, Sat 9.30–4.30, Fri, Sun 1–4.30. Museum: Mon–Sat 9–4.30, Sun 9–1.30

💶 Church: Adult €2.50, under 18 free. Museum: Adult €2.60, child (12–20) €2.60, under 12 €1.90

🚌 A, 12 and all buses to Santa Maria Novella rail station

🎫 Free tours Mon–Sat 10–12.30, 3–5, Sun 3–5 in English, French, German, Spanish, Italian (tours given by volunteers, so times and availability of languages may vary)

📙 Official guidebook €7.75

🏬 Small bookshop in the church sells posters, postcards and some guidebooks

www.smn.it

A detail of St. Thomas Aquinas on one of the stained glass windows (top); one of the turtles that support the obelisks in the square outside (above)

The mosaic on the exterior of San Miniato al Monte

Santo Spirito on the south side of the Arno

A detail of Adoration of the Shepherds at Santa Trinità

SAN MINIATO AL MONTE

✚ 63 D5 • Via Monte alle Croci, 50125
☎ 055 234 2731 ◷ Daily 8–7.30,
Apr–end Oct; daily 8–12.30, 2.30–6, rest
of year 🎫 Free 🚌 12, 13

The church of San Miniato al Monte, on a hill to the south of the city, is one of the finest Romanesque churches in Tuscany. Apart from being a beautiful church in itself, it has wonderful views across the Arno, the old town and Fiesole (▷ 99). A visit requires an uphill walk from town or a bus ride.

Built in 1013, the exterior can be seen from all over the city. White-and-green geometrical marble designs surround a glittering 13th-century mosaic of Christ between the Virgin and St. Minias. Little has changed inside the church since the 11th century. In the middle of the nave, the marble floor is made up of *intarsia* (a kind of inlay) panels decorated with animals and constellations of the zodiac. The Cappella del Crocifisso has a freestanding tabernacle carved by Michelozzo (1396–1472) and terracotta pieces by Luca della Robbia (1400–82). At 5.30pm (4.30pm in winter) you can hear the Benedictine monks, who live in the convent next door, singing Gregorian chants.

SANTO SPIRITO

✚ 62 A4 • Piazza Santo Spirito, 50125
☎ 055 210030 (Church); 055 287043 (Cenacolo) ◷ Church: Mon, Tue, Thu, Fri 10–12, 4–5.30, Wed 10–12, Sat–Sun 4–5.30. Cenacolo: Tue–Sun 9–2
🎫 Church: Free. Cenacolo: Adult €2.10, under 20 €1.60 🚌 D
www.firenzeturismo.it

The beautiful Santo Spirito was the last church designed by Filippo Brunelleschi. He began designing it in 1444 and the work was finally finished in 1481. Its most notable feature is the simple 18th-century façade, now an emblem for the Oltrarno district of Florence, and the huge structure dominates the attractive Piazza Santo Spirito. In spite of its grandeur, it is still a parish church and its broad steps are a convenient outdoor sitting room for the local residents. Inside, grey *pietra serena* stone dominates, with massive columns, arches and vaults creating a harmonious space, and the walls are lined with 38 chapels. This is a great place to escape the crowds. The *Cenacolo* (refectory), next door to the church, has an assortment of carvings and a Crucifixion fresco by Orcagna (c1308–68).

SANTA TRINITÀ

✚ 62 B3 • Piazza Santa Trinità, 50125
☎ 055 216912 ◷ Daily 8–12, 4–7,
🎫 Free 🎟 Free tours Mon–Sat 10–12.30, 3–5, Sun 3–5 in English, French, German, Spanish, Italian (tours given by volunteers, so times and availability of languages may vary) 🚌 A, B

Although it is right in the heart of town, this church is often ignored by those on the popular visitor route. But it's worth visiting for 10 minutes or so for the stunning painting and frescoes in the Sassetti chapel. Inside, the mid-13th-century church is a dark, rather mystical place with pools of light picking out the choicer works of art from the gloom. The interior is square with a series of chapels running down each side. The Sassetti chapel is on the right of the altar and is decorated with exquisite frescoes of the life of St. Francis (1483) by Ghirlandaio. He also painted the superb altarpiece of the *Adoration of the Shepherds* (1485). This painting may seem familiar because of the countless Christmas cards it has adorned. On the left of the altar is the tomb of Benozzo Federighi with a finely carved marble effigy (1454–57) by Luca della Robbia. Along the left aisle, the fourth chapel has an *Annunciation* (1475) by Neri di Bicci and, next to this, there is an altarpiece, the *Coronation of the Virgin* (1430) by Bicci di Lorenzo.

LA SPECOLA

✚ 62 A4 • Via Romana 17, 50125
☎ 055 228 8270 ◷ Thu–Tue 9–1
🎫 Adult €5, child (6–14) €2.50, under 6 free 🚌 D, 11, 36, 37 ♿
www.specola.unifi.it

Known as La Specola because of the observatory (*specola* meaning looking glass or lens) founded in the same building by Grand Duke Pietro Leopoldo, Palazzo Torrigiani was built in 1775 as a zoological museum. It now houses the Department of Natural Sciences of the University of Florence, but the museum (on the third floor) still functions and the zoological collection here is the largest in Italy. Old-fashioned wood and glass cases are filled with every creature imaginable that walks, crawls, flies, swims or slithers: insects, butterflies, crustaceans, reptiles, birds and mammals, both small and large. But it is the collection of anatomical wax models that are the real attraction, although anyone of a squeamish disposition should take a deep breath before embarking on this section. The models in wax are unique and extraordinary. Made between 1775 and 1814 by Clemente Susini, they graphically illustrate every bone, muscle, ligament and blood vessel in the human body, both in close-up section and through lifesized models with their skin peeled off or their internal organs exposed.

On the first floor of the palazzo is the Tribuna di Galileo, built in 1841 in honour of the great scientist Galileo and elaborately decorated in marble and mosaic.

NORTHERN TUSCANY

Northern Tuscany contains some of the region's least-known and most mountainous countryside, a diverse coastline and historic and prosperous cities. Take in the distinctive architectural styles of Pisa and Lucca, enjoy some excellent shopping in towns such as Pistoia and Prato before exploring the wild upland country of the Garfagnana, the Casentino and the Lunigiana.

MAJOR SIGHTS

The small town of Pariana in the foothills of the Alpi Apuane

A view of the cathedral across the rooftops at Barga

Sunset over the countryside around Stia in the Casentino

THE SIGHTS

ALPI APUANE

✚ 282 C3 ℹ Park Information Office, Via Corrado del Greco 11, Seravezza, tel 0584 75821; daily 9–1, 3.30–7.30, May–end Sep
www.parks.it

The Alpi Apuane mountains, a protected regional park, cut a dramatic swathe for 40km (25 miles) down the Versilian Coast. These are no gently rolling hills, but mountains with knife-like ridges and precipitous slopes. Because of their height and position, the Alpi have different habitats, making them a superb destination for nature lovers. The flora is particularly special, as the mountains are one of Italy's richest botanical areas. Bird life is also prolific, with more than 300 species within the park's boundaries. There's a network of trails that penetrate deep into the mountains; the best walking area is inland from the marble towns of Massa and Carrara. There's a park information office at Seravezza where you can reserve a place on guided walks.

BARGA

✚ 283 D3 ℹ Via di Mezzo 45, 55051 Barga, tel 0583 724743 (freephone in Italy 800 028497); Mon–Sat 9–12, 3.30–6, Sun 10–12, 3.30–6 🚉 Barga Gallicano, long uphill walk
www.barganews.com

Barga is off the beaten track, yet easily accessible, making it an ideal trip into the country if you are staying in Lucca or Pisa. You can stroll through the winding streets, shop for local produce (see Don't miss below) or simply enjoy a drink in one of the town's cafés.
Barga sits on a hill above the Serchio Valley with fine views of the Alpi Apuane. It has kept much of its medieval appearance and layout, with remnants of the

old walls and narrow, steep streets stretching down from the Romanesque cathedral. The Duomo dates mainly from the 13th century; it has a lovely exterior and campanile and, inside, a wooden statue of St. Christopher. The climb to the cathedral is fairly steep but worth the effort for the views alone. The town has strong links with Scotland, as many of its residents emigrated to Glasgow. As a result many people speak English. **Don't miss** Have a drink in Caffè Capretz, established in 1870; visit Mazzolini Andrea, a delectable shop on Via di Mezzo selling a wide range of foods, from chestnut flour to mountain pecorino cheese.

CARRARA

✚ 282 B3 ℹ Viale Vespucci 24, Marina di Massa 54037, tel 0585 240063; Mon–Sat 9–1, 3–8, Sun 9.30–12.30

Carrara is tucked beneath the Alpi Apuane and the coast, almost on the border between Tuscany and Liguria. Busy and bustling, it feels like an industrial town, which is due to marble. The stone has been quarried from the Alpi Apuane for thousands of years. You can drive the short distance from town to see the quarries, but the best trip is to the village of Colonnata, 8km (5 miles) from Carrara. The drive takes you up a winding road past quarries to the tiny village, the main square of which is paved with marble. On the way there are plenty of places to stop and buy newly quarried marble.

CASENTINO

✚ 285 J4 ℹ Parco Nazionale delle Foreste Casentinesi, Via Guido Brocchi 7, 52015 Arezzo, tel 0575 50301; Tue, Thu 9–1, 3–5, Mon, Wed, Fri 9–1
🚉 Arezzo
www.parks.it

The wild, richly wooded country north of Arezzo is a rural area known as the Casentino. Its main towns are Bibbiena, focus of Tuscany's tobacco industry, and Poppi, site of the area's main landmark, the 13th-century castle of Conti Guidi. Much of the Casentino lies within the Parco Nazionale delle Foreste Casentinesi, one of Italy's newest parks, which combines preservation of the wildlife and the environment with protection of the area's historic villages, especially La Verna and Camaldoli. It was at La Verna, in 1224, that St. Francis of Assisi is said to have received the stigmata, and this mountaintop monastery is a major pilgrimage place, with many relics of the saint. There's another monastery at Camaldoli, in wooded surroundings popular with weekend hikers. Other Casentino villages include Prato Vecchio, Stia and Badia Prataglia.

CASTELFIORENTINO

✚ 287 F6 ℹ Via Redolfi, 50051 Castelfiorentino, tel 0571 629049; Mon–Thu 9.30–12.30, 3.30–6.30, Fri–Sun 9–12.30, 3.30–7
🚉 Castelfiorentino

The main reason for paying a visit to Castelfiorentino (literally Florentine Castle) is to see the Church of Santa Verdiana (ask at the Tourist Office). This is arguably the finest early 18th-century church in Tuscany, with striking architecture and frescoes. If you are historically minded, you will want to see the underground cell where Verdiana (1178–1242), the town's patron saint, lived for the last 34 years of her life; according to legend, she walled herself in along with two snakes. For art lovers there are two fresco cycles by Benozzo Gozzoli (c1421–97), at the Biblioteca Comunale, depicting the life of the Virgin Mary.

The gardens of Villa Garzoni in Collodi has a number of statues

Fiesole's Roman amphitheatre is part of the Area Archeologica

Porto Mediceo is the 16th-century quarter of Livorno

COLLODI

✚ 283 E4 • Parco di Pinocchio, Via San Gennaro 3, Collodi, 51017 Pescia
☎ 0572 429342 ◷ Daily 8.30–dusk
🎟 Adult €8.50, child (3–14) €6.50
🚌 Pescia
www.pinocchio.it

The name Collodi is the *nom de plume* used by Carlo Lorenzini, creator of Pinocchio, Italy's most famous children's character. This unremarkable village, birthplace of Lorenzini's mother, has been the site of the Parco di Pinocchio since the 1950s. The mazes, tableaux and statues are all related to the book, and presume a good knowledge of the text. Most children will enjoy the park and the excellent toyshop. Adults may prefer to wander through the gardens of the Villa Garzoni next door, laid out in the 18th century around a magnificent villa to a masterly baroque design, complete with topiary, geometric planting, parterres, cascades and fountains. The gardens form a perfect antidote to the excesses of the park.

FIESOLE

✚ 284 G4 🛈 Via Portigiani 3, 50014 Fiesole, tel 055 598720; Mon–Sat 9–6, Sun 10–1, 2–6, Mar–end Oct; closed 5pm rest of year
www.commune.fiesole.fi.it

Perched on a hillside 7km (4 miles) northeast of Florence, Fiesole was originally an Etruscan settlement, which grew in importance under the Romans. Evidence of both periods can be seen in the Area Archeologica east of the main square, Piazza Mino da Fiesole. It has a well-preserved Roman amphitheatre, Roman baths, a Roman temple and some sixth-century BC Etruscan ruins. You will find the cathedral, shops and restaurants on Piazza Mino da Fiesole. From here you can climb Via San

Francesco for sweeping views of Florence below. The Museo Bandini (daily 9.30–7) has ivories, ceramics and paintings on display, while the Church of San Domenico, dating from the 15th-century, has a delicate *Madonna with Saints and Angels* by Fra Angelico.

GARFAGNANA

See pages 100–101.

LIVORNO

✚ 286 C6 🛈 Piazza Civica 1, 57100 Livorno, tel 0586 820288; Tue, Thu 9–1, 3.30–6.30 Mon, Wed, Fri 9–1
🚌 Livorno

Livorno is Tuscany's third largest city, a booming port which has flourished since Roman times and today makes its living as one of the Mediterranean's biggest container docks. It's also a major ferry port, with departures to Corsica, Sardinia and Sicily, as well as the Tuscan islands of Gorgona and Capraia. Heavily bombed in World War II, its rebuilt commercial area is unattractive, so head for the area around the Piazza Grande, the heart of what's left of the old city. This area, the Porto Mediceo, is enclosed by canals and was laid out in 1557. On the Piazza is the Duomo, and just a few minutes' walk away is the Fortezza Vecchia (old fortress) overlooking the harbour. Inland from here is the Fortezza Nuova (new fortress) and August sees a big street festival here. The Museo Civico has nothing on Livorno's most famous son, the 20th-century artist Amedeo Modigliani, but is devoted to Italian Impressionism. It might be more rewarding to spend your time enjoying the excellent seafood for which the city is rightly renowned.

LUCCA

See pages 102–105.

LUNIGIANA

✚ 282 A1 🛈 Piazza della Republicca, 54027 Pontrémoli, Massa Carrara, tel 0187 833278; daily 9–12, 2–6, Jun–end Sep 🚌 Pontrémoli
www.lunigiana.it

There are dramatic landscapes and isolated and remote villages in the Lunigiana, Tuscany's northernmost tip. The two main towns of this area around the Magra valley are Aulla, to the south, and Pontrémoli to the north. Between the two is a succession of tiny villages, often high in the hills, many with castles built to extract tolls from anyone passing through. Aulla suffered huge damage in World War II, so you should perhaps head for some of the surrounding villages sitting among the dense woods of sweet chestnut trees, once the area's staple food. Pontrémoli has a baroque cathedral and a museum (Museo del Comune) with a group of extraordinary prehistoric stylized statues dating from 3000–1000BC.

MONTECATINI TERME

✚ 283 E4 🛈 Viale Verdi 66, tel 0572 772244; Mon–Sat 9–1.30, 3–6, Sun 9–12 🚌 Montecatini

Tuscany's finest spa town lies in the district of the Valdinievole (Valley of Mists) in northern Tuscany. A funicular railway is a scenic link to Montecatini Alto, the old upper town, which has fine views over the valley. The town is dominated by the Parco delle Terme, which has most of the spas. The thermal springs and their healing powers were known to the Romans, and in the 14th century gentlemen came to indulge in water therapy. In the 18th century the magnificent Leopoldine and Tuttuccio baths were built, to be followed in the early 20th century by the art nouveau Excelsior spa (▷ 176).

GARFAGNANA

A spectacular mountain and river valley area that's little known to outsiders, with pretty villages and some of Tuscany's best walking.

RATINGS	
Outdoor pursuits	●●●○
Photo stops	●●●○
Walkability	●●●●

BASICS
✚ 283 D2

🛈 Centro Visite, Parco Regionale delle Alpi Apuane, Piazza delle Erbe 1, 55032 Castelnuovo di Garfagnana, tel 0583 65169; daily 9–1, 3–7, Jun–end Sep; closed 5.30pm, rest of year

🚉 Castelnuovo di Garfagnana

www.garfagnanavacanze.it

North of Lucca, the Serchio valley runs south down the east of the Alpi Apuane (▷ 98), an attractive and largely undiscovered area that's dotted with little towns and laced with excellent walking trails. Even without a car, you can reach towns such as Barga, but with your own vehicle you can drive the numerous tiny roads that run up from the valley floor right into the mountains and through to the next valley system to the east. The area is perfect for wildlife lovers and hikers, since much of it is protected as the regional nature reserve Parco Regionale delle Alpi Apuane. Good bases for exploring the area include the Orecchiella, the most rugged stretch with marked walking trails, Bagni di Lucca and Barga.

THE TOWNS

Only 25km (15 miles) north of Lucca, Bagni di Lucca is a low-key spa town, whose heyday was in the 19th century, when it was among Europe's most popular spas, patronized by English poets Byron, Shelley and Browning. It's still a pleasant place, and has a good range of accommodation. Another good bet for a few days is the town of Barga (▷ 98), some 45km (28 miles) up the Serchio valley, at the start of the most scenic stretch. Peaceful Barga's main sight is its Duomo, dating mainly from the 13th century.

From Barga, it's a 20-minute drive west to the Grotta del Vento underground cave system (▷ 173). Farther north is the valley's main town, Castelnuovo di Garfagnana, a fair-sized market town that's a good base for both hikers and drivers exploring the mountains and villages.

THE ORECCHIELLA

The Orecchiella, wild country with magnificent views over wooded mountains, is easily reached from Barga. The mountains are rounded, with alpine meadows above the treeline—great hiking country that is still traditionally farmed. If you plan to take to the hills and walk, Corfino makes a good base; the park and visitors' office is 7km (4 miles) from there. Northeast from Castelnuovo is the ancient pilgrimage area of San Pellegrino in Alpe (▷ 201), at 1,524m (5,000ft), where you can get insights into the traditional peasant way of life at the Museo Etnografico Provinciale.

The spa town of Bagni di Lucca is set among pretty woodlands (above)

You can find the 12th-century Ponte del Diavolo (The Devil's Bridge) south of Bagni de Lucca (opposite)

Lucca

●

This prosperous town and regional capital is entirely enclosed within superb Renaissance walls, and has a rich heritage of churches and palaces. Some of Tuscany's best shopping and eating is here.

Leaves falling from the trees along the top of the city walls

Dried herbs for sale at a market stall

The Palazzo Mansi houses art from the 15th to 18th centuries

RATINGS	
Chainstore shopping	●●●●
Good for food	●●●●
Historic interest	●●●●●
Photo stops	●●●●●

BASICS
✚ 283 D4
🏠 Piazzale Verdi, 55100 Lucca, tel 0583 583150; daily 9–7, Apr–end Oct; 9–5, rest of year
🚊 Lucca
www.commune.lucca.it

TIPS
● Lucca is easily explored on foot. As the station is only 10 minutes' walk away from the old town and parking is not easy, it is better to come by train rather than car.
● Emulate the locals and get around by bicycle; these can be rented from the tourist office or numerous places around town (look for the word *noleggio*—rental).

The 13th-century mosaic of the Ascension on the exterior of San Frediano (top)

A statue of the Virgin Mary and Child on the outside of San Michele in Foro (opposite)

SEEING LUCCA

Lucca, with its intricate grid of streets neatly enclosed by tree-lined walls, makes a pleasant overnight stop, although it's small enough to make a day trip from Pisa or Florence perfectly feasible. Your best starting point is the Piazza Napoleone, with all the main sights only a few minutes' walk away. Begin at the Duomo just around the corner, and its Museo della Cattedrale, before crossing the square to inspect Santi Giovanni e Reparata. Then cut through to visit the church of San Michele in Foro, with its glorious façade, before heading east to join Via Fillungo (long thread), an expensive shopping street that leads north to the Piazza Anfiteatro and San Frediano, another outstanding church. The main museums lie inside the walls to the west and east of the heart of town. Whatever you do, leave time to walk at least part of the way around the walls, so as to get an overview of this compact and lovely town.

HIGHLIGHTS

DUOMO DI SAN MARTINO

✚ 104 B2 • Piazza San Martino ☎ 0583 490530 🕐 Duomo: Daily 7–7, mid-Mar to end Oct; 7–5, rest of year. Sacristy: Mon–Sat 9.30–6.45, Sun 1–5.45 💶 Duomo: free. Sacristy: Adult €2, child (6–14) €1

Lucca's stunning Romanesque cathedral, with its asymmetrical façade, has 11th- to 13th-century reliefs on and around the three principal doors. Nicola Pisano, a 13th-century Pisan sculptor, first made his mark here; his panels, *Annunciation*, *Nativity* and *Adoration of the Magi*, are around the left-hand door. The interior is best known for the work of Matteo Civitali, a 15th-century sculptor whose masterpiece occupies the middle of the church. This is the Tempietto, an octagonal structure which holds the *Volto Santo* (Holy Face), a cedarwood crucifix much venerated in the city and said to be an exact likeness of Christ. According to legend it was carved by Nicodemus, a witness of the Crucifixion. Look for the tomb of Ilaria del Carretto, the second wife of a local merchant, tenderly carved between 1407 and 1410 by the Sienese master Jacopo della Quercia. You'll find it in the sacristy, where there's also a *Madonna Enthroned with Saints* by Ghirlandaio.

THE SIGHTS

THE WALLS

You can access the walls at any of the bastions and then cycle or walk down the broad tree-lined promenade that runs along the top. The walls were built between 1520 and 1650 and are 12m (40ft) high and 30m (100ft) wide at the base with a moat that is 35m (115ft) wide. After their construction, Lucca was never besieged, so their effectiveness was not put to the test.

CASA DI PUCCINI

⊞ 104 B2 • Via di Poggio 9 ☎ 0583 484028 ⓒ Daily 10–6 🖢 €3
Puccini's father and grandfather were both organists at San Michele in Foro and the family home lies close to the church. It is now a music school with a small museum where you can see the composer's piano and other memorabilia.

TORRE GUINIGI

⊞ 104 B1 • Via Sant'Andrea ☎ 336 203221 ⓒ Daily 9–7 🖢 Adult €4, child (6–12) €2
Once the home of a leading Lucchese family, this battle-mented tower house is topped by a living holm oak, whose roots have grown into the room below the roof. You can climb the 44m (144ft) tower for the best views over the city.

SAN MICHELE IN FORO

⊞ 104 B2 • Piazza San Michele ☎ 0583 48459 ⓒ Daily 7.30–12, 3–6 🖢 Free
The Piazza San Michele, the site of the old Roman forum, has given its name to the church of San Michele in Foro, dating from 1070. The exterior was completed about the middle of the 12th century, a dazzling masterpiece that is an intricate medley of tiny loggias, lavish carvings and decorated columns, all different, the whole topped by the triumphant figure of an archangel. The 12th-century campanile is the tallest in Lucca.

SAN FREDIANO

⊞ 104 B1 • Piazza San Frediano ☎ 0583 493627 ⓒ Daily 7.30–12, 3–6 🖢 Free
San Frediano is the third of Lucca's splendid churches, after the cathedral and San Michele. It was built between 1112 and 1147 on the site of a sixth-century basilica and is fronted by a glittering 13th-century mosaic depicting the Ascension. The interior is crammed with sculptures, the best being the Fonte Lustrale, a 12th-century baptismal font finely carved by three different craftsmen, and the Cappella Trenta altarpiece by Jacopo della Quercia. Don't miss the intricate 12th-century cosmati paving in the presbytery, or the Cappella di Sant'Agostino, frescoed in the early 1500s by a little-known artist, Amico Aspertini.

PIAZZA ANFITEATRO

⊞ 104 B1
This extraordinary piazza, dotted with cafés and bright with flower-sellers' wares, draws more visitors than any of Lucca's churches and it's a great place to take a break. Its shape is that of the Roman amphitheatre that was once here, and you can still see traces of arches and columns incorporated in the old buildings that surround the piazza. Stone from here was carted away for building in the 12th century, after which the space was occupied by medieval slum buildings; these were cleared in 1830.

MUSEO NAZIONALE DI VILLA GUINIGI

⊞ 104 C1 • Via della Quarquonia ☎ 0583 496033 ⓒ Tue–Sat 8.30–7.30, Sun 8.30–1.30 🖢 Adult €4, under 18 free; combined ticket available with Museo di Palazzo Mansi for €6.50 🔠
Lucca's main museum occupies the Villa Guinigi, built for the Guinigi family in the 15th century, and where the exhibits are sensitively displayed. The big and varied collection includes furniture and the

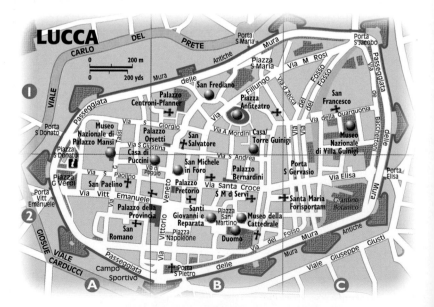

applied arts, archaeological finds, sculpture and painting. The sculpture and archaeology are displayed on the ground floor, while the floor above is devoted to paintings. These represent most major Tuscan schools, ranging from early Lucchese and Sienese works to huge 16th-century panels.

MUSEO NAZIONALE DI PALAZZO MANSI

✚ 104 A1 • Via Galli Tassi ☎ 0583 55570 ⏰ Tue–Sat 8.30–7.30, Sun 8.30–1.30 💷 Adult €4, under 18 free; combined ticket available with Museo di Villa Guinigi for €6.50

The 17th-century palace in which this museum is set is as great a draw as the artworks themselves. You'll pass through a series of ornate rococo rooms, exuberantly frescoed and hung with tapestries, before reaching the rooms with the Pinacoteca Nazionale, the picture collection. Outstanding are portraits by the Mannerists Bronzino (1503–72) and Jacopo Pontormo (1494–1557), smooth and sinuous compositions which contrast with the warm and opulent style of those by the Venetian Tintoretto (1518–94). To learn about the source of Lucca's wealth, spend time in the section that traces the development of the silk and damask industries.

BACKGROUND

There has been a settlement in Lucca since around 1000BC. The city became a Roman colony in 180BC and grew in importance from then on. In Lombard times, around the sixth century, it was the capital of the embryonic Tuscany and by the 11th century banking and silk were starting to prove the mainstay of its economy, helped by its 12th-century recognition as a free Commune. In 1314 the city came briefly under Pisan control, but regained its independence, and defeated Pisa and Pistoia under the leadership of Castruccio Castracani. In the mid-16th century Lucca remained an independent republic and new defensive city walls—those you see today—were erected to replace the earlier Roman and medieval ones. The city remained a republic until the French occupation, when Napoleon Bonaparte presented it to his sister Elisa. After the fall of Napoleon it became a Bourbon duchy and managed to remain independent of the Tuscan Grand Duchy until 1847. Lucca today is one of Tuscany's richest cities, its artistic heritage and high standard of living attracting an increasing number of visitors.

A statue of Giacomo Puccini (1858–1924) outside the Casa di Puccini—he was born in Lucca

Flower stands fill the city's Piazza Anfiteatro

MUSEO DELLA CATTEDRALE

✚ 104 B2 • Piazza Ante ☎ 0583 490530 ⏰ Daily 10–6, mid-Mar to end Oct; Mon–Fri 10–2, Sat–Sun 10–5, rest of year 💷 Adult €3.50, child (6–12) €2

This museum has objects from the cathedral, including illustrated manuscripts, reliquaries, church furnishings and sculpture.

SANTI GIOVANNI E REPARATA

✚ 104 B2 • Piazza Ante ☎ 0583 490530 ⏰ Daily 10–6, mid-Mar to end Oct; Mon–Fri 10–2, Sat–Sun 10–5, rest of year 💷 Adult €5.50, child (6–12) €3

Dating from the eighth century, this was Lucca's first cathedral. Excavations have uncovered Roman mosaics, Roman columns and a fourth-century pavement.

Pisa

Pisa is synonymous with the Leaning Tower, the most famous of a trio of buildings that form one of Italy's loveliest medieval architectural complexes. It is a university city with museums, lovely piazzas and bustling streets.

A view of the Ponte di Mezzo across the River Arno

The Pisan Cross flag flying at the top of the Tower

Taking in the view from up on the Leaning Tower

SEEING PISA

First stop on a tour of the city has to be the Campo dei Miracoli (Field of Miracles), the green space graced by the Leaning Tower (Torre Pendente), the Duomo and the Battistero. Around it are the Camposanto (cemetery) and two museums relevant to the site (if time's short you may want to leave these off your list). From the Campo, Via Carducci and Borgo Stretto, lined with graceful, mainly Renaissance palaces, lead through the most evocative part of the old city to the river. On the way, you could take a detour west to the Piazza dei Cavalieri, one of Pisa's most attractive squares. The streets around here are lively during the morning market. Cross the river to take in the little church of Santa Maria della Spina. Alternatively, head east along the Lungarno to the Museo Nazionale. It's worth considering a night's stay in Pisa if you're flying in late or out early from the region's main airport; otherwise, it is a good day-trip destination, an hour by train from Florence.

HIGHLIGHTS

THE LEANING TOWER OF PISA

✉ Piazza del Duomo, 56126 Pisa ☎ 050 560547 ⏰ Daily 8–8, Apr–end Sep; 9–8, Mar and Oct; 9–5, Nov–end Feb 💶 Adult €15 🎫 By tour only, with timed tickets, lasting 35 minutes ❓ No children under 8 allowed

The Leaning Tower is a fine example of Pisan architecture, but for most visitors its main attraction is the very fact that it leans. You may be surprised to know it always has. Work on the bell tower started in 1173, and by the time three of the eight floors were in place there was a distinct tilt. Despite strenuous efforts, the inclination increased throughout the construction process, and by the time the tower was completed in 1350 the angle was permanent. Unstable ground beneath exacerbated the slant so that by the late 20th century the tower was 4.5m (15ft) off the perpendicular and at a critical angle. In 1990 the tower was shut and 10 steel bands were wrapped around its base to prevent collapse. A 900-tonne lead ingot counterbalance was inserted and the underlying ground drilled to remove water and silt. This operation brought the tower back to its 1838 position, where

RATINGS

Cultural interest	●●●○
Good for kids	●●●●●
Historic interest	●●●○
Photo stops	●●●●●

BASICS

✚ 286 D5
🛈 Piazza del Duomo 1, 56126 Pisa, tel 050 560464; daily 9–7, Jun–end Sep; Mon–Sat 9–6, Sun 10.30–4.30, rest of year
🚆 Pisa Centrale
www.duomo.pisa.it

TIPS

• A combined ticket for the cathedral, baptistery, Museo and Camposanto (but not the Leaning Tower) can be bought at the ticket office of the Leaning Tower or the Museo; two monuments or museums cost €5, all four €10.50.
• Tickets for the Leaning Tower can be purchased in advance at the ticket office or on website www.opapisa.it.
• There are excellent bus and train connections to the city, so leave the car behind.

A detail from the Duomo's bronze doors (top); few realise that the Leaning Tower forms part of the cathedral complex (opposite)

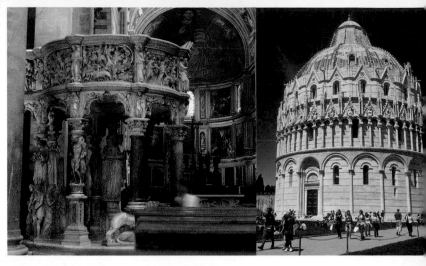

The intricate carving on the Duomo's pulpit (above left); the exterior of the Battistero (above right)

MORE TO SEE

PIAZZA DEI CAVALIERI

This lovely square, the heart of medieval Pisa, was transformed in the 16th century. The Palazzo dei Cavalieri was the headquarters of the Knights of St. Stephen and is decorated with sgraffito, a decorative method of scratching through one layer of paint to reveal a contrasting layer beneath.

MUSEO NAZIONALE DI SAN MATTEO

✉ Piazza San Matteo in Soarta, 56123 ☎ 050 541865 🕐 Tue–Sat 8.30–7.30, Sun 8.30–1 💲 Adult €4, under 18 free

This museum has most of the major artworks from Pisa's churches, with a nucleus of 14th-century paintings.

MUSEO NAZIONALE DI PALAZZO REALE

✉ Lungarno Pacinotti 46, 56123 ☎ 050 926511 🕐 Mon–Sat 9–2.30 💲 Adult €3, under 18 free

The palace was once one of the homes of Tuscany's rulers, the Medici, Lorraine and Savoy families, and displays objects and paintings from their collections.

Fontana dei Putti (1764) by Giovanni Vaccà, with three cherubs bearing the Pisan coat of arms, on the Campo dei Miracoli

it should remain for the foreseeable future. You can climb the 294 steps to the top, 54m (177ft) up, from where Galileo is said to have conducted his experiments on the force of gravity (▷ 33).

DUOMO

✉ Piazza del Duomo, 56126 Pisa ☎ 050 560547 🕐 Mon–Sat 10–12.30, 3–4.30, Sun 3–4.30, Nov–end Feb; Mon–Sat 10–5.30, Sun 1–5.45, Mar and Oct; Mon–Sun 10–7.45, rest of year 💲 Adult €2 (Mar–end Oct), under 10 free; free to all rest of year

A supreme example of Pisan-Romanesque architecture, the Duomo is among Italy's greatest buildings, the subtlety of its grey and white marble the perfect foil for the intricacy of its four-tiered façade. Building started in 1064 and finished in the middle of the 12th century. Spend time admiring the exterior columns and loggias of the front before entering through the Porta di San Ranieri with Bonanno Pisano's bronze doors, cast in 1180. Inside, the five aisles, sheathed in black-and-white marble, provide harmonious surroundings for Giovanni Pisano's marble pulpit, carved between 1302 and 1311, and the apse mosaic (1302) by Cimabue. After a fire in 1595 the pulpit—then considered horribly out of date—was put into storage and was only rediscovered in 1926. It is a wonderful work, the whole surface carved with virtually freestanding figures in a series of tableaux that tell the story of Christ's life. Don't miss the huge incense lamp (1587), for many years thought to have inspired Galileo's theory of the movement of the pendulum.

BATTISTERO

✉ Piazza del Duomo, 56126 Pisa ☎ 050 560547 🕐 Daily 9–4.30, Nov–end Feb; 9–5.30, Mar and Oct; 8–7.30, rest of year 💲 Adult €5, under 10 free

The third structure on the green expanse of the Campo dei Miracoli is the largest baptistery in Italy, built between 1152 and 1350. It's a circular building, its three levels of arcades crowned with an elegant eight-sided dome, whose exterior niches once held statues—you can see these in the Museo dell'Opera del

Duomo. Inside, all is restraint: just a bare dome and plain arcades. The pulpit was carved in 1260 by Nicola Pisano, father of Giovanni.

CAMPOSANTO

✉ Piazza del Duomo, 56126 Pisa ☎ 050 560547 🕐 Daily 9–4.30, Nov–end Feb; 9–5.30, Mar and Oct; 8–7.30, rest of year 👤 Adult €5, under 10 free

The north side of the Campo dei Miracoli is edged by a wall of white marble, part of what used to be the cemetery for Pisa's most eminent citizens. The Camposanto (literally the Holy Field), said to have been built around a cargo of earth brought from the Holy Land, was constructed in the form of a huge Gothic cloister, whose arcades hold memorials and tombs. The entire space was frescoed during the 15th century, creating a building that was considered among the loveliest in Italy. In 1944 an Allied incendiary bomb set fire to the roof, and molten lead poured down the walls, destroying almost all the frescoes. An exhibition room displays photos of the Camposanto as it once looked.

MUSEO DELL'OPERA DEL DUOMO

✉ Piazza del Duomo, 56126 Pisa ☎ 050 835010/560547 🕐 Daily 9–4.20, Nov–end Feb; 9–5.20, Mar and Oct; 8–7.20, rest of year 👤 Adult €5, child (under 10) free

This museum displays religious statuary, paintings, vestments and other treasures from the long history of the Duomo. There's superb sculpture by the Pisano family, including the ravishing *Madonna del Colloquio* by Giovanni (active c1265–1314), and the Pisan Cross, which was carried by the Pisan knights during the First Crusade. Other works include Islamic pieces that throw light on Byzantine influences on Pisan art, and a fine collection of Etruscan and Roman sculpture.

BACKGROUND

A naval base under the Romans, Pisa reached its peak in the 11th and 12th centuries, when this maritime city-state was one of the Mediterranean's greatest powers. It defeated the Saracens and expelled them from Corsica, Sardinia and the Balearic Islands, bringing Pisa to the attention of its powerful neighbour, Genoa. The Genoese victory of 1284 marked the start of decline, with Pisa's commercial empire collapsing and the harbour silting up. In 1406 the city was taken over by Florence, and the Medici embarked on major rebuilding, while turning Pisa into a focus for science and learning. The university they founded numbered Galileo among its teachers. Despite this, the city gradually sank into obscurity and provinciality, its palaces providing inexpensive accommodation in the 19th century for British exiles like the poet Byron and the Shelleys. Although Pisa was heavily bombed during World War II, the second half of the 20th century saw it re-emerge from the shadows as a provincial capital with growing light industry, a thriving university and as the entry point for the thousands of visitors flying into Tuscany via its airport.

SANTA MARIA DELLA SPINA

✉ Lungarno Gambecorte Notel 🕐 Mon–Fri 10–1.30, 2.30–6, Sat–Sun 10–1.30, 2.30–7, Apr–end Oct; closed one hour earlier, rest of year 👤 Adult €1.10

This Pisan-Gothic oratory was built in 1323 to house one of the thorns from Christ's Crown of Thorns. It once stood close to the river and was moved in 1871 to save it from flooding.

Pisa's Duomo predates the cathedrals at Florence and Siena, setting the style for buildings across central Tuscany

The Mugello landscape rivals that of Chianti, but is much less known to visitors

The fruit and vegetable market at Pistoia

THE SIGHTS

MUGELLO

➕ 285 H3 ℹ️ Via P. Togliatti 45, 50032 Borgo San Lorenzo, tel 055 845271; Tue, Thu 9–1, 3–6, Mon, Wed, Fri 9–1 🚉 Borgo San Lorenzo
www.turismo.mugello.toscana.it

Lying hard against the Apennines on Tuscany's border with Emilia-Romagna, the Mugello is a lushly fertile area densely planted with olive groves and vineyards and is popular as a weekend destination for Florentines. Away from the cultivated land around the Mugello, there are thick forests of oak and chestnut trees that form a backdrop to the scenic villages. The main town is Borgo San Lorenzo but if you are planning a stay, it's better to head for one of the villages—perhaps Vicchio, birthplace of Fra Angelico, or Barberino di Mugello, a market town with an attractive central piazza. Barberino is on the way to Passo della Futa, a pass at 900m (2,950ft), from where there are superb views over the valleys and ridges of the area.

PISA

See pages 106–109.

PISTOIA

➕ 284 F4 ℹ️ Palazzo dei Vescovi, Piazza Duomo 4, 51100 Pistoia, tel 0573 21622; daily 9–1, 3–6 🚉 Pistoia
www.pistoia.turismo.toscana.it

Pistoia sits at the foot of the Apennine Mountains, 47km (29 miles) east of Lucca. Its name probably derives from the Latin *pistores*, meaning 'bakers', as it was a town that supplied provisions to the Roman troops. Today much of the city's trade is based on plants and flowers (▷ 13). Pistoia's heart is Piazza del Duomo, with its 14th-century baptistery and sumptuous cathedral, and there are several other churches, as well as a museum. Every Wednesday and Saturday

morning one of Italy's largest markets is held on the piazza.

The cathedral has a striking silver altarpiece, the *Dossale di San Jacopo*, made between 1287 and 1456, and found in the Cappella di San Jacopo. It is covered in a vast number of figures, some of which were carved by Filippo Brunelleschi. The 14th-century Baptistery of San Giovanni has a font made in 1226 and a 16th-century, gold-painted wooden altar. The Church of San Giovanni Fuorcivitas is proud of its terracotta *Visitation* by Luca della Robbia. The Museo Civico's collection includes paintings ranging from Romanesque to 19th-century works.

PRATO

➕ 284 F4 ℹ️ Via Luigi Muzzi 38, 59100 Prato, tel 0574 24112; Mon–Sat 9–1.30, 3–7, Sun 10–1, 2.30–6.30 🚉 Prato
www.prato.turismo.toscana.it

Romantics might be attracted to Prato by the story that this is where the monk and artist Fra Filippo Lippi met and fell in love with a nun, Lacrezia Buti, whom he later married. Prato means 'meadow', but today the town is surrounded by industry. It has a long association with textile manufacturing and has been famous for its fabrics since the 13th century. Most of the sights are within the medieval walls. The mighty, turreted walls of the Castello dell'Imperatore were built by Emperor Frederick II between 1217 and 1248, a time of huge developments in literature, science and poetry.

The cathedral (daily 7.30–12, 3.30–7) was built in the 12th century. The *Pulpit of the Sacred Girdle* by

A detail from the fountain in Prato's main square

Michelozzo and Donatello graces a corner of the façade, and inside are frescoes by Filippo Lippi, including a famous depiction of Salome dancing at Herod's feast. You can see more works from the cathedral in the Museo dell'Opera del Duomo (Mon, Wed–Sat 9.30–12.30, 3–6, Sun 9.30–12.30). The Church of Santa Maria delle Carceri, built in the form of a Greek cross, is regarded as a masterpiece of Renaissance architecture and contains terracotta works by Andrea della Robbia.

SAN MINIATO

➕ 287 E5 ℹ️ Piazza del Popolo 3, 56027 San Miniato, tel 0571 42745; daily 9.30–1, 3.30–7.30, end Mar–end Oct; 9–1, 3–7.30, rest of year 🚉 San Miniato Basso
www.cittadisanminiato.it

San Miniato overlooks the Arno plain and has wide views of the valley. The lower part of the town is busy with leather workshops—something the town is now famous for. Bombing during World War II destroyed much of the old town, but the tower built by Emperor Frederick II

A Liberty-style house number in the beach resort of Viareggio

A fresco at the Villa Poggio a Caiano

The tiled roofs of Vinci, birthplace of the famous artist

was rebuilt. Head up to San Miniato Alto to take in the best of the sights, spread between the Piazza del Popolo and the Piazza della Repubblica up the hill. The cathedral (daily 9–1, 3–5) has a Romanesque façade and a fine bell tower known as Matilda's Tower, after Matilda of Tuscany who was born here in 1046. Art lovers will be attracted by the Museo Diocesano d'Arte Sacra (Tue–Sun 10–1, 3–7), to the side of the cathedral, with works such as a *Crucifixion* by Filippino Lippi. Further up is the Rocca (castle), to which you can climb for extensive views.

VIAREGGIO

➕ 283 C4 ⓘ Via Carducci 10, 55059 Viareggio, tel 0584 962233; Mon–Fri 9–2, 3–6, Sat 9–1.30, 3.30–6.30, Sun 9.30–noon 🚆 Viareggio

Visitors come to Viareggio not for its art or culture, but for the beach. This is the largest resort on Tuscany's Riviera and as it is only an hour's drive from Florence, it attracts large numbers of day-trippers from the city. It is on the coast of northwestern Tuscany, squeezed between the chic resort of Forte dei Marmi to the north and Torre del Lago to the south. Much of the large sandy beach is divided into *stabilimenti balneari* (bathing concessions, ▷ 154), which means you have to pay to use it, but this does ensure that it is kept clean. The beach is edged by an elegant boulevard with a number of Liberty (Italy's version of art nouveau) buildings along it. The town's streets run from the seafront in a strict grid and have plenty of hotels, pizzerias and shops. Be sure to visit the Villa Puccini (Tue–Sun 10–12.30, 2.30–5.30, Dec–end Mar; 10–12.30, 3–6 Apr, May; 10–12.30, 3–6.30 Jun–end Oct), south of Viareggio in Torre

del Lago. Home of the opera composer Giacomo Puccini from 1891 to 1921, it has been preserved as it was during his lifetime and is now a museum, with period furniture and personal memorabilia. A bus service runs regularly from Viareggio—ask at the tourist office.

VILLA MEDICI DI POGGIO A CAIANO

➕ 284 F4 • Piazza de' Medici 12–14, 59016 Poggio a Caiano ☎ 0558 77012 🕐 Daily 8.15–3.30, Nov–end Feb; 8.15–4.30 Mar, Sep, Oct; 8.15–5.30, Apr, May; 8.15–6.30 Jun–end Aug 💷 Adult €2, under 18 free 🎫 Free guided tours of villa, leaving every hour 🏛

This is the best known of the country residences owned by the Medici family. Not only is it a superb building, inspired by ancient Rome and surrounded by parkland, it is also steeped in Italian history. Lorenzo il Magnifico purchased a farmhouse on the site in 1480 and commissioned Giuliano da Sangallo to rebuild it; the first Italian villa to be built specifically as a rural retreat. It became his preferred country hideaway and the place where he wrote his sonnets. His descendants added to the original structure with the entrance loggia and the splendid curving double stairway. Francesco I died here, allegedly poisoned, and Vittorio Emanuele II often used it as a love nest.

The interior of the villa is very striking and its main focus is the double-height Salone, created by Sangallo from the courtyard that occupied the space between the two blocks of the original farmhouse. The 16th-century frescoes that cover the ceiling include a superb depiction of *Caesar Receiving the Egyptian Tribute* by Andrea del Sarto and Pontormo's *Vertumnus and Pomona*, a sun-drenched,

mellow painting of two Roman rural deities, that perfectly evokes the fruitfulness of Tuscany in summer. The frescoes can also be read as a tribute to the Medici family, who appear among the figures, and have references to the life of Lorenzo de'Medici—look out for the giraffe in the *Egyptian Tribute* which was presented to Lorenzo by the Sultan of Egypt. The villa is surrounded by parkland, laid out in a 19th-century English landscaped style, and shelters behind high walls.

VINCI

➕ 284 F5 ⓘ Via della Torre 11, 50059, tel 0571 568012; daily 10–7, Mar–end Oct; 10–6, rest of year www.commune.vinci.fi.it

Vinci is the birthplace of the artist, architect, inventor and all-round genius, Leonardo da Vinci. This pleasant little town is surrounded by slopes thickly clad with olive groves. It's a quiet place mostly free from crowds of visitors, but there is enough in the little town to occupy you for several hours.

The greatest attraction is the Museo Leonardo (daily 9.30–7), in a castle from the early Middle Ages. It contains fascinating scale reproductions of the machines and models that Leonardo invented. The terrace beside the museum has superb views over the hills. You can also visit Chiesa di Santa Croce (check with Tourist Office), the church where Leonardo was baptized. The town has some good bars and cafés where you can relax after your sightseeing.

Don't miss The Casa Natale di Leonardo, 3km (2 miles) from Vinci, is the cottage where Leonardo was born in 1452. There's little to see inside, but the surrounding countryside is attractive.

SIENA

Italy's most perfect medieval city has two focal points: the shell-shaped Campo, one of the world's most beautiful squares, and the Duomo, a superb Gothic building. Around these two are art-filled churches and public buildings, picturesque streets that burst into life for the *Palio* horse-race, and tempting shopping and dining.

MAJOR SIGHTS

Siena

✚ 288 G7 ⓘ Piazza del Campo 56, tel 0577 280551, Mon–Sat 9–7
🚉 Siena (1.5km/1 mile uphill walk, north to the central city)
www.terresiena.it • The official website of Siena's tourist board

A house painted in the warm brown shade of burnt Siena (above); a detail from one of the bronze reliefs on the Duomo's doors (below right)

SEEING SIENA

Siena is a beautifully preserved medieval city, a homogenous sprawl of narrow streets and superb buildings that's centred round the great square of the Campo. This lies at the convergence of the three main streets, the Banchi di Sopra, the Banchi di Sotto and the Via di Città. Each runs along a ridge through the city's three medieval *terzi* (districts), the Terzo di Città to the southwest, the Terzo di San Martino to the southeast and the Terzo di Camollia to the north. This central core was closed to traffic in the 1960s, making exploration pleasurable and straightforward once you've got your bearings. The best way to do this is to use the Campo as your starting point, and then head west and uphill to the Duomo. The Torre del Mangia in the Campo and the Panorama del Facciatone in the Museo dell'Opera del Duomo are ideal viewpoints for seeing the layout of the city. Central Siena is surprisingly small; you'll be able to walk to all the noteworthy sights in well under half an hour, so there's no need to worry about public transport. If it's your first visit, include a night's stay; the city has a whole new perspective once the crowds of day visitors have left.

BACKGROUND

Siena was founded by the Etruscans and then became a Roman city, Saena Julia. In the Middle Ages it grew to be an independent republic and by the 14th century was one of Europe's major cities, a rich banking hub with an important wool industry, whose wealth paid for the construction of great buildings and funded major artists. Siena's prosperity came to an end with the devastation caused by the Black Death in 1348; the population dropped from 100,000 to around 30,000. In 1557 Siena became part of the Medici Grand Duchy of Tuscany, the start of an era that saw the city become little more than a minor provincial town. The upside of this was the preservation of its medieval core, with little building or demolition after the early 1400s. As a backwater, Siena was untouched during World War II and only saw regeneration as tourism developed during the second half of the 20th century, years that also saw the Monte dei Paschi di Siena, the city's oldest bank, founded in 1472, become one of Italy's major financial players.

THE SIGHTS

TIPS

● The tourist office has a good range of city maps and information and will also book English-language guided walking tours around the city.
● The Duomo and museums have *biglietti cumulativi* (combined tickets) valid for several sites. You can pre-book admission to the civic museums by phone or fax (tel 0577 41169; fax 0577 226265). Note that the Pinacoteca is administered by a separate body.
● If you're planning a visit during the *Palio* be sure to book accommodation far in advance—up to a year is recommended.

DON'T MISS

A half-hour at a café in the **Campo** (▷ 116–119).
The views over the city from the **Panorama del Facciatone** (▷ 124).
Browsing through the delicacies on offer at **Manganelli** (▷ 182).
Flag throwing and drumming by the contrade teams as they march through the city on their feast days (▷ 183).
A delectable ice-cream from **Caffè Nannini** at the northern end of the Banchi di Sopra (▷ 231).
The Libreria Piccolomini's **frescoes** in the Duomo (▷ 122–123).

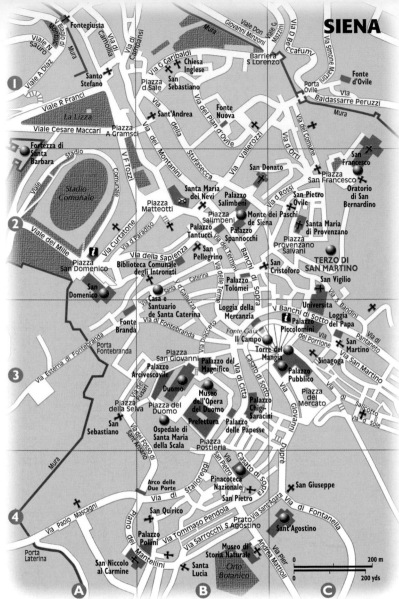

SIENA

THE SIGHTS

The interior of the house of Santa Caterina

You can climb La Fortezza for great views over the city, from where you can see the Duomo in the distance

IL CAMPO

See pages 116–119.

CASA E SANTUARIO DE SANTA CATERINA

🏛 114 B2 • Costa San Antonio 6, 53100
☎ 0577 44177 🕐 Daily 9–6; Chapel of the Crucifix 9–noon 🎟 Free

St. Catherine of Siena lived as a Dominican tertiary—that is, a member of the Dominican order but living outside it—in her family home just south of the church of San Domenico (▷ 127), and you can visit the house today. Caterina Benincasa, as St. Catherine, is joint patron saint of Italy with St. Francis. She was canonized as much for her political as for her mystical role. Born in 1347 the daughter of a dyer, she experienced visions from a very early age and became a nun at 16 against strong family opposition. In the aftermath of the Black Death of 1348, when Siena's population was decimated, she tended the poor and sick, but increasingly saw her God-given role as that of political mediator. She was instrumental through her letters in persuading Pope Urban V to return to Rome from Avignon, having first prevented the Sienese, Pisans and Florentines from rising against him, and afterwards worked tirelessly to reconcile the resulting schism between popes and anti-popes. Her later life was one of visions and prayer—she received the stigmata (marks that correspond to those left on Christ's body after the Crucifixion) in a vision. She died in 1380 and was canonized in 1460.

Her home has been altered over the centuries and now has a Renaissance loggia and a series of oratories—one on the site of

A statue of Santa Caterina found at her home

her cell. In the adjoining church of San Domenico you can see the crucifix in front of which she is said to have received the stigmata, while the Oratorio de (chapel of) Santa Caterina contains frescoes by Il Sodoma and a fine 15th-century statue of the saint by Niccolo di Bartolomeo.

DUOMO

See pages 120–123.

LA FORTEZZA DI SANTA BARBARA

🏛 114 A2 • Fortezza di Santa Barbara, 53100 ☎ Enoteca: 0577 288497 🕐 Tower: Daily 24 hours; Enoteca: Mon 12–8, Tue–Sat noon–1am 🎟 Free

On the northwest edge of the old city looms the Fortezza di Santa Barbara, a huge square fort with massive corner bastions. Initially built by the Holy Roman Emperor Charles V in 1554, it was attacked and destroyed by a mob and rebuilt under Cosimo I in 1561 as a garrison. You can go inside and climb up for great views of the city and hills beyond, but most people visit to sample the wines at the Enoteca Italiana, a state-run enterprise

inside the Fortezza showcasing Italy's largest wine collection. It stocks virtually all of Italy's 1,000-plus wine varieties, more than 400 of which originate in Tuscany. You can sample many by the glass at the bar, and all are on sale to take with you. The Fortezza comes into its own in summer, when it becomes a venue for concerts. Just to the north are the gardens of La Lizza, laid out in the 18th century and still a green haven in this part of town. The gardens are the scene on Wednesdays of Siena's huge weekly market, one of the largest in Tuscany.

MONTE DEI PASCHI DE SIENA

🏛 114 B2 • Piazza Salimbeni 3, 53100
☎ 0577 294599 🕐 By written request

The Monte dei Paschi di Siena is proud to be one of Europe's oldest banks. It was established in the 15th century as a charitable institution, lending money to the poor. The Monte soon became one of Italy's most prestigious banks, a role it retains today. Since the 15th century its headquarters have been two palazzi: the Spanocchi, a Renaissance palace, and the Salimbeni, a superb Gothic structure. In 1972 the architect Pierluigi Spadolino was commissioned to update the complex, which involved the construction of an ultramodern interior within the historic shell. This has created the perfect background for the bank's art collection, most of which is kept in the deconsecrated church of San Donato, reached by an underground passage from the main building. Here are displayed some of Siena's finest Gothic masterpieces, including a crucifix by Pietro Lorenzetti (active 1320–48) and a jewel-like Madonna by Giovanni di Paolo (1403–82).

Il Campo

The Campo is one of Italy's finest squares and is the twice-yearly scene of the thrilling *Palio* horse race. It's a glorious complex of medieval buildings dominated by the Palazzo Pubblico.

Relaxing on the square's fine brick paving

The Palazzo Pubblico dominates the southern side of Il Campo and was built at the end of the 13th century

RATINGS	
Cultural interest	●●●●●
Historic interest	●●●●●
Photo stops	●●●●●
Walkability	●●●●●

TIPS

● The Campo is best seen before the bus tours arrive, so get there early.
● Summer evenings are perfect for a stroll in the Campo.
● Check at the tourist office for details of the occasional summer concerts held in the square.
● If you're planning to attend the *Palio*, arrive early. You won't be able to leave the Campo for at least 2 hours after the race, so be prepared to do without shade, lavatories or refreshment for as much as 6 hours.
● *Contrade* feast days see flag-throwers and drummers in medieval costume processing through the Campo—check times with the tourist office.

Regional flags for sale around the Campo (top)

A view of the Campo from the Torre del Mangia (opposite)

SEEING IL CAMPO

The best approach to the Campo is through one of the narrow, stepped alleys running down from the Via di Città, Siena's main street. Emerging from the shadows, you'll find yourself in the huge scallop-shaped piazza, with the Palazzo Pubblico immediately in front of you. Spend a few minutes taking in the Campo and the sweep of medieval buildings that surround it, before walking down to visit the Palazzo—allow at least an hour for a tour. Once out, cross the courtyard to the entrance to the Torre del Mangia; if you can face the 503 steps there are superb views across the city and countryside from the top. Plan to leave enough time for a drink at one of the cafés around the Campo, perfect for people watching. If you want to eat, however, you'll probably do better away from this visitor hub.

HIGHLIGHTS

PALAZZO PUBBLICO

🏛 114 C3 • Piazza del Campo, 53100 ☎ 0577 292232 🕐 Daily 10–7 💶 Adult €7, under 18 free ❓ Combined ticket with La Torre del Mangia available: Adult €10

The halls and chambers in the Palazzo Pubblico—or town hall—comprise the Museo Civico and give a superb overview of Sienese painting. Here Sienese power, virtue and achievement from its medieval heyday are all proudly celebrated. Everything you see was once the backdrop to council meetings and decisions of state, a reminder of the former importance of the city and its government. After the tour it's worth heading back through the museum to climb the stairs to the rear loggia, which overlooks the Piazza del Mercato and has a superb view towards the countryside to the southeast.

The front rooms

The Sala dei Priori (or Sala di Balia) has a series of scenes from the life of the Sienese-born Pope Alexander III, painted around 1407 by Spinello Aretino. The focus is on Alexander's struggles with Frederick Barbarossa, the German Holy Roman Emperor, and there's a splendid naval battle scene. The next room, the Anticamera del Concistoro,

THE SIGHTS

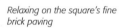

where there are Madonnas by Ambrogio Lorenzetti and Matteo di Giovanni, leads into a trio of rooms, one a richly embellished chapel. Highlights include a gilded bronze *She-Wolf Suckling Romulus and Remus* (Siena was allegedly founded by a son of Remus, ▷ 25) and Gothic frescoes by Taddeo di Bartolo dating from 1407–14. Off the Anticamera is the Sala del Consistoro, its ceiling a riot of writhing Mannerist forms and vivid tones, painted between 1529 and 1535 by Domenico Beccafumi.

Sala del Mappamundo

The Sala del Mappamundo (Room of the World Map), which gets its name from a now-faded circular map, has two remarkable frescoes. Simone Martini's stupendous *Maestà*, a quintessential Sienese Gothic piece, richly decorative in style with an almost translucent quality, was commissioned by the *comune* (city government) in 1315. The *Equestrian Portrait of Guidoriccio da Fogliano*, long believed also to be by Martini—an attribution now disputed—shows a sturdy, mounted knight setting out to besiege a hill town, and encapsulates the late medieval dream of chivalry. The academic quarrel over its artist continues. Some argue that it is a genuine Martini (even if overpainted), while other experts say it is a 16th-century fake. Whatever the truth, it remains one of the most beguiling frescoes in Siena.

Sala della Pace

A doorway leads from the map room into the Sala della Pace (Room of Peace), with Ambrogio Lorenzetti's two *Allegories of Good and Bad Government* (1338). These were commissioned to remind the councillors of their duty, making clear how their government would affect Siena's citizens. The detail of everyday life in both is more compelling than the complexities of the allegorical iconography. The walled city depicted is clearly Siena. Country life, complete with hawking and pig-droving, is going on outside the walls while maidens dance inside. These figures are, in fact, masculine—women dancing in public would have been far too shocking at that date.

IL CAMPO
✚ 114 B3

Since the Middle Ages the Campo has been the focus of Siena's civic and social life, the natural meeting point for all Sienese citizens. It is a gently sloping, rose-red, shell-shaped square, surrounded by a broad arc of palaces, almost all of which date from the 14th to early 15th centuries, with the Palazzo Pubblico on the southeast side providing

Stopping for a chat on the Campo

The Campo bursts with energy when the Palio *is underway*

One of the many narrow alleyways that lead you into Il Campo (left); the Fonta Gaia (below)

the focal point. Completed in 1349, the pavement is divided into nine segments, both to commemorate the rule of the Council of Nine, the medieval governing body, and to represent the folds of the Virgin's cloak. At ground-level virtually every palazzo is a café, bar, restaurant or gift shop, but the upper floors are still occupied by Sienese residents, who rent their windows to spectators at *Palio* time (▷ 183).

LA TORRE DEL MANGIA

✚ 114 C3 • Piazza del Campo, 53100 ☎ 0577 292232 🕐 Daily 10–7 👜 Adult €10, under 18 free; includes entry to Palazzo Pubblico

Built by the *comune* between 1338 and 1348, the Torre del Mangia soars 97m (318ft) above the Campo. It was built as a campanile, whose bell marked the working hours of the day for all citizens. The name goes back to the first watchman, Giovanni di Balduccio, who was renowned as a *mangiaguadagni* (eater of profits). There are 503 steps to the top, the reward being great—if vertiginous—views.

BACKGROUND

Il Campo (literally, The Field) occupies a site at the convergence of the three hilly ridges, the *terzi* (thirds), into which Siena is divided. Also intersecting here are the boundaries of the city's fiercely competitive *contrade* (parishes), making this area the only neutral patch of ground within the city. Here stood the Roman forum, which by the 13th century had become the city's main marketplace, earmarked by the city council in 1293 for expansion into a new public square. To enable construction of the surrounding buildings, a huge buttress was built beneath the lower half of the site, acting as the foundation for the Palazzo Pubblico, the future seat of the city government and financial offices. The Campo was completed by 1349, by which time the Palazzo Pubblico had also almost acquired its present form. The elegant palace is still home to the Sienese council, which occupies the upper floors of the building; the original council chambers, frescoed during Siena's medieval zenith, have been converted into the Museo Civico.

MORE TO SEE

FONTE GAIA
✚ 114 B3

This Renaissance fountain stands at the highest point of the Campo, designed by Jacopo della Quercia in 1419 and named Fountain of Joy for the festivities that took place at its inauguration. Marble panels are 19th-century copies of the originals (now under much-needed restoration in the Ospedale de Santa Maria della Scala).

CAPPELLA DI PIAZZA
✚ 114 C3

A graceful stone loggia at the base of Torre del Mangia, it was commissioned as a thanksgiving at the end of the Black Death in 1348. It was finally finished between 1461 and 1468, which accounts for its totally Renaissance style.

Duomo

Siena's cathedral has been the city's religious focus for 800 years and is a delight for lovers of fine sculpture, fresco, stained glass and decorative marble.

Inside the Libreria Piccolomini

A bronze from the 15th-century baptistery font

Many of the statues on the exterior are now copies

SEEING THE DUOMO

Start your visit in the Piazza where you can admire the Duomo's façade and see the remnants of the unfinished 14th-century nave extension. Inside, spend time examining the marble flooring before moving around the cathedral to take in the altars, chapels and sculptures. Next visit the Libreria Piccolomini through the entrance halfway down the nave on the left, before heading for the Baptistery and crypt. To reach these, go outside and walk down the right-hand side of the Duomo, through the arch and down the steps to the left. The crypt is on the left at the bottom of the first flight; the Baptistery is right at the bottom.

HIGHLIGHTS

DUOMO PAVEMENT

The Duomo's marble paving is one of its greatest treasures, a series of 56 decorative and narrative panels produced between 1369 and 1547. Practically every well-known artist of the day was involved at some stage in their design, the result being a technically superb history of the development of Sienese art. The subject matter is an eclectic mix incorporating allegories, biblical scenes and geometric patterns, and decorations include simple sgraffito (with details engraved) and the variegated marble used for intricate designs. Be aware that during much of the year, some panels will be covered to protect them from visitors' feet.

PULPIT AND STATUES

The Duomo's pulpit is the work of Nicola Pisano, and was created in 1268, soon after his completion of the pulpit for the Baptistery at Pisa (▷ 108–109). This masterpiece of Gothic sculpture is octagonal, the sculpted panels following a similar design to those at Pisa, but executed in a freer and more realistic style. The high relief figures seem to burst from the marble—best seen in the *Last Judgement* panel. A work by Michelangelo is on the Piccolomini Altarpiece in the left aisle. He was commissioned to carve 15 statues, but only four were completed—Saints Peter, Paul, Pius and Gregory—before he was tempted to Florence on a more lucrative commission, the *David*.

TIPS

● A maximum of 35 people are allowed on each crypt visit so book in advance to ensure a place.

● No shorts or sleeveless tops are allowed in the Duomo.

● Only 700 people are allowed in the Duomo at one time so you may have to be patient at peak times.

● A combined ticket is available for the Battistero, Cripta, Museo dell'Opera del Duomo, Museo Diocesano and the Oratorio de San Bernardino for €10.

Part of the lower Duomo's façade, created by sculptor Giovanni Pisano (active c1265–1314, top); a panel from the marble flooring with an image of the She-Wolf, part of the legend of how Siena got its name (opposite)

Volumes in the Libreria Piccolomini include illuminated choir books from the Duomo

BASICS

🏛 114 B3 • Piazza del Duomo, 53100
☎ 0577 283048
🕐 Mon–Sat 10.30–7.30, Sun 1.30–6.30, Mar–end Oct; Mon–Sat 10.30–6.30, Sun 1.30–5.30, rest of year
💶 Duomo: €3; Battistero: €3
🚌 Siena
🎧 Audioguide for €5
📖 Guidebook for €9.50
🎫 Sells large range of books, postcards, posters and gifts
🛍 Near to the shop
www.operaduomo.siena.it

LIBRERIA PICCOLOMINI

This magnificent Renaissance library was built in the 1490s by the future Pope Pius III to hold the collection of books amassed by his uncle, Pius II, Aeneas Silvius Piccolomini. Pius II was the quintessential Renaissance man: well read, open-minded, and with a deep love of the classics, nature and travel. Before becoming pope he travelled widely, and his nephew commissioned the painter Pinturicchio to decorate the library with scenes from his uncle's travels. Vividly glowing and enclosed in classically inspired borders, each fresco depicts an episode from Pius' life, shown against superbly rendered architecture and realistically observed nature and landscape. We see Pius in Basle in Switzerland, Scotland and Germany, being made a cardinal and crowned pope, and officiating at the canonization of Catherine of Siena. Part of the cycle's charm lies in the wealth of

The striking black and white exterior of the cathedral

THE SIGHTS

detail, the animated expressions of the crowds, the lovely Tuscan landscape in the background, and the intricate decorative scheme around each panel. The library contains a Roman statue of the *Three Graces* and illuminated Renaissance books and manuscripts.

BATTISTERO DI SAN GIOVANNI

The Baptistery's chief treasure is the early Tuscan Renaissance baptismal font, commissioned by the cathedral chapter and completed between 1416 and 1434. Jacopo della Quercia was responsible for the overall design, but the authorities also involved two of the real artistic heavyweights of the day: Lorenzo Ghiberti, who produced the *Baptism of Christ* and *John in Prison* panels, and Donatello, who carved *Herod's Feast*. Their work is full of drama, technically superb and overshadows to some extent Jacopo della Quercia's niche statues and surmounting tabernacle.

CRIPTA

The crypt, once part of an entrance to the Duomo, was walled up when the Baptistery was built, and its interior filled with builders' rubble. In 2003 workmen cleared this and opened up the space, discovering a series of wall paintings dating from the 1270s. This was an artistic find of immense importance, as the style of the paintings is far in advance, in terms of movement, fluidity and spatial depth, of anything previously known from that date. Covered for so many centuries, the brown and yellow tones, tawny reds and glowing, deep blues are as fresh as when they were put on.

BACKGROUND

The Duomo, predominantly Romanesque and Gothic in style, was more or less its present size by the first quarter of the 13th century, the start of Siena's period of greatest power and wealth. With money to spare, the authorities visualized expanding the size of the cathedral, and in the 14th century built the Baptistery on the slope at the rear of the cathedral. This was intended to support an entirely rebuilt nave, but proved not strong enough. Plans were then drawn up to completely reorientate the Duomo, converting the existing building into the transept and constructing an enormous new nave northwards in the direction of the Campo—on the right as you face the building. In 1348 the Black Death effectively ended Siena's prosperity and the scheme for the Duomo Nuovo (New Cathedral) was abandoned, leaving the partly built extension as you see it today. Treasures were added to the interior of the Duomo over the years, notably more marble flooring and the Piccolomini Library in 1492. The crypt, behind the Baptistery and beneath the cathedral, was rediscovered and opened up in 2003.

The beautifully ornate ceiling of the Libreria Piccolomini

MORE TO SEE

EXTERIOR

The façade (1284–96) by Giovanni Pisano, with its tall Gothic windows, is decorated with sculpture, carving, pillars and mosaic. The bell tower dates from late 13th century in black and white stone with mullioned windows. There is a lunette by Donatello above Porta del Perdono (Gate of Pardon) on north side.

CAPPELLA DI SAN GIOVANNI BAPTISTA

The left transept chapel has the bronze *John the Baptist* (1457) by Donatello and frescoes by Pinturicchio.

CAPPELLA CHIGI

This chapel was designed by Gianlorenzo Bernini in 1659 to house the 13th-century *Madonna del Voto*, a painting commemorating the dedication of Siena to the Virgin on the eve of the battle of Montaperto, against the Florentines in 1260. The exuberant and over-the-top baroque makes it a great contrast to rest of Duomo.

CHOIR STALLS

These date from mid-14th to mid-16th centuries, with inlay work of the highest quality.

DUCCIO'S WINDOW

The circular stained-glass window above the High Altar was designed by Duccio in 1288, making it one of Italy's earliest.

MUSEO DELL'OPERA DEL DUOMO

The cathedral's museum holds the greatest of all Sienese masterpieces, Duccio's *Maestà*. It also gives you a chance to see the city from a superlative viewpoint.

RATINGS

Cultural interest	● ● ● ◐
Historic interest	● ● ●
Photo stops	● ● ● ● ●
Value for money	● ● ● ●

BASICS

➕ 114 B3 • Piazza del Duomo, 53100
☎ 0577 283048
🕐 Daily 9–7, Mar–end Oct; daily 9–1.30, Nov–end Feb
🎫 Adult €6
🚉 Siena
🎧 Audiotours €5
📖 Official guidebook €6
🚻 Near to the shop
www.operaduomo.siena.it

TIP

● A combined ticket is available for the Battistero, Cripta, Museo dell'Opera del Duomo, Museo Diocesano and the Oratorio de San Bernardino for €10.

The Museo dell'Opera occupies a 15th-century building on the site of what had been intended as the right aisle of the Duomo Nuovo (▷ 123). Since the 19th century it has exhibited works of art from the decoration and furnishings of the Duomo and is administered by the cathedral authorities. Visiting the Museo dell'Opera is easy—follow the signs on the designated route through the museum. At busy times, you may have to wait to get a good look at the *Maestà*.

MAESTÀ

Duccio di Buoninsegna painted the *Maestà* over a four-year period from 1308. It was commissioned as the altarpiece for the high altar of the Duomo and portrays the Virgin, patron of Siena, as Queen of Heaven surrounded by her court of saints. Duccio painted it on both sides, one side with the Virgin's image, the other with a series of small panels telling the story of Christ's Passion. When finished it was the most expensive picture ever to have been commissioned. It remained at the Duomo until 1507 when, out of fashion, it was relegated to a storeroom. Now one of the city's most prized possessions, this glowing masterpiece is rich in intricate detail and brilliant tones standing against a gold ground. Duccio's achievement was to retain this very Sienese style yet abandon the stiffness of his predecessors' work—the *Maestà* is full of movement, accurately observed light and spatial awareness. You can see this at its best in the narrative panels, where the story of the Crucifixion is told for an illiterate population as clearly as it might be in a modern comic strip.

MADONNA DAGLI OCCHI GROSSI

This haunting and primitive *Madonna with the Large Eyes* was the altarpiece of the Duomo before the completion of the *Maestà*. The style is Byzantine, but you can see the beginning of the transition into what was to become Siena's own particular style in the statue's huge eyes. The work is by an unknown artist.

Duccio di Buoninsegna's Maestà is actually decorated on both sides (top); some of the exhibition rooms at the museum have vaulted ceilings (above)

PANORAMA DA FACCIATONE

A narrow passage and steep stairway at the end of the top floor lead you to a high lookout point, which gives a splendid view over the city and the countryside beyond.

OSPEDALE DI SANTA MARIA DELLA SCALA

This compelling complex was Siena's hospital for more than 800 years and is now being developed as a cultural focus for the city. A lively fresco cycle illustrates 15th-century daily life.

The Ospedale was founded in the 11th century as a resting place for pilgrims on the Via Francigena, the route between Rome and northern Europe which skirted Siena. It evolved from this into both a charitable institution, helping Sienese citizens in times of crisis, and a full-scale orphanage and hospital. Richly endowed, the Ospedale foundation was able to spare funds in the 15th century to decorate its church as well as the halls and wards. It became Siena's main hospital and was in use as such until 1995, when a new hospital opened. The frescoes were at once put on view to the public, and there's a plan to establish the huge complex as Siena's foremost museum and cultural space: It is already home to the Museo Archeologico and stages temporary exhibitions. The Pinacoteca Nazionale will eventually move here.

SALA DEL PELLEGRINAIO

This huge hospital ward, built around 1380, was frescoed during the second half of the 15th century with scenes telling the history of the Ospedale and illustrating its role as a charitable institution. The artists were Lorenzo di Pietro, known as Vecchietta, and Domenico di Bartolo. There are eight main frescoes, four down each side wall, and three subsidiary ones across the end. Their content is almost entirely secular, extremely rare at that date, and the paintings are crammed with wonderful details of everyday Sienese life. The left wall is devoted to the Ospedale's history, and on the Scala (ladder) leading to heaven from which the hospital took its name. The right wall depicts scenes illustrating the Ospedale's charitable functions.

CAPPELLA DEL SACRO CHIODO

The hospital chapel, painted by Vecchietta between 1446 and 1449, is named after the *chiodo* (nail), said to be a relic of the Crucifix that was once held here. The subject matter of the paintings is somewhat abstruse, with scenes from the Old Testament illustrating Christain teaching. The frescoes are unusual in Siena in not concentrating on the Virgin Mary, but she is not totally absent from the chapel. The altarpiece is a *Madonna della Misericordia* by Domenico di Bartolo, with the Virgin portrayed sheltering Siena's citizens beneath her cloak.

RATINGS	
Cultural interest	●●●○
Historic interest	●●●●●
Value for money	●●●○

BASICS
✚ 114 B3 • Piazza del Duomo, 53100
☎ 0577 224835; ticket office 0577 224828
🕐 Daily 10.30–6.30
💶 Adult €6, child (11–18) €3.50, under 11 free
📖 Guidebooks available in English, German and Italian for €10
☕ Small café-bar
🏬 Shop selling mostly books
♿ On the ground floor
www.santamaria.comune.siena.it

The frescoed walls of Sala del Pellegrinaio (top); the exterior of the Ospedale (above)

RATINGS

Cultural interest	●●●●●
Value for money	●●●
Walkability	●●●●●

BASICS

✚ 114 B4 • Via San Pietro 29, 53100
☎ 0577 281161; ticket office 0577 46052
◷ Mon 8–2, Tue–Sat 8.15–7, Sun 8–1.30
💵 Adult €4, under 18 free
🎧 Audioguide for €4
📖 A range of guidebooks are available from €8
🏬 Shop sells art books, pictures, posters, prints and postcards
♿ On the ground floor

The altarpiece showing Agostino Novello by Martini was once in the church of Sant'Agostino

PINACOTECA NAZIONALE

Elegant, expressive pictures that trace the development of the Sienese style from the 13th to 16th centuries. You'll find the cream of Sienese Gothic painting here.

SIENESE PAINTING

The Sienese style of painting is a unique form of Gothic, a genre that owes much to Byzantine art and is typified by stylized and static composition, intense colours, intricate detail and burnished gold backgrounds. While Florence eagerly embraced the naturalism of the Renaissance, Siena continued to emulate older styles, and artists produced paintings with gold backgrounds well into the late 15th century. By the 1490s Florentine influence was stronger, and perspective became increasingly realistic. Eventually Mannerism, a 16th-century style that used distorted perspective and bright hues, brought Siena's artists into the mainstream of European painting.

THE ART WORKS

The altarpiece by Simone Martini depicts scenes from the life of the local saint Agostino Novello and was probably painted in 1324. The central panel is of the saint, an Augustinian monk, while the side ones show four of the miracles he performed. The scenes take place in or around Siena itself; the rocks and woodlands, and the scene showing him conversing with an angel, reflect the fact that Agostino was a hermit. The miracles mainly involve children rescued from accidents, subjects chosen to appeal to the peasant congregation.

The Lorenzetti brothers, Pietro and Ambrogio, were prolific artists, innovative in that they explored the possibilities of perspective and greater realism within the conventions of Sienese Gothic. The lovely *Annunciation* by Ambrogio was executed in 1344, and exemplifies these developments: The Virgin's chair is firmly placed in space, rather than appearing flat, and the receding black-and-white pavement adds depth to the composition. Look nearby for two tiny panels by the same artist, *City by the Sea* and *Castles by a Lake*; they are thought to be the first landscapes ever painted.

The *Fall of the Rebellious Angels* by Domenico Beccafumi is a perfect example of the dramatic Mannerist style, of which Beccafumi was the chief Sienese exponent. He painted this in the 1540s and it is heavily influenced by Michelangelo, whose *Last Judgement* in Rome's Sistine Chapel had just been completed. The serpentine figures, unbalanced composition and livid tones are all typical of Mannerism, in contrast to the serene figures of Gothic art.

San Domenico's stark exterior, begun in 1226, dominates the city's northern skyline

The exterior of San Francesco belies its cavernous interior

ORATORIO DI SAN BERNARDINO

✚ 114 C2 • Piazza San Francesco
☎ 0577 283 0481 ⏰ Daily 10.30–1.30, 3–5.30, Mar–end Nov 💰 Adult €3; combined ticket available, see Museo dell'Opera del Duomo

The entrance to the Oratorio di (chapel of) San Bernardino, a Sienese-born preacher saint, is to the right of the church of San Francesco. The Oratorio has two chapels, the upper decorated with scenes from the life of the Virgin, the lower with episodes from the saint's life. Artistically, it is the upper chapel that enthrals, a Mannerist tour-de-force painted between 1496 and 1518 by Il Sodoma and Beccafumi. Below, San Bernardino is portrayed on his preaching travels; he adopted the motto 'Make it clear, short and to the point', a slogan that earned him his role as patron saint of advertising.

SANT'AGOSTINO

✚ 114 C4 • Prato di Sant'Agostino, Via Sant'Agata ⏰ Closed for restoration

Wander down the hill from the Pinacoteca Nazionale (▷ 126) and you'll come to the church of Sant'Agostino. It was built in the 13th century and extensively altered between 1747 and 1755, making it one of Siena's few neoclassical buildings. The 19th-century portico leads into a luminous interior, paved in majolica and containing some excellent paintings. Highlights are a resplendent *Crucifixion* (1506) by Perugino on the second altar in the south aisle, and two lunette medallions by Luca Signorelli (c1441–1523) in the Cappella Bichi in the south transept. Best of all is the Cappella Piccolomini, which contains a lunette fresco by Ambrogio Lorenzetti and Il Sodoma's *Adoration of the Magi*—there is no better illustration of the range of Sienese art than in these two works, separated by over two centuries. Outside, the church's piazza is a pleasant space which gives access to the Orto Botanico, a cool, little-visited garden run by the University that contains every species found in Tuscany and plenty of exotics besides.

SAN DOMENICO

✚ 114 A2 • Piazza San Domenico
☎ 0577 280893 ⏰ Daily 9–1, 3–6.30
💰 Free

The Dominicans founded their monastery in Siena in 1125. A preaching order, they spread God's word through fiery sermons and relied on vast, plain churches to hold the crowds they attracted. Gothic, brick-built San Domenico is such a structure, standing on the outskirts of the city with a good view of the Duomo. It was begun in 1226 and its history is entwined with the cult of St. Catherine of Siena, whose shrine (▷ 115) is near by. The church has some notable paintings in the chapels. St. Catherine's chapel, halfway down the right side of the church, was built in 1488 and lavishly decorated by Il Sodoma. The marble altar (1466) includes a tabernacle that contains the saint's head, while the side walls were painted by Il Sodoma with depictions of Catherine. Back in the main church, the chapels on either side of the high altar have pictures representing the best of local talent: There's a Matteo di Giovanni triptych of the *Madonna and Child with St. Jerome and John the Baptist* to the right, and in the second chapel to the left, the same artist's *St. Barbara, Angels and Saints Mary Magdalene and Catherine*, considered to be one of his most outstanding works.

SAN FRANCESCO

✚ 114 C2 • Piazza San Francesco
☎ 0577 289081 ⏰ Daily 8–12, 3–7
💰 Free

If San Domenico is the church of St. Catherine, Siena's other great preaching stronghold, the Franciscan powerhouse of San Francesco, is linked to San Bernardino. Like San Domenico, the church stands on the edge of the city. It was completed in 1482, but badly damaged by fire in 1655, undergoing reconstruction in the 19th century. What you see today is a bit of a jumble, but there are fragments of frescoes by Pietro and Ambrogio Lorenzetti in two chapels to the left of the high altar, and a superb, glittering polyptych by Lippo Vanni in the sacristy. The church also has some noble marble tombs, including those of the Tolomei family, one of the city's powerful medieval clans.

TERZO DI SAN MARTINO

✚ 114 C2

The ward of the Terzo di San Martino, home to Siena's University, lies east of the Campo, a low-key area where you can expect to escape the crowds. The main street is the Banchi di Sotto, which passes the vast Palazzo Piccolomini, commissioned in the 1460s by Pius II. It's home to the Archivio di Stato, the city's archives, where visitors are welcome to inspect documents dating back to the 13th and 14th centuries.

The *terzo* has two main churches: San Martino, with a stunning *Nativity* by Domenico Beccafumi (1486–1551) and Santa Maria dei Servi, a lovely Renaissance church with some fine artwork and a great view of the city. Beyond here is the Porta Romana, the massive southern gateway into Siena.

SOUTHERN TUSCANY

With its rolling hills, villas and farmhouses, vines, olives and cypresses, the landscape of southern Tuscany is synonymous with the Italian dream. Drive through perfection to explore hilltop towns like San Gimignano, Montalcino and Montepulciano, or head for the atmospheric low country of the Maremma, thriving towns like Arezzo, or the off-shore islands and coast.

MAJOR SIGHTS

Part of the St. Benedict frescoes in Monte Oliveto Maggiore

Abbazia di Sant'Antimo is set in beautiful countryside

A detail of a fresco inside the Abbazia di Sant'Antimo

ABBAZIA Di MONTE OLIVETO MAGGIORE

➕ 288 H8 • 1 Località Monteoliveto Maggiore, 53041 Asciano ☎ 0577 707611 🕐 Daily 9.15–12, 3.15–6, May–end Sep; 9.15–12, 3.15–5, rest of year 🎟 Free 🚻 ♿

This isolated medieval abbey, still the home to a monastic community, stands on a hillside 9km (6 miles) northeast of Buonconvento. This is the heart of the Crete country (▷ 135), the wild limestone landscape distinguished by scree and rock falls that lies south of Siena—a landscape instantly appealing to medieval monastic orders seeking wilderness. The abbey itself, built of rosy brick, is surrounded by groves of olives, holm oak and cypress trees, first planted here by the early monks. It was founded by Bernardo Tolomei, a member of a wealthy Sienese family, and by the mid-15th century it was an immensely rich community with money to spare for artistic projects.

Much of the complex is closed to visitors, but you can go into the Chiostro Grande (Great Cloister) to see how the money was spent. The cloister was frescoed between 1498 and 1508 with scenes from the life of St. Benedict—generally seen as the father of monasticism—by two of the outstanding artists of the day, Luca Signorelli (c1441–1523) and Giovanni Sodoma (1477–1549). The latter was an eccentric figure who kept an extraordinary menagerie of pets, including a talking raven and a badger, both of which appear in some of the fresco panels. The series starts on the east wall; follow it round to trace Benedict's life and enjoy the wealth of detail and the vivid hues. The monastery church has a 15th-century layout, with wooden choir stalls carved by Fra

Giovanni da Verona. Upstairs there's a gorgeous Renaissance library. Today's monks have a library of 40,000 books and other documents, along with a workshop where they restore old books. They also produce wine, honey and olive oil, which you can buy at the monastery shop.

ABBAZIA DI SANT'ANTIMO

➕ 288 H9 • 222 Località Abbazia Sant'Antimo, Castelnuovo dell'Abate, 53024 Montalcino ☎ 0577 835659 🕐 Mon–Sat 6am–9pm, Sun 9–10.30, 3–6 🎟 Free

The honey-toned abbey church of Sant'Antimo, full of architectural appeal, stands untouched by time in a quintessential Tuscan landscape, around 10km (6 miles) from Montalcino (▷ 137). Legend associates its foundation with Charlemagne, said to have built the abbey to thank God for saving his troops from a mysterious disease. In AD814 it was enriched with lands and privileges by Charlemagne's son. It became one of the richest abbeys in Tuscany, in part because it was on many important pilgrimage and trade routes. Parts of the complex are pre-Romanesque, though much dates to the 12th century including the superb church, which has a layout unique in Tuscany, with a basilican plan and radiating chapels. The architecture has a distinctly French Romanesque touch, exemplified by the ambulatory (walkway) behind the main altar; this allowed pilgrims to walk while in prayer.

The abbey is now in the hands of French Augustinian monks, who celebrate mass, complete with Gregorian chants, several times daily. Don't rush a visit here—to truly appreciate the site, it's best to allow time to soak up the peace and serenity of the

spot. If you are feeling energetic, it's a good starting point for a country hike.

ABBAZIA DI SAN GALGANO

➕ 287 G8 • San Galgano 53012, Chiusdino ☎ 0577 756738 🕐 Daily 24 hours 🎟 Free

This huge ruined abbey (69m/226ft long and 29m/95ft wide), standing alone in the heart of the countryside, is one of the best examples of Cistercian Gothic architecture in Italy. The abbey dates back to the 13th century and was built in honour of St. Galganus (San Galgano), who lived on nearby Monte Siepi as a hermit in the 12th century and founded a small church there. It was once the largest Cistercian abbey in Tuscany and one of the two largest in Italy. The abbey's church was repeatedly sacked during the 13th-century in inter-city Tuscan wars and gradually fell into disrepair, the roof finally collapsing in the 18th century. Today the walls and columns still stand, but it is open to the sky and little is left of the monastic buildings.

Close by, on a hill above the main abbey, you can see the Cappella di Monte Siepi, a domed rotunda that was once the saint's hermitage, transformed into a chapel between 1182 and 1185. Inside is the stone into which he is said to have thrust his sword as a symbol of his renunciation of worldly life.

Two more structures were later built here, a 14th-century Gothic chapel and an 18th-century rectory, forming an attractive rural ensemble. The side chapel of the rotunda contains some ghostly traces of frescoes by Ambrogio Lorenzetti; you can just make out Galgano offering his sword to St. Michael.

THE SIGHTS

A poster promoting the attractions of Anghiari

Piazza delle Sorgenti, Bagno Vignoni, is a pool

Buonconvento is one of Tuscany's towns not on a hill

THE SIGHTS

ANGHIARI

✚ 289 K6 🛈 Corso Matteoti 103, 52031 Anghiari, tel 0575 749279; daily 9.30–12.30, 4.30–7.30 🚊 Sansepolcro www.anghiari.it

If you're exploring southeast Tuscany, Anghiari makes a pleasant stop. This little settlement, overlooking a fertile plain planted with tobacco and sunflowers, has all the charms of a typical Tuscan hill town, but with the added bonus of being well off the main visitor routes. Its chief claim to fame is as the scene of a 1440 battle between the Milanese and the Florentines, the subject of what is possibly the best known of all the great Renaissance works of art that have been lost: Frescoed by Leonardo da Vinci for the Palazzo Vecchio in Florence, this was by all accounts a tour de force, depicting semi-naked warriors of breathtaking anatomical realism. Sadly, Leonardo's innovative fresco technique was a disaster and the work didn't survive. Anghiari has an exhibition that will tell you about the battle, but its main pleasures are to be found in exploring the steep streets and stepped alleyways at its heart.

ASCIANO

✚ 288 H8 🛈 Corso Matteoti 18, 53041 Asciano, tel 0577 719510; Mon–Sat 10–1, 3–6, Sun 10–1 🚊 Asciano www.cretesenesi.it

Asciano, first mentioned in records in 715, has Etruscan roots, and its medieval history is one of a town repeatedly fought over by Florence and Siena. It became permanently Sienese in the 13th century, and it was here that one of the city's greatest artists, Domenico di Bartolo, was born in around 1400. It is a beguiling little town, still partly enclosed within its walls. Of the three museums, one is devoted to Etruscan finds from the area, but of greater interest is the Museo d'Arte Sacra (Museum of Religious Art) in a palace in the middle of town. Its collection is surprisingly good for a town of this size and includes works by several major Sienese artists, among them Lorenzetti and Sano di Pietro. The artistic tradition was going strong right through to the 19th century, and the town's third museum has works by local painter Amos Cassioli (1832–92). Make time to inspect the late 13th-century Romanesque-Gothic church of Sant'Agata.

BAGNO VIGNONI

✚ 288 J9 🛈 Strada di Bagno Vignoni, 53027, San Quirico d'Orcia, tel 0577 888975; Wed–Fri 3.30–6.30, Sat–Sun 10.30–1, 3.30–6.30

Bagno Vignoni is one of the region's most unusual sights: a village whose old stone buildings cluster around a large, open-air pool filled with water from natural hot springs. When the air is cool, a mist rises from the warm water and drifts over the village square. The spring was known in Etruscan times, and over the years the waters were enjoyed by Romans and popes, as well as by saints including Catherine of Siena. In medieval times the baths became a resting place for pilgrims on the Via Francigena, the pilgrims' route through Italy to Rome. This is still a great place to stop and rest, with plenty of restaurants; there's a playground near the parking area. You can't bathe in the pool in the square, but you can pay to enjoy the springs in an open-air hotel pool,

A bronze statue of Garibaldi in Anghiari's main square

or take a free dip by following the stream downhill to the pools formed at the confluence with the river below.

BUONCONVENTO

✚ 288 H8 🛈 Museo d'Arte Sacra della Val d'Arbia, Via Soccini 18, 53020 Buonconvento, tel 0577 807181; Tue–Sun 10.30–1, 3–7, Mar–end Oct; Sat–Sun 10–1, 3–5, rest of year 🚊 Buonconvento

This small, brick-built market town was an important trading post in the mid-13th century and a prominent stopping-off point for pilgrims along the Via Francigena. About 27km (17 miles) south of Siena, its well-preserved medieval core is surrounded by walls built between 1371 and 1381. The Museo d'Arte Sacra (also the Tourist Office) is a museum of religious art displaying Sienese paintings from the 14th to the 17th century, including an *Annunciation* by Andrea di Bartolo and the *Madonna del Latte* (Madonna of the Milk), a breastfeeding Madonna by Luca di Tomme. It also has displays of jewellery, wood and marble sculptures.

AREZZO

This thriving provincial capital is best known to art lovers as the home of Piero della Francesca's greatest fresco cycle. You will also find excellent shopping and good food.

Arezzo, crowned with a cathedral and fortress, descends in terraces down its hillside to a fertile plain near the River Arno. The town was founded by the Etruscans and grew in importance during Roman times, with a reputation for producing highly prized red-glazed vases. During the Middle Ages it thrived on gold and jewellery, and the old town from that time has survived. Arezzo remains a world leader in jewellery manufacture, and has a monthly antiques market. The town also hosts Arezzo Wave, one of Italy's biggest rock festivals (▷ 190).

THE LEGEND OF THE TRUE CROSS

One of Italy's most famous fresco cycles is in the church of San Francesco. Commissioned from Piero della Francesca by the Bacci family in the 1450s, the pictures tell the story of the Legend of the True Cross, which links the physical history of Christ's Cross—said to have been made from the Tree of Knowledge in the Garden of Eden, source of Eve's apple—to man's cycle of redemption. Such complicated iconography may not appeal, but the frescoes are sublime. The figures are solid, detached and static, the light translucent and the tones muted. Painted between 1453 and 1466, the frescoes deteriorated badly during the second half of the 20th century and only emerged from extensive restoration in the late 1990s. As a result, access is limited to small groups (see Tip).

OTHER SIGHTS

The Piazza Grande is the town's sloping main square, the scene of the *Giostra del Saraceno* festival (Joust of the Saracen, ▷ 190). The alleys around it are full of dark workshops smelling of wood, where artisans restore antique furniture. Just off the southwest corner is the church of Santa Maria, with a superb arcaded 13th-century façade and shadowy interior. North from here, the cathedral, built over some 250 years from 1278, dominates the city (daily 7–12.30, 3–7). It contains a tiny fresco by Piero della Francesca and some fine stained glass. A short stroll away is the Passeggio del Prato, an attractive park overlooked by the Fortezza Medicea (1538–60), a castle built by the town's Medici rulers. The Museo Archeologico (daily 8.30–7.30), next to the Roman amphitheatre, has good collections of Roman and Etruscan bronzes and pottery.

RATINGS

Good for kids	● ● ●
Historic interest	● ● ● ●
Shopping	● ● ● ●

BASICS

✚ 289 K6

ℹ Piazza della Repubblica 28, 52100 Arezzo, tel 0575 377678; Mon–Sat 9–1, 3–7, Sun 9–1, Apr–end Sep; Mon–Sat 9–1, 3–6.30, rest of year

🚇 Arezzo

www.apt.arezzo.it

TIP

● Admission to the frescoes of *The Legend of the True Cross* (Mon–Sat 9–6, Sun 1–5.30) is strictly by timed ticket— only 25 people are allowed in every 30 minutes. Buy tickets in advance at the ticket office, tel 0575 352727, or buy online at www.pierodellafrancesca.it.

A detail from the Legend of the True Cross, *found on the walls around the altar of San Francesco (top); a monthly antiques market is held in Piazza Grande (above)*

CHIANTI

One of Tuscany's best-known and most popular areas, it is noted for its wooded hills, attractive villages and, especially, its vineyards and their fine red wines.

The Chianti region, between Florence and Siena, is generally explored by driving down the Strada Chiantigiana (SS222), a designated wine road that runs through the heart of the district. This seductive area of rolling hills has produced wine since Etruscan times, and is still providing grapes for Chianti wine. The landscape is likely to be familiar to you, even if you have never visited the region: olive groves, farms, villas and vineyards, some offering tastings. The small towns of the region are unassuming, but make rewarding stops along the way.

CASTELLINA IN CHIANTI
The town was once of great strategic importance as it was on the border between the territories of Siena and Florence. You can still see its fortress at the top of the town and walk along the Via delle Volte, a tunnel-like road that runs around the walls and was formerly used by soldiers. This is a good place to buy both olive oil and wine.

RADDA IN CHIANTI
Radda in Chianti is a hilltop town with great views over the region and fine buildings dating from the 15th and 16th centuries. During the Middle Ages it was capital of the Lega di Chianti, a military league of local towns; the Palazzo Comunale is decorated with local families' shields and faces the town church.

GREVE IN CHIANTI
Greve has plenty of wine shops, cobbled streets and alleyways to explore. The Piazza Matteotti is the town's hub; the surrounding buildings have attractive arcades and it's the scene of the weekly Saturday market. Look for the statue of local hero Giovanni di Verrazzano, who in 1524 was the first European to enter New York harbour.

BADIA A COLTIBUONO
Just 6km (4 miles) from Radda is the Badia a Coltibuono, an 11th-century abbey, with the Romanesque church of San Lorenzo, one of the finest buildings of that date in Tuscany. The abbey estate is now owned by one of Chianti's biggest wine producers, which runs a restaurant (▷ 235) and a shop selling the estate produce. You can then walk along well-marked trails in the surrounding wood.

RATINGS				
Good for food	●	●	●	●
Photo stops	●	●	●	● ●
Walkability	●	●	●	

BASICS

✚ 288 G6 ℹ Viale Giovanni di Verrazzano 59, 50022 Greve in Chianti, tel 055 854 6287; Mon–Sat 10–1, 2.30–7 Easter to end Oct

TIPS

● You'll need a car to explore Chianti, as public transport is limited.
● To get the best of the area make frequent stops: Roads are winding and thickly wooded and much of the appeal lies in the villages and small towns.

Castellina in Chianti (top); a detail from a building in Radda (above); typical Chianti landscape (opposite)

RATINGS

Historic interest	● ● ●
Photo stops	● ● ● ● ●
Walkability	● ● ●

BASICS

✚ 289 K7

🛈 Via Nazionale 42, 52044 Cortona, tel 0575 630352; daily 9–1, 3–7, May–end Sep; Mon–Sat 9–1, 3–6 rest of year

www.cortonaweb.net

A view over the rooftops of Cortona and the valley of Valdichiana (above); the Annunciation *by Fra Angelico (below)*

CORTONA

As one of the highest towns in Italy, Cortona has superb views over Tuscany and Umbria. It also has some great paintings by Fra Angelico and Luca Signorelli.

A visit here provides good exercise as well as rewarding sightseeing, as Cortona is perched on the side of Monte Egidio, making its medieval streets extremely steep. Panoramic views take in the Valdichiana and the region south of here. Substantial parts of the town's Etruscan walls are incorporated into the town's predominantly medieval buildings, and there are churches and good museums to visit along the precipitous cobbled streets. The town's great works of art come from its associations with two painters: the monk Fra Angelico (1387–1455), who lived here for two years in the local Dominican monastery, and native son Luca Signorelli (c1441–1523), in his imaginative power the precursor of Michelangelo.

TWO IMPORTANT MUSEUMS

You'll find the Museo Diocesano (daily 10–7) on Piazza del Duomo. This is home to two masterpieces by Fra Angelico, an *Annunciation* and a *Madonna and Child with Saints*, along with works by Sassetta, Bartolomeo della Gatta and Luca Signorelli. Another highlight is a second-century Roman sarcophagus carved with scenes depicting Dionysus' battle with the Amazons.

The Museo dell'Accademia Etrusca (daily 10–7) recalls the town's more distant past. It has a huge fifth-century bronze lamp, some exquisite jewellery, urns and vases, and an impressive, if incongruous, ancient Egyptian collection.

Other places to see include the 14th-century church of San Domenico, where Fra Angelico worshipped; there is a fresco by him above the main door. The church of San Niccolò, approached through a small walled garden, contains a double-sided painting by Luca Signorelli. The Fortezza Medicea, a ruined Medici fortress, is at the northern end of town. The climb up to it is steep, but it's worth the effort for the views of Lake Trasimeno and Umbria: It is a magical experience to be here at dusk on a fine day. To enjoy the scenery less strenuously, head for the Giardini Pubblichi at the end of Via Nazionale. This street has several smart shops as well as cafés where you can taste local delicacies.

A statue of Leopold II in Piazza Dante, Grosseto

Houses surround the natural harbour of Porto Azzurro on Isola d'Elba

CHIANTI

See pages 132–133.

COLLE DI VAL D'ELSA

➕ 287 G7 🛈 Via Francesco del Campana 43, 53024 Colle di Val d'Elsa, tel 0577 922791; daily 10–1, 3–6.30 🚉 Poggibonsi

Colle di Val d'Elsa is a sleepy little town that is far more attractive than its rather unappealing modern suburbs lead you to expect. Relatively few visitors venture here, but for those that do the old part of town, Colle Alta, on the hill, has its rewards. It has retained much of its medieval layout, with quiet narrow lanes and little alleyways. The main street, Via del Castello, runs the length of the town's ridge, opening out midway into Piazza del Duomo, the main square. There's a small archaeological museum in the square with finds from local Etruscan tombs (Tue–Sun 11–12.30, 4.30–7.30), and on Via del Castello is a palace containing the Museo Civico e d'Arte Sacra, with silverware, sculpture, and medieval and Renaissance paintings (11–12.30, 4.30–7.30).

Colle has a strong industrial heritage and was a major manufacturer of paper from the Middle Ages. The crystal and glass-blowing industry was also important, and today 90 per cent of Italy's crystal is produced here, making Colle an excellent place to buy glassware.

Don't miss Stop at the *borgo*, or vantage point, for excellent views towards Siena.

CRETE SENESE

➕ 288 H7 🛈 Corso Matteotti 18, Asciano, tel 0577 719510; Mon–Sat 10–1, 3–6, Sun 10–1 🚉 Asciano www.cretesenesi.it

The Crete Senese is the name given to a geological area south of Siena, which has some strange, crater-like landslides and bare slopes, where the pale fields of heavy clay are dotted with sheep and punctuated by pencil-slim cypresses. The heartland encompasses the small lowland town of Buonconvento (▷ 130), the abbey of Monte Oliveto (▷ 129) and the village of Asciano (▷ 130).

To see it at its best you should strike out on foot, preferably along one of the ridge routes, although the area still has plenty of quiet *strade bianche* or white roads—unsurfaced dirt roads that are dusty and white in the summer. You could walk from tiny San Giovanni d'Asso, with its 11th-century Romanesque church of San Pietro and 13th-century castle, all the way to Monte Oliveto, a lovely route that takes in the best of this extraordinary landscape.

GROSSETO

➕ 292 G10 🛈 Viale Monterosa 206, 58100 Grosseto, tel 0564 462611; Mon–Fri 8.30–6.30, Sat 8.30–1.30 🚉 Grosseto www.lamaremmafabene.it

Capital of its province, Grosseto is a functional administrative town. Although it suffered heavy bombing during World War II, its massive hexagon of town walls, built by Cosimo I (1519–74) after the Florentines took the town from the Sienese, were spared and are one of the highlights of a visit to this commercial metropolis. You can walk all the way round the walls in about 40 minutes, before inspecting the central Piazza Dante, the main remnant of the old town. It's home to the Duomo, originally 13th century, but heavily altered, both inside and out, during the 19th century. If you're heading into the Maremma (▷ 136), it's worth dropping into the Museo

di Storia Naturale della Maremma (Tue–Sat 9–8), informative on the natural history of this low-lying area. The town's most notable church is San Francesco, which has some lovely cloisters.

ISOLA D'ELBA

➕ 290 C10 🛈 Calata Italia 43, 193 Portoferraio, tel 0565 914671; daily 8–8, Easter–end Sep; Mon–Sat 8–2, 3–6, rest of year ⛴ From Piombino to Portoferraio

Many people visit the island of Elba to explore the place where Napoleon lived in exile from May 1814 to February 1815, but even more come to enjoy the scenery, unspoiled beaches and bustling resort towns. There are plenty of sites to visit, including Napoleon's former villa as well as old, abandoned mines where semi-precious stones can still be found. The island is also an excellent place for walking.

About 10km (6 miles) west of the mainland and an hour's ferry ride from Piombino, Elba is a natural mosaic of coves, beaches, headlands, precipitous coastline, wooded mountains and terraced vineyards. It is the largest island in the Tuscan archipelago, a group of islands once described as the 'necklace that slid from the neck of Venus'. There are several walking trails as well as a cable car to the top of Monte Capanne (1,018m/3,340ft), from where you can enjoy excellent views of the archipelago.

In Portoferraio, the main town, you will find the Villa dei Mulini. This was Napoleon's home while he was exiled and is now a museum (Mon, Wed–Sat 9–7, Sun 9–1) containing furniture of the period and Napoleon's library. Porto Azzurro is a busy resort dominated by a huge fortress once used as a prison.

The beach at Campese on Isola del Giglio

The evening light seen across grassland in the Maremma

The cathedral, Massa Marittima, is decorated with arcades

ISOLA DI GIANNUTRI

🔢 292 G13 ℹ️ Archetto del Palio 1, 58019 Porto Santo Stefano, tel 0564 814208; daily 9–1, 4–7, Easter–end Oct, 9–1, rest of year 🚢 From Porto Santo Stefano to Giannutri

If you're an island enthusiast, Giannutri makes a good day's excursion from Giglio or, in summer, Porto Santo Stefano. It's Tuscany's southernmost island, a flat semi-circular expanse easily walked in a couple of hours, and is part of the Parco Nazionale Arcipelago Toscano, Europe's largest protected marine park. There's little to see except the ruins of a Roman villa at Cala Maestra, but the island has clear waters and excellent scuba diving. Giannutri is privately owned, so there is no accommodation or visitor facilities.

ISOLA DEL GIGLIO

🔢 292 F12 ℹ️ Via Provinciale 9, Giglio Porto, 58012 Isola del Giglio, tel 0564 809400; Wed–Mon 8.30–1.30, 5–8 Jun–end Aug; 9–12.30, 4–7 May, Sep; 10–12, rest of year 🚢 From Porto Santo Stefano to Giglio Porto www.isoladelgiglio.biz

The lovely island of Giglio lies 15km (9 miles) across the sea from Monte Argentario (▷ 138). Packed in summer with people on holiday, it is best visited outside July and August, when the coast and villages are less crowded. If you do visit in high season, you can escape the crowds by heading into the unspoiled interior, a beguiling mix of woodland and barren rocks, which you can explore by rented bicycle or moped—ideal if you don't want to bring a car. It has three main villages: Giglio Porto, where the ferry docks, Giglio Castello, high in the hills 6km (4 miles) from the coast, and Giglio Campese, site of the island's best beach, although the main holiday bases are by the sea. Beaches on Giglio tend to be small, tucked at the bottom of precipitous cliffs; if you're looking for sand, head for Campese, blessed with a 2km (1-mile) sickle of smooth beach. If you want to sightsee, there are castle ruins at Castello, but most people come simply to enjoy the good seafood restaurants, clear sea and glorious surroundings.

LUCIGNANO

🔢 288 J7 ℹ️ Piazza del Tribunnale 22, 52046 Lucignano, tel 0575 838001; Tue, Thu–Sun 10–1, 3–6.30, Mar–end Sep; Tue, Thu–Fri, 10–1, 2.30–5.30, Sat–Sun 10–1, 2.30–6, rest of year 🚌 Monte San Savino or Arezzo

Lucignano is a prosperous, tidy town built around the main church, which is approached by a double stairway. Behind it, you can visit the Museo Comunale, which contains a piece of 14th-century jeweller's work, a reliquary known as the *Albero di Lucignano* (Tree of Lucignano). One glance explains its name— sinuously tree-like in form, glittering with gold and silver, it has crystal and enamel leaves suspended from coral branches. Next door is the church of San Francesco, frescoed during the 13th and 14th centuries.

MAREMMA

🔢 292 G11 ℹ️ Parco Regionale della Maremma, 7–9 Via Besagliari, 58010 Alberese, tel 0564 407098; daily 7.30am–11pm, Jul, Aug; 7.30am–6pm, rest of year 🚌 Alberese www.parcomaremma.it

The Maremma is the name given to the coastal plain that stretches from Cecina (south of Pisa) to Civitavecchia in Lazio, and includes the Monte Amiata range (▷ 138). Unspoiled coastal areas with wide, sandy beaches dominate the western part, while the landscape inland has been covered for centuries in wild, marshy tracts of *maquis*—fragrant scrub containing a variety of herbs, wild flowers and low bushes. The Etruscans started draining the region, but it reverted to malarial swamp until it was finally drained by the Fascist regime under Mussolini. The area between Principina a Mare and Talamone on the Tyrrhenian coast is a nature reserve. The park visitor office is in Alberese, south of Grosseto (▷ 135).

MASSA MARITTIMA

🔢 287 F9 ℹ️ Via Todini 3, 58024 Massa Marittima, tel 0566 902756; Mon–Sat 9.30–12.30, Sun 10–1, 3.30–6.30, Mar–end Oct; Mon–Fri 9.30–12.30, 3.30–6.30, rest of year 🚌 Follonica

This old town has owed much of its prosperity since medieval times to the mining of various minerals in the surrounding metal-rich hills. Today it rewards visitors with some worthwhile artworks, an archaeological museum, another commemorating the town's mining history, and a fine 12th-century cathedral. Some 40km (25 miles) south of Volterra, Massa Marittima overlooks the valley of the River Pecora.

The town is divided in two: The lower town, Città Vecchia (Old Town), has a striking, sloping medieval square, dominated by the cathedral, while the upper town, Città Nuova (New Town), has a 13th-century tower with extensive views. The 13th-century Palazzo del Podestà (Tue–Sun 10–1, 3–7) houses the museum of archaeology with many Etruscan finds, and a small collection of medieval works of art, including a superb *Maestà* by Ambrogio Lorenzetti (active 1319–48).

MONTALCINO

This is an exceptional hill town in a dramatic position at the heart of one of Tuscany's most important wine regions, producing the much-admired Barolo and Brunello reds.

Hilltop Montalcino, 40km (25 miles) south of Siena, overlooks some of southern Tuscany's most ravishing countryside. It's a pleasing town, with narrow streets, a warren of alleys and steps and a central piazza, and it is attracting increasing numbers of visitors. Allow a day to explore the town thoroughly, taste the wine and do some shopping. After your visit, you could drive 20 minutes farther to take in the superb abbey of Sant'Antimo (▷ 129).

THE TOWN

From afar, Montalcino appears to be dominated by its photogenic Rocca, a 14th-century fort (daily 9–8, Apr–end Oct; Tue–Sun 9–6, rest of year) built by the Sienese, which stands just inside the town walls. You can climb its high walls, ramparts and towers to enjoy the panorama over Tuscany—Siena should be visible on a clear day. The Rocca's interior is now a park, and there's an *enoteca* (wine shop, ▷ 186) where you can sample and buy Montalcino's famous Brunello wine and local foods.

Walk downhill from here, through Piazza Garibaldi and into Piazza del Popolo, the town's main square. Here are the Palazzo Comunale, a civic palace built in 1292, and the Fiaschetteria Italiana (daily 7.30–midnight), a pleasingly old-fashioned café and *enoteca* established in 1888, complete with red velvet seats, marble tables and ornate mirrors. Uphill from here is the Museo Civico (Tue–Sun 10–1, 2–5.50), the town's principal museum, in the former convent of Sant'Agostino. Highlights include medieval and late Gothic artworks, wood sculptures from the 14th and 15th centuries and a collection of majolica (a style of glazed pottery that originated during the Renaissance) jugs.

THE WINE

Montalcino produces Brunello, along with Barolo, Italy's premier wine, an intense single-grape wine produced within a tiny area around the town. Brunello, a strong and complex wine, commands huge prices; the lighter and younger Rosso di Montalcino, made with the same grape, is a less expensive option. Also worth trying is the fragrant Moscatello di Montalcino. Wine is on sale all over the town, but you are likely to get the best prices at outlying supermarkets.

RATINGS			
Good for food	● ● ● ○
Photo stops	● ● ● ○
Specialist shopping	● ● ● ○

BASICS

✚ 288 H8
🚶 Via Costa del Municipio 8, 53024 Montalcino, tel 0577 849331; daily 10–1, 2–5.50
🚌 Buonconvento
www.prolocomontalcino.it

TIPS

● Try to park outside the city walls where there are a number of free spaces (those marked with white lines); from there it's a short walk to the town.
● Montalcino is a good base for exploring the Abbey of Sant'Antimo and the villages of the Val d'Orcia.

Wine tasting at the Fiaschetteria Italiana (top); the town, as seen from the top of the fort (above)

THE SIGHTS

The metal cross at the summit of Monte Amiata

Porto Ercole in Monte Argentario was once owned by the Spanish

Castello di Gargonza in Monte San Savino

MONTE AMIATA

✠ 293 J9 ℹ️ Via Adua 25, 53021 Abbadia San Salvatore, tel 0577 775811; daily 9–7 Jun–end Sep; Mon–Sat 9–1, 4–7, rest of year
www.amiataturismo.it

At 1,738m (5,702ft) Monte Amiata is the highest point in southern Tuscany. The mountain is part of an extinct volcano and has a distinctive pyramid shape, visible from many parts of the region. You can go and see the hot springs that gush from its rocks by taking a drive up the winding mountain roads, or by walking through the woodlands along a section of the Anello della Montagna, a marked trail that completely encircles the mountain with views all the way. In winter, its possible to ski.

There are several small towns across its slopes, including the unofficial capital, Abbadia San Salvatore, a medieval town named for its Benedictine Abbey (daily 7.45–6). It was founded in the 8th century and is one of the oldest abbeys in Tuscany. The present abbey church, consecrated in 1036, is Romanesque in style, with a long single nave and raised chancel. Don't miss the crypt, a cavernous space supported by fluted columns whose lintels are superbly carved with Byzantine/Lombard figures, unique in this part of Tuscany.

From Abbadia a road runs virtually to the mountain's summit, from where magnificent views take in the rolling landscape from Bolsena to the southeast to the sea in the west. The Parco Faunistico del Monte Amiata (daily dawn to dusk), near Arcidosso, is a specially-designated nature reserve, where you might see deer, mouflon (a breed of wild sheep) and the Amiata mouse-grey donkey. It's also a good place for hiking.

Other villages worth exploring include Piancastagnaio, south of Abbadia, dominated by a superb 14th-century Aldobrandeschi fortress; Santa Fiora to the west, with remnants of another fortress and two fine churches; and Castel del Piano, the area's commercial hub.

MONTE ARGENTARIO

✠ 292 G12 ℹ️ Corso Umberto 55, Archetto del Palio 1, 58019 Porto Santo Stefano, tel 0564 814208; daily 9–1, 4–7, Easter–end Oct; 9–1, rest of year 🚌 Orbetello

The mountainous promontory of Monte Argentario rears up southwest of Grosseto. A one-time island, it became part of the mainland when its shallow waters silted up and a causeway was formed. You can now reach the mainland through the lagoons of Orbetello. The interior is steep and wooded, while its coast is a succession of headlands, tiny coves and hidden beaches. The promotory has long had a reputation as a chic holiday area, and you'll still see plenty of luxury villas, but prices have dropped and it's not as exclusive as it once was. There are two resorts: the more fashionable and developed Porto Santo Stefano, with its expensive

Flowers outside San Savino's castle

yachts and beautiful people, and Porto Ercole, which still retains its old quarter, its fishing harbour and two Spanish fortresses. From here you can walk up Il Telegrafo, at 635m (2,083ft) Argentario's highest point. The area was once owned by the Spanish and became part of Tuscany in the 19th century, more than 200 years after the painter Caravaggio died of malaria on one of its beaches. Away from the coast, the high rocky terrain makes for superb walking.

MONTE SAN SAVINO

✠ 288 J7 ℹ️ Corso Sangallo 73, 52048 Monte San Savino, tel 0575 849418; Mon–Wed, Sun 9–1, Thu–Sat 9–1, 4–7, May–end Sep; Fri–Sun 9–1, rest of year
www.citymonte.it

On the opposite side of the Valdichiana from Cortona (▷ 134), Monte San Savino is a market town that once marked the border between Florence, Siena and Arezzo. Unlike many places in the area, San Savino has few visitors. This means that, although it is not in the top flight of hill towns, it is remarkably untouched by modern tourism. It has a mix of medieval and Renaissance buildings, local shops, and a bustling air of provincial small-town life that has its own appeal. The town has been associated with majolica (a style of glazed pottery that originated during the Renaissance) production for centuries; you'll see plenty on sale and there are examples in the small ceramic museum. Other sights include the 14th-century Sienese castle, the church of Santa Chiara (there's some fine majolica here too) and the Loggia dei Mercanti, designed by the sculptor/architect Andrea Contucci, known as Sansovino (1460–1529), a native-born son of the town.

MONTEPULCIANO

This dream of a Tuscan hill town is renowned for its red wine. Wander the steep streets to discover fine palaces, intimate corners and tiny squares with lovely views.

THE TOWN

Montepulciano is one of Tuscany's highest hill towns, built along a narrow ridge with alleys dropping steeply away from the central main street. It owes its appearance to the 1511 treaty signed with Florence after long years of Sienese dominance. The Florentines sent Antonio da Sangallo to rebuild the gates and walls, a mission so successful that it provided the impetus for much further building by the same architect. The main square is Piazza Grande, near the town's highest point. It is dominated by the 16th- to 17th-century cathedral (daily 9–12, 3–6), with an altarpiece of the *Assumption* (1401) by Taddeo di Bartolo, a superb, glowing treatment of a frequently recurring Sienese subject. In the baptistery are numerous reliefs, terracottas and other sculptures by various medieval and Renaissance artists. Also on Piazza Grande is the Palazzo Comunale, a 13th-century Gothic palace with a striking resemblance to Florence's Palazzo Vecchio; you can climb the tower for great views. Down the hill, the Museo Civico (Tue–Sun 10–7, Aug; Tue–Sun 10–1, 3–6, rest of year) has a good collection of pottery, medieval sculpture, Etruscan tombs and funerary urns, along with paintings by Sienese artists.

Though not perhaps of the quality of Brunello (▷ 137), the wine of Montepulciano is still a treat. The so-called Vino Nobile was judged so fine by a 16th-century pope that he 'ennobled' it. Sample it in one of the wine shops and restaurants in town, including the elegant Caffè Poliziano with its art-nouveau interior (▷ 237). Montepulciano plays host to various cultural events, including an International Arts Workshop every summer.

SAN BIAGIO

Outside the walls stands the pilgrimage church of San Biagio, Antonio da Sangallo's greatest commission and one of Tuscany's most harmonious Renaissance buildings. Approached by an avenue of cypresses, the church occupied Sangallo from 1518 to his death in 1534 and illustrates all the elements that mark Renaissance architecture. The dome, the use of the three orders of classical columns and the freestanding towers all make this a superbly satisfying building, whose surroundings do much to contribute to its appeal. If you don't have a car, however, you might find the walk there and back a bit far.

BASICS

✚ 288 J8
ℹ️ Via di Gracciano nel Corso 59a, 53045 Montepulciano, tel 0578 75734; daily 9–12.30, 3–8, Easter–end Oct; 9.30–12.30, 3–6, rest of year
🚃 Montepulciano or Chiusi
www.prolocomontepulciano.it

When building work on San Biagio started (top and above), the only bigger church project in Italy was St. Peter's Basilica

Monterchi is on a site once devoted to Hercules by Romans

The medieval town of Pitigliano emerges dramatically out of the volcanic ridge

MONTERCHI

✚ 289 L6 🛈 Piazza Umberto 1, 52035 Monterchi, tel 0575 70092; Mon–Sat 8–2 🚌 Citta di Castello

Monterchi lies between Arezzo (▷ 131) and Sansepolcro (▷ 146) in the High Tiber Valley. A small walled village perched on a hilltop, it has great views towards Umbria and over the surrounding countryside. Small as it is, Monterchi does possess one highly significant work of art: the fresco of the *Madonna del Parto*, painted by Piero della Francesca in the mid-15th century. This depiction of a heavily pregnant, weary-looking Madonna, one of the most unusual portrayals of her in Western art, was once a focus of pilgrimage for pregnant women. It was painted in a nearby chapel, but was removed to an exhibition room on the Via Reglia following restoration (Tue–Sun 9–1, 2–6, Sep–end Jun; 9–1, 2–7, rest of year).

MONTERIGGIONI

✚ 287 G7 🛈 Largo Fontebranda 5, 53035 Castello di Monteriggioni, tel 0577 304810; daily 11–7 www.monteriggionicastello.it

Driving south to Siena it's not easy to miss Monteriggioni, a tiny, perfectly preserved hill town still entirely enclosed by its medieval walls. You have to walk up the hill and through the towered gateway to enter the heart of the village, where you can recover your breath sitting at a café on the spacious square, while contemplating the small church there. Monteriggioni's main draws are its ramparts and its position, set on its hill like a granite crown. It was founded by the Sienese in 1203 to defend the northern approach to Siena from the Florentines. The circular walls were built between 1213

and 1219, destroyed in 1244 by invading Florentines, and rebuilt between 1260 and 1270. The 14 towers were described in Dante's *Inferno* as resembling giants. Today, the population has shrunk, the walls enclose as many gardens as houses, and Monteriggioni makes its living from tourism.

MURLO

✚ 288 H8 🛈 Piazza della Cattedrale, 53016 Murlo, tel 0577 814099; Tue–Sun 10–1, 3–7, Mar–end Oct; Mon–Fri 10–1, Sat–Sun 10–1, 3–5, rest of year www.comune.murlo.siena.it

The beguiling medieval *borgo* (fortified village) of Murlo lies to the south of Siena amid hilly countryside of a stark beauty. Its ring of medieval houses and steep streets lead up to the town hall and church, and it has a first-rate Etruscan museum that displays finds from the sites in the area, particularly from nearby Poggio Civitate. The museum is in the old castle, and its treasures include statues, terracotta tombs and metalwork.

PARCO NATURALE DI MONTI DELL'UCCELLINA

✚ 292 F11 🛈 Park visitor office, Via del Fante, Alberese, tel 0564 407098 ❓ Entry is at Alberese on SS Aurelia 1; at busy times, entry to the park is restricted www.parks.it/parco.maremma

This area of protected parkland, literally the 'mountains of the little bird', allows you to experience a microcosm of classic Maremma scenery: extensive pine forests and endless, sandy beaches. This little-known western part of Tuscany takes in the Uccellina mountains, the Marina di Alberese pinewood, the mouth of the River Ombrone and the Trappola marsh. It is part of the wider Maremma regional

park (▷ 136). The inland waters are great for spotting migratory birds and the characteristic *bovini maremmani*, long-horned cattle that roam the land. Other wildlife to look for includes wild boars, deer, porcupines, pine martens and wildcats. The park is an area to explore at leisure and on foot. There is a 5km (3-mile) walk through the park to the ruined abbey of San Rabano, and other footpaths will take you along the wild coastline or to watchtowers. **Don't miss** The small town of Talamone has magnificent views along the coast from its 15th-century fortress.

PITIGLIANO

✚ 293 J11 🛈 Piazza Garibaldi 51, 58017 Pitigliano, tel 0564 617111; daily 9.30–1, 3–8, Easter–end Oct; Mon–Sat 9.30–1, 3–7, rest of year www.grosseto.turismo.toscana.it

A volcanic ridge, riddled with caves used since Etruscan times, rises dramatically out of the plain where two rivers meet, and on top is Pitigliano's jumble of mellow-toned buildings. This medieval town was once owned by the powerful Orsini family, and the main attraction here is the family residence, the 16th-century Palazzo Orsini (Tue–Sun 10–1, 3–7), which has an excellent collection of Etruscan finds in its finely decorated rooms. Outside, you can explore the cobbled streets and inviting alleyways, the main square and the 14th-century fortress, and enjoy the views of Monte Amiata. Look for the remains of a 14th-century aqueduct in the middle of town, and take in the cathedral with its lovely 18th-century baroque façade and medieval belfry. Pitigliano was home to a thriving Jewish community until World War II; the synagogue is a poignant reminder of the town's Jewish heritage.

THE SIGHTS

PIENZA

A miniature Renaissance city that is set in southern Tuscany's most ravishing landscape. It also has plenty of tempting shops and restaurants.

Pienza lies in rolling countryside in the southeast corner of Tuscany. A compact town, it consists of a maze of small lanes that radiate from the main square. Once within its ancient walls, you will fall under the spell of its timeless atmosphere and crisp beauty, qualities recognized by UNESCO when Pienza was made a World Heritage site in 1996.

HISTORY
Tiny Pienza was the birthplace of Aeneas Silvio Piccolomini (1405–64), and he had a vision of his hometown as a model for Renaissance urban planning and architecture. When he became Pope Pius II in 1459, he put his ambitious plan into action, but he died before the project could be completed and only a handful of buildings, one of which is the cathedral, were finished.

THE SIGHTS
Piazza Pio II has all Pienza's important religious and secular buildings. The cathedral (daily 8–1, 2.30–7), on the south side, has a number of tall windows that allow light to flood in. They illuminate altarpieces by five prominent Sienese artists commissioned by Pope Pius II, including Vecchietta's *Assumption* (1461–62). Palazzo Piccolomini (Tue–Sun 10–12.30, 3–6, Mar–end Oct) is just to the right of the cathedral, where members of the Piccolomini family lived up to the mid-1960s. You must take a guided tour to see the sumptuous state apartments and the Sala d'Armi (armoury room) bristling with all manner of fearsome medieval weaponry. Equally memorable are the views from the rear loggia. The Museo Diocesano (Wed–Mon 10–1, 3–6) brings together paintings, sculptures, tapestries and other medieval and Renaissance artworks from various churches in the area. Its most important pieces include a 14th-century cope (priest's cloak-like vestment) embroidered by English monks, which belonged to Pius, a wooden altarpiece by Pietro Lorenzetti (active 1320–48), and a painted Crucifix dating back to the 12th century. The other building on the square is the Palazzo Comunale (town hall).

Don't miss There are great views towards Monte Amiata (▷ 138) from the lanes along the top of the walls; Pieve di Corsignano is a 10th-century church that escaped Pius' redevelopment.

RATINGS		
Good for kids	● ● ●	
Historic interest	● ● ● ●	
Photo stops	● ● ●	

BASICS

✚ 288 J8

ℹ Corso Rossellino 59, 53026 Pienza, tel 0578 749071; daily 9.30–1, 3–6.30
www.infinito.it/utenti/ufficio.turistico

TIPS

● Leave your car outside the city walls—you will not be able to park inside the city.
● Try to arrive about 9am or after 4pm if you want to avoid tour buses from Siena in the peak summer months. Wednesdays and Thursdays also tend to be quieter than other days of the week.
● Look out for local pecorino (sheep's milk) cheese available in the city's delicatessens.

Pienza's duomo can be seen along the city's walls (top); Pienza is known for its cheese (above)

San Gimignano

Tuscany's most popular day-trip destination bristles with towers and lives up to its nickname of medieval Manhattan. All the ingredients for a rewarding visit are here: well-preserved ramparts, fine buildings and artistic masterpieces.

Only a few towers can still be seen along the city's skyline

Ceramics on sale at a local shop

Frescoes on the courtyard of the Palazzo Comunale

SEEING SAN GIMIGNANO

San Gimignano is surprisingly small—it's possible to walk from one end of town to the other in 15 minutes—but to see and experience this extraordinary town properly you should allow a whole day. Start your visit at the south gate, the Porta San Giovanni, from where Via San Giovanni leads uphill to the interlocking main squares that are the hub of the town. Piazza della Cisterna, named after the 13th-century public well in the middle, is surrounded by a diverse selection of palazzi, towers and mansions. Pass through to Piazza del Duomo with its Collegiata, museum and towers, from where Via San Matteo runs downhill to the Porta San Matteo, the north gate. Beyond this lies the church of Sant'Agostino, famous for its frescoes.

HIGHLIGHTS

THE COLLEGIATA

✉ Piazza del Duomo ☎ 0577 940316 🕐 Mon–Fri 9.30–7.30, Sat 9.30–5, Sun 1–5, Mar–end Oct; Mon–Sat 9.30–5, Sun 1–5, Nov–20 Jan; open for Mass only 21 Jan to 28 Feb 🎫 Adult €3.50, child (6–18) €1.50
Little on the Collegiata's plain brick façade prepares you for the interior, covered with dazzling frescoes enhanced by the zebra-striped marble arcades. On the rear wall your attention is grabbed by Benozzo Gozzoli's 1465 fresco of St. Sebastian. The side walls have scenes from the Old and New Testaments, executed in the mid-14th century. The Old Testament scenes are particularly lively, packed with quirky detail and incidents. There's more spirituality in the New Testament scenes—look for the *Kiss of Judas* and *Christ Carrying the Cross*. Don't miss the Renaissance Cappella di Santa Fina in the right aisle, which is dedicated to San Gimignano's own saint.

PALAZZO COMUNALE

✉ Piazza del Duomo ☎ 0577 990312 🕐 Daily 9.30–7.30, Mar–end Oct; 10–5.30, Nov–end Feb 🎫 Adult €5, child (6–18) €4
The Palazzo Comunale is sometimes referred to as the Palazzo del Popolo. It still houses the council offices, but also contains the Museo Civico, the town's main museum (daily 9.30–7.20, Mar–end Oct;

BASICS

🔲 287 F6
ℹ Piazza del Duomo 1, 53037 San Gimignano, tel 0577 940008; daily 9–1, 3–7, Mar–end Oct; 9–1, 2–6, rest of year
🎫 Combined tickets for the Palazzo Comunale, Pinacoteca, Museo Archeologico and Torre Grossa, Spezeria di Santa Fina, Museo Ornitologico and Galleria d'Arte Moderna: adult €7.50, child (6–18) €5.50
www.sangimignano.com

A detail from the courtyard leading to Palazzo Comunale (top); the distinctive rooftops of San Gimignano (opposite)

The cloister at Sant'Agostino

10–5.50, rest of year). Here too is the access to the Torre Grossa, the only one of the 14 surviving towers you can climb, with the Pinacoteca (art gallery) in the upper rooms. Climb up from the courtyard to reach the Sala del Consiglio, also called the Sala di Dante. It was here that Dante, as a Florentine diplomat, met members of San Gimignano's council. The room contains Lippo Memmi's splendid gold-ground *Maestà* (1316). Upstairs again are paintings by Florentine, Umbrian and Sienese artists. Look for the 14th-century frescoes of wedding scenes in the little room off the stairs, which include a vignette of lovers enjoying a bath before they go to bed.

SANT'AGOSTINO
✉ Piazza Sant'Agostino ☎ 0577 940008 ⏱ Daily 7–12, 3–7, Apr–end Oct; 7–12, 3–6, rest of year 💰 Free

Sant'Agostino was built in the 13th century and is renowned for its fresco cycle on the life of St. Augustine by Benozzo Gozzoli (c1421–97). There's also a magnificent marble altar (1495) by Benedetto di Maiano in the Cappella di San Bartolo on the rear wall of the church, and a serene Renaissance cloister. The frescoes, 17 in all, adorn the walls surrounding the high altar. Painted between 1463 and 1467, they trace Augustine's life from his childhood and schooling, through his conversion to Christianity to his career as one of the most important of the early Fathers of the Church. Augustine's life was spent in the Middle East and Rome, but Gozzoli portrays it against a Florentine background, with a mass of detail that gives a remarkably clear picture of everyday life in the 15th century.

ROCCA DI MONTESTAFFOLI
✉ Rocca ⏱ Daily 24 hours 💰 Free

In 1353 the inhabitants of San Gimignano were ordered by the Florentines to build a fortress at the town's expense 'to remove every cause of evil thinking'. Massive walls, 283m (308 yards) in length, enclosed a pentagonal space and a series of towers at the highest point in the town. By 1558 the Rocca had served its purpose and was largely dismantled, leaving just one tower standing. Today it's the public park, a lovely place for a picnic with the best views in town. Climb the tower for a superb outlook over San Gimignano's central cluster of towers, or walk the walls to view the landscape.

The hillsides surrounding the city

PIAZZA DELLA CISTERNA

✉ Piazza della Cisterna ⏰ Daily 24 hours 🎟 Free

The triangular piazza is a sweeping space paved with herring-bone brick, a superb contrast to the narrow surrounding streets. The well (*cisterna*) in the middle of the piazza gives it its name. The square is surrounded by palaces and dominated by the soaring cluster of towers in the northwest corner. The two most prominent are the twin Ardinghelli towers, guarding the entrance to the adjacent Piazza del Duomo. The northeast corner is home to the Torre del Diavolo, named after its owner attributed its height to the devil's work.

BACKGROUND

Founded by the Etruscans, San Gimignano enters history in the 10th century, when the first feudal castle was built. A settlement grew up around it which, by the 13th century, was walled. The town grew rich on agriculture and as a result of its position on the Via Francigena, the pilgrim and trade route to northern Europe. Its weakness was the propensity of its chief families for feuding. During the years of conflict, the families built 72 protective towers, 14 of which survive. Squabbles continued during the 13th and 14th centuries, only ending with the 1348 Black Death, which wiped out much of the population and crippled the economy. In 1353 San Gimignano became subject to Florentine rule and embarked on centuries of existence as a rural backwater. It was only the advent of post-war tourism and the revival of the town's wine industry that brought prosperity.

An advert for the local wine (above left); relaxing at a café in the Piazza della Cisterna (above right)

A view from the Torre Grossa

THE SIGHTS

RATINGS

Cultural interest	● ● ● ● ●
Good for food	● ● ●
Photo stops	● ● ●

BASICS

✚ 289 L6 ℹ Piazza Garibaldi 2,
52037 Sansepolcro, tel 0575 740536;
daily 9.30–1, 3–6.30
🚍 Sansepolcro

The 16th-century Palazzo delle Laudi (top); a detail of St. John the Baptist from Madonna della Misericordia (above)

SANSEPOLCRO

This handsome, prosperous little town in the upper valley of the Tiber is a must for followers of the Piero della Francesca trail.

At the foot of the Apennine mountains in the Tiber Valley, 8km (5 miles) northeast of Anghiari, Sansepolcro is said to have been founded by two 10th-century monks returning from the Holy Land with relics of Christ's tomb. This pleasant provincial town has one of Italy's biggest pasta factories, but the *centro storico*, its historic heart, is unspoiled. There's a handsome main piazza and on it a fine Romanesque-Gothic cathedral. In the shadowy interior, dimly lit by the alabaster glazing of a rose window, is a 10th-century *Volto Santo* (Holy Face) showing Christ as a patriarchal figure.

PIERO DELLA FRANCESCA

Most people come to Sansepolcro on the trail of della Francesca, one of the Renaissance's most enigmatic, spiritual and memorable artists. He was born in the town around 1420 and, despite absences to work on commissions in Florence, Urbino and Rome, lived the majority of his life here. He worked extremely slowly, his father having occasionally to apologise to his patrons for the length of time his son took, and his painting career was cut short by failing eyesight. Piero's latter years were occupied with writing two treatises, *On Perspective in Painting* and *On the Five Regular Bodies*, which laid out the mathematical theories that lie behind his work.

MUSEO CIVICO

The Museo Civico (daily 9–1.30, 2.30–7.30, Jun–end Sep; 9.30–1, 2.30–6, rest of year) in the old town hall has several of Piero della Francesca's paintings, including two of the most important: the *Madonna della Misericordia* and the *Resurrection*. The *Madonna*, Piero's earliest known painting, was commissioned by the charitable institution Compagnia della Misericordia, which is still in existence. It depicts the Virgin spreading her cloak to shelter a cross-section of humanity. On the wall at a right angle from this painting is the great *Resurrection*, dating from the 1450s. Revolutionary in style when it was painted, it depicts Christ emerging triumphant and muscular from the tomb. The background, a mix of bare and green-leafed trees, alludes to the cycle of death and resurrection. The museum also has a fine banner by Luca Signorelli, a bloodthirsty *Martyrdom of St. Quentin* by Pontormo and an archeological collection.

People taking the waters in the thermal pools at Saturnia

An archway in the older part of Sorano

The cathedral at Sovana has an octagonal dome

SAN QUIRICO D'ORCIA

➕ 288 J8 🚹 Via Dante Alighieri 33, 53027 San Quirico d'Orcia, tel 0577 897211; daily 10–1, 3.30–6.30, Apr–end Oct and 19 Dec–6 Jan

You will find San Quirico d'Orcia 10km (6 miles) west of Pienza. The village once stood on the Via Francigena, the pilgrim route to Rome, and you can see the resulting economic growth this brought in the fine medieval houses that line Via Poliziano. However, you will also find some post-World War II housing sitting alongside the village's 16th-century gardens and exquisite medieval churches.

The main attraction is the Collegiata, a 12th-century church off Piazza Chigi, built on the ruins of an eighth-century church. There are exceptional Lombard-influenced carvings around the doors, and the interior highlights include inlaid Renaissance choir stalls and a *Virgin and Child Enthroned with Four Saints* by Sano di Pietro. On the edge of the village are the peaceful Horti Leonini. These gardens, laid out in 1580, consist of a flower garden and a natural woodland area. If you have time to wander around this partly walled village, you could take a look at the Palazzo Chigi, decorated with Roman frescoes.

SAN VINCENZO

➕ 286 D8 🚹 Via Beatrice Allata 4, 57027 San Vincenzo, tel 0565 701533; Mon–Sat 9–1, 4.30–8, Sun 10–12.30 Jun–end Sep; Mon–Sat 9–1, rest of year

Going south from Livorno (▷ 99) there's a string of resorts along the coast, appealing more to Italian holidaymakers than to foreign visitors. Farther south, pine forests take over from hotels, and beaches become less crowded. The best stretch is at Bolgheri, an internationally

important nature reserve that is a microcosm of the area's habitats. If you want to visit the region, San Vicenzo, 20km (12 miles) to the south, makes a good base. It's a fast-growing resort, with a black-sand beach and a clutch of older buildings to add to its charms. The coast is well wooded with pines, and the beach is big enough to escape the crowds. In summer you'll need to reserve accommodation well in advance.

SATURNIA

➕ 293 H11 🚹 Piazza Garibaldi 51, 58017 Pitigliano, tel 0564 617111; daily 9.30–1, 3–8, Easter–end Oct; Mon–Sat 9.30–1, 3–7, rest of year

If you are feeling stressed or tired, head for this spa town in the inland, hilltop region of the Maremma (▷ 136). Saturnia was named by the Romans after Saturn, the father of the gods, because they believed it to be one of the oldest settlements in Tuscany. It is famous for the sulphurous, hot, blue-green waters of the Gorello falls, which fume and bounce off natural basins of white stone. You can bathe in the waters for nothing, or book into one of the chic hotels to try various treatments such as mud baths.

SORANO

➕ 293 J11 🚹 Piazza Garibaldi 51, 58017 Pitigliano, tel 0564 617111; daily 9.30–1, 3–8, Easter–end Oct; Mon–Sat 9.30–1, 3–7, rest of year

Etruscan roads cut through the tufa all around Sorano, a village 9km (6 miles) northeast of Pitigliano (▷ 140), and the hillsides are riddled with caves and tombs, causing the landslides that have made parts of Sorano uninhabitable. The old part of the village spreads down a steep cliff above a spectacular gorge. It's

full of odd corners and workshops carved out of living rock, with serendipitous discoveries lying around every corner. Above medieval Sorano looms the 18th-century Masso Leopoldino quarter, worth the climb for the views. Visit Fortezza Orsini, once an Aldobrandeschi family stronghold, for its 16th-century military engineering. Sorano has a number of artisan workshops and a small ceramic industry.

SOVANA

➕ 293 J11 🚹 Piazza Garibaldi 51, 58017 Pitigliano, tel 0564 617111; daily 9.30–1, 3–8, Easter–end Oct; Mon–Sat 9.30–1, 3–7, rest of year

On the border with Lazio, the sleepy little town of Sovana has several striking reminders of an illustrious past. It was once a significant Etruscan town and you will see a number of Etruscan, Roman and medieval relics on your visit here. It was also the birthplace of Hildebrand, who became Pope Gregory VII in 1073.

The village is really only a couple of streets. The main street, Via di Mezzo, has the ruins of a medieval fortress at one end. There is a fine Romanesque/Gothic cathedral, which has an even older crypt. One of the town's highlights is the 13th-century parish church of Santa Maria on the Piazza del Pretorio. It has a Romanesque exterior, frescoes by the Sienese school, and a carved ciborium, or altar canopy, dating from the eighth or ninth century. The limestone cliffs that surround Sovana are dotted with tombs and there are a number of signposts for you to follow. Tuscany's most important and elaborate Etruscan tomb, the Tomba Ildebranda, dates from the third century BC. It was discovered in the 1920s and is on the outskirts of the village.

RATINGS	
Cultural interest	● ● ● ○
Historic interest	● ● ● ○
Specialist shopping	● ● ● ● ●

BASICS

✚ 287 F7 ℹ️ Piazza dei Priori 20, 56048 Volterra, tel 0588 87257; daily 10–1, 2–7, Apr–end Oct; 10–1, 2–6, rest of year
🚇 Saline di Volterra
www.volterratur.it

VOLTERRA

Volterra is an unspoiled hilltop town rich in mementos of Etruscan, Roman and medieval times. Its best buy is alabaster, a millennia-old mainstay of the town's economy.

High in the volcanic hills west of Siena, Volterra was one of the Etruscans' largest settlements, the focus of their mining region. The Romans mined here too, ensuring the town's survival as a wealthy settlement into the Middle Ages. Besieged by the Florentines, Volterra lost its independence in 1472 and slid slowly into obscurity. This, and its off-the-beaten-track position, preserved the medieval town virtually intact, and today this agreeable place is still relatively little visited.

THE TOWN

Volterra's medieval heart is the Piazza dei Priori, site of a splendid ensemble of medieval buildings that includes the massive battlemented Palazzo dei Priori, the first town hall to be built in Italy (1208–54), the Palazzo Pretorio, and the Palazzo Vescovile, the bishop's palace. The latter is home to the Museo d'Arte Sacra, where the highlight is the wonderful *Madonna di Villamagna* (1521) by the Mannerist Rosso Fiorentino. Behind the piazza are the 12th-century black-and-white cathedral and a freestanding 13th-century baptistery. Northwest from here, at the bottom of steep streets and outside the medieval walls, are the remains of the Roman theatre, while farther down the hill a narrow country lane runs through the Porta Diana, a third-century BC city gateway. Across town, over the hill, the Parco Archeologico is more like a park than an archaeological site, a lovely green space on hot afternoons. It is overlooked by the Rocca (fort), built by the Medici after they sacked the town.

THE MUSEUMS

Volterra has two unmissable museums: the Museo Etrusco Guarnacci (Via Don Minzoni 13; daily 9–7 Mar–end Oct; 9–2, rest of year), one of Italy's most important archaeological museums, and the Pinacoteca Comunale (Via dei Sarti; daily 9–7, Mar–end Oct; 9–2, rest of year), a fine painting collection in a lovely old palazzo. Etruscan fans should allow a good two hours for the Guarnacci's huge collection, which includes more than 600 funerary urns dating from the fourth to first centuries BC and some extraordinary bronze sculptures. The Pinacoteca presents a good overview of Sienese and Florentine painting. Its highlight is Rosso Fiorentino's *Deposition* (1521), one of the most compelling and dramatic of all Mannerist works.

Urna degli Sposi *(Urn of the Married Couple) at the Museo Etrusco Guarnacci (top); an alabaster workshop in Volterra (above)*

This chapter gives information on things to do in Tuscany other than sightseeing. It is divided into regions, which are shown on the map on the inside front cover, and then by town in alphabetical order. For regions that are cities, such as Florence, entries are listed by category (Shopping, Entertainment, etc) in alphabetical order.

What to Do

SHOPPING

Shopping is taken seriously in Italy, and the provincial capitals of Florence, Siena, Arezzo and Grosseto all have their fair share of stylish shops, while you'll find some nice surprises in even the smallest towns. In design and fashion the big names have conquered the world, but there's more to retail therapy than haute couture and designer labels. Craftsmanship is highly valued and everything from furniture to underwear can be made to order. The back streets are the places to find the tiny stores and workshops selling gifts and self-indulgent purchases.

Out-of-town shopping arcades, outlet stores and factory shops are slowly making an appearance, while towns traditionally associated with a particular product—ceramics, wine, jewellery—have a huge choice at excellent prices. Wine, food and olive oil is sold direct from the estates. In summer, you can taste and buy other local food products at the many *sagre*, food festivals (▷ 157).

MARKETS
There are daily food markets in provincial and regional capitals and other large towns. They generally take place in a purpose-built market hall or in a specific square or street, selling meat, groceries, fish, dairy products, fruit and vegetables. Where there's a daily food market, the weekly market will be devoted to clothes, shoes, household goods, plants, flowers, toys, toiletries and fabrics. In Florence the most prominent are Mercato Centrale, Mercato di Sant'Ambrogio and Mercato Nuovo.

DEPARTMENT STORES
Department stores have been slow to catch on in Italy, even though the main chains have been around for a number of years. In Tuscany you'll find branches of the big four: La Rinascente, Coin, Upim and Standa.

SUPERSTORES
Superstores are becoming much more widespread and generally concentrate on food, household items and linens. They are found on the outskirts of middle- to large-sized towns and cities, along with factory outlets.

Market stand in Florence

Panforte, a cake from Siena

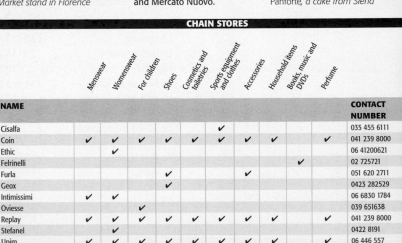

CHAIN STORES										
NAME	Menswear	Womenswear	For children	Shoes	Cosmetics and toiletries	Sports equipment and clothes	Accessories	Household items	Books, music and DVDs	Perfume	CONTACT NUMBER
Cisalfa						✔					035 455 6111
Coin	✔	✔	✔	✔	✔	✔	✔	✔		✔	041 239 8000
Ethic		✔									06 41200621
Felrinelli									✔		02 725721
Furla				✔			✔				051 620 2711
Geox				✔							0423 282529
Intimissimi	✔	✔									06 6830 1784
Oviesse			✔								039 651638
Replay	✔	✔	✔	✔	✔	✔	✔			✔	041 239 8000
Stefanel		✔									0422 8191
Upim	✔	✔	✔	✔	✔	✔	✔	✔		✔	06 446 557

OPENING HOURS

These are fairly standard and apply for most of the year, but be prepared for erratic changes.

- Supermarkets, larger stores and visitor-oriented shops generally stay open all day (*orario continuato*).
- Most stores are open Monday to Saturday 8.30–1 and 4.30 or 5.30–7.
- Clothes shops may not open until 10am.
- Only food shops are open on Monday mornings and they often close on Wednesday afternoons.
- Hours may change from mid-June until the end of August; some shops close completely when their owners

Bags on sale at Mercato Nuovo

are on holiday, while others stay open later for visitors.

- Small shops may close for anything from a week to a month during July and August when Italians are on holiday.
- A pharmacy (*farmacia*) somewhere around the area you are staying in will be open for prescriptions 24 hours a day; this is done on a rotating system and pharmacies post addresses and opening times in their windows.

WHAT TO BUY

FASHION

Fashion is the shopping focus in Italy, and you will find big names and chain stores in every major city and large town. Stores selling popular Italian exports generally carry a larger range than you'd find at home at more competitive prices. Smaller stores sell individual items with a distinct Italian twist.

FOOD AND WINE

Every region has its own local food and wine, available in food stores, markets or delicatessens. Buy such items when you see them—move on 20km (32 miles) and you may be out of the production area.

HANDICRAFTS

Tuscany has a strong artisan tradition that continues to flourish. There is a huge range of regional handicrafts to seek out, such as olive-wood bowls and plates, alabaster ware and glassware, with many products only available in the area where they are made. Florence has an abundance of craft workshops specializing in picture frames, accessories and restored antique furniture.

JEWELLERY

Italy is one of the world's biggest jewellery manufacturers. Production is most prolific in Arezzo and there's a well-established tradition of in-house design across the country. Many jewellers will make pieces to order.

PAPER

Beautiful handmade paper, often marbled or block-printed, is a good buy across the region.

SHOES AND LEATHER

You'll find shoes, belts, bags and accessories at both ends of the price range—but don't neglect the markets, which are great trawling grounds for bargains.

As well as individual designer boutiques and small specialist shops, Italy, like most other Western European countries, has its fair share of chain stores. The most renowned Italian export is Benetton, who have more than 300 stores in their home country. You will encounter branches of chain stores listed in the chart below in shopping districts and malls.

DESCRIPTION OF SHOPS	WEBSITE
All the well-known brands of sportswear, sports equipment and trainers.	www.cisalfa.com
A department store selling mid-range to elegant stock.	www.coin.it
Cool, cheap and original, with a focus on vintage looks and ethnic fabrics.	www.ethic.it
One of the best bookshops in Italy, with regular book launches by writers.	www.lafeltrinelli.it
Handcrafted leather bags and footwear with an ultra modern twist.	www.furla.it
Modern styles with soles that keep water out, but let your feet breathe.	www.geox.com
Cute and indulgent underwear at affordable prices.	www.intimissimi.it
Everything your baby or toddler needs in one store.	www.prenatal.it
Low-end to medium-priced clothes (including swimwear) and homeware.	www.oviesse.it
Affordable, but up-to-date fashion for women.	www.stefanel.it
Department store selling cheap but sturdy fashions and household items.	www.upim.it

ENTERTAINMENT

There is plenty to keep you entertained in the region, from cinema and theatre to classical music and opera.

CINEMA

Cinema is thriving in Italy, but the main problem will be language. It's acknowledged that Italian dubbing is the best in the world, so films are automatically dubbed rather than subtitled. In Florence, you should be able to find a cinema showing VO *(versione originale)* movies; elsewhere, outside film festivals, they are likely to be in Italian.

● Tickets normally cost around €7, with discounts for the early shows on Monday, Tuesday,

On stage at the Arezzo Wave festival

Thursday and Friday and all day Wednesday.
● Very few cinemas accept payment by credit card.
● At busy times, some cinemas sell *posto in piedi* (standing only) tickets; there is no discount for these.
● Smoking is not allowed.

CLASSICAL MUSIC, BALLET AND DANCE

During the winter months most cities and towns of any size will have a regular schedule of classical and orchestral music, though you're unlikely to hear anything avant-garde or contemporary. The same is true of ballet and dance. The best time to see dance is during the summer festivals (see tourist offices for details, ▷ 274).

MUSIC IN CHURCHES

Concerts are staged in some of region's most beautiful churches, where you can hear organ, orchestral and choral recitals in superb surroundings, often with acoustics to match. Look out for posters or ask at local tourist offices.

OPERA

Opera fans should not miss the opportunity to see Italian opera performed on home soil. It might not be what you are used to, as here it's popular entertainment with a great deal of audience participation: Shows can be held up after arias for minutes at a time while the audience show their appreciation (or disapproval).
● The season runs from October to the end of March.
● Top names tend to sing for the first few nights only, so keep an eye on cast-lists.
● Prices vary considerably depending on the venue and company.
● Smoking is not allowed inside the venues.

LIVE MUSIC

Big international bands and stars sometimes take in Florence on their tours. If so, the concerts will be well advertised by posters and tourist information offices will be able to help.

Tuscany hosts two major rock festivals: Arezzo Wave (▷ 190), one of Europe's biggest, in June, and Pistoia Blues in July.

If you're looking for the sounds of traditional Italy, head for the festivals, where there may be a chance to catch local bands and groups.

THEATRE

Unless you speak Italian it's unlikely you'll want to go to the theatre in Italy. Florence has a thriving theatre scene and most provincial capitals have a theatre, busiest during the winter season from September to April.

In summer, there are open-air festivals, taking place in classical theatres and arenas, or the courtyards and gardens of historic buildings—check with the tourist office for upcoming events. When the production is an indoor one, smoking is not allowed.

LISTINGS

There are no nationwide listing magazines, although local listings can be found in Friday editions of newspapers. Magazines in Florence will sometimes cover other events in the region, but your best option outside the city is the local tourist office. For Florence, look out for: *Firenze Oggi* (Florence Today), free in hotels and bars; *Firenze Spettacolo*, on sale Fridays from newsstands; *Informacittà*, on sale monthly and free from tourist offices. The website is www.informacittafirenze.it.

TICKETS

Tickets for events in Florence are available direct from venues or from the company Box Office (Via Alamanni 39, Firenze, tel 055 210804).

For events around the region, including the *Maggio Musicale* (▷ 172), you can contact a central booking office, who'll be able to help you:
Tel 199 109910 (inside Italy)
Tel +39 0953 564767 (outside Italy)
www.firenzeturismo.it.

NIGHTLIFE

The university town of Florence is the liveliest in the region, with activity moving to the coastal resorts during the summer, when the open-air bars and clubs attract huge crowds. The university city of Siena has plenty going on during term-time, though it's primarily aimed at students. The other provincial capitals have a certain amount of nightlife; ask at the tourist offices or look out for fliers in bars. Throughout Tuscany you'll find out-of-town clubs in the midst of the countryside; they're generally open on weekends only.

OPENING HOURS

Things start to heat up around midnight in Florence, but many bars have a prolonged happy hour from 7pm to 9pm, often accompanied by snacks. In smaller towns and rural areas, the opposite is the case, and you may struggle to find a bar open after 11pm.

You'll find many bars have live music

BARS

Bars are open from early till late and serve everything from breakfast, coffee and snacks to beer, wine and aperitifs, with no licensing hours.

Outside Florence, bars are at their busiest between 6.30–9. Evening-only bars often have live music nights and guest DJs, but you'll only find these in Florence and the larger towns. Stylish hotels sometimes have bars that also offer music. Tuscans generally view bars as places to be seen and to meet their friends, and may happily nurse one drink for hours and even at the hottest clubs, relatively little alcohol is drunk.

CLUBS

- There is not much difference between bars with music and small clubs in Italy.
- Many clubs charge an entrance fee, which can include a free drink.
- Some clubs will ask you to buy membership *(tessera)*, which can be purchased on the door. Prices vary and it may be free.
- If there is no entrance fee, you may receive a card, which is stamped when you buy drinks or go to the lavatory and totalled up when you leave.
- There's often a set night for hearing a particular style of music.
- Check the local tourist office for details as nightclubs drop in and out of fashion and new venues regularly open while others close.

FLORENCE

Many central bars and clubs are underground and have no air-conditioning. Some close in summer, when the action moves to the coast; a special late train runs from Florence to Viareggio on weekends in summer and the journey takes a little over an hour. Opening times are erratic and, as everywhere, things can change without warning.

GAY AND LESBIAN NIGHTLIFE

Over the last 10 years Italians have become far more tolerant towards gay and lesbian relationships, but there's still a long way to go in rural areas, and the gay scene remains relatively low profile away from the larger towns. If you're looking for gay bars and clubs, head for the larger cities; Florence is particularly gay-friendly. In summer Torre del Lago, near Viareggio, is the place to go with a vibrant club scene.

- *Babilonia* is a monthly publication that has gay listings for the whole of Italy (€5.20 at newsstands).
- Azione Gay e Lesbica publishes a gay and lesbian map of Tuscany.
- Log on to www.arcigay.it, the official site of Italy's foremost gay and lesbian network, or alternatively try www.gay.it/pinklily.

Having something to eat is a big part of a night out

LISTINGS

Major cities have local listings magazines. Newspapers also have the latest information, particularly for late-night music and the club scene. Tourist offices will be able to help, and bars are a good place to pick up fliers.

SPORTS AND ACTIVITIES

Italy's best-loved sport is soccer, passionately followed by millions of fans. Hot on its heels is basketball, introduced after World War II and now hugely popular. Baseball and American football have also crept in from across the Atlantic, while the Italian passion for cycling is totally home grown. During the long, hot summers, swimming and watersports are popular. Smart hotels have pools and tennis courts, and some will arrange a round of golf for you. Many *agriturismi* (▷ 240) organize activities such as horseback riding, mountain biking and walking.

CYCLING

Hundreds of local clubs take to the roads each weekend, and cyclists out en masse and spectators lining the streets are a common sight all over the country. The largest is the Giro

Ippodromo delle Mulina on the outskirts of Florence

d'Italia, an annual round-Italy race with several stages usually passing through Tuscany. It's staged in the second half of May, and attracts competitors from all over the world.

You can easily rent a bicycle to get around cities or venture out of town onto marked cycle routes—tourist offices provide maps of the trails. If you're in hilly country, think twice before embarking on what could be a tough day in high temperatures. The best cycling is in the province of Siena, where, particularly south of the city, the country is flatter and more open than the hills of Chianti. The Siena APT publishes an

excellent free booklet packed with information and details of several attractive itineraries for all levels of cyclists.

Renting a bicycle is straightforward; ask at local tourist offices for further information, or consider an organized tour.

GYMS

Italian gyms are mainly private, so you'll need to take out temporary membership. Larger city gyms may have a sauna, Turkish bath and solarium and you can book a massage or hydrotherapy treatment.

HORSEBACK RIDING

You can enjoy riding all over Tuscany, either on a riding holiday, or simply by renting a mount from one of the many stables. You'll find stables all over the region, many offering lessons or organized excursions. Local tourist information offices all have details of what's available in their areas, as well as information on staying at *agriturismi* that offer riding.

SOCCER

● The season runs from the end of August until June, with a two-week break from the end of December into January.
● Matches take place on Sunday afternoons.
● Ticket prices range from €15 to €85. The least expensive seats are in the *curva* (curve) at each end of the pitch and the most expensive are along

the side of the pitch, in the *tribuna* (stand).
● Tickets can be purchased from venues, merchandise outlets or agencies.
● General information is at www.lega-calcio.it; Florence's main team, Fiorentina, can be visited at www.acfiorentina.it.

SWIMMING

Many small towns, especially those along the coast, have a public swimming pool. In the main cities, where swimming pools, like gyms, are usually privately run, you may need to buy a temporary membership to enjoy the facilities.

People in the rushing thermal waters at Saturnia

Italian resort beaches are divided into sections, each run as a *stabilimento balneare* (bathing establishment). These are private, and you'll have to pay a hefty fee. Your fee should cover the use of a changing cabin, sun lounger and umbrella. Each *stabilimento* normally has showers, toilets and eating and drinking facilities, some of which are quite grand.

Beach standards are high, with sand cleaned and raked overnight, but water cleanliness can vary. Expect high international standards at major resorts, in remote areas and where the coast is rocky.

Avoid swimming near major cities, ports or industrial coastal areas.

All Italian resorts have a legal obligation to allow free access to a section of the beach, so it is possible to avoid payment if all you want is a quick dip. However, these free access areas are often small and the beaches unkempt.

Inland in Tuscany there are occasional stretches of river where you can swim. These can be idyllic and it's worth checking at tourist offices.

TENNIS

There are plenty of opportunities to enjoy a game of tennis, with courts frequently floodlit so you can play in the cooler

Take your sport further and go abseiling

evenings. Most towns have clubs where you can rent a court throughout the day.

WALKING AND HIKING

Tuscany provides some of Europe's most beautiful walking landscape, seen at its best from mid-April to early June. Don't plan any major hikes for July and August, when temperatures are high and the country dry. In September the weather cools. Access to the countryside is easy: Italy has no laws concerning trespassing so, as long as you follow a path and touch nothing, you can go pretty well anywhere. The major drawback to walking is the lack of well signposted trails or good maps. Notable exceptions are the trails marked out by the CAI (Club Alpino Italiano) that you'll find in the Alpi Apuani, the Orechiella, the Val d'Orcia and parts of Elba. CAI paths are marked with red-and-white signs (usually painted on trees and rocks), but even with them, you'll need a map.

WATERSPORTS

You can rent windsurfers, dinghies, catamarans and such like at the larger resorts along the Tuscan coast. If you're looking to jet- or water-ski, a

resort hotel is probably your best bet, but it's expensive. Scuba divers and snorkellers will find plenty of choice around Monte Argentario and the islands—the main dive bases—where specialized firms offer accompanied day and night dives.

LISTINGS

Events are advertised in listings magazines, Italy's two daily sports newspapers, *La Gazzetta dello Sport* (printed on pink paper) and the *Corriere dello Sport*, and in Friday newspapers. Local tourist offices should be able to help you with any of these activites, or at least point you in the right direction.

Jogging in the Mugello region of Tuscany

HEALTH AND BEAUTY

Given those two major Italian obsessions, the *bella figura*, or looking good, and the digestive system, it's not surprising that Tuscany is well-equipped with spas, health and beauty centres. Recent years have seen the transformation of once serious and utilitarian bathing establishments into sybaritic temples of the body, where it's possible to combine hydrotherapy of all sorts with some serious pampering in opulent surroundings.

SPAS

Tuscan spas are patronized by young and old right across the social spectrum, and 'taking the waters', whether it's immersing the body or delicately sipping a glass or two,

is an integral part of everyday life, ensuring there's something for every taste and pocket.

Tuscany is blessed with mineral-rich, naturally heated springs, and there are *terme*

(spas) all over the region. Many spas still function purely as therapeutic clinics, where doctors will work out a regime for different medical conditions, but an increasing number of *centri benessere* (health and beauty centres) are geared to those who want to be pampered in style. You'll also find free access to hot springs where the water emerges near the spas themselves: Bagno Vignoni (▷ 130) and Saturnia (▷ 189), both in southern Tuscany, are good places for a free swim.

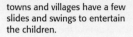

FOR CHILDREN 😊

Children are considered part of mainstream society in Italy and so you'll find few child-specific facilities and amusements, and Tuscan cities are not particularly child-friendly. There is still plenty to do, though, with the bonus that children are indulged, respected and integrated into whatever's going on.

FAMILY FRIENDLY AREAS
Tuscany can keep most outdoor families occupied from exploring tiny towns to cycling, hiking and horseback riding. Some children will be bored after a short time in Florence or the larger towns, so punctuate culture with time in the country or at the beach. Many families find a villa with a pool makes the ideal base or you

Most kids love the bronze boar at the Mercato Nuovo

could vary your trip by mixing a few days in a city with time on an *agriturismo* (▷ 240); most have lots going on.

Good areas for children include the coast and southern Tuscany, while most age groups will enjoy a day out at the Parco di Pinocchio at Collodi (▷ 173).

BEACHES
The seaside holiday is a major part of Italian family life. Resorts are busy during the holiday period of July and August. Small children will be happy at resorts along the Tyrrhenian and Ligurian coasts of Tuscany, where sandy

beaches with shallow bathing, beach games and playgrounds are interspersed with rockier stretches. Bear in mind that few *stabilimenti* (▷ 154) have lifeguards, so children should not be left unattended. Lovely as the islands are, they're not ideal for very young children, who find more to do along the string of broad sandy beaches in the Maremma (▷ 136).

You should also bear in mind the strength of the sun, particularly in the middle of the day, and follow the Italian habit of a long siesta in the shade. If your children are in and out of the water persuade them to cover up with a T-shirt, even when in the water.

ACTIVITIES
For older children there are activities galore in the countryside and along the coast, such as tennis, riding, sailing, swimming, bathing in hot mineral springs and hill walking. If you're near one of Tuscany's natural parks, it's worth checking out what outdoor organized activities are on during your stay; you'll find most on offer during school holiday times (www.parks.it).

For more information, head for the local tourist office and check what's on offer.

PARKS
Although all the major cities have parks, only the biggest have grassy areas large enough for children to play games and run around in. However, many have playgrounds, with a selection of swings and slides, and they are good places for a picnic. Even small Tuscan

towns and villages have a few slides and swings to entertain the children.

CITIES
Tourist information offices will be able to recommend attractions that are likely to appeal to children. Specific attractions in Florence include the Museo dei Ragazzi (the Children's Museum of Florence) and the other activities in the Palazzo Vecchio, Museo Stibbert and the Museo di Storia della Scienza.

In Siena, older children will be fascinated by the different aspects of the *Palio* and will

There are lots of shops and markets that will attract children

enjoy a visit to one of the *contrade* museums—the tourist office will be able to help. Most kids over five will happily spend time browsing in the markets.

DISCOUNTS
In Italy, admission prices for museums, galleries and other attractions are nearly always reduced for children, but you will need proof of identity to be eligible (▷ 265). Family tickets are increasing. Some museums are free to those under five or even up to 18. Prices are normally displayed, but it's always worth asking if they are not advertised.

FESTIVALS AND EVENTS

There's no shortage of festivals celebrating religious holidays, the arts and gastronomic delicacies. Celebrations are organized by Italians for Italians, but they are open to anyone who's willing to participate in the right spirit. That spirit differs enormously according to each festival's focus, so be prepared for intense religious feeling or exuberant high spirits. Major festivals, such as Siena's *Palio*, attract visitors from all over the world, and if you're planning on attending book your accommodation well in advance. You'll find low-key local events throughout the country during the summer. Keep an eye open for posters and ask at tourist offices. For an enthusiastic overview of Italian festivals visit www.hostetler.net.

RELIGIOUS FESTIVALS

These festivals are closely linked to the calendar of the Roman Catholic Church. In Tuscany Christmas is celebrated by elaborate *presepi* (cribs) set up in churches. The start of Lent is the excuse for some serious *Carnevale* (carnival) partying in many towns,

A performance of Madame Butterfly at the Puccini Festival

including Viareggio, which stages Italy's largest carnival outside Venice. Easter sees Florence's major festival, the *Scioppio del Carro* (explosion of the cart), when a cart of fireworks explodes during Easter Mass. Holy Week, the run-up to Easter, is celebrated with religious processions in many small towns—head for Castiglion Fiorentino and Buonconvento to catch the best. *Corpus Domini*, commemorating the cult of the Blessed Sacrament, and the August feast of the Assumption of the Virgin are celebrated across the region. The Day of

the Dead (1 November) is when Italians return to their native towns and villages to tend their relatives' graves and reunite with their whole family. At local levels, every town and village has its own patron saint, whose feast day is celebrated with processions and solemn church services, culminating in late-night partying.

TRADITIONAL FESTIVALS

For an adrenaline rush head for Siena and the passion and spectacle of the *Palio*, a hair-raising bareback horse race preceded by a spectacular procession with flag-throwing. This is Tuscany's biggest, but Arezzo's *Giostra del Saracino* (The Saracen's Joust) along with *Il Gioco del Ponte* (The Bridge Game) and the *Luminaria di San Ranieri* (St. Ranieri's Illumination) in Pisa are historic events that attract thousands. Inhabitants of many small towns celebrate their history by dressing up in traditional costumes and parading through the streets.

ARTS FESTIVALS

Italy has a lively arts festival scene, most active during the summer, when amphitheatres, arenas, churches and piazzas are transformed into venues for cultural events. These festivals cover everything, including Greek theatre, opera, dance, rock and jazz, and many run for well over a month.

Central Italy is particularly active, and if you're in Tuscany during the summer an evening

dose of culture is easy to find. Look out for Florence's *Maggio Musicale Fiorentino*, which ranks high on the international circuit, as does the *Settembre Musica* series. Opera lovers can hear Puccini performed at the composer's villa on the shores of Lago di Massaciuccoli, while farther

Many of the region's festivals celebrate the past

south there's more opera at Batignano, near Grosseto.

FOOD FESTIVALS

For a true taste of Italy seek out the *sagre* (food festivals), where you can sample local products. These small-town festivities provide an insight into rural Italian life. Eating and drinking is often accompanied by a brass band and dancing, rounded off with a firework display. Wine is often a major feature, as it is on *Cantine Aperte* (open wine cellars) day, a May Sunday when wine-producing estates throw open their doors for tastings.

FLORENCE

Florence may be one of the world's richest cultural cities, but it's also a place for serious shoppers, who could easily by-pass the culture and devote an entire visit to retail therapy. You'll probably prefer a little of both, leavening the mix with some cultural entertainment, a bit of partying and perhaps some exercise—all of which Florence will provide.

KEY TO SYMBOLS

⊕	Shopping
♪	Entertainment
♉	Nightlife
♣	Sports
♥	Activities
♡	Health and Beauty
❋	For Children

⊕ SHOPPING

ART AND ANTIQUES

ANTONIO FRILLI GALLERY
Via dei Fossi 26r, 50123
Tel 055 210212
www.frilligallery.com
If you've always wanted figures from famous paintings, such as Rubens' *The Three Graces*, to stand whispering and giggling in your garden, you can find them here. Of course these high-quality hand-made and hand-finished sculptures aren't the real thing, but they come pretty close. Frilli also carries Ionic and Corinthian columns.
⏱ Mon–Sat 9.30–12.30, 3–7; closed Sat pm Jul–end Aug 🚍 A, 36, 37

BARTOLOZZI & MAIOLI
Via Maggio 13r, 50125
Tel 055 239 8633
This antiques shop gives a great insight into the Florentine love of ostentatious adornment. It's like wandering around a theatrical prop department preparing for a new production as craftsmen tap away in the background. You'll find some first-rate pieces in here, but be prepared to spend a lot.
⏱ Mon–Sat 9–1, 3–7; closed Aug 🚍 D, 11, 36, 37

LA CASA DELLA STAMPA
Sdrucciolo de Pitti 11r, 50125
Tel 055 223258
Vivianna is the lithographer who hand-tints many of these beautiful prints. There is a huge selection of Florentine scenes, from the Medici era to the early 19th century, alongside rich studies of butterflies and plants. All are printed on thick paper and can be framed.
⏱ Mon–Sat 9.30–12.30, 3–5 🚍 D, 11, 36, 37

DUCCI
Lungarno Corsini 24r, 50123
Tel 055 214550
www.duccishop.com
A massive selection of tinted lithographs, engravings and prints, both framed and unframed. Also some unusual items that make excellent gifts, as well as and furniture and wooden carvings of shoes and clothing.
⏱ Daily 9.30–7.30; closed Sun in Aug 🚍 A, B, 6, 11, 36, 37

GIOVANNI TURCHI
Via Maggio 50–52r, 50125
Tel 055 217341
A huge selection of period pieces just a stone's throw from the Palazzo Pitti. The store has been in the same family for years, and has items from the local area, Venice and the Veneto. Pieces are less expensive than they would be back home, even including the cost of shipping.
⏱ Mon–Sat 9.30–1, 4–7.30 🚍 D, 11, 36, 37

SHABBY SHOP
Via del Parione 12r, 50123
Tel 055 294826
There are some very unusual pieces of jewellery in this smart (rather than shabby) shop. The collection comes from all over Europe and goes back as far as the 17th century. Some pieces are much more affordable than others, so it's worth having a thorough look.
🕐 Tue–Sat 9.30–1, 3.30–7.30; closed Aug 🚌 A, B, 6, 11, 36, 37

BOOKS AND STATIONERY

ABACUS
Via De' Ginori 28/30r, 50123
Tel 055 219719
www.abacusfirenze.it
The sign on the door says that this bookbindery aspires to 'sturdiness and beauty'. The hand-stitched spines and exquisitely lined covers make the volumes exceptional gifts. Prices are surprisingly low.
🕐 Tue–Sat 9.30–1.30, 3.30–7.30, Mon 3.30–7.30; closed last 2 weeks in Aug 🚌 1, 6, 7, 10

ALINARI
Largo Alinari 15, 50122
Tel 055 23951
www.alinari.it
Alinari has an awesome photographic archive that includes some of the first photos ever taken in Italy. You can order any print for a very reasonable price. Beautiful coffee-table books and the kind of postcards you want to keep rather than send are also for sale.
🕐 Mon–Sat 9–1, 2.30–6.30; closed 2 weeks in Aug 🚌 6, 36, 37

EDISON
Piazza della Repubblica 27r, 50123
Tel 055 213110
Selling not only guides and books in English, but also maps, CDs, magazines and newspapers, Edison is a must for media junkies. The internet café is a great place to sit, surf and watch the world news on huge screens.
🕐 Mon–Sat 9am–midnight, Sun 10am–midnight 🚌 A, 6

FMR
Via Belle Donne 41r, 50123
Tel 055 283312
If you want to impress an Italian, leave a book from FMR lying on your coffee table. Franco Maria Ricci is a fashion icon in the world of print, and also sells superb stationery.
🕐 Mon–Sat 10–1, 3.30–7.30 🚌 A, 6, 11, 22, 36, 37

GIULIO GIANNINI E FIGLIO
Piazza Pitti 37r, 50125
Tel 055 212621
www.giuliogiannini.it
Across from the Palazzo Pitti, at what may be Florence's oldest papermakers, you can buy the most gorgeous muted marbled

Marbled paper is a good buy in Florence

paper, either by the sheet or the box. Also, covered boxes and books for your desk.
🕐 Daily 10–7.30 🚌 D, 36, 37

PAPERBACK EXCHANGE
Via Fiesolana 31r, 50122
Tel 055 247 8154
www.papex.it
A wide selection of art and history books, both new and second-hand, are sold here. Trade in any books you've already read and take your pick from the out-of-print ones, including some in English.
🕐 Mon–Fri 9–7.30, Sat 10–1, 3.30–7.30; closed 2 weeks in Aug 🚌 A, 14, 23

PINEIDER
Piazza della Signoria 13r, 50122
Tel 055 284655
www.pineider.it
Pineider's beautifully crafted tinted papers and inks have been celebrated throughout Europe since the late 18th century—the letters of Napoleon Bonaparte, Lord Byron and Marlene Dietrich were scribed using them. Also exquisite leather-bound notebooks and desk accessories.
🕐 Mon–Sat 10–1.30, 3–7; closed 2 weeks in Aug 🚌 23

SCRIPTORIUM
Via dei Servi 5/7r, 50122
Tel 055 211804
www.scriptoriumfirenze.com
Those who reject ballpoints and palmtops can step back in time at Scriptorium. Leather-bound notebooks, thick quality papers and a huge variety of quills, inks and waxes are sold to clients with an eye for tradition and quality.
🕐 Mon–Sat 10–2, 3.30–7.30, and last Sun in each month 🚌 7, 10, 14, 23

DEPARTMENT STORES

BALLOON
Via del Proconsolo 69r, 50122
Tel 055 212460
www.balloon.it
This Italian chain sells funky casual clothing that looks good on all generations, made from natural fabrics such as silk and cotton.
🕐 Tue–Sat 10–7.30, Mon 3.30–7.30; closed 2 weeks in Aug 🚌 A, 14, 23

COIN
Via dei Calzaiuoli 56r, 50123
Tel 055 280531
www.coin.it
This chain is one of the greatest things about Italy. The fashion department always delivers, with versions of the latest trends that are both affordable and of good quality. Good beauty department too, plus everything for the home.
🕐 Mon–Sat 10–8, Sun 11–8 Apr–end Dec; Mon–Sat 10–7.30, Sun 11–8 Jan–end Mar 🚌 A

MAX & CO
Via Calzaiuoli 89r, 50123
Tel 055 288656
The clothes at this subsidiary of MaxMara are usually variations of classics, but with a contemporary twist. Great for the sort of clothing you might wear at work.
🕐 Tue–Sat 10.30–7.30, Mon 3.30–7.30, Sun 11–7 🚌 A

PRINCIPE
Via del Sole 2, 50123
Tel 055 292764
www.principedifirenze.com
Mature customers are the target at this decidedly old-fashioned store. But any generation will appreciate the classic Italian home and kitchen ware.
🕐 Tue–Sat 9–7.30, Mon 10.30–7.30, last Sun of each month 11–7.30 🚌 A, 6, 11, 36, 37

LA RINASCENTE
Piazza della Repubblica 1, 50123
Tel 055 219113
www.rinascente.it
This classy department store drips designer labels, which extends to the bedding department as well as men's and women's fashion. The cosmetics and perfume counter stocks exclusive Italian brands unavailable back home.
🕐 Mon–Sat 9–9, Sun 10.30–8 🚌 A, 6

SISLEY
Via dei Cerretane 53r, 50123
Tel 055 210683
www.sisley.it
Italian Sisley has a wider selection of stock than their counterparts outside Italy, and tend to be less expensive. The Benetton subsidiary has a wide range of separates and accessories, as well as a number of the season's unmissable buys.
🕐 Mon–Sat 9.30–7.30, Sun 3.30–7.30 🚌 A

STANDA
Via Pietrapiana 42/44r, 50122
Tel 055 234 7856
Standa sells all the sorts of things you need on holiday—

shorts for the kids, beach towels, picnic baskets—all under one roof and at low prices.
🕐 Daily 9–9 🚌 A, 14

CRAFTS AND CERAMICS
ALICE'S MASKS ART STUDIO
Via Faenza 72r, 50123
Tel 055 287370
www.alicemasks.com
Papier-mâché masks in all shapes and sizes are here: animals—mythical and real—as well as more theatrical and surreal characters. They are all hand painted and finished, making great gifts or wall hangings.
🕐 Mon–Sat 9–1, 3.30–7.30 🚌 4, 12, 25, 31, 32, 33

Mask-making is another craft that you'll find in the city

LA BOTTEGHINA DEL CERAMISTA
Via Guelfa 5r, 50129
Tel 055 287367
The bright-hued, lively patterns hand painted on these jugs, bowls and dishes will brighten up any table. Look for the patterned jugs with matching cups, perfect for serving red wine.
🕐 Mon–Fri 10–2, 3.30–7.30, Sat 10–2 🚌 1, 6, 7, 10, 11, 17

MOLERIA LOCCHI
Via Domenico Burchiello 10, 50124
Tel 055 229 8371
www.locchi.com
This shop, next to the Prato dello Strozzino, is reminiscent of a museum, with the most

extraordinary examples of glass you will see outside Venice—with prices to match—created using traditional methods.
🕐 Mon–Fri 8.30–1, 3–6 🚌 12, 13

MOSCARDI
Lungarno Corsini 36r, 50123
Tel 055 214414
Moscardi's wonderful frames hardly need a picture in them. There are also exquisite mirrors of varying sizes, some of which have been treated to give an antique look.
🕐 Mon–Sat 9–1, 3.30–7.30 🚌 B, 11, 36, 37

SANTO SPIRITO
Piazza Santo Spirito 17r, 50125
Tel 055 239 8139
Right across from the church of the same name, this store is worth a visit for some of the most beautiful antique Florentine frames you're likely to find, restored on the premises. New frames are also made. Credit cards are not accepted.
🕐 Mon–Fri 8.30–12.30, 3–7, Sat 8.30–12.30 🚌 D, 11, 36, 37

LA SCAGLIOLA
Piazza Pitti 14r, 50125
Tel 055 211523
Painting on scagliola is one of Italy's oldest crafts. This marble substitute makes beautiful boxes, tabletops, tiles and insets for furniture, and La Scagliola, across from the Palazzo Pitti, has a wonderful selection.
🕐 Daily 10.30–7 🚌 D, 11, 36, 37

FASHION
ECHO
Via dell'Oriuolo 37r, 50122
Tel 055 238 1149
You will not have heard of any of the labels in this shop, but you'll almost certainly be bowled over by the clever designs and the reasonable prices. There's a younger, funkier Echo next door.
🕐 Mon–Sat 10–1.30, 2–7.30 🚌 14, 23

EMILIO CAVALLINI
Via della Vigna Nuova 24r, 50123
Tel 055 238 2789
www.emiliocavallini.com
Come the cooler weather, there's nothing like a whole wardrobe of bright, patterned and textured hosiery to keep your legs warm. Emilio Cavallini is where you can come to get them.
Ⓒ Tue–Sat 10–7, Mon 3–7 🚌 A, B, 6, 11, 36, 37

INTIMISSIMI
Via dei Calzaiuoli 99r, 50123
Tel 055 230 2609
www.intimissimi.it
The simple cotton and silk lingerie and sleepwear here is hard to beat for quality and price. The helpful staff will happily dismantle the shop to ensure you see the entire range.
Ⓒ Daily 9.30–8 🚌 1, 6, 7, 10, 11, 14, 17, 23

PUCCI
Via de' Tornabuoni 21r, 50123
Tel 055 265 8082
www.emiliopucci.com
Exuberant and hugely distinctive prints prevail here. Separates, silk shirts, dresses, shoes, scarves and accessories are all superb, but very pricey. Pucci style devotees can even buy or order a chair or carpet. The couture collection can be seen at Palazzo Pucci, Via de' Pucci 6.
Ⓒ Mon–Sat 10–7, last Sun of each month 2–7 🚌 A, 6, 11, 22, 36, 37

QUELLE TRE
Via de' Pucci 43r, 50123
Tel 055 293284
www.quelletre.it
While some of the clothes border on the bohemian, the wealth of shades, textures and shapes make this shop a superb find for individual dressers and those looking to enliven a sober wardrobe.
Ⓒ Tue–Sat 10–1.30, 3.30–7.30, Mon 3.30–7.30 🚌 1, 6, 7, 10, 11, 14, 17, 23

ZINI
Borgo San Lorenzo 26r, 50123
Tel 055 289850
Zini stocks Italy's most up-and-coming designers. The tailoring and cut of the clothes is impressive, and originality comes in the interesting use of different prints and fabrics.
Ⓒ Daily 10–7.45; closed Sat pm and Sun in Aug 🚌 A

FOOD AND DRINK
BORGO
Borgo San Lorenzo 20r, 50123
Tel 055 215103
www.borgovino.com
This well-stocked wine shop focuses on smaller local winemakers. Cheryl and Franco are

You can pick up excellent wines for good prices in Tuscany

extremely knowledgeable and can help you choose what to buy. Chiantis from €4.20 to €210 for a Super Tuscan. Also *biscotti*, pasta and olive oil.
Ⓒ Mon–Sat 10–7.30 🚌 1, 6, 7, 10, 11, 14

LA BOUTIQUE DEL CIOCCOLATO
Via Miragliano 12r, 50144
Tel 055 361650
If you're a chocoholic it's worth trekking off the beaten track to this chocolate boutique, where owner Sandro Stocchi has created chocolate and cakes in every conceivable shape. Credit cards are not accepted.
Ⓒ Mon–Sat 6am–midnight, Sun 6am–1pm; closed 2 weeks in Aug 🚌 22, 23, 33

CAFÉ DO BRASIL
Via de Servi 89r, 50121
Tel 055 214252
Florentines come here to buy loose tea and to stock up on the freshly roasted Brazilian coffee. You can also choose from a wonderful selection of locally made jams, cookies, sauces and traditional sweets (candies) to take home.
Ⓒ Mon–Sat 10–11.30, 2.30–7.30 🚌 C, 6, 31, 32

DOLCI E DOLCEZZE
Piazza Beccaria 8r, 50121
Tel 055 234 5458
Purveyor of light fluffy cakes, doughnuts and savoury pastries, this bakery is internationally renowned and deservedly so. If you are only in Florence for a day, make sure you come here for your cake stop. Credit cards are not accepted.
Ⓒ Tue–Sun 8–8 🚌 A, 6, 31, 32

ENOTECA MURGIA
Via dei Bianchi 45r, 50123
Tel 055 215686
www.vinodelizia.com
If you need help choosing an olive oil, the staff at this friendly store will take you through all the different types available, and you can taste and try before you buy. They also have a good selection of local wines and Italian liqueurs.
Ⓒ Mon–Sat 9.30–1.30, 3–8 🚌 A, 1, 14, 17, 22, 23

HEMMINGWAY
Piazza Piattellina 9r, 50124
Tel 055 284781
A chocolate heaven that caters to the connoisseur as well as to chocolate scoffers who fancy trying something gourmet. This is where the region's master chocolate makers come to drink coffee and liqueurs, and to talk—and eat—chocolate.
Ⓒ Tue–Sat 4.30pm–11.30pm, Sun 11.30am–8pm 🚌 D, 6

WHAT TO DO

MONACI DI LANURIO

Borgo Ognissanti 44, 50123
Tel 055 284727

Next door to the Ognissanti church, this lovely little shop sells organic food grown and produced by monks and fair trade suppliers. Their *biscotti*, fruit juices, marmalade and tomato sauces all make good gifts.

🕐 Mon–Fri 10–1, 4–7 🚌 A, B

PASTICCERIA MARINO

Piazza Nazario Sauro 19r, 50124
Tel 055 212657

If you are heading south of the river, pull in here for a pastry stop. There is a delicious selection of custard-, chocolate- and marmalade-filled *sfogliatelle*—pastry pockets, rounds and tubes. They also produce a memorable rum baba (a rich sponge cake soaked in rum syrup). Credit cards are not accepted.

🕐 Tue–Sun 6am–8pm 🚌 6, 11, 36, 37

JEWELLERY

ANGELA CAPUTI

Borgo Santi Apostoli 44–46r, 50123
Tel 055 292 993
www.angelacaputi.com

Angela Caputi is the place to look for bright, bold and highly original costume jewellery. Clothing and accessories to go with the pendant or earrings you have just bought are also stocked.

🕐 Mon–Sat 10–1, 3.30–7.30; closed 2 weeks in Aug 🚌 B

BABETTE VON DOHNANYI

Viale Francesco Petrarca 116 int, 50124
Tel 055 223697
www.bd-jewellery.com

Highly unusual glass spheres, strung together with finely spun gold and silver, are sold in the maker's shop close to the Boboli Gardens. Her alternative styles are growing in popularity. Credit cards are not accepted.

🕐 Mon–Fri 10.30–1, 3–7 or by appointment 🚌 12, 13

FRATELLI PICCINI

Ponte Vecchio 23, 50123
Tel 055 294768
www.fratellipiccini.com

Make sure you take in Piccini's if you are jewellery shopping on the Ponte Vecchio. Their gold charms make a delightful gift for someone back home.

🕐 Tue–Sat 10–7 🚌 B, D

GUALTIERI GANDOLFI

Piazza del Limbo 8r, 50123
Tel 055 283318

If you are looking for antique jewellery, this little shop just off Borgo Santi Apostoli has some amazing pieces. Look out for gemstones, glass beads and jet, as well as pieces

There's a number of jewellery shops on the Ponte Vecchio

unique to this region.

🕐 Daily 9.30–1, 3–7.30 🚌 B

ORE DUE

Via Lambertesca 12r, 50122
Tel 055 292143
www.oredue.it

This store close to the Uffizi produces jewellery using the same techniques as the original Florentine goldsmiths. Very traditional styles are set in 18-carat gold. Prices are not over-the-top considering the quality of the materials and craftsmanship.

🕐 Tue–Sat 9.30–7, Mon 3.30–7 May–end Dec; Tue–Sat 9.30–1, 3.30–7, Mon 3.30–7 Jan–end Apr 🚌 B

ORNAMENTA

Via Proconsolo 68, 50122
Tel 055 292879

This little shop sells small amber rings and silver earrings along with more international styles. Great for those who want an inexpensive reminder of their trip. Credit cards are not accepted.

🕐 Daily 9.30–8 🚌 A

PARENTI

Via de' Tornabuoni 93r, 50123
Tel 055 214438
www.parentifirenze.it

Even people who say they don't like jewellery end up ooing and aahing at Parenti's eclectic mix of styles and shapes, ranging from art nouveau to 1970s glitz. And the fair prices mean you can indulge yourself.

🕐 Tue–Sat 9.30–1, 3.30–7.30, Mon 3.30–7.30; closed Aug 🚌 A, 6, 11, 22, 36, 37

PIANEGONDA

Via dei Calzaiuoli 96r, 50123
Tel 055 214941
www.pianegondaitalia.com

This silversmith uses twinkling amethysts, topaz and moonstones alongside bold, sometimes theatrical styles. The pieces are ultramodern but don't lack feminine charm, and prices are reasonable.

🕐 Tue–Sat 10–7.30, Mon 3.30–7.30, last Sun of each month 🚌 A

LEATHER, SHOES AND BAGS

IL BISONTE

Via del Parione 31r, 50123
Tel 055 215722
www.ilbisonte.net

This brand (everything is stamped with the trademark bison) is at the cutting edge of leather bags and accessories. You can buy mobile phone covers, wallets, belts and travel bags, all made out of leather that takes on a beautiful life and colour of its own after use.

🕐 Mon–Sat 9.30–7.30 🚌 A, B, 6, 11, 36, 37

CELLERINI
Via del Sole 37r, 50123
Tel 055 282533
www.cellerini.com
Drop in to view some of the wonderfully simple yet cleverly designed bags and purses here. Cellerini bags are very popular among fashion buffs and will elicit envious glances once you get back home.
🕐 Tue–Sat 9–1, 3–7.30, Mon 3–7.30
🚌 A, 6, 11, 36, 37

MADOVA
Via Guicciardini 1r, 50125
Tel 055 239 6526
www.madova.com
Madova have been making fine-quality leather gloves in every hue for nearly a century; they come with silk, fur, wool or cashmere lining and are reasonably priced.
🕐 Mon–Sat 9.30–7.30 🚌 D, 36, 37

ROMANO
Via degli Speziali 10r, 50123
Tel 055 216535
www.romanofirenze.com
Romano sells a huge variety of shoes, boots and sandals for both men and women and catering to all ages: You'll see trendy young Florentines trying on kitten heels next to matrons looking at shoes seemingly from a bygone age.
🕐 Tue–Sat 10–7.30, Mon 3.30–7.30, Sun 11–7.30 🚌 A

SALVATORE FERRAGAMO
Via de' Tornabuoni 2r, 50123
Tel 055 292123
www.ferragamo.it
Perhaps the leading brand in Italian shoes and bags, Ferragamo is undoubtedly expensive. But the styles are usually timeless and made to last, so you should think of a Ferragamo as an investment. To find out about the legend behind the shoes and see a pair of Ava Gardner's heels, visit the Ferragamo Museum (▷ 78).
🕐 Tue–Sat 10–7.30, Mon 3.30–7.30
🚌 B, 6, 11, 36, 37

SCUOLA DI CUOLO DI SANTA CROCE
Piazza Santa Croce 16, 50122
Tel 055 244533
www.leatherschool.it
Come to this workshop, at the back of the Santa Croce church, to learn how to spot quality and craftsmanship in leather working. If you make a purchase at the on-site shop, they'll personalize the goods for you with a stamp.
🕐 Mon–Sat 9–6, Sun 10.30–4.30 Apr–end Oct 🚌 B, C, 23

UMBERTO LEATHER
Via Guicciardini 114r, 50125
Tel 055 293091
www.umbertoleather.com

Leather goods from the Scuola di Cuolo di Santa Croce

Close to the glove shop Madova is Umberto Leather. Excellent for robust but classic satchels and briefcases that last a lifetime.
🕐 Mon–Sat 9.30–7.30 🚌 D, 36, 37

MARKETS

CASCINE
Parco delle Cascine, Viale Abramo Lincoln, 50144
It's worth an early start to experience the hustle and bustle of this market, in Florence's biggest park, by the Ponte della Vittoria. There are meats, fruit and vegetables, bric-a-brac, clothes and shoes. Credit cards are not accepted.
🕐 Tue 8–1 🚌 B, 1, 9, 12, 13

MERCATO CENTRALE
Piazza del Mercato Centrale, San Lorenzo, 50123
The outside stands are where to buy leather—make sure it's made in Italy and always be prepared to bargain—as well as clothes and the usual gifts. Inside is the real Mercato Centrale, a cavernous space full of mouthwatering Florentine delicacies. Feast your eyes on the wonderful fruit and vegetable stalls as well as the *salumeria* (delicatessen) counters brimming with meats and cheeses. There are also stands where you can get a simple lunch. Credit cards are not accepted.
🕐 Mon–Sat 8.30–7 in summer; 8.30–2 in winter 🚌 4, 12, 25, 31, 32, 33

MERCATO DEI LIBERI ARTIGIANI
Loggia del Grano, Via de Neri, 50122
This market of free traders *(liberi artigiani)* sells clothes and jewellery. There are some superb bargains for those with the patience to search, otherwise there's not that much. Credit cards are not accepted.
🕐 Thu 8–7 🚌 B, 23

MERCATO NUOVO (PORCELLINO)
Loggia Mercato Nuovo, Via Porta Rossa, 50123
Full of inexpensive reproductions of Florentine classics—great for gifts. The Italian leather bags and shoes are often a good buy. Look for the statue of the slavering boar, its gleaming snout made of bronze. Credit cards are not accepted.
🕐 Daily 9–7 🚌 A, 6, 11, 36, 37

MERCATO DELLE PULCI
Piazza dei Ciompi, 50121
This flea market is probably Florence's best, with all manner of household goods, antiques and vintage clothing. For the label-conscious there are second-hand designer clothes and plenty of shoes. Credit cards are not accepted.
🕐 Mon–Sat 8–7 🚌 A, 14

MERCATO DI SANT'AMBROGIO

Piazza Lorenzo Ghiberti, 50121

If you are staying in the Santa Croce area, this is your local produce market, off Via de' Macci, but by the time you get there the real business will have been done by the early-risers. Bargain hunters prepared to haggle should check out the cheap clothing stalls. Credit cards are not accepted.

🕐 Daily 7–2 🚌 A, C

SANTO SPIRITO

Piazza Santo Spirito, 50125

There are stands daily at Santo Spirito, selling bedding, shoes, clothing and haberdashery, but the alternative Sunday markets are particularly worth visiting. On the second Sunday of the month there's an ethnic flea market, while the third Sunday is devoted to organic foods, Tuscan clothing and herbal remedies. Credit cards are not accepted.

🕐 Second and third Sun 8–6 🚌 D, 11, 36, 37

SILKS, FABRICS AND LINENS

ANTICO SETIFICIO FIORENTINO

Via Lorenzo Bartolino 4, 50124

Tel 055 231861

www.anticosetificiofiorentino.com

This 'old Florentine silk factory' makes fine fabrics for some of Italy's most sought-after designers. Much of the fabric is produced using traditional methods, and their most coveted cloth is woven on 18th-century looms.

🕐 Mon–Fri 9–1, 2–5 🚌 D

CASA DI BAMBOLA

Borgo San Frediano 135r, 50124

Tel 055 214367

www.casadibambola.com

Casa di Bambola is perhaps best known for its lampshades, but also sells finely embroidered linens. They have some beautiful cotton curtains and cushions, all with openwork stitching.

🕐 Mon–Sat 9–1, 3–7.30 🚌 D

ERMINI

Via Borgo San Lorenzo 3r, 50123

Tel 055 292200

This bizarre fabric shop, across from Piazza San Giovanni, seems stuck in a time warp. Only serious customers are welcome, but come to buy suiting and linen at good prices. There are also more lavish fabrics for upholstery.

🕐 Mon–Sat 9–1, 3.30–7.30; closed 2 weeks in Aug 🚌 1, 6, 7, 10, 11, 14, 17, 23

LORETTA CAPONI

Piazza Antinori 4r, 50123

Tel 055 213668

Loretta Caponi has cornered the market in Florentine lace

A window display at Casa di Bambola

and luxury embroidered linens. A lot of work goes into these pieces so be prepared to pay. There is exquisite clothes for young children and beautiful lingerie is also for sale.

🕐 Tue–Sat 9–1, 3.30–7.30, Mon 3.30–7.30 🚌 A, 6, 11, 22, 23, 36, 37

PAM

Via Bartolommeo Scala 2r, 50126

Tel 055 681 3375

www.pamfirenze.it

Rather out of the way, but stocks a wide and impressive selection of bed linen, table-cloths and bath sets, made from damask, Irish linen, silk and perçale. Some are beauti-fully hand embroidered and

everything is immaculately hand finished.

🕐 Mon–Fri 8.30–1, 3–7.30 🚌 3, 8, 23, 31, 31

PASSAMANERIA TOSCANA

Via dei Federighi 1r, 50124

Tel 055 239 8047

www.ptfsrl.com

A great place to pick up all those little Florentine decorative touches and flourishes. They have tassels, tiebacks, fringes, coats of arms and trims, as well as brocade cushions, damask runners and wall hangings. Check out their mosquito nets. Former US First Lady (now Senator) Hillary Clinton is a well-known customer.

🕐 Mon–Sat 10–1, 3.30–7.30 🚌 D

VALLI

Via Strozzi 4r, 50123

Tel 055 282485

Valli's shop window showcases fabrics designed by Valentino, Armani and others. It has a very luxurious array of gleaming and plush fabrics, most of which you can't find back home.

🕐 Tue–Sat 9.30–7, Mon 3–7 🚌 A, 6, 11, 22, 36, 37

VALMAR

Via Porta Rossa 53r, 50123

Tel 055 284493

www.valmar-florence.com

This store is like a big sewing box, with ribbons, trims and buttons tumbling out of trays and baskets. It takes time to work your way through everything, but you're sure to find some unique bits and bobs for great finishing touches. You can even take in your own fabric and they will create something for you.

🕐 Mon–Sat 9–7.30 🚌 A, 6, 11, 36, 37

🎵 ENTERTAINMENT

CINEMA

CINEHALL ODEON

Piazza Strozzi, 50123

Tel 055 214068

www.cinehall.it

To avoid the frustrating (if comic) experience of seeing an English-speaking film dubbed into Italian, head to the Cinehall Odeon. Films are regularly shown here with their original soundtrack intact. English-language films are usually shown on Mondays, Wednesdays and Thursdays Reduced prices on Wednesday and in the afternoons.

🎬 €5–€7.50 🚌 A, 6, 11, 22, 36, 37

CINEMA FULGOR
Via Maso Finiguerra 24r, 50123
Tel 055 238 1881
www.staseraalcinema.it/cinemafulgor
This wonderful art deco cinema is between Ognissanti and the banks of the Arno. It's a great place to watch the likes of Robert De Niro (usually dubbed) amid the 1930s cinema surroundings.

🎬 €5–€7 🚌 A, 11, 36, 37

CINEMA GOLDONI
Via Serragli 109, 50124
Tel 055 222437
The Goldoni is one of only three Florentine cinemas to show films in their original language. Give them a call to find out about the latest blockbusters and art-house movies to be screened.

🎬 €4.50–€7 🚌 36, 37

MULTISALA VARIETY
Via del Madonnone 84r, 50100
Tel 055 677902
www.staseraalcinema.it/cinemavariety/frameset.html
There are five screens to choose from in this modern multiplex. The Variety has the latest sound system in the large Sala Sole. There is a discount ticket on Wednesday and on weekday afternoons.

🎬 €5–€7 🚌 14, 34

CLASSICAL MUSIC

AMICI DELLA MUSICA
Via della Pergola 12/32, 50121
Tel 055 607440
www.amicimusica.fi.it
The prestigious Teatro della Pergola hosts regular classical concerts by the Amici della Musica organization. Leading musicians from around the world appear in the grandiose Sala Grande and the more intimate Saloncino della Pergola during the concert season (Oct–end Mar).

🎬 €12–€18 🚌 C, 14, 23

BASILICA DI SAN LORENZO
Piazza San Lorenzo 9, 50123
Tel 055 216634
It may have changed quite a few times since its consecration in AD393, but the Basilica di San Lorenzo remains one of the most evocative Florentine classical music venues. The celebrated home-grown

Many churches in Florence host classical music concerts

orchestra, the Filarmonica di Firenze Gioacchino Rossini, regularly plays here.

🎬 Free 🚌 1, 6, 7, 10, 11, 17

BATTISTERO DI SAN GIOVANNI
Piazza San Giovanni, 50123
Tel 055 230 2885
www.operaduomo.firenze.it
Florence's Baptistery makes a wonderful setting for classical concerts. Look out especially for events organized by the O flos colende orchestra. The Musicus Concentus organization occasionally puts on more innovative concerts.

🎬 Free 🚌 1, 6, 11, 14, 17, 23

CHIESA DI SANTA MARIA
Via del Corso, 50122
Tel 333 307 4339
If you would like to sample the distinctive sound of Florentine organ music, then this is the place to visit. A wonderfully evocative setting in which to hear music similar to that heard by Dante here in the 13th century.

🎬 €11 🚌 A, 14

GIARDINI DI BOBOLI
Piazza Pitti, 50121
Tel 055 211158
During the summer months, the wonderful Palazzo Pitti courtyard and the Giardini di Boboli, once occupied by the Medici and the alleged setting for Boccaccio's *Decameron*, becomes the backdrop for ballet and classical concerts.

🎬 €33 🚌 D, 11, 36, 37

SANTO STEFANO
Piazza Santo Stefano, 50122
Tel 055 783374/055 210804
www.orcafi.it
The Orchestra da Camera Fiorentina stage many of their seasonal concerts at this church by the Ponte Vecchio. As might be expected from a chamber orchestra, concerts frequently feature works by Vivaldi, Haydn, Bach and Mozart. Tickets available at Via Luigi Alamanni 39.

🎬 €15–€20 🚌 B

TEATRO COMMUNALE
Corso Italia 16, 50123
Tel 055 27791; 055 213535 (ticket office)
www.maggiofiorentino.com
Il Teatro Communale is Florence's major venue for all things orchestral, balletic and operatic. The winter concert season is January through March; opera and ballet season is September through March. Expect popular operatic and ballet repertoire and a wide range of concert works by seminal composers from Bach to Wagner.

🎬 €22–€150 🚌 A, B

WHAT TO DO

TEATRO GOLDONI
Via Santa Maria 12, 50125
Tel 055 233 5518
www.maggiofiorentino.com
This famous old theatre has a
capacity of 1,500 for opera and
ballet productions, as well as
various classical concerts.
💶 €30–€50 🚌 11, 36, 37

TEATRO VERDI
Via Ghibellina 99, 50122
Tel 055 212320
www.orchestradellatoscana.it
This is the home of the
Orchestra della Toscana, which
covers a broad repertoire of
classical music styles, from
baroque to contemporary.
The theatre also hosts many
other concerts by international
musicians throughout the
year, most notably during the
Maggio Musicale Fiorentino
(▷ 172).
💶 €10–€15 🚌 A, 14, 23

CONTEMPORARY LIVE MUSIC

ASTOR CAFFÈ
Piazza Duomo 20r, 50123
Tel 055 239 9000
This stylish café/bar near
the Duomo serves up
Mediterranean dishes accompanied by a house, jazz and
easy-listening soundtrack. Grab
a seat for an *aperitivo* and
munch on the buffet snacks
before the DJ sets and occasional live music get going in
the back room.
🕐 Daily 9am–2am 💶 Free 🚌 A, 1, 6,
7, 10, 11, 14, 17, 23

AUDITORIUM FLOG
Via Michele Mercati 24b, 50139
Tel 055 487145
www.flog.it
This is Florence's best alternative music venue. As well as
Italian indie acts like 99 Posse,
the Flog attracts some well-
known international artists
and many tribute bands.
Every night there is something
different: from rock 'n' roll to
ska and reggae to electronic
trance.
🕐 Tue–Sun 9.30pm–2am 💶 €5–€25
🚌 4, 8, 14

BLOB CLUB
Via Vinegia 21r, 50122
Tel 055 211209
Grab a sofa upstairs to get the
best view of the live music
action below. If you prefer hot
and sweaty jumping, then join
the throng on the floor sway-
ing and nodding to the mainly
rock cover bands.
🕐 Daily 6pm–2am 💶 Annual membership €10, taken out on door 🚌 23

CAFFÈ LA TORRE
Lungarno Cellini 65r, 50125
Tel 055 680643
www.caffelatorre.it
After a few aperitifs and some
free nibbles, try some of this
trendy, art-filled café's cocktails

*Jazz music is a popular choice at
the city's bars and clubs*

while soaking up the eclectic
live music. Expect anything
from smooth samba to drum
and bass two-step between
7.30 and midnight. The Sunday
brunch menu is well worth
sampling.
🕐 Daily 11am–3.30am 💶 Free 🚌 12,
13, 23

ELLIOT BRAUN
Via Ponte alle Mosse 117r, 50144
Tel 055 352352
www.elliotbraun.it
Drink the delicious house
aperitif, Apericena, before
tucking into the *cucina Laziale*
(cooking from the Rome area).
Among the entertainment is
poetry reading, live music

(especially Wednesday),
dancing, cabaret and lessons
for aspiring bar staff.
🕐 Daily 6pm–2am 💶 Free 🚌 2, 17,
29, 30, 35

JAZZ CLUB
Via Nuova de' Caccini 3, 50121
Tel 055 247 9700
If you like live jazz and a
relaxed atmosphere, head
for this central Florence club.
Shows start at 10.15pm.
Credit cards are not accepted.
🕐 Fri–Wed 9pm–2am, Thu 7pm–2am
💶 Annual membership €7.50, taken
out on door 🚌 C, 14, 23

LOONEES
Via Porta Rossa 15, 50123
Tel 055 212249
The understated entrance
hints at hidden depths, which
the friendly basement bar
delivers. The bands mainly play
American and British classic
covers that the international
crowd laps up. Not ground-
breaking but fun. Credit cards
are not accepted.
🕐 Daily 10pm–3am 💶 Free 🚌 A, 6,
11, 36, 37

MAYDAY
Via Dante Alighieri 16r, 50122
Tel 055 238 1290
Locals swarm around this live
music bar, so you will hear a
lot of the Florentine dialect.
Live guitar-based acts take the
stage from around midnight
into the early hours. Credit
cards are not accepted.
🕐 Mon–Sat 8pm–2am 💶 Free 🚌 A,
14, 23

MUSICUS CONCENTUS
Sala Vanni, Piazza del Carmine 19,
50124
Tel 055 210804
www.musicusconcentus.com
Musicus Concentus pushes
the boundaries of contemporary jazz with its innovative
schedule of concerts. Expect
everything and anything from
classical and world music to
the latest electronic wizardry.
🕐 See wesbite for details 💶 €15
🚌 D

PALASPORT FIRENZE
Viale Pasquale Paoli 1, 50137
Tel 055 661497/8
www.boxoffice.it
This medium-sized venue near Campo Marte hosts some of Italy's most celebrated rock/pop acts, like Pino Daniele and Ligabue. Check in advance for well-known British and American bands who may be swinging into the Palasport.
🕐 See wesbite for details 💶 €20–€65 🚍 3, 10

PINOCCHIO LIVE JAZZ
Viale Giannotti 13, 50126
Tel 055 683388
www.pinocchiojazz.it
Jazz fans will love this place where some of Italy's top artists can be heard. Members nod approvingly in this smoky venue while the musicians play their instruments into the night.
🕐 Sat 10pm–3am, Nov to mid-Apr
💶 €9 for membership fee, plus €8 entrance fee 🚍 31, 32

PORTO DI MARE
Via Pisana 128, 50143
Tel 055 715794
Live Italian rock and pop music, great food and unusual themed nights pull in the crowds to this relaxing bar. Enjoy the classic tunes plucked from past Sanremo Festival playlists.
🕐 Tue–Sun 8pm–3am, Mon 10pm–3am 💶 Free 🚍 6, 25, 27, 80

RIO GRANDE
Via degli Olmi 1, 50144
Tel 055 331371
Rio Grande is Florence's finest for Latin-American fun, spread over four dance floors. Book a table to feast on the spicy Churrascaria fare and enjoy the samba dancing, live music and unrelenting percussion. Later on you can learn some merengue moves.
🕐 Wed–Sat 9pm–4am 💶 €15 🚍 1, 9, 12, 13, 16, 26, 27, 80

SASCHALL
Lungarno Aldo Moro 3, 50136
Tel 055 650 4112
www.saschall.it
Florence's leading music venue hosts big name rock/pop acts and well-known musicals. Expect to see international artists like Tori Amos as well as Italian stars. Check the website for the latest events.
🕐 Performances usually start 9pm
💶 €5–€45 🚍 3, 14, 31, 32, 34

THEATRE
TEATRO DELLA LIMONAIA
Via Gramsci 426, Sesto Fiorentino, 50019
Tel 055 440852
www.teatro-limonaia.fi.it

Teatro Comunale has a wide range of theatrical productions

Fresh, edgy, contemporary productions are the mainstay of the Limonaia. Alongside quality theatrical collaborations with the likes of the National Theatre in London, the venue also holds various classical concerts amid the lush park surroundings.
💶 €8–€10 🚍 2, 28a

TEATRO LE LAUDI
Via Leonardo da Vinci 2r, 50132
Tel 055 572831
Alongside classic literary plays and classical concerts, this theatre also stages family-friendly productions like *Le Avventure di Pinocchio* (The Adventures of Pinocchio)
and *Cappuccetto Rosso* (Little Red Riding Hood).
💶 €8–€15 🚍 10, 11, 13, 17, 20, 33

TEATRO PERGOLA
Via della Pergola 12/32, 50121
Tel 055 226 4335
www.pergola.firenze.it
Well-known theatre productions are regularly held in the sumptuous main hall and the elegant Saloncino, its second hall. As well as staging Italian classics by the likes of D'Annunzio and De Filippo, English-, Irish- and French-language playwrights, including Oscar Wilde, Steven Berkoff, Victor Hugo and Georges Feydeau, are also showcased.
💶 €13–€17 🚍 C, 14, 23

TEATRO PUCCINI
Via delle Cascine 41, 50144
Tel 055 362067
www.teatropuccini.it
If you wish to improve your knowledge of the Italian language and culture, this is ideal. The Puccini has a full schedule of theatrical productions, which have included the satirical monologues of Paolo Hendel and the classic comedies.
💶 €17–€20 🚍 17, 17c

🌙 NIGHTLIFE
BARS AND PUBS
CADILLAC
Via degli Alfani 57r, 50121
Tel 055 234 3993
This is a café by day and cocktail bar by night. Students and visitors flock here for tasty snacks and vibrant cocktail concoctions. Art exhibits and photos adorn the walls of this bustling bar. Happy hour is between 5pm and 9.30pm, and there are lots of drink promotions throughout the evening. Credit cards are not accepted.
🕐 Mon–Sat 8am–2am, Sun 5pm–1am
🚍 C, 31, 32

WHAT TO DO

CAFFÈ CONCERTO PASZKOWSKI
Piazza della Repubblica 31–35r, 50123
Tel 055 210236
In the summer, the seating outside this bar is swamped with posing Florentines. Where once this was the meeting place of the 19th-century intelligentsia, it's now the domain of the well-groomed Florentine.

🕐 Tue–Sun 7am–1am 🚌 A, 6, 22

FIDDLER'S ELBOW
Piazza Santa Maria Novella 7a, 50123
Tel 055 215056
The original Florentine Irish pub, popular with students and visitors. Gulp the best Guinness in town and catch up on the soccer action on the widescreen TVs.

🕐 Daily midday–1am 🚌 A, 1, 14, 17, 36, 37

GIRASOL LATIN BAR
Via del Romito 1r, 50129
Tel 055 474948
A huge totem pole welcomes visitors to this swinging South American bar. All Latin musical genres get an airing in the downstairs dance area, where none other than Compay Segundo (of Buena Vista Social Club fame) has made an appearance.

🕐 Daily 7pm–2am 🚌 12, 14, 23, 28, 33, 80

KIKUYA
Via dei Benci 43r, 50122
Tel 055 234 4879
www.kikuya.it
Drink pints of Dragoon, Red Stripe and Bombardier beer while soaking up the English pub atmosphere in this ever-popular central haunt. Kikuya shows widescreen soccer and serves decent sandwiches. Happy Hour is 7–10pm, except on Saturday. The cocktails are particularly generous. Also hosts occasional live music. Credit cards are not accepted.

🕐 Daily 7pm–2am 🚌 B, C, 23

KIWI
Via Fratelli Bronzetti 12, 50137
Tel 055 611160
The friendly staff set this multi-faceted bar apart from the crowd. If you don't wish to listen to the karaoke classics or watch widescreen soccer in the back bar, there's plenty of space both outside and in to drink and chat.

🕐 Daily 7pm–3am 🚌 11, 17

LIDO
Lungarno Pecori Piraldi 1, 50122
Tel 055 234 2726
This bar along the River Arno has the feel of a colonial ship—you can even rent boats from here. Cocktails and innovative

Stop for a drink and people watch at the Caffè Paszkowski

snacks are consumed to a soundtrack of lounge, drum-and-bass and nu jazz beats.

🕐 Tue–Sun 6pm–2am 🚌 8, 12, 14, 31, 32, 33, 80

OFFICINA MOVE BAR
Via Il Prato 58r, 50123
Tel 055 210399
A good choice for some snacks and late-night alcohol-fuelled fun if you plan to be in the Porta a Prato quarter. Subtle lighting and intimate seating arrangements set the scene for a flirtatious adventure. Credit cards are not accepted.

🕐 Daily 3pm–3am 🚌 1, 2, 9, 17, 27, 29 30, 35

REX CAFÉ
Via Fiesolana 25r, 50122
Tel 055 248 0331
This popular bar has a spell-binding interior of retro lighting and paint-splashed walls, as well as some eye-catching, constantly changing art exhibits. The global house music complements the array of drinks from around the world, which include mojitos (mint, lime juice, rum and soda) and Green Days (kiwi fruit, vodka and soda). Credit cards are not accepted.

🕐 Daily 5.30pm–3am; closed mid-May to mid-Sep 🚌 A, C, 14, 23

SHOT CAFÉ
Via dei Pucci 5a, 50123
Tel 055 282093
A great place to start a night out near the Duomo. Not sur-prisingly, this bar has a wide range of shots to knock back. Visitors and party animals get here early, as there are cheap drinks between 5 and 8pm. Credit cards are not accepted.

🕐 Daily 7am–2am 🚌 8, 12, 14, 33

SLOWLY CAFÉ
Via Porta Rossa 63r, 50123
Tel 055 264 5354
This relaxing contemporary bar is full of vibrant decorative touches. The easy-listening and chilled music sounds com-plement the subdued lighting and all-round welcoming vibe. There's a wide selection of cocktails at the bar and very good fish dishes served in the dining area.

🕐 Daily noon–3pm, 7pm–2am 🚌 6, 11, 36 37

CAFÉS
ANTICO CAFFÈ TORINO
Viale Matteotti 2r A/B, 50125
Tel 055 588247
Elegant antiques fill the two rooms of this wonderfully evocative café. Soft piano-bar music accompanies the coffee, cocktails, freshly-squeezed juices and delicious pastries. A relaxing place to unwind.

🕐 Daily 7am–3am 🚌 8, 80

CAFFÈ NOTTE
Via delle Caldaie 28r, 50125
Tel 055 223067
There are plenty of board games to occupy you on the large wooden benches in this Oltrarno café-bar. The jovial staff are happy to recommend one of their fine grappas, or create a lethal cocktail before your increasingly bleary eyes. Credit cards are not accepted.
Tue–Thu, Sun 8am–2am, Fri–Sat 8am–3am; closed Aug ☐ D, 11, 36, 37

DOLCE VITA
Piazza del Carmine 5, 50124
Tel 055 284595
One of the trendy places where young Florentines go, in the Oltrarno district. A great place for a refreshing *aperitivo* or a cocktail and to mingle with the pre-club beautiful people.
Tue–Sat 5pm–2am, Sun 6pm–2am ☐ D, 6

MEZZANOTTE E DINTORNI
Via Kassel 9, 50126
Tel 055 653 1651
Come here for an early evening drink or one of the house's divine cocktails. The friendly staff will also serve you substantial tasty meat and vegetable dishes to fill the stomach for the night ahead.
Mon–Sat 7pm–2am, Sun 6pm–2am ☐ 3, 8, 23

PANINERIA POKER
Via Pisana 329a, 50143
Tel 055 754969
A great place to grab some late-night snacks and a few drinks. As well as a good selection of *panini*, they also serve pasta dishes at an affordable price. Credit cards are not accepted.
Tue–Fri noon–2am, Sat–Sun 2pm–3am, Mon noon–3.30pm ☐ 6, 12

PORFIRIO RUBIROSA
Viale Strozzi, 18r, 50123
Tel 055 490965
An elegant café-bar popular with young Florentines and business people. Sit back, sip cocktails and watch the locals at play.
Mon–Sat 7pm–2am ☐ A, 6, 22

CLUBS

CENTRAL PARK
Via del Fosso Macinate, 2, 50144
Tel 055 353505
www.discocentralpark.it
This is a house music complex, complete with garden, eight bars, four dance floors, restaurant and a VIP terrace. Italian house dominates but there's also plenty of room for lounge and smooth piano-bar music.
Daily 8.30pm–4am ☐ €17, free for visitors (show your passport) and students ☐ 1, 9, 12, 80

Dolce Vita is across the river from the old town

CLUB MONTECARLA
Via dei Bardi 2, 50125
Tel 055 234 0259
Exotic leopard-skin patterned upholstery, chintz and belle-époque furnishings give this unique club a sophisticated kitsch vibe. Drink mojitos and other cocktails, amid bright cushions and peculiar artworks. Drinks are a little pricey but the friendly atmosphere wins you over. Credit cards are not accepted.
Daily 9pm–5am ☐ Members only, membership available for €5 on door ☐ C, D

CRISCO
Via Sant'Egidio 43r, 50122
Tel 055 248 0580
www.crisco.it
This is one of Florence's leading gay clubs, near the Duomo in Santa Croce. This is a city famed for its cross-dressing, so expect the most glamorous transvestites you've ever seen. Credit cards are not accepted.
Sun–Mon, Wed–Thu 10.30pm–3am, Fri–Sat 10.30pm–6am ☐ €12 ☐ A, 14, 23

JARAGUA
Via Erta Canina 12r, 50125
Tel 055 234 3600
www.jaragua.it
Italy's first exclusively Latino music club is a lot of fun and free to get into. The spicy South American food also makes it popular. If you don't know how to dance salsa or merengue, there are lessons available as well as many willing tutors on the dance floor. Credit cards are not accepted.
Tue–Sun 9.30pm–3am ☐ Free ☐ C, D

MARACANA
Via Faenza 4r, 50123
Tel 055 210298
www.maracana.it
Six levels, a carnival stage and a party crowd make this vibrant club popular with lovers of all things Brazilian. It's the place to watch carnival dancers, to samba and sip caipirinhas (the classic Brazilian cocktail of ice, lime, sugar and Caçasa). The bar staff juggle bottles while some of the crowd attempt dance-floor acrobatics.
Tue–Sun 8.30pm–4am ☐ €12 ☐ 31, 32

TENAX
Via Pratese 46, 50127
Tel 055 308160
www.tenax.org
This is Florence's premier house music club, attracting big international names like Dimitri from Paris, Thievery Corporation, Grace Jones and

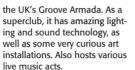

the UK's Groove Armada. As a superclub, it has amazing lighting and sound technology, as well as some very curious art installations. Also hosts various live music acts.

◉ Daily 11pm–4am 🎫 €15 🚌 5, 29, 30, 56

UNIVERSALE

Via Pisana 77r, 50143
Tel 055 221122
www.universalefirenze.it
This former cinema is now dedicated to dance music, cocktails and Italian food. Wednesday and Thursday focus on commercial house while Saturday nights see a more eclectic music policy of funk and jazz. Special culinary events and top DJs arranged for Sundays.

◉ Wed–Sun 8pm–3am; closed May–end Oct 🎫 €15 🚌 6, 12

YAB

Via Sassetti 5, 50122
Tel 055 215160
www.yab.it
Theatrical surroundings and renowned DJs make this one of Florence's most fashionable clubs. House music dominates the schedule, with hard house on Fridays and happy house on Saturdays. Monday's Smoove Night sees hip-hop tunes and electric acrobatics on the dance floor. Credit cards are not accepted.

◉ Mon–Tue, Thu–Sat 11pm–4am 🎫 €14 🚌 A, 1, 6, 14

🎭 SPORTS AND 🎯 ACTIVITIES

BASKETBALL

BASKET FIRENZE
Palazzetto S. Marcellino, Via Chiantigiana, 50126
Tel 055 436 0301
www.firenzebasket.net
Fans of basketball should get themselves down to the compact Palazzetto S. Marcellino. Founded in 1948, I Biancorossi (The White and Reds) of Basket Firenze play their home games here, competing in the

second flight of the Italian men's league. Credit cards are not accepted.

◉ Sun 6.30pm 🎫 Free 🚌 31, 32

GOLF

CLUB MONTELUPO
Via Le Piagge 4, 50056 Fibbiana, Montelupo Fiorentino
Tel 0571 54 1004
www.golfmontelupo.it
This par 36, 9-hole course lies below the Chianti Montalbano hills on the banks of the Arno. Enjoy the wonderful scenery and the excellent facilities which include a pro shop, practice area and putting greens. Coaching available: one half-hour lesson €22 or six

Ballooning is a wonderful way to see the countryside

lessons for €100.

◉ Daily 9am–dusk 🎫 €30 for 9 holes 🚗 Take the Firenze-Pisa-Livorno expressway and leave at Montelupo Fiorentino or Empoli Est exit. Look for directions to Fibbiana

HORSE RACING

LE CASINE
Ippodromo delle Mulina, Viale dell'Aeronautica/Viale del Pegaso 1, 50144
Tel 055 422 6076
www.softvision.it
The Ippodromo delle Mulina is the place to go and see horse racing in Florence. If you feel like placing a bet on the *galoppo* (flat racing) or *trotto* (chariot racing) many *tabbachi*

(tobacconists) have easy-to-use betting facilities.

◉ Race season is Jun, Jul, Nov–end Mar 🎫 Free 🚌 17c

HOT-AIR BALLOONING

BALLOONING IN TUSCANY
Podere La Fratta, 53020 Montisi
Tel 0577 845211
www.ballooningintuscany.com
If you have euros to spare and three companions, why not book a balloon ride over Tuscany? This small company organizes personalized balloon trips with champagne breakfast. It's an hours' drive south of Florence but the views are worth it.

◉ Contact for details 🎫 €200 (minimum 4 adults) 🚗 A1 towards Siena, Montisi exit

ICE SKATING

ICE SKATING IN THE CITY
Piazza Santa Croce, 50122/ Fortezza da Basso, 50129
In December and January each year, a temporary ice rink is constructed in Piazza Santa Croce or the Fortezza da Basso. As you glide around you can admire the architecture of the magnificent Cocchi-Serristori and dell'Antella palaces or the imposing military structure of the fortress.

◉ Dec, Jan 🎫 €5 🚌 C, 12, 14, 23, 28, 33, 80

MOUNTAIN WALKING

AZIMUT GROUP
La Casa del Popolo 25 aprile, Via Bronzino 117, 50142
Tel 055 700460
www.azimut.fi.it
For outdoor adventure in the Tuscan hills or further afield, the Azimut group is a good port of call to arrange mountain walking or climbing. Should you require more speed with your outdoor adrenalin rushes, they also run alpine skiing and mountain biking trips. Credit cards are not accepted.

◉ Telephone calls only Mon–Fri 4–10pm 🎫 Membership: Adult €13, child €6 🚌 6, 26, 27 80

SOCCER

FIORENTINA VIOLA
Viale Manfredo Fanti 14, 50137
Tel 055 262 5537
www.fiorentina.it
Watch the reborn Viola (the team's kit is violet) at the open-bowl, 47,000-capacity Stadio Communale Artemio Franchi (named in remembrance of the ex-Fiorentina director). Soccer is *the* sport in Italy, so expect fervent support for the club formerly known as Fiorentina. Credit cards are not accepted.
🕐 Alternate Sun, Sep–end May 🎟 €5
🚌 3, 10, 11, 17, 20, 34

TENNIS

CENTRO SPORTIVO DLF
Via Paisiello 131, 51144
Tel 055 363052
Le Cascine's sports complex, in the largest park in Florence, has nine tennis courts. These can be booked up to 3 days ahead.
🕐 Daily 8am–11pm 🎟 Outdoor court €9.50; indoor €15.50

VOLLEYBALL

PALAVOLA FIRENZE
Palestra Paolo Valenti, Via Taddeo Alberotti 26, 50139
Tel 055 896 9042
Italian women's volleyball (*palavola*) can be seen at Palazzetto dello Sport in Campo di Marte. Italy has some of the world's best players and the game has a large and enthusiastic following, so check in advance for ticket availability. Credit cards are not accepted.
🕐 Alternate Sun, Oct–end May
🎟 Free 🚌 8, 14, 28

WATER SPORTS

CANOTTIERI COMUNALI FIRENZE
Lungarno Ferrucci 4, 50126
Tel 055 681 2151
www.canottiericomunalifirenze.it
Try your hand at canoeing, boating and rowing at this club on the River Arno. As well as kayaking sessions, there are a number of courses available for all ages. There's also the chance to try Dragon boating, Polynesian canoeing or even a game of canoe polo.
🕐 Mon–Sat 8.30am–9pm, Sun 8.30–1; ring the information number for the latest details about upcoming courses and other activities 🎟 Joining fee €95
🚌 8, 31, 32

🏥 HEALTH AND BEAUTY

CELSUS
Viale Gramsci 27r, 50125
Tel 055 234 2733
For a total overhaul, book a day at Celsus. They will buff, massage and smooth you towards perfection. Their lash-tinting and brow-shaping is particularly recommended.

You can buy handmade cosmetics at Officina Profumo

🕐 Mon–Sat 8.30–7 🎟 Body treatments from €50; eyelash tints from €20
🚌 C, D

COIFFEUR RENATO
Via San Gallo 199r, 50129
Tel 055 483548
www.renatocoiffeur.com
This is one of Florence's smartest hairdressers and the perfect place to come for a treat. The interior of the salon is a stylish mix of old and contemporary and the experienced staff are charming and professional.
🕐 Tue–Sat 9–6 🎟 €20 for a blow-dry
🚌 1, 7, 8, 13, 25, 33

GENNY
Via de' Pucci 4, 50122
Tel 055 214823
Where better to be pampered than at the Florentine home of decadence and glamour: the beautiful Palazzo Pucci. You can enjoy shiatsu massage, hydromassage, hydrotherapy, reflexology and a variety of beauty treatments for face, body and nails.
🕐 Mon–Fri 9–7, Sat 9–1 🎟 Back massage €40 🚌 4, 23

KLAB WELLNESS CENTRE
Via Giambattista Lulli 62a, 50144
Tel 055 333621
www.klab.it
Even if you don't feel like a session on an exercise bike or joining one of the aerobics classes, you can enjoy a hydro massage before slipping into the Turkish bath for a deep, relaxing clean. A Scottish Shower, alternating hot and cold jets of water targeted at specific areas of the body (said to be effective in the battle against cellulite) is also available.
🕐 Mon–Fri 9am–10.30pm, Sat 9–6, Sun 10–2 🎟 Hydro massage from €25
🚌 22, 23, 33

OFFICINA PROFUMO
Via della Scala 16, 50123
Tel 055 216276
www.smnovella.it
This pharmacy, Farmaceutica di Santa Maria Novella, was originally run by Dominican friars and established during the 1220s. It was opened to the public in 1612. The formulae of some of its better-known preparations, such as the Pasta di Mandorle (almond hand-cream) and perfumes, date back to the days of Catherine de' Medici. You can also buy from its wide range of luxury cosmetics.
🕐 Mon–Sat 9.30–7.30, Sun 10.30–6.30
🎟 Almond hand-cream from €20
🚌 A, 6, 11, 36, 37

✪ FOR CHILDREN

GIARDINO DI BOBOLI
See page 74.

GIARDINI DEI SEMPLICI
Via Micheli 3, 50121
Tel 055 2757402
www.unifi.it
The Giardini dei Semplici was laid out between 1545–46 and is the third oldest botanical garden in the world. It covers 2ha (5 acres), three quarters of which is occupied by the original 16th-century garden. Some 6,000 different plants grow here, from Italy and all over the world. The greenhouses are home to tropical flowers and plants, ferns, palms, orchids and citrus trees. It's a great place to let the kids loose in.
🕐 Tue 9–1, 3–6, Wed–Fri 9–1 Apr–end Oct; Tue–Fri 9–1 Nov–end Mar
💶 Adult €3, child (6–14) €1.50, under 6 free 🚌 1, 7, 25

MUSEO DEI RAGAZZI
Piazza della Signoria, 50122
Tel 055 276 8558/8224
www.museorazzi.it
Florence's interactive childrens' museum is primarily aimed at school groups, but runs activities in English on weekends. The main themes are Renaissance life, with workshops explaining how the Palazzo was built; a chance to play with lenses and test out Galileo's ideas; and 'Clothing and the Body', in which an actress dresses for a 16th-century day while discussing clothing and changing attitudes to the body with her maid and husband.
🕐 Fri–Wed 9–7, Thu 9–2 💶 Adult €6, under 18 €2 🚌 A, B 🔲 Guided tours only and visits must be booked ahead

MUSEO STIBBERT
Via Vittorio Emmanuelle II, 50134
Tel 055 475520
www.museoragazzi.it
This is an interactive exhibition of historic weaponry and military costume. You can try on the contrasting designs of Ottoman sultans' and Medici

(sidebar) **WHAT TO DO**

MARCH/APRIL

SCOPPIO DEL CARRO
Easter Sunday
Florence's *Scoppio del Carro* (Explosion of the Cart) dates back to the 11th century, when a carousel of fireworks was lit to spread the good news of Easter. A ceremonial cart stuffed with incendiaries is wheeled into Piazza del Duomo, and a wire is run to the statue of the Virgin on top of the Duomo and into the cathedral. At about 11pm the wire is lit and a mechanical dove slides down to the cart causing an explosion, igniting the fireworks.

MAY/JUNE

MAGGIO MUSICALE FIORENTINO
May and June
Biglietteria Teatro Communale, Via Solferino 15, 50123
Tel 055 211 1158
www.maggiofiorentino.it
This is Florence's major music festival, held in venues inside and outside across the city. Founded in 1933, it's Italy's longest-running music festival with a good mix of opera, ballet and classical music.
🚌 B, D, 1, 9, 13

GIOCO DI CALCIO
Sundays in June
Ufficio Valorizzazione Tradizioni Popolari Fiorentine, Piazzetta di Parte Guelfa 1r, 50123

captains' uniforms, weaponry and regalia.
🕐 Mon–Wed 10–1, Fri–Sun 10–5 💶 Adult €5, child (6–12) €2, under 6 free 🚌 4 🔲 Guided tours only, lasting 1 hour, departing every half hour

MUSEO DI STORIA DELLE SCIENZA
See page 78.

MUSEO ZOOLOGICO (LA SPECOLA)
See page 96.

Gioco di Calcio

Tel 055 261 6050/1/6
www.globeit.it/caf/storia.html
A no-holds-barred version of soccer that is played between the four city quarters, originally used to keep the city militia in fighting shape and to meld the various factions into a united force. The final day is celebrated with a costumed procession and a flotilla of candlelit boats with fireworks on the River Arno.
💶 €10–€25 🚌 C, 23

OCTOBER

MUSICA DEI POPOLI
October
Via Maestri del Lavorol Festival, 50134
Tel 055 422 0300
www.flog.it/mus_pope.htm
In October each year, artists from around the globe descend on Florence for this international folk music festival. Italy's finest world music event has been running for more than 25 years and attracts many to its main venue, the Auditorium Flog.
🚌 4, 8, 14

PARCO DELLE CASCINE
Piazza Vittorio Veneto, 50144
Cows and wild boars roamed these parklands when it was owned by Alessandro and Cosimo I dei Medici. Children will love the wide-open spaces, fountains, monuments, horse riding, swimming pool and playgrounds. Bring a picnic, rent rollerblades and check out the amphitheatre's attractions.
🕐 Open 24 hours 🚌 1, 17, 17c, 19, 26, 80

NORTHERN TUSCANY

There's a happy mix of prosperous towns and villages and unspoiled countryside in northern Tuscany, with plenty of culture to go with it. Incomes are high, reflected in the excellent shopping to be found in provincial hubs such as Pisa and Lucca, and leisure is taken seriously, with a wide variety of outdoor activities available and high standards of entertainment of all sorts.

KEY TO SYMBOLS

- ⊞ **Shopping**
- 🎭 **Entertainment**
- 🍸 **Nightlife**
- 🏃 **Sports**
- ⭐ **Activities**
- ♥ **Health and Beauty**
- ★ **For Children**

ALPI APUANE

⭐ GROTTA DEL VENTO

Grotta del Vento, 55020 Vergemoli
Tel 0583 722024
www.grottadelvento.com
This cave is one of the openings to the complex underground system that runs under the Alpi Apuane Nature Park. A guided tour takes in stalactites, stalagmites, small lakes and underground rivers.
🕐 Daily 10–6, Apr–end Sep; Sun 10–6, rest of year 💰 Adult €7.50, under 10 €5, for one-hour tour 🚗 SS12 from Lucca to Borgo a Mozzano, then left onto SS445 to Gallicano, from here turn off to Fornovolasco

BAGNI DI LUCCA

♥ TERME JEAN VARRAUD

Piazza S. Martino 11, 55021 Bagni di Lucca
Tel 0583 87221
www.termebagnidilucca.it
One of the most popular of the springs in this spa town, known since the 13th century for its therapeutic waters. The best things about Terme Jean Varraud are its two natural steam grottoes, each at a stable temperature of between 40°C (102°F) and 47°C (115°F).
🕐 Mon–Sat 8.30–12.30, Nov–end May; Mon–Sat 8.30–12.30, 2.30–6 Jun–end Oct 💰 Treatments from €16; swimming pool from €10

CASENTINO

⭐ CASENTINESI

Headquarters: Via G. Brocchi 7, 52015 Pratovecchio
Tel 0575 50301
This national park, Parco Nazionale delle Foreste Castentinesi, is on the Apennine ridge between Tuscany and Romagna. It has a wide choice of walking, cycle riding and horseback-riding routes. Among the beech and silver fir forests are buildings of religious and historical interest such as the Camaldoli monastery. There are 11 visitor offices around the park.
🕐 Headquarters: Mon–Fri 9–1, also Tue, Thu 3–5.30 🚗 Take the Incisa Valdarno exit on A1, then SS69 following signs to the National Park.

COLLODI

★ PARCO DI PINOCCHIO

Via San Gennaro 3, 51014 Collodi
Tel 0572 429342
www.pinocchio.it
Pinocchio Park brings the story of the famous wooden puppet alive, with mosaics, statues and fountains incorporating all the story's characters. Attractions include puppet shows, a maze, a playground, exhibitions and a children's restaurant. Credit cards are not accepted.
🕐 Daily 8.30–dusk 💰 Adult €8.50, child (3–14) €6.50, under 3 free

FIESOLE

ESTATE FIESOLANA
Piazza del Mercato 5, Fiesole, 50014 Firenze
Tel 055 597 8303/800 41 42 43
www.estatefiesolana.it
Sunset concerts and operatic productions are held at the 1st-century Teatro Romano in the Fiesole hills above Florence, a cool, tranquil venue during the heat of summer.
Jun–end Sep €20–€52 7

GARFAGNANA

IL CORNIOLO
Località Le Prade 25, 55033 Castiglione Garfagnana, Lucca
Tel 0583 68705
www.ilcorniolo.it
This country estate in the Parco dell'Orecchiella makes an ideal base for riding. Sergio is an English-speaking qualified riding instructor who teaches and accompanies groups (direct number tel 340 350 2796). There are various schedules available. Accommodation is available as the estate is an *agriturismo* (▷ 240). Children under 7 not accepted.
By arrangement €25 for 2 hours; €60 for day excursion

GARFAGNANA ADVENTURES
Braccicorti, Località Braccicorti, Pontecosi, Pieve Fosciana 55036, Lucca
Tel 0583 683355
www.garfagnanaadventures.com
This company, run by a married couple, will get you moving. They run a number of tours of the area by mountain or road bike, will take you kayaking on lakes or skiing over mountain tops. There are also some tours of the towns.
By arrangement Half day bike tour €65

PARCO ALPI APUANE
Piazza delle Erbe 1, 55032 Castelnuovo Garfagnana, Lucca
Tel 0583 65169
www.garfagnanavacanze.it
The visitors' office is an essential stopping place for advice on walking, rock climbing and mountain biking in the area.

Maps are available and you can tailor activities to suit your abilities and your schedule—anything from a short stroll to a 10-day circular walk among the surrounding mountains, staying in refuges.
Daily 9–1, 3–7, Jun–end Sep; Tue–Sun 9–1, 3–5.30, rest of year

LUCCA

LA CACIOTECA
Via Fillungo 242, 56100 Lucca
Tel 0583 496346
A tiny food shop selling a host of local and traditional seasonal produce. Staff are friendly and helpful, even if your command of Italian is weak. Try the ham, goat's

The flower market at the Piazza del Anfiteatro, Lucca

cheese, olives and Lucchese wines for a quick picnic.
Mon–Sat 7am–8pm, plus every 3rd Sun of month

CARIOLA
Piazza San Michele 10, 56100 Lucca
Tel 0583 467677
On Lucca's main square, this is one of the best of the many ceramics shops in Lucca. Cariola's goods are not mass produced and relatively reasonably priced, with a wide range of designs, both traditional and modern.
Tue–Sun 9–1, 3.30–7.30, Mon 3.30–7.30

CARLI
Via Fillungo 95, 56100 Lucca
Tel 0583 491119
First opened in 1655 and furnished as it was in the 18th century, Carli is one of Lucca's oldest jewellers. Visit for antique watches and silver, or just to see the high-vaulted room frescoed in 1800.
Tue–Sun 9.30–1, 3.30–7.30, Mon 3.30–7.30

CERAMISTI D'ARTE
Via Mordini 74/78, 56100 Lucca
Tel 0583 492700
The Tuscan artists Stefano Seardo and Fabrizio Falchi sculpt and paint at this workshop. Visit to pick up hand-painted decorative tiles, terracotta sculptures and marble mosaics made from the prized Massa Carrara marble. Everything is produced according to ancient Italian ceramic techniques.
Tue–Sun 9.30–1, 3–7, Mon 3.30–7.30

CIOCCOLATERIA CANIPAROLI
Via San Paolino 96, 56100 Lucca
Tel 0583 53456
Lucca's most innovative chocolate maker has chocolates that are so artistic they should be displayed rather than consumed. However, they are too delicious to pass up. The range combines traditional shapes and indulgent flavours. Be sure to sample the popular *praline di cioccolato* (chocolates with soft fillings).
Tue–Sun 9–1, 3.30–8; closed Jul, Aug

ENOTECA VANNI
Piazza del Salvatore 7, 55100 Lucca
Tel 0583 491902
www.enotecavanni.com
Enoteca Vanni has been supplying Lucca and its visitors with typical local foods since 1965 and has some of the best wines, spirits and extra virgin olive oils in the region. Nowhere better to stock up on gourmet gifts or picnic items.
Tue–Sat 9–1, 4–8, Mon 4–8

WHAT TO DO

🌐 GALLERIA VANNUCCI
Via del Battistero 50/52, 56100 Lucca
Tel 0583 955815
Among the best of Lucca's antiques shops, Galleria Vannucci has local 17th- and 18th-century furnishings and drawings in its two rooms. The records for some of the goods are particularly interesting, as they can be traced back to Lucca's busy period of antiques dealing in the 18th century.
🕐 Tue–Sun 9–1, 3–7, Mon 3–7

🌐 LUCCA IN TAVOLA
Via San Paolino 130–132, 56100 Lucca
Tel 0583 581022
Visiting gourmets love this wine shop, one of the most popular in the city. Drop by for a wine tasting if not to buy a few cases to take home (they will organize shipment if you want to do this). The famed DOC Vino Rosso delle Colline Lucchesi is a good choice. They also stock olive oils, herbs and other delicacies typical of the region.
🕐 Daily 9.30–7.30 Apr–end Oct; Tue–Sun 9–1, 3.30–7.30, rest of year

🌐 MERCATO D'ANTIQUARIO
Piazza San Giusto, Piazza Antelminelli and surrounding streets
This large antiques market has a wide range of furnishings, rare coins and old jewellery on the 3rd Sunday of every month. On the 3rd Saturday and 4th Sunday of the month, there is a crafts market.
🕐 9am–7pm

🌐 MERCATO DEI LIBRI
Via Beccheria, 56100 Lucca
Just behind the church of San Giusto and running towards both Piazza Napoleone and Piazza San Michele, Lucca's book stands sell anything and everything that is printed. Look for old prints of Lucca and other Italian cities, modern postcards and even comic books in all sorts of languages.
🕐 Daily 10–6

🌐 MERCATO DI LUCCA
Via dei Bacchettoni, 56100 Lucca
Just inside the city's walls, between the San Jacopo and Elisa gates, Lucca's market sells clothing, fresh and silk flowers, food, table linen and household implements and is very good value, especially for clothes and shoes. Get here early for the best bargains.
🕐 Wed, Sat 9–1

🌐 MARSILI COSTANTINO
Piazza San Michele 38 and Via del Moro 18–22, 56100 Lucca
Tel 0583 491751
Marsili gives you a tasty introduction to Lucca's local vineyards, with some lesser-

Concerts are often held in churches around Lucca

known but delicious wines as well as famous varieties like Brunello, Rosso di Montalcino, Montecarlo and Colline Lucchesi. Take time to try some of the many herb liqueurs and *digestifs* that are produced, following traditional local recipes.
🕐 Daily 9–7.30 Jun–end Sep; Tue–Sat 9–1, 3.30–7.30, Mon 3.30–7.30, rest of year

🌐 PASTICCERIA TADDEUCCI
Piazza San Michele 34, 56100 Lucca
Tel 0583 494933
Popular for its delicious version of *buccellato* (sweet aniseed-flavoured bread with raisins), Pasticceria Taddeucci has been producing this classic Lucchese

delicacy for four generations without change. It gets its name from the Latin *buccellatum* ('sailor's cookie'). It's best eaten at breakfast or for an afternoon snack.
🕐 Daily 8–7.30, Apr–end Sep; Fri–Wed 9–1, 3–7, Mon 3–7, rest of year

🌐 SANT'ANNUNZIATA
Via delle Tagliate 656, 56100 Lucca
Tel 0583 491778
Sant'Annunziata carries on the silk-weaving traditions for which Lucca was famous and on which its riches were built in the 11th to 17th centuries. The delicate, hand-woven fabrics are influenced by Renaissance paintings and are produced in natural fibres and modern textiles.
🕐 Tue–Sat 9.30–1, 4–8, Mon 4–8

🎭 CENTRALE
Via Poggio 36, 55100 Lucca
Tel 0583 55405
This is a two-screen cinema showing the latest Hollywood blockbusters. There are special shows on public holidays. Credit cards are not accepted.
👜 Adult €7, child €5, reduced price of €5 for all on Mon

🎭 CINEMA ITALIA
Via Biscione 32, 55100 Lucca
Tel 0583 467264
One-screen cinema showing the latest Hollywood releases for two weeks at a time. Most showings in original language. Credit cards are not accepted.
👜 Adult €7, child €5, reduced price of €5 for all on Fri

🎭 TEATRO ASTRA
Piazza del Giglio 7, 55100 Lucca
Tel 0583 496480
Showing the most up-to-date cinematic releases in Lucca, Teatro Astra's one screen is popular among students for its quick turnover of films. It also takes pride of place in Lucca's film festivals. Credit cards are not accepted.
🕐 Closed Thu 👜 Adult €7, child €5, gallery seats €8, reduced price of €5 for all on Wed

WHAT TO DO

🎭 TEATRO DEL GIGLIO
Piazza del Giglio 13/15, 55100 Lucca
Tel 0583 467521
www.teatrodelgiglio.it
From September to November this 19th-century opera house stages classical dramas. Dance, opera and classical music performances take place from November to March. It also houses the Centro Studi G. Puccini (The Puccini Studies Centre). Credit cards are not accepted.
💺 Adult €25, child €12

🎭 TEATRO MODERNO
Via Vittorio Emanuele II 17, 55100 Lucca
Tel 0583 53484
One-screen cinema with each film generally running for two weeks. Evening showings only, but does have student discounts.
💺 Adult €7, under 7 €5, reduced price of €5 for all on Wed

🍷 THE GOLDEN FOX
Viale Regina Margherita 207, 55100 Lucca
Tel 0583 491619
www.thegoldenfox.it
This establishment so prides itself on being an English pub that it imported its entire interior from England. English, Scottish and Irish beers are on tap. Credit cards are not accepted.
🕐 Tue–Sun 8pm–1am

🍷 MCCULLOUGHS
Piazza Curtatone 135, 55100 Lucca
Tel 0583 469067
Stop by for a Celtic or Gaelic-themed evening with live music and dancing. This lively Irish pub has Guinness on tap as well as a good selection of Irish and Scottish whiskies. Credit cards are not accepted.
🕐 Daily 8pm–1am

🍷 NICOLAS
Viale S. Concordio 887, 55100 Lucca
Tel 0583 582378
Known for its live music, Nicolas gives local musicians the chance to perform to an audience. The play list has everything from jazz and blues to pop and reggae as well as traditional Italian singers. Credit cards are not accepted.
🕐 Tue–Sun 8pm–2am

🍷 OSTERIA DEL NENI
Via Pescheria 3, 55100 Lucca
Tel 0583 492681
www.leosteriedilucca.it
This traditional wine bar gives you a family-run introduction to the best Chianti and Lucca regional wines. A wide range of snacks is available.
🕐 Daily 12–3, 7.30–11

✪ TORRE GUINIGI
Via Sant'Andrea, 55100 Lucca
Tel 336 203221

Views from the top of the Torre Guinigi

Climb the 40m (130ft) Guinigi tower, which was built by the family of the same name, once one of the richest in Lucca. The tower was part of their 14th-century villa that now houses the Guinigi Museum. On top, there's an ancient oak tree to play on and great views. Credit cards are not accepted.
🕐 Daily 9–7 💺 Adult €4, child €2

MONTECATINI TERME

♥ TERME EXCELSIOR
Viale Verdi 61, 51016 Montecatini Terme, Pistoia
Tel 0572 778487
www.termemontecatini.it
There are nine different spas here, but this is the central one and open all year. The emphasis is on health and wellbeing, with a medical team available to give advice before starting treatments. Patients with liver and rheumatism problems are said to benefit from taking the waters, and you can indulge in a wide range of beauty treatments.
🕐 Therapy Centre: daily 8–12.30, 4–7, Easter–end Oct; 8–12.30, rest of year. Beauty Centre: Mon–Sat 8.30–8, Sun 9–2 💺 Body massage €52

MUGELLO

🏎 AUTODROMO DEL MUGELLO
Autodromo del Mugello, Mugello
Tel 055 849 9111
www.mugellocircuit.it
Motor sports events are staged regularly at this historic track owned by Ferrari. The biggest motorcycle races, including the Italian Grand Prix for 125cc and 250cc bikes, as well as the Superbike World Championships, draw large crowds who fill the natural amphitheatre around the track, which is one of the most scenic in the world. Credit cards are not accepted.
🕐 Contact for latest meetings
💺 €5–€25 including parking 🚗 Take 302 Faentina road passing Scarperia for Mugello or A1 (Bologna–Firenze) motorway and exit at Barberino di Mugello

PECCIOLI

✪ PARCO PREISTORICO
Via dei Cappuccini 20, 56037 Peccioli
Tel 0587 636030
www.parcopreistorico.it
The medieval town of Peccioli, above the Era Valley, is not just olive groves, vineyards and grassy hills. It is known for its prehistoric park, complete with reproductions of dinosaurs, cavemen and their habitats. There is also a large picnic area. Credit cards are not accepted.
🕐 Daily 9–nóon, 2–dusk; closed Christmas and New Year 💺 Adult €4, child €4 (child €3, Aug–end Mar)
🚗 Take the Altopascio exit on A11 motorway, then follow signs to Peccioli

PIETRASANTA

⭐ TRENINO DELLE VACANZE

Tel 0584 747737 (Fratelli Verona)
This *trenino delle vacanze* (holiday train) has fantastic views of the Versilia Coast, as it runs from the town along the coast of Marina di Pietrasanta during summer. The hour-long route takes in the towns of Le Nocette, Motrone, Tonfano, Fiumetto and Pietrasanta. You can buy tickets on board. Credit cards are not accepted.
🕐 Daily at 5.30pm and 9pm, Jun–end Sep 💷 Adult €5, child €3

PISA

🏬 FEDERICO SALZA

Borgo Stretto 46, 56100 Pisa
Tel 050 580244
www.salza.lt
This Pisan outlet of a popular Turin confectioner sells beautifully fashioned chocolates and pastry goods. Look for the chocolate Leaning Tower of Pisa. It is a stone's throw from Piazza dei Miracoli and a must for any sweet-toothed visitor.
🕐 Daily 8am–8.30pm, Jun–end Oct; Tue–Sun 8am–8.30pm, rest of year

🏬 GALLERIA BARSANTI

Piazza Duomo 6, 56100 Pisa
Tel 050 560535
Galleria Barsanti is both an art gallery and a sculpture studio. Items are made of local marble and alabaster, and you can buy anything from kitsch unicorn sculptures to delicate copies of Etruscan masks. It's a huge shop, a short stroll from the Leaning Tower of Pisa.
🕐 Daily 9–7.30

🏬 LENZI GHINO GIACOMO

Via Provinciale Vicarese 371, 56010 San Giovanni alla Vena, Pisa
Tel 050 799011
www.ceramichelenzi.it
In this factory shop selling classic Tuscan ceramics, they pride themselves on producing basins, vases and pottery the traditional way. Choose from vases and crockery splashed with green and white—they are beautifully decorated pots

for storing oil, wine and herbs and make great gifts.
🕐 Mon–Sat 9–1, 3–8 🚗 Follow directions west out of Pisa towards Vicopisano and Cascina; San Giovanni alla Vena is midway between the two

🏬 LIBRERIA FOGOLA

Corso Italia 82, 56100 Pisa
Tel 050 502547
This neat, tiny bookshop has very helpful staff as well as internet access. Books covering every subject under the sun are either on the shelves or can be ordered. English-language books and tourist information available.
🕐 Mon–Sat 9.30–7.30

Borgo Stretto in Pisa is a good shopping street

🏬 PAOLO CAPRI

Via di Marino 2, 56100 Pisa
Tel 050 577111
Designer Paolo Capri's showroom is a popular outlet for jewellery, watches and frames, where most of the items are created by Florentine silversmiths. There is also a wide range of giftware that takes its inspiration from local traditions and culture.
🕐 Tue–Sat 9–1, 4–7, Mon 4–7

🏬 PAUL DEBONDT

Via Turati 22, 56125 Pisa
Tel 050 501896
A Dutch artisan and former Artistic Chocolate World Champion, Paul Debondt

creates custom chocolate designs for clients. This Pisa outlet has everything from animal-shaped chocolates filled with almond paste to simple, rich truffles. The *ganascia* chocolates, made with fresh cream and butter, are what Debondt is known for. The shop is closed over the summer as it's too hot for the chocolate.
🕐 Tue–Sat 10–1, 4–8, Oct–end Apr

🏬 I PISANI

Via di Signano 25/A, 56017 San Giuliano Terme, Pisa
Tel 050 817025/815013
www.ipisani.it
This delicatessen sells a selection of the tastiest food, produced by the best local artisans. Shop for truffles, extra virgin olive oils, cheeses, salami, sauces and much more. The English-speaking staff can provide recommended recipes as well as all the cooking advice you might require.
🕐 Mon–Fri 9–1, 2–6 🚗 7km (4 miles) from Pisa on the Brennero Road (SS12) towards Lucca

🎬 ARISTON

Via Filippo Turati 27, 56127 Pisa
Tel 050 43407
A three-screen cinema showing the latest releases in original language with Italian subtitles. There is generally a choice of a children's film, a romantic comedy and an action drama. Refreshments and snacks available. Credit cards are not accepted.
💷 Adult €7, child €4.60

🎬 ARSENALE

Via Scaramucci 4, 56127 Pisa
Tel 050 502640
www.arsenalecinema.it
This is an art-house cinema with four daily showings of two films, with an extensive library of old cinema and video. All screenings are in the original language. Credit cards are not accepted.
💷 Adult €4.50

🎬 CINEMA TEATRO NUOVO
Piazza della Stazione 1, 56127 Pisa
Tel 050 41332
Popular with visitors and locals, this art-house cinema has one screen showing films in their original language. Occasionally, films are not subtitled. Credit cards are not accepted.
👋 Adult €6.70, child €4.60

🎬 LANTERI
Via San Michele dei Scalzi 46, 56127 Pisa
Tel 050 577100
This big-screen cinema mostly shows the latest releases. Films are screened in the original language with Italian subtitles. There is free parking next door. Credit cards are not accepted.
👋 Adult €6.70, child €4.60

🎬 ODEON
Piazza San Paolo all'Orto 18, 56127 Pisa
Tel 050 540168
www.multisalaodeon.com
A modern multiplex showing the latest releases on four screens. Films are shown in the original language. Credit cards are not accepted.
👋 Adult €7, child €4.50, reduced price of €5.50 for all on Fri

🎬 TEATRO SANT'ANDREA
Via del Cuore, 56127 Pisa
Tel 050 542364
www.archicoop.it/santandrea
The attractive Romanesque Chiesa di Sant'Andrea was abandoned for 20 years before local volunteers converted it into a theatre in 1986. You can see local and touring performances here. Credit cards are not accepted.
🕐 Season: Nov–end May 👋 Adult €5–€25, child €3–€18

🎬 TEATRO VERDI
Via Palestro 40, 56127 Pisa
Tel 050 941111
www.teatrodipisa.pi.it
Inaugurated in 1867, this theatre is one of the most beautiful in central Italy and has a notable ceiling fresco.

See opera, drama and dance in the 900-seat auditorium.
🕐 Season: Sep–end May 👋 €6–€43

🍷 ABSOLUT
Via Mossotti 10, 56100 Pisa
Tel 050 2201262
www.absolut.gay.it
By day this is an internet café, by night a laid-back gay and lesbian bar. There's also live music and cabaret. Credit cards are not accepted.
🕐 Tue–Sun 10pm–2am

🍷 BORDERLINE
Via G. Vernaccini 7, 56100 Pisa
Tel 050 580577
This pub, part of a chain, has a good reputation for live music.

Tennis is an option for those who want to get more active

Popular with the university crowd, the bar is decorated in the style of the Wild West and hosts live performances (mostly rock, blues and folk) most nights.
🕐 Mon–Sat 8pm–2am

🍷 LA LOGGIA
Piazza Vitt. Emanuele II 11, 56100 Pisa
Tel 050 46326
www.barlaloggia.com
This ice cream shop, frequented by visitors and locals, becomes a bar at night, known for its international beers. After 7pm, drop by for some tasty Tuscan cooking.
🕐 Daily 7am–4am; closed first 2 weeks in Jan

🍷 OFFSIDE
Ospedaletto, Uscita Pisa Nord Est, Via Emilia, 56100 Pisa
Tel 340 4964845
www.off-side.pisa.it
Themed evenings here range from Friday's gay and lesbian night to live music gigs on Wednesday and Saturday nights. Cocktails and dance club are on Sundays, and karaoke—the best night—is on Thursday. Credit cards are not accepted.
🕐 Mon, Wed–Thu 8pm–2am, Fri–Sat 8pm–4am, Sun 6pm–4am

⭐ PARCO REGIONALE DI MIGLIARINO-SAN ROSSORE-MASSACIUCCOLI
Via Aurelia Nord 4, 56122 Pisa
Tel 050 525500
Walking and biking routes in this national park along the coast include 16th-century pine forests, rich in wildlife. There's good bird-watching at Lake Massaciuccoli.
👋 Free 🚗 From Pisa follow signs to Gombo and take the Viale delle Cascine to San Rossore; then the Viale dei Pini to Migliarino and head to Massaciuccoli for Lake Massaciuccoli

🎾 TENNIS CLUB PISA
Piazzale dello Sport 7, 56122 Pisa
Tel 050 530313
www.tennisclubpisa.it
This club has five outdoor clay courts, three of which have lighting for night games, and two indoor courts. The clubhouse has a bar, changing facilities and shop. You must book a court the day before.
🕐 Daily 9am–10pm 👋 €15 per hour

💙 SAN GIULIANO TERME
Largo Shelley 18, 56017 San Giuliano Terme
Tel 050 818047
www.termesangiuliano.com
This 18th-century building, once used by the Grand Dukes of Tuscany, is set in a beautiful park of olive trees in the Pisan foothills. The spa is known for its facial and body treatments as well as regimes to revitalize the respiratory and

immune systems. The hotel has a bar and restaurant.

🕒 Mon–Sat 8–1, 3–6 💶 €60 for a 50-minute massage, weekend packages of six treatments start at €279 🚗 7km (4 miles) from Pisa on the Brennero Road (SS12) towards Lucca

🕸 ARSENALE MEDICI
Lungarno Simonelli, 56100 Pisa
Tel 050 21441

Occupying a 12th-century Medici storehouse along the Arno, the Arsenale Medici houses 12 Roman wooden ships, one of which dates back to the first century BC. Many of the ships' contents are also on display, including clay vases, skeletons and vessels containing wine, olives and walnuts some 20 centuries old. Credit cards are not accepted.

🕒 Tue–Sun 10–6 ✋ Adult €3, child €2

🕸 MUSEO DI STORIA NATURALE E DEL TERRITORIO
Via Roma 103, 56011 Calci
Tel 050 937751

Journey into the lives and secrets of all kinds of animals in this former convent. Skeletons of marine mammals hang from invisible wires, while models of dolphins and killer and sperm whales lines in the long corridor. There are also 19th-century stuffed amphibians, reptiles, mammals and birds, many rare or extinct. Credit cards are not accepted.

🕒 Tue–Sat 9–5, Sun 10–6 ✋ Adult €5, child (6–18) €2.50, under 6 free 🚌 SS12 to Lucca, then turn off to the right at San Giuliano Terme

PISTOIA

🏛 BRUNO CORSINI
Piazza San Francesco 42, 51100 Pistoia
Tel 0573 20138

They have been making chocolates here since 1918 and there's a tempting range to try, including chocolates with chili peppers. Handmade personalized Easter eggs can be ordered, and you can watch Corsini's hedgehog confetti or

snowballs being made from hard spun sugar.

🕒 Mon–Sat 8–1, 4–7.30; closed 9–26 Aug

🏛 FIASCHI
Via Atto Vannucci 20, 51100 Pistoia
Tel 0573 31701

Pistoia is famous for its textiles and Fiaschi has a wide range of household linens with fine hand-embroidered tablecloths, napkins and silk and pure cotton nightgowns. Children's clothes are available too, and a selection of boxes decorated with lace and ribbons. Nearly all the stock is made locally.

🕒 Tue–Sat 9–1, 3.30–7.30, Mon 3.30–7.30; closed Aug

Treat yourself to something sweet

TIRRENIA

🕸 CICLILANDIA
Piazza dei Fiori, 56018 Tirrenia
Tel 050 33573
www.ciclilandia.it

Ciclilandia (Cycleland) is one of Tuscany's more unusual amusement parks: mountain bikes, cycle-carriages, cycle go-carts, and cycling lessons for youngsters, all watched over by traffic police. The Pirates' Castle has a different kind of fun with its tunnels, bridges, slides and rubber forests. Credit cards are not accepted.

🕒 Daily 9–midnight, mid-Jun to mid-Sep; Mon–Sat 2.30–7.30, Sun 10–12.30, 2.30–7.30, rest of year ✋ Entrance is free, bike rental €3.60 for half an hour

🕸 PARCO GIOCHI FANTASILANDIA
Viale Tirreno, 42, 56018 Tirrenia
Tel 050 30326

Split into two sections, Fantasy Land has a free area with electric car track, miniature train and mechanical bull. The other section has waterslides and swings. There's also a park specifically equipped for young children, with tricycles and pedal cars, and picnic tables. Credit cards are not accepted.

🕒 Mon–Fri 2.30–dusk, Sat–Sun 8.30–dusk, Mar–end Sep ✋ Paying section: Joint adult and child €4 🚗 Take the Pisa Centro exit on A12, then follow signs to Tirrenia

VIAREGGIO

🏛 GABRIEL CRYSTALS
Viale Carducci 23b, 55049 Viareggio
Tel. 0584 430335
www.gabrielcrystals.com

A dazzling collection of glass and crystal is displayed in this large showroom, with a fountain in the middle. There's beautiful hand-blown glass from Murano and crystal from France and Bohemia.

🕒 Daily 10–1, 5–midnight, Easter–end Oct; Tue–Sat 9.30–1, 3.30–8, Sun 3.30–8, rest of year

🏛 MERCATO DI VIAREGGIO
Piazza Cavour, 55049 Viareggio

Large, partially covered market that has a fresh fish section with produce straight from the Versilia Coast. Stands in the central covered section sell a vast selection of shoes. Most stands are there daily, but the main market day is Thursday.

🕒 Daily dawn–dusk

🕸 VIAREGGIO BEACH

There are miles of wide sandy beach at Viareggio, and the long promenade has plenty of places to buy a refreshing ice cream. If you want to get away from the sun, take refuge in the pine-shaded park, Pineta di Ponente. See pages 111 and 154 for more information.

🕒 Daily dawn–dusk ✋ Charges to use certain areas of the beach apply

WHAT TO DO

FEBRUARY/MARCH

VIAREGGIO CARNEVALE
February and March
Piazza Mazzini 22 c/o Palazzo delle
Muse, 55049 Viareggio
Tel 0584 962568
www.viareggio.ilcarnevale.com
Viareggio's carnival is among
Italy's biggest and best, with
floats holding 200 people that
wend their way along the
waterfront four Sundays in a
row. Gigantic moving puppets
portray current events and
poke fun at famous people.
It's all accompanied by music,
dancing and food, and the
National Lottery awards a
huge prize to the best float.
🖐 Free 🚆 Trains run from Pisa to
Viareggio every hour 🚗 Take the
Versilia exit off A12

JUNE/JULY/AUGUST

A CORTO DI CINEMA
Second week in June
Cinema Italia, Via Biscione 32,
55100 Lucca
Tel 0583 467264
www.cinefestival.it/acortodicinema
This festival of short films is
open to professional and
amateur film directors of all
nationalities, with a €600
top prize. All films have
English subtitles and the
shortlisted films are shown at
the Cinema Italia before the
winner is announced.
🖐 Free

PALIO DI SAN RANIERI
17 June
Tel 050 560464 (Pisa Tourist Board)
www.comune.pisa.it
A race on the River Arno is
held in celebration of Pisa's
patron saint. The teams
consist of eight oarsmen, a
steersman and a climber who
races to the top of a 10m-high
(33ft) mast with the winning
banner at the finish. The race
can be seen along the Arno
between the railway bridge
and the Palazzo Medici. Try
to get a spot at the Palazzo

Medici for the mast-climbing
finale.

**LUMINARIA AND GIOCO
DEL PONTE**
Last Sunday in June
Pisa
Pisa's main festival focuses
on tug-of-war games between
12 teams from the north and
south banks of the River Arno,
who push a 7-tonne carriage
over the Ponte di Mezzo—
while dressed in Renaissance
costumes. The highlight of the
Luminaria are the blazing
torches that light the houses
and streets on either side of
the river.

**OPERA, THEATRE AND MUSIC
FESTIVAL**
15 June to 15 July
Tel 0583 493040
www.ccm.uc.edu/lucca
Summer sees the squares,
churches and halls of Lucca
filled with sounds by some of
the world's best amateur and
semi-professional singers and
musicians. It is sponsored by
the Music College of the
University of Cincinnati.
🖐 Most concerts free; opera €15

SUMMER FESTIVAL LUCCA
July
Piazza Napoleone and Piazza
Anfiteatro, 55100 Lucca
Tel 0584 46477
www.summer-festival.com
Past acts at the Lucca
Summer Festival, one of
Tuscany's most popular music
festivals, have included Paul
Simon, David Bowie, Oasis
and Rod Stewart. There are
plenty of Italian bands too.
🖐 Adult €5–€20, child €3–€15

FESTIVAL PUCCINI
July and August
Teatro all'Aperto, 55048 Torre del Lago
Puccini, Lucca
Tel 0584 359322
www.puccinifestival.it
Just a few steps from Villa

*Tosca, performed at the
Puccini Festival*

Puccini (where Giacomo
Puccini wrote his most
famous works), Torre del
Lago's opera festival draws
40,000 spectators every year
to its performances of Puccini
classics.
🖐 €29–€95 🚗 A20, just outside
Lucca on A11/SS1

BARGA JAZZ FESTIVAL
Last week in August
Barga and Lucca
Tel 0583 711044
www.bargajazz.com
This international festival
revolves around a jazz orches-
tra competition. Performances
are held at the Teatro dei
Differenti and on Piazza
Angelio in Barga as well as in
Lucca's Palazzo Ducale and in
Castelnuovo Garfagnana's
Piazza Umberto.
🖐 Adult €10, child €7.50 🚗 Barga

SEPTEMBER

LUMINARIA DI SANTA CROCE
13 September
Lucca
Lucca's treasured *Volto Santo*
(believed to be a true effigy
of Christ) is carried in procession through the candlelit
streets of the town. The statue
is adorned with silver slippers
and a diamond-studded
crown, and the whole town
turns out in homage to
the effigy.

SIENA

Locally produced items should be high on the shopping list in Siena, a prosperous city whose shops cater equally to visitors, locals and students. This is reflected in the entertainment, which ranges from classical concerts to funky student clubs. Siena's great festival is the *Palio*, but your visit may coincide with a smaller festival, with flag-throwing and costumed processions, at any time of year.

KEY TO SYMBOLS

- Shopping
- Entertainment
- Nightlife
- Sports
- Activities
- Health and Beauty
- For Children

SHOPPING

ART AND ANTIQUES

ANTICHITÀ MONNA AGNESE
Via di Città 99, 53100
Tel 0577 280205
One of Siena's better antiques stores, stocking furniture and silver amid other items. There is another, smaller shop on the opposite side of the street at No. 45, which deals in antique jewellery.
Mon–Sat 10–1, 4–7.30

BOOKS

LIBRERIA SENESE
Via di Città 62–66, 53100
Tel 0577 280845
Libreria Senese has a good selection of English-language books and magazines, including local guides. For a memento of your visit, you might want to pick up one of the many glossy picture books on Tuscany and Italy.
Mon–Sat 9–8, Sun 10–8

FASHION

CORTECCI ABBIGLIAMENTO
Via Banchi di Sopra 27, 53100
Tel 0577 280096
www.corteccisiena.it
The two branches of this shop stock a large collection of men's and women's designer labels including Gucci, Armani, Yves Saint Laurent, Christian Dior, Roberto Cavalli and Dolce & Gabana. This branch has the more classic collections, while the other branch, at Il Campo 30, stocks labels aimed at a younger market.
Tue–Sat 9.30–1, 3.30–8, Mon 3.30–8

TESSUTI A MANO
Via San Pietro 7, 53100
Tel 0577 282200
Drop into this workshop and boutique to pick up beautiful, hand-woven accessories and fashionable garments. Designer Floretta Bacci can often be found sitting at a pair of large looms, weaving her incredible, much sought-after scarves, shawls and items of clothing.
Mon–Sat 10.30–7

FOOD AND DRINK

ANTICA SALUMERIA SALVINI
Località Costafabbri, on SS73 Ponente 46, 53100 Siena
Tel 0577 394399
A traditional Sienese delicatessen selling home-made products that are mainly organic or additive free. Many of the goods are made according to local recipes and methods. Stock up from a wide selection of sausages and cooked meats, cheeses and wines. You can also sample the produce.
Mon–Sat 7.30–2, 5–8 On the SS73; follow the signs from Siena to Soricille and Follonica and Costafabbri is 2km (1.2 miles) from Siena

WHAT TO DO

DROGHERIA MANGANELLI
Via di Città 71, 53100
Tel 0577 280002
A must for gourmets. It is a member of the Slow Food Movement, an organization that promotes organic food, grown and cooked using traditional methods. Drogheria Manganelli has been selling local produce since 1879, including cured meats, cheeses, vinegars, wine, olive oil, *ricciarelli* (almond cookies), home-made cakes and pasta sauces.
🕐 Mon–Sat 9–8

MORBIDI
Via Banchi di Sopra 75, 53100
Tel 0577 280268
One of the best-known Sienese delicatessens, Morbidi sells Tuscan salamis and the more unusual *finochiona* (salami made with fennel). Try one of the local cheeses such as pecorino or the oval-shaped *fresco di Monnalisa*. Other possible picnic ingredients are artichoke pâté and various cooked vegetables and pastas.
🕐 Mon–Sat 9–8

OPIFICIO DEL BOSCO DI GROSSO MARIA
Podere Porcignano 100, 53030
Radicondoli
Tel 0577 793134
www.opificiodelbosco.com
This family-run business in the Chianti hills, just off the road to Follonica, produces jams, oils and spirits. Using traditional methods and local ingredients, many of which are gathered from the local woods, the products are wholesome and delicious. The store is also a member of the Slow Food Movement (see Drogheria Manganelli). Sample the food in the adjacent restaurant.
🕐 Wed–Mon 9–9 🚗 In the Parco delle Carline on SS73 west of Siena towards Follonica

PASTICCERIA LE CAMPANE
Via delle Campane 9, 53100
Tel 0577 282290
A bakery known for its Sienese cakes and sweets: The fragrant, freshly baked *ricciarelli* (almond cookies) are the star attraction. From September to November the family bakes *pan co'santi* (fruitcake); their excellent *cantucci* (almond cookies traditionally served with sweet wine) are enjoyed year round.
🕐 Mon–Tue, Thu–Sat 8–1.30, 5–8, Wed, Sun 8–1.30

TERRE DI SIENA
Via Duprè 32, 53100
Tel 0577 223528
This delightful little shop is off the beaten track and popular with locals because of the

Drogheria Manganelli is a great place to pick up food items

value for money it gives. A wide range of local wines, cheeses, salami, oil, honey, sweetmeats, pasta, jams and conserves are on sale. Tastings of these local products are organized downstairs in the cellar, and locally made crystal glasses and terracotta dishes are also for sale.
🕐 Daily 10–7.30

GIFTS

CERAMICHE ARTISTICHE SANTA CATERINA
Via di Città 74, 53100
Tel 0577 283098
A family business run by the founder, Marcello Neri, his wife and son. The family works in the traditional Sienese style of ceramics using only black, white and *terra di Siena*, or 'burnt siena' glazes. Their art is inspired by the local architecture, especially the Duomo, and you can watch them at work in their studio at Via Mattioli 12.
🕐 Daily 9.30–8

HOME FURNISHINGS

SIENA RICAMA
Via di Città 61, 53100 Siena
Tel 0577 288339
This embroidery and needlepoint shop is run by Signora Fontani, who makes all the goods herself. Drawing inspiration from medieval designs, local art, frescoes and manuscripts, the embroidered or cross-stitched items include clothing, soft furnishings, lampshades and tapestries.
🕐 Mon–Fri 9.30–1, 2.30–7, Sat 9.30–1

🎵 **ENTERTAINMENT**

CINEMA

MODERNO
Via Calzoleria 44, 53016 Siena
Tel 0577 289201
This single-screen cinema shows the latest releases in their original language. Most films come from Hollywood and are screened in English. There is no bar or refreshments, and credit cards are not accepted.
🕐 Closed Jul, Aug 💰 Adult €6.70, child €4.65

THEATRE

TEATRO DEI RINNOVATI
Palazzo Comunale Piazza Il Campo, 53100
Tel 0577 292265
www.comune.siena.it
Rinnovati is one of Siena's most popular theatres. From November to March it focuses on touring theatre productions, live music and orchestras. Credit cards are not accepted.
💰 €5–€37

TEATRO DEI ROZZI

Piazza Indipendenza 15, 53100
Tel 0577 46960
www.comune.siena.it

This restored theatre in the Accademia Rozzi stages dance, opera and drama productions during the winter season, November to April. Credit cards are not accepted.

👋 €5–€37

👁 NIGHTLIFE

BIRRERIA IL BARONE ROSSO

Via dei Termini 9, 53100
Tel 0577 286686
www.barone-rosso.com

Providing food, drink and live music in the heart of Siena's medieval streets, lively Il Barone Rosso is a popular haunt for Sienese beer drinkers, with Guinness on tap. Credit cards are not accepted.

🕐 Daily 9pm–3am

ENOTECA I TERZI

Via dei Termini 7, 53100
Tel 0577 44329

Lively bar in a gorgeous building that attracts the crowds all afternoon and evening. There's a small but comprehensive selection of Italian and international wines, a lunch menu and snack food.

🕐 Mon–Sat 12.30–3, 6–11

L'OFFICINA

Piazza del Sale 3, 53100
Tel 0577 286301

There's live music here on Thursdays, with various DJs playing all sorts from salsa to house music, the rest of the week. The bar stocks more than 900 varieties of beer, and there are TVs screening sports. Credit cards are not accepted.

🕐 Daily 8pm–3am

🟢 SPORTS AND 🟢 ACTIVITIES

STADIO COMUNALE

Via Mille 3, 53100
Tel 0577 280937

Crowded with passionate and vocal residents on match days,

this soccer ground is home to AC Siena. The less expensive seats are in the *Curva Robur* and *Curva San Domenica*—the two 'curves' or stands at the end of the stadium behind the goals.

🕐 Season: end Aug–end May
👋 Men €22, women €16.50, child (10–14) €16.50, under 10 free; most expensive seat is €190

PISCINA DI SIENA

Località Acquacalda, 53100
Tel 0577 271567

This is an open air pool where you can cool off after a hard day's sightseeing.

🕐 Daily 9.30–7, Jun–end Aug
👋 Adult €5.20, child €3.10

JULY/AUGUST

SETTIMANE MUSICALE

July
Tel 0577 22091
www.chigiana.it

A prestigious classical music festival run by the Accademia Chigiana, Siena's renowned conservatoire. Concerts take place all over the city, and the festival usually includes a major opera production.

IL PALIO

2 July and 16 August
Il Campo, 53100 Siena
Headquarters: Piazza Gramsci 7, 53100
Tel 0577 280551
www.ilpaliodisiena.com

The *Palio*—a bareback horse race around the Campo in Siena in honour of the Virgin Mary—is arguably Italy's most famous festival. The high speed, confined space and lack of rules make it hazardous for horse and rider alike, but exhilarating for spectators. The race is over in a moment, but it takes weeks to prepare the accompanying pageantry, feasting and drama. This is a festival the

Sienese are immensely proud of, evoking passion on an extraordinary scale.

👋 Free

SIENA JAZZ

July 24 to August 7
Fortezza Medicea Anfiteatro, 53100
Tel 0577 271401
www.sienajazz.it

Since 1977 Siena Jazz has presented jazz performances, seminars and master classes. Concerts are held in Piazza il Campo, Enoteca Italiana and Piazza Jacopo della Quercia.

👋 Free

SEPTEMBER

TERRE DI SIENA

26–29 September
Cinema Nuovo Pendola, Via S. Quirico 13, 53016
Tel 0577 43012
www.sienafilmfestival.it

This international film festival screens two films per night for three nights at the end of September. These are mostly art-house films, some of which are in English. Credit cards are not accepted.

👋 Adult €6.20, child €4.65

⊗ FOR CHILDREN

MUSEO DEL BOSCO DI ORGIA

Località Borgolozzi, Fraz. Orgia, 53010 Sovicille
Tel 0577 342097

Children enjoy Siena's Museum of the Woods, with its presentation of items used by the people who once lived in the nearby woodlands and their folk stories. Walks and trails provide an introduction to the animals (such as wild boars) and vegetation of the forest. Credit cards are not accepted.

🕐 Fri–Sat 9.30–12.30; other days by request only 👋 Adult €2, child €1
🚗 15-minute drive from Siena on SS73, then onto SS37 and SP52 to Sovicille

SOUTHERN TUSCANY

WHAT TO DO

Southern Tuscany's the area to track down local produce and crafts, and you'll find plenty in hill towns such as San Gimignano, Montepulciano, Montalcino and Pienza. Arezzo is good for mainstream shopping, as well as some excellent music and festivals, most of which you'll find throughout the area in summer, while the beautiful countryside has excellent outdoor opportunities.

KEY TO SYMBOLS	
🌐	**Shopping**
🎭	**Entertainment**
🍸	**Nightlife**
⚽	**Sports**
✪	**Activities**
♡	**Health and Beauty**
✾	**For Children**

AREZZO

🌐 ALMA BARDI ANTICHITÀ
Corso Italia 97, 52100 Arezzo
Tel 0575 20640
In a town well known for its antiques, Alma Bardi Antichità and its silver and jewels attract a loyal following of customers searching for something different. You will find reasonably priced items perfect for gifts and mementos.
🕐 Tue–Sun 9–1, 3–7, Mon 3–7

🌐 L'ALVEARE
Via Niccolò Aretino 19, 52100 Arezzo
Tel 0575 20769
This tiny store specializes in local produce. As its name suggests (l'alveare means 'beehive') the shop sells neatly packaged Aretine honey. Arezzo is part of a beekeeping region that stretches from Arezzo to Grosseto and produces delicious honey of fine quality.
🕐 Tue–Sat 9–1, 4–8, Mon 4–8

🌐 LA BELLE EPOQUE
Piazza San Francesco 18, 52100 Arezzo
Tel 0575 355495
La Belle Epoque deals exclusively in antique fabrics. The fragile laces and embroidered linens are dainty and make exquisite decorative items.
🕐 Mon–Sat 10–1, 5–8

🌐 DA ARETÈ
Piazza Grande 38, 52100 Arezzo
Tel 0575 352803
www.areteterracotte.it
This busy ceramics shop sells a vast range of local terracotta, as well as arts and crafts. Look for the beautifully decorated, minuscule copies of Aretine buildings in terracotta, which make great gifts of Arezzo.
🕐 Daily 9.30–7.30, Easter–end Oct; Tue–Sun 10.30–7.30, rest of year

🌐 EMPORIO ARMANI
Corso Italia 306, 52100 Arezzo
Tel 0575 355262
This is a popular branch of Emporio Armani with prices at an appealing 30 per cent discount compared with prices overseas. Some of the fashion items are discounted by as much as 70 per cent during the sales.
🕐 Mon 4–8, Tue–Sat 9–1, 4–8, first Sun of month 9–1, 4–8

🌐 FIERA ANTIQUARIA
Piazza San Francesco, 52100 Arezzo
One of Italy's leading antiques fairs, Fiera Antiquaria spills across Piazza San Francesco, Piazza Grande and the Logge Vasari. With more than 600 dealers, there are items ranging from 19th-century furniture to 17th-century glass and objects dating back to the Renaissance. The fair appeals to serious collectors as well as browsing visitors.
🕐 First Sun of the month 7.30–7, Apr–end Sep; 7.30–3, rest of year

GRACE GALLERY

Via Cavour 30, 52100 Arezzo
Tel 0575 354963

Grace Gallery has pride of place among the many antiques shops that line Arezzo's cobbled side streets. Specializing in furnishings and paintings, it also has a superb array of trompe l'oeil curiosities, bronzes and eccentricities. Browsers are welcome. There is also a second branch at Piazza Grande 30.

🕐 Mon–Sat 9–1, 3–7, Sun 9–12

PANE E SALUTE

Corso Italia 11, 52100 Arezzo
Tel 0575 20657

Come here for the bakery's *focaccia*, available in plain, wholegrain or olive. The deliciously light olive oil bread is perfect for picnic lunches. A round, flat loaf called *pane medieval* is the house classic.

🕐 Mon–Sat 7.30–1.30, 4–8

TESSITURA ARTIGIANA CASENTINESE

Via Sanarelli 49, 52017 Stia
Tel 0575 583659
www.tacs.it

A big retail outlet and factory where you can purchase locally produced fashions made from Casentino (the mountainous area nearby) textiles, and watch their 13 phases of production. The scarves make excellent gifts.

🕐 Mon–Fri 9–12, 2–6, Sat 9–12
🚌 Take SS71 Umbria Casentinese road northwest towards Bibbiena, then follow signs for Stia

EDEN

Via Guadagnoli 2, 52100 Arezzo
Tel 0575 353364

This popular cinema is famous for its role in Roberto Benigni's *Life is Beautiful* (▷ 273). Most films are screened in the original language with subtitles. A bar sells drinks and snacks. Credit cards are not accepted.

🖐 Adult €6.50, child €4

JOLLY

Via del Trionfo 27, 52100 Arezzo
Tel 0575 910395

Jolly is a multi-screen cinema showing the latest blockbusters. Most of the films are screened in their original language with subtitles. There's also a bar serving drinks and snacks. Credit cards are not accepted.

🖐 Adult €6.50, child €4

TEATRO PETRARCA

Via Guido Monaco 8/14, 52100 Arezzo
Tel 0575 23975

Named after Arezzo's most famous poet and scholar, Teatro Petrarca is renowned for its perfect acoustics and its

The monthly antiques market in Arezzo

performances of theatre, opera, ballet and classical music. Europe's largest choir competition, Guido d'Arezzo, takes place here at the end of August. Credit cards are not accepted.

🖐 Adult €11–€26, child €9–€21

GRACE

Via Madonna del Prato 125, 52100 Arezzo
Tel 0575 403669
www.grace.it

Run by three friends, this trendy club and sushi restaurant has an interior verging on the kitsch, with art deco seating and 1970s lighting. A variety of theme nights

includes performances by local acts. Credit cards are not accepted.

🕐 Fri–Sat 12.30am–5am 🖐 €16

LA FERROVIA ITALIANA

Piazza della Repubblica 1/a, 52100 Arezzo
Tel 0575 39881
www.trenitalia.com

The LFI (La Ferrovia Italiana) railway, with its fleet of electric locomotives, links Arezzo with Stia, Bibbiena and Sinalunga. Take a ride for wonderful views over the surrounding countryside. If you are in the area at the right time, try to reserve seats on a steam train (tel 0575 300712, usually May and Sep, €35).

🕐 Mon–Sat 16 services a day, Sun 4 services a day 🖐 €1–€2.60, depending on distance

SKATERPARK DI AREZZO

Calamandrei Industrial Estate, Via Ferraris, 52100 Arezzo

This skate park, 3km (2 miles) from downtown Arezzo, welcomes anyone who turns up. Locals come here to skateboard, rollerblade and BMX bike on the numerous multi-purpose ramps.

🕐 Daylight hours 🖐 Free

BUONCONVENTO

BOTTEGA DEL PANE

Via Roma 36, 53022 Buonconvento
Tel 0577 809016
www.dolcezzedinanni.com

The staff here are proud to tell you how they supply the Queen of England at Christmas with their freshly baked Tuscan goodies, such as *cantucci* (hard almond cookies for dunking in the sweet wine Vin Santo), *ricciarelli* (soft almond cookies) and *panforte* (fruitcake) in various flavours. The unusual *amaretti* (macaroons) flavoured with lemon, orange or coffee are definitely worth a try.

🕐 Mon–Sat 7.30–1, 5–7.30

🏛 IL POZZO DI SANTA LUCIA

Via Roma 42, 53022 Buonconvento
Tel 0577 809090
A carefully chosen selection of household furnishings, super-sharp cooking knives, a variety of cooking utensils carved in olive wood, candles, tableware and bright ceramics can be found here: all perfect for gifts.
🕐 Mon–Sat 9.30–1, 4–8

CHIANTI

🏛 ENOTECA DEL CHIANTI CLASSICO

Ptta S. Croce 8, 50022 Greve in Chianti
Tel 055 853297
www.chianticlassico.it
This well-established wine shop in Greve, capital of Chianti Classico, has a series of small rooms filled with bottles on wooden shelves. On display are 300 different examples of Chianti Classico, as well as a large selection of Super Tuscans and other Tuscan wines like the sweet Vin Santo.
🕐 Daily 9.30–1, 3–7.30, May–end Oct; Thu–Tue 9.30–1, 3–7.30, rest of year

🏛 MANIERA

Fornance di Meleto, 53013 Gaiole in Chianti
Tel 0577 744023
www.maniera.it
American John Ryan and his Italian wife Daniela Tozzi display their fine handcrafted Tuscan goods in a converted old brick kiln—household linens, pottery, wooden furniture, glass, tableware, table silver from Florence, travertine marble plates and bowls, brass door knockers and fashion accessories. Special orders can be arranged.
🕐 Daily 10–7, Mar–end Sep; 10–6, Oct–7 Jan; closed 8 Jan–end Feb
🚌 1km (0.5 miles) from Gaiole just off the Siena road SS408; take turning to Rietine and Maniera is on the right after 500m (545 yards)

CORTONA

🏛 IL COCCIAIO

Via Nazionale 56, 52044 Cortona
Tel 0575 604405
www.terrabruga.com

One of Cortona's oldest and most creative ceramics shops is full of locally produced terracotta. The brilliant yellow sunflowers that blanket the local fields in summer are rendered on the best-selling ceramic pieces.
🕐 Daily 10–1, 3–8

🏛 IL GIRASOLE

Via Casali 2/4, 52044 Cortona
Tel 0575 601616
www.il-girasole.com
Il Girasole sells Tuscan arts and crafts. Owner Alessandra Federici scours the countryside to gather her stock of gifts and housewares from makers around the region. You will

The pretty Isola d'Elba is known for its minerals

find ceramics, bronze and jewellery among the local crafts represented.
🕐 Daily 9.30–7.30

🏛 LORENZINI

Piazza Repubblica 18, 52044 Cortona
Tel 0575 603296
A wonderful collection of hats for ladies and gentlemen—warm felts for the winter and straw hats for the summer. Many are by Borsalino, a famous name in Italy. You'll also find a big range of umbrellas and shoes.
🕐 Daily 9.30–8, May–end Sep; 10–1, 2.30–7.30, Mar–end May, Oct–end Dec; closed Jan–end Feb

ISOLA D'ELBA

🏛 GIANNINI

Viale Italia 2, 57036 Porto Azzurro, Isola d'Elba
Tel 0565 95307
Elba is famous for its minerals, which are still mined and worked here. This big show-room displays an amazing collection of objects made from stones, crystals and semi-precious gemstones, including jewellery and ornaments such as little carved animals and crystal trees.
🕐 Daily 9–midnight, May to mid-Oct; 9–1, 3–7, rest of year

🏛 MUTI E LUPI

Via Palestro 13, 57038 Rio Marina, Isola d'Elba
Tel 0565 962304
This is where you'll find the true original version of *schiaccia briaca*, an olive oil bread made with dried fruits and pine nuts, with the addition of some of the local wine, Aleatica, to give it its name and red appearance. The wine itself is also sold here, along with other home-made breads and cakes.
🕐 Daily 7.15–1.30, 4–8.30, Jun–end Sep; Mon–Sat 7.15–1.30, rest of year

MONTALCINO

🏛 ENOTECA LA FORTEZZA DI MONTALCINO

Piazzale Fortezza, 53024 Montalcino
Tel 0577 849077
www.enotecalafortezza.it
In this wine bar and shop inside the courtyard of the medieval fort, you can sample a glass of the famous local red wine, Brunello, with some simple food—cold meats or cheese with hunks of crusty bread—while gentle music plays in the background. More than 125 producers of Brunello are represented here, along with other Tuscan and national wines. Wine and olive oil tastings can be arranged. The least expensive glass of Brunello is €6.
🕐 Daily 9–8, Apr–end Oct; 9–6, rest of year

LE TELE ANTICHE
Via Mazzini 27, 53024 Montalcino
Tel 0577 849338
www.LeAnticheTele.com
Beautiful fabrics for household
furnishings and linens are still
handwoven in the traditional
way in various parts of
Tuscany, and here a tempting
range is attractively displayed.
Owner Alexia, a skilled needle-
woman, will sew to order and
ship worldwide.
🕐 Tue–Sun 9.30–1, 4.30–8,
Easter–end Nov; closed Sun Dec–
Easter and May 27 to Jun 7

VILLA I CIPRESSI
Via Ricasoli 26, 53024 Montalcino
Tel 0577 848019
www.villacipressi.lt
Beekeeper Hubert Ciacci
has beehives on his nearby
estate, and his mother runs
this little retail outlet selling
their products: honey, candles,
cosmetics, soaps and various
delicious foods based on
honey.
🕐 Daily 10–8, Mar–end Nov; Sat–Sun
only, rest of year

MONTEPULCIANO

BOTTEGA DEL RAME
Via dell'Opio nel Corso 64, 53045
Montepulciano
Tel 0578 717038
Three generations of the
Mazzetti family have been
making copper kitchen utensils
and decorative items—as you
can see in their workshop
near the shop at Piazza Teatro
4. They also sell lamps and
walking sticks with unusual
handles. Tax free shopping
and worldwide shipping
can be arranged for non-EU
customers.
🕐 Daily 9.30–1, 2.30–7.30

CANTINA DEL REDI
Via di Collazzi 5, 53045 Montepulciano
Tel 0578 757166
www.cantinadelredi.com
Look for the sign outside the
Palazzo Redi on Via Ricci gia
della Mercanzia, which leads
to the top entrance of this
cantina (wine cellar). Follow

the ramp winding through the
cellars dating from 3,000 years
ago, carved out of the rock. In
the dim light you can see the
huge oak barrels filled with
the famous local wine—Vino
Nobile di Montepulciano—
which you can taste when
you arrive at the bottom.
🕐 Daily 10.30–1, 3–7, mid-Mar to end
Dec; Sat–Sun, 10.30–1, 3–7, rest of year
✋ Free

MALEDETTI TOSCANI
Via di Voltaia nel Corso 40, 53045
Montepulciano
Tel 06578 757130
This spacious shop not only
sells newspapers, but leather
goods to die for: a big range of

*Wine-tasting and buying wine
are popular in Montalcino*

albums and assorted books
bound in heavy leather and a
collection of luggage to last a
lifetime. It also sells pens, ink,
seals and wax and photo-
graphs of the surrounding
countryside.
🕐 Daily 7am–10pm, Mar–end Oct;
7am–1pm, rest of year

MONTEVARCHI

PRADA FACTORY OUTLET
Località Levanella SS 69, 52025
Montevarchi
Tel 055 919 6528
Montevarchi is home to the
Prada factory and its bargain
outlet: bags, ties, lingerie and
shoes at discounts of as much
as 80 per cent. When you

arrive, take a ticket from the
machine and wait your turn to
enter. If you can't find what
you want in the Prada range,
the store also stocks Miu Miu,
Helmut Lang and Jil Sander.
🕐 Mon–Sat 9.30–7.30, Sun 2–7.30
🚃 Turn off A1 at junction Valdarno
and follow the signs

PIENZA

BOTTEGA DEL NATURISTA
Corse Il Rossellino 16, 53026 Pienza
Tel 0578 748081
You'll be offered tastings of
pecorino in this shop, the
locally produced cheese made
with sheep's milk. There are
many varieties, but look out for
two in particular: a soft fresh
type or a more mature one,
sometimes seasoned in wine,
or wrapped in walnut leaves
and ashes. When you've made
your selection, they'll vacuum-
pack your purchases. There
is also a tempting range of
honey, dried herbs, vinegars
and locally produced salamis
and cured meats.
🕐 Daily 9.30–7

BOTTEGA ARTIGIANA
DEL CUOIO
Corso Il Rossellino 58, 53026 Pienza
Tel 0578 748730
Owner Valerio Truffelli sews
all his leather goods by hand
in his little shop. He makes
almost anything to order,
but you can buy ready-made
belts, purses and notebooks.
The cowhide skins come from
near Pisa, an area famous for
tanning. A man's belt will cost
you in the region of €27.
🕐 Mon–Sat 9.30–1, 3–8, Sun 9.30–1,
Easter–end Nov; daily 9.30–1, rest of
year

POPPI

PARCO ZOO DELLA
FAUNA EUROPEA
Zoo Fauna Europa, 52015 Poppi
Tel 0575 504541 or 504542
www.parcozoopoppi.it
Opened in 1972 by vet Dr.
Roberto Mattoni, this zoo
exhibits specifically European
animals, including deer,

wolves, bears, birds of prey, and species in danger of extinction, such as the Asinara donkey. There are also pony rides, a botanical garden and a children's play area to add to the experience. A restaurant, bar, picnic area and free parking are available. Credit cards are not accepted.

🕐 Daily 9–7 💵 Adult €5, child (3–11) €4.50 🚍 30-minute drive from Arezzo along SS71; follow signs for Bibbiena, then Parco Nazionale Casentinese or Parco Zoo Poppi

RAPOLANO TERME

🌀 ANTICA QUERCIOLAIA THERMAL BATHS
Via Trieste 22, 53040 Rapolano Terme
Tel 0577 724091
www.termeaq.it
Antica Querciolaia has been a spa resort since Etruscan times. Its spring provides thermal baths and an adjoining park with three open-air pools. You can watch the water erupting from the famous intermittent fountain every 10 minutes and try a mud wrap or inhalation treatment.

🕐 Daily 9–7 💵 €49 for a 1-hour treatment. Swimming pool: €11 Mon–Fri, €13 Sat–Sun 🚍 Rapolano is on the SS326; turn off at the A1 intersection Valdichiana and follow the signs

SAN GIMIGNANO

🏛 ANTICO LATTERIA
Via San Matteo 19, 53037
San Gimignano
Tel 0577 941952
The friendly, family-run 'Old Dairy' is known for its regional gastronomic delicacies and locally produced wines. It's an excellent place to get goodies for a picnic or to pick up gourmet food gifts.

🕐 Daily 9–7.30

🏛 BAR CAFFE GELATERIA COMBATTENTI
Via San Giovanni 124, 53037
San Gimignano
Tel 0577 940391
www.sangimignano.com/aco008e.htm
The self-proclaimed oldest bar in San Gimignano, this spot

has been a bar, café and meeting place since 1924. Try the vintage grappa from beautiful hand-blown glass bottles.
🕐 Tue–Sun 7am–1am

🏛 BAZAR DEI SAPORI
Via San Giovanni 8, 53037
San Gimignano
Tel 0577 942021
Saffron was originally cultivated in various parts of the Siena province between the 12th and 15th centuries, but was eventually abandoned in favour of more profitable crops. This is one of 20 shops that make up Associazione Il Croco, an organization that promotes this precious spice.

Pottery from Tinacci Tito & M. Grazia SNC

It is sold here in the raw form, along with other local produce such as ham.
🕐 Daily 9–8

🏛 CASE E COSE
Via San Giovanni 99, 53037
San Gimignano
Tel 0577 942116
On San Gimignano's main street, Case e Cose is filled with locally made arts and crafts. In addition to the ceramics, they sell bowls, chopping boards and other objects made from olive wood. The service is friendly and browsers are welcome.
🕐 Daily 9.30–7

🏛 TENUTA TORCIANO
Via Crocetta 18, Ulignano, 53030
San Gimignano
Tel 0577 950055
www.torciano.com
In the hills just outside San Gimignano, this shop is attached to a vineyard that has been run by the Giachi family since 1720. They have wine tastings and educational courses as well as selling their own olive oils. Try some local dishes with the excellent wine at the small restaurant.

🕐 Daily 9–12, 3–6 🚍 Exit Siena/Florence highway at Poggibonsi Nord and follow signs for San Gimignano; once out of Poggibonsi look for the signs to Ulignano; after 6km (4 miles) there will be signs for the shop itself

🏛 TINACCI TITO & M. GRAZIA SNC
Via San Giovanni 41/A, 53037
San Gimignano
Tel 0577 940345
www.tinacci.com
A large showroom of Tuscan arts, crafts and design, ranging from expensive objects to inexpensive gifts, all housed in renovated wine cellars in the old town. Choose from a wide range of ceramics, terracotta, wooden furniture and other items such as masks, religious articles and leather goods.
🕐 Daily 8–8

🎬 CINE ESTATE
Rocca di Montestaffoli, 53073
San Gimignano
Tel 0577 940008
On Saturdays and Sundays, and three nights a week, the public park hosts an outdoor cinema. Performances include Hollywood blockbusters and European art-house films in the original language.

🕐 Jun–end Aug; days vary 💵 Adult €6, child €5

🍸 AVALON
Viale Roma 135, 53037 San Gimignano
Tel 0577 940023
www.avalon-pub.com
Avalon appeals to all tastes with its *birreria* (pub), *enoteca*

WHAT TO DO

(wine bar) and pizzeria, spread across three buildings in the old town. There is occasional live music and entertaining karaoke nights.

⏱ Wed–Mon 12.30pm–2.30pm, 7pm–1.30am; pub only open 7pm–1.30am

⭐ COLLINE METALLIFERE

Tourist Office at Via Roncolla 38, 56045 Pomarance
Tel 0588 63187

The Colline Metallifere hill range, named after the rich deposits of iron, lead, copper and pyrite that give the area its unusual colour, has various walking and cycling routes which take you through gentle rolling countryside.

🚌 Take SS68 towards Volterra, turn right at Saline di Volterra onto SS439 towards Larderello

⭐ MUSEO CRIMINALE MEDIOEVALE

Via del Castello 1/3, 53037 San Gimignano
Tel 0577 942243

San Gimignano's Torture Museum is a rather gruesome presentation of a private collection of medieval instruments used for torture. All manner of items for all manner of misdeeds over the ages, including the Inquisition, are covered. Probably not for the fainthearted or very young. It's near the Piazza della Cisterna. Credit cards are not accepted.

⏱ Mon–Sat 10–7, Sun 10–8 ✋ Adult €8, child €5.50

⭐ MUSEO ORNITOLOGICO

Chiesa di San Francesco, Via Quercecchio, 53037 San Gimignano
Tel 0577 941388

This local ornithological collection showcases around 330 species of bird. It is particularly interesting for its presentation of extinct species and information on species on the verge of extinction. The owners have obviously put a lot of love and attention into this museum. Credit cards are not accepted.

⏱ Daily 11–8, Apr–end Sep ✋ Adult €1.50, child €1

SANSEPOLCRO

🏛 CASA DEL FORMAGGIO

Via Mazzini 88/a, 52037 Sansepolcro
Tel 0575 741222

Sansepolcro is renowned for its lace, its pasta and the artist Piero della Francesca, who was born here around 1420. However, no visit to the town is complete without stocking up on some fragrant pecorini (cheeses made from sheep's milk) at Casa del Formaggio in the middle of town.

⏱ Mon–Sat 8–1, 4.30–8; closed Wed pm

Craftsman at work with alabaster in Volterra

SATURNIA

💚 TERME DI SATURNIA

58050 Saturnia
Tel 0564 600311
www.termedisaturnia.it

The thermal spring water feeding the pools at a constant temperature of 37°C (99°F) is said to benefit skin conditions, and joint and muscular aches. You can get treatments and medical advice. There is also a gym with trained staff, snack bar and changing rooms.

⏱ Pool: daily 9.30–7.30, Apr–end Oct; 9.30–5.30, rest of year. Treatment centre: daily 8–9pm–booking advisable Sat and Sun (tel 0564 600301). Gym: daily 9–6.30 ✋ Entry €16 per day; sunbed €6.50; full body massage €80

SINALUNGA

🎭 CIRO PINSUTI TEATRO

Via Umberto I, 53048 Sinalunga
Tel 0577 631200
www.sinalunga.it/teatro

This small theatre, a copy of Milan's La Scala, is named after the best-known son of this well-preserved Etruscan town—the 19th-century composer Ciro Pinsuti. Local choirs, orchestras and jazz musicians perform here. Credit cards are not accepted, but you can reserve ahead.

⏱ Season: Nov–end Apr ✋ Adult €5–€12, child €8

TALLA

🏛 CASEIFICIO PRATOMAGNO

Via di Bicciano 29a, 52010 Talla
Tel 0575 597330
www.caseificiopratomagno.com

Just a 30-minute, picturesque drive from Arezzo, this shop in the town of Talla is worth the trip. They stock a range of pecorini (sheep's milk cheeses; from €8), extra virgin olive oils (from €6.50), honey (from €3.10), *prosciutto* (cured ham; from €10) and wines (from €3). Tours can be arranged.

⏱ Mon–Fri 9–1.30, 3–7.30, Sat 9–1.30

🚌 From Arezzo follow signs to Casentino then Talla, or from A1 intersection at Valdarno and again follow signs for Casentino then Talla

VOLTERRA

🏛 ENOTECA SCALI

Via Guarnacci 13, 56048 Volterra
Tel 0588 81170

Owner Massimo is passionate about wine and stocks more than 700, ranging from top-of-the-line to a simple bottle of Chianti to drink with a picnic lunch. There is also a wide selection of local cheeses, cured meats, salamis and fresh bread. Tempting jars fill the wooden shelves with balsamic vinegars, sauces, truffles and dried pasta, plus more than 80 different olive oils.

⏱ Daily 9–8, Mar–end Dec

FABULA ETRUSCA

Via Lungo le Mura del Mandorlo 10,
56048 Volterra
Tel 0588 87401
www.fabulaetrusca.it

Etruscan women loved their gold jewellery, and a *fabula* was the brooch that was used to hold together their clothes. Here their jewellery is copied in 18ct gold by a team of craftsmen working on the premises. Custom-made designs can be commissioned or there is a wide range of ready-made items, with prices ranging from €50 for earrings.

🕐 Daily 10–7, May–end Oct; Mon–Sat 10–7, rest of year

IL GIRASOLE

Via Buonparenti 15, 56048 Volterra
Tel 0588 85312

There's no sign outside but your eye will be caught by two brightly filled windows. Inside there are plenty of ideas for gifts. Children will love the locally made handcrafted wooden theatres and other toys. For adults there are photo frames, quill pens and inks, seals and sealing wax, stencils, paper goods and a range of aromatherapy products.

🕐 Mon–Sat 9–8, Jun–end Sep; 9–1 3.30–7, rest of year

ROSSI ALABASTRI

Via del Mandorlo, 56048 Volterra
Tel 0588 86133
www.rossialabastri.com

This is the oldest alabaster workshop in Volterra. This soft stone has been mined and worked here for more than 3,000 years. The Etruscans used it to carve their funerary urns, but now you can get anything from simple dishes to large statues that show off the marvellous translucent quality of the stone. Watch Rossi's craftsmen creating fine objects using traditional tools. Worldwide shipping can be arranged.

🕐 Mon–Sat 9–1, 2.30–6.30, Sun 9–1

WHAT TO DO

FESTIVALS AND EVENTS

MAY

MOSTRA DEL CHIANTI
Last Sunday in May for one week
Contact Tourist Office, Via Sonnino,
50025 Montespertoli
Tel 0571 657579

Montespertoli sits on a hill in the middle of the Chianti region and has spectacular views of Florence. One of the wine capitals of Tuscany, it is the perfect place to taste the best of the year's vintage. The Piazza San Pietro in the heart of the town is taken over by wine lovers and professional buyers who flock to this well-established event.

JUNE

ESTATE SAN GIMIGNANO
Mid-June to August
Piazza del Duomo 1, 53037
San Gimignano
Tel 0577 940008

A summer arts festival with good music, including open-air opera recitals, classical concerts and film screenings in the ruins of the Rocca fortress. See Cine Estate (▷ 188).
🖐 €14–€40

JULY

AREZZO WAVE
First week of July
Corso Italia 236, 52100 Arezzo
Tel 0575 911005
www.arezzowave.com

Arezzo Wave is one of Italy's most important and enduring rock festivals, which explains the 250,000-strong audience

it attracts. Around 150 different events take place during the week.
🖐 Free

VOLTERRA TEATRO
12–20 July
La Fortezza, 56048 Volterra
Tel 0588 80392
www.volterrateatro.it

Held in Volterra and the surrounding towns, this is Italy's leading avant-garde theatre festival. It includes experimental drama, dance and film, with a good variety of international acts performing in English.
🖐 Adult €10, child €8

AUGUST/SEPTEMBER

BRAVIO DELLE BOTTE
Last Sunday in August
www.valdichiana.it/montepulciano

This race, dating from 1372, sees a 2-man team from each of Montepulciano's eight *contrade* (districts) rolling 80kg (176lb) wine barrels, mainly uphill, through the town's streets to the Piazza Grande. Meanwhile there's plenty of dancing and drinking going on in the crowd that gathers to encourage the rollers.

GIOSTRA DEL SARACINO
Last Sunday in August and first Sunday in September
Piazza Grande, 52100 Arezzo
Tel 0575 377262
www.giostradelsaracino.arezzo.it

A vibrant medieval celebration of chivalry and jousting which can be traced back to the 14th century, when the Christian military carried out combat training for the Crusades. The four opposing teams from the four quarters of Arezzo (Crucifera, Foro, Sant'Andrea, Santo Spirito) compete for the Lancia d'Oro (the Golden Lance) trophy.
🖐 Free

This chapter describes six walks and three drives that explore the beautiful countryside and medieval towns of Tuscany. The location of each walk and drive is marked on the map on page 192, where you will also find the key to individual maps.

Out and About

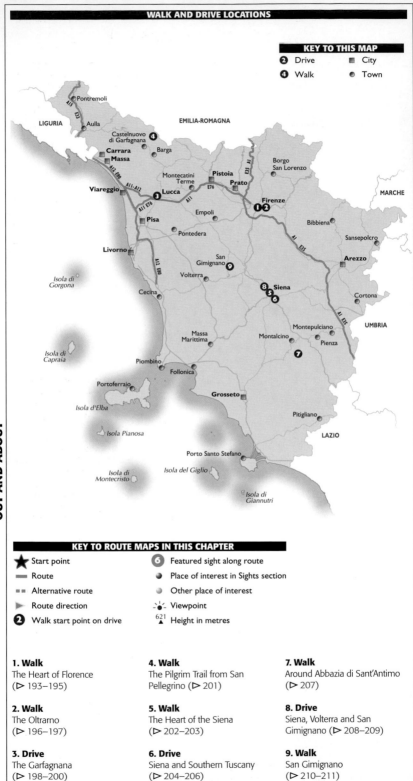

WALK AND DRIVE LOCATIONS

LIGURIA

Pontremoli

Aulla

Castelnuovo di Garfagnana **4**

Carrara

Massa

Barga

Viareggio

Montecatini Terme

3 Lucca

EMILIA-ROMAGNA

Pistoia

Prato

E76

A11

Borgo San Lorenzo

Firenze 12

MARCHE

Pisa

Empoli

Pontedera

Bibbiena

Sansepolcro

Livorno

Isola di Gorgona

San Gimignano **9**

Volterra

Cecina

8 9 5 6 Siena

Arezzo

Cortona

UMBRIA

Isola di Capraia

Massa Marittima

Montalcino

Montepulciano

Pienza

7

Piombino

Follonica

Portoferraio

Grosseto

Isola d'Elba

Isola Pianosa

Pitigliano

LAZIO

Porto Santo Stefano

Isola di Montecristo

Isola del Giglio

Isola di Giannutri

1. Walk
The Heart of Florence
(▷ 193–195)

2. Walk
The Oltrarno
(▷ 196–197)

3. Drive
The Garfagnana
(▷ 198–200)

4. Walk
The Pilgrim Trail from San
Pellegrino (▷ 201)

5. Walk
The Heart of the Siena
(▷ 202–203)

6. Drive
Siena and Southern Tuscany
(▷ 204–206)

7. Walk
Around Abbazia di Sant'Antimo
(▷ 207)

8. Drive
Siena, Volterra and San
Gimignano (▷ 208–209)

9. Walk
San Gimignano
(▷ 210–211)

OUT AND ABOUT

THE HEART OF FLORENCE

This walk starts and ends with two of Florence's great churches and is a good way to get a general feel for the city. Weaving in and out of the main visitor route, it takes in some of the lesser-known churches, palaces and small museums of the city's historic heart.

THE WALK

Distance:	2km (1.2 miles)
Allow:	1.5 hours
Start at:	Duomo
End at:	Piazza Santa Maria Novella

★ **Begin at Piazza del Duomo** (▷ 84–89), Florence's religious heart and one of the city's three main squares.

❶ The Piazza is home to Florence's Duomo, one of Italy's most familiar landmarks, while the Battistero holds a significant place in Florence's spiritual history. The views from the top of Giotto's campanile are spectacular. On the corner with Via de' Calzaiuoli is the 14th-century Loggia del Bigallo, built for the Misericordia, a charitable institution whose members cared for plague victims in the 13th and 14th centuries. The finely carved porch served as a drop-off point for unwanted babies.

On the southwest side of the square is Via de' Calzaiuoli (street of the shoemakers), built on the site of a Roman road. Follow this pedestrian-only, shop-lined street—the medieval city's main thoroughfare—to Piazza della Signoria, passing the unusual church of Orsanmichele (▷ 79) on your right along the way.

Piazza della Signoria (▷ 83) is the second of the city's three large squares and has been its political and civic focus since medieval times. Leave the square on Via Vacchereccia, which emerges near the top of Via Por Santa Maria, once lined with medieval palaces that were destroyed by German bombing in 1944. A right turn brings you out to the Mercato Nuovo.

❷ The Mercato Nuovo is also known as Il Porcellino (the Little Pig), after the famous bronze statue of a boar, a copy (1612) by Pietro Tacca of the marble classical original. Its snout is worn shiny by the daily caresses of thousands of visitors. There has been a market on this site since the early 11th century. The elegant loggia was built by Cosimo I in 1547; it now shelters stands selling gifts and leather goods.

Pass the market, turn left and walk down Via Porta Rossa. On the left is the Palazzo Davanzati or the Museo della Casa Fiorentina Antica (▷ 75), complete with top-floor loggia. At the end of the street is Piazza Santa Trinità (▷ 96).

❸ The Piazza and its church are artistically rich. In the

Florence's Duomo provides spectacular city views

middle of the square is the tall Column of Justice, a monolith brought from the Baths of Caracalla in Rome and given to Cosimo I in 1560 by Pope Pius IV. On the left stands the fine Palazzo Bartolini-Salimbeni, built between 1520 and 1523 by Baccio d'Agnolo, and beyond this the splendid Palazzo Spini-Feroni, one of the best-preserved private medieval palaces in Florence, now housing Ferragamo's flagship store and shoe museum (▷ 78).

Take the left exit down Borgo Santi Apostoli, which leads to a tiny sunken square.

❹ Piazza del Limbo is so-called because it stands on the site of a cemetery for unbaptized babies, which were believed to spend eternity in limbo. The church of Santi Apostoli is also here. This is one of the oldest churches in the city, founded in the 11th century, with a series of marble columns, capitals and a carved tomb by Benedetto da Rovezzano (1474–1554) inside. He also designed the entrance door.

OUT AND ABOUT

Return to Piazza Santa Trinità and take Via del Parione to the right of the church of Santa Trinità, then turn right down Via Parioncino. You will emerge onto Via del Purgatorio. Walk to your left to the intersection with Via della Vigna Nuova. With your back still to Via del Purgatorio, the Palazzo Rucellai will be in front of you.

5 Palazzo Rucellai's exterior was designed by Leon Battista Alberti and built by Bernardo Rossellino between 1446 and 1451. The lovely Loggia dei Rucellai, now home to a fashion store, is on your right.

Turn left here onto Via della Vigna Nuova. Cross over Via della Vigna Nuova, turn right up Via dei Palchetti (at the corner of Palazzo Rucellai), then right again onto Via dei Federighi. This leads onto Piazza San Pancrazio.

6 Piazza San Pancrazio is home to the deconsecrated church of San Pancrazio, now the Museo Marini dedicated to the work of the Florentine sculptor Marino Marini (1901–80). Just around the corner from here, on the right at Via della Spada 18, is the tiny Cappella di San Sepolcro. Built in 1467 for the Rucellai family, it has a superbly carved

Light filters through a narrow lane leading to Piazza del Limbo

marble inlay model of the Sanctuary of the Holy Sepulchre in Jerusalem.

From Cappella di San Sepolcro, walk back a little way along Via della Spada and turn left down Via del Moro, which is full of antiques shops. At Piazza Goldoni turn right and continue along Borgo Ognissanti. No. 60r is one of Florence's more unusual buildings, a well-preserved example of art-deco architecture.

7 The wide Piazza d'Ognissanti is just a few doors down, site of the church and

adjacent convent that give the square its name. When facing the church, the 15th-century Palazzo Lenzi—now the French Consulate—is on the left-hand side. Across the river you can see San Frediano in Cestello, one of the many churches in Florence with a façade left unfinished.

Backtrack a little and turn left up Via della Porcellana, lined with workshops, then turn right down the Via della Scala. At the top is the huge Piazza Santa Maria Novella.

8 The church of Santa Maria Novella (▷ 95) is the superb Gothic building that stands at the north end of the square.

The Medici family crest on the church of the Ognissanti

The striking black-and-white marble façade of the Gothic church of Santa Maria Novella

Morning is the best time to explore Florence, as all the churches and museums are open. During the afternoon, and on Mondays, many of the smaller churches are closed so you can't see their remarkable interiors.

WHERE TO EAT

There are plenty of bars and cafés to choose from in this part of town. One of the nicest is Caffè Rivoire (Piazza della Signoria 5r, tel 055 214412; Tue–Sun 8am–midnight), which has a gorgeous terrace. The Cantinetta dei Verazzano (Via dei Tavolini 18–20r, tel 055 268590; Mon–Sat 8am–9pm), just off Via Calzaiuoli, serves coffee and cakes along with excellent wines and snacks.

PLACES TO VISIT

Museo della Casa Fiorentina Antica (▷ 75)
Via Porta Rossa 13
🕐 Daily 8.15–1.50; closed 1st and 2nd Sun and 1st, 3rd and 5th Mon of the month

Santi Apostoli
Piazza del Limbo
🕐 Mon–Sat 10–12, 4–6, Sun 4–6

Museo Marini
Piazza San Pancrazio
🕐 Wed–Mon 10–5; closed Sat Jun, Jul, Sep and all of Aug

Cappella di San Sepolcro
Via della Spada 18
🕐 Mon–Sat 10–noon

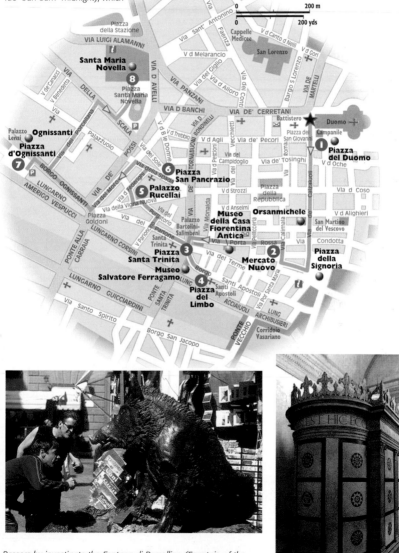

Passers-by investigate the Fontana di Porcellino (Fountain of the Piglet) in the Mercato Nuovo (above); a carved model of the Sanctuary in Cappella di San Sepolcro (right)

THE OLTRARNO

The Oltrarno is the part of Florence to the south of the river. The walk begins amid the bustle of the city, yet only a short distance to the west is a tranquil district where you can catch glimpses of everyday local life. Soon city turns to countryside, and you will find yourself in a landscape of mellow villas, olive groves and cypress trees.

THE WALK

Distance:	5km (3 miles)
Allow:	3 hours
Start/end at:	Ponte Vecchio

★ **Set off from the south side** of the Ponte Vecchio (▷ 91). With your back to the bridge, turn right and walk parallel to the river down Borgo San Jacopo.

❶ The buildings on Borgo San Jacopo are in a mixture of architectural styles, and include several medieval tower houses such as Torre dei Belfredelli on the left at No. 9, and the Torre dei Barbadori opposite. Farther on, the 11th-century Church of San Jacopo Soprarno has a graceful, three-arched portico, and often hosts concerts.

Just after a little marble fountain on the left, the street ends in Piazza de' Frescobaldi. To the left is Via Maggio, lined with elegant palaces and expensive antiques shops. Cross this road and turn left onto the narrow Via del Presto di San Martino. This emerges alongside the church of Santo Spirito (▷ 96).

❷ Santo Spirito is on the tranquil, tree-lined piazza of the same name. This is the bustling heart of a lively and vibrant district of artisans' workshops, narrow streets and medieval houses. A small morning market is held here each Monday to Saturday, as well as a flea market on the second Sunday of each month.

With your back to the church, leave the square by the bottom (southern) corner, passing the grand 16th-century Palazzo Guadagni on the corner, and turn left into Via Mazzetta. This leads to Piazza San Felice.

❸ Piazza San Felice has a tall marble column dating from 1572, and a 14th-century church. On the first floor of No. 8, on the left towards Via Maggio, is the Casa Guidi, where the poets Robert and Elizabeth Barrett Browning lived between 1847 and 1861.

Cross the square and walk into Piazza de' Pitti, passing Palazzo Pitti (▷ 80–81) on the right. It was in the row of houses opposite the palace, at No. 22, that Dostoyevsky wrote *The Idiot* (1868). Walk straight on along Via de' Guicciardini and turn right into Piazza Santa Felicità.

The Ponte Vecchio dates from 1345, giving a taste of the medieval city as well as lovely river views

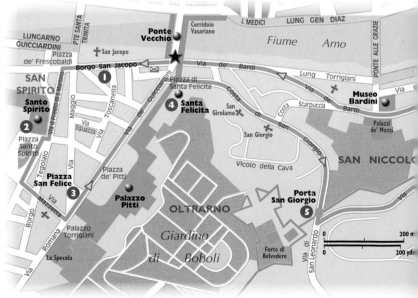

❹ Santa Felicità (▷ 92) is in the square of the same name. One of the oldest churches in Florence, its dome was lopped off in the mid-16th century to make way for the Corridoio Vasariano, which links the Pitti and Uffizi palaces. Inside is Pontormo's (1494–1557) painting of the *Deposition*.

Behind the church, Costa di San Giorgio leads out of the piazza. You will now be walking steeply uphill, with some wonderful views over the river and the rest of the city. Towards the top on the right (No. 19) is a house where the 16th-century scientist Galileo Galilei once lived. At the top of the hill, the street passes under the old city gate of Porta San Giorgio. The entrance to Forte di Belvedere is on the right.

❺ Bernardo Buontalenti (1536–1608) designed the huge, star-shaped Forte di Belvedere in 1590 as part of the city's defences. The ramparts themselves, partially grassed, are popular as a public park with locals and visitors alike, and the terraces provide magnificent views over the city and surrounding countryside.

After the gate, turn left along Via Belvedere, which follows the 13th-century defensive walls. From here the road heads down to the small gateway of Porta San Miniato. Turn right and head up Via Monte alle Croce. Enoteca Fuori Porta, one of the city's best-known wine bars, is on the right. A little further up, take the steep Via di San Salvatore al Monte on the left, which crosses the busy Viale Galileo. Cross the road and continue on up the last few steps to the sober Franciscan Church of San Salvatore al Monte. From here, Via delle Porte Sante to the right leads to San Miniato al Monte.

❻ The Romanesque church of San Miniato al Monte (▷ 96) has a dazzling marble exterior and a terrace with panoramic views. Benedictine monks still live in the monastery next door.

With your back to the church, cross over Via delle Porte Sante and onto Viale Galileo. Turn right and continue downhill until you reach Piazzale Michelangelo

❼ There are endless photographic possibilities at Piazzale Michelangelo (▷ 90), with Florence and the hills beyond as a backdrop.

From here, the No. 12 bus (the bus stop is on the Viale Michelangelo) will take you down to Ponte alle Grazie. It is then a short walk back to the Ponte Vecchio along the river. Or take the path from the Piazzale down to the 14th-century Porta San Niccolò. Turn left onto Via di San Niccolò and follow this to Piazza de' Mozzi, where the 13th-century Palazzo dei Mozzi and the Museo Bardini (▷ 74) face each other. From here, Via de' Bardi leads to the Ponte Vecchio.

Writing a postcard home on the Ponte Vecchio

The marble façade of San Miniato al Monte

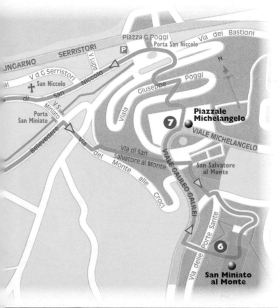

WHEN TO GO

This is a long walk with several steep climbs, so avoid the midday sun and take a hat and plenty of water. The views over the city at dusk are stunning and if you happen to reach San Miniato by 4.30pm in winter or an hour later in summer, you can hear the monks singing Gregorian chants at evening Mass.

WHERE TO EAT

There are bars and cafés on Piazza Santo Spirito, at the top of the hill near Piazzale Michelangelo and on Via di San Niccolò.

Enoteca Fuori Porta
Via Monte alle Croce 10r
☎ 055 234 2483
🕓 Mon–Sat 12.30pm–12.30am

PLACES TO VISIT

Casa Guidi
Via Maggio 8
☎ 055 354457
🕓 Mon, Wed, Fri 3–6, Apr–end Nov
💰 Donation

San Salvatore al Monte
🕓 Daily 7–7
💰 Free

THE GARFAGNANA

This drive takes you through the cool mountains of the Garfagnana, the region north of Lucca that stretches between the rugged country of the Parco Regionale delle Alpi Apuane in the west and the softer slopes of the Riserva Naturale dell'Orecchiella in the east. Towns and villages are sprinkled about the hills, and there are plenty of paths if you feel like stopping and exploring on foot.

OUT AND ABOUT

THE DRIVE

Distance: 170km (106 miles)	
Allow: 8 hours	
Start/end at: Lucca	

★ **Leave Lucca** (▷ 102–105) through the Porta San Donato and pick up the SR12 going towards Abetone. At the next turning follow the signs for Castelnuovo di Garfagnana. After 4km (2.5 miles) you will see the Lucchesi hills in front of you. Shortly after this, turn left at the brown signpost indicating 'Garfagnana' (▷ 100–101) and cross the bridge over the Serchio river onto the road that runs parallel to the SR12 on the river's opposite bank. Pass through two tunnels and, after about 4km (2.5 miles), turn left again. Stay on this road, which goes through Diecimo; papermaking factories bear witness to an old local industry. Drive on to the village of Borgo a Mozzano, where there is a bell tower on the left-hand side. Just after this you'll see a sign saying 'Barga 18'; go over a bridge. The Ponte del Diavolo is to your right, but you can't drive over it.

❶ Ponte del Diavolo (The Devil's Bridge), as it's locally known, spans the river. This distinctive bridge dates from the 12th century. According to legend, the builder sought help from the Devil to build it and in return the Devil demanded the soul of the first being to cross the river. The builder is said to have outwitted the Devil by making sure that a dog went over the bridge first.

After about 8km (5 miles) take a right-hand turn towards Barga, cross the river, turn left into Calavorno, then continue through Piano di Coreglia to reach Fornaci di Barga. Just at the entrance to this village take the right-hand fork to Barga; the road

Just outside Borgo a Mazzano is the distinctive 12th-century hump-back bridge known locally as The Devil's Bridge (above) Bigarelli da Como's 13th-century sculpture on the pulpit of Barga's cathedral (below)

climbs and the scenery becomes craggier and more alpine in appearance.

❷ Barga is a hilltop town with a Romanesque cathedral that towers over the village (▷ 98). Don't miss the panoramic views of the mountains from the terrace by the cathedral entrance.

Continued on page 200

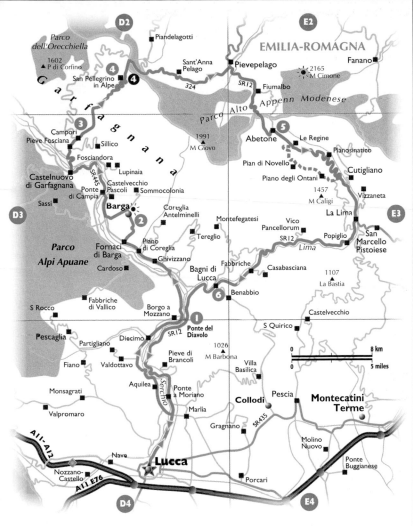

D2

Parco
dell'Orecchiella

Piandelagotti

E2

EMILIA-ROMAGNA

1602
▲ P di Corfino

Sant'Anna
Pelago

Pievepelago

Fanano

San Pellegrino
in Alpe

4

4

324

SR12

Fiumalbo

● 2165
M Cimone

Parco Alto Appenn Modenese

3

Campori

Pieve Fosciana

Sillico

1991
M Giovo

Abetone

Le Regine

5

Pianosinatico

Fosciandora

Lupinaia

Pian di Novello

Cutigliano

Castelnuovo
di Garfagnana

SR445

Castelvecchio
Pascoli

Ponte
di Campia

Sommocolonia

Piano degli Ontani

1457
M Caligi

Vizzaneta

Sassi

Barga

2

Coreglia
Antelminelli

Montefegatesi

Vico
Pancellorum

La Lima

San
Marcello
Pistoiese

E3

D3

Tereglio

SR12

Popiglio

Parco
Alpi Apuane

Fornaci
di Barga

Piano
di Coreglia

Lima

Cardoso

Ghivizzano

Fabbriche

Bagni di
Lucca

Casabasciana

1107
La Bastia

Fabbriche
di Vallico

Benabbio

Castelvecchio

S Rocco

Borgo a
Mozzano

6

Pescaglia

Partigliano

Diecimo

1

SR12

**Ponte del
Diavolo**

S Quirico

0   8 km

Fiano

Valdottavo

Pieve di
Brancoli

1026
M Barbona

Villa
Basilica

0   5 miles

Monsagrati

Aquilea

Ponte
a Moriano

Collodi

Pescia

**Montecatini
Terme**

Valpromaro

Marlia

SR435

Gragnano

A11-A12

Nave

Molino
Nuovo

Nozzano-
Castello

Lucca

Ponte
Buggianese

A11 E76

Porcari

D4

E4

OUT AND ABOUT

WHEN TO GO

Spring and autumn are the best times to visit; August is the most crowded time, and in winter snow and ice can make driving hazardous.

WHERE TO EAT

Barga's historic Caffè Capretz (Piazza Salvo Salvi 1, tel 0583 723001; closed Tue) is close to the Tourist Information Office. Here you can sit outside on a sunny day and enjoy a cappuccino and a pastry. Further along the route at San Pellegrino in Alpe is Albergo L'Appennino da Pacetta (Piazza San Pellegrino 5, tel 0583 649069; daily 12–3, 6.30–9.30), a relaxed family restaurant and inn with a sister café on the other side of the

road (tel 0583 649069). All the food is homemade, from the cakes and pasta to the bread and jam. There are also several places in Bagni di Lucca where you can grab a quick coffee.

PLACES TO VISIT

**Museo Etnografico
Provinciale**
Via del Voltone, San Pellegrino in Alpe
☎ 0583 649072
🕐 Tue–Sun 9–12, 2–5, Apr–end May; 9.30–1, 2.30–7, Jun–end Sep (also Mon Jul, Aug); Tue–Sat 9–1, Sun 9–12, 2–5, rest of year

Thermal waters running from the mouth of a fountain in spa resort Bagni di Lucca

THE GARFAGNANA 199

A church tower high above the wooded mountainside in the Garfagnana, near the resort town of Bagni di Lucca (left) The door of the Romanesque duomo that towers over the town of Barga (above)

Continued from page 198

Continue through Barga and follow the sign for Castelnuovo di Garfagnana. Cross another river and drive through Castelvecchio Pascoli; near the village is the house of poet Giovanni Pascoli (1855–1912). Continue through Ponte di Campia and follow the SR445 for about 9km (6 miles) through thickly wooded hills to reach Castelnuovo di Garfagnana (▷ 101). This is the largest town in the area, and has an office of the Alpi Apuane Regional Park providing regional maps and books. When you reach the crossroads take the SP72 signed for San Pellegrino in Alpe. Drive through Campori.

As you leave Campori ❸, the road begins to wind steeply upwards, cutting through hills cloaked with chestnut trees. For many years the economy of the Garfagnana depended

on chestnuts, cheese and spelt (a type of wheat).

After 13km (8 miles) you will reach San Pellegrino in Alpe.

❹ San Pellegrino is a little mountain village that has attracted pilgrims and artists for centuries, including Michelangelo and the English poet Percy Bysshe Shelley. It is a good spot for a walk (▷ 201) and a bite to eat, and is also the home of the Museo Etnografico Provinciale, an excellent folk museum.

Drive on from San Pellegrino and join the 324, which snakes downhill. Follow the road as it passes through Sant'Anna Pelago and Pievepelago. At the cross-roads, turn right taking the SR12 towards Abetone. Here you cross the river and start to climb again. Drive for 7km (4 miles) until you reach Abetone ❺, a ski resort with a distinctly alpine feel.

From Abetone the SR12 winds down to Le Regine. You can continue on the SR12 here, or take an alternative route through the mountain woods and villages by turning off to the right just outside Abetone, at the brown sign indicating 'Piano degli Ontani'. Drive along this quiet little road for about 2km (1 mile), then take the left-hand fork and continue through the woods to reach Pian di Novello, a small skiing village. From here the road twists steeply downhill, through Piano degli Ontani, eventually rejoining the SR12, where you turn right and follow the road to La Lima. Bear right in La Lima, still on the SR12, then drive through Popiglio, following the road for 17km (11 miles) until you reach Bagni di Lucca. Cross the small bridge on the right-hand side to reach the heart of the town.

❻ Bagni di Lucca gained a reputation as a spa town in the 19th century, attracting many illustrious visitors who came to take the waters, including the poets Lord Byron, Shelley, and Robert and Elizabeth Barrett Browning.

Cross back over the bridge and continue along the SR12, which passes the Ponte del Diavolo and takes you back to Lucca.

THE PILGRIM TRAIL FROM SAN PELLEGRINO

This is an easy, but rewarding, circular walk high in the mountains of the Garfagnana. It starts and ends in the hamlet of San Pellegrino in Alpe, a settlement that grew up around the relics of St. Pellegrino and has attracted countless pilgrims since the eighth century. You can enjoy striking views over the mountains at several points along the trail.

THE WALK

Distance: 4km (2.5 miles)

Allow: 1 hour

Start/end at: Middle of San Pellegrino in Alpe, with the L'Appennino da Pacetto inn on your left and the museum on your right

Paths: Wide, firm trails and one section of quiet road

Parking: Free parking in the main village of San Pellegrino in Alpe

Begin in the heart of the village, in the square between the museum and the inn. With the museum on your right, walk forward until you find a red-and-white sign on the side of a building with the words 'In giro Monte Spicio' (roughly meaning 'this way to walk round Monte Spicio'). Go up the steps. Pass the mobile phone mast on the right-hand side and follow the wide path flanked by trees. Follow this wooded path for a little more than 1km (0.5 mile).

The landscape now begins to open up, taking on the appearance of moorland, with heather dotting either side of the trail. It can get foggy up here, but on clear days you can glimpse some good views to the right.

Continue to follow the main trail, ignoring any side routes, until the path intersects with a wide gravel trail. You'll know you've reached it as there is a green post marking the point where the paths cross.

If you turn right here you come to a tiny stone building known as Capella di San Pellegrino. Pellegrino, who was said to be the son of the king of Scotland, came to this area on a pilgrimage in the seventh century and stayed to provide refreshment and accommodation for other pilgrims.

Choose a clear day to enjoy the stunning views from the hamlet of San Pellegrino in Alpe

Look down for beauty as well as up in San Pellegrino in Alpe

To return to the main route, turn left and follow the wide trail. Keep walking until you reach a bend in the path.

On the left-hand side of this bend is a rocky outcrop with an excellent viewpoint. This makes a good photo stop, and you can also appreciate just how high up you are.

Continue following the wide trail, walking down until you reach a tarmac road. At this point you are on the border between Tuscany and Emilia-Romagna. Turn left and walk downhill along the tarmac road. It's generally quiet, but still keep a sharp lookout for any passing cars. Follow this road all the way to San Pellegrino. There are some exceptional views of the mountains as you approach the village.

WHEN TO GO

This area can be covered with snow early in the winter so, despite the easy trails, you should do this walk only in good weather as the trails can get blocked by the snow.

WHERE TO EAT

Albergo L'Appennino da Pacetta

Piazza San Pellegrino 5

☎ 0583 649069

🕐 Wed–Sun 9–12, 2–6

OUT AND ABOUT

THE HEART OF SIENA

Siena is small enough for you to gain a rapid understanding of the city's layout. This walk takes you through the less-visited southern parts of the city, passing most of the main sights, and finishes on Piazza San Domenico.

THE WALK

Distance: 2.8km (1.7 miles)
Allow: 2–3 hours
Start at: Piazza del Duomo
End at: Piazza San Domenico

★ **Start your walk on Piazza del Duomo** where you'll find the Duomo (▷ 120–123), the Museo dell'Opera del Duomo (▷ 124) and the Ospedale di Santa Maria della Scala (▷ 125).

❶ The Duomo has a spectacular marble floor made up of 56 panels. In the aisles on either side of the nave are the *Ten Sibyls* by various artists and earlier panels showing an *Allegory of Virtue* by Pinturicchio (c1454–1513); a *Wheel of Fortune* can be seen in the nave. Best of all are the panels in the central hexagon and the pavements in front of the high altar. These are mainly the work (1518–47) of Domenico Beccafumi and depict scenes from the Old Testament.

The Piazza del Duomo is the first of two adjoining squares; from here walk down the steps to enter Piazza San Giovanni with the Battistero di San Giovanni. The Baptistery contains works by Donatello and other important artists (▷ 123). Face the Baptistery and take the road to the right of it, Via dei Fusari, and then continue, where the road name changes to Via Girolamo. At the intersection with Via del Fosso di San Ansano is Piazza della Selva. Turn left onto the quiet Via del Fosso di San Ansano until you reach an archway.

❷ The Arco delle Due Porte formed part of the city's 11th-century walls. Turn left at the arch onto Via di Stalloreggi and look for the house (No. 91–93) where Duccio di Buoninsegna (c1255–1319) painted his glorious *Maestà*, now on display at the Museo del Opera dell'Duomo (▷ 124).

Looking across the Piazza del Campo to the Torre del Mangia

At the intersection with Via San Pietro turn right. On your left are the Pinacoteca Nazionale (▷ 126) and the Church of San Pietro. Continue down Via San Pietro and turn left onto Via Sant'Agata. Cross the gravel area to your right.

❸ The 13th-century Chiesa di Sant'Agostino (▷ 127) contains two splendid examples of Sienese painting by Giovanni Sodoma (1477–1549) and Ambrogio Lorenzetti (active 1319–48).

Back on Via Sant'Agata, continue walking as far as the intersection with Via Giovanni Dupre and turn left onto that road—it has attractive alleyways branching off to either side. Keep your eyes open for Via del Mercato, which will curve away to your right, and Piazza del Mercato. Take Via Malcontenti out of the square and onto Via di Salicotto, and turn left. Turn right onto Vicolo delle Scotte.

❹ Sinagoga, Siena's synagogue, is on your left. The Jewish ghetto was founded by Cosimo I de' Medici in 1571 and the Sinagoga was once at the heart of the city.

Cross Via del Porrione, so named after the Latin emporium or market place, referring to the Roman markets that stood close by. On the right is Loggia del Papa (Loggia of the Pope). Walk to the end of the road and turn left onto Banchi di Sotto. On your left stands the Palazzo Piccolomini.

Look for Vicolo dei Pollaiuoli or Via dei Rinaldini on the left; either will bring you to Piazza del Campo. Here you can admire the views of this famous square from one of its cafés or visit the Museo Civico in the Palazzo Pubblico (▷ 116–117).

Leave the Campo by Via di Città and turn right, where you will see the Gothic Loggia della Mercanzia (1428–44). Continue past the intersection with Banchi di Sotto and onto Banchi di Sopra, a major street that follows the path of the Via Francigena, an old pilgrim route between Rome and northern Europe. You will pass the Palazzo Tolomei along this road to your left.

❺ Palazzo Tolomei is part of the original fortress-home of the Tolomei family, one of a number of powerful medieval banking families. There is also a statue of the she-wolf that suckled Romulus and Remus (▷ 25). Opposite is the Romanesque Church of San Cristoforo in Piazza Tolomei.

Continue up Banchi di Sopra; ahead is Piazza Salimbeni.

❻ Piazza Salimbeni has three fine palaces: Palazzo Tantucci (to the left, 1548); the 14th-century Palazzo Salimbeni (to the rear); and Palazzo Spannocchi (to the right, 1470; only open to the public during the Palio). The Salimbeni family were prominent bankers and silk and grain traders, while Ambrogio Spannocchi was treasurer to the Sienese Pope Pius II. They now form the home of Monte dei Paschi di Siena (▷ 115).

OUT AND ABOUT

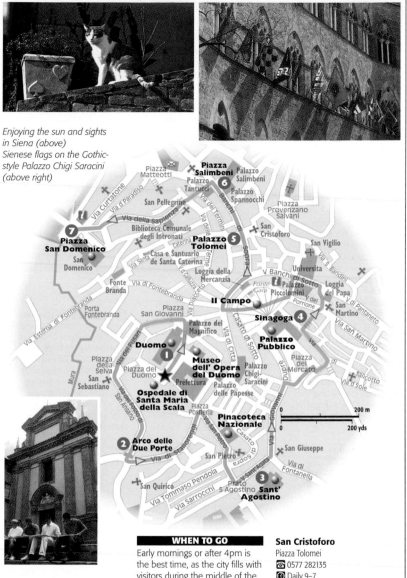

Enjoying the sun and sights in Siena (above)
Sienese flags on the Gothic-style Palazzo Chigi Saracini (above right)

Piazza
Matteotti
Piazza Salimbeni 6
Palazzo Salimbeni
Palazzo Tantucci
Palazzo Spannocchi
Piazza Provenzano Salvani
Via Curtatone
Via d'Paradiso
San Pellegrino
Via dei termini
Via della sapienza
Biblioteca Comunale degli Intronati
San Cristoforo
San Vigilio
Piazza San Domenico 7
San Domenico
Casa e Santuario de Santa Caterina
Palazzo Tolomei 5
Via di Sopra
Via S. Bandini
Universita
Via Santa Caterina
Loggia della Mercanzia
V Banchi di Sotto
Fonte Branda
Via di Fontebranda
Fonte Gaia
Palazzo Piccolomini
Loggia del Papa
Porta Fontebranda
Via Esterna di Fontebranda
Piazza San Giovanni
Il Campo
V del Porrione
San Martino
Via di Pantaneto
Via San Martino
Mura
Palazzo del Magnifico
Sinagoga 4
Palazzo Pubblico
Duomo 1
Via di Città
Via del Casato di Sotto
Via Duprè
Piazza del Mercato
Piazza della Selva
San Sebastiano
Piazza del Duomo
Prefettura
Museo dell' Opera del Duomo
Palazzo Chigi-Saracini
Palazzo delle Papesse
Via d'salicotto
Via d'sole
Ospedale di Santa Maria della Scala
Piazza Postierla
Pinacoteca Nazionale
San Giuseppe
Arco delle Due Porte 2
Via di Stalloreggi
San Pietro
Casato di sopra
Via di Fontanella
Via Sant'Agata
San Quirico
Via Tommaso Pendola
Via Sarrocchi
Prato S Agostino
Sant' Agostino 3

200 m
200 yds

Leave the piazza on Via della Sapienza. Along this road you will pass the Church of San Pellegrino alla Sapienza and the Biblioteca Comunale degli Intronati. Via della Sapienza leads to Piazza San Domenico.

7 Piazza San Domenico is home to the Church of San Domenico, notable for its associations with St. Catherine of Siena and its frescoes by Sodoma (▷ 127).

Sketching on the steps of San Pietro church on Via San Pietro

WHEN TO GO

Early mornings or after 4pm is the best time, as the city fills with visitors during the middle of the day. Note that the Sinagoga is only open on Sundays.

WHERE TO EAT

Caffé Nannini at Banchi di Sopra 95–99 (daily 7.30am–11pm, ▷ 231) is a good place for a break, as is Bar Il Palio on Piazza del Campo (tel 0577 282055; daily 8am–2am).

PLACES TO VISIT

Sinagoga
14 Via delle Scotte
☎ 055 234 6654
⏰ Sun 10–1, 2–5
💶 Free

San Cristoforo
Piazza Tolomei
☎ 0577 282135
⏰ Daily 9–7
💶 Free

San Pellegrino alla Sapienza
Via delle Sapienza
⏰ Daily 5–7
💶 Free

Biblioteca Comunale degli Intronati
Via delle Sapienza 5
☎ 0577 282972
⏰ Mon–Sat 9–6
💶 Free

Battistero di San Giovanni
Piazza San Giovanni
☎ 0577 283048

SIENA AND SOUTHERN TUSCANY

From Siena, this drive takes you south past the ancient abbeys of Sant'Antimo and Monte Oliveto Maggiore and the hilltop towns of Pienza, Montepulciano and Montalcino. Some of Italy's finest wines are produced in this region, so look for wine bars and shops where non-drivers can try a glass or two.

THE DRIVE

Distance: 190km (118 miles)
Allow: 11 hours (spread over 2 days, staying at Pienza or Montepulciano)
Start/end at: Siena

★ **Leave Siena** on the bypass, or *tangenziale*, heading south towards Rome and take the last exit onto the Via Cassia. In 3km (2 miles) you will see signs indicating 'Buonconvento 25'. After another 8km (5 miles) turn left, staying on the SR2 for Buonconvento. When you come to a crossroads, stay on the SR2. Bear right after the bridge to enter the town.

❶ Buonconvento (▷ 130), unusual in this area in that it is not perched on a hill, has a medieval old town and a small museum, the Museo d'Arte Sacra. It was once an important stop on the Via Francigena, the pilgrims' route that stretched from Canterbury to Rome.

Leave Buonconvento, following the SR2 through the town's outskirts. Turn right and take the SP45 towards Montalcino. The scenery becomes more pleasing and you will soon see Montalcino on the hill ahead of you. You will start to notice a

large number of signs for *enoteche* (wine bars and shops), many of which offer free tastings.

After about 9km (6 miles), bear right at the top of the hill and join the SP14, following signs for Montalcino. With the city wall to the right you arrive at the roundabout (traffic circle) at the top of the hill. There is free parking on the left and pay parking to the right, next to La Fortezza.

❷ Montalcino (▷ 137) is particularly famous for its rich ruby-red Brunello wine, characterized by an intense aroma and delicate, warm flavour with a hint of vanilla.

After exploring Montalcino, head for Abbazia di Sant'Antimo ❸ by following the brown signs from the roundabout (traffic circle) at the top of the hill and getting on the SP55. The road now starts to wind downhill and in about 2km (1 mile) you should spot the abbey, nestling below the hills on the right-hand side (▷ 129). Turn right to reach the abbey, a good starting point for a walk.

From here, return to the road and drive up the hill to Castelnuovo dell'Abate. Turn right at the top of the hill, following the sign indicating 'Stazione Monte Amiata' on the SP22. You

will now pass the Val d'Orcia, from where the road begins to twist downhill. Pass over a level crossing (grade crossing) by Monte Amiata station and cross the River Orcia before coming into the hamlet of Monte Amiata, after which the road begins to climb again. When you reach the intersection, go to the left towards Castiglione d'Orcia. From here the road climbs even more steeply, with rewarding views. When you come to an intersection, take a left turn and pick up the SR323. Continue towards Castiglione d'Orcia.

❹ Castiglione d'Orcia has two churches worth seeing: the Romanesque Church of Santa Maria Maddelena, and the Church of Santo Stefano with its 16th-century façade and Madonnas by Simone Martini (1284–1344) and Pietro Lorenzetti (active 1320–48). At the heart of town is Piazza Vecchietta, named after the artist Lorenzo di Pietro (1412–80), who was known as Il Vecchietta and is claimed as a son by the town. It is overlooked by the Palazzo Comunale, where there's a fresco of the Madonna and

Continued on page 206

OUT AND ABOUT

You can do this drive any time of year, but July and August are the hottest and busiest months, while the countryside is at its best in spring and autumn.

The Fiaschetteria Italiana, a lovely old café in Montalcino, serves coffee, light meals and wine (Piazza del Popolo 6, tel 0577 849043; 7.30am–midnight). There are plenty of cafés and restaurants in Bagno Vignoni; try La Parata (Piazza Moretta 40,

tel 0577 887508; Thu–Tue 10.30–2.45, 7.30–9.30). It serves *panini* and cakes, along with local cheese and olive oil, and you can sit outside on fine days. In Montepulciano you can enjoy cakes, snacks and a glass of wine at the art-nouveau Caffè Poliziano (Via di Voltaia nel Corso 27–29, tel 0578 758615; daily 7am–midnight), which also serves meals in its restaurant.

Museo d'Arte Sacra
Via Socini 18, Buonconvento
☎ 0577 807181
🕐 Tue–Sun 10.30–1, 3–7, Mar–Oct; Sat–Sun 10–1, 3–5, rest of year
💶 €3.10

Abbazia di Sant'Antimo
Castelnuovo dell'Abate, Siena 53024
☎ 0577 835659
🕐 Daily 6–9.30
🎟 Free

OUT AND ABOUT

Looking out over the rooftops and towers of wine-producing Montalcino to the vineyards below (far left); the evening sunlight silhouettes a statue of the Madonna on the summit of Monte Amiata (left); the once-dominant castle of Castiglione d'Orcia (above)

Continued from page 204

Child with two saints in the Sienese school style, taken from the nearby village of Rocca d'Orcia.

Drive through the village, then head downhill. After 5km (3 miles) turn left at the intersection to take the SR2. Continue until you reach the intersection for Bagno Vignoni. Park just outside town, on top of the hill.

❺ Bagno Vignoni has been used as a spa since Etruscan times and is dominated by an enormous outdoor pool of warm, sulphurous water (▷ 130).

Go back downhill from the town, turn left at the end of the road and then take the next right onto the SP53 for Pienza. Turn left onto the SP18 and drive uphill, and you will see the red sandstone town of Pienza (▷ 141). Park at the bottom of the hill.

❻ Pienza is a UNESCO World Heritage Site. Its focal point is the Piazza Pio II, bordered by the Palazzo Piccolomini, the Palazzo Borgia and the cathedral. The cathedral has a pure Renaissance exterior and late-Gothic style interior, and contains several altarpieces by Sienese masters.

Leave Pienza and continue uphill until you come to an intersection.

Turn right here for the 146 and Montepulciano. Follow the road until you reach the town (▷ 139) and park outside the walls.

❼ Montepulciano has sweeping views and a maze of steep, winding streets and alleyways. Besides the Renaissance church of San Biagio, the town has many wine shops where you can purchase bottles of Vino Nobile, the famous local wine. Aged in oak barrels for two years (three years for Riserva), this dry wine has a delicate bouquet with violet scents.

From Montepulciano, drive downhill. Turn right for Pienza on the 146 and after 7km (4 miles) turn right onto the SP15, a twisting road heading towards Torrita di Siena. Turn left

The cloisters in Pienza's 13th-century church of San Francesco (above)
The opaque waters of the hot springs at Bagno Vignoni (left)

just in front of a bar on the corner to join the SP57. Follow the road to an intersection where you take a sharp left past Petroio and then drive on for another 4km (2.5 miles), after which you turn right for Montisi.

The road now descends in tight bends, passing through the woods until you reach an intersection. Turn left here and follow the SP14 through Montisi and on to the outskirts of San Giovanni d'Asso. When you come to the next intersection, turn right towards the remote Abbazia di Monte Oliveto Maggiore. Follow this road to Montefresco, then turn left at the intersection and drive for another 3km (2 miles). At the next intersection go left, then shortly turn off to visit the late 13th-century abbey (▷ 129).

❽ Abbazia di Monte Oliveto Maggiore, a Benedictine abbey, stands in a wooded park on a scenic rise and is still inhabited by monks. Pause to admire the famous frescoes in the main cloister.

Leave the abbey and continue along the 451 until you reach Buonconvento. From here, pick up the SR2, which will take you back to Siena.

OUT AND ABOUT

AROUND ABBAZIA DI SANT'ANTIMO

This walk starts at the serene Abbazia di Sant'Antimo, one of the finest Romanesque churches in Italy, dating back to the ninth century. It takes you past quiet woodlands and olive groves to the lovely hamlet of Villa a Tolli, where time seems to have stood still for centuries.

THE WALK

Distance: 6.4km (4 miles)

Allow: 1.5–2 hours

Start/end at: Abbazia di Sant'Antimo, near Castelnuovo dell'Abate

Paths: Wide trails and a steady, steep climb

Parking: Free parking at Abbazia di Sant'Antimo

From the parking area, walk towards the abbey. When you are in line with the abbey entrance, you will see a large brown sign on the right-hand side with details of this walk. Turn right and follow the wide, stony track that was once the main Roman road.

After about 300m (330 yards) you'll come to a small stone hut where the path forks. There is a red-and-white mark painted on the hut, and this sign is used to denote the correct trail throughout the walk. Take the left-hand fork and continue ahead. If you are on the walk in spring this path will be laced with wild flowers. The landscape now closes in and your path is surrounded by woodland, with a farm on the left-hand side.

Keep following the trail, watching out for patches of heather where trees have been cut down. This was used locally to make brooms and is still commonly known as broom *(scopa)* in Italian.

Continue until you reach another fork and take the right-hand path. You will be walking through denser woodland now, full of glossy Mediterranean trees such as juniper. The path begins to climb and becomes rockier underfoot. Follow it to another fork, where again you will take the right-hand path. You should see a sign that points to Villa a Tolli.

Wind uphill, watching for the occasional red-and-white mark on the trees. This is a steep climb, which will eventually bring you to an olive grove on the left-hand side, and then to a broad trail.

On your left is a farmhouse, La Magia. Turn right, following the wide gravel trail. Eventually the trail winds to the right and you will see the tiny church and bell tower at Villa a Tolli.

The interior of the beautiful Romanesque abbey

Walk into the village, where there are workers' cottages and several wineries. If the owners are around they will be happy to show you where they keep the huge vats of wine and maybe sell you a bottle.

From the village it is possible to continue following the trail all the way to Montalcino. Otherwise, retrace your steps to walk back to the abbey, turning left at La Magia, left at the next trail, then taking the right-hand fork to walk downhill.

From here you get superb views of the abbey, sheltered beneath curving hills topped with shapely cypress trees.

WHEN TO GO

The best time to go is late spring or early summer (late April, May or early June) as many of the wild flowers will be in bloom and the songbirds, especially the nightingales, will be in full voice. Alternatively, go in September or October to see the wine harvest.

WHERE TO EAT

There are a number of cafés in Castelnuovo and Montalcino, but you won't be able to get anything to eat or drink on the route itself, so take a picnic.

OUT AND ABOUT

Woods and pastures surrounding the Abbazia di Sant'Antimo

SIENA, VOLTERRA AND SAN GIMIGNANO

This drive is through the kind of rolling countryside that typifies Tuscany. You travel along quiet roads through gently undulating hills, past olive groves, cypress trees and immaculately preserved hilltop towns and villages, many of which are generally overlooked by visitors.

THE DRIVE

Distance:	154km (96 miles)
Allow:	8 hours
Start/end at:	Siena

Volterra's 14th-century Fortezza Medicea is now used as a prison

★ **From Siena**, follow the bypass, or *tangenziale*, towards Florence. As the road climbs take the Siena Acquacalda exit and follow the road past some houses to a roundabout (traffic circle). Turn left here onto the Via Cassia to Monteriggioni (▷ 140).

❶ Monteriggioni's fortifications can be seen high on the hill. You have to park at the bottom of the town and continue on foot to the top. It's worth the climb to see this extraordinarily well-preserved medieval fortified town, encircled by tower-studded walls.

From Monteriggioni follow the signs indicating 'Firenze 46'. At the T-junction, turn left at the sign for Colle di Val d'Elsa.

❷ The landscape now becomes flatter and is covered with vineyards; this area is known as Chianti Colle Senesi. When you reach a roundabout (traffic circle) you will see a large sign on the left saying CALP, indicating the works of one of the world's biggest producers of rock crystal.

Drive into Colle di Val d'Elsa, going uphill to reach the Colle Alta, the old part of town. Follow the parking signs and park in Via della Porta Vecchia.

❸ Colle di Val d'Elsa (▷ 135) is defined by three levels: Borgo (Borough), Castello (Castle) and Piano (Plain). It is renowned for the production of fine, handcrafted crystal. The Borough is entered through the Porta Nuova, gateway to a string of fine 16th- and 17th-century noble houses: the town hall, Palazzo Usimbardi, Palazzo Buoninsegni and the magnificent, but unfinished,

Palazzo Campana, which marks the entrance to the castle, the oldest part of Colle di Val d'Elsa. The Piazza del Duomo is overlooked by the 14th-century Palazzo Pretorio, now seat of the Museo Archeologico (Archaeological Museum), the 17th-century cathedral, and the Bishop's Palace, housing the Museo Civico e d'Arte Sacra (Museum of Sacred Art). Via delle Volte, the most evocative corner of the town, leads off the square.

From Colle take the SR68, following signs for Volterra. After 6km (4 miles) the road climbs into the heart of the country. Go through Castel San Gimignano, after which there are glorious views of vine-dotted hills, olive groves, dark cypresses and fields of sunflowers. In the distance, you can see the thermal electric plant at Larderello, 33km (21 miles) from Volterra. Look for steam rising from the underground thermal springs that spurt from these hills. After about 8km (5 miles) you should begin to see Volterra on the horizon as you reach the top of the hill, and shortly after that (1km/0.5 mile) you come to Volterra.

❹ Volterra (▷ 148) was founded by the Etruscans, and has splendid medieval buildings and a Roman theatre.

Leave Volterra and follow the signs for Pontedera. After 4km (2.5 miles) you will see a yellow sign on the left-hand side for San Cipriano ❺. Photographers will find this little church an ideal spot for capturing the extensive views. Alternatively, keep going and follow the SP15 as it winds its way steeply downhill, taking the right-hand fork and going over a modern bridge, until you reach an intersection. Take the exit for Firenze and follow the SP4 for about 9km (6 miles). Turn right and follow the signs for San Gimignano. You will see the town perched on a hill in the distance; drive up and park outside the town walls.

❻ San Gimignano (▷ 142–145) is frequently referred to as the medieval Manhattan, because of its striking crown of towers. It's worth stopping to spend some time wandering around the unspoiled (if busy) streets.

Leaving San Gimignano, drive around the town walls to reach an intersection, where you turn right for Poggibonsi ❼. Go straight over the next roundabout towards Poggibonsi. When you reach the uninspiring industrial town, go left at the next roundabout, and get onto the Superstrada Firenze-Siena to return to Siena.

OUT AND ABOUT

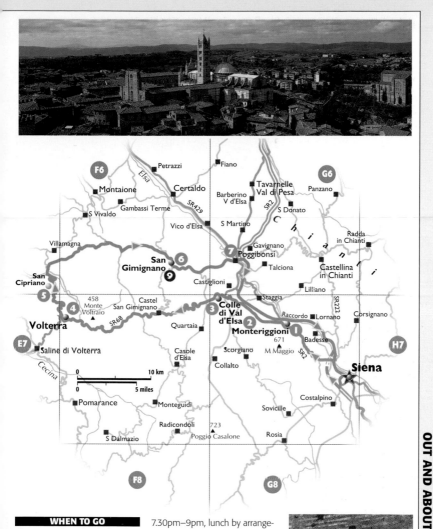

F6 · Petrazzi · Fiano · G6

Montaione · Certaldo · Tavarnelle Val di Pesa · Panzano

S Vivaldo · Gambassi Terme · Barberino V d'Elsa · S Donato

SR429 · Vico d'Elsa · S Martino · Chianti

Villamagna · Gavignano · Radda in Chianti

San Gimignano 6 · Poggibonsi 7 · Talciona · Castellina in Chianti

San Cipriano 5 · 9 · Castiglioni · Lilliano

458 Monte Voltraio · Castel San Gimignano · Staggia · SR222

4 · SR68 · Colle di Val d'Elsa 3 · Raccordo · Lornano · Corsignano

Volterra · Quartaia · Monteriggioni 2 · 1 · Badesse

E7 · Saline di Volterra · Casole d'Elsa · Scorgiano · 671 M Maggio · SR2 · H7

Cecina · Collalto · Siena

0 10 km · 0 5 miles · Costalpino

Pomarance · Monteguidi · Sovicille

Radicondoli · 723 Poggio Casalone · Rosia

S Dalmazio

F8 · G8

WHEN TO GO

The scenery is so lovely that this drive is good any time of the year, but to miss the crowds (particularly in San Gimignano) try to avoid summer, visiting in early spring or late autumn.

WHERE TO EAT

There are several places to choose from in Volterra, including Trattoria da Bado (Borgo San Lazzero 9, tel 0588 86477; Thu–Tue 12–2, 7–9.30), which serves typical Tuscan dishes. Alternatively, if you just want a snack, there is an Internet Café on Via Porte Lago, which has a glass floor revealing the remains of a Roman grain silo. Just outside the town, off the SR439, is Villa Palagione, an elegant villa that is a lovely rural spot for a meal (tel 0588 391129; daily

7.30pm–9pm, lunch by arrangement; closed Nov–end Mar). You have several choices of restaurants, cafés and pizzerias in San Gimignano. The Gelateria di Piazza (daily 9am–11pm; closed mid Nov to mid Feb) in Piazza della Cisterna has a reputation for serving the best ice cream in Italy.

PLACES TO VISIT

Museo Archeologico
Piazza del Duomo, Palazzo del Duomo, 53034 Colle di Val d'Elsa
🕐 Tue–Sun 11–12.30, 4.30–7.30
📷 €3

Museo Civico e d'Arte Sacra
Via del Castello 31, 53034 Colle di Val d'Elsa
☎ 0577 923888
🕐 11–12.30, 4.30–7.30
📷 €3

The Duomo, the Campanile and the Tuscan hills beyond seen from from Siena's Torre del Mangia (top)
Siena's Porta San Marco, gateway to the city (above)

OUT AND ABOUT

SAN GIMIGNANO

The old hilltop town of San Gimignano, with its celebrated skyline, is one of the highlights of a visit to Tuscany. This walk introduces you to the town's main museums and churches, including the former cathedral. It also takes you off the well-trodden visitor route to explore some of the quieter streets where you can best soak up the town's medieval beauty.

OUT AND ABOUT

THE WALK

Distance: 2.5km (1.5 miles)
Allow: 1–2 hours
Start/end at: Third (and last) parking area outside the city walls, called Parking No. 3 on Via Bagnaia

★ **From the parking area**, cross the road, go up some steps and enter the city walls. Turn right following Via Folgore da San Gimignano and Via XX Settembre. Turn left into Via San Matteo.

❶ Via San Matteo will make you feel as if you are stepping back 600 years, surrounded as you are by medieval palaces and towers. The same ornamental motifs are repeated in endless variations on the façades: Window arches are decorated with friezes of arrowheads, and doors are framed by typically Tuscan arches, where the keystone is shaped like a teardrop. Halfway down the street on the left you pass the church of San Bartolo, a tiny Romanesque building of rose-pink and yellow brick.

Continue along Via San Matteo to enter Piazza del Duomo.

❷ The Piazza's beauty is striking, but the original purpose of the towers found here was grim. In the vagaries of medieval inter-family conflict, the towers were both status symbol and offensive and defensive fortress. Noble families, the *magnati*, crowned their palaces with these symbols of their wealth, each aiming to build higher than the next one—several of San Gimignano's towers exceed 50m (165ft). Fourteen towers survive of the original 72 that were once packed into this tiny city.

Walk to the left-hand corner of the piazza and descend into Piazza della Cisterna.

Some of the remaining towers that make up San Gimignano's skyline

❸ Piazza della Cisterna, with its herringbone brick paving, gets its name from the 13th-century well (*cisterna*) in the middle.

With your back to Piazza del Duomo, leave Piazza della Cisterna by the right-hand corner, passing under the 12th-century Arco dei Becci. From here you can walk all the way down Via San Giovanni, which has some of the best shops, to the Porta San Giovanni, one of the city gates ❹. Turn right at the gate and right again at the sign for Madonna dei Lumi at the top of the steps on the left-hand side, where you will pass the Trattoria Chiribiri on the right. This means you are climbing back to the heart of San Gimignano along Via Berignano, a quiet residential street with unusual views of the towers crowning the highest point of the city. Here you will pass the La Mondragola restaurant (▷ 238). At the end of this street turn right then take the first left up Via della Costarella. At the top, turn right through the archway leading into the frescoed courtyard of the Palazzo del Popolo.

❺ The Palazzo del Popolo, dating from 1323, contains the Museo Civico (▷ 143–144). The most beguiling exhibits are the wedding scene frescoes, dating from the 1320s, by Memmo di Filippuccio and his assistants. They show a happy couple taking a bath together in a huge wooden tub and the groom stealing into bed alongside his sleeping bride. The energetic can climb the adjacent Torre Grosso for outstanding views.

Exit the Palazzo del Popolo and turn right, then immediately left under an arch into a small courtyard with the Collegiata on the right. This is Piazza Luigi Pecori.

❻ The Piazza has a loggia that is now the entrance to the Baptistery that shelters an *Annunciation* fresco by Ghirlandaio (1482). Musicians often perform on the opposite side of the square, next to the Palazzo della Propositura (Provost's house). There is also a small museum of religious art in the square.

Leave the square and turn left to reach the steps of the Collegiata (▷ 143) in Piazza del Duomo. Go through the Baptistery to enter the Collegiata.

Looking down on Piazza della Cisterna from the Torre Grossa

❼ Collegiata is modelled on the cathedral of Siena with its striped walls and star-covered vaults. The interior is a feast of frescoes. *The Last Judgement* scenes (1393–96) by Taddeo di Bartolo are the greatest attraction here since they depict an imaginative and grotesque range of punishments being meted out on the damned by devils who are clearly relishing their task. Less gruesome are the scenes from Genesis (1367) by Bartolo di Fredi , which include an appealing depiction of the creation of Adam and Eve.

Turn left out of the Collegiata and left again at the church into Piazza del Erbe, and then walk along Via della Rocca. Look out for the signs to 'rocca e parco di Montestaffoli'. This will lead you to the 14th-century Fortezza di Montestaffoli, which has good views of the city and surrounding countryside from its walls.

Backtrack to Piazza del Duomo, and leave by Via San Matteo. At the end you emerge by Porta San Matteo; turn right down Via Cellolese and left into Piazza Sant'Agostino.

❽ One of the last to be completed, Sant'Agostino (▷ 144) is another frescoed church. Benozzo Gozzoli's (c1421–97) scenes in the choir, illustrating the life of St. Augustine, are fresh and vivid, full of the gentle landscapes that this painter so loved.

To return to your car, leave the square beside the church of San Pietro and walk back down Via Folgore da San Gimignano to the gate in the city walls.

WHEN TO GO

San Gimignano fills up with day visitors between 11am and 6pm, so it's best to try to be here early in the morning or late in the afternoon. Thursday is a good day to come as this is market day.

WHERE TO EAT

The town is full of restaurants, pizzerias and bars. Try Osteria del Carcere (Via del Castello 13, tel 0577 941905; daily 12.30–2, 7.30–9.30), or Osteria delle Catene (Via Mainardi 18, tel 0577 941966; daily 12.30–2, 7.30–9.30), both of which serve simple, traditional dishes. Or visit Gelateria di Piazza (Piazza della Cisterna 5, tel 0577 942244; daily 9am–11pm mid Feb to mid Nov). This place serves excellent ice cream and they are previous winners of the Coppa

San Gimignano's atmospheric streets are perfect for a stroll

d'Oro (Gold Cup) in the Italian Championships.

PLACES TO VISIT

Santo Bartolo
Via San Matteo
🕐 Daily 8–7
💶 Free

Sant Agostino
🕐 Daily 7–12, 3–7 Apr–end Oct, 7–12, 3–6 Nov–end Mar
💶 Free

ORGANIZED TOURS

Numerous companies specialize in organized tours across the region. Whether you're an art lover, gourmand, fitness freak or thrill seeker, there will be something to suit. Below are a few of the many tours led by expert tour guides who can help you get to grips with Tuscany's abundant attractions and long history.

A horse-drawn trap mingles with pedestrians on Florentine streets

Michelangelo's Holy Family in Florence's Uffizi Gallery

The Tuscan countryside makes a stunning arena for a cycle ride

FLORENCE TOURS

ASSOCIAZIONE GUIDE TURISTICHE FIORENTINE
Tel 055 422 0901
www.florenceguides.it
This company provides a number of differently themed walks around the city, as well as archaeological tours of Fiesole.

CITY SIGHTSEEING ITALY
Tel 055 264 5363
www.city-sightseeing.it
Take an open-top bus tour around Florence and Fiesole (▷ 99). City itineraries last from one to two hours.

FLORENCE BY BIKE
Tel 055 488992
www.florencebybike.it
A growing company that rents bicycles and scooters within the city and has cycling tours of Chianti.

WALKING TOURS OF FLORENCE
Tel 055 264 5033
www.artviva.com
Providing a large range of themed walks around the city and tours around many Tuscan towns, such as Pisa, San Gimignano and Siena.

ART AND ARCHITECTURE

ACE STUDY TOURS
Tel 01223 835055 (UK)
www.study-tours.org
A long-established charity that organizes guided art and architecture trips and makes donations to restoration projects throughout the world.

ROAD TO ITALY
Tel 800/848-8163 (Canada)
www.roadtoitaly.com
Escorted breaks to Tuscany—the company will also put together bespoke packages.

CYCLING AND WALKING

THE ACCIDENTAL TOURIST
Tel 055 699376
www.accidentaltourist.com
This company organizes cycling and walking tours in the Tuscan countryside, as well as food and nature themed tours.

CHARNES TOURS
Tel 866 6650324 (US)
www.charnestours.com
A US-based company running fully supported one- or multiday bicycle and walking tours in Tuscany.

HEADWATER
Tel 01606 720099 (UK)
www.headwater.com
Guided walking, cycling and culinary holidays in many Italian regions, including the countryside of Tuscany.

RAMBLERS HOLIDAYS
Tel 01707 331133 (UK)
www.ramblersholidays.co.uk
Ramblers run a choice of guided walking and sightseeing country and city holidays throughout the region.

FOOD, EVENTS AND CULTURE

Tourist offices have details of a large number of cooking schools that suit a wide range of budgets and time scales.

EVERLAST TOUR AND TRAVEL
Tel 06 4741644
www.italytourtravel.com
Everlast, based in Rome, caters to a range of interests. It runs gastronomic, cultural, language, cycling and walking tours as well as Formula 1 Grand Prix excursions.

JMB OPERA HOLIDAYS
Tel 01905 830099 (UK)
www.jmb-travel.co.uk
Specializing in opera, JMB's tours include tickets to music festivals and concerts in some of the great opera houses in Italy.

KUDU TRAVEL
Tel 01722 782982 (UK)
www.kudutravel.com
A company running a choice of individual guided walking tours specializing in culture, gourmet food and wine, music and wildlife

PAGE AND MOY
Tel 08700 106212 (UK)
www.page-moy.com
A leading specialist with a varied choice of escorted and independent special interest tours, city breaks and trips to Grand Prix motor racing.

TASTING PLACES
Tel 020 7460 0077 (UK)
www.tastingplaces.com
Offers a choice of week-long escorted culinary trips, where you get an informal yet intensive exploration of regional cooking.

This chapter lists places to eat and places to stay, broken down by region, then alphabetically by town, or in the cities by establishment.

Eating and Staying

EATING OUT IN TUSCANY

Eating is definitely one of life's pleasures in Tuscany, as it is all over Italy. Tuscan food is fresh, seasonal and, above all, local. There's no such thing as Italian cooking, but rather regional cuisine, and you'll eat the best of Tuscan produce cooked to Tuscan recipes. Expect to find magnificent meat, beans and pulses, hearty bread and fruity olive oil.

A meal is all part of the Tuscan experience, whether dining formally or having a picnic

FRESH REGIONAL PRODUCE

Most Tuscan cooks are obsessed with freshness and food shopping is a daily social event in smaller towns. This is beginning to change in Florence and the larger towns, as huge supermarkets provide convenient 'one-stop' shopping for an increasingly busy population. But even here you will notice the range, freshness and quality of what's available. Outside the big cities, you're also unlikely to find restaurants serving anything other than local food, so don't expect to find much in the way of specialities from other Italian regions, let alone any serving international cuisine.

BREAD AND BEANS

Bread is the traditional staple and restaurants that pride themselves on their local cooking will feature it heavily—served up as *crostini* (bread with a savoury topping) covered in olive paste, fresh tomatoes or drizzled with oil, adding body to old-fashioned soups such as *ribollita* (thick vegetable soup), and providing the perfect foil to locally-cured *prosciutto crudo* (raw cured ham) and *finocchiona* (fennel-flavoured salami).

Tuscans are dubbed *mangiafagioli* (bean-eaters) with some justification—beans are very popular throughout the year, from the first tender broad beans eaten raw with pecorino (cheese made from sheep's milk) to the dried white beans with sage that accompany grilled meats.

MEALS

Many working Italians eat breakfast *(prima colazione)* in a bar—a cappuccino, strong coffee with plenty of hot milk, and a sweet pastry or a jam- or custard-filled croissant. Hotels usually serve a buffet breakfast with fruit juice and a selection of cereal, cold meat and cheeses.

Lunch *(pranzo)* and dinner *(cena)* both follow the same pattern—though it's unlikely that you will want to tackle the full menu twice a day. The first course is the *antipasto* (starter, literally 'before the meal'), a selection of *crostini* (bread with a savoury topping), cold meats and salami, seafood or vegetable dishes. *Il primo* (first course) consists of pasta, soup or risotto. This is followed by the *secondo* (second course), a portion of a meat or a fish dish, served on its own—if you want vegetables *(contorni)* or a salad *(insalata)* order them separately. This is followed by a selection of desserts *(dolci)* or cheese *(formaggio)*. The former is often fruit, fruit salad *(macedonia)* or an ice cream *(gelato)*, though more sophisticated places will have a wider range. There's no pressure to go through the whole menu, and it's acceptable to order a *primo* and salad, or an *antipasto* and *secondo*.

Italians drink water *(acqua minerale)* with every meal, either sparkling *(frizzante* or *con gas)* or still *(senza gas)*, accompanied by a relatively modest amount of wine or a beer. Excessive drinking is frowned upon in Italy. Bread is included with every meal.

MEALTIMES AND SMOKING

If you are heading for breakfast in a bar, most open for business around 7–7.30. Restaurants normally open for lunch around 12.30 or 1 and stop serving at 3; they close for the afternoon and re-open for dinner around 7.30–8.

Smoking is due to be banned in all public places in 2005, bringing Italy into line with EU regulations. However there is strong opposition and it remains to be seen how strictly the law will be enforced. In the meantime, some restaurants will have non-smoking sections.

WHERE TO EAT

- *Trattorie* are usually family-run places. They are generally more basic than restaurants. Sometimes there is no written menu and the waiter will reel off the list of the day's specials (see the menu reader on pages 216–217 for help). They are normally open during lunchtime and in the evening.
- *Ristoranti* are not always open for lunch. The food and surroundings are usually more refined than those of a *trattoria*. Both *trattorie* and *ristoranti* add a cover charge (*coperto*), which includes bread and a service charge to the bill.
- *Pizzerie* specialize in pizzas, but often serve simple pasta dishes as well. Look out for the sign *forno al legno*, meaning that the pizzas are cooked in a wood-fired oven.
- *Osterie* can either be old-fashioned places specializing in home-cooked food or extremely elegant, long-established restaurants.

PAYING THE BILL

- Pay by requesting the bill (*il conto*), and check to see whether service is included.
- Scribbled bills on scraps of paper are illegal; if you don't get a proper one, say that you need a receipt (*una ricevuta*), which all restaurants, bars and shops are legally obliged to issue. Both they and you can be fined if you do not take this with you.
- Smaller establishments normally expect to be paid in cash; you'll be able to use a credit card in more expensive establishments.
- If service isn't included, it's customary to leave a small tip—some loose change will do.
- All restaurants have one official closing day a week, but many places open every day during the summer.

SNACKS AND ICE CREAM

- Bars serve hot and cold drinks, alcohol and snacks throughout the day. It's customary to eat or drink standing up; you will pay a surcharge if you sit down either inside or at a table outside. In busier city bars make your request and pay at the cash desk, then take the receipt (*scontrino*) and go to the bar where you will be served.
- Snacks include *pannini* (filled rolls), *tramezzini* (sandwiches made on soft white bread), mini-pizzas and *toast* (toasted sandwiches). Smarter bars will bring olives, crisps (chips) or nuts with your drink if you're sitting down.
- All bars have toilets (*bagni*) but you may have to ask for the key (*chiave*).
- *Alimentari* (general grocers) sell breads and will often make you up a *pannino* (filled roll).
- Pizza, Italy's contribution to fast food, is available everywhere and served by the slice from tiny *pizzerie* to take out—look for the sign *pizza al taglio*. There are also a few international pizza chains to be found around the region.
- *Tàvole calde* are stand-up snack bars that serve freshly prepared hot food; some have seating as well.
- *Forni* (bakers) sell *foccace*, a flat oil and herb bread, which makes a great snack.

- *Rosticcerie* serve spit-roasted food, particularly chicken, pasta and vegetable dishes to eat in or take out.
- *Gelateria* sell a range of ice cream, served in a cone (*cono*) or a tub (*coppa*) of varying sizes. The best ice cream is made on the premises, known as *produzione propria*.
- Larger towns and cities have branches of McDonalds and Burger King.
- International cuisine is very limited in Italy. Chinese restaurants are becoming increasingly popular in middle- to large-sized towns, but Florence is about your only option in Tuscany for a wider choice.

WHAT TO DRINK

- Coffee (*caffè*) is served in bars and cafés. Choose from a small black coffee (*caffè* or *espresso*), a cappuccino (with frothy milk), *caffè con latte* (very milky coffee), *caffè macchiato* (an espresso with a drop of milk) or a *caffè corretto* with a slug of spirits. If you want weaker coffee, ask for a *caffè lungo* or an *Americano*. Decaffeinated coffee goes by the generic name Hag.
- Tea (*tè*) is generally served black; ask for *latte freddo* (cold milk) if you want milk. In summer *tè freddo* (iced tea), livened up with lemon or peach, is popular.
- Hot chocolate (*cioccolata calda*), often served with whipped cream (*panna*), is available during the winter months.
- Beer (*birra*) is widely drunk, either bottled or draught (*alla spina*). Preferred Italian brands include Nostra Azzura, Peroni and Moretti, and imported beers are widely available.
- Wine is served in bars as well as in restaurants. Ask for white (*bianco*), red (*rosso*) or the less common rosé (*rosato*). House wine is either *vino de la casa* or *vino sfuso*, and can be very good. Bottled wines are locally produced, except in smarter restaurants; best are DOCG wines (Denominazione d'Origine Contollata e Garantita)—the label guarantees its origins. Many producers are marketing some superb wines as *vino da tàvola*, which are well worth sampling.
- You may also see a wine called a Super Tuscan. These wines are made from non-traditional grapes, and are expensive, but highly regarded.
- Spirits are known by their generic names, and you will find all the usual ones on sale. Italians are also fond of *aperitivi* such as Martini, Campari, Cinzano and the artichoke-based Cynar, and firmly believe in settling the stomach after eating with a *digestivo*. Fiery grappa is the most common, but herb-based liqueurs (*amari*), such as Averna and Montenegro, are drunk everywhere and there are dozens of local varieties: Amaretto, based on almonds, Strega, made from herbs and saffron, and Limoncello, a lemon liqueur. Stock and Vecchia Romagna are Italy's preferred brandies.
- Soft drinks such as cola and lemonade compete with others, such as *spremuta di aranci* (freshly pressed orange juice), *granita* (fruity crushed ice), *sugo di albicocca* (bottled apricot juice) and *frullata*, a type of milk shake.

To fully appreciate Tuscan cuisine you will need to venture away from the beaten track and sample local dishes. If you don't speak Italian this can be a daunting prospect, but knowledge of a few key words will help you to work out what's on the menu, order what you want and avoid any embarrassing blunders. This menu reader will help you to translate common words and familiarize yourself with dishes and ingredients that you are likely to see on a menu.

Aubergines (eggplant, left), cheese for sale (middle) and freshly picked green olives (right)

Piatti–Courses
antipasti starter
primi piatti first course
secondi piatti main course
contorni vegetables/side dish
dolci desserts
spuntini snacks

Carne–Meat
agnello lamb
cacciagione game
cinghiale wild boar
coniglio rabbit
fegato liver
maiale pork
manzo beef
pancetta bacon
pollo chicken
prosciutto cotto cooked ham
prosciutto crudo cured raw
　　ham, saltier and stronger
　　than Parma
salsiccia sausage
tacchino turkey
trippa alla Fiorentina tripe
　　with onions
vitello veal

Pesce–Fish
alici anchovy
baccalà dried salt cod
branzino sea bass
fritto misto mixed fried fish
merluzzo cod
sarde sardines
sogliola sole
tonno tuna
trota trout

Frutti di Mare–Seafood
aragoste lobster
calamari squid
canestrelli scallops
cozze mussels
gamberetti prawns (shrimps)
ostriche oysters
vongole clams

Verdure–Vegetables
asparagi asparagus
carote carrots
cavolo nero strong dark
　　cabbage used in Tuscan
　　winter soups
cicoria bitter green leaves
　　stewed with garlic and
　　olive oil
cipolla onion
fagioli beans
fagiolini green beans
latuga lettuce
melanzane aubergines
　　(eggplant)
patate potatoes
peperone red/green pepper
　　(capiscum)
piselli peas
pomodori tomatoes
spinaci spinach
zucca pumpkin

Metodi di Cucina– Cooking Methods
affumicato smoked
al forno baked
alla griglia grilled, often over
　　an open wood fire

arrosto roasted
bollito boiled
casalingha home-made
cotto cooked
crudo raw
fritto fried
ripieno stuffed
stufato stewed

La Pasta–Pasta
cannelloni baked meat- or
　　cheese-filled tubes
fettucine wide strips
fusilli spiral shapes
lasagne layers of pasta, meat
　　sauce and béchamel or
　　tomato sauce
pappardelle rippled strips
penne quill shapes
ravioli pasta parcels filled with
　　meat, cheese or spinach
tagliatelle thin ribbons or strips
tortellini little 'hats' with meat
　　or cheese filling

Salsi/Sugi–Sauces
amatriciana bacon, tomato,
　　chilli and onion
arrabbiata tomato and hot chili
brodo broth
burro e salvia melted butter,
　　parmesan and sage
cacciatore sauce for meat:
　　tomato, onion, garlic,
　　mushrooms, wine
carbonara pancetta bacon, egg,
　　cream and black pepper
passata sieved tomatoes

EATING

pesto basil, garlic, pinenuts, olive oil and pecorino cheese
puttanesca tomato, garlic, hot chili, anchovies, capers
ragù minced meat, tomato and garlic
salsa sauce
salsa verde parsley, garlic, anchovies, capers, lemon juice, salt, pepper, olive oil
salsa di pomodoro tomato
sugo another term for sauce

Altri Piatti–Other Dishes
antipasto misto mixed cold meats: salami, ham etc.
frittata omelette
gnocchi small dumplings made from potato and flour or semolina
minestrone thick vegetable soup with pasta
risotto rice cooked in stock
risotto alla Milanese risotto with saffron
zuppa soup

Formaggi–Cheeses
fontina smooth, rich cheese
un formaggio di capra goat's cheese
un formaggio nostrano local cheese
parmigiano parmesan
pecorino hard cheese made with sheep's milk

Bevande–Drinks
acqua minerale mineral water
birra beer

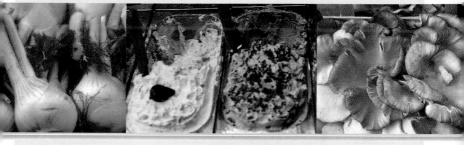

Fennel (left), vanilla and pistachio ice cream (middle) and oyster mushrooms (right)

Specialità–Special Dishes
acqua cotta thin vegetable soup, sometimes served with a poached egg
bistecca alla fiorentina thick steak grilled over a wood or charcoal fire
crostini rounds of toasted bread topped with olive oil, garlic and a variety of other toppings
fagioli al fiasco haricot beans stewed in olive oil
fagioli all'uccelletto cannelloni beans stewed slowly with garlic, sage and tomatoes
pappardelle al suga di lepre rippled strips of pasta with a hare sauce
peperonata sweet pepper and tomato stew
polpetti meatballs
ribollito literally meaning 're-boiled', vegetable soup thickened with bread and served the day after it's prepared
scaloppini thinly-sliced veal cooked in white wine
stracotto beef stew

Contorni–Side Dishes
insalata mista mixed salad
insalata verde green salad
pane bread
patate fritte chips (french fries)

Dolci–Cakes/Desserts
cantuccini very hard almond biscuits, served with wine at the end of a meal
cassata Sicilian fruit ice cream
cioccolata chocolate
crema custard
gelato ice cream
macedonia fruit salad
panforte hard spiced fruit cake from Siena
panna cream
una pasta a cake/pastry
semifreddo chilled semi-frozen dessert
tiramisù chocolate/coffee sponge (ladyfinger) dessert
torta tart, often latticed and filled with jam
zabaglione egg, sugar and Marsala dessert
zabaione di Verduzzo custard pudding with Friuli wine
zuccotto ice cream cake
zuppa inglese trifle

Frutti–Fruit
arancia orange
ciliege cherries
fragole strawberries
lamponi raspberries
mele apples
melone melon
pere pear
pesca peach
pesca noci nectarine
uve grapes

caffè corretto coffee with liqueur/spirit
caffè freddo iced coffee
caffelatte milky coffee
caffè lungo weak coffee
caffè macchiato coffee with a drop of milk
caffè ristretto strong coffee
digestivo after-dinner liqueur
frizzante fizzy
ghiaccio ice
liquore liqueur
porto port wine
secco dry
spumante sparkling wine
succo di arancia orange juice
tè tea
tè al latte tea with milk
tè freddo iced tea
vini da tavola table wines
vini pregiati quality wines
vino bianco white wine
vino rosato rosé wine
vino rosso red wine

Condimenti–Seasonings
aglio garlic
aromatiche herbs
basilico basil
capperi capers
pepe pepper
peperoncino chili
prezzemolo parsley
rosemarino rosemary
sale salt
salvia sage
senape mustard
zucchero sugar

EATING

13 GOBBI

Via del Porcellana 9r, 50123 Firenze
Tel 055 284015

This friendly restaurant is a great place to bring kids. Alongside an unusual assortment of foods there are more standard choices for those who prefer plain food. There are also fabulous desserts, such as *cioccolata con pere* (pears in chocolate sauce) and good Tuscan wine. When the weather is fine, reserve a table in the small courtyard to eat alfresco.

🕐 Tue–Sat 12.30–2.30, 7.30–10.30, Mon 7.30–10.30
🍽 L €40, D €65, Wine €16
🚌 B, C, 6, 11, 36, 37

ACQUERELLO

Via Ghibellina 156r, 50122 Firenze
Tel 055 234 1330

Sardinian restaurants are rare in Florence, but this is one of the best. There are lots of fish and seafood dishes to enjoy, including marinated anchovies, pasta with mussels, grilled lobster and cooked prawns. Otherwise, try the *petto di pollo alla Vernaccia* (chicken breasts in a white wine sauce). Sardinian wines such as Vermentino or Cannonau are available, along with Sardinian beer.

🕐 Daily 7pm–2am; closed Aug
🍽 D €40, Wine €10
🚌 A, 14

ALLE MURATE

Via Ghibellina 52r, 50122 Firenze
Tel 055 240618
www.caffeitaliano.it

An elegant, sophisticated restaurant, known for serving popular Tuscan dishes with an imaginative twist. Choose dishes beautifully prepared from a variety of fish and meat, including duck and turbot, or try home-made pasta such as *puglian orecchiette* (little ear-shaped pasta) with a meat sauce and *scamorza* cheese (rather like mozzarella). There's a selection of more than 300 wines. The soft lighting and candles make for an intimate dining experience.

🕐 Tue–Sun 7.30–11; closed 2 weeks over Christmas
🍽 D €100, Wine €18
🚌 A, 14

L'ANTICO RISTORO DI CAMBI

Via Sant'Onofrio 1r, 50124 Firenze
Tel 055 217134
www.anticoristorodicambi.it

Popular with the local lunchtime crowd, this eatery

is in the Oltrarno district south of the river, near the Ponte Vespucci. The food is generally light with an emphasis on fresh produce. Try one of the excellent salads or a platter heaped with such delicacies as buffalo mozzarella, basil, cured meats and pecorino (sheep's milk) cheese.

🕐 Mon–Sat 12.30–2.30, 7.30–10.30
🍽 L €30, D €65, Wine €12
🚌 D, 6

ASTOR CAFFÈ

Piazza Duomo 20r, 50123 Firenze
Tel 055 239 9000

For something different try this modern, American-style café-bar near the Duomo, a superb place to eat lunch or to grab a snack. Mediterranean cuisine dominates—try the excellent fish dishes and innovative salads, which make a change from the traditional *insalate* (salads) that are usually served in the city. In the evening DJs and sometimes bands perform in the back room (▷ 166).

🕐 Mon–Sat 9am–1am (buffet served until 10pm); closed 2 weeks in Aug
🍽 L €40, Wine €15 (food only served at lunchtime)
🚌 A, 1, 6, 7, 10, 11, 14, 17, 23

BALDOVINO

Via San Giuseppe 22r, 50122 Firenze
Tel 055 241773
www.baldovino.com

This bustling, friendly *trattoria*, not far from Piazza Santa Croce, is run by a Scotsman, whose famous friends from the world of entertainment often drop in when they're in town. Children are always welcome, and most enjoy the great pizzas from the wood-burning oven. The constantly changing menu includes plenty of soups, beef dishes, various grilled meats and some inventive plates of *pastasciutta* (pasta with a sauce), including *tagliatelle agli asparagi* (pasta with an asparagus sauce). The wine list includes many Tuscan classics.

🕐 Daily 12–2.30, 7–midnight Mar–end Oct; Tue–Sun 12–2.30, 7–midnight, rest of year
🍽 L €35, D €55, Wine €15
🚌 C, 14

LA BARAONDA

Via Ghibellina 67r, 50122 Firenze
Tel 055 234 1171

The charming dark wood and tiled interior of this excellent restaurant is the setting for many a memorable Florentine meal. The friendly staff will guide you through the menu, which consists of first-class *cibo da casa* (home-style food) based on seasonal Tuscan produce. A bottle of Brunello wine complements the Tuscan cuisine.

🕐 Thu–Tue 7–midnight
🍽 L €45, D €50, Wine €10
🚌 A, 14

BAR GELATERIA ERMINI

Via Gioberti 125, 50121 Firenze
Tel 055 244464

Close to Piazza Beccaria, in a popular shopping area, this *gelateria* is a good place to take a break and cool down. Ask for one of the cones as the portions are more generous than those served in the *coppette* (small cups). You can't go wrong with a *palla*

EATING

BECCOFINO

Piazza degli Scarlatti 1r, 50125 Firenze
Tel 055 290076
www.beccofino.com

This popular *enoteca* (wine bar) attracts an international crowd, who enjoy such delights as *gnocchi al nero di seppia* (small dumplings in squid ink) and *faraona alle olive* (roast guinea fowl with black olives). For a lighter meal, try a salad, pasta or risotto dish from the alternative menu. The 500-strong wine list has a superb range of Tuscan and Piedmontese wines.

🕙 Tue–Sat 7–11.30, Sun 12.30–3
🍴 L €50, D €95, Wine €15
🚌 6, 11, 36, 37

(scoop) of *bacio* ice cream, which contains pieces of nuts and chocolate. Credit cards are not accepted.

🕙 Mon–Tue, Thu–Sat 8am–midnight; Sun 8–8
🍦 Ice cream cone €1.50
🚌 6, 8, 12, 31, 32, 33, 80

BAR PERSEO

Piazza della Signoria 16r, 50122 Firenze
Tel 055 239 8316

The fresh fruit varieties are the best of all the mountains of delicious ice cream on view at Bar Perseo: the *fragola* (strawberry) and mango are both hard to resist. As well as the ice cream, they serve drinks and a good selection of quick bites, including filled *panini* and *ciabattas*. The chicken breast salad is popular, and vegetarians will enjoy the croissants with a filling of *carciofi* (artichoke). Your snack will cost you a lot more, however, if you sit at one of the tables on the street. Credit cards are not accepted.

🕙 Daily 7am–midnight; closed 3 weeks in Nov
🍴 Cappuccino €3; ice cream cone €3; filled *panini* from €3
🚌 A, B

BELLE DONNE

Via delle Belle Donne 16r, 50100 Firenze
Tel 055 238 2609

This tiny, informal restaurant, near Piazza Santa Maria Novella, is densely packed with convivial shared tables, decorated with masses of fruit, vegetables and flowers. Choose your Tuscan dish from the blackboard—salads and vegetables are the highlights.

🕙 Daily 12–2.30, 7–8.30
🍴 L €20, D €40, Wine €12
🚌 6, 9, 11

BORGO ANTICO

Piazza Santo Spirito 6r, 50125 Firenze
Tel 055 210437

Enjoy some Neapolitan pizza in a setting reminiscent of Naples itself. There are plenty of meat dishes for the main course, and a fine northern/southern Italian fusion in the

risotto scamorza e zucchine (risotto with smoked cheese and courgettes/zucchini). Reserve a table to avoid disappointment—especially if you want to eat outside.

🕙 Daily noon–midnight
🍴 L €20, D €60, Wine €13
🚌 D, 11, 36, 37

THE BRISTOL

Hotel Helvetia & Bristol,
Via dei Pescioni 2, 50123 Firenze
Tel 055 287814

This fine restaurant at the five-star Hotel Helvetia & Bristol (▷ 244) attracts international stars and Florentine nobility. In the restaurant and Winter Garden cocktail bar the gilding, chandeliers and draperies give an exclusive, old-world charm. There isn't anything too innovative on the menu, but it is expertly prepared, traditional Tuscan cuisine and well-known Italian dishes.

🕙 Daily 12.30–3, 7–10.30
🍴 L €75, D €125, Wine €20
🚌 A, 6, 11, 22, 36, 37

CAFFÈ AMERINI

Via della Vigna Nuova 63r, 50123 Firenze
Tel 055 284941

This is a good spot to take a break during the day, but avoid early afternoon when it's particularly busy. Try one of the excellent snacks, which include filled *panini*, *piadine* (flat bread) and a variety of savoury pastries packed with tasty fillings. Those with a sweeter tooth will be tempted by the array of cakes.

🕙 Mon–Sat 8–8
🍴 Filled *panino* €4
🚌 A, 6

CAFFÈ ITALIANO

Via Condotta 12, 50122 Firenze
Tel 055 289020
www.caffeitaliano.it

It's a pleasure to linger in the high-vaulted rooms of the Palazzo da Cintoia, which are

full of wonderful antiques. Classic Tuscan fare includes *cinghiale* (wild boar) and an excellent choice of pasta dishes and chunky soups. The wine list includes lots of Chiantis and Super Tuscans.

🕙 Tue–Sun noon–1am
🍴 L €50, D €90, Wine €15
🚌 A

CAFFÈ MEGARA

Via della Spada 11–17, 50123 Firenze
Tel 055 211837

This is a great place to grab a *merenda* (snack break) while reading one of newspapers provided. In the heart of the clothes shopping district, the Megara also shows catwalk videos. The adventurous menu includes exotic meats, such as kangaroo and ostrich, prepared *carpaccio* style (very thinly sliced and raw), as well as vegetarian dishes.

🕙 Daily 8am–2am
🍴 Pasta dishes for around €7, Wine €8
🚌 A, 6, 11, 22, 36, 37

EATING

CAFFÈ RICCHI

Piazza Santo Spirito 8–9r, 50125 Firenze
Tel 055 215864
www.caffericchi.it

The Oltrarno's beautiful people make up the bulk of the crowd here. You can eat alfresco in the leafy Piazza Santo Spirito, or inside in the contemporary dining rooms. The menu is crammed with traditional Tuscan dishes made from fresh fish, such as *maltagliati* (pasta with oysters) and *viareggina* (spaghetti with small clams). Caffè Ricchi also serves meat dishes, plus salads.

🕐 Mon–Sat 7.30pm–2am; closed 1 week mid-Aug

🍴 D €70, Wine €15

🚍 D, 11, 36, 37

CAMMILLO

Borgo San Jacopo 57r, 50125 Firenze
Tel 055 212427

A well-established *trattoria* that attracts an international crowd and a host of Italian celebrities enticed by the excellent home-made pasta, various *baccalà* (salted cod) dishes and expertly cooked meats. Try some of the Masiero family's delicious virgin olive oil with bread. Wine lovers have a great choice of Tuscan and Piedmontese wines.

🕐 Thu–Tue 12–2.30, 7.30–10.30; closed Aug, 2 weeks over Christmas

🍴 L €45, D €80, Wine €9.50

🚍 D, 11, 36, 37

IL CANTASTORIE

Via della Condotta 7–9r, 50122 Firenze
Tel 055 239 6804

Paintings of old Florentine scenes and subdued lighting adorn the exposed stone and stuccoed walls of this eatery, which has many loyal customers who love its rustic interior. The friendly staff are

happy to help you choose from the excellent soups and grilled meats. Although the type of food served here is

SPECIAL

CAFFÈ RIVOIRE

Piazza della Signoria 5r, 50122 Firenze
Tel 055 214412

A Florentine institution, opened in the 1870s, that is a must if you are a first-time visitor or chocolate lover—the Rivoire produces arguably the best chocolate in town. Try one of their exquisite ice creams or the famous Rivoire hot chocolate at one of the tables in the Piazza della Signoria or Loggia dei Lanzi. But remember, you pay for the privilege of sitting down to enjoy your treat.

🕐 Tue–Sun 8am–midnight; closed 2 weeks in Jan

🍴 Sit down: cappuccino €5, ice cream from €5.50

🚍 A, B

often called *cucina povera* (poor person's food), it is rich in taste and texture. There is a limited choice of Chianti and other Tuscan wines.

🕐 Daily 12–2.30, 7–11

🍴 L €25, D €50, Wine €12

🚍 A, 23

CANTINA BARBAGIANNI

Via Sant'Egidio 13, 50122 Firenze
Tel 055 248 0508
www.barbagianni.it

The decorations here include contemporary artworks, and there is an equally inventive menu. Among the highlights are a green pepper risotto with strawberries and mint, and duck with blueberries. And it's likely that you've never tasted anything like some of the unusual salad combinations. The layout of the restaurant consists of a lot of small tables, so the place is not suited to large groups. Reservations advisable.

🕐 Mon–Sat 7.30–midnight; closed last 2 weeks in Jul

🍴 D €60, Wine €12

🚍 14, 23

CANTINETTA ANTINORI

Palazzo Antinori, Via dei Tornabuoni 3, 50123 Firenze
Tel 055 292234
www.antinori.it

This elegant *cantinetta* (little cellar) is famed for its excellent wines. The wonderful food

uses the best seasonal produce: *bruschetta* (garlic toast), pork, truffles, salted fish, hearty soups and pâté dominate in winter, and lighter pasta dishes, imaginative salads and fresh fish in the warmer months.

🕐 Mon–Fri 12.30–2.30, 7–10.30; closed Aug

🍴 L €45, D €85, Wine €12

🚍 A, 6, 11, 22, 36, 37

CAPOCACCIA

Lungarno Corsini 12–14r, 50123 Firenze
Tel 055 210751
www.capocaccia.com

This stylish café-bar is one of the places to be seen in Florence. It's famous for its sumptuously filled *panini* and American-influenced brunch menu. Eat out in style in the frescoed *salone* or in the bar area overlooking the Arno. There are more than 200 different wines available, including Brunello.

🕐 Tue–Sun noon–2am, Mon noon–4pm

🍴 Filled *panini* €4.50–€12, smoked salmon and salad €15

🚍 B

CARABÈ

Via Ricasoli 60r, 50121 Firenze
Tel 055 289476
www.gelatocarabe.com

A Sicilian *gelateria,* Carabè sells ice cream that harks back to the original recipes that arrived in southern Italy from the ancient Arabic world. Tastes such as pistachio, fig and apricot provide some stimulating alternatives to the more usual selection. Try, too, the refreshing *granite* (crushed ice with fruits and sometimes with added cream) and *sorbetti* (sorbets). Credit cards are not accepted.

🕐 Daily 10am–1am

🍴 Ice cream cone €1.70–€5.50

🚍 1, 6, 11, 14, 17, 22

EATING

CAVINI
Piazza delle Cure 19, 50133 Firenze
Tel 055 587489
www.gelateriacavini.it
This *gelateria* (ice-cream parlour) in Campo di Marte has been going strong since the 1920s. Traditional ice creams such as strawberry vie with new tastes each month. Past creations have included papaya and *semifreddo alla zabaione*, which contains marsala wine. More eccentric combinations include cheese and pears. A wide variety of cakes and pastries also sold.
Ⓒ Tue–Sun 9am–1am
Ⓦ Small cup of ice cream €1.25
Ⓔ 7

IL CESTELLO
Piazza Ognissanti 3, 50123 Firenze
Tel 055 264201
Enjoy an *aperitivo* in the Westin Excelsior Hotel's lavish Bar Donatello before dining in style in a grand salon, with views of the River Arno. Chef Giuseppe Dalla Rosa uses the finest seasonal ingredients in his fusion of international haute cuisine and traditional Mediterranean and Tuscan influences. Alternative menus exploring specific cuisines, including *cucina pugliese* (from Puglia in southern Italy), are regularly available. There is an excellent wine list.
Ⓒ Daily 12–2.30, 7.30–11
Ⓦ L €60, D €120, Wine €20
Ⓔ A, B, 6, 11, 36, 37

COCO LEZZONE
Via del Parioncino 26, off Lungarno Corsini, 50123 Firenze
Tel 055 287178
Coco is a fashionable and well-known restaurant with an interesting mix of functionalism and gourmet cuisine. The cool white-tiled dining room is a reminder that the building used to be a dairy. It is also furnished with communal tables, so you must be prepared to share your space. The cuisine is Tuscan, with particularly good meat dishes. Try the enormous *bistecca alla fiorentina* (grilled steak, which is best ordered in advance) or pork chine. The service is quick, and at busy times you may be asked to move on to make way for new customers. Credit cards are not accepted.

SPECIAL
CIBREO
Via de' Macci 122r, 50122 Firenze
Tel 055 234 1100
Fabio Picchi's renowned restaurant is one of Florence's gastronomic shrines, and as such is expensive. Starters include couscous with yoghurt and *insalatina di trippa* (tripe salad). The fish and meat dishes are both innovative and delicious—such as the tuna steaks, while for vegetarians there are dishes piled with porcini mushrooms. There are also great Tuscan wines to choose from. Ask about the latest performances at the Teatro del Sale-Cibreocittà (an adjoining theatre with dining space).
Ⓒ Tue–Sat 12.30–2.30, 7–11; closed Aug, 1st week in Jan
Ⓦ L €80, D €140, Wine €16
Ⓔ A, C

Ⓒ Mon, Wed–Sat 12–2.30, 7–10.30, Tue 12–2.30; closed Aug
Ⓦ L €30, D €60, Wine €10
Ⓔ 11, 31, 32, 36, 37

COQUINARIUS
Via delle Oche 15r, 50122 Firenze
Tel 055 230 2153
This is one of central Florence's better wine bars, full of dark wood and stylish posters. It's a great place to sample lots of different cheeses, cold cuts, smoked fish, *carpacci* meats (raw, thinly cut and dressed with lemon and oil) and *stuzzichini* (Italian bar snacks). There are also soups and large salads to choose from, plus a large selection of wines, a range of teas and some wickedly rich hot chocolate concoctions.
Ⓒ Mon–Sat 9am–11pm; closed Aug
Ⓦ L €20, D €45, Wine €10
Ⓔ A, 14, 23

DA BENVENUTO
Via della Mosca 16r, 50122 Firenze
Tel 055 214833
A popular restaurant in the Santa Croce quarter serving good quality Tuscan food. The walls are adorned with an eclectic collection of artworks, and the clientele is an equally intriguing array of local characters. As for the menu, pasta

with a meaty sauce represents good value, or ask about the season's beef and pork dishes, which are served with herbs and accompanied by side dishes of potatoes and crunchy vegetables.
Ⓒ Mon–Sat 12–2.30, 7–10.30
Ⓦ L €25, D €45, Wine €7
Ⓔ B, 23

DON CHISCIOTTE
Via Cosimo Ridolfi 4r, 50129 Firenze
Tel 055 475430
A truly wonderful culinary experience awaits you at this popular eatery near the Fortezzo da Basso, serving mostly fish and some meat dishes to satisfy the most knowledgeable Tuscan gourmet. Try the *insalata calda di frutta di mare sul panzanella Toscana* (warm seafood salad on Tuscan bread) or the *timballo di melanzane ripieno di pappa di pomodoro* (aubergine/eggplant mousse stuffed with bread and tomatoes). The service is attentive and the wine list includes top quality Tuscan wines as well as some great choices from overseas.
Ⓒ Tue–Sat 1–2.30, 8–10.30; closed Aug
Ⓦ L €40, D €100, Wine €6
Ⓔ 7, 10, 20, 25, 31, 32, 33

SPECIAL
ENOTECA PINCHIORRI
Via Ghibellina 87, 50122 Firenze
Tel 055 242777
www.enotecapinchiorri.com
This French-influenced establishment is one of Italy's best. The rose-scented courtyard and elegant dining areas are ideal settings to complement the exquisite nouvelle cuisine and wonderful wine list. Try one of the imaginative dishes of liver or pigeon, and the sumptuous desserts are a delight. The service is impeccable but the prices are high, and you will need to reserve a table.
Ⓒ Thu–Sat 12.30–2, 7.30–10, Tue 7.30pm–10pm; closed Aug and Christmas
Ⓦ L €130, D €210, Wine €25
Ⓔ A, 14

EATING

FRANCESCANO

Largo Bargellini 16r, 50122 Firenze
Tel 055 241605

The quality of the food at the Francescano, near Santa Croce church, distinguishes it from other restaurants in this part of town. Surrounded by marble and unusual artworks, its regulars enjoy the Tuscan dishes created from fresh ingredients. Begin with the cheese and cold meat platter and assorted vegetable starters. If you haven't tried the hearty Tuscan *ribollita* (soup made with beans and black cabbage), this is a good place to enjoy a bowl.

🕐 Wed–Mon 12–3, 7–11; closed Aug
🍴 L €30, D €50, Wine €10
🚌 C, 14

FUOR D'ACQUA

Via Pisana 37r, 50124 Firenze
Tel 055 222299

As its name implies (it means out of water), this restaurant is famed for its wonderful fish creations, such as the marine salads with balsamic vinegar dressing or the beautifully prepared *calamari* (squid). The wine list is dominated by white wines, but there are also some decent reds to choose from.

🕐 Mon–Sat 8–11; closed Aug
🍴 D €110, Wine €15
🚌 D, 6

GELATERIA DE' MEDICI

Via dello Statuto 3–5, 50129 Firenze
Tel 055 475156

What this elegant *gelateria* lacks in seating it more than makes up for in exciting the taste buds of its loyal clientele. Home-made *frutti di bosco* (woodland fruits), *fragole* (strawberry) and a rum-chocolate combination are just the start. Credit cards are not accepted.

🕐 Daily 9.30am–12.30am
🍴 Cups and cones from €1.50
🚌 4, 8, 20, 28

GELATERIA DEI NERI

Via dei Neri 20/22r, 50125 Firenze
Tel 055 210034

Neri's display of *gelati* (ice creams), *semifreddi* (a type of frozen mousse) and *sorbetti* (sorbets), decorated with fresh fruit flourishes, is spectacular. All the delicious ices are made on the premises, so freshness is guaranteed. A variety of

wafers is available to go with your choice. Credit cards are not accepted.

🕐 Daily 11.30–11.30, Apr–end Oct; Thu–Tue 11.30–11.30, rest of year
🍴 Small cup of ice cream €2.50
🚌 C, D, 23

LE GIUBBE ROSSE

Piazza Repubblica 13r, 50123 Firenze
Tel 055 212280
www.giubberosse.it

This celebrated café was once the haunt of the Florentine *avanguardia* (avant garde); the red-jacketed waiters and stylish interior hint at this illustrious cultural past. Bring a book, order one of the pasta dishes or a *panino*, and observe the scene on the elegant piazza. For just a taste of history, order a drink at the bar and linger there. It also has a restaurant.

🕐 Daily 8am–2am; restaurant 12–3.30, 6.30–11
🍴 Pasta dishes €4, D €50, Wine €12,
🚌 A, 6, 22

GUSCIO

Via dell'Orto 49a, 50124 Firenze
Tel 055 224421

Both fish- and meat-eaters are very well served at this popular *trattoria*. Various beef and goose dishes are served daily, and locally produced sausages often figure in sauces. Ask the waiter to suggest a suitable vintage from the superb wine list. Among the tempting desserts is ice cream topped with a warm chocolate sauce.

🕐 Tue–Sat 7.30pm–11pm; closed Aug
🍴 D €55, Wine €10
🚌 D

INCANTO

Piazza Ognissanti 1, 50123 Firenze
Tel 055 27161

The restaurant of the Grand Hotel (▷ 243) has a lavish interior yet contemporary feel. The menu changes with the seasons and is always very well balanced. Look out for crustacean treats, like the wonderfully piquant marinated *gamberi* (prawns), and the various *ragù* (rich meat sauces), but save some space for one of the fabulous *dolci* (desserts). Wine buffs will not be disappointed by the list of more than 300 labels.

🕐 Daily 12.30–3, 7–11
🍴 L €42, D €140, Wine €30
🚌 A, B

IL LATINI

Via de' Palchetti 6r, 50123 Firenze
Tel 055 210915
www.illatini.com

This rustic *osteria* serving hearty helpings of Tuscan classics attracts a loyal crowd to the long communal tables. Highlights include a traditional *zuppa di farro* (a meat, grain and vegetable soup) and the wild boar *dolceforte* (wild boar stewed in honey, dried fruit and pinenut sauce). Save room for the heavenly tiramisu—even if you can't manage to finish a whole portion of this rich dessert. The Latini family produce some fine wines and their own delicious olive oil.

🕐 Tue–Sun 12.30–2.30, 7.30–10.30
🍴 L €24, D €50, Wine €10
🚌 A, 6

OLIVIERO

Via delle Terme 51r, 50123 Firenze
Tel 055 287643
www.ristorante-oliviero.it

Excellent service and superb Tuscan food are the main characteristics of Francesco Altomare's eatery. Meat-lovers have a lot to choose from, including guinea fowl and rabbit. Delicious soups, wonderfully fresh vegetables and some innovative pasta creations make up the rest. The dessert list includes *zuppa inglese* (trifle). Rare wines and spirits are available.

🕐 Mon–Sat 7.30pm–1am; closed Aug
🍴 D €90, Wine €17
🚌 A, B, 6, 11, 36, 37

OSTERIA ANTICA MESCITA SAN NICCOLÒ

Via San Niccolò 60r, 50125 Firenze
Tel 055 234 2836

The San Niccolò serves up a superb range of antipasti dishes in its rustic wooden interior, including lots of salami, *crostini* and *bruschette* (savoury toasts). These are

EATING

followed by traditional dishes such as *trippa* (tripe) and *lingua* (tongue). Vegetarians can choose from the heaped salads and the couscous with vegetables.

🕓 Mon–Sat 12–3, 7–1am
🍽 L €25, D €36, Wine €6.50
🚇 C, D, 23

OSTERIA DEL CINGHIALE BIANCO

Borgo San Jacopo 43r, 50125 Firenze
Tel 055 215706
www.cinghialebianco.it

The White Boar restaurant, near Ponte Santa Trinità, has an attractive white-painted two-level interior. The cooking is traditional Tuscan, and there is boar on the menu, which is served with polenta. If that doesn't appeal to you, there are also chicken, rabbit or veal dishes.

🕓 Mon–Tue, Thu–Fri 6.30–11, Sat–Sun 12–2.30, 6.30–11
🍽 L €40, D €70, Wine €16
🚇 3, 13, 32

OSTERIA FARNIENTE

Via della Mattonaia 19r, 50121 Firenze
Tel 055 246 6473

This unusual *osteria* (inn) is a modern take on the traditional rustic eatery, and in that vein, each dish has a contemporary twist. Order a bottle of one of the excellent Super Tuscan wines (▷ 215), munch on the *crostini* (toasted crusty bread) with black Umbrian truffle paste, and let one of the friendly waiters guide you through the menu. Ones to look out for include their famous soups and hearty meat dishes.

🕓 Tue–Sun 12.30–3, 7–midnight
🍽 L €30, D €50, Wine €12
🚇 6, 31, 32

OSTERIA SANTO SPIRITO

Piazza Santo Spirito 16r, 50125 Firenze
Tel 055 238 2383

The Santo Spirito is a trendy eatery that excels in creating adventurous, mountainous salads, including a wonderful parmesan and *prosciutto* (cured ham) salad with pinenuts and mixed leaves. There is also a superb choice of cheeses and a decent wine list.

🕓 Daily 12.30–2.30, 7.30–11.30
🍽 L €20, D €60, Wine €12
🚇 D, 11, 36, 37

PALLOTTINO

Via Isola delle Stinche 1r, 50122 Firenze
Tel 055 289573
www.trattoriapallottino.com

In business for nearly 100 years, this traditional *trattoria* has small dining rooms, wooden tables and candles. It is near Santa Croce and is known for its cheese and salami platters. Also excellent pasta dishes with both creamy and tomato-based sauces.

🕓 Tue–Sun 12.30–2.30, 7.30–10.30; closed 2 weeks in Aug
🍽 L €30, D €40, Wine €8
🚇 B, 13, 23

RISTORANTE ENOTECA PANE E VINO

Piazza di Cestello 3r, 50125 Firenze
Tel 055 247 6956

This inviting restaurant is a popular evening choice in the San Niccolò district. Seasonal Tuscan dishes predominate, so the menu changes frequently. However, expect such delights as *zucca* (pumpkin) in a buttery sage sauce, *ravioli di pesce* (fish-filled ravioli), pasta with a wild boar sauce and *petto di faraona* (guinea-fowl breast). There is an excellent wine list and, unusually, an ample dessert menu.

🕓 Mon–Sat 7pm–11pm; closed Aug
🍽 D €60, Wine €13
🚇 C, 23

PAOLI

Via dei Tavolini 12r, 50122 Firenze
Tel 055 216215

The restaurant dates back to the 19th century, and Tuscan and other Italian dishes are served in a beautifully frescoed dining room reminiscent of a medieval tavern. Most are

served with fresh vegetables; try the sole or pasta with kidneys. Paoli is centrally placed between the Duomo and Piazza della Signoria, making reservations essential.

🕓 Wed–Mon noon–2.30, 7–10.30; closed most of Aug
🍽 L €52, D €84, Wine €16
🚇 A, 1, 6, 7, 11, 14

PERCHÈ NO!

Via dei Tavolini 19r, 50122 Firenze
Tel 055 239 8969

This *gelateria* has the welcome bonus of tables where you can sit and enjoy your choice of ice cream. There are always new varieties to try, but for a taste of the Mediterranean you can't beat the Malaga, which is dotted with rich wine grapes. Ask for *due palline* (two scoops) of *meringa gelata* (meringue ice cream) and wait for the server to ask for confirmation and reply 'Perchè no!' (meaning Oh, why not!). Credit cards are not accepted.

🕓 Wed–Mon 11am–12.30am, Tue 11am–7.30pm, Mar–end Oct; Wed–Mon 12–7.30pm, Nov–end Feb
🍦 Ice-cream cone from €2
🚇 6, 17, 23

PILLORI D'ARNO

Borgo Ognissanti 65r, 50123 Firenze
Tel 055 292195

The Pillori d'Arno may look functional, but the edges are softened by the staff of this café-bar in Ognissanti, who are very friendly. Take a break from the area's antiques shops and join the various assorted characters who drift in to sample the excellent coffee, pastries and snacks. The *barista* (bar staff) will prepare you a great *spremuta d'arancia* (freshly squeezed orange juice). If you're hungry, order one of the excellent filled *panini*. Credit cards are not accepted.

🕓 Daily 7am–9pm
🍽 Sit down: filled *panino* €3, cappuccino €2.10
🚇 A, B

EATING

PITTI GOLA E CANTINA
Piazza Pitti 16, 50125 Firenze
Tel 055 212704
Sample the Pitti's excellent selection of wines, and feast on the fabulous meat and cheese platters and grilled vegetables. Wine bottles and other paraphernalia fill the wooden interior, and an eclectic Italian musical soundtrack plays in the background. The young staff prepare the simple but wholesome fare in front of your eyes at the bar, and serve some of Italy's finest cold cuts accompanied by huge chunks of bread. Choose a table outside overlooking the Palazzo Pitti or grab a stool by the bar.
🕐 Tue–Sun 10am–11pm
🍽 Cheese and meat platter €22, Wine from €4 per glass
🚍 D, 11, 36, 37

RELAIS LE JARDIN
Hotel Regency, Piazza D'Azeglio 5, 50121 Firenze
Tel 055 245247
www.regency-hotel.com
The dark wood and carpeted interiors, and lush, well-kept gardens make the Hotel Regency's restaurant a welcoming place. Head chef Rino Pennucci's immaculately prepared and presented haute cuisine menu is constantly evolving, as traditional Italian dishes are given a modern twist. Book early to reserve a candlelit table.
🕐 Daily 12.30–3.30, 7.30–11.30
🍽 L €50, D €180, Wine €25
🚍 C, 6, 31, 32

RISTORANTE PERSEUS
Piazza Mino da Fiesole 9, 50014 Firenze
Tel 055 59143
This is one of the best places in Florence to sample the famous *bistecca alla fiorentina* (Florentine T-bone steak from special Tuscan cattle). Choose either a huge chunk of beef by weight—a 1kg (2lb) slab will feed two hungry mouths—or a thinner version cooked with balsamic vinegar. These classic dishes are accompanied by delicious salads, Tuscan cannellini beans and cooked vegetables. For dessert, try the pannacotta with forest fruits or a slab of delicious cheesecake. There's a good wine list and a lovely terrace where you can dine alfresco facing the Teatro Romano.

🕐 Daily 12.30–3, 7.30–11.30, Apr–end Oct; Wed–Mon 12.30–3, 7–11, rest of year
🍽 L €30, D €55, Wine €13
🚍 7

SABATINI
Via dei Panzani 9a, 50123 Firenze
Tel 055 282802
www.ristorantesabatini.it
This elegant restaurant is a respected Florentine institution. The cuisine mixes solid Tuscan dishes with international influences. They serve a

great *bistecca alla fiorentina* (Florentine steak), while seafood enthusiasts can try the risotto with scampi. Excellent wine list and professional and unobtrusive service.
🕐 Tue–Sun 12.30–2.30, 7.30–10.30
🍽 L €60, D €120, Wine €25
🚍 A, 1, 4, 7, 10, 11, 22, 23, 36, 37

IL SANTO BEVITORE
Via di Santo Spirito 64–66r, 50125 Firenze
Tel 055 211264
www.ilsantobevitore.com
A *enoteca* (wine bar) that has great food and is good value, serving platters of salami, *prosciutto* and various cheeses. Main courses include *risotto alla zucca* (pumpkin risotto), a soup of the day and *bucatini con le sarde* (long tubes of pasta with a sardine sauce). An amiable place full of wood, marble and bonhomie.
🕐 Mon–Sat 12.30–2.30, 7.30–11.30
🍽 L €30, D €45, Wine €8
🚍 11, 36, 37

TARGA DI CAFFÈ CONCERTO
Lungarno Cristoforo Colombo 7, 50136 Firenze
Tel 055 677377
www.targabistrot.net
For international cuisine at its finest amid sleek contemporary surroundings, try Caffè Concerto alongside the River Arno. Typically southern European ingredients are used

innovatively. The menu includes *tortiglioni con pesce spada* (pasta with swordfish) and a scampi risotto. There are plenty of cheeses to sample, a detailed wine list and some delectable *dolci* (desserts). Book well in advance.
🕐 Mon–Sat 12.30–2.30, 7.30–11; closed 1–20 Aug and over Christmas
🍽 L €55, D €90, Wine €14
🚍 31, 32

TAVERNA DEL BRONZINO
Via delle Ruote 25r, 50129 Firenze
Tel 055 495220
Taverna del Bronzino serves a wealth of Tuscan culinary delights alongside more international dishes, including deep-fried lamb chops served with vegetables. Fish and meat dishes change frequently according to the seasons. If it's on the menu, and you are a fish lover, try the expertly prepared sea bass. The Florentine artist Bronzino (1503–72) would surely have approved of the masterpieces created daily in his former workshop.
🕐 Mon–Sat 12.30–2.30, 7.30–11.30; closed Aug
🍽 L €40, D €100, Wine €16
🚍 7, 10, 20, 25, 31, 32, 33

TRATTORIA ADA
Viale Mazzini 25–27r, 50132 Firenze
Tel 055 244140
This pleasant, bright *trattoria* in the Campo di Marte area is a relaxing place to try Florentine fare at its best. Expect traditional recipes alongside more contemporary creations. They also serve the famous *bistecca alla fiorentina* (Florentine steak). There's ample seating outside.
🕐 Mon–Sat 12.30–3, 7.30–10.30
🍽 L €30, D €52, Wine €8
🚍 12, 13

TRATTORIA ANTELLESI
Via Faenza 9r, 50123 Firenze
Tel 055 216990
Antellesi serves excellent Tuscan food at affordable prices. Starters include pâté with *crostini* (toasted crusty bread), as well as an inventive salad that combines nuts, fruits, various leaves and pecorino (sheep's milk) cheese. Equally enticing are the stuffed lamb, beef stew, veal escalope and *bistecca alla fiorentina* (Florentine

EATING

steak). Vegetarians will love the artichoke risotto. Antellesi has a decent wine list, and serves pannacotta with *frutti del bosco* (fruits of the forest).

🕐 Wed–Mon 12–2.45, 7–10.45
🍽 L €25, D €50, Wine €10
🚌 4, 7, 10, 12, 13, 25, 31, 32, 33

TRATTORIA ANTICHI CANCELLI

Via Faenza 73r, 50123 Firenze
Tel 055 218927

Hearty Tuscan food is the mainstay of this *trattoria*, which provides good value for money in central Florence. Feast on hearty soups and *bruschetta* (toast) topped with deliciously sweet tomatoes and extra virgin olive oil. The menu changes according to the season, and there's always a substantial meat or fish dish. Vegetarians have a variety of *contorni* (side dishes) along with the classic *spaghetti al pomodoro e basilico* (with tomato and basil) to choose from. The house wine is very reasonable.

🕐 Daily 12–2.30, 7–10.30
🍽 L €20, D €40, Wine €8
🚌 4, 7, 10, 12, 13, 25, 31, 32, 33

TRATTORIA DEI QUATTRO LEONI

Via del Vellutini 1r, 50125 Firenze
Tel 055 218562
www.4leoni.com

The Four Lions is a welcoming, informal place spread across two high-ceilinged, brick-arched rooms. You can sit outside in spring and summer under a large awning. The food is generally straightforward Florentine cuisine with a few inventive twists, such as cabbage salad with avocado. Good fish options on Friday. Booking is recommended.

🕐 Thu–Tue 12–2.30, 7–11, Wed 7–11
🍽 L €40, D €60, Wine €10
🚌 6, 11

TRATTORIA PALLE D'ORO

Via Sant'Antonino 43r, 50123 Firenze
Tel 055 288383

From the outside it looks decidedly inauspicious, but this Santa Maria Novella *trattoria* consistently proves to be very good value. Expect hearty soups, *gnocchi* (small dumplings made of flour and potato) dishes, decent fish and filling pasta. For dessert, the

pannacotta, cheesecake or tiramisu are all great choices.

🕐 Mon–Sat 12–3, 7.30–11
🍽 L €15, D €26, Wine €10
🚌 1, 6, 7, 10, 11, 17

TRATTORIA PONTE VECCHIO

Lungarno Archibusieri 8r, 50125 Firenze
Tel 055 292289
www.trattoriapontevecchio.com

A stone's throw from the Ponte Vecchio and its crowds, this *trattoria* is inevitably popular with visitors and you cannot fault the Tuscan cuisine. One

of the house specials is pasta with mushrooms.

🕐 Daily 12–3.30, 7–10
🍽 L €30, D €860, Wine €15
🚌 D

TRE SOLDI

Via d'Annunzio 4r, 50137 Firenze
Tel 055 679366

This no-nonsense *trattoria* is welcoming and unpretentious. It's well worth the trip to Campo di Marte—especially if you are going to see Florentia play soccer at the nearby stadium. The food is great value and includes some highly inventive dishes, including *insalatina calda al ginepro* (a warm vegetable salad with junipers) and *gnocchetti di zucca* (small dumplings with a pumpkin sauce). The wine menu is mostly Tuscan reds.

🕐 Sun–Thu 12–3, 8–10, Fri 12–3; closed Aug
🍽 L €30, D €50, Wine €8
🚌 3, 6, 20, 34

ZÀ-ZÀ

Piazza del Mercato Centrale 26r, 50123 Firenze
Tel 055 215411

An old-fashioned, inexpensive *trattoria* near the Mercato Centrale, which is very popular with visitors. The Tuscan food is excellent, and the fixed price menus are great value. The inviting stone-walled interior is especially appealing in the

summer heat; arrive at opening time or reserve a table.

🕐 Daily 11–11
🍽 L €26, D €70, Wine €9.50
🚌 1, 6, 7, 10, 12, 25

ZIBIBBO

Via di Terzollina 3r, 50129 Firenze
Tel 055 433383
www.zibibbonline.com

Zibibbo has a deservedly good reputation. They specialize in fish dishes, but don't ignore the tasty vegetable *contorni* (side dishes) and typically Tuscan creations like tagliatelle with duck *ragù* (tomato sauce). There's a superb choice of fish, including *tagliatelle ai gamberi e zucchine* (prawns and zucchini) and *spaghetti al pesce spada* (with swordfish), and there are plenty of Tuscan wines to select. Good selection of desserts including chocolate cake. Subtle lighting gives the place a comfortable feel.

🕐 Mon–Sat 12.30–3, 7–11; closed Aug
🍽 L €50, D €80, Wine €14
🚌 14c

EATING

NORTHERN TUSCANY

The restaurants are listed alphabetically (excluding Il and Le) by town, then by name. The prices given are for a two-course lunch (L) and a three-course dinner (D) for two people, without drinks. The wine price is for the least expensive bottle. See pages 173–179 for alternative places to eat. See page 2 for a key to the symbols.

BARGA

OSTERIA ANGELIO
Piazza Angelio, 55051 Barga
Tel 0583 724547
If you are a jazz fan, you'll love this intimate restaurant owned by Gian-Marco, a charismatic jazz buff and fluent English speaker. He serves rustic country fare at reasonable prices.

The menu has few dishes and rotates seasonally depending on local produce, but usually includes grilled meats (such as sausage with beans, rosemary and sage), cold cuts and some vegetarian pasta dishes. During the summer you can eat on the terrace. Reservations are recommended during the jazz festival (▷ 180).
🕙 Tue–Sun 12–3, 6–11
🍴 L €20, D €30, Wine €8

CAMAIORE

RISTORANTE LA MEA
Viale Provinciale, Valpromaro 1, 55041 Camaiore
Tel 0584 956047
This large, family-run place serves a variety of home-made Tuscan dishes with produce fresh from the local market. Popular dishes include *crostini alla toscana* (hot chicken liver and wild boar pâtés on toasted crusty bread), *ravioli con funghi* (wild mushroom ravioli) and a range of grilled and roasted meats, such as guinea fowl. Save some room for the *dolci della casa*—desserts made to traditional family recipes. Credit cards are not accepted.
🕙 Daily 12–2, 7–10, Jun–end Sep; Wed–Mon 12–2, 7–10, rest of year
🍴 L €20, D €40, Wine €5

FAUGLIA

LA GATTAIOLA
Vicolo San Lorenzo 2–4, 56043 Fauglia
Tel 050 650852
You can see as far as Pisa's Leaning Tower and Lucca's city walls from the small hill town of Fauglia. Local Tuscan cuisine is served and the house specials come recommended by the friendly staff: *risotto con funghi* (wild mushroom risotto), *arrosto d'agnello* (roast lamb with garlic) and a range of home-made pastas sprinkled with truffle shavings. Reservations advisable.
🕙 Tue–Sun 12.30–3, 7.30–10.30
🍴 L €45, D €60, Wine €8
🚗 From Pisa, take the Collesalvete/ Rome road, SS206; follow the signs to Fauglia (18km/11 miles from Pisa)

FIESOLE

LA LOGGIA
Via Doccia 4, Fiesole 50014
Tel 055 567 8200
www.villasanmichele.com
Its evocative former monastery setting and some of the finest cuisine in the area are what attract diners to this Fiesole restaurant in the hotel Villa San Michele (▷ 248). You can eat in the covered courtyard or the vaulted open-air section, which has stunning views of Florence below. Expect plenty of fresh produce and home-made pasta: The mushroom tagliatelle and scampi dishes are delights. Later in the evening a pianist plays in the cocktail area at the far end of the terrace. Reservations are essential.
🕙 Daily 1–2.30, 7–9.30; closed mid-Nov to mid-Mar
🍴 L €100, D €180, Wine €30
🚗 7
🚗 A1 from Florence (or Via Giuseppe Mantellini—the road to Fiesole); turn right at the sign at the bottom of the hill

RISTORANTE I POLPA
Piazza Mino da Fiesole 21–22, 50014 Fiesole
Tel 055 50485
Come to eat at this friendly restaurant and to enjoy a magnificent night-time view over the city of Florence. Not only is there an open wood-burning grill, but the oven is lit too, for cooking *crostini*—the toasted crusty bread with a variety of toppings that make tasty starters. Reservations are advisable.
🕙 Thu–Tue 7–10
🍴 D €40, Wine €9
🚗 7

GARFAGNANA

ALBERGO L'APPENNINO DA PACETTA
Piazza San Pellegrino 5, 55035 San Pellegrino in Alpe, Lucca
Tel 0583 649069
www.albergolappennino.com
This friendly, family-run hotel has been receiving visitors since 1221, and its excellent restaurant prides itself on a warm welcome. Everything is home-made, from the pasta to the jam used in the cakes and pastries. Good, hearty mountain food is represented by *polenta con cinghiale* (ground maize cooked to a thick porridge served with a wild boar sauce).
🕙 Daily 12–3, 6.30–9.30
🍴 L €30, D €40, Wine €5.50
🚗 From Castelnuovo di Garfagnana follow SP72, and signs for San Pellegrino in Alpe

ALBERGO RISTORANTE DA CARLINO
Via Garibaldi 15, 55032 Castelnuovo Garfagnana, Lucca
Tel 0583 644270
Carnivores will find they are pampered here with generous hunks of freshly grilled meats appearing on wooden platters. Some of the beef is local, some comes from Ireland. There's local trout on the menu, and *sformatino di verdura*, a sort of vegetable soufflé, will please vegetarians. You can eat in the wood-beamed room inside or on the terrace in the summer. Credit cards are not accepted.
🕙 Daily noon–3, 7.30–midnight
🍴 L €22, D €50, Wine €5

EATING

OSTERIA VECCHIO MULINO

Via Vittorio Emanuele 12, 55032
Castelnuovo Garfagnana
Tel 0583 62192

Owner Andrea is part of the
Italian Slow Food movement—
suppliers of organic food,
produced using traditional
methods. His *osteria* is tiny
and usually packed, so you
might consider stopping for an
early lunch or to buy ingredients for a picnic. If you eat in,
wave after wave of delicious
dishes are brought on wooden
platters. These might include
slivers of *bazzone* (local ham
from pigs that forage in the
woods) or *pane di patate*
(bread made with potatoes).
Shelves line the crowded walls
with a large selection of wines.
 ⏰ Mon–Sat 7.30am–8.30pm
 🍴 L €25, Wine €5

LUCCA
ANTICO CAFFÈ DELLE MURA

Piazzale Vittorio Emanuele 2,
55100 Lucca
Tel 0583 467962

This restaurant is set into
Lucca's splendid city walls.
Specializing in Tuscan cuisine
such as *tortelli lucchese* (pasta
stuffed with meats, cheese
and vegetables), timbale with
vegetables and basil sauce,
and fillet of pork in an onion
dressing, the menu also has
a good selection of seasonal
fish dishes. Tables are set up
in summer under the pillars
in front of the restaurant, and
reservations are recommended
for these.
 ⏰ Wed–Mon 10.30am–7.30pm
 🍴 L €50, Wine €12

BARSOTTI DA GUIDO

Via C. Battisti 28, 55100 Lucca
Tel 0583 467219

This small *trattoria*, a few
paces from Piazza San
Salvatore in the middle of
Lucca, serves predominantly
Tuscan and Lucchese cuisine

with the usual mixture of cold
cuts, grilled meats (including
wild boar sausage, beef and
veal), roasts and home-made

pastas. Light salads play a key
role. There is no English version of the menu but staff are
happy to translate. Small but
well-chosen wine list.
 ⏰ Mon–Sat 12–3, 7–11
 🍴 L €30, D €50, Wine €7

BUCA DI SAN ANTONIO

Via della Cervia 3, 56100 Lucca
Tel 0583 55881

One of the oldest restaurants
in Lucca, Buca di San Antonio

is also one of the most popular. The menu is all à la carte,
with an emphasis on Lucchese
cuisine, and changes with the
seasons. Dishes generally
include grilled and roasted
meats such as stuffed oven-
cooked rabbit and pork with
rosemary and garlic. The waiters can provide you with
recommendations from the
wine list, which is extensive.
Reservations are advisable
for dinner.
 ⏰ Tue–Sat 12.30–2.30, 7.30–10.30,
Sun 12.30–2.30
 🍴 L €40, D €60, Wine €10

DANTE

Via delle Gavine 72, San Macario,
55100 Lucca
Tel 0584 956046

This small restaurant serves
dishes typical of the Lucca
area, including home-made
ravioli stuffed with wild

mushrooms, *pollo al mattone*
(chicken cooked on a brick, a
traditional way of oven-cook-
ing meat) and a wide range of
grilled meats. The à la carte
menu also has wine recom-
mendations to accompany
your selection. The restaurant
is relatively quiet and reservations are only necessary in
especially busy months.
 ⏰ Tue–Sun 12–2, 7.30–10, Mon
7.30–10
 🍴 L €35, D €50, Wine €10
 🚗 Take the Viareggio road and follow
signs to San Macario (10km/6 miles
from Lucca)

OSTERIA IL PERGOLONE

Via di Tiglio 622, Località Palaiola,
Pieve di Compito, 55012 Cappanori,
Lucca
Tel 0583 960089
www.ilpergolone.com

There's an emphasis on home
cooking at this family-run
osteria on the edge of a small
lake. In the compact dining
room you can choose predominantly Lucchese dishes from
either of the two menus (one
meat, one fish). Taking pride
of place on the meat menu are
antipasto misto di cinghiale
(a mix of wild boar starters)
and *coniglio alla cacciatora*
(rabbit stew). The fish menu
varies according to the season,
but tends to include lobster,
langoustines and a variety of
freshly caught seafood.
 ⏰ Thu–Tue 12.30–2.30, 7–11
 🍴 L €16, D €30, Wine €6.50
 🚗 Take the SS439 from Lucca towards
Pontedera

RISTORANTE CANULEIA

Via Canuleia 14, 55100 Lucca
Tel 0583 467470

A small and friendly restaurant
that is within walking distance
of the amphitheatre. It specializes in Italian fast food, or
what the owners like to call
'spaghetti express'. It also has
a generous *menu turistico*,
which includes *zuppa di farro*
(a grain soup traditional to
the Garfagnana region) and
spaghetti vodka. Eat alfresco
in the garden or in the small
dining room. Reservations
are recommended.
 ⏰ Mon–Sat 12–2.30, 7.45–9.30
 🍴 L €36, D €60, Wine €8

RISTORANTE CELIDE
Viale Giusti 7, 56100 Lucca
Tel 0583 91091

Just outside Lucca's city walls, Ristorante Celide specializes in seafood caught fresh off the nearby Versilia Coast. House dishes such as *catalana frutti e verdura* (lobster with seafood and vegetables) come with wine recommendations and the bar is well stocked with after-dinner *digestifs*. Dining is split between two rooms: one whitewashed, with arched ceiling supports, the other quieter and full of leafy plants and paintings by local artists.

🕐 Mon–Sat 12.30–3, 7.30–11
🍴 L €35, D €60, Wine €6

RISTORANTE GAZEBO
Via Nuova per Pisa 1952, 55050 Massa Pisana, Lucca
Tel 0583 379737
www.locandalelisa.com

In the conservatory of the Locanda l'Elisa hotel (▷ 249), Il Gazebo prides itself on using local produce in its classic regional dishes. The food is delicious and it makes a good choice for a romantic meal. Main courses like *costolette d'agnello al rosmarine con purea di patate al tartufo* (lamb cutlet with rosemary served on mashed potato with truffles) reflect the chef's aim to serve traditional country food. Reservations essential.

🕐 Daily 12.30–2.30, 7.30–10; closed Jan
🍴 L €35, D €100, Wine €20
🚌 Take the A11 from Lucca, leave at the Lucca exit and follow the SS12 towards San Giuliano Terme/Pisa (3km/2 miles from Lucca)

RISTORANTE LA MORA
Via Lodovica 1748, 55029 Sesto di Moriano, Lucca
Tel 0583 406402
www.ristorantelamora.it

Although it is 10km (6 miles) from the city, this is one of Lucca's best known and most expensive restaurants. La Mora serves a *menu gastronomico* of about a dozen dishes in leisurely succession. Based on local Garfagnanan and Lucchese cuisine, dishes include *tortelli lucchese* (oven-cooked pasta stuffed with meats, cheese and vegetables) and *coniglio garfagnana* (rabbit stewed with rosemary and garlic). Be sure to save room for dessert, of which there are usually two or three. Spacious conservatory dining room with great views of the garden. Reservations required.

🕐 Tue–Thu 12–2.30, 7.30–10
🍴 L €30, D €70, Wine €10
🚌 Take the SS12 from Lucca towards Abetone

TRATTORIA DA LEO
Via Tegrimi 1, 55100 Lucca
Tel 0583 492236
www.trattoriadaleo.it

At this popular family-run *trattoria* you can eat in the dining room, with its pastel walls and wooden furnishings, or on the simple but shaded terrace. The owners pride themselves on making guests feel at home, sometimes pulling up a chair and chatting when the meal is over. The menu includes dishes such as *ribollita* (Tuscan bean soup), *vitello arrosto con patate arroste* (roast veal with roast potatoes) and *ravioli agli spinaci fatti in casa* (home-made spinach pasta).

🕐 Mon–Sat 12.30–2.30, 7.30–10.30, Sun 12.30–2.30, Sep–end Jun; daily 7.30pm–10.30pm Jul, Aug
🍴 L €20, D €40, Wine €10

MONTECATINI TERME
ENOTECA GIOVANNI
Via Garibaldi 25/27, 51016 Montecatini Terme, Pistoia
Tel 0572 71695

Many visitors come to Montecatini Terme for health reasons, and there is a fresh, light approach to food at this elegant restaurant. The menu has a good selection of fish, vegetable and meats dishes. There is also a comprehensive list of national and international wines. Soft lighting and gentle background music plays in the restaurant or you can eat outside in the square in the summer. Reservations recommended for evening dining.

🕐 Tue–Sun 12.30–2.30, 8–10; closed 2 weeks from 14 Feb and from 15 Aug
🍴 L €40, D €120, Wine €16

RISTORANTE LA TORRE
Piazza Giusti 8, Montecatini Alto, 51016 Montecatini Terme, Pistoia
Tel 0572 70650

There is a funicular that will take you from Montecatini Terme to Montecatini Alto and this restaurant. It is in the pretty little main square with outside eating, where you can keep an eye on the village scene. There's a good Tuscan menu: try the *zuppa di fagioli* (bean soup) or the *grigliata mista* (mixed grilled meats). The wine list has more than 400 different wines. Inside there is a frescoed room, as well as a tower dating back to 1100, with space only for a candlelit table for two: A reservation for this is essential.

🕐 Wed–Mon 12–3, 7–11
🍴 L €24, D €60, Wine €13
🚌 Follow signs for Montecantini Alto and wind uphill for 3km (2 miles)

PISA
BENY
Piazza Chiara Gambacorti 22, 56100 Pisa
Tel 050 25067

A small restaurant that specializes in fish bought fresh from the market that morning. The chalkboard menu is entirely dependent on the season and can change at short notice, but generally includes sea bass, langoustines and various seafood pastas. Beny, the owner, will give you food and wine recommendations. The restaurant sees an increasing number of foreign visitors, but no English is spoken, so bring your dictionary if you want a translation of the ingredients.

🕐 Mon–Fri 1–2.30, 8–11, Sat 7.30–11; closed 1 week in Aug
🍴 L €45, D €80, Wine €13

LA BUCA
Via G. Tassi 6/B, Via S. Maria 171, 56100 Pisa
Tel 050 560660
www.labuca.org

Within walking distance of Piazza dei Miracoli, La Buca is in a popular spot in the heart of Pisa. It draws the crowds with its pleasant outdoor terrace and the set-price lunch menu, which offers Tuscan cuisine at a reasonable cost.

Dinner is a little more formal with à la carte menus and attentive waiters, but the dishes are nothing unusual for Pisa with lots of pizza and pasta choices.

Sat–Thu 12–3, 7–11

L €25, D €40, Wine €9

DA BRUNO
Via Luigi Bianchi 12, 56100 Pisa
Tel 050 560818
www.pisaonline.it/trattoriadabruno
The self-proclaimed best restaurant in Pisa, Da Bruno is a long-established *trattoria* serving traditional Pisan cuisine. The two dining rooms have wood-beamed ceilings, long, elegant tables, and whitewashed walls covered with photographs of famous people who have dined here. The menu includes rustic country dishes such as *baccalà con i porri* (salt cod cooked with leeks and tomatoes) and a variety of grilled fish dishes. Reservations advisable.

Wed–Sun 12–3, 7–11, Mon 12–3

L €40, D €50, Wine €18

DA UGO
Statale Aurelia 1, Migliorino Pisano, 56100 Pisa
Tel 050 804455
A popular restaurant just outside the city, Da Ugo serves Italian and traditional Tuscan meat and fish dishes. What's on offer depends on what was fresh at the market, but generally includes pasta, rice dishes, such as *risotto con funghi porcini* (risotto with porcini mushrooms), and a range of home-made desserts. A good wine list complements the dishes, while the staff are relaxed and eager to help. Reservations are advisable.

Tue–Sat 12–3, 7.30–10.30, Sun 12–3

L €30, D €50, Wine €6

Take Via Aurelia towards Genova; 10-minute drive from Pisa

OSTERIA LA MESCITA
Via Cavalca 2, 56100 Pisa
Tel 050 544294
Influenced by seasonal and local produce, this family-run

restaurant and wine bar serves light but traditional Tuscan cuisine. The menu changes weekly depending on what's on offer in the market. The wine cellar has more than 300 varieties.

Tue–Sun 12.30–3, 7.45–10.45; closed 3 weeks in Aug

L €30, D €70, Wine €12

LA PERGOLETTA
Via delle Belle Torri 36, 56127 Pisa
Tel 050 542458
La Pergoletta occupies one of the most attractive medieval towers in a street famous for its beautiful towers. The owner has devised a menu which gives the best of Tuscany's rustic cuisine with a modern twist. Dishes include *minestra di farro* (soup with farro grain), *arrosto d'agnello* (roast lamb with rosemary and garlic) and a fresh fish of the day. Reservations recommended.

Tue–Fri, Sun 1–2.30, 8–10.30, Sat 1–2.30; closed 1st 2 weeks in Aug

L €30, D €60, Wine €8

RISTORANTE EMILIO
Via Cammeo 44, 56100 Pisa
Tel 050 562141
Close to the Campo dei Miracoli (▷ 106–109), this is a good place to stop for lunch. On a day of hot afternoon sun, the two dining rooms feel fresh with their whitewashed walls, wooden furnishings, marble flooring and leafy plants. The cuisine is mostly Tuscan with both fish and meat playing an important role. There is also a good local wine list. Reservations recommended; open for dinner by prior arrangment only.

Daily noon–3.30pm

L €30, Wine €5.20

OSTERIA DEI CAVALIERI
Via San Frediano 16, 56100 Pisa
Tel 050 580858
This small, whitewashed *osteria*, close to the university quarter, is popular with visitors and locals for its generously priced menu and friendly welcome. The cuisine is Tuscan and Lucchese with dishes such as *ribollita* (bean soup), *tortelli lucchese* (oven-cooked pasta stuffed with meats, cheese and vegetables) and a range of *grigliata* (grilled wild boar sausage, chicken, beef or veal). Vegetarian dishes are available on the à la carte menu. Reservations may be necessary in high season.

Mon–Fri 12.30–2, 7–11.30, Sat 7.45–10; closed last week Jul, 1st week Aug

L €25, D €55, Wine €8

RISTORANTE SANTA MARIA
Via Santa Maria 104/106, 56100 Pisa
Tel 050 561881
www.pisaonline.it/Ristorante-SantaMaria
The Santa Maria has a well-priced but straightforward menu of pizzas, cold cuts, grilled meats and seasonal Tuscan dishes. The restaurant is split between a self-service area, perfect for grabbing a

quick lunch, and a pizzeria in an ancient-looking dining room with exposed medieval brick walls, arched doorways and a beamed ceiling. The wine list is varied and bottles are stacked behind the well-stocked bar.

Daily 9–4, 6–12.30

L €16, D €40, Wine €7

LO SCHIACCIANOCI
Via Vespucci 104a, 56125 Pisa
Tel 050 21024

A tiny *trattoria* specializing in fish from the nearby coast, pasta and traditional Tuscan meat dishes. It's simple, old-fashioned and relaxed. Giovanni and his wife recommend the best of that day's seafood pasta, grilled meats or fish (commonly octopus, shellfish and sea bass). Other dishes include *ribollita* (thick bean soup) and mushroom ravioli. The wine list has labels from all over Italy.

Mon–Sat 12–3, 7.30–10.30

L €30, D €40, Wine €8

LA TANA GUIDO
Via San Frediano 6, 56126 Pisa
Tel 050 580540

La Tana Guido is a family-run pizzeria in the heart of the university area, catering mainly to students and visitors, who flock here for the generous servings of pizza and sociable atmosphere. There's also a range of *grigliata* (grilled meats) and *arosta* (roast chicken or pork flavoured with garlic) on the menu. The wine list is reasonable and there is seating for 150 diners.

Mon–Sat 12–2.30, 7–10.30

L €12, D €28, Wine €8

LA TAVERNA DI PILLO
Via del Borghetto 39, 56100 Pisa
Tel 050 571467
www.latavernadipillo.it

Pillo's owners, Sandra and Paolo, run this well-respected restaurant, whose house specials include oven-baked fish from the Tyrrhenian Sea, ravioli stuffed with wild mushrooms, rice with seafood and a range of grilled meats covered with garlic and herbs. The principally local wine list is well chosen to match the varied menu.

Fri–Wed 12.30–2.30, 8.15–10.30, Nov–end May; 12.30–3.30, 7–10.30, rest of year

L €30, D €50, Wine €7

PISTOIA
TRATTORIA DELL'ABBONDANZA
Via dell'Abbondanza 10, 51100 Pistoia
Tel 0573 368037

Care has been taken here to create a fresh, attractive environment, with swags of dried flowers and fruit hanging from the white-painted beams, and tile-topped tables with dark green mats. There's a bustle about the place, as a team of cooks prepare fried chicken, roasted rabbit and *la trippa*— tripe cooked in the Florentine way. The *trattoria* is in a tiny traffic-free street just off the old market in town, and in fine weather tables are put outside.

Fri–Tue 12.15–3, 7.15–10, Thu 7.15–10; closed 1st 2 weeks in May and in Oct

L €18, D €40, Wine €4

TIRRENIA
DANTE E IVANA
Viale del Tirreno 107c, Tirrenia 56018 Pisa
Tel 050 384882
www.danteeivana.it

Named after the owner and his wife, Dante e Ivana is a first-class fish restaurant serving carefully selected produce. There is no menu—the dishes depend on what Dante has found in the market that morning. Lobster is the house delicacy, and other mainstay dishes include sea bass sautéed with oregano and tomato. This is a winebar/restaurant, so the wine list is extensive.

Tue–Sat 12.30–2.30, 7.30–midnight (kitchen closes 9.30pm)

L €45, D €95, Wine €12

Follow the signs for Tirrenia from Pisa

VIAREGGIO
GIORDANO BRUNO
Viale Europa 7, 55049 Viareggio, Lucca
Tel 0584 392201

Former soccer player Bruno Giordano owns this combination of wine bar and pizzeria in a building with views to the sea and the mountains behind. Inside it is crisp and cool with modern furnishings. Giordano is passionate about food and wine and organizes wine tastings on a regular basis from his selection of more than 1,300 different labels, of which 500 are non-Italian. Afterwards you can enjoy a pizza cooked in a wood-burning oven or sample some of the delights of the interesting menu. In summer the big doors are removed to let in the sea breezes, and there is a roof terrace.

Daily 8pm–2am

D €64 (Pizza €8), Wine €12

TRATTORIA LA DARSENA
Via Virgilio 150, 55049 Viareggio
Tel 0584 392785

Hidden away on a back street in the less glamorous part of Viareggio, La Darsena is a bustling, bright and popular

family-run fish restaurant; booking is essential. The fish and seafood is always very fresh and prepared in a typically no-nonsense way. Start your meal with the endless stream of house antipasti. Follow this with a delicious *spaghetti alle vongole* (with clams), *allo scoglio* (with mixed seafood) or with red mullet sauce. Main courses include octopus and potato stew and *fritto misto* (mixed, deep fried seafood). The wine list is dominated by whites; the *vino della casa* is inexpensive and cheerful.

Tue–Sun 12–2.30, 7.30–10.30

L and D €30, Wine €8

RISTORANTE PIZZERIA LEONE
Via della Foce 23–27, 55049 Viareggio, Lucca
Tel 0584 32198

Away from the activity of the seafront you can sit outside here and watch the bustle of the old port. Although the pizzas are excellent, fish is the priority and locals pack in to eat the changing dishes of the day. The surroundings are simple, so all the attention is on the food and welcoming, helpful service. A delicious Prosecco (sparkling white wine) from the Veneto area marries well with the food.

Tue–Sat 7–midnight, Sun 12–3pm

D €60, Wine €8

SIENA

AL MANGIA

Piazza del Campo 42–46, 53100 Siena
Tel 0577 281121
www.almangia.it
The Al Mangia occupies a great spot overlooking the Piazza del Campo. The restaurant is now run by the fourth generation of the Senni family. Tastefully decorated, Al Mangia serves typical local meat and fish dishes, including quail's egg salad with palm hearts and

locally smoked duck breast with *crostini* (toasted crusty bread). Because of its location, reservations recommended.
🕐 Daily 12–3.30, 7–10, Mar–end Oct; Thu–Tue 12–3.30, 7–10, rest of year
🍽 L €70, D €90, Wine €16

AL MARSILI

Via del Castoro 3, 53100 Siena
Tel 0577 47154
www.ristorantealmarsili.it
This restaurant is in a medieval building dating from the 14th century and with a dining room lovingly furnished with traditional heavy wood. Besides the large main dining area there are smaller brick niches, with banqueting tables for larger parties. The Tuscan cuisine includes *gnocchetti* (little potato dumplings) with duck, home-made *crespelle*

(crêpes) and vegetarian options. The wine bar is in a cellar carved out of rock below the Marsili Palace. Reservations are advisable.

🕐 Tue–Sun 12.30–2.30, 7.30–10.30
🍽 L €30, D €60, Wine €12

ANTICA OSTERIA DA DIVO

Via Franciosa 29, 53100 Siena
Tel 0577 284381
This eatery is celebrated as much for its architecture as for its food: The medieval building, with some walls left as bare rock, is very striking. You may find the back and basement rooms (former Etruscan tombs) a little morbid, but the romantic hidden corners and tunnels make the place popular. Try the *pici al ragù di lepre* (pasta with rabbit sauce) or duck breast with saffron croquettes.
🕐 Wed–Mon 12–2.30, 7–10, Nov–end Aug; daily, Sep and Oct
🍽 L €25, D €70, Wine €14

ANTICA TRATTORIA BOTTEGANOVA

Strada Chiantigiana 29, Frazione di Botteganova, 52025 Siena
Tel 0577 284230
www.anticatrattoriabotteganova.it
You will find this popular restaurant 2km (1 mile) outside the old town walls. There's a *menu degustazione* that allows you to sample a large number of dishes. Otherwise you can settle for fresh pasta, grilled or roasted meat and fish, and Italian classics such as a guinea fowl terrine with Sicilian pistachios and a chestnut-honey sauce. Vegetarian dishes available.
🕐 Mon–Sat 12.30–2, 8–10; closed 1 week in Jan, 1 week in summer
🍽 L €55, D €110, Wine €18
🚌 From the Porta Ovile in Siena, follow the SS408 towards Montevarchi

IL BIONDO

Via del Rustichetto Angolo Piazza Posta, 53100 Siena
Tel 0577 280739
Down a quiet side street lined with medieval buildings, Il Biondo is popular with business people at lunchtime and visitors in the evening. In summer, try to reserve a table on the outside terrace overlooking the small piazza. The menu is strong on local cuisine, particularly fish, pasta and desserts. This place is worth splurging on if you like good food. Reservations recommended.
🕐 Thu–Tue 12–2.30, 7.30–10.30
🍽 L €45, D €65, Wine €7

BUCA DI PORSENNA

Via delle Donzelle 1, 53100 Siena
Tel 0577 44431
Buca di Porsenna, named after an Etruscan king who fought the Romans, is in a medieval building with the restaurant spread out over three levels. The secluded tables in the clay

cellars, where the walls are lined with red brick, are best. The connection to medieval times extends as far as the menu, which includes old recipes alongside modern Tuscan food. Reservations are recommended.
🕐 Wed–Mon 12–2.30, 7.30–10.30
🍽 L €25, D €50, Wine €6

CAFFÈ NANNINI

Banchi di Sopra 95–99, 53100 Siena
Popular with visitors and locals, Caffè Nannini is a richly decorated café serving coffees and teas, ice cream, sandwiches, cakes, a variety of delicious *cantucci* (almond cookies), *ricciarelli* (Sienese marzipan cakes), *panforte* (rich fruit cake) and more.
🕐 Daily 7.30am–11pm
🍽 L €20, coffee €1, cakes from €2.50

IL CAMPO
Piazza del Campo 50–51, 53100 Siena
Tel 0577 280725
This is the original restaurant on the Piazza del Campo and a great spot for people-watching, day or night. A consequence of this is that service may suffer at very busy times. The menu is a mix of Italian and European cuisine. No reservations, so just hang around until a table is free.
🕐 Daily noon–10.30
🍴 L €25, D €60, Wine €10

CANE & GATTO
Via Pagliaresi 6, 53100 Siena
Tel 0577 287545
This small restaurant seating just 24 is renowned for its service and food. There is no written menu: You just sit down and wait to be served several courses of traditional cuisine, including antipasti, soup, pasta, risotto, meat, salad, dessert and fruit. Each course comes with a wine to complement it. Special requests are also taken. Reservations are essential. Although not scheduled, Cane e Gatto will open at lunchtime if reservations are made in advance.
🕐 Fri–Wed 8pm–10.30pm
🍴 D €120, Wine €14

IL CANTO
Strada di Certosa 82, 53100 Siena
Tel 0577 288180
www.certosadimaggiano.com
The celebrated restaurant of the Hotel Certosa di Maggiano (▷ 252) is in a former monastery dating from 1314. Meals are created from the hotel's farm produce, and every meal comes with a hearty serving of fresh home-made bread. Visit the rustic kitchen for breakfast or sit by the pool in summer. Dinner is served in the small dining room or under the expansive arches of the central cloister.
🕐 Thu–Mon 12.30–2.30, 8–10, Wed 8–10; closed Dec 10–Feb 10
🍴 L €80, D €130, Wine €20

MEDIO EVO
Via dei Rossi 40, 53100 Siena
Tel 0577 280315
www.medioevosiena.com
A family-run restaurant in a 13th-century house in the heart of Siena. The main restaurant is downstairs in a

medieval vaulted dining room complete with banners and coats of arms. Upstairs is a banqueting hall that accommodates 80 people. The

kitchen serves Tuscan dishes based on local produce, including meat, game, mushrooms, pasta and desserts. The wine list has more than two dozen local wines. Reservations recommended in high season.
🕐 Fri–Wed 12.30–3, 7.30–10
🍴 L €45, D €65, Wine €8

OSTERIA CASTELVECCHIO
Via di Castelvecchio 65, 53100 Siena
Tel 0577 49586
You will find Osteria Castelvecchio halfway up a steep incline in an old palace, dating from eighth century. It's a pleasant eatery with subdued lighting and graffiti on the walls, with the owner's passion for wine reflected in the wine list. The menu changes daily, and includes modern interpretations of local dishes, as well as some recipes resurrected from Etruscan and medieval times. The tasting menu of many small dishes costs €25. Reservations are advisable.
🕐 Mon–Sat 12–2.30, 7.30–9.30
🍴 L €25, D €45, Wine €8

OSTERIA LA CHIACCHERA
Costa di Sant'Antonio 4, 53100 Siena
Tel 0577 280631
The 'Chatterbox' is a small restaurant with old wooden furniture and terracotta floors. One of the least expensive places to eat in Siena, it has a menu redolent of the area's peasant heritage, with simple but filling dishes such as *pici boscaiola* (fat noodles with tomatoes and mushrooms) or, for the more adventurous, tripe. It is also one of the few places where you can eat late into the evening. There's a

short and inexpensive wine list. Reservations advisable. Credit cards are not accepted.
🕐 Wed–Mon 12–3, 7–midnight
🍴 L €15, D €30, Wine €10

OSTERIA LE LOGGE
Via del Porrione 33, 53100 Siena
Tel 0577 48013
In a former medieval pharmacy, this charming restaurant is just off the Campo. There are tables outside in the summer, plus two dining areas, but if the weather's good the door will be wide open to let the air in. The menu is full of simple, classic Tuscan dishes, such as *malfatti all'osteria* (ricotta and spinach dumplings in a cream sauce) and *anatra al finocchio* (roast duck with fennel). Reservations are advised.
🕐 Mon–Sat 12.30–2.30, 7.30–10.30
🍴 L €40, D €80, Wine €10

RISTORANTE CASALTA
Via Matteotti 22, Strove, 53035 Monteriggioni
Tel 0577 301171
www.ristorantecasalta.it
Barbara gives you a warm welcome while her husband, Lazaro, is busy cooking a changing repetoire of basically Tuscan receipes in a light, modern style. Try *gamberoni con lardo con fagioli* (grilled prawns on a white bean purée) or *petto di faraona ripieno di spinaci e fegato grasso* (breast of guinea fowl stuffed with spinach and foie gras). You eat in a series of lightly painted rooms or outside in the courtyard in summer. It's worth asking advice on selecting a suitable wine for your menu as there is an extensive list of Italian and foreign wines. Booking for dinner is recommended.
🕐 Wed–Mon 1–2, 8–10; closed 10 Jan–10 Feb
🍴 L €40, D €90, Wine €15
🚗 Turn off the Florence/Siena superstrada at Monteriggioni; follow signs for Colle di Val d'Elsa; turn left through Abbadia Isola and on to Strove; it is just beyond the church on the right (15km/9 miles from Siena)

RISTORANTE ENZO
Via Camollia 49, 53100 Siena
Tel 0577 281277
This smart restaurant has a more modern, creative approach to food than many

EATING

others in these parts. Although in an old building, it has modern glass doors leading into a contemporary white room. The menu's highlights include

a good selection of fish, tasty yellow pumpkin *gnocchi* (potato dumplings) with porcini mushrooms and truffles, and a delicious terrine of nettles. Reservations are recommended.

🕐 Mon–Sat 12.30–2.30, 8–10.30; closed last 2 weeks in Jul
🍴 L €45, D €60, Wine €12

RISTORANTE GUIDO
Vicolo del Pettinaio 7, 53100 Siena
Tel 0577 280042
www.emmeti.it/guido
Close to Piazza del Campo, in a spacious brick cavern adorned with old photographs and elegant art nouveau lights, Ristorante Guido is justifiably well liked for its superb food. Dishes such as *rustici alla Guido* (home-made pasta

with asparagus, truffles and fresh mushrooms), *filet mignon alla Guido* (fillet steak with asparagus and porcini mushrooms), and locally reared veal. Reservations are advisable.

🕐 Daily 12.30–2.30, 7.30–10
🍴 L €35, D €70, Wine €15

RISTORANTE PIZZERIA EZIO
Via V. Emanuele II 32, 53100 Siena
Tel 0577 48094
The menu at this restaurant in Siena's historic heart includes

pizza and traditional Italian meats and fish as well as international dishes and good vegetarian options. The cakes and desserts are all home-made and there's a good selection of international and local wines.

🕐 Thu–Tue 12–2.30, 7–11
🍴 L €22, D €50, Wine €11

SAPORDIVINO
Via Banchi di Sopra 85, 53100 Siena
Tel 0577 56011
www.ghcs.it
Dine beneath a crystal ceiling in the courtyard of the Palazzo Gori, in the Grand Hotel Continental (▷ 252). The traditional menu uses local ingredients and has a large selection of cheeses and cold meats, plus an extensive wine list with more than 300 labels from both local and international vineyards. If you are lucky, you might come across one of the wine tasting sessions that are held regularly.

🕐 Daily 11am–1am
🍴 L €50, D €100, Wine €25

SOTTO LE FONTI
Via Esterna Fonteblanda 14, 53100 Siena
Tel 0577 226446
www.sottolefonti.it
This medieval building has been renovated to re-create an old-fashioned restaurant. The menu is based on Sienese

dishes such as salami, game, or lamb chops with juniper; cakes and desserts are all home-made. There's an extensive wine list, plus a range of spirits and beers. Reservations advisable in high season.

🕐 Daily 12–2.30, 7–10.30
🍴 L €30, D €40, Wine €8

LA TAVERNA DEL CAPITANO
Via del Capitano 6/8, 53100 Siena
Tel 0577 288094
This independent restaurant in the old town near the Duomo

and Pinacoteca specializes in Sienese and regional food, with everything from light lunches to full meals. Menu choices include *gnocchi al pecorino* (potato dumplings with cheese), Florentine steak, cured salt fish and a good selection of home-made desserts. The long wine list has an extensive selection of Chiantis. Reservations are advisable.

🕐 Wed–Mon 12.30–3, 7.30–10; closed Feb
🍴 L €30, D €50, Wine €13

LA TAVERNA DI SAN GIUSEPPE
Via Giovanni Duprè 132, 53100 Siena
Tel 0577 42286
www.tavernasangiuseppe.it
A lively group of young people run this *trattoria*. It specializes in classical Tuscan food, with an emphasis on meat, although vegetarians are well catered for with a rich vegetable soup, *ribollita*. Meals end with a delicious selection of desserts—watch the waiters using a torch to burn the sugar topping for crème brulée. Set in a pleasantly lit room you will be eating at traditional dark wooden tables.

🕐 Mon–Sat 12.15–2.30, 7–10; closed last 2 weeks in Jan and July
🍴 L €20, D €50, Wine €8

LA TORRE
Via Salicotto 7, 53100 Siena
Tel 0577 287548
Just off Piazza del Campo, La Torre is highly recommended by locals. It has an open-plan kitchen so customers can watch their food being prepared. All pasta is home-made and comes with a choice of sauces followed by other well-prepared Tuscan standards such as *piccione al forno* (oven-baked pigeon). Despite its omission from the menu, coffee is served—it's delivered from the bar next door. Reservations essential.

🕐 Fri–Wed 12.15–3, 6.45–9.15
🍴 L €23, D €40, Wine €8

AREZZO

BACCO E ARIANNA
Via Cesalpeno 10, 52100 Arezzo
Tel 0575 299598
On the ground floor of an old building in the heart of town, Bacco e Arianna is a great wine bar, serving a good selection of food. Since the owner is an enthusiastic connoisseur, this is one of the best places in Arezzo for sampling local wines by the glass. Local cheeses and cured meats are served alongside Tuscan dishes and desserts.
Tue–Thu 10–7, Fri–Sat 10am–midnight, Sun 10–6
L €30, D €44, Wine €8

BUCA DI MICHELANGELO
Via Roma 51, 52033 Caprese Michelangelo
Tel 0575 793921
In an old stone house at Caprese Michelangelo, 25km (15 miles) from Arezzo, this eatery is in a quiet area with panoramic views over the Tevere Valley forests and is well suited to those who like a long walk to build up an appetite. The house where Michelangelo was born is only a brief stroll away. Tuscan dishes fill the menu, and on Sundays a hearty Tuscan multi-course lunch is served. The wine list has a few local labels.
Daily 1–2.30, 8–9.30, Jun–end Sep; Fri–Wed 1–2.30, 8–9.30, Feb–end May, Oct–end Dec
L €40, D €75, Wine €10
Take SS71 from Arezzo towards Bibbiena, turn right to Anghiari, then left to Caprese Michelangelo

BUCA DI SAN FRANCESCO
Via San Francesco 1, 52100 Arezzo
Tel 0575 23271
www.bucadisanfrancesco.it
Right in the heart of Arezzo, this family-run restaurant is in the basement of a 14th-century medieval palace; the dining room floor is made of stone slabs dating from Etruscan times. The menu reflects the traditional cuisine of the area with dishes such as *ribollita* (a thick bean and

cabbage soup) and Chianti beef stew. Charlie Chaplin, Salvador Dalì and President Truman all dined here. Reservations are advisable.
Wed–Sun 12–2.30, 7–9.30, Mon 12–2.30; closed 2 weeks in Jul
L €25, D €50, Wine €9

BUONO & SANO
Largo 1 Maggio 23, 52100 Arezzo
Tel 0575 26405
Providing a change from Tuscany's usual meat-heavy menus, Buono & Sano serve organic, vegetarian food and has a non-smoking policy. The restaurant has an increasing following of local vegetarians, as well as meat-eaters looking for a lighter option. The chef devises meat-free versions of local dishes, and the restaurant's recipe book shot it to stardom. They also have a small range of vegetarian wines and beers. Credit cards are not accepted.
Mon–Thu 12–2.30, Fri–Sat 12–2.30, 7.30–9.30; closed Aug
L €16, D €40, Wine €7.50

LE TASTEVIN
Via de Cenci 9, 52100 Arezzo
Tel 0575 28304
This popular eatery claims Oscar-winner Roberto Benigni (*Life is Beautiful*, ▷ 273) as a regular. One room resembles

a traditional *trattoria*, while the second, adorned with pictures of film stars, is a jazz bar. The food is traditional with some modern additions such as truffle and asparagus

risotto. There's outside seating in summer and reservations are recommended.
Tue–Sun 12.30–2.30, 7.30–11.30
L €40, D €65, Wine €10

LA TORRE DI GNICCHE
Piaggia San Martino 8, 52100 Arezzo
Tel 0575 352035
This small bar seats just 30, but in the summer you can sit on the terrace overlooking the Piazza Vasari. A menu is available but regular customers here trust the staff to decide between the snacks, sandwiches and local main dishes that change regularly with the seasons. They have a good selection of local cheeses, and a wine list that includes the local Colli Aretini.
Thu–Tue noon–3, 6–1am
L €12, D €40, Wine €12

BAGNO VIGNONI

IL LOGGIATO
Piazza delle Sorgenti 36, 53020 Bagno Vignoni, Siena
Tel 0577 887174
Described as a wine bar, this establishment feels more like a farm kitchen of 100 years ago. Owner Sabrina and her friends have lovingly collected objects in common use then and gathered them together here—baskets and herbs hang from the ceiling and a big wooden bread chest stands in the corner. All the dishes served are fresh and home-made: warming soups, cakes, pastries, local meats and cheeses. Gentle jazz music plays softly in the background. Opening times

EATING

tend to be as individual as the place.

🕒 Fri 6pm–midnight, Sat–Sun 9am–midnight, Mar–end Dec

🍴 L & D €24, Wine €10

OSTERIA DEL LEONE

Piazza del Moretto, 53020 Bagno Vignoni, Siena

Tel 0577 887300

This friendly restaurant is more sophisticated than the traditional simple *osteria*, but still serves delicious regional dishes such as *sfogliatella con fonduta di pecorino* (light pastry topped with melted fresh sheep's cheese) and generous helpings of local grilled meats. There's a dedicated menu for vegetarians and all the food is fresh and seasonal. There are four welcoming little rooms with dark wood furniture, or you can eat outside in the garden lit by flares at night.

🕒 Tue–Sun 12.30–2.30, 7–10

🍴 L €24, D €50, Wine €10

BUONCONVENTO

RISTORANTE DA MARIO

Via Soccini 60, 53022 Buonconvento, Siena

Tel 0577 806157

This family-run *trattoria* is popular with the locals, who come to enjoy the home cooking, and visitors are warmly welcomed. Try the freshly made *pici* (hand rolled Tuscan pasta) or the *zuppa di farro* (soup made from spelt, a type of grain that was grown by the Etruscans). Mario's daughters, Anna and Nara, who now run the kitchen, only serve seasonal

food. There's a little garden at the back for summer eating.

🕒 Sun–Fri 12–2.30, 7.30–9.30; closed Aug

🍴 L €18, D €40, Wine €4

CHIANTI

RISTORANTE BADIA A COLTIBUONO

53013 Gaiole in Chianti, Siena

Tel 0577 749424

www.coltibuono.com

The Abbey of Coltibuono is now the family home of well-known cookery writer Lorenza

de' Medici, but her son Paolo Stucchi Prinetti runs this attractive restaurant. You can eat outside and enjoy the spectacular views from the garden and shady terrace. Most of the recipes used are Lorenza's, with a lighter approach to traditional Tuscan cooking, and uses fresh ingredients from the garden. Extra virgin olive oil and Chianti wine also come from the family estates. It's worth making a reservation, as the restaurant is some distance from Gaiole, and very popular.

🕒 Daily 12.15–2.30, 7.15–9.30, May–end Oct; Tue–Sun, 12.15–2.30, 7.15–9.30, Mar–end Apr, Nov; closed Jan, Feb

🍴 L €32, D €72, Wine €8

🚗 Take SP429 from Radda in Chianti towards Montevarchi (6km/3.5 miles from Radda)

RISTORANTE DA ANTONIO

Via del Chianti 28/32, 53019 Castelnuovo Berardenga, Siena

Tel 0577 355321

In front of you as you enter is the open-plan kitchen and a team of chefs in tall white hats preparing delicious fish dishes. Crisp, snowy white is used throughout this elegant restaurant to create a cool minimal atmosphere and show off the beautifully presented food and wine. The owners go daily to Viareggio to get their fish fresh from the market there and menus vary accordingly. No meat served. Reservations advisable, especially for dinner.

🕒 Tue–Sat 1–2.30, 8–10.30, Sun 11–2.30; closed Nov

SPECIAL

IL CARLINO D'ORO

Località San Regolo 33, 53013 Gaoile in Chianti, Siena

Tel 0577 747136

The family have been running this little *osteria* for 43 years; you can look into the kitchen and watch Mamma seasoning her chicken with local fresh herbs before spit roasting it on the big open hearth. It is always packed—mostly with locals, some of whom work on the adjoining Brolio wine estate. Arrive early to be sure of a table; otherwise reservations are essential. It is only open for lunch, except on weekends in the summer.

🕒 Tue–Sun 12–2, also Fri–Sun 7.30–9, Apr–end Sep; Tue–Sun 12–2, rest of year

🍴 L €24, D €60, Wine €5

🚗 Follow SP484 between Radda in Chianti and Castelnuovo Berardenga. At Castello di Brolio take turning to Pianella–San Regolo is then less than 1km (0.5 mile)

🍴 L €80, D €120, Wine €14

🚗 Follow the signs for Castelnuovo Berardenga on SP484, off the Siena/Sinalunga road (SP326); it is on the road to San Giusme on the edge of town

TRATTORIA DEL MONTAGLIARI

Via Montagliari 29, 50020 Panzano, Greve in Chianti, Firenze

Tel 0558 52014

www.montagliari.it

This *trattoria* on an idyllic wine estate was founded in 1720, 5km (3 miles) from Greve. The large dining room has a beamed ceiling, check-patterned tablecloths and old prints on the walls, plus tables outside in summer. Go for the *pappardelle al cinghiale* (wide pasta ribbons with rich wild boar sauce), the homemade ravioli or the *faraona al vinsanto* (guinea fowl with an intense wine sauce). The estate produces Chianti Classico and Riserva, Vin Santo and Amaro—all of which you can buy in the estate shop.

🕒 Tue–Sun 12.30–2.30, 7.30–9.30; closed 7 Jan–7 Feb

🍴 L €25, D €50, Wine €7.50

🚗 On the SS222 from Siena to Florence

EATING

CORTONA

IL FALCONIERE

Località San Martino 370, 52044 Cortona

Tel 0575 612679

www.ilfalconiere.it

When you eat at this old country hotel, you can choose between the elegant period charm of the dining room, the wrought-iron and glass conservatory or the outdoor terrace with a view over the Val di Chiana. The modern Italian menu includes home-made pasta and locally produced olives and grapes. The wine list highlights the local Baracchi vineyard. Reservations advisable.

🕐 Daily 1–2, 8–10, Mar–end Oct; Thu–Tue 1–2, 8–10, Nov–end Feb

🍴 L €45, D €130, Wine €20

🚗 Just north of Cortona, on the main road towards Arezzo, is a turning on the right to San Martino

LA LOCANDA NEL LOGGIATO

Piazza di Pescheria 3, 52044 Cortona

Tel 0575 630575

A family-run restaurant, La Locanda nel Loggiato is in a pretty medieval lodge overlooking the little square in Cortona. Choose from indoor or outdoor dining: Inside, the atmosphere is calm and relaxed, while outside you can observe the comings

and goings of village life. The high quality of the restaurant's local cuisine attracts people from the area as well as visitors, so reservations are necessary during the summer months.

🕐 Thu–Tue 12.30–3, 7.30–10.30

🍴 L €20, D €35, Wine €6

ISOLA D'ELBA

IL CANOCCIA

Via Palestro, 57038 Rio Marina, Isola d'Elba, Livorno

Tel 0565 962432

In the two simple rooms here, the rough whitewashed walls are hung with nautical prints and pictures. You will find classically cooked fish dishes using only the finest, freshest ingredients—food you can only find at a restaurant within striking distance of the sea. The local wines of the island make the ideal accompaniment. Reservations advisable in the evenings.

🕐 Daily 12.30–2.30, 7.30–midnight, May–end Sep; Tue–Sun, rest of year

🍴 L €24, D €60, Wine €12

LA LATERNA MAGICA

Lungomare Vitaliani 5, 57036 Porto Azzurro, Isola d'Elba, Livorno

Tel 0565 958394

You feel as if you are on a yacht at this restaurant—it is built out over the water of the harbour of this pretty village. The menu is extensive, with an emphasis on fish; one section has choices of local traditional food. Try *acciugata con cavolo nero* (Tuscan black cabbage stewed with garlic and anchovies), or *zerri marinati* (pickled local fish). Pizzas are also available. With such a setting, reservations are definitely advisable in the evenings.

🕐 Tue–Sun 12–2.30, 7–9; closed Jan

🍴 L €24, D €54, Wine €10.50

ISOLA DEL GIGLIO

DA MARIA

Giglio Castello, 58012 Isola del Giglio, Grosseto

Tel 0564 806062

At the top of the hill at the far end of the medieval walled village, Da Maria has been a *trattoria* for three generations. In the tranquil white-walled rooms, you feel as though you are a family guest rather than a customer. You get home cooking at its best, with fish to the fore; what is served will depend on what has been caught in the sea that day. The *trattoria* is small, so it's advisable to make a reservation.

🕐 Daily 12.30–2.30, 7.30–9.30; closed Jan–end Mar

🍴 L €20, D €50, Wine €10

MONTALCINO

GRAPPOLO BLU

Via Scale di Moglio, 53024 Montalcino, Siena

Tel 0577 847150

Down some steps from the main piazza is Luciano's great

little restaurant. Terracotta floors, scrubbed tables and rush-seated chairs marry happily with the white walls and beamed ceiling—true Tuscan style. Eat *zuppa di fagioli* (Tuscan bean soup) *crostini* (toasted crusty bread with a variety of different toppings), and *stinco all'aceto balsamico* (shin of beef in balsamic vinegar)—but leave room for the meltingly delicious *crostata di limone* (lemon tart). With a local wine, it's all excellent value.

🕐 Sat–Thu 12–3.30, 7.30–10; closed mid-Jan to mid-Feb

🍴 L €25, D €45, Wine €8

OSTERIA AL GIARDINO

Piazza Cavour 1, 53024 Montalcino, Siena

Tel 0577 849076

The air of cool modernity in this white-walled *osteria* contrasts with the hearty, warming Tuscan cooking, as in the *pinci all'aglione* (home-made pasta with a spicy tomato sauce) or *coniglio all'etrusca* (locally farmed rabbit in a special sauce). For dessert there's a tiramisu to die for. In summer you can eat on the terrace in the tree-filled piazza outside.

🕐 Thu–Tue 12.15–2.30, 7.30–9.45; closed mid-Jan to mid-Feb

🍴 L €30, D €70, Wine €15

RE DI MACCHIA

Via S. Saloni 21, 53024 Montalcino, Siena

Tel 0577 84611

The entrance right on the main street brings you straight into this delightful little restaurant. There are two small rooms with an open fireplace, pleasing lighting and prints, and tables set with attractive patterned cloths and fine tableware. Chef Roberta can be seen in the kitchen preparing *pasticcio ai funghi porcini* (a local type of lasagne with porcini mushrooms) or stewing beef in a sauce made with Brunello—the rich local red wine. There's an extensive list of Italian wines, but you should try the Brunello or Rosso di Montalcino. Reservations advisable as there are only six tables.

🕒 Fri–Wed 12–2, 7–9.30; closed Jan
🍴 L €24, D €50, Wine €10

RISTORANTE DI POGGIO ANTICO
Località Poggio Antico, 53024 Montalcino, Siena
Tel 0755 849200
This internationally renowned restaurant is set in the Poggio Antico wine estate, so the Brunello you may drink is from the vineyards around you (there is an extensive list of other national and international wines too). Chef Roberto Minnetti creates delicious dishes using traditional ingredients cooked in a fresh, modern way. There is a tasting menu of four courses of Tuscan cooking, an international menu of six courses, or you can eat à la carte. The view from the terrace stretches across the Val d'Orcia to Monte Amiato.

🕒 Daily 12.30–2.30, 7.30–10, Apr–end Oct; Tue–Sat 12.30–2.30, 7.30–10, Sun 12.30–2.30, rest of year
🍴 L €50, D €90, Wine €18
🚌 Take the Grosseto road, SP14, south from Montalcino; follow sign to restaurant after 4km (2.5 miles), then 1km (0.5 mile) down the cypress-lined drive

MONTEPULCIANO

CAFFÈ POLIZIANO
Via di Voltaia nel Corso 27–29, 53045 Montepulciano, Siena
Tel 0578 758615
This bar/café, with its warm paisley-covered walls hung with prints, marble-topped tables and upholstered benches around the walls, seems to be in a time warp. It's been like this since 1868, serving a huge range of hot chocolates and teas as well as all the usual drinks. Light lunches of omelettes, pastas

and salads are served in the spacious ground-floor rooms. Downstairs is an elegant restaurant open only in the evening for dinner. A terrace at the back has views as far as Lake Trasimeno in Umbria.

🕒 Daily 7am–midnight. Restaurant Mon–Sat 7pm–10.30pm; closed Feb
🍴 L €14, D €60, Wine €14.50

IL CANTUCCIO
Via delle Cantine 1, 53045 Montepulciano, Siena
Tel 0578 757870
www.ristoranteilcantuccio.com
This typically Tuscan restaurant at the bottom of town serves straightforward food—mixed salami, *crostini* (toasted crusty bread with various toppings), plainly grilled meats, *salsicce* (sausages) and gently simmered beans. *Panzanella* (summer salad with bread, tomatoes and herbs) and *coniglio arrosto* (roast rabbit) are sometimes on the menu. The house wine is fine, but you might prefer the Vino Nobile di Montepulciano on its home ground. For friendly service and good value, Il Cantuccio can't be beaten. It is very busy at lunchtime with day visitors but quieter in the evenings.

🕒 Tue–Sun 12–2.30, 7.30–10
🍴 L €30, D €50, Wine €9

LA GROTTA
Località San Biagio, 53045 Montepulciano, Siena
Tel 0578 757607

Facing the church of San Biagio, this well-established restaurant has such delights as *ravioli di piccione alla pafferano* (ravioli stuffed with pigeon in a saffron sauce) and *anitra al ginepro e miele* (duck cooked with juniper berries and honey). Excellent service and a large wine list, including a good choice of the local robust red Vino Nobile di

Montepulciano. There's a shady garden for summer eating. Reservations advisable.

🕒 Thu–Tue 12.30–2.15, 7.30–9.30; closed Jan, Feb
🍴 L €50, D €90, Wine €12

MONTE SAN SAVINO

LA TERRASSE
Via di Vittorio 2/4, 52048 Monte San Savino
Tel 0575 844111
www.ristorantelaterrasse.it
In the historic heart of Monte San Savino, 19km (12 miles) from Arezzo, La Terrasse stands in front of the Florentine Gate, which marks the main entrance to the medieval village. Inside, the restaurant is decorated in shades of yellow. In good weather opt for the outside terrace, a wonderful place to dine alfresco. The menu includes local and national dishes, and the wine list is international.

🕒 Thu–Tue 12–2.30, 7–10.30; closed 5–20 Nov
🍴 L €30, D €50, Wine €6

MURLO

BOSCO DELLA SPINA
Località Lupompesi Murlo, 53016 Siena
Tel 0577 814605
www.boscodellaspina.com
This family-run restaurant is set in a columned building in the Sienese hills, 25km (16 miles) south of Siena. In fine weather, you can sit on the terrace, from which you get expansive views over the valley. Inside, the open fireplace and modern Tuscan wood furniture give the place its character. The menu concentrates on traditional Tuscan food and home-baked pastries, using ingredients that have been grown on the attached farm. There's an extensive wine list, mainly of local varieties. Reservations advised.

🕒 Wed–Mon 12.30–2.15, 8–10; closed 7 Jan–15 Feb
🍴 L €45, D €60, Wine €10
🚌 From Siena follow SS2 (Via Cassia) towards Roma, at Monteroni d'Arbia turn right to follow signs for Vescovado di Murlo; Lupompesi is just outside Vescovado

PIENZA

CAFFÈ DELLE VOLPE

Via delle Case Nuove 7, 53026 Pienza, Siena
Tel 347 404 3450

The emphasis here is on natural healthy food and drink. Owner Paolo whizzes up fresh fruit or vegetable juices and serves them with filled crêpes or assorted *panini* (filled rolls). He also serves good ice creams and a big range of teas. Enhance the experience by eating outside in the little flower-filled square. Credit cards are not accepted.

🕐 Daily 8am–midnight, May–end Sep; Tue–Sun 8am–midnight, Oct–end Apr
🍴 *Panini* for around €12

DAL FALCO

Piazza Dante 3, 53026 Pienza, Siena
Tel 0578 748551
www.ristorantedalfalco.toscana.nu

There's a tree-shaded piazza outside Pienza's walls, from where an archway leads through to Falco. The terracotta floors, whitewashed walls and dark wood add charm, but the strip lighting detracts from the atmosphere. The food is truly Tuscan: expect *crostini* (toasted crusty bread) with liver, olives and tomato, steaming pasta and plainly grilled meat. They do great *salsicce* (home-made sausages) and delicious *formaggio al prosciutto* (grilled cheese wrapped in parma ham).

🕐 Sat–Thu 12.30–3, 7–10
🍴 L €20, D €40, Wine €10

LATTE DI LUNA

Via San Carlo 2, 53026 Pienza, Siena
Tel 0578 748606

Roberto and his family own and run this popular restaurant justly famed for its *maialino* (roast sucking pig) and memorable *semifreddo al aranci* (a soft ice cream with an intense orange taste). There is a small outside terrace. It's very lively and always packed, so reservations are definitely advisable.

🕐 Wed–Mon 12–2.30, 7.30–10; closed Feb and Jul
🍴 L €24, D €50, Wine €10

SAN GIMIGNANO

BAR LE TORRI

Piazza del Duomo 10, 53037
San Gimignano
Tel 0577 940746

This is a large and airy café, but in good weather you can take advantage of the outdoor seating on the Piazza del Duomo. Light lunches, such as sandwichs or salads, are served, and the pastries here are highly recommended.

🕐 Tue–Sun 7am–midnight, Jun–end Aug; 7am–10pm, Sep–end Dec, Feb–end May
🍴 L €9, D €9, Wine €10

BEL SOGGIORNO

Via San Giovanni 91, 53073
San Gimignano
Tel 0577 940375
www.hotelbelsoggiorno.it

Within the city walls, Bel Soggiorno shares a 13th-century building with a hotel of the same name. The restaurant has been run by the same family for five generations, who serve dishes following Etruscan and medieval recipes. Traditional furnishings and a glass wall giving views over the rolling hills add to the charm. Reservations advisable.

🕐 Thu–Tue 7.30–10
🍴 D €80, Wine €8

DORANDÒ

Vicolo dell'Oro 2, 53037
San Gimignano
Tel 0577 941862
www.ristorantedorando.it

In a 14th-century building in the historical heart of San Gimignano, the Dorandò lies between Piazza del Duomo and Piazza della Cisterna. Some of the menu's dishes are based on recipes from the

Middle Ages and the Etruscan era, with an intriguing history lesson included, but each has been given a modern twist. The desserts are delicious. Although there are three dining rooms, advance reservations are essential.

🕐 Daily 12.30–2.30, 7.30–9.30, Easter–end Oct; Tue–Sun 12.30–2.30 7.30–9.30, rest of year; closed Jan–end Feb
🍴 L €50, D €80, Wine €8

LA GROTTA GHIOTTA

Via Santo Stefano 10, 53037
San Gimignano
Tel 0577 942074

La Grotta Ghiotta is a small restaurant—there are just a dozen seats and one big communal table—owned and run by brother-and-sister team Roberto and Sylvia. They specialize in products exclusively from San Gimignano, and the restaurant is highly recommended for the excellent quality of the food, the low prices and the escape it provides from the bustle of the crowds. The menu includes a wonderful array of cured ham, olives, local cheeses, honey and fresh bread, and there's a good wine list.

🕐 Daily noon–9; closed Jan
🍴 L €20, D €30, Wine €5

LA MANDRAGOLA

Via Berignano 58, 53037
San Gimignano
Tel 0577 942110
www.sangimignano.com/lamandragola

A large, busy restaurant in the old part of town, serving Tuscan dishes that include home-made breads and locally harvested mushrooms and truffles. The furnishings are more modern than in most local restaurants, which makes the dining room look large. Outdoor terrace seating is available in good weather. Local wines fill the list, making the restaurant popular with

visitors on wine tours. Reservations advisable.

🕐 Daily 12–2.30 7.30–10, Easter–end Oct; Fri–Wed 12–2.30 7.30–10, rest of year
🍴 L €30, D €50, Wine €9

OSTERIA DELLE CANTENE

Via Mainardi 18, 53037 San Gimignano
Tel 0577 941966

The interior of Osteria delle Cantene is an interesting mix of handmade medieval

EATING

brickwork and contemporary paintings and lighting. The menu includes classic as well as unusual local dishes, with an emphasis on saffron, the spice on which San Gimignano built its wealth. Try the saffron soup or wild boar with black cabbage, accompanied by wine from their local selection. Book ahead in high season.

🕐 Thu–Tue 12.30–2, 7.30–9.30
🍴 L €30, D €52, Wine €8

IL PINO
Via Cellesa 68, 53037 San Gimignano
Tel 0577 942225
A family-run restaurant close to the Porto di San Matteo in the heart of the town, with brick arches and candlelit rooms giving it a medieval atmosphere. Classical San Gimignano dishes are prepared with locally sourced ingredients, including *bruschetta* (garlic toast) with wild boar, *crostini* (toasted crusty bread) with salmon and mascarpone, saffron soup, and pork fillet with Chianti and juniper sauce. Local vineyards are represented on the wine list. Reservations advisable.

🕐 Fri–Wed 12.30–2.30, 7.30–10; closed 16 Nov to 16 Dec
🍴 L €50, D €80, Wine €9

LE TERRAZZE
Piazza della Cisterna 23, 53037 San Gimignano
Tel 0577 940328
www.hotelcisterna.it

This restaurant is in the Cisterna Hotel, and its main draw is the views over San Gimignano. Although there is no outdoor seating, one wall in the 14th-century dining room is all glass, providing the illusion of alfresco dining all year round—as well as magnificent, panoramic views. Traditional Tuscan and San Gimignano cuisine and a wide selection of wines, both local and national.

🕐 Fri–Mon 12.30–2.30, 7.30–9.30, Wed–Thu 7.30–9.30; closed Jan, Feb
🍴 L €30, D €60, Wine €10

SANSEPOLCRO
RISTORANTE VENTURA
Via N. Agguinti 30, 52037 Sansepolcro, Arezzo
Tel 0575 742560
This is a well-established local *trattoria* that is popular with residents. It's menu is based

on serving traditional Tuscan food, such as hearty meat dishes, bean dishes, pasta and soups. The interior has a rustic style.

🕐 Tue–Sat 12.30–2.15, 7.30–9.30, Sun 12.30–2.15
🍴 L €30, D €60, Wine €12

SAN VINCENZO

GAMBERO ROSSO
Piazza della Vittoria 13, 57027 San Vincenzo, Livorno
Tel 0565 701021
Fulvio Pierangelini's restaurant is one of only a handful of establishments in Tuscany to possess two Michelin stars. It is in a light and airy room overlooking the marina at San Vincenzo. Although the menu has some meat dishes, most people come here to sample the exquisite fish and seafood which is prepared with imagination and skill. The set, multi-course *menu dégustazione* of Gambero Rosso classics (including a spicy seared tuna salad, velvety chick pea cream soup with prawns and fish sautéed with artichoke hearts) is excellent value at €85, or you can choose à la carte. Booking is essential.

🕐 Wed–Sun 12.30–2.30, 7.30–10
🍴 L and D €85 (set menu), €100 (à la carte), Wine €20

VOLTERRA
L'INCONTRO
Via Matteotti 18, 56048 Volterra, Pisa
Tel 0588 80500
L'Incontro means 'the meeting' and this is where many locals and visitors gather. A glorious smell of chocolate and a tempting counter full of home-made pastries and chocolates greet you. There's a little wine bar at the back where simple

meals are served: soups, salads, cold cuts and cheese.

🕐 Thu–Tue 7.30am–1am (lunch 12.30–3.30)
🍴 L €14, Wine €10

TRATTORIA IL SACCO FIORENTINO
Piazza XX Settembre 18, 56048 Volterra, Pisa
Tel 0588 88537
This elegant, tranquil restaurant is owned and run by a young couple: Cristina is the hostess and Paolo cooks. The menu has dishes to suit all tastes, but the emphasis is on fish and game: *bocconcini di*

cinghiale al Chianti is wild boar stewed in a rich sauce made with Chianti wine. Vegetarians could choose *pecorino al forno con radicchio roso e noci* (red-leaved chicory covered with fresh pecorino cheese and walnuts cooked in a hot oven).

🕐 Thu–Tue 12–2.30, 7–9.30; closed 7 Jan for 3 weeks
🍴 L €18, D €40, Wine €8

STAYING IN TUSCANY

Choose from world-class hotels in historic buildings, ultra-chic boutique hotels or family-run *pensiones* that haven't changed much in 30 years; or rent a villa, stay on a farm or track down a village room. On the whole, accommodation is more expensive in Tuscany than in many other parts of the country, and is in high demand from May until September. So shop around, and book in advance for the best deals.

Helvetia & Bristol, Florence (left), Casa Bellavista, Cortona (middle) and Villa Nencini, Volterra (right)

HOTELS

Tuscan hotels *(alberghi)* are graded by the regional authorities on a star rating of one to five. These refer to the facilities provided—air conditioning, telephone and television, elevator, swimming pool—rather than the character or comfort.

● You can expect five-star hotels to be grand, with superb facilities and a high level of service; they will sometimes be in converted buildings, such as palaces, combining antique furnishings with 21st-century luxury.

● Four-star establishments will be almost as good as five-star and the accommodation first class.

● Three-star hotels are more idiosyncratic. Prices can vary enormously between them, as can the public areas, and staffing levels will be considerably lower, with often only one person manning the entire hotel. You can expect all three-star rooms will have a television, a telephone and sometimes air conditioning.

● One-and two-star hotels are relatively inexpensive, but are clean and comfortable, and rooms almost always have private bathrooms in two-star places. Breakfast is usually included, but simpler hotels rarely have restaurants, and some do not provide breakfast. Breakfast can be very poor too, so consider a bar breakfast instead.

PENSIONES

There's little difference between simpler hotels and *pensiones*. Both are usually family-run, and will provide spotlessly clean, comfortable rooms at a fair price. Some *pensiones* have failed to move with the times, and rooms may be dated, but this is also the case in smaller hotels. Seaside resorts are generally rich in this type of accommodation and they'll be a good choice of full-board packages, excellent value if you want a week at the sea. The downside is often that single nights are unavailable and you'll have to take some or even all meals.

LOCANDE

You may see the term *locande*, meaning inn. Italy used to have a large number of these, but they have virtually disappeared and the word today is more likely to refer to something fairly chic and expensive.

AGRITURISMI

The *agriturismo* scheme was started to enable farmers and landowners to conserve redundant farm buildings by converting them into holiday accommodation. This can take the form of a small and luxurious hotel, an apartment, or simply a handful of rooms in a converted barn. Accommodation is often on a weekly only basis, but many owners will rent rooms by the night, and meals can be provided. *Agriturismi* are often in beautiful surroundings and frequently provide activities such as riding, escorted walking and mountain biking. Many have swimming pools and serve their home-grown produce at meal times. The movement is particularly strong in Tuscany. You'll need a car as *agriturismi* can be well off the beaten track, and most require advance booking. All tourist offices carry a full list of *agriturismi* in the area.

INDEPENDENCE

Cooking for yourself is an excellent option for cutting costs and giving yourself freedom. In Tuscany there's both a range of city apartments and a great number of old farmhouses and villas to choose from. Tour operators sell villa packages, which include flights and car rental, but if you

STAYING

want to be independent, contact the local visitor offices well in advance, or look at their websites. There are also websites devoted to private house rentals. If you're using Italian internet sites do your research on-line, then phone to book.

RIFUGI

If you're in the mountains hiking or climbing, you can stay in a network of *rifugi*—mountain huts—owned by the Club Alpino Italiano. Most are fairly sparse, and you'll probably find yourself in a dormitory bunk bed and washing in cold water, but all are very reasonably priced and surrounded by

PRICING

● Italian hotels are legally required to post rates for high and low season on the back of every bedroom door.
● You should agree on a price before making a reservation.
● Rates vary according to the season, sometimes by as much as 25 per cent. Some hotels have high *(alta)* and low season *(bassa stagione)* rates; others charge the same rate year round *(tutto l'anno)*.
● Hotels often quote their most expensive rates. So if you want a particular hotel ask if they have a less expensive room.

La Scaletta, Florence (left), Grand Hotel Duomo, Pisa (middle) and Grand Hotel Continental, Siena (right)

wonderful countryside with spectacular views. For further details contact local tourist offices or go to www.cai.it and click on *rifugi*.

ROOMS TO RENT

In popular areas you may see signs saying rooms, *camere* or *zimmer*. These are rooms to rent in private houses and are a good option if money is tight or you can't find a hotel. Local tourist offices keep a list.

RESERVATIONS

Florence is so popular that you will need to book in advance at whatever time of the year you decide to visit. Elsewhere, Italians are on holiday during August, so remember you'll be competing with them for beds. If you're booking in advance from home, make certain you get written confirmation and take it with you. Without this, you may turn up and find all knowledge of your booking denied. If you make an internet booking, be sure to print out your booking confirmation and take it with you.

FINDING A ROOM

● If you haven't booked in advance, start your search around the main piazza or in the *centro storico* (old town). In hilltop villages and towns it is also worth looking outside the *centro storico* or town walls. The tourist information office will have lists and may be willing to book for you.
● Yellow signs direct you to hotels both in the middle and on the outskirts of towns and villages.
● It's perfectly acceptable to ask to see the room before you decide to stay somewhere.
● Check-out time is normally noon, but hotels will usually store your luggage until the end of the day.

● City hotels sometimes have reduced weekend rates.
● Smaller hotels can be open to gentle bargaining, particularly during quieter times. However, don't be surprised if you don't get anywhere.
● Hotels are often willing to put another bed in a room for an extra 35 per cent, ideal for families with children.

FURTHER SOURCES OF INFORMATION

AGRITURISMI

Agriturist (Corso V Emanuele 101, 00168 Roma, tel 06 8521342; www.agriturist.com) publishes *Vacanza in Fattoria*, a guide to farm holidays in English.
Touring Club Italiano (TCI) publishes *Agriturismo e vacanze in campagna* annually at €40, plus a number of other useful publications. Visit www.touringclub.it.

CAMPING

TCI (see above for details) publishes an annual guide to campsites, *Campeggio e Villaggi Turistici* (€20).

VILLAS

There are a number of companies who organize villa rental, including:
Cottages to Castles has information for visitors from the UK, US, New Zealand and Australia (www.cottagestocastles.com).
Magic of Italy has villa rental packages (tel 0870 8880228, www.magictravelgroup.co.uk).
Vacanze in Italia (tel 413/528-6610, www.homeabroad.com) has farmhouses, villas and apartments, mainly in the countryside for US visitors.

The hotels below are listed alphabetically, excluding Il and Le. Prices are for a double room for one night, including breakfast. All the hotels listed accept credit cards unless otherwise stated.

See page 2 for a key to the symbols.

ALBERGO FIRENZE
Via del Corso-Piazza dei Donati 4, 50122 Firenze
Tel 055 214203
www.hotelfirenze-fi.it
Between the Duomo and the Piazza della Signoria, this is an inexpensive place to stay if you are not seeking luxury but want to be right at the the heart of the city. The rooms are plain but neat and almost all have a private bathroom.
🛏 €94
🛈 57
🚌 23

ALESSANDRA
Borgo S.S. Apostoli 17, 50129 Firenze
Tel 055 283438
www.hotelalessandra.com
This two-star hotel is in a small street that runs parallel to the Arno and its location is its main selling point. The guest rooms are spacious, clean and neat, but as not all have a private bathroom and a couple don't have air conditioning, it is best to check on these facilities when making a reservation.
🛏 €140–€150
🛈 27 (9 non-smoking)
🚌 6, 11, 36, 37

ANNALENA
Via Romana 34, 50125 Firenze
Tel 055 222419
www.hotelannalena.it
This building has housed a wide cross-section of guests throughout history, from tragic young widows during the Medici era to Mussolini's Fascist police. The accommodation is simple and clean; one room has a terrace and the others look out over the garden. Each room has a private shower or bath as well as TV and telephone. A peaceful

haven after a busy day at the art galleries, the hotel is also close to good restaurants in the area.
🛏 €120–€177
🛈 20
🔳
🚌 D, 11, 36, 37

BALCONY
Via dei Banchi 3r, 50123 Firenze
Tel 055 283133
www.hotelbalcony.it
A welcoming and dependable no-frills hotel close to Piazza Santa Maria Novella, within walking distance of almost everything in Florence. The rooms are basic but clean and all have a private bathroom (bath or shower), telephone, TV and minibar. There is a communal area with a TV and library, as well as a compact terrace with fine views of the Duomo.
🛏 €70–€120
🛈 14
🔳
🚌 A, 6, 11, 14, 17

BELLETTINI
Via de' Conti 7, 50123 Firenze
Tel 055 213561
www.hotelbellettini.com
Close to the church of San Lorenzo and the Duomo, this hotel dates from the 15th century, making it one of the oldest in Florence as well as one of the friendliest and best run in the city. The interior has some attractive Tuscan touches and the rooms come in a variety of sizes, making the hotel perfect for families. The facilities include optional private bathroom, TV, telephone, safe and internet access. Breakfast includes the owner's home baking and should not be missed.
🛏 €125–€159
🛈 28, 5 suites
🔳
🚌 1, 6, 7, 10, 11, 14, 17, 23

BRUNELLESCHI
Piazza Sant'Elisabetta 3, 50122 Firenze
Tel 055 290311
www.hotelbrunelleschi.it
In a peaceful spot behind Via dei Calzaiuoli, this excellent four-star hotel is a conversion of a medieval tower. There are amazing views of the Duomo

from the roof terrace and some of the guest rooms. The interior has exposed brick walls in most public areas, with guest rooms cool and calm in white and cream with red accents in the flooring and soft furnishings. The hotel has a restaurant, a bar, laundry and internet services, and a private museum displaying objects found during the conversion.
🛏 €240–€360
🛈 96 (20 non-smoking)
🔳
🚌 1, 6, 7, 11, 14

CASCI
Via Cavour 13, 50129 Firenze
Tel 055 211686
www.hotelcasci.com

A family-run hotel that was once the home of Italian composer Gioacchino Rossini, and especially good for families. Although thoroughly modernized, it still has some of its original 14th-century features. The present owners, the Lombardi family, provide immaculate, functional rooms just a short stroll from the Duomo. Triple-glazed windows cut down the noise from outside. The rooms are simple but relaxing and scrupulously clean; many have a balcony and all have private bathrooms, telephone, cable TV and minibar.
🛏 €100–€150
🛈 25 (8 non-smoking)
🔳
🚌 1, 6, 7, 10, 11, 17, 31, 32

CHIAZZA
Borgo Pinti 5, 50121 Firenze
Tel 055 248 0363
www.chiazzahotel.com
The Chiazza is in the Santa Croce area, close to the Duomo. It has been refurbished and is a stylish, relaxing

STAYING

budget option. The guest rooms are modern and immaculate and the breakfast room functions as a small bar in the evening. Some of the rooms look out onto the city's terracotta-tiled rooftops.

💶 €60–€120
🛏 14
🚭
🚌 14, 23

CRISTINA
Via della Condotta 4, 50122 Firenze
Tel 055 214484

The small, friendly Cristina is a great place for families as the owners go out of their way to make children and parents feel relaxed and at home. The rooms are clean and spacious and four have private bathrooms. Most have high ceilings and simple dark wood furniture. Being such excellent value for money, the hotel is popular, so make reservations well in advance. Credit cards are not accepted.

💶 €75–€95
🛏 9
🚌 A, 14, 23

DE ROSE PALACE HOTEL
Via Solferino 5, 50123 Firenze
Tel 055 239 6818
www.hotelderose.it

This hotel is well named, as its pink and peach shades create a rosy glow throughout. Although it lies to the west of the city, it is still within walking distance of Florence's attractions. The guest rooms are comfortably furnished and have private bathrooms, telephone, TV and hairdryer. The public rooms are somewhat grander. The De Rose is great value for money.

💶 €120–€210
🛏 18 (10 non-smoking)
🚭
🚌 B, D

EXCELSIOR
Piazza Ognissanti 3, 50123 Firenze
Tel 055 264201
www.westin.com

The Excelsior is characterized by old-fashioned opulence. Walking into the magnificent reception area you get a sense of the splendour found throughout the hotel. The marble-laden rooms have frescoes and numerous antiques and artworks; many have views of the Arno and the city.

The fine Il Cestello restaurant (▷ 221) and the downstairs Bar Donatello make it far too easy never to step outside. Residents have the use of a nearby gym.

💶 €546–€790, excluding breakfast
🛏 161
🚭
🚌 B, C, 9

GALILEO
Via Nazionale 22a, 50123 Firenze
Tel 055 496645
www.galileohotel.it

A bright and cheerful hotel right on Via Nazionale that is ideal for those who want to make the most of every minute they are in Florence. The rooms are clean and relaxing and have all the amenities you might require, including private bathroom, telephone and TV. The public rooms welcome you in and helpful staff complete the picture.

💶 €100–€200
🛏 31 (7 non-smoking)
🚭
🚌 4, 12, 25, 31, 32, 33

GALLERY HOTEL ART
Vicolo dell'Oro 5, 50123 Firenze
Tel 055 27263
www.lungarnohotels.com/gallery/

This is Florence's finest hotel for sleek modernity and stylish comfort. The public spaces display an intriguing mix of exhibits, including ethnic art and sculpture, and there's a superb library. With designer furniture, quality detailing, subtle lighting and state-of-the-art technology the rooms are relaxing. The penthouse has linen sheets and cashmere blankets. The small Fusion Bar Shozan serves light meals and drinks, and has views over the Ponte Vecchio.

💶 €275–€363
🛏 64 (44 non-smoking)
🚭
🚌 B

GIGLIO
Via Cavour 85, 50129 Firenze
Tel 055 486621
www.hotelgiglio.fi.it

The Giglio is a small family-run hotel between the Duomo and Piazza San Marco. The family also owns the restaurant Il Cinghiale Bianco, which guarantees you a reservation as a hotel guest. The guest rooms have been upgraded and have

hardwood and terracotta tiled floors. They are small but relaxing and have private bathroom, telephone and internet access, safe and minibar.

💶 €95–€155
🛏 19 (6 non-smoking)
🚭
🚌 1, 6, 7, 10, 11, 17

GOLDONI
Borgo Ognissanti 8, 50123 Firenze
Tel 055 284080
www.hotelgoldoni.com

Hotel Goldoni is great value for money. Mozart was a guest here in 1700 and many more have enjoyed the hotel's excellent position, near to the Galleria degli Uffizi, the Ponte Vecchio and the River Arno. The rooms have a chic, Parisian feel to them and are very well maintained; there

are some appealing period pieces of furniture throughout the hotel. Each guest room has a private bathroom, telephone, TV and internet point.

💶 €110–€190
🛏 20 (5 non-smoking)
🚭
🚌 A, B, 6, 11, 36, 37

GRAND HOTEL
Piazza Ognissanti 1, 50123 Firenze
Tel 055 288781
www.starwood.com/grandflorence

The Grand may be smaller than its sister hotel, the Excelsior, but it is definitely more romantic. It is a popular place with visiting celebrities so there is a chance you'll see someone you think you know. The luxurious rooms have the most fabulous bathrooms in Florence and the most sumptuous bed linen. You are also treated to great Tuscan cooking at the hotel's Incanto restaurant (▷ 222).

💶 €561–€820, excluding breakfast
🛏 107 (29 non-smoking)
🚭 🛎
🚌 B, C, 9

HELVETIA & BRISTOL
Via dei Pescioni 2, 50123 Firenze
Tel 055 287814
www.thecharminghotels.com

Once a port of call for English ladies on the Grand Tour, the Helvetia & Bristol is still redolent of 19th-century refinement. It has hosted European royalty and eminent artistic figures such as the composer Stravinsky and the writer Pirandello. Each guest room is different, with rich hues creating a warm environment. Modern-day amenities such as private bathroom, TV and telephone are carefully blended into the prevailing period style. You can dine in the enchanting Winter Garden or eat contemporary Tuscan fare in the Bristol restaurant (▷ 219).

🖐 €286–€517, excluding breakfast
🛈 67 (30 non-smoking)
🆘
🚉 A, B, 6, 11, 22, 36, 37

HERMITAGE
Vicolo Marzio 1, 50122 Firenze
Tel 055 287216
www.hermitagehotel.com
The emphasis here is on a warm and friendly welcome, something that draws visitors back time and again. The hotel is right next to the River Arno with the light, airy roof terrace overlooking the Ponte Vecchio. The guest rooms have TV and a safe and the hotel has a baby-sitting service, parking (at an extra cost), restaurant, bar and an email service.

🖐 €161–€220
🛈 28 (18 non-smoking)
🆘
🚉 B

HOTEL CIMABUE
Via B. Lupi 7, 50129 Firenze
Tel 055 475601
www.hotelcimabue.it
A family-owned, and -run, small hotel that claims to be

the best value two-star hotel in Florence, and is excellent value. Every bedroom is individually furnished with antiques; five of the rooms have painted ceilings. There is a charming bar-cum-breakfast room as you enter. Nearby parking can be arranged for €15–€18 per day.

🖐 €75–€140
🛈 16
🆘
🚉 1, 6, 17

HOTEL ORTO DE'MEDICI
Via San Gallo 30, 50129 Firenze
Tel 055 483427
www.ortodeimedici.it
This elegant townhouse was converted to a hotel in the 1950s and the original painted ceilings, wallpapers and parquet floors give the feeling of being a guest in a private house. A painted veranda leads to a large terrace with views of San Marco where drinks and breakfast are served. Attentive, friendly staff are eager to please.

🖐 €99–€237
🛈 31 (all non smoking)
🆘
🚉 1, 7, 10, 17, 25

HOTEL RITZ
Lungarno della Zecca Vecchia 24, 50123 Firenze
Tel 055 234 0650
www.florenceitaly.net
The Ritz is on the north bank of the Arno, with many of the rooms having good views. Bright hues prevail, and the many reproductions of Old Masters give the illusion you are staying in the Uffizi. It is comfortably furnished, has attractive bedrooms, and the bonus of free email services.

🖐 €110–€180
🛈 30
🆘
🚉 14, 23

JOHANNA
Via Bonifacio Lupi 14, 50129 Firenze
Tel 055 481896
www.johanna.it
The owners of this hotel and its sister hotel, the Johanna II, employ knowledgeable and enthusiastic staff who help to create a relaxed feeling. The rooms are small but attractively furnished and there is a communal room with fridge. Amenities include private

bathroom, coffee-making facilities, TV and telephone.

🖐 €85
🛈 11
🚉 8, 11, 12, 20,

LIANA
Via Vittorio Alfieri 18, 50121 Firenze
Tel 055 245303
www.hotelliana.com
In a former British embassy palace, the Liana has all the elegance and atmosphere of a 19th-century residence at very reasonable rates. The reception area has ornate ceilings, marble floors and a splendid staircase. The rooms, which vary in size and quality, retain a period feel. The excellent amenities include telephone, private bathroom, minibar, safe and TV. Breakfast and drinks can be taken in the lovely gazebo or in the lush gardens.

🖐 €85–€160
🛈 24 (10 non-smoking)
🆘
🚉 6, 8, 13, 31, 32, 33, 80

LOCANDA DEI GUELFI
Via Guelfa 45, 50123 Firenze
Tel 055 626 6053
www.locandadeiguelfi.com
This renovated guesthouse is on the third floor of an 18th-century palazzo, close to Santa Maria Novella. The rooms are simply furnished and there is access to a rooftop terrace that gives you views right across Florence to the surrounding hills.

🖐 €75–€85, excluding breakfast
🛈 5
🆘
🚉 4, 12, 25, 31, 32, 33

LUNGARNO
Borgo San Jacopo 14, 50125 Firenze
Tel 055 27261
www.lungarnohotels.com
The Lungarno gives you the choice of being more independant by staying in one of its apartments. The conservative

LOGGIATO DEI SERVITI

Piazza Santissima Annunziata 3, 50122 Firenze
Tel 055 289592
www.loggiatodeiservitihotel.it

You can relax under vaulted ceilings, amid dark-wood antiques and rich fabrics in the former monastery of the Serviti. The refurbished guest rooms are enlivened by bright curtains and throws. Many look onto the Brunelleschi-designed arcades of the Piazza Santissima Annunziata (▷ 90). The building's façade mirrors that of Brunelleschi's Ospedale degli Innocenti opposite. Rooms have telephone, private bathroom, minibar, safe, hairdryer and TV. The breakfast room and bar have views of the Accademia gardens.

🕙 €130–€205
🛏 29
🚭
🚌 C, 6, 31, 32

yet rich decorative interiors are reminiscent of a country house: Privacy and luxury sum up the style. The exposed walls and original architecture of this 13th-century tower blend beautifully with clean, bright decoration. Tall windows frame Florentine vistas and a tranquil central courtyard. Standard rooms have excellent facilities, and each apartment is equipped with kitchen, cable TV, a workstation with high-speed internet access and an espresso machine. Contemporary dining is available at the Fusion Bar Shozan and Gallery restaurant just over the river.

🕙 €308–€396
🛏 64 rooms (13 non-smoking), 4 apartments in adjoining building
🚭
🚌 D, 11, 36, 37

MALASPINA

Piazza Indipendenza 24, 50129 Firenze
Tel 055 489869
www.malaspinahotel.it

The elegant Malaspina was built in the 14th century, which is bourne out by its grand exterior. The rooms are quite modern but retain traditional touches and are scrupulously

clean. The soundproofed rooms have TV, minibar, safe and telephone.

🕙 Closed 5–25 Aug
🕙 €150–€200
🛏 31 (9 non-smoking)
🚭
🚌 7, 10, 20, 25, 31, 32, 33

MARIO'S

Via Faenza 89, 50123 Firenze
Tel 055 216801
www.hotelmarios.com

This family-run hotel is an example of the great value for money that can still be found in an expensive city. The small size of the hotel makes it possible to feel as if you are staying in someone's home, and with the care and attention paid to the rooms and to your needs, the illusion of being a house guest continues. Rooms are simply furnished, as are the public spaces, adorned with antiques and interesting old photographs. There is also a bar-lounge area. A small apartment is available.

🕙 €115–€165
🛏 16 (all non-smoking)
🚭
🚌 4, 7, 10, 12, 13, 25, 31, 32, 33

MAXIM

Via dei Calzaiuoli 11, 50122 Firenze
Tel 055 217 474
www.hotelmaximfirenze.it

The one-star Maxim is just around the corner from the Duomo. This means it's great for the sights, but it can be noisy: Try to get a room that faces into the courtyard. The guest rooms are basic but do have private bathrooms, which is unusual for this price range. There are more rooms available in the large apartment above the hotel, which are mainly used by groups.

🕙 €88–€114
🛏 23, 16 in apartment
🚭
🚌 1, 7, 14, 23

MONNA LISA

Borgo Pinti 27, 50121 Firenze
Tel 055 247 9751
www.monnalisa.it

This 15th-century palace is a wonderful mix of old and contemporary. The overall 19th-century style is enhanced by paintings of the period and works by the sculptor Giovanni Dupré (1817–82). The reception area has stuccoed walls and a magnificent staircase leading to the upstairs rooms. Many of these have elaborate ceilings, Florentine wall hangings and dark antique furniture with modern velvet covers and cushions. Facilities include private bathroom, hairdryer, TV, telephone, minibar and safe. Arguably the loveliest thing about this hotel is the flower-filled garden, a perfect spot for a glass of wine.

🕙 €180–€350
🛏 55
🚭
🚌 14, 23

PALAZZO MAGNANI FERONI

Borgo San Frediano 5, 50124 Firenze
Tel 055 239 9544
www.florencepalace.it

This is a grand place to stay on the south side of the River Arno. It has an inner courtyard, vaulted ceilings and a lavish use of marble. The owners are very hospitable and will make all manner of arrangements for you: They can even arrange for a shoemaker or a tailor to visit you in the privacy of your own room. Facilities include TV, telephone, minibar and safe.

🕙 €210–€750
🛏 12 (5 non-smoking)
🚭 📺
🚌 D, 11, 36, 37

PALAZZO RUSPOLI

Via de' Martelli 5, 50129 Firenze
Tel 055 267 0563
www.palazzo-ruspoli.it
Ideally placed close to the
Duomo and San Lorenzo,
Palazzo Ruspoli is an immaculate and comfortable place to
stay with its attractive paint-
work and patterened soft
furnishings. The excellent facilities include private bathroom,
telephone, TV and hairdryer.
💶 €130–€220
🛏 20
📶 in 10 rooms
🚻 1, 6, 7, 11, 17

PENSIONATO PIO X

Via dei Serragli 106, 50122 Firenze
Tel 055 224037/225044
For those on a very tight
budget, this former convent
run by the Church is clean and
welcoming. There are two single rooms; other beds are in
small dormitories of three or
four, two of which have private
bathrooms. The layout of the
communal showers allows
some privacy. The minimum
stay is two nights and the maximum is five. Note that you
must be in by midnight. Credit
cards are not accepted.
💶 €20, excluding breakfast
🛏 55 beds
🚻 D, 11, 36, 37

PLAZA HOTEL LUCCHESI

Lungarno della Zecca Vecchia 38,
50122 Firenze
Tel 055 26236
www.plazalucchesi.it
A riverside hotel, in the Santa
Croce area, east of Ponte alle
Grazie, that has more understated sophistication than you
will find at some of the city's
other establishments. Rooms
are light and relaxing, decorated in subdued shades.
Private bathroom, TV, minibar,
telephone and safe included.
Some rooms are smaller and
have showers, not baths.
💶 €258–€335
🛏 97 (40 non-smoking)
📶
🚻 B, C, 12, 13

PORTA FAENZA

Via Faenza 77, 50123 Firenze
Tel 055 284119
www.hotelportafaenza.it
Don't reject this hotel because
of its proximity to the busy Via
Nazionale and the rail station—
its soundproofing blocks out

the noise of the city admirably.
The rooms are sparsely yet
tastefully furnished with large
tiled bathrooms. Rooms also
have telephone, TV, safe and
hairdryer. There is a rustic
breakfast room where you
will find good service.
💶 €85–€130
🛏 25
📶
🚻 4, 7, 10, 12, 13, 25, 31, 32, 33

PORTA ROSSA

Via Porta Rossa 19, 50123 Firenze
Tel 055 287551
The Porta Rossa, established
in 1386, is one of the oldest
hotels in Italy. A long line of
famous guests have stayed
in the converted medieval
palazzo, including writers Lord
Byron and Stendhal as well
as some of today's Hollywood
stars. All guest rooms have
private bathroom, telephone
and minibar, and public areas
include a cafeteria and a billiard room. There's also a
laundry service.
💶 €141–€176
🛏 80 (10 non-smoking)
📶
🚻 6, 11

RESIDENZA

Via dei Tornabuoni 8, 50123 Firenze
Tel 055 218684
www.laresidenzahotel.com
This is a modest, pleasant
hotel right in the heart of the
city. The roof terrrace allows
you to take in views of the
Piazza Santa Trinità and the
hotel has a restaurant, bar
and laundry service. The
guest rooms have telephone,
satellite TV and minibar.
💶 €120–€180
🛏 24 (8 non-smoking)
📶
🚻 B, 22

RIVOLI

Via della Scala 33, 50126 Firenze
Tel 055 282853
www.hotelrivoli.it
The Rivoli is a beautifully
renovated Franciscan
monastery, close to Santa
Maria Novella. The public
spaces have cross vaults,
arches and pillars, which are
links to the building's serene
and austere past. Rooms
are simple with large marble
bathrooms; some have a balcony or terrace. Services and
amenities include 24-hour

room service, laundry service,
TV, radio and telephone. On
fine days, breakfast is served
on the flower-filled patio.
💶 €150–€320
🛏 69 (12 non-smoking)
📶 🌊 Outdoor heated hottub
🚻 A, 11, 36, 37

SAVOY

Piazza della Repubblica 7,
50123 Firenze
Tel 055 27351
www.roccofortehotel.it
A 19th-century building in
Piazza della Repubblica is one

of Florence's top boutique
hotels. It has parquet flooring
and natural fabric carpets
throughout; sleek furniture,
cool photography and sculpture give the rooms a designer
edge. The private bathrooms
have deep bathtubs and are
adorned with marble and
mosaics. L'Incontro restaurant
is downstairs, where you can
eat in the company of the
Florentine glitterati, and have a
nightcap in the handsome bar.
💶 €264–€495, excluding breakfast
🛏 107 (64 non-smoking)
📶 🍽
🚻 A, 6, 22

LA SCALETTA

Via dei Guicciardini 13, 50125 Firenze
Tel 055 283028
www.lascaletta.com
For those who want to stay on
the quieter south side of the
River Arno, La Scaletta is
peaceful, yet close to the
Palazzo Pitti (▷ 80–81) and
the Boboli Gardens (▷ 74),
which you can see from its
lovely terrace. The rooms are
unfussy and clean and the
public spaces are relaxing
enough to invite you to linger.
Facilities include telephone,
private bathroom and TV.
💶 €100–€135
🛏 14
📶
🚻 D

STAYING

SCOTI

Via dei Tornabuoni 7, 50123 Firenze
Tel 055 292 128
www.hotelscoti.com

Scoti is in a 15th-century building opposite the Palazzo Strozzi in a bustling shopping street. It's a great place to stay—excellent value, with period character, and a good central base from which to explore the city. The bedrooms are simple and light. There are no private bathrooms, but the shared ones

are very clean. The lounge area has 18th-century frescoes of landscapes.

🛏 €65–€90
🛋 11
🕿
🚌 A, 6, 11, 22, 36, 37

SOGGIORNO ANTICA TORRE

Piazza della Signoria 3, 50122 Firenze
Tel 055 216402
www.anticatorre.com

Part of this hotel is based around an 11th-century tower, and despite refurbishments and countless renovations, the original ceilings have been kept intact, and are complemented by handsome parquet floors. The guest rooms are beautifully furnished and have a distinctly Florentine feel to them. Each has a private bathroom (with shower or bath), minibar, TV and telephone.

🛏 €114–€150, excluding breakfast
🛋 6
🕿
🚌 A, B

SORELLE BANDINI

Piazza Santo Spirito 9, 50125 Firenze
Tel 055 215308

A *pensione* that's excellent value for money, if you don't mind joining the many and varied visitors who end up

here in the Oltrano. Because of its prices, it is often fully reserved far in advance. Credit cards are not accepted.

🛏 €108–€130
🛋 12
🚌 D, 11, 37

TORRE GUELFA BORGO

Borgo Santi Apostoli 8, 50123 Firenze
Tel 055 239 6338
www.hoteltorreguelfa.com

This 13th-century tower, once home to the wealthy Acciaiuoli family, is now home to one of Florence's best hotels, known

for its service and views. The loftiness of the tower is obvious from the inside with the high ornate ceilings giving the guest rooms an airy feel. Some have balconies and canopied beds, and include telephone, private bathroom and TV. The rooftop terrace is perhaps the biggest reason why most guests return year after year.

🛏 €160–€190
🛋 20
🕿
🚌 B, D, 11, 37

VILLA LA MASSA

Via della Massa 24, Bagno a Ripoli, 50012 Firenze
Tel 055 62611
www.villalamassa.it

The Medici family once owned this villa, which is about 10 minutes' drive from central Florence. It has been given a new lease of life as a haven for lovers of luxury. Famous past guests include Winston Churchill and Elizabeth Taylor. Guest rooms are furnished with heavy embroidered brocade and Florentine antiques, and have huge marbled bathrooms and views over the well-tended grounds. Tuscan cuisine is served at the Verocchio restaurant, with a terrace overlooking the lush riverbank. Tennis, golf and horseback riding available,

and there is a free bus service to and from the Ponte Vecchio.

🕿 Closed Nov–end Feb
🛏 €370–€450
🛋 37
🕿 🏊 Outdoor
🚌 48
🚗 Take A1 from Firenze and exit Firenze Sud before following signs for Bagno a Ripoli and Candeli

VILLANI

Via delle Oche 11, 50122 Firenze
Tel 055 239 6451
www.hotelvillani.it

The Villani has a good cross-section of visitors: Academics, Italian families, students from around the world and couples are all attracted by the value for money available here. The guest rooms have private bathroom and TV, and while quite small, are pleasantly furnished. The hotel's position beside the Duomo also means that the main attractions are just a short stroll away.

🛏 €100–€120
🛋 13 (6 non-smoking)
🕿
🚌 A

TORNABUONI BEACCI

Via dei Tornabuoni 3, 50123 Firenze
Tel 055 212645
www.tornabuonihotels.com

This handsome hotel is great for shopping and sightseeing but its position on a busy road means that it can be noisy. Since the late 1920s it has attracted writers, academics and aesthetes, including novelist John Steinbeck and actor Frederic March. The large, leafy roof garden and antiques-filled library-cum-lounge are quiet retreats from the nearby shopping frenzy. Take to the roof, order an *aperitivo* from the bar and watch as the sun sets the Florentine rooftops aflame. The design of the guest rooms is simple and uncluttered, and each is equipped with private bathroom, telephone, hairdryer, satellite TV, minibar and safe.

🛏 €150–€230
🛋 40
🕿
🚌 A, 6, 11, 22, 36, 37

STAYING

STAYING

FIESOLE

PENSIONE BENCISTÀ

Via B. da Maiano, 50014 Fiesole
Tel 055 59163

You'll find this old-fashioned, family-run *pensione* in a fabulous position on a hill just under Fiesole overlooking Florence. The building was once a monastery. It has many interesting nooks and crannies and is filled with solid antiques; comfortable rather than luxurious, it maintains a real old-world feel. The bedrooms are individually furnished and a long, flower-filled terrace (where breakfast is served in the summer) takes full advantage of the views as does the dining room.

⊙ Often closed Dec and Jan
€170–€190 half board (obligatory)
42 rooms (all non-smoking)

VILLA FIESOLE

Via Beato Angelico 35, 50014 Fiesole
Tel 055 597252
www.villafiesole.it

The Villa Fiesole Hotel gives visitors a taste of luxury just a short bus ride from Florence. The 19th-century villa has a splendid greenhouse, which contains the breakfast room, a lounge area and several bedrooms. The guest rooms have every modern comfort as well as private bathroom, TV and telephone. It's exceptional value for money.

€135–€300
32 (4 non-smoking)
Outdoor
7
Take A1 from Firenze (or Via Giuseppe Mantellini—the road to Fiesole), then follow the signs as you enter Fiesole

LUCCA

ALBERGO SAN MARTINO

Via della Dogana 7/9, 55100 Lucca
Tel 0583 469181
www.albergosanmartino.it

This three-star hotel in Lucca's old town is only a brief stroll

from the cathedral from which it takes its name. The bedrooms are well furnished and have a TV and refrigerator. One of the services available is an English speaker who

comes to the hotel at 6pm every day to give guests a talk on what to see and do in Lucca. The talk comes with complimentary afternoon tea or summer drinks. Parking and bicycle rental available.

€100–€130
9 (all non-smoking)

ALBERGO CELIDE

Viale Giusti 25, 55100 Lucca
Tel 0583 954106
www.albergocelide.it

Celide sits just outside the city's ramparts. Popular with business people, the guest rooms here come with a range of modern facilities such as internet connection and cable TV. Downstairs is an intimate café-bar and upstairs the roof garden has panoramic views. Facilities also include a TV room, a courtesy bus into town if you don't feel like the walk, and 24-hour reception. There's a cocktail bar and restaurant next door.

€104–€145
61 (20 non-smoking)

DA ELISA ALLE SETTE ARTI

Via Elisa 25, 55100 Lucca
Tel 0583 494539
www.daelisa.com

This budget lodging option has accommodation on an *affittacamere* basis, which means that guests rent rooms by the night. Rooms in the 19th-century building have chandeliers and patterned floor tiles. There are three bathrooms for the six rooms. Free parking is available near by and bicycle rental can be arranged.

€42–€50, excluding breakfast
6

HOTEL ILARIA

Via del Fosso 26, 55100 Lucca
Tel 0583 47615
www.hotelilaria.com

Although the building looks rather old on the outside, the rooms are modern, with bright tiling or carpets, pastel walls and beamed ceilings. Each bedroom has a private shower or bath. The large apartment is suitable for groups and for longer stays. Ilaria's restaurant

SPECIAL

LOCANDA L'ELISA

Via Nuova per Pisa 1952, 55050
Massa Pisana, Lucca
Tel 0583 379737

In attractive mountainous surroundings within easy reach of Lucca, the Hotel

Locanda l'Elisa is in a converted 18th-century villa thought to have been built under the direction of Napoleon's sister, Elisa Baciocchi. The 10 suites are decorated with period furnishings and lavish fabrics, and feel surprisingly intimate after the grandeur of the entrance. The stately conservatory houses a well-reputed restaurant (▷ 228). Guests have use of the lush and heavily scented flower garden, bar, conference hall and laundry service.

🍽 €230–€390
🛏 10
♿ 🏊 Outdoor
🚗 Follow the blue signs marked Pisa on SS12; the hotel is on the left, 5.5km (3.5 miles) from Lucca

has a list of more than 300 wines. Both bar and restaurant serve traditional cuisine. Private parking is available.

🍽 €200–€230
🛏 40 (10 non-smoking)
♿

PICCOLO HOTEL PUCCINI

Via di Poggio 9, 55100 Lucca
Tel 0583 55421
www.hotelpuccini.com

This small, friendly, three-star hotel is in the busy central square at the very heart of Lucca. The house in which the opera composer Giacomo Puccini was born, now a museum, is just opposite the hotel. The guest rooms, although small, are well priced.

Each bedroom has a TV, telephone, hairdryer and safe. Parking is available by arrangement. The hotel operates a courtesy car for trips to and from the airport or train station.

🍽 €83
🛏 14

LA ROMEA

Via Sant'Andrea, 56127 Lucca
Tel 0583 464175
www.laromea.com

Bed and breakfast is provided here on the first floor of a late 14th-century palace, just a short walk from the Torre Guinigi. Each guest room has a decorative theme: The earth room has a view of the Torre dell'Ore; the sky-blue room has a frescoed ceiling and lovely wooden floor. All are equipped with TV and hairdryer. Private parking is available.

🍽 €120–€160
🛏 3 rooms, 2 suites (all non-smoking)
♿ 🏊 Outdoor

VILLA LA PRINCIPESSA

Via Nuova per Pisa 1616, 55050 Massa Pisana, Lucca
Tel 0583 370037
www.hotelprincipessa.com

At the base of the hills surrounding Lucca, just 3km (2 miles) from the city, this vine-covered villa is the former home of Castruccio Castracani, lord and duke of Lucca and said to be the inspiration for Machiavelli's Prince. Today this four-star hotel is one of the most elegant lodgings in all of Tuscany. The luxurious guest rooms are decorated with antiques and period furnishings and come equipped

with telephone, satellite TV and minibar. There is a lounge, bar and restaurants.

🍽 €250–€300
🛏 42
♿ 🏊 Outdoor

🚌 On the SS12, follow the blue signs for Pisa, the hotel is on right after 3.5km (2 miles)

VILLA ROMANTICA

Via Barbantini 246, 55100 Lucca
Tel 0583 496872
www.villaromantica.it

A few minutes' walk from the famous walls of Lucca, Villa Romantica is a grand Liberty (also known as art nouveau) townhouse surrounded by trees and flower-filled urns. Rooms are decorated in the fashion of the period with bright walls and busy fabrics. For a romantic experience, reserve the suite with four-poster bed, living room and terrace. There's a bus service to central Lucca (4 times an hour), free private parking and bicycles for rent.

🍽 €98–€138 excluding breakfast
🛏 3
♿ 🏊 Outdoor

MONTECATINI TERME

GRAND HOTEL DU PARK ET REGINA

Viale Diaz 8, 51016 Montecatini Terme, Pistoia
Tel 0572 79232
www.regina-hotel.it

Shades of the Belle Époque are in evidence at this stately old spa hotel. It's right in the middle of town and close to the thermal spas (▷ 99). There are spacious public rooms, a restaurant serving both Tuscan and international cuisine, a garden and parking. Continuing the spa and relaxation theme, there is also a beauty spa providing sauna, massages and solarium.

🍽 €130
🛏 78
♿ 🏊 Outdoor

PIETRASANTA

ALBERGO PIETRASANTA
Via Garibaldi 35, 55045 Pietrasanta, Lucca
Tel 0584 793726
www.albergopietrasanta.com
This handsome hotel, just inland from the popular Versilia beaches, is in a 17th century palazzo on a pedestrian street in the middle of attractive, lively Pietrasanta. The elegant interior (fine plasterwork, chandeliers, vast fireplaces and antique furniture) is a good backdrop for the owner's extensive collection of modern Italian art. The comfortable and spacious bedrooms have warm parquet floors and smart fabrics; those at the top have round windows and are particularly attractive. Breakfast is served in a big conservatory and there is a pretty garden, as well as a Turkish bath.
🗓 Closed early Jan–end Mar
💶 €200–€300
🛏 19
♿ 🕎

PISA

GRAND HOTEL DUOMO
Via Santa Maria 94, 56100 Pisa
Tel 050 561894
www.grandhotelduomo.it
This hotel is just a step away from the Leaning Tower. It has splendid views over the monuments on Campo dei Miracoli from the roof garden, which also provides alfresco dining on summer evenings. Guest rooms are spacious and clean and come with satellite TV. The restaurant serves a range of Tuscan dishes, and there's a bar and private parking.
💶 €137–€180
🛏 93
♿

HOTEL FRANCESCO
Via Santa Maria 129, 56126 Pisa
Tel 050 554109
www.hotelfrancesco.com
This is a small hotel and restaurant close to the Leaning Tower and botanical gardens, right in the midst of historical Pisa. Rooms are whitewashed, with wooden furnishings and—in most cases—panoramic

views. Make a reservation for the one room that has a private terrace. Breakfast is served alfresco on the hotel's main terrace. Bedrooms have TV and minibar. Facilities

include a family-run pizzeria, bicycle rental and a courtesy airport shuttle.
💶 €100–€125
🛏 13 (all non-smoking)
♿

HOTEL LA PACE
Viale Gramsci 14 (Galleria B), 56125 Pisa
Tel 050 29351
www.hotellapace.it
This relaxing hotel has a quiet yet central spot close to the rail station and Pisa's main shopping area. Guest rooms are well furnished and neat, with decorative schemes in various shades of red, yellow and pink. All bedrooms come equipped with TV. A quirky touch in the reception area, contrasting with the otherwise elegant surroundings, is the two traditional English phone booths. The hotel has room service and a restaurant.
💶 €90–€100
🛏 66
♿

HOTEL RELAIS DELL'OROLOGIO
Via della Faggiola 12/14, 56126 Pisa
Tel 050 830361
www.hotelrelaisorologio.com
An old manor house, with the restored remains of a 14th-century tower, is a short walk from the Piazza dei Miracoli and the bustling university quarter. Low, wooden-beamed ceilings, tartan rugs, spacious sitting rooms, antique furnishings and original fireplaces typify the interior, yet the guest rooms have every modern convenience, including Jacuzzis in some rooms. There's a well-regarded restaurant, where

ROYAL VICTORIA
Lungarno Pacinotti 12, 56100 Pisa
Tel 050 940111
www.royalvictoria.it
The Royal Victoria first opened in 1837, when the Piegaja family (whose descendants still run it) bought an old medieval tower and turned it into a hotel. It has expanded since then, and the hotel's history, frescoed ceilings and near-original furnishings ensure that the visitor's book (which includes such illustrious names as Charles Dickens) is always full. The hotel has a bar, concierge service, free parking and bicycle rental.
💶 €75–€125
🛏 48 (all non-smoking)
♿ 20 rooms

you can chose to take breakfast or have it in the garden, which also hosts evening receptions. An airport bus service is available on request.
💶 €290–€330
🛏 21 rooms, 2 suites, 2 junior suites (13 non-smoking)
♿ 🕎 Solarium

HOTEL ROSETO
Via Pietro Mascagni 24, 56100 Pisa
Tel 050 42596
www.hotelroseto.it
This hotel, near the rail station, is brightly decorated and large windows, tiled floors and high ceilings give the rooms a cool, airy and spacious feel. The leafy roof garden, with space for some guests to take breakfast and for evening drinks, is one of the biggest attractions. There's also a breakfast room and bar.
💶 €70, excluding breakfast
🛏 16
♿

HOTEL VERDI
Piazza Repubblica 5/6, 56100 Pisa
Tel 050 598947
Small and friendly, this hotel shares its name with the nearby Teatro Verdi. It was built on the site of an old convent destroyed during World War II, and parts of the original architecture can still be seen, including the hallway that once linked the convent

STAYING

to the Church of Sant'Andrea. The rooms are fresh and neatly furnished with some original touches. There is a lounge area with a bar, and free parking.

€115
32 (all non-smoking)

VILLA KINZICA HOTEL
Piazza Arcivescovado 2, 56100 Pisa
Tel 050 560419
www.hotelvillakinzica.it
The Villa Kinzica comes as a pleasant surprise as it is within walking distance of the Leaning Tower but still charges reasonable rates for the location. The hotel is in a renovated Italian villa with some of the original fireplaces and frescoed ceilings, yet it has modern furnishings and pastel-hued decorations. Many of the rooms at the front have views over the Piazza dei Miracoli. There's a restaurant, concierge and room service.

€108
30 (15 non-smoking)

SAN CASCIANO IN VAL DI PESA

SPECIAL

VILLA IL POGGIALE
Via Empolese 69, 50026 San Casciano in Val di Pesa, Firenze
Tel 055 828311
www.villailpoggiale.it
The Villa Il Poggiale sits in typical Tuscan countryside between San Casciano and Empoli. Occupying a beautiful Renaissance villa overlooking a smooth, green lawn, it has the feeling of a private house. A pastel interior keeps things cool throughout the spacious and elegant public rooms and the individually-furnished bedrooms. There are family portraits, antiques and (modern) four poster beds, chandeliers and filmy white curtains. Outside, you can relax under the loggia at the front of the villa, on the west-facing terrace or by the pool.

Closed Feb
€130–€140
21 (5 non-smoking)
Outdoor
2km (1.2 miles) from San Casciano on Empoli road

SANTA MARIA DEL GIUDICE

HOTEL VILLA RINASCIMENTO
Via del Cimitero 532, 55058 Santa Maria del Giudice, Lucca
Tel 0583 378292
www.villarinascimento.it
Hotel Villa Rinascimento is a great choice for visitors with cars, as it's perched on the hillside above the small village of Santa Maria del Guidice. Surrounded by olive groves and vineyards, guests can choose between rooms in the restored Renaissance stone villa and those in the wooden chalets. The whitewashed guest rooms have beamed ceilings and wooden floors. A bar is also available.

€90–€145
34
17 rooms Outdoor
On SS12, 8km (5 miles) from Lucca

TIRRENIA

GRAND HOTEL GOLF
Via dell'Edera 29, 56018 Tirrenia, Pisa
Tel 050 957018
www.grandhotelgolf.it
The hotel is named after its two golf courses, one 9-hole and one 18-hole, which are open all year. The hotel and its vast grounds also have plenty for non-golfers, including a stretch of private beach, a piano bar and a restaurant specializing in local cuisine. Balconied bedrooms have good panoramas over the coast and the cultivated pine forests for which the Tyrrhenian Coast is famous.

€137–€170
77 rooms, 18 suites
Outdoor
Take the Pisa Centro exit on the A12 and follow signs for Tirrenia

HOTEL MEDUSA
Via Oleandri 37/39, 56018 Tirrenia, Pisa
Tel 050 37125
www.hotelmedusa.com
Just a 30-minute drive from Pisa but beside the sea, the Medusa has the best of both worlds. The hotel has a comfortable feel to it with soft sofas for relaxation in the lounge area and chairs out on the terrace. Good Tuscan cooking is served in the restaurant and alfresco dining is possible if you book early. The hotel also has a bar, parking and beach chair reservations.

€65–€99
32

Take the Pisa Centro exit on the A12 and follow signs for Tirrenia

VIAREGGIO

HOTEL MIRAMARE
Lungomare Carducci 27, 55049 Viareggio, Lucca
Tel 0584 48441
www.miramarehotel.net
This hotel is extremely good value for one that is right on the waterfront. Bedrooms on the higher floors have the best views and are quieter. Parking is not easy in Viareggio, but is available in a nearby garage for €15 per day. The hotel also has an arrangement with a beach concession for €5–€8 per person per day. The restaurant is open July to September. The entire hotel is a non-smoking establishment.

€90–€130
26

HOTEL PLAZA E DE RUSSIE
Piazza d'Azaglio 1, 55049 Viareggio, Lucca
Tel 0584 44449
www.plazaederussie.com
The Plaza E de Russe was Viareggio's first hotel. It has been here since 1871 and retains some original marble floors and Murano glass chandeliers. The interior is of the highest standards of comfort and luxury. The roof restaurant has spectacular views of the sea, mountains and up the coast to the Cinque Terre. You can use the facilities of the adjacent beach concession, which has a swimming pool filled with sea water.

€137–€197
50
Outdoor

SIENA

ALBERGO CANNON D'ORO

Via Montanini 28, 53100 Siena
Tel 0577 44321
www.cannondoro.com
A good choice if you are on a budget as it is within the walls of the old city, and inexpensive by Sienese standards. The reception area is hung with old prints of the city. The bedrooms, on the two floors above (no elevator), are simply furnished but spotlessly clean and reasonably quiet as the area is virtually traffic free. The breakfast room is small—many visitors prefer to go to the nearest bar. The hotel is reached via a quiet alley off the busy shopping street, just off the Campo.
€65–€100
30

CERTOSA DI MAGGIANO

Strada di Certosa 82, 53100 Siena
Tel 0577 288180
www.certosadimaggiano.com
The Certosa is in a former monastery dating from 1314 and is one of the most luxurious hotels in town. Its 17 guest rooms were once monastic cells but are now lavishly furnished with rich linens and wall coverings. The public areas have 18th-century paintings of 12 Roman emperors, and there's an antique alderwood bookcase in the library.
€382
17 (all non-smoking)
Outdoor

GRAND HOTEL CONTINENTAL

Via Banchi di Sopra 85, 53100 Siena
Tel 0577 56011
www.royaldemeure.com
A former noble house, this hotel is a part of Siena's cultural heritage. It has been faithfully restored including the magnificent frescoes, a wall painting of St. Christopher dating from the 15th century, and ornamental motifs from the 19th century. A covered courtyard is now a winter garden and you can eat in style at the Sapordivino restaurant. Full leisure facilities are available at the nearby Park Hotel via a courtesy bus service.

€444–€540
51 (10 non-smoking)

GRAND HOTEL VILLA PATRIZIA

Via Fiorentina 58, 53100 Siena
Tel 0577 50431
www.villapatrizia.it
The pale yellow villa is surrounded by a well-kept Renaissance garden and a tennis court. The hotel has a restaurant and meals are served in the garden when the weather is good. Inside are several large, comfortably furnished reception rooms, and the bedrooms are very well equipped. The hotel is on the northern edge of the city and would make an ideal base not just for visiting Siena but also the surrounding area.
€150–€200
33 (3 non-smoking)

HOTEL ARCOBALENO

Via Fiorentina 32/40, 53100 Siena
Tel 0577 271092
www.hotelarcobaleno.com
Arcobaleno is a family-run three-star hotel in a 19th-century Tuscan country villa just outside the city walls. The pastel shades used in the interior are a refreshing respite from everything medieval. Breakfast is served on a pleasant covered terrace or in the hotel's restaurant. All guest

ANTICA TORRE

Via di Fieravecchia 7, 53100 Siena
Tel 0577 222255
www.anticatorresiena.it
This independent three-star hotel gets its name from the 16th-century medieval tower it occupies. The rooms and corridors can seem claustrophobic, but are full

of medieval charm. The breakfast room is in a brick-lined 600-year-old former pottery, and the best rooms are on the top floors, up the steep, narrow staircase, with views over Siena to the green hills beyond.
€90–€110, excluding breakfast
8 (2 non-smoking)

rooms have private bathroom, TV, telephone and internet connection. This is an intimate place with a warm welcome.
€68–€150
19 (6 non-smoking)

HOTEL ATHENA

Via P. Mascagni 55, 53100 Siena
Tel 0577 286313
www.hotelathena.com
This four-star hotel in a quiet area close to the Duomo contains a curious mix of 1960s and 70s design, with a classical Etruscan pillar in the middle of the lobby. Its rooms with three or four beds are great value for groups who don't mind sharing. Relax and enjoy the views in the tranquil terrace bar and restaurant. Free parking is available
€110–€196
100 (15 non-smoking)

STAYING

HOTEL CHIUSARELLI

Viale Curtatone 15, 53100 Siena
Tel 0577 280562
www.chiusarelli.com

Visitors have been coming here since the 1860s, but only some painted ceilings remain from those days. There are spacious public rooms and a large veranda room overlooking the garden where a generous buffet breakfast is served. Bedrooms have simple modern furnishings; those at the back overlooking the soccer stadium of the Siena team are quieter. No elevator.

€90–€117

49

HOTEL DUOMO

Via Stalloreggi 34/38, 53100 Siena
Tel 0577 289088
www.hotelduomo.it

This 17th-century palace is now a three-star hotel in a quiet part of the old town and is just a 5-minute walk from the Piazza del Campo. The bedrooms are modern, but the dining room has retained more of the building's original character. All guest rooms have private bathrooms. Rooms on the upper floors have good views over the city and beyond. Free parking.

€100–€130

23

HOTEL IL GIARDINO

Via B. Peruzzi 33, 53100 Siena
Tel 0577 285290
www.hotelilgiardino.it

Il Giardino is a family-run hotel just outside the city walls on a hill in its own grove of olive trees. Well-kept, spacious rooms have period decorations and furnishings, making it good value for Siena. There are great views over the city and surrounding countryside, and breakfast is served on the terrace. An extra bed can be put in your room for €25. Free parking is available.

€90–€130

20 (12 non-smoking)

Outdoor

HOTEL ITALIA

Via Cavour 67, 53100 Siena
Tel 0577 44248

The owners are continually redecorating and modernizing this hotel. The bedrooms are attractively furnished and bathrooms have bright hand-painted tiles and a full range of accessories. There's a cheerful breakfast room, limited parking and helpful, friendly staff at the reception desk. It's a 10-minute walk into the old city, which you will enter through Porta Camollia just as the medieval pilgrims did.

€90–€119

66

HOTEL MINERVA

Via Garibaldi 72, 53100 Siena
Tel 0577 284474
www.albergominerva.it

A ten-minute walk from Piazza del Campo and the rail station, the three-star Hotel Minerva has views over the whole city and the hills beyond. It's good value, especially as single rooms are priced from just €78, and the guest rooms are modern and fully equipped.

€90–€108

59 (all non-smoking)

HOTEL SANTA CATERINA

Via E. S. Piccolomini 7, 53100 Siena
Tel 0577 221105
www.hscsiena.it

This converted 18th-century villa still has much of its original decoration and antique furniture. The pleasant shady garden has fine views across Southern Tuscany to Monte Amiata (▷ 138), and breakfast is served here on summer mornings. Ask for a room overlooking the garden as those over the street can be noisy. There is parking for only six cars so it's advisable to reserve a space well in advance.

€105–€155

21 (8 non-smoking)

PALAZZO RAVIZZA

Via Piano dei Mantellini 34, 53100 Siena
Tel 0577 280462
www.palazzoravizza.it

This four-star *pensione* has been owned by the same family for more than 200 years. The 18th-century palace was converted into a hotel in 1929 but it has kept its character through the likes of the checkerboard marble floors and columns. The guest rooms are furnished with antiques, and the best suites come with Jacuzzis.

€130–€160

40

HOTEL VILLA LIBERTY

Viale Vittorio Veneto 11, 53100 Siena
Tel 0577 44966
www.villaliberty.it

This little hotel opposite the Medici fort is in a converted Liberty (the Italian version of art nouveau) villa—hence the name. There is an intimate, well furnished bar and sitting room on the ground floor and a small garden at the back. Care has been taken to make the bedrooms comfortable, and bathrooms are well equipped, clean and modern. Smoking is not allowed in public rooms. There is ample free parking in adjacent streets.

€90–€120

18

PALAZZO BRUCHI DI MASIGNANI

Via Pantaneto 105, 53100 Siena
Tel 0577 287342
www.palazzobruchi.it

The effervescent, English-speaking owner runs this bed-and-breakfast in an 18th-century building in the heart of Siena. There is a warm, relaxing atmosphere, the rooms are individually furnished with antiques, and large windows overlook the garden courtyard or the old city walls. You will need to specify which view you want when making your reservation. The Bruchi represents very good value. Credit cards are not accepted.

€65–€120

9

STAYING

PALAZZO RAVIZZA

Via Piano dei Mantellini 34, 53100 Siena
Tel 0577 280462
www.palazzoravizza.it
The same family has owned
the palazzo since the 18th
century, and converted it into
a hotel in the 1920s. In spite
of renovation it has kept some
of its period features, such
as the checkerboard marble
floors and columns and
painted ceilings. The guest
rooms are furnished with
antiques and the best suites
come with Jacuzzis. There is a
garden behind with fine views,
parking is available and there
is a restaurant.
€130–€200
40

PICCOLO HOTEL ETRURIA

Via delle Donzelle 3, 53100 Siena
Tel 0577 288088
www.hoteletruria.com
This is a popular two-star hotel
in the heart of Siena. The guest
rooms are basic but all have
telephone, TV, bathroom with
shower and safe. There's the
bonus that pets are welcome.
Make your reservation as far
in advance as you can, as this
is hotel is good value.
€75–€80, excluding breakfast
20

SANGALLO PARK HOTEL

Strada di Vico Alto 2, 53100 Siena
Tel 0577 334149
www.sangalloparkhotel.it

Sangallo Park is on the Vico
Alto hill, just outside the city
walls. It has all modern amenities, but lacks the romance
of many hotels in the historic
heart of Siena. But it does
have panoramic views over
the town from the rooms at
the front and the restaurant
where breakfast is served,
as well as a quiet setting and
relaxing gardens.

€70–€140
50
Outdoor
From Siena follow signs for
Ospedale/Policlinico Le Scotte and turn
left just before entrance; the hotel is on
the left, 1.5km (1 mile) from Siena

LO STELLINO

Via Fiorentina 95, 53100 Siena
Tel 0577 51987
www.sienaholidays.com
Just outside the old town walls
near the station, this is one of
the least expensive places to
stay in Siena. Guest rooms are
modern and pleasantly light
and airy; each has a telephone
and TV. There are some rooms
for three or four to share. If
you want to cook for yourself,
there is a kitchen available to
guests. The small café next
door is open for breakfast.
€60–€70, excluding breakfast
15

TRE DONZELLE

Via delle Donzelle 5, 53100 Siena
Tel 0577 280358
You find this well-run 2-star
hotel just a minute's walk
from the Campo. It only has
27 rooms, so you will need to
book well ahead. Only 4 of the
rooms have private bathrooms
and there is no lift or breakfast,
but the rooms are kept spotlessly clean and you couldn't
be more central.
€47–€60
27

VILLA CATIGNANO

Località Catignano 1, 53010 Siena
Tel 0577 356744
www.villacatignano.it
Built at the end of the 17th
century by the writer and artist
Quinto Settano, these apartments are still owned and run
by his family. The villa has
views of Siena's medieval towers in the distance and is set in
a classical Italian garden with
statues, olive groves and an
avenue of cypress trees leading to the pool. The nearest
shop is a kilometre (about half
a mile) away so stock up on
food in advance.
€78, excluding breakfast
8 apartments in villa, 19 in
farmhouse
Outdoor
8km (5 miles) from Siena; follow
signs for Catignano 3km (2 miles)
from the SS408 road between Siena
and Florence

VILLA PICCOLA SIENA

Via Petriccio Belriguardo 7, 53100 Siena
Tel 0577 588044
www.villapiccolasiena.com
A welcoming, family-run bed-
and-breakfast with elegantly
decorated rooms, each with
internet access and TV. It's
good value because it is
1.5km (1 mile) from the old
town. A shuttle bus from the
station can be booked by prior
arrangement. The family have
a small car they rent to guests
for €65 per day as well as
mountain bicycles.
€90–€130
13 (6 non-smoking)

Take the Siena North exit from A1
towards Siena, at first traffic lights the
hotel will be in front of you, to the right

VILLA SCACCIAPENSIERI

Via Scacciapensieri 10, 53100 Siena
Tel 0577 41441
www.villascacciapensieri.it
A colonial air pervades this
four-star hotel in a grand
19th-century villa with high
ceilings, beams and dark
wooden furniture. It is on
a hill 2km (1.25 miles) outside
the city walls and there are
panoramic views over Siena
and the countryside from the
hotel's well-designed gardens.
Bicycles are available to rent,
and a regular bus service from
the gates makes this a good
place to stay for anyone who
prefers not to be in the heart
of town. Tennis courts are
available for rent.

16 Mar to 14 Nov
€180–€235
31
Outdoor
Take the Siena Nord and follow the
signs for Nuovo Opsedale/Policlinico
Le Scotte and then follow signs for
the hotel

SOUTHERN TUSCANY

ANGHIARI

RELAIS LA COMMENDA

Località Commenda 6, 52031 Tavernelle di Anghiari, Arezzo
Tel 0575 723356
www.relaislacommenda.com
This bed-and-breakfast is just outside Anghiari, in a former monastery surrounded by cypress, oak, beech and olive woods. Rooms inside the stone interior are large and boldly decorated, with yellow walls, blue furnishings and red rugs. There are beamed ceilings, wooden floors and open fires in most rooms, including the large lounge for guests. The surrounding countryside is great for walkers, and there are a number of activities that can be arranged, such as archery, cooking courses, sailing and windsurfing.
🛏 €170–€200
🛋 4 suites, 3 apartments
🏊 Outdoor
🚗 From Arezzo, take the SS Aretina until Ville, then follow directions to Anghiari. The Relais is on the right; 27km (17 miles) from Arezzo

AREZZO

HOTEL CONTINENTALE

Piazza Guido Monaco 7, 52100 Arezzo
Tel 0575 20251
www.hotelcontinentale.com
The hotel was built in 1948 and has bright furnishings,

lavish bathrooms and a large panoramic roof garden. The guest rooms are modern and equipped with satellite TV and minibar. Breakfast is served on the roof terrace if the weather is fine. Other facilities include a restaurant and free parking.
🛏 €98, excluding breakfast
🛋 73
🔲

HOTEL MINERVA

Via Fiorentina 4, 52100 Arezzo
Tel 0575 370590
www.hotel-minerva.it
The Minerva has grown up around its traditional Tuscan

restaurant, which was known as the Spiedo d'Oro when it first opened in 1968. It is in here that the buffet breakfast is served. There is also a courtesy airport shuttle service and parking.
🛏 €100–€135
🛋 128
🔲
🚗 From the Autostrada A1 Arezzo exit, follow directions to the centre of Arezzo for 5km (3 miles) and then signs for the hotel

BAGNO VIGNONI

HOTEL POSTA MARCUCCI

Via Ara Urea 43, Bagno Vignoni 53027, San Quirico d'Orcia, Siena
Tel 0577 887112
www.hotelpostamarcucci.it
A peaceful spa hotel in the beautiful countryside of the Val d'Orcia with old-fashioned comforts and furnishings. Guests can reach the large thermal pool by a passageway: Unwind under the stream of water as it enters the pool at 43°C (110°F), or sit on the benches in the water to relax. You can also indulge in a massage. There's a restaurant, and spacious public rooms. Two

meals are obligatory on Saturdays and public holidays.
🛏 €138
🛋 35
🔲

BUONCONVENTO

HOTEL GHIBELLINO

Via Dante Alighieri 1, 53022 Buonconvento, Siena
Tel 0577 809112
www.paginegialle.it/hotelghibellino
Although it is modern both inside and out, this hotel is notable for the use of traditional local materials. The guest rooms have wooden floors, and headboards carved especially for the hotel by local craftsmen. Subdued lighting throughout creates a calm environment, and there is a solarium/roof terrace to soak up the sun.
🛏 €83
🛋 23
🔲

CHIANTI

ALBERGO LA FONTE DEL CIECO

Via Ricasoli 18, 53013 Gaiole in Chianti, Siena
Tel 0577 744028
www.lafontedelcieco.it
Mother and daughter, Tania and Francesca, have lovingly restored this early 20th-century townhouse into a hotel. The seven bedrooms are all named after local wild flowers and decorated with wrought-iron bedsteads, terracotta floors and wooden beamed and tiled ceilings. Soft pastel shades are used throughout. The bathrooms are very well equipped, with plenty of soft towels. There is a small garden and a view onto the main square.
🛏 €90–€100
🛋 7 (all non smoking)

HOTEL VILLA LA GROTTA

Località Brolio, 53013 Gaiole in Chianti, Siena
Tel 0577 747125
www.hotelvillalagrotta.it
This four-star hotel is in a 19th-century villa, with additional rooms in an adjacent farmhouse. Each room is uniquely furnished, in keeping with the period villa. Turkish bath and spa treatments are available on site but the main attraction

is the countryside, including the wine estate of Borro.

🏨 €230

🛏 12

💺 🏊 Indoor and outdoor

🚗 From the A1 exit at signs for Valdichiana, follow the signs for Siena, turn off and go through Castelnuovo Berendega and follow signs for Broloi

DEL CHIANTI

Piazza Matteotti 86, 50022 Greve in Chianti, Firenze
Tel 0558 53763

Greve is one of the most quintessential Chianti villages, and this old hotel—parts of the building are nearly 1,000 years old—is right on the central piazza. Bedrooms are light and airy, with wrought-iron headboards and cool white draperies, while downstairs there are terracotta floors, white walls and a tasteful mix of the modern and antique. The vine-shaded eating area under a pergola in the garden is a real bonus.

🔆 Closed Nov to mid-Dec and mid-Jan to end Mar

🏨 €90–€100

🛏 16

💺 🏊 Outdoor

RELAIS FATTORIA VIGNALE

Via Pianigiani 8, 53017 Radda in Chianti, Siena
Tel 0577 738300
www.vignale.it

Fattoria (farmhouse) Vignale started life as the manor house of a big wine estate. Today it's among Italy's top hotels, which is reflected in its clientele. The conversion has been done extremely well: Expect

traditional Tuscan architecture, well-polished antiques, fireplaces big enough to live in, and huge, opulent sofas. The bedrooms, some with private terraces, are luxurious and sybaritic, with service to match. The vaulted wine cellars house a taverna, and there's a more

elegant restaurant just a short distance (200m/220 yards) from the main building.

🔆 Mid-Mar to end Nov

🏨 €160–€240

🛏 40 (all non-smoking)

💺 🏊 Outdoor

CORTONA

CASA BELLAVISTA

Località Creti 40, 52044 Cortona
Tel 0575 610311
www.casabellavista.it

This bed-and-breakfast is within easy reach of Cortona, as well as Arezzo, with views towards the peak of Monte Amiata (▷ 138). Here you can experience a traditional Tuscan home complete with a pet rooster. Breakfast, made according to family recipes, is served in the dining room. The public rooms include a library, study and lounge.

🔆 Closed Jan, Feb

🏨 €90–€115

🛏 3

🏊 Outdoor

🚗 Take the Valdichiana exit from A1 and follow signs for Foaino della Chiana and then Fratta–S. Caterina; take a right next to the ruined building and follow the road uphill for 1km (0.5 mile); 35km (22 miles) from Arezzo, 12km (7 miles) from Cortona

HOTEL ITALIA

Via Ghibellina 5/7, 52044 Cortona
Tel 0575 630254/630564

The three-star Hotel Italia has modestly priced accommodation in a palace dating from the 1600s, just a few steps from Cortona's main square. The hotel's restaurant, Taverna Il Ghibellino, serves typical Tuscan cuisine in the subterranean stone cellar dining room. The large roof terrace is a great place to relax and enjoy the panoramic views over Valdichiana and south towards the neighbouring Umbria and Lake Trasimeno.

🏨 €92–€97

🛏 26 (all non-smoking)

💺

RELAIS VILLA BALDELLI

San Pietro a Cegliolo 420, 52044 Cortona
Tel 0575 612406
www.villabaldelli.com

This country villa, built during the 17th century of *pietra serena* (the local hard, grey stone), is now a four-star hotel. It sits in peaceful parkland with

a golf driving range. Rooms are simple but elegant with pinkish walls, beamed ceilings, wrought-iron beds and

wooden furnishings. The shared lounge has a large, original fireplace. Amenities include a bar and wine-tasting room, and traditional breakfasts are served on the terrace in summer. Walks, horseback riding and excursions can be arranged and there is an on-site golf academy.

🏨 €200–€300

🛏 15

💺 🏊 Outdoor

🚗 Take the Valdichiana exit on A1 and follow signs for Cortona; at Camuca take SS71 in the direction of Arezzo; the Relais is on the right just after Sodo

ISOLA D'ELBA

HOTEL VILLA OMBROSA

Spiaggia de Le Ghiaie, 57037 Portoferraio, Isola d'Elba
Tel 0565 914363
www.villaombrosa.it

Just over the headland from the port there is a fine pebble beach with clear blue water and, above it, this charming family-owned hotel. It's an ideal base for visiting the island without bringing a car. A room with a sea view costs a supplement, depending on the season, and you must pay for two meals daily in July, August and September.

🏨 €72–€88

🛏 38

🚗 Turn right from the ferry terminal and follow the port, then follow signs for Centro Storico and then signs for Spiaggia Le Ghiaie; the hotel is 460m (500 yards) along the bay on the left

VILLA OTTONE

Località Ottone, 56037 Portoferraio, Isola d'Elba
Tel 0565 933042
www.villaottone.com

This white-fronted villa dates from the 19th century. It stands on the shoreline of the bay at

Portoferraio, some 10km (6 miles) from the main town. The guest rooms are split between the villa, decorated with frescoes, and a newer building. Those in the latter are not to be underestimated—the more expensive rooms have Jacuzzis. The hotel has a private beach, restaurant, bar, gardens and tennis courts. The terrace is a great spot to sit and watch the sun set over the bay and the complex is well placed for touring the island.

💰 €168–€296 (half board only)
ℹ️ 80
🅿️ 🏊 Outdoor
🚗 From Portoferraio (10km/6 miles from the hotel), take the Porto Azzura road, turn left at the sign for Bagnaia Maggazina; the hotel is 4km (2.5 miles) along on the left

ISOLA DEL GIGLIO
IL SARACENO
Via del Saraceno 69, 58013 Giglio Porto, Isola del Giglio
Tel 0564 809006
The granite building is set on the rocks just above the clear blue sea with views looking back to Monte Argentario. Steps lead you down from the hotel to the water, and places for sitting and sunbathing have been created among the rocks. The restaurant has an outside terrace. Rooms are minimally furnished with white walls, wooden furniture and nautical charts. A bonus is the parking space: It is worth bringing a car if you are staying for a few days so that you can explore the rest of the island.

📅 Apr–end Oct
💰 €90–€120
ℹ️ 44
🅿️

LUPOMPESI
BOSCO DELLA SPINA RESIDENCE
Lupompesi Murlo, 53016 Siena
Tel 0577 814605
www.boscodellaspina.com
Designed by the owners and in the peaceful hills, the four-star Bosco della Spina Residence is on the edge of the Maremma forest, and near the medieval village of Lupompesi. It makes a good base for exploring the smaller villages and archaeological sites of the province of Siena. The building is a successful mix of old and new,

and the suites are individually designed. All the rooms have good views—those overlooking the gardens are best.

📅 Closed 7 Jan to 14 Feb
💰 €120–€180
ℹ️ 14 suites
🅿️ 🏊 Outdoor
🚗 20km (12 miles) south of Siena; from Siena, take the SS2 and follow signs for Rome/Buonconvento and then turn left for Murlo

MONTALCINO
DEI CAPITANI
Via Lapini 6, Montalcino, 53024 Siena
Tel 0577 847227
www.deicapitani.it
Almost all the rooms in this beautifully converted late

medieval building have sweeping views over the Val d'Orcia. Bedrooms are lofty, with cool tones, lovely beamed ceilings and plenty of space; some are in the annex to the main building. It's a family-run hotel that prides itself on personal service, so expect smiles and helpfulness. The breakfast buffet will keep you going all day, and if the private parking's full, the hotel staff will help you find a space in town.

📅 Closed 15 Jan to 15 Feb
💰 €103–€150
ℹ️ 29
🅿️ 🏊 Outdoor

IL GIGLIO
Via Soccorso Saloni 5, Montalcino, 53024 Siena
Tel 0577 848167
This three-star hotel is right in the heart of town, just around the corner from the Piazza del Popolo, and is excellent value for money. The style of the interior is rustic, making use of the stone and woodwork from the original building. Most of the guest rooms have panoramic views and each has a bathroom with shower, TV, telephone and minibar. The hotel has a laundry service,

and a restaurant with a good choice of local wines. Staff will arrange wine tours, and there is a shuttle bus service to the station or the airport.

💰 €78–€85
ℹ️ 12

MONTE ARGENTARIO
HOTEL LA CALETTA
Via Civinini 10, 58019 Port Santo Stefano, Grosseto
Tel 0564 812939
www.hotelcaletta.it
You'll get good value for your money at this hotel, which is in a quiet position right on the water's edge at the far end of town. The guest rooms are relaxing, with white walls and blue furnishings, and all look on to the sea. There is a small beach outside with sunbeds and umbrellas for guests, and a scuba diving shop next to it. Many guests return annually, often on a plan that includes two or all meals—the hotel has an excellent restaurant that's popular with locals. Parking is available near by.

💰 €70–€104
ℹ️ 26
🅿️

HOTEL DON PEDRO
58018 Porto Ercole, Grosseto
Tel 0564 833914
www.hoteldonpedro.it
Set on a hill overlooking the village of Porto Ercole, this is a family-owned hotel. You can watch the boats coming and going from the old port below your balcony or the roof solarium. Fresh furnishings create a cool contrast to the bright light and heat outside; ask for a room on the upper floors for a better view and less noise from the road below. The restaurant, with good views, serves a varied menu with the emphasis on locally caught fish. Parking is available.

📅 Apr–end Nov
💰 €90–€145
ℹ️ 50
🅿️

IL PELLICANO

Cala dei Santi, 58018 Porto Ercole,
Grosseto
Tel 0564 858111
www.pellicanohotel.com

The guest accommodation at this luxury hotel is set among the pine trees in the expansive grounds. The terraced gardens are scented with Mediterranean plants and stretch down to the sea. Great care has been taken with every detail, from specially designed hand-painted tiles in the bathrooms to chic sunbeds. Relax by the pool or down by the sea, or perhaps play a game of tennis before a light buffet lunch on the terrace. You can be pampered at the Beauty and Spa Centre. The internationally acclaimed restaurant has an extensive wine list.

🕐 Apr–end Oct
🍴 €359–€577
🛏 50
🏊 🏖 Heated outdoor 🐴

MONTEPULCIANO

ALBERGO DUOMO

Via San Donato 14, 53045
Montepulciano
Tel 0578 757473
www.albergoduomo.it

Apart from the breakfast room, the Albergo Duomo has little in the way of public rooms. However, its position makes up for this small deficiency: It is directly opposite the Duomo and at the town's highest point. Run by the same family for many years, the lovely old building has been sensitively restored in true Tuscan style—the beamed ceilings have been retained and the furniture kept simple. Room sizes vary; try for one of the huge first-floor rooms at the front.

🍴 €90–€120
🛏 13

IL MARZOCCO

Piazza Savonarola 18, 53045
Montepulciano
Tel 0578 757262
www.albergoilmarzocco.it

This Renaissance palace was turned into a hotel in 1870 and the same family have run it since the early 1900s, with the result that you feel as though you are a guest in an old family house. Many of the furnishings are original, with spacious public rooms and a billiard table. The best

bedrooms have terraces and marvellous views. Simple home cooking is served in the restaurant.

🍴 €90
🛏 16

PIENZA

RELAIS IL CHIOSTRO DI PIENZA

Corso Rossellino 26, 53026 Pienza
Tel 0578 748400
www.relaisilchiostrodipienza.com

Walk through the luminous cloister of a 15th-century former monastery to one of the southern Tuscany's most remarkable hotels. The restoration has been beautifully done, leaving the vaulted ceilings, beams and architectural details untouched, but adding in 21st-century comfort. The bedrooms are big, the beds slumber-inducing, and antique pieces enhance the public areas. A good restaurant, dreamy terraces and cascades of geraniums add to the magic, and it's all a minute's walk from Pienza's main piazza.

🕐 Closed 7 Jan to 15 Mar
🍴 €180–€200
🛏 37
🏊 🏖 Outdoor

SAN GIMIGNANO

ALBERGO RELAIS SANTA CHIARA

Via Matteoti 15, 53037 San Gimignano
Tel 0577 940701
www.rsc.it

A short walk from the town, the four-star Relais Santa Chiara combines contemporary architecture with superb views. To ensure the best view, request a room with a balcony when making a reservation. The hotel has no restaurant, but a generous breakfast is served. There is also a cocktail bar, a garden and parking. Guest rooms are equipped with satellite TV and minibar.

🍴 €148–€195
🛏 41 (all non-smoking)
🏊 🏖 Outdoor

L'ANTICO POZZO

Via San Matteo 87, 53037
San Gimignano
Tel 0577 942014
www.anticopozzo.com

This superbly restored 15th-century townhouse is now a three-star hotel in the heart of San Gimignano. The interior is medieval in character, and contains a well-preserved

lobby with a high, vaulted ceiling. There's a bar in the old brick cellar and the first-floor courtyard has great views of the town's stone towers and cobbled streets. Each room comes with satellite TV, minibar and safe.

🕐 Closed Dec to mid-Jan
🍴 €130–€155
🛏 18
🏊

CASOLARE LE TERRE ROSSE

Località San Donato 2, 53037
San Gimignano
Tel 0577 907046
www.hotelterrerosse.com

You'll find this attractive Tuscan farmhouse set in lush, green countryside just 5km (3 miles) from San Gimignano. The interior is fresh and bright, and guest rooms are spacious and modern. Assorted antique furniture combined with plush sofas and huge terracotta urns creates a distinctive contemporary style. The pleasant inner courtyard has a bar and restaurant where guests can enjoy a relaxing aperitif and dine. Parking is available.

🍴 €85–€125
🛏 42
🏊 🏖 Outdoor
📍 From San Gimignano, take the road towards Volterra; after 5km (3 miles), the hotel is on the right

HOTEL PESCILLE

Località Pescille, Strada Provinciale 47,
53037 San Gimignano
Tel 0577 940186
www.pescille.it

The rolling countryside 3km
(2 miles) from San Gimignano
is home to an old farmhouse
turned three-star hotel. It has
views of the famous medieval
towers and walls of the town.
The hotel garden with its olive
trees and cypresses is perfect
for a pleasant evening stroll. It
also has a solarium, tennis
courts, bar and internet access.
Guest rooms are modern and
sleek, while the building still
presents a picture of authentic,
old-fashioned Tuscany.

€95–€125

50

Outdoor

From San Gimignano, take the road
signed for Castel San Gimignano/
Volterra, the hotel is on the left

SANSEPOLCRO

ALBERGO FIORENTINO

Via Pacioli 60, 52037 Sansepolcro,
Arezzo
Tel 0575 740370
www.albergofiorentino.com

There's been a hotel here since
1807 and the public rooms are
virtually unaltered. Bedrooms
have been modernized, are
simply furnished and represent

good value for such a central
position. The restaurant serves
a Tuscan-based menu. There is
parking available (€9 per day),
but no elevator.

€65

21

SATURNIA

HOTEL TERME DI SATURNIA

58050 Saturnia, Grosseto
Tel 0564 600111
www.termedisaturnia.it

Here the baths of Rome live
on in the 21st century, with
modern seekers of opulence
in white robes enjoying this
luxury spa resort. The complex

has undergone major work to
enlarge and improve it; travertine marble on the walls and
wooden floors create a cool,
minimalist feeling. The huge
adjoining thermal pool is
fed by a volcanic sulphurous
spring at a constant temperature of 37°C (98.6°F). The
emphasis is on health and
wellbeing with medical facilities on hand. The hotel
restaurant serves light, healthy
food with renowned local
wines such as the Morellino
of Scansano. There is also a
golf driving range.

€340

140

SOVANA

SCILLA

Via di Sotto 3, Sovana, 58010 Grosseto
Tel 0564 616531
www.scilla-sovana.it

Sovana is at its best in the
evenings, so an overnight stay
at this tiny and charming hotel
in the heart of the village is
recommended, but you must
book ahead. The building is
old, so rooms tend to be small,
but they are well equipped,
furnished and decorated. In
summer you can sit outside
on the restaurant's leafy terrace, which serves great food,
and in cold weather there's a
log fire in the hotel.

First 10 days in Feb and all Nov

€92–€100

8

SUBBIANO

HOTEL RISTORANTE
LA GRAVENNA

Località Gravenna 101, 52010 Subbiano
Tel 0575 420682/48588
www.lagravenna.it

La Gravenna is a panoramic
drive up through the hills to
the verdant mountain town
of Subbiano on the left bank
of the River Arno. All guest
rooms have private bathrooms,
there's a bar and restaurant,
with an extensive wine list and
a good reputation. Free parking is available. Walking treks
and horse riding can be
arranged by the friendly staff.

€78

37

SS71 in the direction of Bibbiena
and then follow signs for Subbiano and
Gravenna; 12km (7 miles) from Arezzo

VOLTERRA

ALBERGO VILLA NENCINI

Borgo Santo Stefano 55, 56048
Volterra, Pisa
Tel 0588 86386

There are magnificent views
from this hotel, which stands
in its garden just outside the
medieval walls of Volterra.
Built as a villa in the 17th
century, the main building still
has the original vaulted brick
ceiling in the reception area;
breakfast is served in the old
cellar. Most of the bedrooms
are comfortably furnished
with wooden furniture and
old prints on the walls. The
private bathrooms are clean
and modern. There is no air
conditioning, but Volterra is up
in the hills and there is always
a cooling breeze at night.

€68–€83

37

HOTEL SAN LINO

Via San Lino 26, 56048 Volterra, Pisa
Tel 0588 85250
www.hotelsanlino.com

A converted convent is now
this agreeable hotel. The convent's courtyard, with pool
and terrace, is overlooked by
the bedrooms decorated in
warm pastel shades. There is
a spacious restaurant where a

substantial buffet breakfast is
served, a bar and internet
access. The staff are a helpful
and charming team.

Closed 15 Jan to 15 Feb, and Nov

€73–€81

44

HOTEL GROUPS IN TUSCANY

Name of hotel group	Description	Website
Best Western	The world's largest group, with 4,000 independently owned hotels in 80 countries.	www.bestwestern.it
Boscolo Hotels	Seventeen luxury hotels in some of the most sophisticated cities in Italy.	www.boscohotels.com
Charming Hotels	The Charming Hotels group was founded in 1995, but its popularity has grown rapidly and they now have 60 luxury hotels world-wide.	www.thecharminghotels.com
Golden Tulip (inc Tulip Inns)	This Netherlands-based company has around 440 hotels in 51 countries, branded as either Golden Tulip (four-star) or Tulip Inns (three-star).	www.goldentulip.com
Ibis	Part of the French Accor group, Ibis is a fast-growing hotel chain, with more than 670 business and budget hotels world-wide.	www.ibishotel.com
Jolly Hotels	Jolly has been running hotels in Italy since 1949, and now has establishments in 26 Italian cities.	www.jollyhotels.it
Minotel	This company has 700 hotels worldwide in more than 30 countries	www.minotel.com
Novotel	Part of the French group Accor, Novotel have 373 hotels in 63 countries.	www.novotel.com
Orient Express Hotels	There are three luxurious hotels under the Orient Express brand in Italy, including Villa San Michele.	www.orient-express.com
Relais & Chateaux	An international group that runs a number of smart hotels in rural areas	www.relaischateaux.com
Rocco Forte Hotels	Rocco Forte have luxury hotels in key locations around the world, and runs the Savoy in Florence.	www.roccofortehotels.com
Sina Hotels	Founded by the Bocca family in 1959, the Sina Hotels Group now has four- and five-star hotels in key cities throughout Italy.	www.sinahotels.com
Sofitel	Part of the French group, Accor, Sofitel is the company's premium brand, with 160 establishments around the world.	www.sofitel.com
Starwood Hotels	Starwood is the name behind the hotel chains Sheraton, Westin and St. Regis, owning, leasing or managing around 750 hotels in 79 countries.	www.starwood.com
Utell International	The world's largest representative company, handling hotel reservations for nearly 5,000 luxury, business and budget hotels, resorts and apartments world-wide.	www.utell.com

STAYING

Planning

BEFORE YOU GO

CLIMATE
The best months to visit are May, June and September, when you should find long sunny days, but avoid the real heat of July and August. Winters are cold, with snow in the mountains. November is dank and wet, but things improve around Christmas, when you can hope for some crystal-clear, cold, sunny weather.

WEATHER REPORTS
BBC World News, www.bbc.co.uk, and CNN, www.CNN.com, broadcast regular global weather updates in English. There are also a number of dedicated websites, such as Weather Channel at www.weather.com.

PASSPORTS
All visitors to Italy need a passport, which should be valid for at least another six months from the date of entry into Italy. Officially, visitors from EU

It can be tricky when cycling in the rain through the crowds in Piazza della Signoria

countries only need a national identity card (if your home country has them). In practice, you will need a passport. If you lose your passport, you should contact your embassy or consulate (▷ 270).

Keep a note of your passport number or carry a photocopy of the information page separately from your passport.

VISAS
If you are an EU national, or from Australia, Canada, New Zealand or the United States, you do not need a visa for stays of up to 90 days. To extend your visit you can, one time only, apply to any

WEATHER STATIONS

Firenze 43m 141ft

Grosseto 7m 23ft

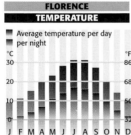

FLORENCE
TEMPERATURE

- Average temperature per day
- per night

GROSSETO
TEMPERATURE

- Average temperature per day
- per night

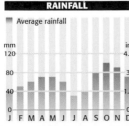

RAINFALL

- Average rainfall

RAINFALL

- Average rainfall

TIMES ZONES		
CITY	**TIME DIFFERENCE**	**TIME AT 12 NOON GMT**
Amsterdam	0	noon
Auckland	+11	11pm
Berlin	0	noon
Brussels	0	noon
Cairo	+1	1pm
Chicago	-7	5am
Dublin	-1	11am
Johannesburg	+1	1pm
London	-1	11am
Madrid	0	noon
Montreal	-6	6am
New York	-6	6am
Paris	0	noon
Perth, Australia	+7	7pm
San Francisco	-9	3am
Sydney	+9	9pm
Tokyo	+8	8pm

Italy is one hour ahead of GMT. The clocks are moved forward an hour for daylight saving time on the last Sunday in March. The clocks go back an hour on the last Sunday in October. The chart shows the time differences from Italy.

police station for an extension of a further 90 days. This extension cannot be used for studying or employment, and you will have to prove that you can support yourself financially. In any case contact the Italian embassy in your home country before travelling because visa rules can change at short notice. If you are a citizen of a country other than those mentioned above, contact the Italian embassy in your country to check requirements.

TRAVEL INSURANCE
Take out your insurance as soon as you book your trip to ensure you are covered for delays. Most policies cover cancellation, medical expenses, accident compensation, personal liability and loss of personal belongings (including money). Your policy should cover the cost of getting you home in case of a medical emergency.

An annual travel policy may be the best value if you intend to make several trips a year away from home, but long trips abroad may not be covered. If you have private medical cover, check your policy, as you may be covered while you are away.

HEALTH

● No vaccinations are necessary for a trip to Italy, unless you are coming into the country from an infected area. If you have any doubts, contact your doctor before you leave.

● You should always make sure you have adequate health insurance—see Travel Insurance on page 262.

● European citizens should carry an E111 or a European Health Insurance Card (EHIC), available from post offices, health offices and social security offices. Italy has a reciprocal health agreement with the rest of the EU, Iceland, Liechtenstein and Norway, which allows free or reduced-cost dental and medical (including hospital) treatment on presentation of the E111 or EHIC.

● If you are on regular medication, you should ensure that you have adequate supplies for your trip. Make a note of the chemical name (rather than the brand name) in case you need replacement supplies.

● See pages 268–269 for more details on health matters.

WHAT TO TAKE

● Your driver's licence.

● Photocopies of all important documents: passport, insurance details, credit card, debit card, passport numbers and registration numbers for mobile phones, cameras and other expensive items.

● Alternatively, scan documents and send them to a web-based email account that can be accessed worldwide.

● Lightweight cottons and linens to wear during the summer, and depending on the time of year that you travel, rain-proof gear and an umbrella.

● Clothes that cover your shoulders and knees if you intend to visit churches or other religious buildings.

● Comfortable shoes for walking, especially in the hills.

● A torch (flashlight) and binoculars.

● An Italian phrase book—any attempt at Italian is appreciated.

● A first-aid kit.

CUSTOMS

The import of wildlife souvenirs from rare and endangered species may be either illegal or require a special permit. Before you make any such purchase, you should check customs regulations.

See below for more details on what can be brought through customs.

DUTY-FREE AND DUTY-PAID GUIDELINES

Anything that is clearly for personal use can be taken into Italy free of duty, but it is worth carrying receipts for valuable items in case you need to prove that they were not bought in Italy.

Duty-paid allowances for US citizens

You can take home up to $800 worth of duty-paid goods, provided you have been out of the country for at least 48 hours and have not made another international trip in the previous 30 days. This limit applies to each member of your family, regardless of age, and allowances may be pooled. For the most up-to-date information, see the US Department of Homeland Security's website: www.customs.treas.gov.

- 1 litre of alcohol
- 100 cigars (non-Cuban)
- 200 cigarettes
- 1 bottle perfume (if trademarked in the US)

Duty-paid guidelines for EU citizens

You cannot buy goods duty free if you are journeying within the EU. You can take home unlimited amounts of duty-paid goods, as long as they are for your own personal use. In the UK, H. M. Customs and Excise considers anything over the following limits to be for commercial use.

- 3,200 cigarettes
- 3kg of tobacco
- 400 cigarillos
- 200 cigars
- 110 litres of beer
- 10 litres of spirits
- 90 litres of wine
- 20 litres of fortified wine (such as port or sherry)

Whatever your entitlement, you cannot take home goods for payment (including payment in kind) or for resale. These goods are considered for commercial use and duty is payable. For the most up-to-date information, see the H. M. Customs and Excise website: www.hmce.gov.uk.

PLANNING

ADDRESSES IN FLORENCE

Florence has a dual address system. Each street has a double set of numbers: A black or blue number denotes a private residence or hotel, and a red number indicates a shop, restaurant or business. In a written address, the letter 'r' after the street number stands for *rosso* (red) and means it's a business address. You may see 'Int' in an address. This stands for 'internal', and indicates a building that is inside a courtyard.

ELECTRICITY

The electric current in Italy is 240 volts, and appliances are fitted with sockets that have two round pins. If your appliances are manufactured for 240 volts, you just need a plug adaptor. If your voltage is different, as it will be from the US, you need an adaptor and transformer.

LAUNDRY

Most visitors trust their hotel with their laundry and cleaning; if you do this, your clean clothes are returned to your room and the (often high) charge is added to your bill. Self-service launderettes *(lavandaria automatica)* are few and far between in Italy, but are emerging in the larger cities. A

wash costs around €4. Dry cleaning *(lavasecco)* starts from around €3 for a shirt up to €7.50 for larger items such as jackets and coats, but the quality of the service varies immensely.

LOCAL WAYS

● A few words of Italian will always go down well (▷ 275–278), even if you can only manage hello and goodbye.
● Use *buongiorno* for hello up to midday, and *buonasera* in the afternoon and evening.
● Italians tend to use please and thank you less frequently than other nationalities.
● Show respect and dress appropriately when visiting places of worship. Cover your shoulders and knees.
● Don't intrude on religious services unless you wish to take part.
● Before taking photographs in churches and museums, always check that it is permitted and never use the flash.
● Italians tend to drink alcohol only with meals, and public drunkenness is frowned upon.
● In cafés, never attempt to use the tables if you have paid bar prices.
● If you only want a one-course meal, eat in a pizzeria. It's considered bad form to eat less than two courses in a restaurant.

LOST PROPERTY

● A lost property office is an *ufficio oggetti smarriti*.
● In Florence:
ATAF city buses: Via Circondaria 17G, tel 055 328 3942, Mon–Fri 8–12.30, 4–6.
Trains: Santa Maria Novella, platform 16, tel 055 235 6120, daily 6am–midnight.
Florence airport: tel 055 306 1711, daily 8am–10pm.
● Siena rail station: tel 0577 207360, daily 8–8.
● Pisa rail station: tel 050 849400, daily 7am–10.30pm.

MEASUREMENTS

Italy uses the metric system. Distances are measured in metres and kilometres, fuel is sold by the litre and food is weighed by the kilogram. Italians also use the *ettogrammo* (100g), usually abbreviated to *etto*.

CLOTHING SIZES

Clothing sizes in Italy are in metric. Use the chart below to convert the size you use at home.

UK	Metric	USA	
36	46	36	
38	48	38	
40	50	40	
42	52	42	SUITS
44	54	44	
46	56	46	
48	58	48	
7	41	8	
7.5	42	8.5	
8.5	43	9.5	
9.5	44	10.5	SHOES
10.5	45	11.5	
11	46	12	
14.5	37	14.5	
15	38	15	
15.5	39/40	15.5	
16	41	16	SHIRTS
16.5	42	16.5	
17	43	17	
8	36	6	
10	38	8	
12	40	10	
14	42	12	DRESSES
16	44	14	
18	46	16	
20	46	18	
4.5	37.5	6	
5	38	6.5	
5.5	38.5	7	
6	39	7.5	SHOES
6.5	40	8	
7	41	8.5	

TOILETS

There are public toilets at rail stations and in larger museums, but otherwise they are rare. You will probably end up using the facilities in a bar or café. Owners may let you use their facilities if you are not a customer, but obviously they prefer you to buy something first. Many bars keep the toilets locked, so you will need to ask for the key. Facilities can be basic: Toilet paper may not be provided, and sometimes there is only one lavatory for both men and women. In some places there is a dish for gratuities—you should tip around €0.25. Where separate facilities exist, make sure you recognize the difference between *signori* (men) and *signore* (women).

PLANNING

CONVERSION CHART

FROM	TO	MULTIPLY BY
Inches	Centimetres	2.54
Centimetres	Inches	0.3937
Feet	Metres	0.3048
Metres	Feet	3.2810
Yards	Metres	0.9144
Metres	Yards	1.0940
Miles	Kilometres	1.6090
Kilometres	Miles	0.6214
Acres	Hectares	0.4047
Hectares	Acres	2.4710
Gallons	Litres	4.5460
Litres	Gallons	0.2200
Ounces	Grams	28.35
Grams	Ounces	0.0353
Pounds	Grams	453.6
Grams	Pounds	0.0022
Pounds	Kilograms	0.4536
Kilograms	Pounds	2.205
Tons	Tonnes	1.0160
Tonnes	Tons	0.9842

PLACES OF WORSHIP

If you are Roman Catholic you will have no problem finding somewhere to celebrate your faith in Tuscany. There are Catholic churches in even the smallest towns and villages, and religious festivals are celebrated enthusiastically throughout the year.

● There is an Anglican Church of St. Mark's at Via Maggio 16, 50125 Florence (tel 055 294764), which holds daily services.

● St. James is an Episcopalian church at Via Bernardo Ruccelai 9, 50123 Florence (tel 055 294417), where services are held on Sundays.

● To find synagogues and Jewish communities in Tuscany, go to www.kosherdelight.com or www.maven.co.il.

● There are few mosques in Italy. For information contact the Unione delle Comunite ed Organizzazione Islamiche in Italia (UCOII; Via Padova 38, 20127 Milano, tel 01 83660253).

SMOKING

● Smoking is very common in Italy, and is still permitted in many hotels and restaurants. But non-smoking areas are becoming more popular.

● Smoking is not permitted on public transport, inside airport buildings and in most public offices and buildings.

● Smoking is due to be banned in all public places in 2005, bringing Italy into line with EU regulations. However there is strong opposition and it remains to be seen how strictly the law will be enforced.

● Cigarettes and other tobacco products can only legally be sold in *tabacchi* (tobacconists) to those over 16. The stand-alone *tabacchi* are open during normal shop hours (▷ 272) and there are vending machines outside many *tabacchi*. Those attached to bars stay open longer.

VISITING WITH CHILDREN

Children are welcomed in almost all restaurants and at most hotels. Items such as baby food are available in many food stores or supermarkets. On the down side, the lack of public toilets and changing facilities can make things difficult for anyone with very young children.

● You should keep a particular eye on your children when wandering around the very busy streets of Florence.

● Italian children stay up late—if parents are eating out, the kids go too. This means that most hotels do not have a baby-sitting or listening service.

● Slap a high-factor sunscreen, or even better use sun-block, on your children and keep them covered up in the sun.

● Children are susceptible to heat stroke, so seek shade in the middle of the day and keep their heads and necks protected.

● Most hotels will put up to three or four beds in a room so families can stay together; the add-on cost is around 30 per cent of the room price.

● Hotels are often unheated until the end of October.

● If you are bottle-feeding your baby, you might want to take the formula with you.

● Children aged 4 to 12 qualify for a 50 per cent discount on trains; under 4s travel free.

● Entrance to state-run museums is free to EU citizens under 18 and over 60. But you must bring proof of identity, especially for children, to be eligible. If you don't, you'll have to pay the full charge.

VISITORS WITH DISABILITIES

Wheelchair access is improving in the larger cities, as it is in the smaller towns, where many of the museums have been adapted. It is always worth asking individual establishments what access is like. However, the narrow, cobbled streets and lack of pavements (sidewalks) in many of the old towns can prove difficult.

● Holiday Care in the UK publishes information on accessibility for visitors with disabilities (Holiday Care, 7th Floor, Sunley House, 4 Bedford Park, Croydon, Surrey CR0 2AP, tel 0845 124 9971, fax 0845 124 9972, www.holidaycare.org.uk).

● In the US, SATH (Society for Accessible Travel and Hospitality) has lots of tips for visitors with visual impairment or reduced mobility (www.sath.org).

● Tourist offices should be able to help you.

● See page 58 for more details for visitors with a disability.

MONEY

Italians traditionally use cash, but this is changing. Credit and debit cards are widely accepted, but not for small sums. Food bought in a store is paid for in cash and market traders don't take cards.

BEFORE YOU GO

● It is advisable to use a combination of cash, traveller's cheques and credit cards rather than relying on any one means of payment during your trip.
● Check with your credit card company that you can withdraw cash from ATMs (cash machines). You should also check what fee will be charged for this and what number you should phone if your card is stolen (see panel).
● Traveller's cheques are a relatively safe way of carrying money, as you are insured if they are stolen. Remember to keep a note of their numbers separately from the cheques themselves.

EXCHANGE RATES

The exchange rate per euro for visitors from the UK, US and Canada is subject to daily fluctuation. At the time of printing €1 is worth approximately £0.70, US$1.25 and C$1.60.

CREDIT AND DEBIT CARDS

MasterCard, Diners Club and Visa are widely accepted, as well as Eurocheque cards, but some smaller establishments still do not take credit cards (carta di credito). Look for the credit card symbols in the shop window or check with the staff.

You can also use your credit card to make cash withdrawals, although your credit card company will charge it as a cash advance. Contact your company to get a PIN number.

ATMS

ATMs (cash machines), called bancomats in Italy, are plentiful, and many are accessible 24

LOST OR STOLEN CREDIT CARDS

American Express
06 7228 0371

Diners Club
800 864064

MasterCard/Eurocard
800 870866

Visa/Connect
800 877232

American Express traveller's cheques
800 872000

---

hours a day. Most have instructions in a number of languages, including English. You avoid commission and the exchange rates are better when you withdraw cash with a debit card (Cirrus/Maestro/Delta) from an ATM rather than using a bureau de change. Check with your bank before leaving home that you will be able to take cash out with your card while in Italy.

TRAVELLER'S CHEQUES

Traveller's cheques are accepted almost everywhere. To avoid additional exchange rate charges, take cheques in euros, pounds sterling or US dollars.

CURRENCY EXCHANGE

Banks in your home country will have differing exchange and commission rates. Check for details and shop around before you buy.

In Italy, traveller's cheques, personal cheques and foreign money can be changed at banks, rail stations and airports, and very often at major hotels (generally at a poorer rate).

BANKS AND POST OFFICES

The largest banks in Italy are Unicredito and Intesa-BCI, and Monte dei Paschi di Siena is the largest in Tuscany. Most major

---

banks have ATMs and exchange facilities, although they are often very busy. Banks are usually open from 8.30 until 1 or 1.30, and again for a short time in the afternoon. Some open on Saturday morning. Central post offices usually have a currency exchange that is open throughout the day until 6.30.

BUREAUX DE CHANGE

There are bureaux de change (cambio) in all the main cities, usually open throughout the day until around 7.30. They often change money commission-free, but the exchange rates are not as good as those from banks.

CURRENCY RESTRICTIONS

Import and export of local and foreign currency is limited to €10,329.14, but check with your embassy before departure if you need to bring large sums into the country. Amounts greater than this should be declared and validated in Italy.

WIRING MONEY

Wiring money is a lengthy process and the bureaucracy involved means that it is probably not worthwhile unless you are planning to spend quite a long time in Italy. You can get money wired out to any bank from home, but if your bank is already in contact with certain banks in Italy it will make the process a lot easier. Ask your bank at home for a list of affiliated banks. Always ask for a separate letter, telex or fax confirming that the money has been sent and ask that it be sent to Swift. It can take up to a week, sometimes more, for the money to transfer.

American Express Moneygram and Western Union Money Transfer are faster from the US, but more expensive. Citibank can transfer money for a flat fee of $10 to anywhere in the world

---

PLANNING

BANKS IN MAIN TUSCAN TOWNS			
Florence	Cassa di Risparmio di Firenze, Via Bufalini 6, 50122 Firenze	tel 055 26121	www.bancafirenze.it
	Banca d'Italia, Via dell'Oriuolo 37–39, 50122 Firenze	tel 055 245472	www.bancaditalia.it
	Banca Nazionale del Lavoro, Via Ghibellina 6, 50122 Firenze	tel 055 244851	www.bnl.it
Siena	Monte dei Paschi di Siena, Via Banchi di Sotto 21, 53100 Siena	tel 0577 281211	www.mps.it
Pisa	Cassa di Risparmio di Pisa, Piazza del Duomo 7, 56126 Pisa	tel 055 551314	www.caripisa.it
Lucca	Banca del Monte di Lucca, Piazza Martino 4, 55100 Lucca	tel 0583 450	www.fondazionebmlucca.it

(www.c2it.com). Do not wire more money than you need; you can only export just over €10,300.

DISCOUNTS
● Seniors (over 65) can get discounts on some museum entry charges on production of an identity document, but this is often restricted to EU residents only.
● An International Student Identity Card (ISIC; www.isic.org) may help you obtain free or reduced entry to museums and attractions as well as other discounts.
● See pages 45 and 53–55 for information on transport passes.

TAXES
● Sales tax is at 7 per cent and is known as IVA. It is added to services such as meals you have in restaurants and hotel accommodation. This is non-refundable. For all other goods and services, such as shop purchases, 16 per cent is added.
● Visitors from non-EU countries are entitled to a reimbursement of the 16 per cent tax paid on

purchases to the value of more than €90.15, which needs to be spent in the same store.
● The store must provide a properly completed invoice itemizing all goods, the price paid for them, and the tax charged, as well as full address details of both the vendor and purchaser. The goods must then be taken out of the EU within three months.
● The goods and the invoice(s) should be taken to the booth at Italian customs on your departure from the EU, prior to checking in your baggage. This is where your claim will be processed.

10 EVERYDAY ITEMS AND HOW MUCH THEY COST	
Sandwich	€2.50
Bottle of water	€0.50
Cup of tea or coffee	€1.50–€4
0.5 litre of beer	€3.20–€6.50
Glass of wine	€0.85–€4.50
Daily newspaper	€0.90–€3
Roll of camera film	€5
20 cigarettes	€2.50
An ice cream cone	€2
A litre of petrol (gas)	€1.05

● Tax can also be reclaimed through Global Refund Tax Free Shopping, a service offered by major retailers worldwide; visit www.globalrefund.com.

TIPPING	
Italians do not tip heavily. Service is often included in your hotel or restaurant bill, although a little extra is appreciated if the service has been good. The following is a general guide:	
Pizzerias or trattorias	round up to the nearest euro
Restaurant	10 per cent
Bar service	up to €0.25
Taxis	round up to nearest €0.50
Porters	€0.50 to €1 per bag
Chambermaids	€0.50 to €1 per day
Cloakroom attendants	€0.50
Toilets	€0.20–€0.50

BANKNOTES AND COINS

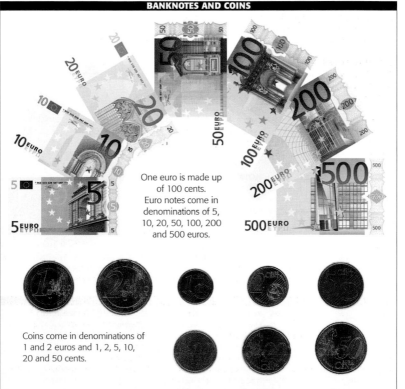

One euro is made up of 100 cents. Euro notes come in denominations of 5, 10, 20, 50, 100, 200 and 500 euros.

Coins come in denominations of 1 and 2 euros and 1, 2, 5, 10, 20 and 50 cents.

HEALTH

HOW TO FIND A DOCTOR
- To get in touch with a doctor (*un medico*), ask at your hotel or consult the *Pagine Gialle* (Yellow Pages) under Unità Sanitaria Locale.
- If you need emergency treatment, go directly to the Pronto Soccorso (casualty department/ER) of the nearest hospital.
- If you are staying in Florence, you can contact the Tourist Medical Centre, Via Lorenzo il Magnifico 59, tel 055 475411. Doctors here speak English, French and German, but the service is private. A visit will cost €45 and no appointment is necessary. They provide a drop-in service six days a week (Mon–Fri 11am–noon, 5–6, Sat 11am–noon) and a 24-hour callout service is available on the same telephone number.
- If you are staying outside Florence, your hotel or local tourist office will help you find a multilingual doctor.

EMERGENCY TREATMENT
The telephone number 118 is for the ambulance service. The number 112 is for help when you are anywhere in Europe—in Italy, you will be put through to the police (*Carabinieri*).

HOW TO GET TREATMENT WITH THE E111/EHIC
- If you need medical treatment while you are away, take your E111/EHIC to the Unità Sanitaria Locale (USL) office, which will give you a certificate of entitlement.
- Take this to any doctor or dentist on the USL list to receive free treatment. If they need to refer you to a hospital, they will give you a certificate that entitles you to free treatment.
- If you go to hospital without being referred by a doctor, you should give the form to them.
- If you do not have a USL

It's a good idea to protect your children and yourself from the sun

USEFUL NUMBERS
Ambulance
118
Tourist Medical Centre (24 hours)
055 475411

certificate, you will have to pay for treatment and it may be difficult to get the money back afterwards—and then you will probably only receive a partial refund.
- If you are charged in full for prescriptions, keep the price tags or receipts—you will not get a refund without them.
- It is advisable to carry a photocopy of your form, as some doctors and hospitals will keep the original.

HOW TO GET TREATMENT WITH INSURANCE
- If you have health insurance at home it is possible that it will cover you for medical treatment abroad. Check your policy before you leave home.
- Take a copy of your insurance documents to the doctor or hospital—they may be able to bill

your insurance company direct.
- If you have to pay for treatment, keep all your receipts for your insurance claim.

PHARMACIES
Pharmacies (*farmacia*) sell toiletries as well as a wide range of over-the-counter medicines. Pharmacists are well trained and can deal with minor ailments. Most pharmacies are open during normal shop hours, but a rotation system operates in major cities so that there is at least one open at all times—a copy of the rotation is displayed in pharmacy windows.

A green cross outside a shop denotes a pharmacy

SELECTED HOSPITALS WITH EMERGENCY DEPARTMENTS		
CITY	**ADDRESS**	**TELEPHONE**
Florence	Santa Maria Nuova, 1 Piazza Santa Maria Nuova	055 27581
Grosseto	Misericordia, Via Senese	0564 485111
Lucca	Campo di Marte, Via del Ospedale	0583 9701
Pisa	Santa Chiara, Via Buonanno Pisano	050 992111
Poggibonsi, near San Gimignano	Località Compostaggia	0577 9941
Siena	Policlinico Le Scotte, Viale Bracci	0577 585807

DENTAL TREATMENT

If you have an E111 or EHIC, contact the USL (▷ 268). If you do not have one of these, contact a private dentist (in the Yellow Pages under *Dentista*, or ask at your hotel). Again, take a copy of your insurance details and keep your receipts.

OPTICIANS

Opticians can usually carry out minor repairs to your glasses, such as replacing screws, on the spot, for little or no charge. Lenses can often be replaced overnight. If you really cannot survive without your glasses or contact lenses, bring a copy of your prescription with you so that you can have replacements made up if necessary. If possible, pack a spare pair of glasses for emergencies.

FOOD AND WATER

Italy's tap water is generally safe to drink, but you should look out for signs that say *acqua non potabile*, which means the water is not drinkable. Local meat, dairy products, poultry, seafood, fruit and vegetables are all safe to eat.

SUNSHINE

From April to the end of September the sun is extremely strong and you will need to wear a high-factor sunblock (factor 15 or above is recommended).

HAZARDS

Insect bites are irritating rather than dangerous. There are no malaria-carrying insects in Italy, but there is an ongoing mosquito problem across the country, even in inland towns. Use plenty of insect repellent or a mosquito net at night in the summer months, and be vigilant near water and woodland areas.

COMPLEMENTARY MEDICAL TREATMENT

Alternative medicine, such as homeopathy and reflexology, is becoming increasingly more popular. Local pharmacies can help you find practitioners in your area and most sell homeopathic remedies. It is not offered as part of the national health service and is not regulated. You should therefore be very careful in your choice.

An easily recognized ambulance in Vicchio

HEALTHY FLYING

● Visitors to Italy from as far as the US, Australia or New Zealand may be concerned about the effect of long-haul flights on their health. The most widely publicized concern is Deep Vein Thrombosis, or DVT. Misleadingly called 'economy class syndrome', DVT is the forming of a blood clot in the body's deep veins, particularly in the legs. The clot can move around the bloodstream and could be fatal.

● Those most at risk include the elderly, pregnant women and those using the contraceptive pill, smokers and the overweight. If you are at increased risk of DVT see your doctor before departing. Flying increases the likelihood of DVT because passengers are often seated in a cramped position for long periods of time and may become dehydrated.

To minimize risk:
Drink water (not alcohol)
Don't stay immobile for hours at a time
Stretch and exercise your legs periodically
Do wear elastic flight socks, which support veins and reduce the chances of a clot forming

EXERCISES

1 ANKLE ROTATIONS	2 CALF STRETCHES	3 KNEE LIFTS

Lift feet off the floor. Draw a circle with the toes, moving one foot clockwise and the other counterclockwise

Start with heel on the floor and point foot upward as high as you can. Then lift heels high keeping balls of feet on the floor

Lift leg with knee bent while contracting your thigh muscle. Then straighten leg pressing foot flat to the floor

Other health hazards for flyers are airborne diseases and bugs spread by the plane's air-conditioning system. These are largely unavoidable but if you have a serious medical condition seek advice from a doctor before flying.

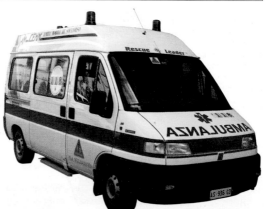

FINDING HELP

EMERGENCY NUMBERS
FROM ANYWHERE IN ITALY
Ambulance (Ambulanza)
118
Fire Brigade
(Vigili del Fuoco)
115
Police (Carabinieri)
112
Police (Polizia)
113
Roadside Rescue
(Europ Assistance Vai)
803803
Automobile Club d'Italia
(ACI)
803116

CONSULATES IN FLORENCE		
	ADDRESS	**TELEPHONE**
Belgium	Via dei Servi 28	055 282094
France	Piazza Ognissanti 2	055 230 2556
Netherlands	Via Convour 81	055 475249
USA	Lungarno Amerigo Vespucci 38	055239 8276
UK	Lungarno Corsini 2	055 284133

Visitors from Australia, Canada, Ireland and New Zealand should contact their embassies in Rome.

PERSONAL SECURITY

Tuscany is much like any other region in the West when it comes to crime. You should be safe against personal attack, but petty crime, especially pickpocketing, is fairly common. Visitors who are not on their guard are main targets, so take some sensible precautions:

● Take care around rail stations, on public transport and in crowded areas in the larger cities where pickpockets and handbag (purse) thieves may be operating. Be particularly wary of groups of children who may try to distract your attention while stealing from you.

● Passports, credit cards, travel tickets and cash should not be carried together in your bag or pocket. Only carry with you what you need for the day and make use of safe deposit facilities in hotels.

● An increasing number of robberies are taking place from cars at rest stops along main roads. You should treat with caution offers of help if you find yourself with a flat tyre, as sometimes the tyre will have been punctured deliberately.

● Lock your vehicle and never leave valuables in it even if you will only be away for a short time or are near by.

● Never carry money or valuables in your back pocket. Always keep them secure in a money belt or similar.

● Do not flaunt your valuables; leave valuable jewellery in a hotel safe.

● Never put your camera or bag down on a café table or on the back of a chair, from where it could be snatched.

● Carry bags or cameras on the side of you that is farthest away from the road, to minimize the risk from scooter-borne bag snatchers.

● Wear your shoulder bag across your body rather than just over your shoulder, from where it can be easily snatched.

● If you have a safe in your hotel room, do not use your date of birth as the code. It is on your passport and your hotel registration.

LOST PROPERTY

ATAF has lost property offices for articles left on buses or trams, as do Trenitalia for anything left on their trains (▷ 55, 56).

● If you will be making an insurance claim, you need to report the loss to the police to get a statement *(denuncia)*.

● If your passport is lost or stolen, report it to the police and your consulate. The whole process of getting a replacement is easier if you have kept a copy of your passport number or a photocopy of the information page in a safe place.

Recognize carabinieri officers by the white sash

● If your credit or bank card is stolen, report it to the police and phone the appropriate emergency number to cancel your card. All are open 24 hours a day.

● If your traveller's cheques are stolen, notify the police, then follow the instructions given with the cheques.

REPORTING THEFT

Report thefts to a police station, where you will need to make a statement. It is unlikely that you will get your belongings back, but you need the statement *(denuncia)* to make a claim on your insurance. You can find the address and contact details of your nearest police station in the Yellow Pages *(Pagine Gialle)* under Commissariato, Commando di polizia or Stazione dei carabinieri.

POLICE

There are three branches of the police in Italy, any of whom should be able to help you if you are in difficulty.

● The *carabinieri* are military police, easily recognizable by the white sash they wear across their bodies. They deal with general crime, including drug control.

● The *polizia* is the state police force, whose officers wear blue uniforms. They too deal with general crime, and if you are unfortunate enough to be robbed (or worse) they are the ones you will need to see.

● The *vigili urbani*, traffic police, wear dark blue uniforms and white hats.

EMBASSIES AND CONSULATES

Lists of embassies and consulates are available from tourist offices. You can also look under Ambasciate or Consolati in the phone book or visit www.embassyworld.com.

PLANNING

COMMUNICATION

CALL CHARGES

Free phone numbers *(numeri verde)* usually begin with 800; national call rate numbers begin with 848 or 199. Hotels tend to overcharge for long-distance and international calls, so it is best to make calls from a public phone, using a telephone card. Rates are lowest on Sunday throughout the day and between 10pm and 8am on weekdays and Saturday.

PUBLIC TELEPHONES

If you are calling from a public telephone you must deposit a coin or use a phone card to get a dialling tone. Note that some pay phones will only accept coins and others only phone cards. Phones that take only coins tend to be less reliable than phone-card phones. Call-centre phones are a better bet than the often poorly maintained public telephones. Here you are assigned a booth to make your call and you pay the attendant when you have finished.

PHONE CARDS

Prepaid *carte telefoniche* (phone cards) are used widely. You can buy them from post offices, tobacconists, newsstands and bars. Tear off the corner of the card and insert it in the slot of the public phone. When you dial, the amount on the card appears in the window. After you hang up, the card is returned so you can use it until it runs out. The Time phone card is good value, allowing you to call Europe and the United States at €0.28 per minute during peak time; however, if you are calling between 10pm and 8am, or all day Sunday, conventional phone cards are cheaper.

MOBILE PHONES

It can be very expensive to use your mobile phone abroad and you will often be charged to receive calls as well as to make them. If you travel abroad frequently and intend to use your phone, consider swapping your SIM card for a card from an alternative provider—either a foreign network or a dedicated provider of international mobile phone services. You can buy these at mobile phone shops before you leave.

COUNTRY CODES FROM ITALY	
Australia	00 61
Belgium	00 32
Canada	00 1
France	00 33
Germany	00 49
Greece	00 30
Ireland	00 353
Netherlands	00 31
New Zealand	00 64
Spain	00 34
Sweden	00 46
UK	00 44
USA	00 1

AREA CODES FOR MAJOR CITIES	
Florence	055
Pisa	050
Siena	0577

Text messages can be cheaper than voice calls, but check your service provider's charges for making calls and text messages.

CALLING ABROAD

A call from outside Italy is dialled as 00 39 + 055 (code for Florence) + phone number. A call from Florence to the UK is dialled as 00 44 + the area code omitting the first 0 (eg 01780 becomes 1780) + the number. A call from Florence to the US would be dialled as 001 + the area code + the number. For all calls within Italy, local and long distance, dial the regional code *(prefisso)*, which begins with 0—as 055 for Florence.

LAPTOPS

If you intend to use your own laptop in Italy, remember to bring a power converter to recharge it and a plug socket adaptor. A surge protector is also a good idea. To connect to the internet you need an adaptor for the phone socket.

If you use an international internet service provider, such as AOL or Compuserve, it's cheaper to dial up a local node rather than the number at home. Dial-tone frequencies vary from country to country, so set your modem to ignore dial tones.

INTERNET CAFÉS

You'll find internet cafés across Tuscany and they are reasonably

cheap—around €5 an hour. You need a web-based email account if you want to send or receive email from abroad (gmail, hotmail, yahoo and many more).

POSTAL SERVICES

Poste Italiane have 14,000 post offices *(posta, ufficio postale* or *PT)* across Italy. Mail services have been notoriously unreliable, but the introduction of a priority service *(posta prioritaria)* has provided a more efficient alternative, relieving the pressure on the old state mail service, which has improved.

Stamps *(francobolli)* are also available from tobacconists denoted with an official *tabacchi* sign, a large 'T'—they can weigh letters but if you need to send a heavy letter or a package, it's best to go to a post office.

For information on all Italy's mail services, contact Poste Italiane (tel 800 222666, www.poste.it). In general, post offices are open Mon–Fri 8.15–2, Sat 8.15–noon or 2, or in larger towns and cities they are open until 7pm.

POSTCARDS

These are classed as low-priority mail, so if you want them to arrive at their destination within a couple of weeks, send them *prioritaria*.

OPENING TIMES AND TICKETS

BANKS
Most are open Monday to Friday 8.30–1.30. Larger branches might open on Saturday.

CAFÉS AND BARS
The hours kept by cafés and bars vary considerably between establishments and according to the season.

CHURCHES
Most churches open early in the morning for Mass, often around 7am. They close at lunchtime, opening again around 4 and closing at 7pm. Some of the larger churches are open all day, but some may be closed to visitors during services. Check the Sights section of this book for specific opening times, or contact the church.

MUSEUMS AND GALLERIES
Opening times for museums and galleries vary greatly, according to season and location. Some are open all day, while others close at lunchtimes. Many close one day each week, usually Monday. Check the Sights section of this book, or contact the museum or gallery for the most up-to-date information.

PHARMACIES
Pharmacies are usually open the same hours as shops, but take turns staying open during the afternoon and late into the evening. Look for the list in the shop window providing details of other pharmacies in the area and their opening times.

POST OFFICES
These are usually open Monday to Friday 8.15–2, Saturday 8.15–noon or 2. Larger offices are open until 7pm.

RESTAURANTS
Restaurants serving lunch open at noon and usually close in the afternoon. They reopen, along with those that only serve dinner, some time after 7pm until late. Pizzerias usually only open in the evening. Many restaurants close for the whole of August—look for the sign *chiuso per ferie*.

SHOPS
Traditionally, shops open in the morning between 8 and 9 and close for lunch at around 1. They reopen in the afternoon at 3.30 or 4 and close at 8. Most are closed Sundays and Monday mornings. Shops in larger cities are starting to stay open all day.

NATIONAL HOLIDAYS
Shops and banks generally close on public holidays and the road and rail networks are usually very busy. There is limited public transport service on 1 May (Labour Day) and the afternoon of Christmas Day. However, with the exception of Labour Day, 15 August (the Assumption) and Christmas Day, most bars and restaurants remain open. See panel for more National Holidays.

ENTRANCE FEES
Admission to churches is usually free. However, you may be asked for a small donation or charged a fee to see inside a church, or part of a church, that is of artistic or historic interest. You should expect to pay around €2, but it can be as much as €8. Museums charge for admission; entrance fees are usually €5–€10, but discounts for certain visitors are almost always available (see below). Entrance fees sometimes include a guided tour.

COMBINED TICKETS
If you are intending to do a lot of sightseeing, it is worth enquiring about combined tickets. Siena (▷ 112–127) has a ticket incorporating all of its museums, providing significant savings, as does Pisa (▷ 106–109) and San Gimignano (▷ 142–145). In Florence, the Palazzo Vecchio and the Cappelle Brancacci have joint tickets and you can buy combined tickets for various museums at the Palazzo Pitti (▷ 80–81): Palatino, Argenti, Arte Modern and the Boboli Gardens, which is €10.50 for adults; the Boboli and the Argenti is €3 for adults. Most major towns or regions have combined tickets for museums and areas of cultural interest. Further details are available from tourist offices.

BOOKING TICKETS
Florence has a dedicated organization that promotes the city's art history. They have a booking service, where you can buy tickets to a wide number of attractions in the city. The service is called Firenze Musei (Via Ricasoli 7, tel 055 294883, Mon–Fri 8.30–6.30, Sat 8.30–12.30, www.firenzemusei.it) and it covers: Cappelle Medicee, Galleria dell'Accademia, Galleria degli Uffizi, Giardino di Boboli, Museo Archeologico, Museo Nazionale del Bargello, Museo di San Marco, plus the Galleria Palatina, Galleria d'Arte Moderna and Museo degli Argenti at the Palazzo Pitti. Tickets can be bought in various combinations.

DISCOUNTS
Where there is an admission charge for a church, discounts are rarely available, but all other museums and attractions have concessions for students (with an international student card), European Union citizens over 65, and children under 5 or 6, who are generally admitted free. Occasionally children under 10 have free admission too. There tend to be discounts available for those up to the age of 18 and this is sometimes extended to those under 20 (see also page 265). Some attractions have free entry for visitors with a disability and a carer.

NATIONAL HOLIDAYS
If a public holiday falls on a weekend, it is celebrated on that Saturday or Sunday. If the holiday falls on a Tuesday or Thursday, many people take the Monday or Friday off to make a *ponte* (bridge) to the weekend. Saints' days are celebrated locally in individual cities, such as 24 June, St. John's Day, in Florence.

1 Jan	New Year's Day
6 Jan	Epiphany
Mar/Apr	Easter Monday
25 Apr	Liberation Day
1 May	Labour Day
2 Jun	Republic Day
15 Aug	Assumption of the Virgin (*Ferragosto*)
1 Nov	All Saints' Day
8 Dec	Feast of the Immaculate Conception
25 Dec	Christmas Day
26 Dec	St. Stephen's Day

PLANNING

MEDIA

TELEVISION
Italy has three state-run television stations (RAI-1, -2 and -3), which broadcast some worthy entertainment, three stations run by Prime Minister Berlusconi's Mediaset group (Italia Uno, Rete Quattro and Canale Cinque), and a number of local channels. RAI-3 has international news broadcasts, including an English-language section. Most hotels, from mid-range upwards, have satellite television, so you can keep up-to-date with the news and sport on channels such as BBC World or CNN. There are few Tuscan channels.

RADIO
RAI Radios 1, 2 and 3 (89.7FM, 91.7FM and 93.7FM), the state-run stations, have a mixture of light music, chat shows and news—all in Italian. Radio Italia Network (90–108FM) is the best national radio station for dance music, and Radio Deejay (99.7–107FM) broadcasts a variety of popular music and chat shows. You can get BBC radio stations including Radio 1, Radio 2, 5 Live and 6 Music on the internet via www.bbc.co.uk. The BBC World Service frequencies in Italy are MHz 12.10, 9.410, 6.195 and 0.648. To find US radio stations online visit www.radio-locator.com.

NEWSPAPERS
You can buy major international newspapers at three times their home cover price. They are usually available the day after publication, from about 2pm, at larger newsstands, particularly *The Times*, *The Financial Times*, *The Guardian*, *The European*, *The New York Times*, *The Wall Street Journal* and *The International Herald Tribune*.

Florence's most popular paper is *La Nazione*. It publishes regional versions for most Tuscan towns. Other papers include *La Repubblica* and *Corriere della Sera*. There are two daily sports papers published in Italy—*La Gazzetta dello Sport* (printed on pink paper) and the *Corriere dello Sport*—mainly dominated by soccer and motor sport news.

MAGAZINES
English language magazines are hard to find, but if you read a little Italian, *Panorama* and *L'Espresso* are good for news, while *Oggi* is slightly more light-hearted with more of a focus on celebrity gossip and lifestyle. *L'Espresso*, renowned for its restaurant reviews and accreditations, is highly respected in Italy.

FILMS AND BOOKS

FILMS
- *Hannibal* (2001), the sequel to *The Silence of the Lambs*, contains some scenes shot in Florence's palaces and along the banks of the River Arno.
- To get an idea of the rolling Tuscan countryside, watch Kenneth Branagh's adaptation of Shakespeare's *Much Ado About Nothing* (1993). Starring Branagh as Benedict and Emma Thompson as Beatrice, this classic play is brought to life in the hilltop Villa Vignamaggio, with its knot gardens and vineyards, typical of Greve in Chianti.
- *Under the Tuscan Sun* (2003) stars Diane Lane as a writer who visits Tuscany and decides to embrace the region's people and lifestyle. It was shot in various Italian locations, including Cortona and Florence. The film is based on the book of the same name by Frances Mayes.
- Set in 1930s Italy and shot in Terni in Umbria and Arezzo in Tuscany, *La Vita e Bella* (Life is Beautiful, 1997) is a dark yet heart-warming tale of a Jewish bookkeeper who struggles to hold his family together during German occupation and help his

Anthony Hopkins (seated) in Piazza Signoria in Florence filming Hannibal

son survive the horrors of a Jewish concentration camp.
- Franco Zeffirelli co-wrote and directed *Tea with Mussolini* (1999). It follows the fortunes of a group of expatriates living in Florence at the start of World War II. The all-star cast includes Cher, Maggie Smith, Judi Dench, Joan Plowright and Lily Tomlin.
- Bernardo Bertolucci's *Stealing Beauty* (1995), with Liv Tyler, was filmed around Castelnuovo, Gaiole in Chianti and Siena.

- *The English Patient* (1996), directed by Antony Minghella, was partly shot around Siena, Pienza, Pisa and Monastero di Sant'Anna in Camprena.

BOOKS
There are many good books covering Italy's long, vibrant and eventful history.
- Anyone interested in Italian politics and society should read *The Dark Heart of Italy* (2003) by Tobias Jones, which discusses Italian life under Berlusconi's administration.
- E. M. Forster's novel *A Room with a View* (1908) is a critique of 19th-century middle class Britons abroad in Florence. The author's *Where Angels Fear to Tread* (1905) is set in San Gimignano.
- *Up at the Villa* (1941) by W. Somerset Maugham follows the fortunes of an English widow in Florence.
- There is a huge number of travel biographies on the shelves, but particularly good is *Vanilla Beans and Brodo: Real Life in the Hills of Tuscany* (2002) by Isabella Dusi, which gives an insight into rural Tuscan life.

TOURIST OFFICES

Most major towns have a tourist office and there are information desks at the airports. Known as Azienda Promozione del Turismo (APT), they tend to keep normal shop opening hours (▷ 272). They have maps and information and provide help and advice in finding accommodation. They may also book accommodation and tours for you.

The Ente Provinciale per il Turismo (EPT) is usually devoted more to the bureaucracy of tourism rather than providing information for visitors. Villages sometimes have a small office known as a Pro Loco, but these often have limited opening hours. All cities have a central office with extended opening hours.

The table below shows the addresses and contact details for the main regional tourist offices across Italy.

OVERSEAS TOURIST OFFICES		
Italian State Tourist Offices Overseas (ENIT)		www.enit.it
Australia	Level 26, 44 Market Street, Sydney NSW 2000	tel 02 9262 1666
New Zealand	36 Grant Road, Thorndon, Wellington	tel 04 736065/4735339
Canada	1 Place Ville Marie, Montréal, Québec H3B 3M9	tel 514 8667667
UK	1 Princes Street, London W1 8AY	tel 020 7408 1254
US	630 5th Avenue, Suite 1565, Rockefeller Center, NY 10111	tel 212/245-5618

TOURIST OFFICES				
Florence	Via Manzoni 16	tel 055 23320	fax 055 234 6285	www.firenzeturismo.it
Lucca	Piazza S. Maria	tel 0583 919931	fax 0583 91663	www.lucca.turismo.toscana.it
Pisa	Via Pietro Nenni	tel 050 929777	fax 050 929764	www.pisa.turismo.toscana.it
Siena	Piazza del Campo 56	tel 0577 280 551	fax 0577 281041	www.terresiena.it

WEBSITES

www.aboutflorence.com
Plenty of information to help you plan your visit, or to use when you are there. There are maps and plenty of information to give you an insight to the city (in English, Spanish and Japanese).

www.cafe.ecs.net
A useful and interactive site that has a directory of internet cafés in Italy. You are invited to contact the site with comments (in Italian and English).

www.castellitoscani.com
Comprehensive information about all the castles in Tuscany with maps and directions (in English).

www.firenze.net
Lots of information about Florence on a range of subjects such as museums, shopping, entertainment and restaurants (in English and Italian).

www.firenzemusei.it
This site encompasses the major museums in the city, with background on the collections as well as practical information (in English, Italian and Spanish).

www.firenzeturismo.it
The official site of the APT in Tuscany (in English and Italian).

www.florence.ala.it
Lots of information and links to accommodation sites and museums as well as maps and cultural details (in English).

www.florencehotelsnetwork.com
A searchable database of hotels and apartments for rent in Florence (in English).

www.fodors.com
A comprehensive travel-planning site that lets you research prices and book air tickets, aimed at the American market (in English).

www.museionline.it
This site covers museums all over Italy but allows you to search by different categories as well as by region (in English and Italian).

www.parks.it
A very useful site if you want to explore outside the cities, as it lists the parks, reserves and protected areas in the country, including Tuscany (in English, French, German and Italian).

www.theAA.com
If you are planning to drive to Tuscany or rent a car while you are there, visit this site for up-to-date travel advice (in English).

www.turismo.toscana.it
A very good site that covers all manner of things that you might want to do on holiday (in English, German and Italian).

www.welcometuscany.it
A good general website, with lots of information, particularly on themed topics, such as cooking courses, sports and romantic Tuscany (in English).

PLANNING

WORDS AND PHRASES

Once you have mastered a few basic rules, Italian is an easy language to speak: It is phonetic, and unlike English, particular combinations of letters are always pronounced the same way. The stress is usually on the penultimate syllable, but if the word has an accent, this is where the stress falls.

Vowels are pronouned as follows:

a	casa	as in	mat (short 'a')
e	vero	as in	base
e	sette	as in	vet (short 'e')
i	vino	as in	mean
o	dove	as in	bowl
o	otto	as in	not
u	uva	as in	book

Consonants as in English except:
c before **i** or **e** becomes **ch** as in **ch**urch
ch before **i** or **e** becomes **c** as in **c**at
g before **i** or **e** becomes **j** as in **J**ulia
gh before **i** or **e** becomes **g** as in **g**ood
gn as in oni**on**
gli as in mi**lli**on
h is rare in Italian words, and is always silent
r usually rolled
z is pronounced **tz** when it falls in the middle of a word

All Italian nouns are either masculine (usually ending in o when singular or i when plural) or feminine (usually ending in a when singular or e when plural). Some nouns, which may be masculine or feminine, end in e (which changes to i when plural). An adjective's ending changes to match the ending of the noun.

NUMBERS

0 zero	9 nove	18 diciotto	70 settanta
1 uno	10 dieci	19 diciannove	80 ottanta
2 due	11 undici	20 venti	90 novanta
3 tre	12 dodici	21 ventuno	100 cento
4 quattro	13 tredici	22 ventidue	1000 mille
5 cinque	14 quattordici	30 trenta	million milione
6 sei	15 quindici	40 quaranta	quarter quarto
7 sette	16 sedici	50 cinquanta	half mezza
8 otto	17 diciassette	60 sessanta	three quarters tre quarti

CONVERSATION

Good morning
Buongiorno

Good afternoon/evening
Buonasera

Goodbye
Arrivederci

How are you?
Come sta?

Fine, thank you
Bene, grazie

My name is…
Mi chiamo…

What's your name?
Come si chiama?

Hello, pleased to meet you
Piacere

I'm here on holiday
Sono qui in vacanza

What is the time?
Che ore sono?

I don't speak Italian
Non parlo italiano

Do you speak English?
Parla inglese?

I don't understand
Non capisco

Please repeat that
Può ripetere?

Please speak more slowly
Può parlare più lentamente?

Write that down for me, please
Lo scriva, per piacere

SHOPPING

Could you help me, please?
Può aiutarmi, per favore?

How much is this?
Quanto costa questo?

I'm looking for…
Cerco…

Where can I buy…?
Dove posso comprare…?

How much is this/that?
Quanto costa questo/quello?

When does the shop open/close?
Quando apre/chiude il negozio?

I'm just looking, thank you
Sto solo dando un'occhiata

I'll take this
Prendo questo

Do you accept credit cards?
Accettate carte di credito?

I'd like a kilo of…
Vorrei un chilo di…

MONEY

Is there a bank/currency exchange office near by?
C'è una banca/un ufficio di cambio qui vicino?

Can I cash this here?
Posso incassare questo?

I'd like to change sterling/dollars into euros
Vorrei cambiare sterline/dollari in euro

Can I use my credit card to withdraw cash?
Posso usare la mia carta di credito per prelevare contanti?

I'd like to cash this traveller's cheque
Vorrei incassare questo travellers cheque

POST AND TELEPHONES

Where is the nearest post office/mail box?
Dov'è l'ufficio postale più vicino/la cassetta delle lettere più vicina?

One stamp, please
Un francobollo, per favore

I'd like to send this by air mail/registered mail
Vorrei spedire questo per posta aerea/posta raccomandata

Can you direct me to a public phone?
Dov'è il telefono pubblico più vicino?

Can I dial direct to…?
Posso chiamare…in teleselezione?

Do I need to dial 0 first?
Devo comporre prima lo zero?

Where can I find a phone directory?
Dove posso trovare un elenco telefonico?

Where can I buy a phone card?
Dove posso comprare una carta telefonica?

Has anyone telephoned me?
Ci sono state telefonate per me?

GETTING AROUND

Where is the train/bus station?
Dov'è la stazione ferroviaria/degli autobus (dei pullman—long distance)?

Does this train/bus go to…?
È questo il treno/l'autobus (il pullman—long distance) per…?

IN THE TOWN

on/to the right **a destra**	south **sud**	museum **museo**	island **isola**
on/to the left **a sinistra**	east **est**	monument **monumento**	river **fiume**
around the corner **all'angolo**	west **ovest**	palace **palazzo**	lake **lago**
opposite **di fronte a…**	free **gratis**	gallery **galleria**	bridge **ponte**
at the bottom (of) **in fondo (a)**	donation **donazione**	town **città**	no entry **vietato l'accesso**
straight on **sempre dritto**	open **aperto**	old town **centro storico**	push **spingere**
near **vincino a**	closed **chiuso**	town hall **municipio**	pull **tirare**
cross over **attraversi**	daily **giornalmente**	boulevard **corso**	entrance **ingresso**
in front of **davanti**	cathedral **duomo/cattedrale**	square **piazza**	exit **uscita**
behind **dietro**	church **chiesa**	street **via**	toilets—men/women **gabinetti—uomini/donne**
north **nord**	castle **castello**	avenue **viale**	

Does this train/bus stop at…?
Questo treno/autobus (pullman–long distance) ferma a…?

Please stop at the next stop
La prossima fermata, per favore

Do I have to get off here?
Devo scendere qui?

Where can I buy a ticket?
Dove si comprano i biglietti?

Is this seat taken?
È occupato?

Please can I have a single/return ticket to…
Un biglietto di andata/andata e ritorno per…

When is the first/last bus to…?
Quando c'è il primo/l'ultimo autobus per…?

I would like a standard/first class ticket to,,,
Un biglietto di seconda/prima classe per…

Where is the information desk?
Dov'è il banco informazioni?

Where is the timetable?
Dov'è l'orario?

Where can I find a taxi?
Dove sono i tassì?

Please take me to…
Per favore, mi porti a…

How much is the journey?
Quanto costerà il viaggio?

Please turn on the meter
Accenda il tassametro, per favore

I'd like to get out here please
Vorrei scendere qui, per favore

SHOPS

Baker's **Panetteria**	Fishmonger's **Pescheria**	Lingerie shop **Biancheria intima**
Bookshop **Libreria**	Florist **Fiorista**	Newsagent's **Giornalaio**
Butcher's **Macelleria**	Gift shop **Regali**	Perfume shop **Profumeria**
Cake shop **Pasticceria**	Grocer's **Alimentare**	Photographic shop **Fotografo**
Clothes shop **Abbigliamento**	Hairdresser's **Parrucchiere**	Shoe shop **Calzature**
Delicatessan **Salumeria**	Jeweller's **Gioielleria**	Sports shop **Articoli sportivi**
Dry-cleaner's **Lavasecco**	Launderette **Lavanderia**	Tobacconist's **Tabaccheria**

USEFUL WORDS

yes **sì**	excuse me! **scusi!**	when **quando**	who **chi**
no **no**	where **dove**	now **adesso**	may I/can I **posso**
please **per piacere**	here **qui**	later **più tardi**	you're welcome **prego**
thank you **grazie**	there **là**	why **perchè**	

COLOURS

black **nero**	red **rosso**	green **verde**	sky blue **azzurro**	gold **oro**
brown **marrone**	orange **arancia**	blue **blu**	purple **viola**	silver **argento**
pink **rosa**	yellow **giallo**	light blue **celeste**	white **bianco**	grey **grigio**

HOTELS

I have made a reservation for…nights
Ho prenotato per…notti

How much per night?
Quanto costa una notte?

Double/single room/twin
Camera doppia/singola/a due letti

With bath/shower
Con bagno/doccia

I'll take this room
Prendo questa camera

Is breakfast included in the price?
La colazione è compreso?

I am leaving this morning
Parto stamattina

Please can I pay my bill?
Posso pagare il conto?

Please order a taxi for me
Mi chiama un tassì, per favore

Is this the way to…?
È questa la strada per…?

Excuse me, I think I am lost
Mi scusi, penso di essermi perduto/a

Can you help me, please?
Può aiutarmi, per favore?

I have lost my passport/wallet/purse/handbag
Ho perso il passaporto/il portafogllio/il borsellino /la borsa

Is there a lost property office?
C'è un ufficio oggetti smarriti?

Where is the police station?
Dov'è il commissariato?

I don't feel well
Non mi sento bene

Could you call a doctor please
Può chiamare un medico, per favore

Is there a doctor/pharmacist on duty?
C'è un medico/farmacista di turno?

Where is the hospital?
Dov'è l'ospedale?

I am allergic to…
Sono allergico/a a…

Can I have a painkiller?
Posso avere un analgesico?

Waiter/waitress
Cameriere/cameriera

What time does the restaurant open?
A che ora apre il ristorante?

I'd like to reserve a table for… people at…
Vorrei prenotare un tavolo per…persone a…

A table for…, please
Un tavolo per…, per favore

We have/haven't booked
Abbiamo/non abbiamo prenotato

Are there tables outside?
Ci sono tavoli all'aperto?

I'd like…
Vorrei…

Can I have the bill, please?
Il conto, per favore?

Is service included?
Il servizio è compreso?

Where is the tourist information office/tourist information desk, please?
Dov'è l'ufficio turistico/il banco informazioni turistiche?

Do you have a city map?
Avete una cartina della città?

Please could you point them out on the map?
Me li può indicare sulla cartina?

What is the admission price?
Quant'è il biglietto d'ingresso?

Is there a discount for senior citizens/students?
Ci sono riduzioni per anziani/studenti?

What time does it open/close?
A che ora apre/chiude?

Is photography allowed?
Si possono fare fotografie?

Could you reserve tickets for me?
Mi può prenotare dei biglietti?

HOLIDAYS		
New Year's Day **Capodanno**	Assumption **Ferragosto**	26 December **Santo Stefano**
Epiphany **Epifania**	All Saints' Day **Ognissanti**	New Year's Eve **San Silvestro**
Easter **Pasqua**	Christmas **Natale**	

TIMES/DAYS/MONTHS			
Monday **lunedì**	evening **sera**	summer **estate**	July **luglio**
Tuesday **martedì**	night **notte**	autumn **autunno**	August **agosto**
Wednesday **mercoledì**	day **giorno**	winter **inverno**	September **settembre**
Thursday **giovedì**	month **mese**	January **gennaio**	October **ottobre**
Friday **venerdì**	year **anno**	February **febbraio**	November **novembre**
Saturday **sabato**	today **oggi**	March **marzo**	December **dicembre**
Sunday **domenica**	yesterday **ieri**	April **aprile**	
morning **mattina**	tomorrow **domani**	May **maggio**	
afternoon **pomeriggio**	spring **primavera**	June **giugno**	

ARCHITECTURAL GLOSSARY

Aisle: the interior corridors of a church, running either side of the nave

Apse: the semi-circular end of a church or chapel

Architrave: a moulded frame around a door or window

Atrium: an inner courtyard, open to the sky

Baldacchino/baldacchin: a canopy, usually over a throne or altar

Baroque: architectural style popular in the 17th-century. It is characterized by its elaborate decoration of convex and concave curves

Byzantine: architectural style developed after AD330, when Byzantium became capital of the Eastern Empire. It is characterized by its Eastern influences and highly decorated style

Campanile: a bell tower, often separate from the main building

Capital: top of a column

Chancel: the eastern end of a church, where the high altar is found

Chiaroscuro: exaggerated light and shade effects in a painting

Classical: architectural style characterized by its use of elements from Ancient Greece or Rome, including finely proportioned, simple shapes, and which has its roots in the 5th century BC. It has seen many revivals, including in the 16th century and Neoclassicism, which was popular between the late 18th and early 19th centuries

Cloister: a courtyard, often in a monastic building, surrounded by a covered passageway with an open arcade or colonnade on the interior side

Coffering: ceiling decoration made up from patterns of recessed squares or other shapes

Colonnade: a row of columns supporting a beam

Column: an upright, usually used as a decorative support, but can be freestanding as a monument

Confessio: an underground area of a church, usually below the altar, which houses relics

Crossing: the area of a church where the transepts, nave and chancel intersect

Crypt: area below a church, usually for graves

Cupola: a domed roof

Etruscans: a race of people who inhabited Tuscany from around the 10th century BC. Their architecture was similar in style to that of the Greeks of the same period

Fresco: a painting made directly onto damp plaster so that the image becomes permanent

Frieze: a decorated band, often along the top of a wall

Gothic: architectural style popular between the late 12th century and the mid-16th century, recognizable by its pointed arches and ribbed vaulting on the ceiling

Greek cross: a church layout, whose ground plan resembles a cross with four equal arms (see also Latin cross)

Grotesque: style based on ancient Roman decoration found in underground ruins

Latin cross: a church layout, whose ground plan resembles a cross with three short arms and one longer one

Loggia: a room or gallery that is open on one or more sides

Mannerism: an architectural style, popular between 1530 and 1600, that was characterized by breaking the rules of Classicism and using Classical forms in a way other than was traditionally acceptable

Nave: the long arm of a Latin cross church; the opposite end to the apse

Pediment: in Classical architecture, a low gable and entablature forming a triangular shape. Usually on the outside of a building, but also above doorways and fireplaces

Peristyle: columns ranged around a building or courtyard

Portico: a roofed area, usually the focus of a building's façade, supported by columns and topped with a pediment (see above)

Reliquary: an elaborate container holding part of a deceased holy person's body

Rococo: architectural style popular in the 18th century, characterized by low-relief decoration, usually in white and gold

Romanesque: an architectural style popular in the 11th–12th centuries, combining Classicism with influences from Byzantium and Islam

Sacristy: in a church, where the vestments and sacred vessels are kept

Sepulchre: a tomb cut from rock, or built from stone or brick

Stucco/stuccowork: a slow setting plaster, used to form intricate decoration

Transept: the short arms of a Latin cross church

Triptych: a picture or carving on three panels, often used as an altarpiece

Trompe l'oeil: paintings that appear to show a room or landscape by use of perspective

Tympanum: between the lintel over a door and the arch above it. Also used to describe the flat area inside a pediment (see above)

Vaulting: an arched ceiling or roof

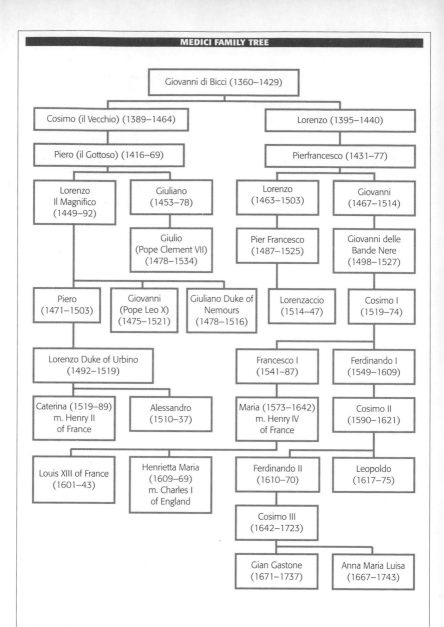

Little could the Medici's 14th-century founding father have suspected the extent to which his family would dominate Florence and Tuscany, nor how his descendants would include popes and cardinals and marry into some of Europe's most prestigious noble and royal families. Among others, Medici offspring would provide spouses for such illustrious names as Charles I of England and Scotland, Philip II and Philip IV of Spain, Henri II and Henry IV of France, Emperor Ferdinand II, the Elector of Palatine, and Mary, Queen of Scots. Although the direct Medici male line died out in the 18th century (with the death of the decadent and debauched Gian Gastone de'Medici), Medici blood still flows in the royal and aristocratic veins of countless European families.

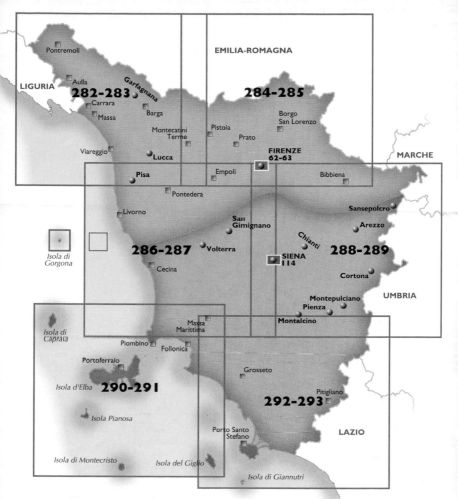

LIGURIA

EMILIA-ROMAGNA

Pontremoli

Aulla
Garfagnana

282-283

284-285

Carrara

Barga

Massa

Pistoia

Prato

Borgo
San Lorenzo

Montecatini
Terme

MARCHE

Viareggio

Lucca

FIRENZE
62-63

Empoli

Bibbiena

Pisa

Pontedera

Livorno

Sansepolcro

San
Gimignano

Arezzo

Isola di
Gorgona

286-287

Volterra

Chianti

**SIENA
114**

288-289

Cecina

Cortona

UMBRIA

Montepulciano

Massa
Marittima

Pienza

Montalcino

Isola di
Capraia

Piombino

Follonica

Portoferraio

Isola d'Elba

290-291

Grosseto

Pitigliano

Isola Pianosa

292-293

LAZIO

Isola di Montecristo

Porto Santo
Stefano

Isola del Giglio

Isola di Giannutri

	Toll motorway (Turnpike)	
	Motorway (Expressway)	
	Motorway junction	
	National road	
	Regional road	
	Other road	
	Railway	
	Regional boundary	
	Provincial boundary	
	City	
	Town / Village	
	National park	
	Featured place of interest	
	Airport	
621	Height in metres	
	Ferry route	
	Mountain pass	
	Viewpoint	

282-293

0   10 km

0   5 miles

Maps

Borgo

Tarsogno

Albareto

SS523

Berceto

1492
Monte Cervellino

Passo della Cisa
1039

SS62

Corniglio

Passo del Bratello
953

Passo Cirone
1255

Trevignano

Palanzan

A15

E33

Vecciatica

Vairo

Cervara

1287
Monte Ribone

Lugagnano

Nirone

Pontremoli

Valditacca

Trefiumi

Rigoso

Succiso

Zeri

Lusignana

1640
Monte Gottero

L
u
n
i
g
i
a
n
a

Parco Nazionale dell'Appennino Toscano-Emiliano

Passo di Lagastrello
1200

2017
▲Alpe Succ

Coloretta

Rossano

Filattiera

Antessio

Mulazzo

Bagnone

Camporaghena

Passo del Cerre 126

Pieve

Montereggio

Groppoli

Malgrate

Tavernelle

Comano

Sassalbo

Villagrossa

Villafranca in Lunigiana

Licciana Nardi

943

Cornice

Villecchia

Tresana

Merizzo

Pognana

2

A12

Brugnato

Calice al Cornoviglio

Giovagallo

Pieve di Monti

Fivizzano

SS63

E80

Mattarana

Borghetto di Vara

Barbarasco

Fornoli

Groppo

Sannaco

Casola in Lunigiana

Antogna

Cassana

Beverino

Bolano

Aulla

Rometta

Soliera

SR445

LIGURIA

Pignone

SS1

Vara

Piano di Follo

Gragnola

Codiponte

Levanto

Corvara

Bastremoli

Ponzanello

Vezzanello

Minucciano

Ricco del Golfo di Spezia

Buonviaggio

Vezzano Ligure

Ponzano Magra

Marciaso

Monzone

Vinca

Mor Pisar 194

Parc

Monterosso al Mare

Vernazza

Cinque Terre

San Benedetto

SS62

Sarzana

Fosdinovo

P d Mesco

Corniglia

LA SPEZIA

Arcola

Caniparola

Castelnuovo Magra

Gragnana

Alp

Manarola

Romito

Lama

Ortonovo

Colonnata

Riomaggiore

Parco delle Cinque Terre

Golfo della Spezia

Lerici

Magra

Carrara

Forno

Ameglia

Canevara

Portovenere

Le Grazie

Fiascherino

Montemarcello

Massa

Isola Palmaria

P Bianca

Marina di Carrara

Isola del Tino

A12

Marina di Massa

E80

Stret

Serave

Vallec

Forte dei Marmi

Olbia
Palau
Golfo Aranci

Marina di Pietrasanta

4

Lido di Camaio

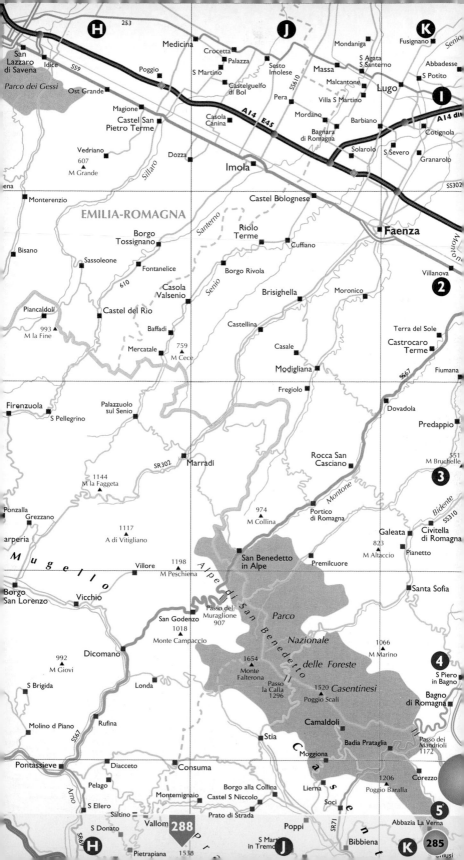

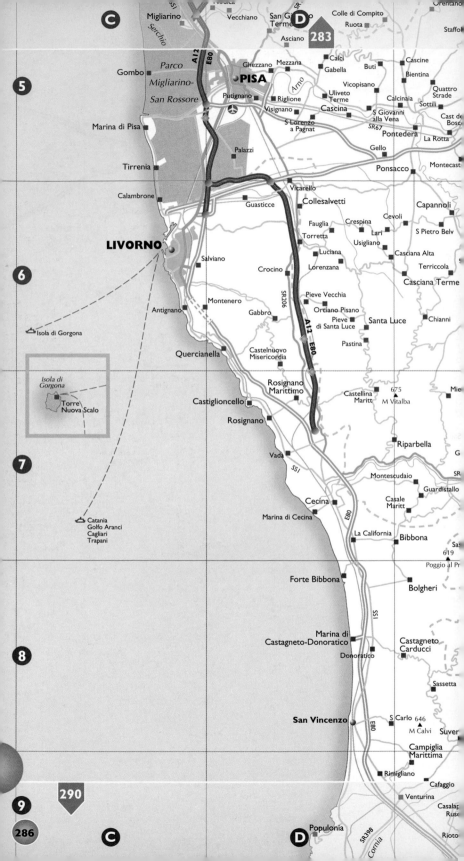

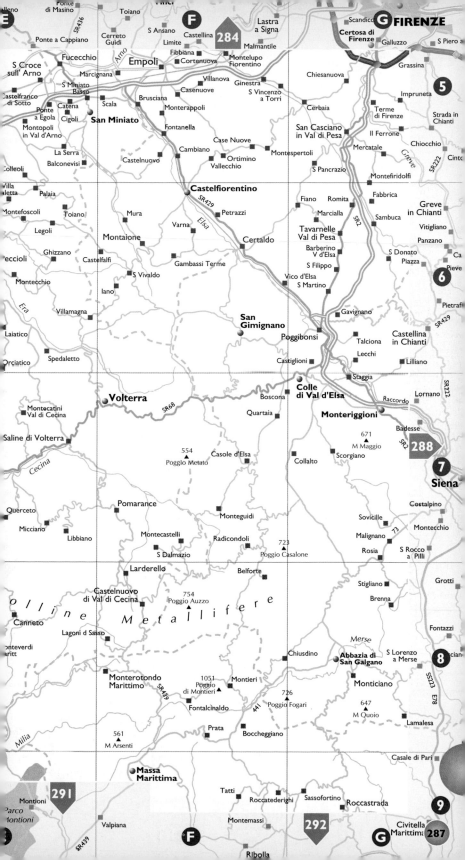

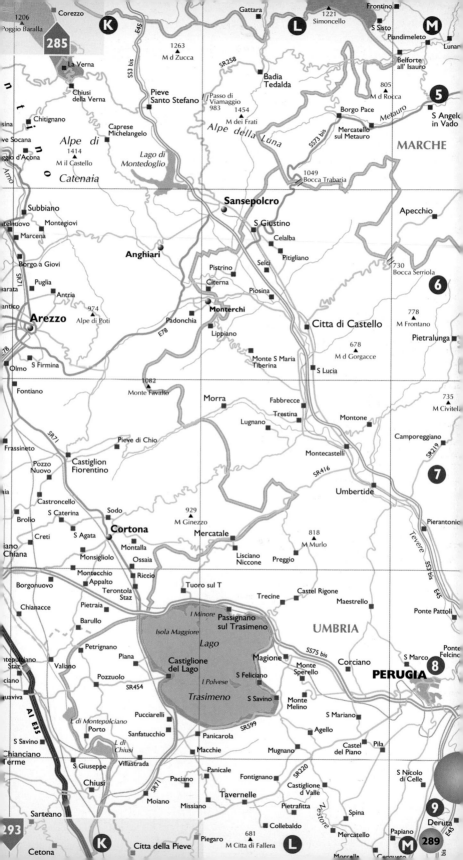

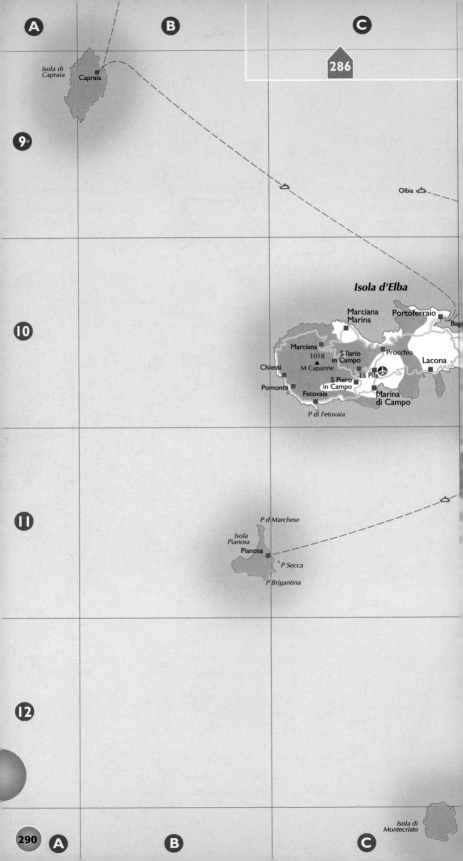

286

9°

Isola di
Capraia

Capraia

Olbia

Isola d'Elba

10

Marciana
Marina

Portoferraio

Bag

Marciana

1018
M Capanne

S Ilario
in Campo

Procchio

Lacona

Chiessi

S Piero
in Campo

La Pila

Pomonte

Fetovaia

Marina
di Campo

P di Fetovaia

11

P d Marchese

Isola
Pianosa

Pianosa

P Secca

P Brigantina

12

Isola di
Montecristo

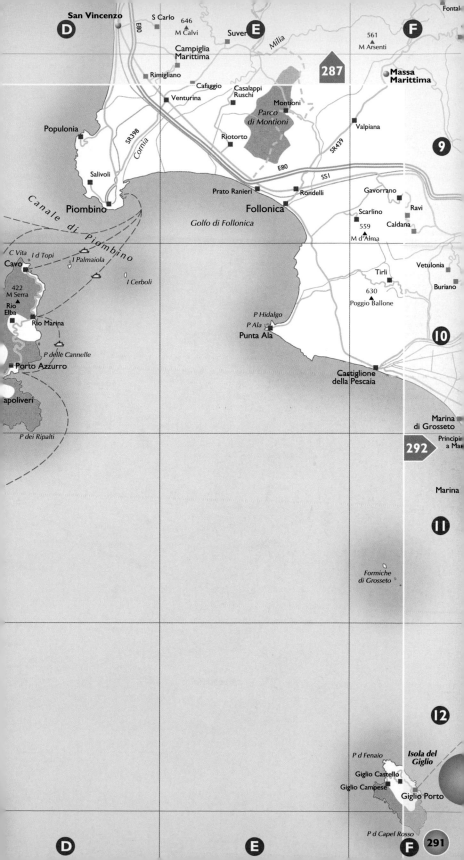

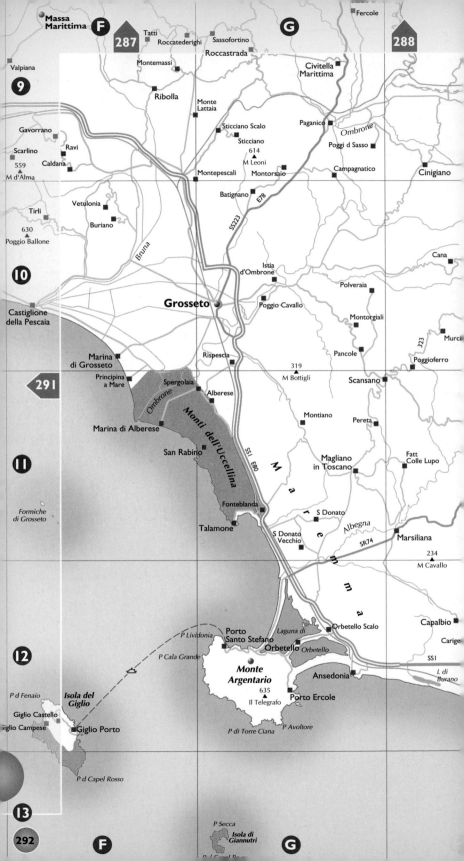

Fercole

Tatti
Roccatederighi
Sassofortino

Roccastrada

Montemassi

Civitella
Marittima

9 Valpiana

Ribolla

Monte
Lattaia

Paganico

Ombrone

Gavorrano

Sticciano Scalo

Poggi d Sasso

Ravi

Scarlino

Caldana

Sticciano

559
M d'Alma

614
M Leoni

Montepescali

Montorsaio

Campagnatico

Cinigiano

Tirli

Vetulonia

Batignano

E78

Buriano

SS223

630
Poggio Ballone

Cana

10

Bruna

Istia
d'Ombrone

Polveraia

Castiglione
della Pescaia

Grosseto

Poggio Cavallo

Montorgiali

323

Murci

Pancole

Poggioferro

Marina
di Grosseto

Rispescia

Principina
a Mare

319
M Bottigli

Scansano

291

Spergolaia

Ombrone

Alberese

Montiano

Pereta

Marina di Alberese

Monti dell'Uccellina

Fatt
Colle Lupo

San Rabino

Magliano
in Toscano

11

M

*Formiche
di Grosseto*

SS1

E80

a

Fonteblanda

S Donato

Albegna

Talamone

e

S Donato
Vecchio

SR74

Marsiliana

m

234
M Cavallo

m

a

Orbetello Scalo

Capalbio

*Formiche
di Grosseto*

P Lividonia

Porto
Santo Stefano

Laguna di

Carige

12

P Cala Grande

Orbetello

Orbetello

SS1

P d Fenaio

*Monte
Argentario*

Ansedonia

*L di
Burano*

Giglio Castello

**Isola del
Giglio**

635
Il Telegrafo

Porto Ercole

Giglio Campese

Giglio Porto

P di Torre Ciana

P Avoltore

P d Capel Rosso

13

P Secca

292

F

P d Capel Rosso

**Isola di
Giannutri**

G

Page numbers in bold indicate the main reference. Entries beginning with Italian words for Saint are indexed under S first, and then according to the second part of the name, e.g, Santa Croce is indexed before San Domenico.

ACKNOWLEDGMENTS

Abbreviations for the credits are as follows:
AA = AA World Travel Library, t (top), b (bottom), c (centre), l (left), r (right), bg (background)

UNDERSTANDING TUSCANY

4cl AA/Ken Paterson; 4c AA/Clive Sawyer; 4r AA/Simon McBride; 5c AA/Ken Paterson; 5r AA/Ken Paterson; 5br AA/Ken Paterson; 6tr AA/Jerry Edmanson; 7cl AA/Simon McBride; 7c AA/Simon McBride; 7cr AA/Terry Harris; 8tl AA/Simon McBride; 8tr AA/Simon McBride; 8cr AA/Richard Ireland; 8cr AA/Ken Paterson; 8br AA/Simon McBride; 8br AA/Terry Harris; 9tl AA/Terry Harris; 9tr AA/Clive Sawyer; 9cl AA/Terry Harris; 9cr AA/Jerry Edmanson; 9cl AA/Ken Paterson; 9bl AA/Terry Harris; 9br AA/Clive Sawyer; 10tr AA/Clive Sawyer; 10cr AA/Ken Paterson; 10cr AA/Simon McBride; 10bc AA/Richard Ireland.

LIVING TUSCANY

11 AA/Clive Sawyer; 12/13bg AA/Terry Harris; 12tl AA/Ken Paterson; 12tc AA/Jerry Edmanson; 12tr AA/Ken Paterson; 12cl Paul Harcourt Davies/Hidden Worlds; 12cr Moviestore Collection; 12bl APT Costa degli Truschi, Piazza Cavour 6, 57125 Livorno; 12bl/c Florence Tourist Board; 13tl/c AA/Ken Paterson; 13tr AA/Ken Paterson; 13cl AA/Ken Paterson; 13cc AA/Clive Sawyer; 13cr AA/Terry Harris; 13cr AA/Clive Sawyer; 14/15bg Brand X Pictures; 14tc Marco Di Lauro/Getty Images; 14tr AA/Terry Harris; 14cl AA/Terry Harris; 14cc AA/Terry Harris; 14cl AA/Clive Sawyer; 14bl AA/Clive Sawyer; 15tl D. Donadoni/Marka; 15tc APT Costa degli Truschi, Piazza Cavour 6, 57125 Livorno; 15tr AA/Max Jourdan; 15cc AA/Jerry Edmanson; 15cr Franco Origlia/Getty Images; 16/17bg AA/Clare Garcia; 16tl AA/Terry Harris; 16tc www.tinacci.com; 16tr AA/Simon McBride; 16cl AA/Terry Harris; 16cr AA/Terry Harris; 16b AA/Terry Harris; 17tl AA/Terry Harris; 17tr AA/Simon McBride; 17c Torsten Silz/AFP/Getty Images; 17r AA/Clare Garcia; 18/19bg AA/Max Jourdan; 18tl/c AA/Ken Paterson; 18tr AA/Terry Harris; 18cl AA/Clive Sawyer; 18cc AA/Terry Harris; 18cr AA/Simon McBride; 18bl AA/Richard Ireland; 18bc AA/Clive Sawyer; 19tl www.cosetoscane.com; 19tc AA/Ken Paterson; 19tc AA/Terry Harris; 19tr AA/Ken Paterson; 19cl www.cosetoscane.com; 19cc AA/Simon McBride; 19cr AA/Terry Harris; 19br www.cosetoscane.com; 20/21bg AA/Simon McBride; 20l AA/Terry Harris; 20tc AA/Terry Harris; 20tc AA/Clive Sawyer; 20tr AA/Ken Paterson; 20cc AA/Simon McBride; 20cr AA/Terry Harris; 21t Franco Origlia/Getty Images; 21cl AA/Dario Castagno; 21cr AA/Pete Bennett; 21br AA/Terry Harris; 22bg AA/Simon McBride; 22tl Michael Steele/Getty Images; 22tr AA/Simon McBride; 22c Massimo Sestini/Grazia Neri.

THE STORY OF TUSCANY

23 AA/Terry Harris; 24/25bg AA/Ken Paterson; 24cl AA/Ken Paterson; 24cr AA; 24bl Archivi Alinari, Florence; 24c AA/Richard Ireland; 25cl AA/Jim Holmes; 25cr AA/Terry Harris; 25bl AA/Ken Paterson; 25c AA/George Scharf; 25cr AA/Ken Paterson; 25bc AA/Clive Sawyer; 25br AA/Ken Paterson; 26/27bg AA/Terry Harris; 26cl AA/Richard Ireland; 26cr Bargello, Florence/www.bridgeman.co.uk; 26bl AA/Simon McBride; 26c AA/Jerry Edmanson; 26br AA/Jerry Edmanson; 27c AA; 27cr AA/Clive Sawyer; 27bl Scala, Florence 1990 - courtesy of the Ministero Beni e Att. Culturali; 27bc AA/Terry Harris; 27r AA/Simon McBride; 27br AA/Clive Sawyer; 28/29bg AA/Simon McBride; 28cl AA/Terry Harris; 28bl AA/Clive Sawyer; 28/29b Mary Evans Picture Library; 29cl/cr AA 29c AA/Clive Sawyer; 29br AA/Simon McBride; 30/31bg AA/Simon McBride; 30cl AA; 30c AA/Ken Paterson; 30b Giraudon/Bridgeman Art Library/www.bridgeman.co.uk;

31cl/c AA; 31bl AA/Terry Harris; 31bc AA/Ken Paterson; 31r AA/Ken Paterson; 31br AA/Simon McBride; 32/33bg Digital Vision; 32c AA/Clive Sawyer; 32bl AA/Clive Sawyer; 32br AA/Clive Sawyer; 33cl David Levine/www.travelbrochure-graphics.org; 33cr AA; 33bc AA/Simon McBride; 33br AA/Terry Harris; 34/35bg AA/Ken Paterson; 34cl AA/Isla Love; 34bl AA/Ken Paterson; 34br Scala, Florence 1990 - courtesy of the Ministero Beni e Att. Culturali; 35cl/c/cr AA; 35bc Mary Evans Picture Library; 35br Archivi Alinari/Bridgeman, Florence; 36/37bg Archivio Storico Piaggio "Antonella Bechi Piaggio"; 36c Daimler Chrysler; 36bl David Levine/www.travelbrochuregraphics.org; 36bc Archivio Storico Piaggio "Antonella Bechi Piaggio"; 36br Emilio Cavallini; 37c Gucci; 37bl Illustrated London News; 37bc AA/Clive Sawyer; 37br Museo Salvatore Ferragamo; 38bg AA/Simon McBride; 38cl Stefano Goldberg/RPBW; 38cl AA/Simon McBride; 38cr Ippodromi & Citta, Firenze; 38bl AA/Simon McBride; 38br Paolo Cocco/AFP/Getty Images.

ON THE MOVE

39 AA/Max Jourdan; 40-43t Digital Vision; 40c Aeroporto di Firenze; 42b AA/Richard Ireland; 43c AA/Simon McBride; 44-47t AA/Jerry Edmanson; 44b AA/Ken Paterson; 45b AA/Terry Harris; 46c AA/Terry Harris; 48-52t Digital Vision; 49cl AA/Terry Harris; 49c esseBi Italia; 50c esseBi Italia & Automobile Club D'Italia; 50b AA/Terry Harris; 52c AA/Jim Holmes; 52b AA/Richard Ireland; 53-55t Digital Vision; 53c AA/Terry Harris; 55c AA/Jerry Edmanson; 56-57t AA/Terry Harris; 56c AA/Terry Harris; 57c AA/Terry Harris; 58t AA/Simon McBride.

THE SIGHTS

59 AA/Ken Paterson; 60–148tbg Simon McBride; 61cr AA/Simon McBride; 61bl AA/Jerry Edmanson; 64tl AA/Terry Harris; 64c AA/Simon McBride; 65t AA/Terry Harris; 65cr AA/Terry Harris; 66t AA/Ken Paterson; 66cl AA/Simon McBride; 66cr AA/Simon McBride; 67t Finsiel/Archivi Alinari, Florence ; 67bl AA/Ken Paterson; 68 AA; 69t Bridgeman Art Library/Alinari/www.bridgeman.co.uk; 69cl Clive Sawyer; 69c www.bridgeman.co.uk; 69cr AA/Simon McBride; 70/71 Archivi Alinari/Bridgeman, Florence; 72tl www.bridgeman.co.uk; 72br AA/Simon McBride; 73 Bridgeman/Alinari Archives; Reproduced with the permission of Ministero per i Beni e le Attività Culturali; 74tl AA/Clive Sawyer; 74tc AA/Simon McBride; 74tr AA/Clive Sawyer; 74b AA/Ken Paterson; 75tl AA/Jerry Edmanson; 75tr AA/Clive Sawyer; 76t www.bridgeman.co.uk; 76b AA/Ken Paterson; 77 AA/Simon McBride; 78tl AA/Clive Sawyer; 78tr AA/Clive Sawyer; 78cl Ferragamo Museum; 79tl AA/Clive Sawyer; 79tc AA/Clive Sawyer; 79tr AA/Clive Sawyer; 79c AA/Terry Harris; 80t AA/Simon McBride; 80cl Scala, Florence 1990 - courtesy of the Ministero Beni e Att. Culturali; 81t Archivi Alinari/Bridgeman, Florence; 81b AA/Simon McBride; 82t AA/Jerry Edmanson; 82c AA/Clive Sawyer; 83t AA/Clive Sawyer; 83cr AA/Jerry Edmanson; 84 AA/Ken Paterson; 85t AA/Clive Sawyer; 85cl AA/Simon McBride; 85cc AA/Clive Sawyer; 85cr AA/Simon McBride; 85br AA/Clive Sawyer; 86tc AA/Clive Sawyer; 86cl AA/Clive Sawyer; 86cr AA/Clive Sawyer; 87c AA/Simon McBride; 87cr AA/Clive Sawyer; 87br AA/Simon McBride; 88t AA/Simon McBride; 88c AA/Jerry Edmanson; 88b AA/Terry Harris; 89t AA/Clive Sawyer; 89c AA/Simon McBride; 90tl AA/Clive Sawyer; 90tr AA/Clive Sawyer; 90b AA/Clive Sawyer; 91tl AA/Clive Sawyer; 91tr AA/Clive Sawyer; 91b AA/Terry Harris;

92tl AA/Terry Harris; 92tc AA/Clive Sawyer; 92tr AA/Terry Harris; 93t AA/Clive Sawyer; 93cr AA/Clive Sawyer; 94t AA/Terry Harris; 94b AA/Terry Harris; 95t AA/Ken Paterson; 95cr AA/Jerry Edmanson; 96tl AA/Clive Sawyer; 96tc AA/Richard Ireland; 96tr AA/Jerry Edmanson; 98tl AA/Clive Sawyer; 98tc AA/Terry Harris; 98tr AA/Clive Sawyer; 99tl AA/Ken Paterson; 99tc AA/Clive Sawyer; 99tr AA/Terry Harris; 100 AA/Terry Harris; 101 AA/Ken Paterson; 102t AA/Clive Sawyer; 102cl AA/Clive Sawyer; 102c AA/Ken Paterson; 102cr AA/Tony Souter; 103 AA/Ken Paterson; 105t AA/Terry Harris; 105b AA/Richard Ireland; 106 AA/Clive Sawyer; 107t AA/Terry Harris; 107cl AA/Terry Harris; 107c AA/Terry Harris; 107cr AA/Terry Harris; 108tl AA/Terry Harris; 108tr AA/Terry Harris; 108br AA/Terry Harris; 109 AA/Terry Harris; 110tl AA/Terry Harris; 110tr AA/Ken Paterson; 110br AA/Clive Sawyer; 111tl AA/Ken Paterson; 111tc AA/Ken Paterson; 111tr AA/Ken Paterson; 113l AA/Terry Harris; 113r AA/Jerry Edmanson; 115tl AA/Terry Harris; 115tr AA/Terry Harris; 115b AA/Terry Harris; 116t AA/Jerry Edmanson; 116cl AA/Clive Sawyer; 116cr AA/Terry Harris; 117 AA/Simon McBride; 118tl AA/Simon McBride; 118b Luca Lozzi/Getty Images; 119l AA/Simon McBride; 119r AA/Simon McBride; 120 AA/Terry Harris; 121t AA/Terry Harris; 121cl AA/Terry Harris; 121c AA/Terry Harris; 121cr AA/Terry Harris; 122t AA/Terry Harris; 122b AA/Terry Harris; 123 AA/Terry Harris; 124t AA/Terry Harris; 124cl AA/Clive Sawyer; 125t AA/Terry Harris; 125b AA/Terry Harris; 126 Scala, Florence 1990 - courtesy of the Ministero Beni e Att. Culturali; 127tl AA/Terry Harris; 127tr AA/Terry Harris; 129tl AA/Simon McBride; 129tc AA/Simon McBride; 129tr AA/Simon McBride; 130tl AA/Terry Harris; 130tc AA/Simon McBride; 130tr AA/Terry Harris; 130br AA/Terry Harris; 131t AA/Clive Sawyer; 131cr AA/Terry Harris; 132 AA/Ken Paterson; 133t AA/Ken Paterson; 133br AA/Richard Ireland; 134t AA/Clive Sawyer; 134b AA/Terry Harris; 135tl Vision; 135tr AA/Ken Paterson; 136tl Paul Harcourt Davies/Hidden Worlds; 136tc AA/Ken Paterson; 136tr AA/Ken Paterson; 137t AA/Terry Harris; 137cr AA/Clive Sawyer; 138tl AA/Ken Paterson; 138tc AA/Ken Paterson; 138tr AA/Tony Souter; 138bl AA/Tony Souter; 139t AA/Clive Sawyer; 139br AA/Simon McBride; 140tl AA/Terry Harris; 140tr AA/Ken Paterson; 141t AA/Simon McBride; 141cr AA/Simon McBride; 142 AA/Ken Paterson; 143t AA/Simon McBride; 143cl AA/Ken Paterson; 143c AA/Richard Ireland; 143cr AA/Simon McBride; 144tl AA/Simon McBride; 144b AA/Clive Sawyer; 145cl AA/Ken Paterson; 145cr AA/Ken Paterson; 145b AA/Simon McBride; 146t AA/Terry Harris; 146b AA/Terry Harris; 147tl AA/Ken Paterson; 147tc AA/Terry Harris; 147tr AA/Terry Harris; 148t Archivio Fotografico Consorzio Turistico Volterra; 148b Archivio Fotografico Consorzio Turistico Volterra.

WHAT TO DO

149 AA/Simon McBride; 150/151t AA/Terry Harris; 150cl AA/Richard Ireland; 150cr AA/Terry Harris; 151cl AA/Terry Harris; 152/153t AA/Clive Sawyer; 152cl Photowave; 153cl Digital Vision; 153cr AA/Clive Sawyer; 154/155t AA/Terry Harris; 154cl Ippodromi & Citta; 154cr AA/Ken Paterson; 155cl Photodisc; 155cr AA/Terry Harris; 156/157t AA/Simon McBride; 156cl AA/Ken Paterson; 156cr Photodisc; 157cl Festival Puccini; 157cr AA/Terry Harris; 158-172t AA/Clive Sawyer; 158c AA/Terry Harris; 159c AA/Clare Garcia; 160c AA/Dario Miterdiri; 161c AA/Terry Harris; 162c AA/Terry Harris; 163c Scuola del Cuoio; 164c AA/Richard Ireland; 165c AA/Simon McBride; 166c Digital Vision; 167c Maggio Fiorentino; 168c AA/Terry Harris; 169c AA/Richard Ireland; 170c Ballooning in Tuscany; 171c AA/Terry Harris; 172cr AA/Simon McBride; 173-180t AA/Terry Harris; 173c AA/Clive Sawyer; 174c AA/Terry Harris; 175c AA/Terry Harris; 176c AA/Ken Paterson; 177c AA/Terry Harris; 178c Photodisc; 179c Photodisc; 180cr Festival Puccini; 181-183t AA/Terry Harris; 181c AA/Simon McBride; 182c AA/Terry Harris; 184-190t AA/Ken Paterson; 184c AA/Terry Harris; 185c AA/Terry Harris; 186c AA/Ken Paterson; 187c AA/Terry Harris; 188c Tinacci Tito & M. Grazia; 189c AA/Richard Ireland; 190c Photowave.

OUT AND ABOUT

191 AA/Simon McBride; 193 AA/Simon McBride; 194t AA/Terry Harris; 194c AA/Clive Sawyer; 194b AA/Terry Harris; 195bl AA/Terry Harris; 195br AA/Terry Harris; 196 AA/Clive Sawyer; 197cl AA/Ken Paterson; 197cr AA/Simon McBride; 197b AA/Terry Harris; 198t AA/Terry Harris; 198b AA/Terry Harris; 199 AA/Ken Paterson; 200tl AA/Terry Harris; 200tr AA/Terry Harris; 201t AA/Terry Harris; 201b AA/Terry Harris; 202 AA/Terry Harris; 203tl AA/Simon McBride; 203tr AA/Terry Harris; 203c AA/Terry Harris; 204 AA/Clive Sawyer; 205bl AA/Ken Paterson; 205br AA/Ken Paterson; 206t AA/Simon McBride; 206c AA/Ken Paterson; 207t AA/Simon McBride; 207b AA/Simon McBride; 208 Archivio Fotografico Consorzio Turistico Volterra; 209t AA/Clive Sawyer; 209b AA/Terry Harris; 210 AA/Ken Paterson; 211t AA/Simon McBride; 211c AA/Simon McBride; 212tl AA/Clive Sawyer; 212tc AA/Simon McBride; 212tr AA/Terry Harris.

EATING AND STAYING

213 AA/Simon McBride; 214cl AA/Clive Sawyer; 214cc AA/Clive Sawyer; 214cc AA/Simon McBride; 214cr AA/Clive Sawyer; 216cl AA/Dario Miterdiri; 216cc AA/Simon McBride; 216cr AA/Jerry Edmanson; 217cl AA/Ken Paterson; 217cc AA/Simon McBride; 217cr AA/Tony Souter; 219c AA/Richard Ireland; 220l AA/Terry Harris; 223c AA/Terry Harris; 225c AA/Terry Harris; 225r AA/Terry Harris; 226 AA/Terry Harris; 227l AA/Richard Ireland; 227ct AA/Richard Ireland; 231l AA/Terry Harris; 231r AA/Terry Harris; 233cl AA/Terry Harris; 234c AA/Terry Harris; 235l AA/Terry Harris; 235c AA/Richard Ireland; 236l AA/Terry Harris; 236r AA/Terry Harris; 238r AA/Richard Ireland; 239ct AA/Terry Harris; 239tr AA/Richard Ireland; 239br AA/Richard Ireland; 240cr AA/Richard Ireland; 241c AA/Terry Harris; 250 AA/Terry Harris; 251 AA/Terry Harris; 253 AA/Terry Harris; 255bl AA/Terry Harris; 257 AA/Terry Harris; 258tr AA/Richard Ireland; 259l AA/Terry Harris.

PLANNING

261 AA/Clive Sawyer; 262tc AA/Simon McBride; 263 AA/Terry Harris; 264 AA/Simon McBride; 265 AA/Terry Harris; 267 ECB; 268t AA/Clive Sawyer; 268b AA/Terry Harris; 269b AA/Terry Harris; 270 AA/Terry Harris; 271 AA/Clive Sawyer; 273 AA/Simon McBride; 274 AA/Terry Harris.

Project editor
Clare Garcia

Interior design
David Austin, Glyn Barlow, Kate Harling, Bob Johnson,
Nick Otway, Carole Philp, Keith Russell

Additional design work
Katherine Mead, Jo Tapper

Picture research
Alice Earle

Cover design
Tigist Getachew

Internal repro work
Susan Crowhurst, Ian Little, Michael Moody

Production
Lyn Kirby, Helen Sweeney

Mapping
Maps produced by the Cartography Department of AA Publishing

Main contributors
Rebecca Ford, Tim Jepson, Sally Roy, Nicky Swallow,
James Taylor, The Content Works, Frances Wolverton

Copy editor
Audrey Horne

See It Florence and Tuscany ISBN 1-4000-1511-1

Published in the United States by Fodor's Travel Publications and simultaneously in Canada by
Random House of Canada Limited, Toronto. Published in the United Kingdom by AA Publishing.

Fodor's is a registered trademark of Random House, Inc., and and Fodor's See It
is a trademark of Random House, Inc.
Fodor's Travel Publications is a division of Fodor's LLC.

Colour separation by Keenes
Printed and bound by Leo, China

Special Sales: Fodor's Travel Publications are available at special discounts for bulk purchases for
sales promotions or premiums. Special editions, including personalized covers, excerpts of existing
guides, and corporate imprints, can be created in large quantities for special needs. For more
information, contact your local bookseller or write to Special Marketing, Fodor's Travel Publications,
1745 Broadway, New York, NY 10019. Inquiries from Canada should be directed to your local Canadian
bookseller or sent to Random House of Canada, Ltd., Marketing Department,
2775 Matheson Blvd. East, Mississauga, Ontario L4W 4P7.

A01609
Maps in this title produced from:
mapping © Mairs Geographischer Verlag / Falk Verlag, D-73751 Ostfildern, Germany
and with reference to mapping © GEOnext - ISTITUTO GEOGRAFICO DE AGOSTINI, Novara

Relief map images supplied by Mountain High Maps® Copyright © 1993 Digital Wisdom, Inc
Weather chart statistics supplied by Weatherbase © Copyright 2004 Canty and Associates, LLC
Communicarta assistance with distance/time charts gratefully acknowledged

Important note: Time inevitably brings changes, so always confirm prices, travel facts,
and other perishable information when it matters. Although Fodor's cannot accept
responsibility for errors, you can use this guide in the confidence that we have taken
every care to ensure its accuracy.

Fodor's Key to the Guides

AMERICA'S **GUIDEBOOK LEADER** PUBLISHES GUIDES FOR **EVERY KIND OF TRAVELER**. CHECK OUT OUR MANY SERIES AND FIND YOUR **PERFECT MATCH**.

FODOR'S GOLD GUIDES
America's favorite travel-guide series offers the most detailed insider reviews of hotels, restaurants, and attractions in all price ranges, plus great background information, smart tips, and useful maps.

COMPASS AMERICAN GUIDES
Stunning guides from top local writers and photographers, with gorgeous photos, literary excerpts, and colorful anecdotes. A must-have for culture mavens, history buffs, and new residents.

FODOR'S CITYPACKS
Concise city coverage in a guide plus a foldout map. The right choice for urban travelers who want everything under one cover.

FODOR'S WHERE TO WEEKEND
A fresh take on weekending, this series identifies the best places to escape outside the city and details loads of rejuvenating activities as well as cool places to stay, great restaurants, and practical information.

FODOR'S AROUND THE CITY WITH KIDS
Up to 68 great ideas for family days, recommended by resident parents. Perfect for exploring in your own backyard or on the road.

FODOR'S TRAVEL HISTORIC AMERICA
For travelers who want to experience history firsthand, this series gives in-depth coverage of historic sights, plus nearby restaurants and hotels. Themes include the Thirteen Colonies, the Old West, and the Lewis and Clark Trail.

FODOR'S FLASHMAPS
Every resident's map guide, with 60 easy-to-follow maps of public transit, parks, museums, zip codes, and more.

FODOR'S LANGUAGES FOR TRAVELERS
Practice the local language before you hit the road. Available in phrase books, cassette sets, and CD sets.

THE COLLECTED TRAVELER
These collections of the best published essays and articles on various European destinations will give you a feel for the culture, cuisine, and way of life.

FODOR'S HOW TO GUIDES
Get tips from the pros on planning the perfect trip. Learn how to pack, fly hassle-free, plan a honeymoon or cruise, stay healthy on the road, and travel with your baby.

KAREN BROWN'S GUIDES
Engaging guides—many with easy-to-follow inn-to-inn itineraries—to the most charming inns and B&Bs in the U.S.A. and Europe.

OTHER GREAT TITLES FROM FODOR'S
Baseball Vacations, The Complete Guide to the National Parks, Family Vacations, Golf Digest's Places to Play, Great American Drives of the East, Great American Drives of the West, Great American Vacations, Healthy Escapes, National Parks of the West, Skiing USA.